"The detail is comprehensive and chilling."   —*Time*

"Intimate and engaging."   —*The New Yorker*

"Sorkin succeeds in translating a highly complex . . . series of events into a gripping and intelligible read. Through months of interviews and behind the scenes access, he renders normally stony-faced executives and politicians in three dimensions, affording the reader a rare sense of their real personalities and private conflicts."   —Forbes.com

"Sorkin has succeeded in writing *the* book of the crisis, with amazing levels of detail and access."   —Reuters

"Sorkin has pulled off a rare feat. He has turned more than 500 hours of interviews and documentary evidence . . . into an engrossing fly-on-the-wall account of one of the most tumultuous years in U.S. history."   —Bloomberg.com

"The preternaturally ambitious, 32-year-old DealBook editor [Andrew Ross Sorkin] has an insane work ethic in addition to a powerful, high-profile job and a bestselling book. Ever since we read it we've been thinking to ourselves: How can we be more Sorkin-like?"   —*New York Magazine*

"This crisis has passed, but neither the country's financial system nor its economy have recovered. [*Too Big To Fail*] should be required reading for anyone trying to fix—or simply understand—either."
—Adam Lashinsky, *San Francisco Chronicle*

"This moment-by-moment account of the collapse and rescue of Wall Street reads like a novel, exploring the minds of characters ranging from Lehman Brothers' then-CEO Richard Fuld to former Treasury Secretary Henry Paulson."
—Lisa Von Ahn, Reuters

"The drama of the collapse produced many novelistic moments, but until Sorkin's *Too Big To Fail*, none of the several books offered the drama of such earlier classic Wall Street takedowns as *Barbarians At the Gate* or *Liar's Poker*. Sorkin's book . . . is a phenom. An absolute tour de force."
—Robert Kuttner, *The American Prospect*

"Gives the reader a front-row view into the day-to-day decisions made by the nation's top bankers and government officials. . . . Sorkin's book reads like a Dan Brown thriller."   —*The Free Lance-Star* (Fredericksburg)

"As close to a definitive account as we are likely to get."
—Dominic Lawson, *The Sunday Times* (London)

ABOUT THE AUTHOR

BRENT MURRAY

Andrew Ross Sorkin is the award-winning chief mergers and acquisitions reporter and columnist for the *New York Times*. He is also the editor and founder of DealBook, an online daily financial report. He has twice won a Gerald Loeb Award, one of the highest honors in business journalism; once for breaking news and and a second time for authoring *Too Big to Fail*. The World Economic Forum named him a Young Global Leader and he was added to The Directorship 100, recognizing the nation's most influential people on corporate boardrooms. *Too Big to Fail* has been on the hardcover bestseller list for more than twenty-three weeks.

TOO BIG TO FAIL

*The Inside Story of How Wall Street and Washington
Fought to Save the Financial System—
and Themselves*

Andrew Ross Sorkin

PENGUIN BOOKS

PENGUIN BOOKS

Published by the Penguin Group

Penguin Group (USA) Inc., 375 Hudson Street, New York, New York 10014, U.S.A. • Penguin Group (Canada), 90 Eglinton Avenue East, Suite 700, Toronto, Ontario, Canada M4P 2Y3 (a division of Pearson Penguin Canada Inc.) • Penguin Books Ltd, 80 Strand, London WC2R 0RL, England • Penguin Ireland, 25 St Stephen's Green, Dublin 2, Ireland (a division of Penguin Books Ltd) • Penguin Group (Australia), 250 Camberwell Road, Camberwell, Victoria 3124, Australia (a division of Pearson Australia Group Pty Ltd) • Penguin Books India Pvt Ltd, 11 Community Centre, Panchsheel Park, New Delhi – 110 017, India • Penguin Group (NZ), 67 Apollo Drive, Rosedale, Auckland 0632, New Zealand (a division of Pearson New Zealand Ltd) • Penguin Books (South Africa) (Pty) Ltd, 24 Sturdee Avenue, Rosebank, Johannesburg 2196, South Africa

Penguin Books Ltd, Registered Offices: 80 Strand, London WC2R 0RL, England

First published in the United States of America by Viking Penguin, a member of Penguin Group (USA) Inc. 2009
Published in Penguin Books with a new afterword 2010
This edition published 2011

10   9   8   7   6   5

PHOTOGRAPH CREDITS
Insert page 1 (*top*): Lehman Brothers Holdings; (*center*): Hiroko Masuike/World Picture Network; (*bottom*): Scott J. Ferrell/Congressional Quarterly/Getty Images. Pages 2 (*top*), 3 (*top*), and 13 (*bottom*): Chip Somodevilla/Getty Images News. Pages 2 (*center*) and 6 (*top*): © Corbis. Page 2 (*bottom*): Brendan Smialowski/The New York Times/Redux. Pages 3 (*bottom*), 4 (*top*), and 10 (*center*): United States Department of Treasury. Page 4 (*bottom left*): Ethan Miller/Getty Images Entertainment. Pages 4 (*bottom right*), 7 (*center right*), and 9 (*center and bottom*): Photographer: Andrew Harrer/Bloomberg. Page 5 (*top left*): Scott Halleran/Getty Images Sport; (*top right*): Sullivan & Cromwell; (*bottom*): Magic Photography. Page 6 (*bottom*): Keith Waldgrave/Solo/Zuma Press. Page 7 (*top*): Goldman, Sachs & Co.; (*center left*): Axel Schmidt/DDP/Getty Images. Pages 7 (*bottom*) and 8 (*top left and right*): J. P. Morgan. Page 8 (*bottom*): Yoshikazu Tsuno/AFP/Getty Images. Page 9 (*top*): Mario Tama/Getty Images News. Page 10 (*top*): Wachtell, Lipton, Rosen & Katz; (*bottom*): Reuters. Pages 12 (*all*) and 14 (*bottom*): Morgan Stanley. Page 13 (*top*): Mark Wilson/Getty Images News; (*center*): Chester Higgins Jr./The New York Times/Redux. Page 14 (*top*): Win McNamee/Getty Images News. Page 16 (*top*): Alex Wong/Getty Images News; (*bottom*): Robert Kindler.

ISBN 978-0-670-02125-3 (hc.)
ISBN 978-0-14-311824-4 (pbk.)
ISBN 978-0-14-312027-8 (pbk. movie tie-in)
CIP data available

Printed in the United States of America
Set in Dante • Designed by Carla Bolte

To my parents, Joan and Larry, and my loving wife, Pilar

Size, we are told, is not a crime. But size may, at least, become noxious by reason of the means through which it was attained or the uses to which it is put.

— Louis Brandeis, *Other People's Money: And How the Bankers Use It*, 1913

AUTHOR'S NOTE

T his book is the product of more than five hundred hours of interviews with more than two hundred individuals who participated
directly in the events surrounding the financial crisis. These individuals
include Wall Street chief executives, board members, management teams,
current and former U.S. government officials, foreign government officials, bankers, lawyers, accountants, consultants, and other advisers. Many
of these individuals shared documentary evidence, including contemporaneous notes, e-mails, tape recordings, internal presentations, draft filings, scripts, calendars, call logs, billing time sheets, and expense reports
that provided the basis for much of the detail in this book. They also spent
hours painstakingly recalling the conversations and details of various
meetings, many of which were considered privileged and confidential.

Given the continuing controversy surrounding many of these events—
several criminal investigations are still ongoing as of this writing, and
countless civil lawsuits have been filed—most of the subjects interviewed
took part only on the condition that they not be identified as a source. As
a result, and because of the number of sources used to confirm every scene,
readers should not assume that the individual whose dialogue or specific
feeling is recorded was necessarily the person who provided that information. In many cases the account came from him or her directly, but it may
also have come from other eyewitnesses in the room or on the opposite
side of a phone call (often via speakerphone), or from someone briefed
directly on the conversation immediately afterward, or, as often as possible, from contemporaneous notes or other written evidence.

Much has already been written about the financial crisis, and this book
has tried to build upon the extraordinary record created by my esteemed
colleagues in financial journalism, whose work I cite at the end of this

volume. But what I hope I have provided here is the first detailed, moment-by-moment account of one of the most calamitous times in our history. The individuals who propel this narrative genuinely believed they were—and may in fact have been—staring into the economic abyss.

Galileo Galilei said, "All truths are easy to understand once they are discovered; the point is to discover them." I hope I have discovered at least some of them, and that in doing so I have made the often bewildering financial events of the past few years a little easier to understand.

THE CAST OF CHARACTERS
AND THE COMPANIES THEY KEPT

FINANCIAL INSTITUTIONS

American International Group (AIG)

Steven J. Bensinger, chief financial officer and executive vice president

Joseph J. Cassano, head, London-based AIG Financial Products; former chief operating officer

David Herzog, controller

Brian T. Schreiber, senior vice president, strategic planning

Martin J. Sullivan, former president and chief executive officer

Robert B. Willumstad, chief executive; former chairman

Bank of America

Gregory L. Curl, director of corporate planning

Kenneth D. Lewis, president, chairman, and chief executive officer

Brian T. Moynihan, president, global corporate and investment banking

Joe L. Price, chief financial officer

Barclays

Archibald Cox Jr., chairman, Barclays Americas`

Jerry del Missier, president, Barclays Capital

Robert E. Diamond Jr., president, Barclays PLC; chief executive officer, Barclays Capital

Michael Klein, independent adviser

John S. Varley, chief executive officer

Berkshire Hathaway

Warren E. Buffett, chairman and chief executive officer
Ajit Jain, president, re-insurance unit

BlackRock

Larry Fink, chief executive officer

Blackstone Group

Peter G. Peterson, co-founder
Stephen A. Schwarzman, chairman, chief executive officer, and
co-founder
John Studzinski, senior managing director

China Investment Corporation

Gao Xiqing, president

Citigroup

Edward "Ned" Kelly, head, global banking for the institutional clients
group
Vikram S. Pandit, chief executive
Stephen R. Volk, vice chairman

Evercore Partners

Roger C. Altman, founder and chairman

Fannie Mae

Daniel H. Mudd, president and chief executive officer

Freddie Mac

Richard F. Syron, chief executive officer

Goldman Sachs

Lloyd C. Blankfein, chairman and chief executive officer
Gary D. Cohn, co-president and co-chief operating officer
Christopher A. Cole, chairman, investment banking

John F. W. Rogers, secretary to the board
Harvey M. Schwartz, head, global securities division sales
David Solomon, managing director and co-head, investment banking
Byron Trott, vice chairman, investment banking
David A. Viniar, chief financial officer
Jon Winkelried, co-president and co-chief operating officer

Greenlight Capital

David M. Einhorn, chairman and co-founder

J.C. Flowers & Company

J. Christopher Flowers, chairman and founder

JP Morgan Chase

Steven D. Black, co-head, Investment Bank
Douglas J. Braunstein, head, investment banking
Michael J. Cavanagh, chief financial officer
Stephen M. Cutler, general counsel
Jamie Dimon, chairman and chief executive officer
Mark Feldman, managing director
John Hogan, chief risk officer
James B. Lee Jr., vice chairman
Timothy Main, head, financial institutions, investment banking
William T. Winters, co-head, Investment Bank
Barry L. Zubrow, chief risk officer

Korea Development Bank

Min Euoo Sung, chief executive officer

Lazard Frères

Gary Parr, deputy chairman

Lehman Brothers

Steven L. Berkenfeld, managing director
Jasjit S. ("Jesse") Bhattal, chief executive officer, Lehman Brothers
Asia-Pacific

Erin M. Callan, chief financial officer

Kunho Cho, vice chairman

Gerald A. Donini, global head, equities

Scott J. Freidheim, chief administrative officer

Richard S. Fuld Jr., chief executive officer

Michael Gelband, global head, capital

Andrew Gowers, head, corporate communications

Joseph M. Gregory, president and chief operating officer

Alex Kirk, global head, principal investing

Ian T. Lowitt, chief financial officer and co-chief administrative officer

Herbert H. ("Bart") McDade, president and chief operating officer

Hugh E. ("Skip") McGee, global head, investment banking

Thomas A. Russo, vice chairman and chief legal officer

Mark Shafir, global co-head, mergers and acquisitions

Paolo Tonucci, treasurer

Jeffrey Weiss, head, global financial institutions group

Bradley Whitman, global co-head, financial institutions, mergers and acquisitions

Larry Wieseneck, co-head, global finance

Merrill Lynch

John Finnegan, board member

Gregory J. Fleming, president and chief operating officer

Peter Kelly, lawyer

Peter S. Kraus, executive vice president and member of management committee

Thomas K. Montag, executive vice president and head, global sales and trading

E. Stanley O'Neal, former chairman and chief executive officer

John A. Thain, chairman and chief executive officer

Mitsubishi UFJ Financial Group

Nobuo Kuroyanagi, president and chief executive officer

Morgan Stanley

Walid A. Chammah, co-president

Kenneth M. deRegt, chief risk officer

James P. Gorman, co-president

Colm Kelleher, executive vice president, chief financial officer, and
   co-head, strategic planning

Robert A. Kindler, vice chairman, investment banking

Jonathan Kindred, president, Morgan Stanley Japan Securities

Gary G. Lynch, chief legal officer

John J. Mack, chairman and chief executive officer

Thomas R. Nides, chief administrative officer and secretary

Ruth Porat, head, financial institutions group

Robert W. Scully, member, office of the chairman

Daniel A. Simkowitz, vice chairman, global capital markets

Paul J. Taubman, head, investment banking

Perella Weinberg Partners

Gary Barancik, partner

Joseph R. Perella, chairman and chief executive officer

Peter A. Weinberg, partner

Wachovia

David M. Carroll, president, capital management

Jane Sherburne, general counsel

Robert K. Steel, president and chief executive

Wells Fargo

Richard Kovacevich, chairman

THE LAWYERS

Cleary Gottlieb Steen & Hamilton

Alan Beller, partner

Victor I. Lewkow, partner

Cravath, Swaine & Moore

Robert D. Joffe, partner

Faiza J. Saeed, partner

Davis Polk and Wardwell

Marshall S. Huebner, partner

Simspon Thacher & Bartlett

Richard I. Beattie, chairman
James G. Gamble, partner

Sullivan & Cromwell

Jay Clayton, partner
H. Rodgin Cohen, chairman
Michael M. Wiseman, partner

Wachtell, Lipton, Rosen & Katz

Edward D. Herlihy, partner

Weil, Gotshal & Manges

Lori R. Fife, partner, business finance and restructuring
Harvey R. Miller, partner, business finance and restructuring
Thomas A. Roberts, corporate partner

NEW YORK CITY
Michael Bloomberg, mayor

NEW YORK STATE INSURANCE DEPARTMENT
Eric R. Dinallo, superintendent

UNITED KINGDOM

Financial Services Authority

Callum McCarthy, chairman
Hector Sants, chief executive

Government

James Gordon Brown, prime minister
Alistair M. Darling, chancellor of the Exchequer

U.S. GOVERNMENT

Congress

Hillary Clinton, senator (D-New York)

Christopher J. Dodd, senator (D-Connecticut), chairman of the Banking Committee

Barnett "Barney" Frank, representative (D-Massachusetts), chairman of the Committee on Financial Services

Mitch McConnell, senator (R-Kentucky), Republican leader of the Senate

Nancy Pelosi, representative (D-California), Speaker of the House

Department of the Treasury

Michele A. Davis, assistant secretary, public affairs; director, policy planning

Kevin I. Fromer, assistant secretary, legislative affairs

Robert F. Hoyt, general counsel

Dan Jester, adviser to the secretary of the Treasury

Neel Kashkari, assistant secretary, international affairs

David H. McCormick, under secretary, international affairs

David G. Nason, assistant secretary, financial institutions

Jeremiah O. Norton, deputy assistant secretary, financial institutions policy

Henry M. "Hank" Paulson Jr., secretary of the Treasury

Anthony W. Ryan, assistant secretary, financial markets

Matthew Scogin, senior adviser to the under secretary for domestic finance

Steven Shafran, adviser to Mr. Paulson

Robert K. Steel, under secretary, domestic finance

Phillip Swagel, assistant secretary, economic policy

James R. "Jim" Wilkinson, chief of staff

Kendrick R. Wilson III, adviser to the secretary of the Treasury

Federal Deposit Insurance Corporation (FDIC)

Sheila C. Bair, chairwoman

Federal Reserve

Scott G. Alvarez, general counsel
Ben S. Bernanke, chairman
Donald Kohn, vice chairman
Kevin M. Warsh, governor

Federal Reserve Bank of New York

Thomas C. Baxter Jr., general counsel
Terrence J. Checki, executive vice president
Christine M. Cumming, first vice president
William C. Dudley, executive vice president, Markets Group
Timothy F. Geithner, president
Calvin A. Mitchell III, executive vice president, communications
William L. Rutledge, senior vice president

Securities and Exchange Commission

Charles Christopher Cox, chairman
Michael A. Macchiaroli, associate director, Division of Trading and
    Markets
Erik R. Sirri, director, Division of Market Regulation
Linda Chatman Thomsen, director, Division of Enforcement

White House

Joshua B. Bolten, chief of staff, Office of the President
George W. Bush, president of the United States

PROLOGUE

Standing in the kitchen of his Park Avenue apartment, Jamie Dimon poured himself a cup of coffee, hoping it might ease his headache. He was recovering from a slight hangover, but his head really hurt for a different reason: *He knew too much.*

It was just past 7:00 a.m. on the morning of Saturday, September 13, 2008. Dimon, the chief executive of JP Morgan Chase, the nation's third-largest bank, had spent part of the prior evening at an emergency, all-hands-on-deck meeting at the Federal Reserve Bank of New York with a dozen of his rival Wall Street CEOs. Their assignment was to come up with a plan to save Lehman Brothers, the nation's fourth-largest investment bank—or risk the collateral damage that might ensue in the markets.

To Dimon it was a terrifying predicament that caused his mind to spin as he rushed home afterward. He was already more than two hours late for a dinner party that his wife, Judy, was hosting. He was embarrassed by his delay because the dinner was for the parents of their daughter's boyfriend, whom he was meeting for the first time.

"Honestly, I'm never this late," he offered, hoping to elicit some sympathy. Trying to avoid saying more than he should, still he dropped some hints about what had happened at the meeting. "You know, I am not lying about how serious this situation is," Dimon told his slightly alarmed guests as he mixed himself a martini. "You're going to read about it tomorrow in the papers."

As he promised, Saturday's papers prominently featured the dramatic news to which he had alluded. Leaning against the kitchen counter, Dimon opened the *Wall Street Journal* and read the headline of its lead story: "Lehman Races Clock; Crisis Spreads."

Dimon knew that Lehman Brothers might not make it through the weekend. JP Morgan had examined its books earlier that week as a potential lender and had been unimpressed. He also had decided to request some extra collateral from the firm out of fear it might fall. In the next twenty-four hours, Dimon knew, Lehman would either be rescued or ruined. Knowing what he did, however, Dimon was concerned about more than just Lehman Brothers. He was aware that Merrill Lynch, another icon of Wall Street, was in trouble, too, and he had just asked his staff to make sure JP Morgan had enough collateral from that firm as well. And he was also acutely aware of new dangers developing at the global insurance giant American International Group (AIG) that so far had gone relatively unnoticed by the public—it was his firm's client, and they were scrambling to raise additional capital to save it. By his estimation AIG had only about a week to find a solution, or it, too, could falter.

Of the handful of principals involved in the dialogue about the enveloping crisis—the government included—Dimon was in an especially unusual position. He had the closest thing to perfect, real-time information. That "deal flow" enabled him to identify the fraying threads in the fabric of the financial system, even in the safety nets that others assumed would save the day.

Dimon began contemplating a worst-case scenario, and at 7:30 a.m. he went into his home library and dialed into a conference call with two dozen members of his management team.

"You are about to experience the most unbelievable week in America ever, and we have to prepare for the absolutely worst case," Dimon told his staff. "We have to protect the firm. This is about our survival."

His staff listened intently, but no one was quite certain what Dimon was trying to say.

Like most people on Wall Street—including Richard S. Fuld Jr., Lehman's CEO, who enjoyed one of the longest reigns of any of its leaders—many of those listening to the call assumed that the government would intervene and prevent its failure. Dimon hastened to disabuse them of the notion.

"That's wishful thinking. There is no way, in my opinion, that Washington is going to bail out an investment bank. Nor should they," he said decisively. "I want you all to know that this is a matter of life and death. I'm serious."

Then he dropped his bombshell, one that he had been contemplating for the entire morning. It was his ultimate doomsday scenario.

"Here's the drill," he continued. "We need to prepare right now for Lehman Brothers filing." Then he paused. "And for Merrill Lynch filing." He paused again. "And for AIG filing." Another pause. "And for Morgan Stanley filing." And after a final, even longer pause he added: "And potentially for Goldman Sachs filing."

There was a collective gasp on the phone.

As Dimon had presciently warned in his conference call, the following days would bring a near collapse of the financial system, forcing a government rescue effort with no precedent in modern history. In a period of less than eighteen months, Wall Street had gone from celebrating its most profitable age to finding itself on the brink of an epochal devastation. Trillions of dollars in wealth had vanished, and the financial landscape was entirely reconfigured. The calamity would definitively shatter some of the most cherished principles of capitalism. The idea that financial wizards had conjured up a new era of low-risk profits, and that American-style financial engineering was the global gold standard, was officially dead.

As the unraveling began, many on Wall Street confronted a market unlike any they had ever encountered—one gripped by a fear and disorder that no invisible hand could tame. They were forced to make the most critical decisions of their careers, perhaps of their lives, in the context of a confusing rush of rumors and policy shifts, all based on numbers that were little more than best guesses. Some made wise choices, some got lucky, and still others lived to regret their decisions. In many cases, it's still too early to tell whether they made the right choices.

In 2007, at the peak of the economic bubble, the financial services sector had become a wealth-creation machine, ballooning to more than 40 percent of total corporate profits in the United States. Financial products—including a new array of securities so complex that even many CEOs and boards of directors didn't understand them—were an ever greater driving force of the nation's economy. The mortgage industry was an especially important component of this system, providing loans that served as the raw material for Wall Street's elaborate creations, repackaging and then reselling them around the globe.

With all the profits that were being generated, Wall Street was minting a new generation of wealth not seen since the debt-fueled 1980s. Those who worked in the finance industry earned an astounding $53 billion in total compensation in 2007. Goldman Sachs, ranked at the top of the five leading brokerages at the onset of the crisis, accounted for $20 billion of that total, which worked out to more than $661,000 per employee. The company's chief executive officer, Lloyd Blankfein, alone took home $68 million.

Financial titans believed they were creating more than mere profits, however. They were confident that they had invented a new financial model that could be exported successfully around the globe. "The whole world is moving to the American model of free enterprise and capital markets," Sandy Weill, the architect of Citigroup, said in the summer of 2007, "Not having American financial institutions that really are at the fulcrum of how these countries are converting to a free-enterprise system would really be a shame."

But while they were busy evangelizing their financial values and producing these dizzying sums, the big brokerage firms had been bolstering their bets with enormous quantities of debt. Wall Street firms had debt to capital ratios of 32 to 1. When it worked, this strategy worked spectacularly well, validating the industry's complex models and generating record earnings. When it failed, however, the result was catastrophic.

The Wall Street juggernaut that emerged from the collapse of the dot-com bubble and the post-9/11 downturn was in large part the product of cheap money. The savings glut in Asia, combined with unusually low U.S. interest rates under former Federal Reserve chairman Alan Greenspan (which had been intended to stimulate growth following the 2001 recession), began to flood the world with money.

The crowning example of liquidity run amok was the subprime mortgage market. At the height of the housing bubble, banks were eager to make home loans to nearly anyone capable of signing on the dotted line. With no documentation a prospective buyer could claim a six-figure salary and walk out of a bank with a $500,000 mortgage, topping it off a month later with a home equity line of credit. Naturally, home prices skyrocketed, and in the hottest real estate markets ordinary people turned into specu-lators, flipping homes and tapping home equity lines to buy SUVs and power boats.

At the time, Wall Street believed fervently that its new financial products—mortgages that had been sliced and diced, or "securitized"—had diluted, if not removed, the risk. Instead of holding on to a loan on their own, the banks split it up into individual pieces and sold those pieces to investors, collecting enormous fees in the process. But whatever might be said about bankers' behavior during the housing boom, it can't be denied that these institutions "ate their own cooking"—in fact, they gorged on it, buying mountains of mortgage-backed assets from one another.

But it was the new ultra-interconnectedness among the nation's finan-cial institutions that posed the biggest risk of all. As a result of the banks owning various slices of these newfangled financial instruments, every firm was now dependent on the others—and many didn't even know it. If one fell, it could become a series of falling dominoes.

There were, of course, Cassandras in both business and academia who warned that all this financial engineering would end badly. While Profes-sors Nouriel Roubini and Robert J. Shiller have become this generation's much-heralded doomsayers, even as others made prescient predictions as early as 1994 that went unheeded.

"The sudden failure or abrupt withdrawal from trading of any of these large U.S. dealers could cause liquidity problems in the markets and could also pose risks to others, including federally insured banks and the finan-cial system as a whole," Charles A. Bowsher, the comptroller general, told a congressional committee after being tasked with studying a developing market known as derivatives. "In some cases intervention has and could result in a financial bailout paid for or guaranteed by taxpayers."

But when cracks did start to emerge in 2007, many argued even then that subprime loans posed little risk to anyone beyond a few mortgage firms. "The impact on the broader economy and the financial markets of the problems in the subprime markets seems likely to be contained," Ben S. Bernanke, the chairman of the Federal Reserve, said in testimony before Congress's Joint Economic Committee in March 2007.

By August 2007, however, the $2 trillion subprime market had collapsed, unleashing a global contagion. Two Bear Stearns hedge funds that made major subprime bets failed, losing $1.6 billion of their investors' money. BNP Paribas, France's largest listed bank, briefly suspended customer withdrawals, citing an inability to properly price its book of subprime-related bonds. That was another way of saying they couldn't find a buyer at any reasonable price.

In some ways Wall Street was undone by its own smarts, as the very complexity of mortgage-backed securities meant that almost no one was able to figure out how to price them in a declining market. (As of this writing, the experts are still struggling to figure out exactly what these assets are worth.) Without a price the market was paralyzed. And without access to capital, Wall Street simply could not function.

Bear Stearns, the weakest and most highly leveraged of the Big Five, was the first to fall. But everyone knew that even the strongest of banks could not withstand a full-blown investor panic, which meant that no one felt safe and no one was sure who else on the Street could be next.

It was this sense of utter uncertainty—the feeling Dimon expressed in his shocking list of potential casualties during his conference call—that made the crisis a once-in-a-lifetime experience for the men who ran these firms and the bureaucrats who regulated them. Until that autumn in 2008, they had only experienced *contained* crises. Firms and investors took their lumps and moved on. In fact, the ones who maintained their equilibrium and bet that things would soon improve were those who generally profited the most. This credit crisis was different. Wall Street and Washington had to improvise.

In retrospect, this bubble, like all bubbles, was an example of what, in his classic 1841 book, Scottish author Charles Mackay called "Extraordinary Popular Delusions and the Madness of Crowds." Instead of giving birth to a brave new world of riskless investments, the banks actually created a risk to the entire financial system.

But this book isn't so much about the theoretical as it is about real people, the reality behind the scenes, in New York, Washington, and overseas—in the offices, homes, and minds of the handful of people who controlled the economy's fate—during the critical months after Monday, March 17, 2008, when JP Morgan agreed to absorb Bear Stearns and when United States government officials eventually determined that it was necessary to undertake the largest public intervention in the nation's economic history.

For the past decade I have covered Wall Street and deal making for the *New York Times* and have been fortunate to do so during a period that has seen any number of remarkable developments in the American economy. But never have I witnessed such fundamental and dramatic changes in business paradigms and the spectacular self-destruction of storied institutions.

This extraordinary time has left us with a giant puzzle—a mystery, really—that still needs to be solved, so we can learn from our mistakes. This book is an effort to begin putting those pieces together.

At its core *Too Big to Fail* is a chronicle of failure—a failure that brought the world to its knees and raised questions about the very nature of capitalism. It is an intimate portrait of the dedicated and often baffled individuals who struggled—often at great personal sacrifice but just as often for self-preservation—to spare the world and themselves an even more calamitous outcome. It would be comforting to say that all the characters depicted in this book were able to cast aside their own concerns, whether petty or monumental, and join together to prevent the worst from happening. In some cases, they did. But as you'll see, in making their decisions, they were not immune to the fierce rivalries and power grabs that are part of the long-established cultures on Wall Street and in Washington.

In the end, this drama is a human one, a tale about the fallibility of people who thought they themselves were too big to fail.

CHAPTER ONE

The morning air was frigid in Greenwich, Connecticut. At 5:00 a.m. on March 17, 2008, it was still dark, save for the headlights of the black Mercedes idling in the driveway, the beams illuminating patches of slush that were scattered across the lawns of the twelve-acre estate. The driver heard the stones of the walkway crackle as Richard S. Fuld Jr. shuffled out the front door and into the backseat of the car.

The Mercedes took a right onto North Street toward the winding and narrow Merritt Parkway, headed for Manhattan. Fuld stared out the window in a fog at the rows of mansions owned by Wall Street executives and hedge fund impresarios. Most of the homes had been bought for eight-figure sums and lavishly renovated during the second Gilded Age, which, unbeknownst to any of them, least of all Fuld, was about to come to a crashing halt.

Fuld caught a glimpse of his own haggard reflection in the window. The deep creases under his tired eyes formed dark half-moons, a testament to the four meager hours of sleep he had managed after his plane had landed at Westchester County Airport just before midnight. It had been a hellish seventy-two hours. Fuld, the CEO of Lehman Brothers, the fourth-largest firm on Wall Street, and his wife, Kathy, were still supposed to be in India, regaling his billionaire clients with huge plates of *thali*, piles of *naan*, and palm wine. They had planned the trip for months. To his jet-lagged body, it was 2:00 in the afternoon.

Two days earlier he had been napping in the back of his Gulfstream, parked at a military airport near New Delhi, when Kathy woke him. Henry M. Paulson, the Treasury secretary, was on the plane's phone. From his office in Washington, D.C., some seventy-eight hundred miles away, Paulson told him that Bear Stearns, the giant investment bank, would either be sold or go bankrupt by Monday. Lehman was surely going to feel the reverberations. "You'd better get back here," he told Fuld. Hoping to return as quickly as possible, Fuld asked Paulson if he could help him get clearance from the government to fly his plane over Russia, shaving the flight time by at least five hours. Paulson chuckled. "I can't even get that for me," Paulson told him.

Twenty-six hours later, with stops in Istanbul and Oslo to refuel, Fuld was back home in Greenwich.

––––––

Fuld replayed the events of the past weekend over and over again in his mind: Bear Stearns, the smallest but scrappiest of Wall Street's Big Five investment houses, had agreed to be sold—*for $2 a fucking share!* And to no less than Jamie Dimon of JP Morgan Chase. On top of that, the Federal Reserve had agreed to take on up to $30 billion of losses from Bear's worst assets to make the deal palatable to Dimon. When Fuld first heard the $2 number from his staff in New York, he thought the airplane's phone had cut out, clipping off part of the sum.

Suddenly people were talking about a run on the bank as if it were 1929. When Fuld left for India on Thursday, there were rumors that panicky investors were refusing to trade with Bear, but he could never have imagined that its failure would be so swift. In an industry dependent on the trust of investors—investment banks are financed literally overnight by others on the assumption that they will be around the next morning—Bear's crash raised serious questions about his own business model. And the short-sellers, those who bet that a stock will go down, not up, and then make a profit once the stock is devalued, were pouncing on every sign of weakness, like Visigoths tearing down the walls of ancient Rome. For a brief moment on the flight back, Fuld had thought about buying Bear himself. Should he? *Could* he? No, the situation was far too surreal.

JP Morgan's deal for Bear Stearns was, he recognized, a lifesaver for the banking industry—and himself. Washington, he thought, was smart to have played matchmaker; the market couldn't have sustained a blow-up of that scale. The trust—the confidence—that enabled all these banks to pass billions of dollars around to one another would have been shattered. Federal Reserve chairman Ben Bernanke, Fuld also believed, had made a wise decision to open up, for the first time, the Fed's discount window to firms like his, giving them access to funds at the same cheap rate the government offers to big commercial banks. With this, Wall Street had a fighting chance.

Fuld knew that Lehman, as the smallest of the remaining Big Four, was clearly next on the firing line. Its stock had dropped 14.6 percent on Friday, at a point when Bear's stock was still trading at $30 a share. *Was this really happening?* Back in India, a little over twenty-four hours ago, he had marveled at the glorious extent of Wall Street's global reach, its colonization of financial markets all over the world. Was all this coming undone?

As the car made its way into the city, he rolled his thumb over the trackball on his BlackBerry as if it were a string of worry beads. The U.S. markets wouldn't open for another four and a half hours, but he could already tell it was going to be a bad day. The Nikkei, the main Japanese index, had already fallen 3.7 percent. In Europe rumors were rampant that ING, the giant Dutch bank, would halt trading with Lehman Brothers and the other broker-dealers, the infelicitous name for firms that trade securities on their own accounts or on behalf of their customers—in other words, the transactions that made Wall Street Wall Street.

Yep, he thought, *this is going to be a real shit-show.*

———

Just as his car merged onto the West Side Highway, heading south toward Midtown Manhattan, Fuld called his longtime friend, Lehman president Joseph Gregory. It was just before 5:30 a.m., and Gregory, who lived in Lloyd Harbor, Long Island, and had long since given up on driving into the city, was about to board his helicopter for his daily commute. He loved the ease of it. His pilot would land at the West Side Heliport, then a driver would shuttle him to Lehman Brothers' towering offices in Times Square. Door to door in under twenty minutes.

"Are you seeing this shit?" Fuld asked Gregory, referring to the carnage in the Asian markets.

While Fuld had been making his way back from India, Gregory had missed his son's lacrosse game in Roanoke, Virginia, to spend the weekend at the office organizing the battle plan. The Securities and Exchange Commission and the Federal Reserve had sent over a half dozen goons to Lehman's office to babysit the staff as they reviewed the firm's positions.

Fuld was deeply worried, Gregory thought, and not without reason.

But they had lived through crises before. *They'd survive*, he told himself. *They always did*.

The previous summer, when housing prices started to plummet and overextended banks cut back sharply on new lending, Fuld had proudly announced: "Do we have some stuff on the books that would be tough to get rid of? Yes. Is it going to kill us? Of course not." The firm seemed impregnable then. For three years Lehman had made so much money that it was being mentioned in the same breath as Goldman Sachs, Wall Street's great profit machine.

As Fuld's Mercedes sped across a desolate Fiftieth Street, sanitation workers were hauling crowd-control barriers over to Fifth Avenue for the St. Patrick's Day parade later that day. The car pulled into the back entrance of Lehman headquarters, an imposing glass-and-steel structure that may as well have been a personal monument to Fuld. He was, as Gregory often put it, "the franchise." He had led Lehman through the tragedy and subsequent disruptions of 9/11, when it had had to abandon its offices across the street from the World Trade Center and work out of hotel rooms in the Sheraton, before buying this new tower from Morgan Stanley in 2001. Wrapped in giant LED television screens, the building was a bit gauche for Fuld's taste, but with New York City's unstoppable real estate market, it had turned into a hell of an investment, and he liked that.

The daunting thirty-first executive floor, known around the firm as "Club 31," was nearly empty as Fuld stepped out of the elevator and walked toward his office.

After hanging his coat and jacket in the closet next to his private bathroom, he began his series of daily rituals, immediately logging on to his Bloomberg terminal and switching on CNBC. It was just after 6:00 a.m. One of his two assistants, Angela Judd or Shelby Morgan, would typically arrive in the office within the hour.

When he checked the futures market—where investors make bets on how stocks will perform when the markets open—the numbers hit him in the face: Lehman shares were down 21 percent. Fuld reflexively did the calculations: He had just personally lost $89.5 million on paper, and the market hadn't even opened.

On CNBC, Joe Kernen was interviewing Anton Schutz of Burnham

Asset Management about the fallout from the Bear Stearns deal and what it meant for Lehman.

"We've been characterizing Lehman Brothers as the front, or ground zero, for what's happening today," Kernen said. "What do you expect to see throughout the session?"

"I expect these investment banks to be weak," Schutz replied. "The reason is there's just this tremendous fear of mismarking of assets on balance sheets, and how could JP Morgan have gotten away with paying so little for Bear Stearns, and why did the Fed have to step up with $30 billion to take on some of the bad assets. I think there's a lot of question marks out here, and we're in need of a lot of answers."

Fuld watched with a stone face, mildly relieved when the conversation veered away from Lehman. Then it veered back. "What do you do if you're one of the thousands and thousands of Lehman employees watching every tick here today?" asked Kernen. "This is people on pins and needles."

Pins and needles? That didn't begin to describe it.

At 7:40 a.m. Hank Paulson called to check in. Dow Jones Newswire was reporting that DBS Group Holdings, the largest bank in Southeast Asia, had circulated an internal memo late the previous week ordering its traders to avoid new transactions involving Bear Stearns and Lehman. Paulson was concerned that Lehman might be losing trading partners, which would be the beginning of the end.

"We're going to be fine," Fuld said, reiterating what he had told him over the weekend about the firm's solid earnings report, which he planned to announce Tuesday morning. "That'll quiet down all this shit."

"Keep me updated," Paulson said.

———

An hour later tumult ruled on every trading floor in the city. Fuld stayed glued to the two Bloomberg screens on his desk as Lehman's stock opened: down 35 percent. Moody's reaffirmed its A1 rating on the investment bank's senior long-term debt, but the rating agency had also lowered its outlook to stable from positive. On the flight back from India, Fuld had debated with Gregory and Lehman's chief legal officer, Tom Russo, about whether to preannounce the firm's earnings today, before the market opened, instead of tomorrow, as originally planned. There was no compelling reason to wait. The earnings were going to be good. Fuld had been so confident that, before leaving for Asia, he had recorded an upbeat internal message to employees. But Russo had talked him out of moving up the earnings announcement, fearing that it might look desperate and ratchet up the anxiety.

As Lehman's stock continued to plummet, Fuld was second-guessing not only this decision but countless others. He had known for years that Lehman Brothers' day of reckoning could come—and worse, that it might sneak up on him. Intellectually, he understood the risks associated with cheap credit and borrowing money to increase the wallop of your bet—what is known on the Street as "leverage." But, like everyone else on Wall Street, he couldn't pass up the opportunities. The rewards of placing aggressively optimistic bets on the future were just too great. "It's paving the road with cheap tar," he loved to tell his colleagues. "When the weather changes, the potholes that were there will be deeper and uglier." Now here they were, potholes as far as the eye could see, and he had to admit, it was worse than he'd ever expected. But in his heart he thought Lehman would make it. He couldn't imagine it any other way.

———

Gregory took a seat in front of Fuld's desk, the two men acknowledging each other without uttering a word. Both leaned forward when CNBC ran a crawl along the bottom of the screen asking: "Who Is Next?"

"Goddamit," Fuld growled as they listened incredulously to one talking head after another deliver their firm's eulogy.

Within an hour, Lehman's stock had plunged by 48 percent.

"The shorts! The shorts!" Fuld bellowed. "That's what's happening here!"

Russo, who had canceled his family's vacation to Brazil, took the seat next to Gregory. A professorial sixty-five-year-old, he was one of Fuld's few other confidants in the firm besides Gregory. On this morning, however, he was fanning the flames, telling Fuld the latest rumor swirling around the trading floor: A bunch of "hedgies," Wall Street's disparaging nickname for hedge fund managers, had systematically taken down Bear Stearns by pulling their brokerage accounts, buying insurance against the bank—an instrument called a credit default swap, or CDS—and then shorting its stock. According to Russo's sources, a story making the rounds was that the group of short-sellers who had destroyed Bear had then assembled for a breakfast at the Four Seasons Hotel in Manhattan on Sunday morning, clinking glasses of mimosas made with $350 bottles of Cristal to celebrate their achievement. Was it true? Who knew?

The three executives huddled and planned their counterattack, starting with their morning meeting with nerve-racked senior managers. How could they change the conversation about Lehman that was going on all over Wall Street? Every discussion about Bear, it seemed, turned into one about Lehman. "Lehman may have to follow Bear into the confessional before Good Friday," Michael McCarty, an options strategist at Meridian Equity Partners in New York, told Bloomberg Television. Richard Bernstein, the respected chief investment strategist for Merrill Lynch, had sent out an alarming note to clients that morning: "Bear Stearns's demise should probably be viewed as the first of many," he wrote, tactfully not mentioning Lehman. "Sentiment is just beginning to catch on as to how broad and deep the credit market bubble has been."

By midmorning Fuld was getting calls from everybody—clients, trading partners, rival CEOs—all wanting to know what was going on. Some demanded reassurance; others offered it.

"Are you all right?" asked John Mack, the CEO of Morgan Stanley and an old friend. "What's going on over there?"

"I'm all right," Fuld told him. "But the rumors are flying. I've got two banks that won't take my name"—Wall Street–speak for the stupefying fact that the banks wouldn't trade with Lehman. The newest rumor was that Deutsche Bank and HSBC had stopped trading with the firm. "But we're fine. We've got lots of liquidity, so it's not a problem."

"Okay, we'll trade with you all day," Mack assured him. "I'll talk to my trader. Let me know if you need anything."

Fuld began reaching out to his key deputies for help. He called the London office and spoke to Jeremy Isaacs, who ran the firm's operation there. When he got off the phone with Fuld, Isaacs told his team, "I don't think we're going bust this afternoon, but I can't be one hundred percent sure about that. A lot of strange things are happening. . . ."

———

Despite his recent infatuation with leverage, Fuld believed in liquidity. He always had. You always needed a lot of cash on hand to ride out the storm, he would say. He liked to tell the story about how he once sat at a blackjack table and watched a "whale" of a gambler in Vegas lose $4.5 million, doubling every lost bet in hopes his luck would change. Fuld took notes on a cocktail napkin, recording the lesson he learned: "I don't care who you are. You don't have enough capital."

You can never have enough.

It was a lesson he had learned again in 1998 after the hedge fund Long-Term Capital Management blew up. In the immediate aftermath, Lehman was thought to be vulnerable because of its exposure to the mammoth fund. But it survived, barely, because the firm had a cushion of extra cash— and also because Fuld aggressively fought back. That was another take-away from the Long-Term Capital fiasco: You had to kill rumors. Let them live, and they became self-fulfilling prophecies. As he fumed to the *Washington Post* at the time, "Each and every one of these rumors was proved to be incorrect. If SEC regulators find out who started these stories, I'd like to have fifteen minutes with them first."

One of the people on Fuld's callback list that morning was Susanne Craig, a hard-nosed reporter at the *Wall Street Journal* who had been covering Lehman for years. Fuld liked Craig and often spoke to her on "background." But this morning she had called trying to convince him to be interviewed on the record. She pitched it as a way for him to silence the critics, to explain all the advance planning Lehman had done. Fuld, who hated reading about himself, thought it might be a good idea to participate. He regretted the way he had handled the media during the Long-Term Capital crisis. He wished he'd been more proactive from the start. "I want to do it right this time," he told her.

By noon, Fuld and his lieutenants had formulated a plan: They would give interviews to the *Wall Street Journal,* the *Financial Times*, and *Barron's*. They'd provide a little ticktock and color to Craig, about what was going on inside the firm, in the hopes that her editors would splash the story on the front page. They set up back-to-back sessions with the reporters starting at 3:00 p.m. The talking points were clear: The rumors were bogus. Lehman had ample liquidity, right up there with Goldman Sachs and Morgan Stanley. If the firm did need to make a payout, it was good for the money.

For the interview with Craig, Fuld was joined in a conference call by

Gregory, Russo, and Erin Callan, the company's new chief financial officer. "We learned we need a lot of liquidity and we also know we need to deal with rumors as they arise, not long after," Fuld told the reporter. He also stressed the fact that, with the Fed window now open, Lehman was on much stronger footing: "People are betting that the Fed can't stabilize the market, and I don't think that is a very good bet."

"We have liquidity," Gregory reiterated. "But while we don't need it right now, having it there alone sends a strong message about liquidity and its availability to everybody in the market." That remark skirted the catch-22 involved with the Fed's decision to make cheap loans available to firms like Lehman: Using it would be an admission of weakness, and no bank wanted to risk that. In fact, the Fed's move was intended more to reassure investors than to shore up banks. (Ironically, one of Lehman's own executives, Russo, could take partial credit for the strategy, as he had suggested it in a white paper he presented in Davos, Switzerland, at the annual capitalist ball known as the World Economic Forum, just two months earlier. Timothy F. Geithner, the president of the Federal Reserve Bank of New York, had been in the audience.)

After wrapping up the interview, Gregory and Callan returned to their offices and worked the phones, calling hedge funds that were rumored to be scaling back their trading with Lehman and doing everything they could to keep them on board.

The blitz paid off: In the last hour of trading, Lehman's stock made a U-turn: After falling nearly 50 percent earlier in the day, it closed down at only 19 percent, at $31.75. It was now at a four-and-half-year low, the gains of the boom years erased in a single day. But the executives were pleased with their efforts. Tomorrow they would release their earnings, and maybe that would keep the good momentum going. Callan would be walking investors through the report in a conference call, and she went back to Gregory's office to rehearse her lines.

Exhausted, Fuld got into his car to head back home and get a good night's sleep. Once again he found himself wishing that the renovations on the sixteen-room, full-floor apartment he and Kathy bought at 640 Park Avenue for $21 million were finished, but Kathy had decided to gut it. He settled into the backseat of the Mercedes, put down his BlackBerry, and enjoyed a few minutes of respite from the world.

No one would ever have voted Dick Fuld the most likely to rise to such levels on Wall Street.

As a freshman at the University of Colorado at Boulder in 1964, he seemed lost, struggling academically and unable to decide on a major. Looking for answers, he joined the Reserve Officers' Training Corps, the college-based, officer-commissioning program.

One morning during ROTC training, the commanding officer, a university senior, lined up all the students in the huge university quadrangle for a routine inspection.

"Fuld, your shoes aren't shined," the officer barked.

"Yes they are, sir," he began to answer. But before he could get the words out of his mouth, the officer stomped on Fuld's left shoe and sullied it. He ordered Fuld to go back to the dorm and shine it, which he did without complaint. When Fuld returned, the officer then stepped on his right foot—and again sent him back to the dorm.

By the time Fuld returned, the officer had turned his attention to the next person in line, a diminutive student. He placed his heavy army-issue boot on the young man's ankle and pressed hard, causing him to fall to the ground and cry out in pain. For good measure he thrust his knee in the boy's face, breaking his eyeglasses.

Fuld didn't know his classmate, but he had seen enough.

"Hey, asshole," he said to the commanding officer. "Why don't you pick on someone your own size?"

"Are you talking to me?" the senior asked, stepping up to within inches of Fuld's face.

"Yes," Fuld shot back without hesitation.

They soon came to blows, and in the end, both Fuld and the officer lay bloodied on the floor after other cadets had separated them. The eighteen-year-old Fuld was promptly hauled in front of the head of the ROTC program at the university and informed that he was being expelled. "You got into a fight with your commanding officer," an ROTC official told him. "That's not behavior becoming of a cadet."

"I understand that, sir, but I'd like you to hear my side of the story," Fuld protested. "You have to understand what happened."

"No, there's only one side to the story. You got into a fight with your commanding officer. That's all that matters. I can't have you in the program."

The ROTC was only the latest in a series of disappointments for Fuld, but it was also a sign that he was slowly coming into his own.

———

Richard Severin Fuld Jr. grew up in the wealthy suburb of Harrison in Westchester County, New York, where his family owned United Merchants & Manufacturers, a textile company whose annual revenue ultimately grew to $1 billion. United Merchants had been co-founded by his maternal grandfather, Jacob Schwab, in 1912 as the Cohn-Hall-Marx Company.

Because Fuld's father didn't want his son to go into the family business, Jacob Schwab, his grandfather, reached out to his longtime banking firm, a Wall Street outfit called Lehman Brothers, and secured his grandson a part-time summer position in its tiny Denver trading outpost in the summer of 1966. It was a three-person office, and Fuld did the chores—he spent most of his day copying documents (and this was the pre–copy machine era) and running errands. But the job was a revelation. Fuld loved what he saw. On the trading floor men yelled and worked with an intensity that he had never experienced before. *This is where I belong,* he thought. Dick Fuld had found himself.

What attracted him was not the fulfillment of some lifelong dream about playing with other people's money, but rather something far more visceral, something that instantly clicked. "I truly stumbled into investment banking," he acknowledged years later. "Once I got exposed to it, I discovered that I actually understood it, and all the pieces fit."

There was one person in the company, though, whom he didn't really like: Lewis L. Glucksman, a rough-hewn, sloppily dressed muckety-muck from headquarters who occasionally dropped by the Denver office, intimidating and speaking gruffly to the crew. As keen as he was on landing a job in finance, Fuld swore he'd never work for this tyrant.

After graduating from college a semester late, in February 1969, he rejoined Lehman as a summer intern, this time working at the firm's magnificent 1907 Italian Renaissance building at One William Street in the heart of Wall Street. He lived with his parents and commuted into the city. He worked on the desk that traded commercial paper—basically short-term IOUs used by companies to finance their day-to-day operations.

For Fuld, the job was perfect except for one significant detail: He reported to Glucksman, who picked up rattling him right where he had left off in Denver.

Fuld didn't mind all that much. He considered the job at Lehman temporary; he had eventually picked international business as his major at Colorado and was determined to get his MBA. Halfway through his summer internship, he walked up to Glucksman and asked if he would write a letter of recommendation for him.

"Why the fuck do you want to do that?" Glucksman growled. "People go to graduate school to get in a position to get a job. I'm offering you a job."

Fuld, however, wanted to stick to his plan.

"We don't get along," Fuld shot back. "You scream at me."

"Stay here and you won't have to work for me," Glucksman told him.

Fuld agreed to remain at Lehman as he pursued his degree from New York University at night. He continued doing menial tasks, one of which was operating the firm's latest technology—a video camera. One day he was taping an interview with Glucksman, when in the middle of the recording session, Glucksman asked, "Who's behind the camera?" Fuld poked his head out.

"What the hell are you doing?" he asked. "Come see me in my office first thing tomorrow morning."

When Fuld appeared in his office the following day, Glucksman told him that it was ridiculous that he was doing "all this menial bullshit. Why don't you just come work for me?"

"Do I get a raise?" asked Fuld.

The two became fast friends, and Fuld began his ascension at the firm. His salary was $6,000 a year, roughly 1/10,000 of what he'd take home as the firm's CEO some three decades later. By the end of the year, he was able to move out of his parents' house and rent a one-bedroom at 401 East Sixty-fifth Street for $250 a month. He drove to work in an orange Pontiac GTO, giving a lift to colleagues, including a young Roger C. Altman, who would later become the deputy Treasury secretary.

In Fuld, Glucksman saw himself as a young trader: "He didn't let his emotions get the best of his judgment," said Glucksman, who died in 2006.

"Dick understood buys when they were buys and sells when they were sells. He was a natural."

Every morning, as he walked onto the cramped trading floor, Fuld could feel his heart pounding with excitement. The noise. The swearing. Surviving by your wits alone. Trusting only your gut. He loved it all. As it happened, he had arrived at Lehman just as the firm was undergoing a major transformation that would benefit him enormously.

———

Since it was founded in 1850, Lehman Brothers has been a banker to an outsized share of twentieth-century business icons. Emanuel Lehman, who with his brothers, Henry and Mayer, emigrated from Bavaria in southern Germany just years earlier, had originally gone into business in Montgomery, Alabama, where they traded cotton, the country's cash crop before the Civil War. Twenty years later the three brothers set up shop in Manhattan, where they helped establish the New York Cotton Exchange. In New York, Lehman quickly morphed from a trading house to an invest-ment bank, helping finance start-ups such as Sears, Woolworth, Macy's, and RCA. (The rough equivalent today would be the bank behind Apple, Google, Microsoft, and Intel, if such a bank existed.)

Fuld's first year at the firm coincided with the death of its legendary senior partner, Emanuel's grandson, Robert Lehman, who had seen it through the crash of 1929 and turned it into a financial powerhouse in post-Depression America. The aristocratic, Yale-educated Lehman had reigned during the firm's glory years and was a banker to some of the biggest and most important U.S. corporations early in the American Cen-tury.

By the 1960s the firm's advisory banking business was second only to that of Goldman Sachs. But because Robert Lehman and the other partners hated the fact that corporate clients would have to go to Goldman for their financing needs, Lehman decided to start its own commercial paper-trad-ing operation, hiring Lewis Glucksman from the powerful Wall Street investment bank of A. G. Becker to run it.

When Fuld came on board, Glucksman's trading operation was begin-ning to account for a majority of the profits at Lehman. The trading space was noisy and chaotic, with overflowing ashtrays, cups of tepid coffee, and papers piled on the tops of terminals and under the telephones. Glucksman had the windows blacked out in a bid to re-create a Las Vegas casino atmosphere, with traders focused only on the Quotron and Telerate machines that were standard-issue on Wall Street then. Phones were thrown; wastebaskets were kicked. And as in a Vegas casino, a miasma of cigarette smoke hung everywhere. It was a galaxy away from the genteel world of the bankers, but it was increasingly what Lehman Brothers was all about.

———

Although Fuld stands no more than five feet ten inches tall, he has an intimidating presence, a definite asset in the kill-or-be-killed environment that Glucksman fostered. He has jet-black hair and a broad, dramatically angular forehead that hoods dark, deep-set, almost morose eyes. A fitness buff and a weightlifter, Fuld looked like someone you didn't want to take on in a fight, and he had the intensity to match. With his gaze fixed on the green early-generation computer screens in front of him, he would grunt out his trades in staccato, rapid-fire succession.

Within Lehman, Fuld earned a reputation as a single-minded trader who took guff from no one. One day he approached the desk of the floor's supervisor, Allan S. Kaplan (who would later become Lehman's vice chairman), to have him sign a trade, which was then a responsibility of supervisors. A round-faced man, cigar always in hand, Kaplan was on the phone when Fuld appeared and deliberately ignored him. Fuld hovered, furrowing his remarkable brow and waving his trade in the air, signaling loudly that he was ready for Kaplan to do his bidding.

Kaplan, cupping the receiver with his hand, turned to the young trader, exasperated. "You always think you're the most important," he exploded. "That nothing else matters but your trades. I'm not going to sign your fucking trades until every paper is off my desk!"

"You promise?" Fuld said, tauntingly.

"Yes," Kaplan said. "Then I'll get to it."

Leaning over, Fuld swept his arm across Kaplan's desk with a violent twist, sending dozens of papers flying across the office. Before some of them even landed, Fuld said, firmly but not loudly: "Will you sign it now?"

By this time, Fuld was known within the firm—and increasingly outside of it—as "The Gorilla," a nickname he didn't discourage. Years later, as the firm's chief executive, he even kept a stuffed gorilla in his office, where it remained until Lehman had to evacuate its Lower Manhattan headquarters across the street from what had been the World Trade Center on September 11, 2001.

———

Several years after he started at Lehman, Fuld noticed a fresh face on the mortgage desk. While Fuld was dark and brooding, the new guy was pale and affable. He quickly introduced himself—a gesture Fuld appreciated—sticking out his hand in a manner that suggested a person comfortable in his own skin: "Hi, I'm Joe Gregory." It was the start of an association that would endure for nearly four decades.

In terms of temperament, Gregory was Fuld's opposite—more personable, perhaps, and less confrontational. He looked up to Fuld, who soon became his mentor.

One day Fuld, who even as CEO upbraided executives over how they dressed, took his friend aside and told him he was sartorially objectionable. For Fuld, there was one acceptable uniform: pressed dark suit, white shirt, and conservative tie. Glucksman, he explained, could get away with soup stains on his tie and untucked shirt tail, but neither of them was Glucksman. Gregory set off to Bloomingdale's the following weekend for a wardrobe upgrade. "I was one of those people who didn't want to disappoint Dick," Gregory later told a friend.

Like Fuld, Gregory, a non–Ivy Leaguer who graduated from Hofstra University, had come to Lehman in the 1960s almost by accident. He had planned to become a high school history teacher, but after working a summer at Lehman as a messenger, he decided on a career in finance. By the 1980s Gregory and three other fast-track Lehman executives were commuting together from Huntington on the North Shore of Long Island. During the long early-morning ride, they discussed the trading strategies they'd try out on the floor that day. Within the firm the group was known as the "Huntington Mafia": They arrived with a consensus. They often stayed around after work and played pickup basketball at the company's gym.

Both Fuld and Gregory advanced quickly under Glucksman, who was himself a brilliant trader. Fuld was clearly Glucksman's favorite. Each morning Fuld and James S. Boshart—another rising star—would sit around with Glucksman reading his copy of the *Wall Street Journal*, with Glucksman providing the color commentary. His bons mots were known as Glucksmanisms. "Don't ever cuff a trade!" he'd say, meaning don't bother picking up the phone if you don't know the latest stock quote.

Glucksman's unkemptness, they had come to realize, was a political badge of sorts, for Glucksman seethed with resentment at what he regarded as the privileges and pretenses of the Ivy League investment bankers at the firm. The battle between bankers and traders is the closest thing to class warfare on Wall Street. Investment banking was esteemed as an art, while trading was more like a sport, something that required skill, but not necessarily brains or creativity. Or so the thinking went. Traders had always been a notch lower in the pecking order, even when they started to drive revenue growth. The combative Glucksman encouraged this us-against-them mentality among his trading staff. "Fucking bankers!"was a constant refrain.

Once, Glucksman heard that Peter Lusk, a successful banker in Lehman's Los Angeles office in the 1970s, had spent $368,000 to decorate his office with crystal chandeliers, wood-paneled walls, and a wet bar. Glucksman immediately got on a plane to the West Coast and went straight to Lusk's office, which was unoccupied when he showed up. Horrified by the decor, he rummaged around a secretary's desk, found a piece of paper, scribbled a message in block letters, and taped it on the door: "YOU'RE FIRED!"

He didn't leave it at that. Glucksman returned to the secretary's desk, grabbed another piece of paper, and wrote an addendum to his previous message, taping it right below: "And you will pay Lehman Brothers back every cent you spent on this office."

In 1983 Glucksman led one of Wall Street's most memorable coups, which ended with an immigrant—Glucksman was a second-generation Hungarian Jew—deposing one of the most connected leaders in the industry: Peter G. Peterson, a former commerce secretary in the Nixon administration. During their final confrontation, Glucksman looked Peterson in the eye and told him he could go easy or he could go hard, and Peterson, who went on to co-found the powerful Blackstone Group, went easy. Glucksman, who became more diplomatic with age, never liked talking about the clash. "That's kind of like talking about my first wife," he remarked years later.

Glucksman's tenure as the head of Lehman was short-lived. Eight months later, on April 10, 1984—a day Fuld called the darkest of his life— the company's seventeen-member corporate board voted to sell out to American Express for $360 million. It had been Peterson's loyalists who had initiated contact with American Express, making the deal, in effect, a countercoup. And it prevailed for more than a decade, until the original insurgents fought back and won.

Shearson Lehman, as the newly combined investment arm was known, involved merging Lehman with AmEx's retail brokerage operation, Shearson. The idea was to combine brains and brawn, but the relationship was troubled from the start. Perhaps the biggest mistake the corporate parent made was not immediately firing the Lehman managers who had made it clear that they thought the whole deal had been a big mistake. At the time of the merger, Fuld, who was already a member of Lehman's board, had been one of just three directors to oppose the sale. "I loved this place," he said in casting his dissenting vote.

Glucksman, Fuld, Gregory, and the rest of Glucksman's inner circle would spend the next decade fighting to preserve Lehman's autonomy and identity. "It was like a ten-year prison sentence," recalled Gregory. To encourage their solidarity, Glucksman summoned Fuld and his other top traders to a meeting in the firm's conference room. For reasons no one quite understood, Glucksman was holding a few dozen number 2 pencils in his hand. He handed each trader one and asked him to snap it in half, which everyone did, easily and without laughing or even smirking. He then handed a bunch of them to Fuld and asked him to try to break them all in half. Fuld, "The Gorilla," could not do it.

"Stay together, and you will continue to do great things," Glucksman told the group after this Zenlike demonstration.

Lehman's traders and executives chafed at being part of a financial supermarket—the very name suggested something common. To make things worse, the new management structure bordered on byzantine. Fuld was named co-president and co-chief operating officer of Shearson Lehman Brothers Holdings in 1993, along with J. Tomilson Hill. They reported to a Shearson chief executive, who reported to American Express' chief, Harvey Golub. A Fuld protégé, T. Christopher Pettit, ran the investment banking and trading division. No one really knew who was in charge, or, for that matter, if anyone was in charge at all.

When a red-faced AmEx finally spun off Lehman in 1994, the firm was undercapitalized and focused almost entirely on trading bonds. Stars like Stephen A. Schwarzman, the future CEO of Blackstone, had left the company. No one expected it to survive for long as an independent firm; it was just takeover bait for a much larger bank.

American Express CEO Harvey Golub anointed Fuld, who was Shearson Lehman's top trader and had risen to be co-president and chief executive of the newly independent entity. Fuld had his work cut out for him. Lehman was reeling, with net revenue plunging by a third when the Shearson units were sold; investment banking was down by nearly the same amount. They were bailing water.

And the infighting continued. By 1996 Fuld had pushed out Pettit when he made noises about increasing his status. (Pettit died three months later in a snowmobile accident.) For years, Fuld operated the firm alone, until he appointed Gregory and another colleague, Bradley Jack, to the role of co-COO in 2002. But Jack was quickly pushed out by Gregory, who had the confidence of Fuld, in part because of his talent and, perhaps more important, because he appeared nonthreatening.

"You're the best business fixer I have," Fuld told him, vowing that with Gregory's help he would do away with the backbiting that had nearly torn the firm apart in the 1980s. Fuld began by slashing payroll. By the end of 1996, the staff had shrunk by 20 percent, to around 7,500 employees. At the same time that he was downsizing, he was adopting a smoother management style. To his own surprise Fuld proved to be good at massaging egos, wooing new talent, and, perhaps most shocking for a trader, schmoozing clients. As Fuld recast himself as the public face of the firm, Gregory became the chief operating officer: "Inside" to Fuld's "Mr. Outside." Yes, Fuld had become one of the "fucking bankers," intently focused on one goal: boosting the newly public company's stock price. Lehman shares were increasingly doled out to employees; eventually the workforce owned a third of the firm. "I want my employees to act like owners," Fuld told his managers.

To encourage teamwork, he adopted a point system similar to the one that he used to reward his son, Richie, when he played hockey. Fuld taped his son's games and would inform him, "You get one point for a goal, but two points for an assist." He had some other choice paternal advice for his son that he also applied at Lehman: "If one of your teammates gets attacked, fight back like hell!" At Lehman, senior executives were compensated based on the performances of their team.

If you were loyal to Fuld, he was loyal to you. Almost everyone at Lehman had heard the story about his vacation with James Tisch, the chief executive of Loews, and his family. The group went hiking together in Bryce Canyon National Park in Utah. Nearly a mile down from the rim of the canyon, Tisch's ten-year-old son, Ben, had an asthma attack and began panicking when he realized he had left his inhaler back on top of the canyon.

Fuld and Tisch took charge, helping the boy to make the hike back. "Ben, lead the way," Fuld instructed, trying to build up the boy's confidence.

Halfway up they encountered another hiker who looked at Ben and said, "My, aren't we wheezy today."

Fuld, without slowing, turned on him and shouted with a memorable ferocity: "Eat shit and die! Eat shit and die!"

Exhilarated by Fuld's defense of him, Ben nearly ran up the rest of the way.

Perhaps Fuld's greatest moment as a leader came after the 9/11 attacks. As the world was literally crumbling around him he instilled a spirit of camaraderie that helped keep the firm together. The day after the towers were hit, Fuld attended a meeting at the New York Stock Exchange to discuss when it should reopen. Asked if Lehman would be able to trade, he told the room, almost on the verge of tears, "We don't even know who's alive."

In the final reckoning, Lehman lost only one employee. But the firm's global headquarters at 3 World Financial Center was so severely damaged it was unusable. Fuld set up makeshift offices for his 6,500 employees at a Sheraton hotel on Seventh Avenue in Midtown; a few weeks later he personally negotiated a deal to buy a building from one of his archrivals, Morgan Stanley, which had never moved into its new headquarters. Within a month Lehman Brothers was up and running in a new location as if nothing at all had happened. But there was one casualty of the move: Fuld's stuffed gorilla was lost in the shuffle and never replaced. Gregory later pointed out that both Fuld and the firm had outgrown it.

———

For all his talk about change, however, Fuld did not so much overhaul Lehman's corporate culture as tweak it. He instituted a subtler version of the paranoid, combative worldview propagated by Glucksman. The martial metaphors remained: "Every day is a battle," Fuld barked at his executives. "You have to kill the enemy." But traders and bankers were no longer at each other's throats, and for a while, at least, Lehman was less riven by internal strife. "I tried to train investment bankers to understand the products they were selling," Glucksman said long after Fuld had gone on to be CEO. "We were one of the first firms to put investment bankers on the trading floor—and Dick has gone far beyond where I was when I left the firm."

Fuld eventually decided that Lehman was too conservative, too dependent on trading bonds and other debts; seeing the enormous profits that Goldman Sachs made by investing its own money, he wanted the firm to branch out. It fell on Gregory to execute the boss's vision. Though he was not by nature a details guy or a risk manager, Gregory played a pivotal role in the firm's increasingly aggressive bets, pushing Lehman into commercial real estate, mortgages, and leveraged lending. And in a galloping bull market, its profits and share price soared to unprecedented heights; Gregory was rewarded with $5 million in cash and $29 million in stock in 2007. (Fuld made a package worth $40 million that year.)

Gregory also handled Fuld's less desirable conversations. Whenever a personnel matter called for discipline, the rebuke usually came from Gregory; the person on the receiving end invariably referred to the "new asshole" he had just been provided. Around the office, Gregory was known as "Darth Vader." Though Fuld was unaware of it, Gregory's heavy-handed tactics were regular fodder at the water cooler.

In 2005 Gregory made one of his harshest personnel decisions, one that would become legend within the firm. He inexplicably sidelined his protégé and longtime favorite, Robert Shafir, Lehman's global head of equities, who had helped him build that business, for what seemed like no reason.

Gregory, who said he'd find him another role at the firm, then kicked him off the firm's executive committee. In case Shafir hadn't gotten the message, Gregory then gave him an office right across from the conference room where the executive committee met, a cruel reminder of his diminished status. In the middle of all this, Shafir's daughter was diagnosed with cystic fibrosis, and he took some time off, hoping that when he returned to the firm, Gregory might have a job for him.

But when Shafir failed to resign after a few months, Gregory called him into his office. "What do you think about moving to Asia?" he asked him after an awkward silence.

Shafir was dumbstruck. "Asia? You have to be kidding, Joe. You know about my kid, you know I can't go to Asia."

Shafir left the firm for Credit Suisse, perhaps the most notorious victim of what people inside Lehman referred to as a "Joeicide."

Some of Gregory's hiring decisions, meanwhile, struck people as highly unorthodox. In 2005, he took the firm's head of fixed income, Bart McDade, who was an expert in the world of debt, and made him the head of equities, a business he knew very little about. In 2007, as the property bubble neared the breaking point, Gregory was asked repeatedly why so many of the executives he placed in the commercial real estate business had no background in that area. "People need broad experience," Gregory explained. "It's the power of the machine. It's not the individual."

Of all the individuals whom Gregory anointed, none was more controversial than Erin Callan, a striking blonde who favored *Sex and the City*-style stilettos. When he chose the forty-one-year-old Callan as the firm's new chief financial officer in September 2007, Lehman insiders were stunned. Callan was obviously bright, but she knew precious little about the firm's treasury operations and had no background in accounting whatsoever. Another woman at the firm, Ros Stephenson—perhaps the only Lehman banker besides Fuld who could get Kohlberg Kravis Roberts kingpin Henry Kravis on the phone—was furious about the appointment and took her complaint directly to Dick Fuld, who, as always, backed Gregory.

Callan yearned to prove to her colleagues that she was a seasoned street fighter, just like Fuld. If anything, her path to the very top of the financial industry had been even more improbable than his. One of three daughters of a New York City police officer, she graduated from NYU Law School in

1990 and took a job working for the big Wall Street firm of Simpson Thacher & Bartlett as an associate in its tax department. Lehman Brothers was a major client.

After five years at Simpson, she took a chance one day and phoned her contact at Lehman: "Would it be weird for someone like me to work on Wall Street?" she asked.

No, it would not. Hired by Lehman, she caught a break early on when a change in the tax law sparked a boom in securities that were taxed as if they were debt. Callan, with her tax law expertise, became adept at structuring these complex investments for clients like General Mills. Savvy, confident, and a skillful pitchwoman, she quickly catapulted up the ranks, overseeing the firm's global finance solutions and global finance analytic groups within a few years. Hedge funds were becoming top Wall Street clients, and in 2006 Callan was entrusted with the critical job of overseeing the firm's investment banking relationships with them.

In this role, she solidified her reputation as a player by helping Fortress Investment Group become the first American manager of hedge funds and private-equity funds to go public; she later oversaw the initial public offering of another fund, the Och-Ziff Capital Management Group. For Lehman's most important hedge fund client, Ken Griffin's Citadel Investment Group, she orchestrated the sale of $500 million worth of five-year bonds, a groundbreaking offering by a hedge fund.

She soon caught the eye of Joe Gregory, an executive who believed strongly in the value of diversity. He recognized that the world was changing and that Lehman, as well as the rest of the financial community, could no longer be a sanctuary for white men only. Promoting someone who was young and smart—*and* a woman—would be good for Lehman and would reflect well on him. It didn't hurt that Callan looked great on television.

———

On the night of March 17, in her apartment at the Time Warner Center, Erin Callan endlessly tossed and turned. The next day was going to be the biggest of her career, a chance to single-handedly extinguish the flames threatening to engulf Lehman—and to prove her critics inside the firm wrong.

In just a few hours Callan would represent Lehman Brothers—to the market, to the world. She would run the crucial conference call detailing the firm's quarterly results. Scores of financial analysts from around the nation would be listening in; many of them would be ready to shred Lehman at the slightest sign of weakness. After presenting Lehman's numbers, there'd be questions, and given all that was going on, there'd probably be a few very tough ones that would force Callan to think on her feet. Her answers might literally make or break the firm.

Finally giving up on getting any sleep, she rolled out of bed and grabbed the *Wall Street Journal* outside her apartment door. The page-one story did nothing to alleviate her nerves; its headline read: "Lehman Finds Itself in Center of a Storm," and it featured her as one of the main Lehman executives fighting back rumors about the firm's failing health. But she liked the press.

Despite her fatigue, Callan was fired up, adrenaline coursing through her slender body. She dashed downstairs, coffee in hand, dressed in an elegant black suit picked out by her personal shopper at Bergdorf Goodman. She had blown her hair out for an appearance later that day on *Closing Bell with Maria Bartiromo* on CNBC.

She waited for her driver under the awning of the Time Warner Center. She was hoping her place there would be only temporary. With her new job title and expected income, she had been looking to upgrade and was in negotiations to buy her dream home: a 2,400-square-foot apartment on the thirty-first floor of 15 Central Park West, one of the most coveted addresses in New York City. The limestone building, designed by Robert A. M. Stern, was the new home to such storied financiers as Goldman Sachs' Lloyd Blankfein, Citigroup's legendary Sanford Weill, hedge fund maestro Daniel Loeb, and the rock star Sting. She was planning to borrow $5 million to pay for the $6.48 million space. As she entered the backseat of the company car, she reflected on how much was at stake this morning—including the new apartment she wanted.

In his office at Lehman, Dick Fuld steadied his nerves and got ready to watch Treasury secretary Paulson live on CNBC. He reached for the remote and turned up the volume. Matt Lauer of the *Today* show was conducting the interview, simulcast on both NBC and CNBC.

"I don't want to make too much of words," Lauer began, "but I would like to talk to you about the president's words that he used on Monday after meeting with you. He said, 'Secretary Paulson gave me an update, and it's clear that we're in challenging times.'"

Paulson, looking sleep deprived, was standing in the White House pressroom, straining to listen to the question coming through in his right ear.

Lauer continued: "I want to contrast that to what Alan Greenspan wrote in an article recently," he said. A photo of Greenspan flashed on the screen accompanying his quote: "The current financial crisis in the U.S. is likely to be judged in retrospect as the most wrenching since the end of the Second World War."

"Doesn't 'we're in challenging times' seem like the understatement of the year?" Lauer asked, in his polite but persistent style.

Paulson stammered for a moment, then recovered and continued with what he clearly hoped was a soothing message. "Matt, there's turbulence in our capital markets, and it's been going on since August. We're all over it, we're looking for ways to work our way through it. I've got great confidence in our markets, they're resilient, they're flexible, but this has taken some time and we're focused on it."

Fuld waited with growing impatience for Lauer to ask about the implications of the Bear Stearns bailout. "The Fed took some extraordinary steps over the weekend to deal with the Bear Stearns situation," Lauer finally said. "It has some people asking: 'Does the Fed react more strongly to what's happening on Wall Street than they do to what's happening to people in pain across the country, the so-called people who live on Main Street?'"

An exasperated Fuld thought Lauer's question was just another example of the popular media's tendency to frame complex financial issues in terms of class warfare, pitting Wall Street—and Paulson, Goldman's former CEO—against the nation's soccer moms, the *Today* show's audience.

Paulson paused as he searched for his words. "Let me say that the Bear Stearns situation has been very painful for the Bear Stearns shareholders, so I don't think that they think that they've been bailed out here." He was obviously trying to send a message: The Bush administration isn't in the business of bailouts. Period.

Then Lauer, quoting from the front page of the *Wall Street Journal*, asked, "'Has the government set a precedent for propping up failing financial institutions at a time when its more traditional tools don't appear to be working?' In other words, they're saying, is this now the wave of the future, Mr. Secretary? That financial institutions that get in trouble in the future turn to the government to get bailed out?"

It was a particularly poignant question; only nights before Paulson had railed on a conference call with all the Wall Street CEOs about "moral hazard"—that woolly economic term that describes what happens when risk takers are shielded from the consequences of failure; they might take ever-greater risks.

"Well, again, as I said, I don't believe the Bear Stearns shareholders feel they've been bailed out right now," Paulson repeated. "The focus is clearly, all of our focus is on what's best for the American people and how to minimize the impact of the disruption in the capital markets."

———

When she sat down at her desk Callan turned on her Bloomberg terminal and waited for Goldman Sachs to announce its results for the quarter, which the market would take as a rough barometer of the shape of things to come. If Goldman did well, it could give Lehman an added boost.

When Goldman's numbers popped up on her screen, she was delighted. They were solid: $1.5 billion in profits. Down from $3.2 billion, but who wasn't down from a year ago? Goldman handily beat expectations. So far, so good.

That morning, Lehman Brothers had already sent out a press release summarizing its first-quarter results. As Callan knew, of course, the numbers were confidence inspiring. The firm was reporting earnings of $489 million, or 81 cents per share, off 57 percent from the previous quarter but higher than analyst forecasts.

The first news-service dispatches on the earnings release were positive. "Lehman kind of confounded the doomsayers with these numbers," Michael Holland, of Holland & Company, the private investment firm, told Reuters. Michael Hecht, an analyst with Bank of America Securities, called the quarterly results "all in all solid."

At 10:00 a.m., a half hour after the market opened, Callan entered the boardroom on the thirty-first floor. Though Lehman's results were already calming market fears, a great deal was still riding on her performance.

Surely everyone listening in would ask the same questions: How was Lehman different from Bear Stearns? How strong was its liquidity position? How was it valuing its real estate portfolio? Could investors really believe Lehman's "marks" (the way the firm valued its assets)? Or was Lehman playing "mark-to-make-believe"?

Callan had answers to all of them. She had prepped and studied and gone through dry runs. She had even rehearsed the numbers for a roomful of Securities and Exchange officials—hardly the easiest crowd—over the weekend, and they had left satisfied. She knew the numbers cold; she knew by heart the story that needed to be told. And she knew how to tell it.

The markets roared their approval of the earnings report. Shares of Lehman surged while the credit spreads tightened. Investors now perceived the risk that the firm would fail had diminished. All that had to happen now was for Callan to supply the punctuation. She took a sip of water. Her voice was raspy after talking nonstop for four straight days.

"All set?" asked Ed Grieb, Lehman's director of investor relations.

Callan nodded and began.

"There's no question the last few days have seen unprecedented volatility, not only in our sector but also across the whole marketplace," she said into the speakerphone, as dozens of financial analysts listened. Her voice was calm and steady. For the next thirty minutes she ran through the numbers for Lehman's business units, carefully elucidating the specifics, or, in the jargon of Wall Street, providing the "color." She put particular emphasis on the firm's efforts to reduce leverage and increase liquidity. She spelled it all out in painstaking, mind-numbing detail.

It was a stellar presentation. The analysts on the call seemed impressed by Callan's candor, her command of the facts, her assuredness, and her willingness to acknowledge the outstanding problems.

But she wasn't finished yet; next came the questions. First up was Meredith Whitney, an analyst with Oppenheimer, who had made her name as an unsparing banking critic the previous fall with the accurate prediction that Citigroup would be forced to cut its dividend. Callan, as well as every other Lehman executive in the room, held their breaths as they waited for Whitney to start probing. "You did a great job, Erin," Whitney said, to everyone's amazement. "I really appreciate the disclosure. I'm sure everyone does."

Callan, trying hard not to show her relief, knew then that she had pulled it off. If Whitney was buying it, all was well. As they spoke, shares of Lehman continued spiking. The markets were buying it, too. The stock would end the day up $14.74, or 46.4 percent, to $46.49, for the biggest one-day gain in the stock since it went public in 1994. William Tanona, an analyst with Goldman Sachs, raised his rating on Lehman to "buy" from "neutral."

When the session ended, the excitement at Lehman was palpable. Gregory rushed over to give Callan a big hug. Fuld was ecstatic. "The only complaint I have is that you shouldn't have hung up on the call. Because as long as you were on there, the stock kept coming up," he told her. Later, as she went down to the bond-trading floor, she passed by the desk of Peter Hornick, the firm's head of collateralized debt obligation sales and trading. He held out his palm, and she slapped him a high five.

For a brief, shining moment, all seemed well at Lehman Brothers.

———

Outside Lehman, however, skeptics were already voicing their concerns. "I still don't believe any of these numbers because I still don't think there is proper accounting for the liabilities they have on their books," Peter Schiff, president and chief global strategist of Euro Pacific Capital, told the *Washington Post*. "People are going to find out that all these profits they made were phony."

Across town, a prescient young hedge fund manager named David Einhorn, who had just gotten off a red-eye flight from Los Angeles and had raced to his office to listen to the call that morning, was coming to the same conclusion: *Lehman was a house of cards.* He was one of those "hedgies" investors Fuld had railed about. And he was so influential, he could move markets just by uttering a sentence. He had already bet big money that the firm was more vulnerable than Callan was letting on, and he was getting ready to share his opinion with the world.

CHAPTER TWO

In a leafy enclave of northwest Washington, D.C., Hank Paulson was pacing back and forth in his living room, his cell phone sitting in its usual place, against his ear. It was Easter Sunday, exactly one week after the takeover of Bear Stearns, and Paulson had promised his wife, Wendy, that they'd take a bicycle ride in Rock Creek Park, the large public space that bisects the capital, just down the road from their home. She had been annoyed with him all weekend for spending so much time on the phone.

"Come on, just for an hour," she said, trying to coax him out of the house. He finally relented; it was the first time in more than a week that he would try to take his mind off work.

Until his phone rang again.

Seconds later, after hearing what the caller had to say, the Treasury secretary exclaimed, "That makes me want to vomit!"

It was Jamie Dimon on his speakerphone from his wood-paneled office on the eighth floor of JP Morgan's headquarters in Midtown Manhattan, overlooking a barren Park Avenue. He had just told Paulson something the Treasury secretary didn't want to hear: Dimon had decided to "recut" his $2-a-share deal for Bear Stearns and raise the price to $10.

The news wasn't completely unexpected. Paulson, who could be relentless, had phoned Dimon virtually every day that week (interrupting his early-morning treadmill jog at least once), and based on those conversations, he knew a higher price for Bear was a possibility. In the days since announcing the deal, both men had become justifiably worried that disgruntled Bear shareholders would vote down the deal in protest of the low price, creating another run on the firm.

But Dimon's decision still roiled Paulson. He had expected that if Dimon did raise the price, he'd hike it by no more than a few dollars—up to $8 a share, say, but not into double digits.

"That's more than we talked about," replied Paulson, who was now whispering into the phone in his unmistakable raspy voice, hardly able to believe what he was hearing. Just a week earlier, when Dimon had indicated that he was prepared to pay $4 a share, Paulson had privately instructed him to lower the price: "I could see something nominal, like one or two dollars per share," he had said. The fact was, Bear was insolvent without the government's offer to backstop $29 billion of its debt, and Paulson did not want to be seen as a patsy, bailing out his friends on Wall Street.

"I can't see why they're getting anything," he told Dimon.

So far, nobody other than Dimon knew that the Treasury secretary of the United States of America was behind the original paltry sale price, and Paulson wanted to keep it that way. Like most conservatives, he still honored the principle of "the invisible hand"—that widely held, neoclassical economic notion that official intervention was at best a last resort.

As a former CEO himself, Paulson understood Dimon's position perfectly well. He, too, wanted to restore calm to the markets, for it had been a nail-biter of a week. After the $2-a-share purchase price had been announced, Bear's shareholders and employees had practically revolted, threatening to upend not just the deal but also the entire market. And in the hastily arranged merger agreement, Dimon had found a glaring error, which he blamed on his lawyers, Wachtell, Lipton, Rosen & Katz: Bear's shareholders could vote against the deal, and JP Morgan would still be on the hook to guarantee its trades for an entire year.

Dimon recounted to Paulson how Ed Moldaver, a longtime broker at Bear—"an asshole," in Dimon's estimation—had publicly mocked him during a meeting Dimon had called to explain the transaction to Bear employees. "This isn't a shotgun marriage," Moldaver scowled in front of hundreds of Bear staffers. "This is more like a rape."

In Washington, Paulson now revealed to Dimon that he was facing a similar revolt, for most people in government thought everyone on Wall Street was greedy and overpaid, and bailing them out was about as popular a notion as raising taxes. "I'm getting it from all sides," he confided.

To make matters worse, it was a presidential election year. On Monday, a day after the Bear Stearns deal was announced, Democratic candidate Senator Hillary Clinton, who at the time had a slight lead in national polls, criticized the bailout, going so far as to link the Bush administration's rescue of Bear Stearns to the problems in Iraq.

Barney Frank, the Democratic chairman of the House Financial Services Committee, was every bit as harsh. He, too, turned the deal into an indictment of Paulson's boss, President Bush. "All these years of deregulation by the Republicans and the absence of regulation as these new financial instruments have grown have allowed them to take a large chunk of the economy hostage," Frank complained. "And we have to pay ransom, like it or not."

While attacking the rescue plan was one of the few completely bipartisan affairs in town, the Republicans hated it for different reasons. The conservatives believed that the marketplace would take care of everything, and that any government intervention was bound to make things worse. "First, do no harm!" they'd say, quoting Hippocrates' *Epidemics*. A little blood might be spilled, but creative destruction was one of the costs of capitalism. Moderate Republicans, meanwhile, were inundated with complaints from their constituents, who wondered why the parties responsible for decimating their 401(k)s deserved any taxpayer money at all.

Everyone was calling it a "bailout"—a word Paulson hated. As far as he was concerned, he had just helped save the American economy. It was a bailout in the literal sense of bailing water out of a sinking boat, not a handout. He didn't understand why no one in Washington could see that distinction.

At some level, though, he knew there would be hell to pay, no matter how correct his prognosis proved to be. While the president publicly praised him and the deal, Bush, privately, was livid. The president understood the necessity of the bailout, but he also appreciated how it would be politicized. "We're gonna get killed on this, aren't we?" he had asked Paulson, knowing full well that the answer was yes.

Paulson didn't need to be reminded where the president stood on the issue. The Wednesday before the Bear deal, Paulson had spent the afternoon in the Oval Office advising Bush on the speech he would give that coming Friday to the Economic Club of New York at the Hilton Hotel.

Bush had included a line in his remarks asserting that there would be no bailouts.

"Don't say that," Paulson insisted, looking over the draft.

"Why?" Bush asked. "We're not going to have a bailout."

Paulson broke the bad news to him: "You may need a bailout, as bad as that sounds."

All in all, the situation had become Paulson's worst nightmare: The economy had turned into a political football, his reputation was on the line, and he was stuck playing by Washington rules.

———

Henry Paulson's understanding of how things worked in the nation's capital was part of the reason he had turned down the job of Treasury secretary not once, but twice in the spring of 2006. He knew Washington; his first job after college had been at the Defense Department, and he had worked in the Nixon White House for a number of years after that. So he appreciated the risks that the job presented. "I will get down here and I won't be able to work with these people, and I'll leave with a bad reputation. Look at what people said about Snow and O'Neill!" he said. His predecessors, John Snow and Paul O'Neill, had both come to Washington as wizards of their respective industries but had departed with their legacies tarnished.

He agonized for months before making his decision. As far as he was concerned, he already had the best job in the world: CEO of Goldman Sachs, the most revered institution on Wall Street. As its chief executive, Paulson traveled around the world, focusing much of his attention on China, where he had become something of an unofficial U.S. Ambassador of Capitalism, arguably forging deeper relationships with Chinese leaders than had anyone in Washington, including the secretary of State, Condoleezza Rice.

Joshua Bolten, President Bush's new chief of staff, was pushing especially hard for Paulson to come on board. He had convinced the president that Paulson's close ties in China could be a huge plus, given the rapid and geopolitically significant rise of the Chinese economy. Professionally, Bolten knew Paulson well. A former Goldman Sachs insider himself, he had worked for the firm as a lobbyist in London in the 1990s and served briefly as the chief of staff to Jon Corzine, when he headed the firm.

But Bolten wasn't making any headway with Paulson—or the Paulson family, for that matter. It didn't help that Paulson's wife, Wendy, could not stand the president's politics, even though her husband had been a "pioneer" for Bush in 2004—a designation given to those who raised more than $100,000 for the president's reelection campaign. His mother, Marianna, was so aghast at the idea that she cried. "You started with Nixon and you're going to end with Bush? Why would you do such a thing?" she sobbed. Paulson's son, a National Basketball Association executive, and daughter, a reporter for the *Christian Science Monitor*, were also initially against his making the move.

Another key doubter was Paulson's mentor, John Whitehead. A former Goldman chairman and a father figure to many at the bank who had served in the State Department under Reagan, Whitehead thought it would be a big mistake. "This is a failed administration," he insisted. "You'll have a hard time getting anything accomplished."

In an interview in April, Paulson was still dismissing talk that he was a candidate for Treasury secretary, telling the *Wall Street Journal*, "I love my job. I actually think I've got the best job in the business world. I plan to be here for a good while."

Meanwhile, Bolten kept pushing. Toward the end of April, Paulson accepted an invitation to meet with the president. But Goldman's chief of staff, John F. W. Rogers, who had served under James Baker in both the Reagan and G.H.W. Bush administrations, urged him not to attend the meeting unless he was going to accept the position. "You do not go to explore jobs with the president," he told Paulson. Rogers's point was impossible to dispute, so Paulson awkwardly called to send his regrets.

Paulson and his wife, however, did attend a luncheon at the White House that month for President Hu Jintao of China. After the meal they took a stroll in the capital, and as they walked past the Treasury Building, Wendy turned to him.

"I hope you didn't turn it down because of me," she said. "Because if you really wanted to do it, it's okay with me."

"No, that's not why I turned it down."

Despite his reluctance, others believed Paulson's decision was not quite final, and Rogers, for one, thought his boss secretly did want the job. On the first Sunday afternoon of May, he found himself fretting in his home in Georgetown, wondering whether he had given Paulson bad advice. He finally picked up the phone and called Bolten. "I know Hank told you no," he told him, "but if the president really wants him, you should ask him again."

When Bolten called and repeated his pitch, Paulson wondered whether his resistance to the overtures was really a matter of a fear of failure. At Goldman he was known as someone who "runs to problems." Was he now running away from them?

Paulson is a devout Christian Scientist and, like most members of the faith, he deeply admires the writings of Mary Baker Eddy, who, seeking to reclaim early Christianity's focus on healing, founded the First Church of Christ, Scientist, in Boston in 1879. "Fear is the fountain of sickness," she wrote. Fear "must be cast out to readjust the balance for God."

Paulson was already having second thoughts about turning down the Treasury job when James Baker followed up on Bolten's call. Baker, the GOP's éminence grise, confided to him that he had told the president that Paulson was by far the best candidate for the position. Deeply flattered, Paulson assured him that he was giving the idea serious consideration.

That same week, John Bryan, the chief executive of Sara Lee and a longtime friend, Goldman director, and client of Paulson's from when he was an investment banker in Chicago, offered him this advice: "Hank, life is not a dress rehearsal," he said. "You don't want to be sitting around at eighty years old telling your grandchildren you were once asked to be secretary of the Treasury. You should tell them you did it."

Paulson finally accepted the position on May 21, but because the White House did not plan to announce the appointment until the following week after running a background check, he was left in the awkward predicament of attending the annual meeting of Goldman partners that weekend in Chicago without being able to tell anyone that he was resigning. (Ironically enough, the guest speaker that day was the junior senator from Illinois, Barack Obama.) But with the newspapers—not to mention his colleagues—still speculating about whether he would join the administration, Paulson hid upstairs in his hotel room throughout the event.

On Wall Street, there are two kinds of bankers: the silky smooth salesmen who succeed based on wits and charm, and those who persist with bulldog tenacity. Paulson was of the latter type, as the White House soon discovered. Before he officially accepted the job, Paulson made certain to see to a few key details. If thirty-two years at Goldman Sachs had taught him anything, it was how to cut the best deal possible. He demanded assurances, in writing, that Treasury would have the same status in the cabinet as Defense and State. In Washington, he knew, proximity to the president mattered, and he had no intention of being a marginalized functionary who could be summoned at Bush's whim but couldn't get the chief executive to return his calls. Somehow he even got the White House to agree that its National Economic Council, headed by Allan Hubbard, a Harvard Business School classmate of Paulson's, would hold some of its meetings at the Treasury Building, and that the vice president, Dick Cheney, would attend them in person.

Hoping to silence any suggestion that he would favor his former employer, he voluntarily signed an extensive six-page "ethics" agreement that barred him from involving himself with Goldman Sachs for his entire tenure. His declaration went far beyond the regular one-year time period required for government employees. "As a prudential matter, I will not participate in any particular matter involving specific parties in which The Goldman Sachs Group, Inc. is or represents a party for the duration of my tenure as Secretary of the Treasury," he wrote in a letter that served as the agreement. "I believe that these steps will ensure that I avoid even the appearance of a conflict of interest in the performance of my duties as Secretary of the Treasury." It was an avowal that would certainly hinder his power, given Goldman's role in virtually every aspect of Wall Street, and one that he would later desperately try to find ways around.

One additional condition came with the appointment: Paulson would have to divest his huge holding of Goldman Sachs stock—some 3.23 million shares, worth about $485 million—as well as a lucrative investment in a Goldman fund that held a stake in the Industrial and Commercial Bank of China. Because new Internal Revenue Service rules allowed executives who entered into government service to sell their interests without a penalty, Paulson saved more than $100 million in taxes. It was perhaps one of the most lucrative deals he ever struck, but for many months prior to the crisis, he watched chagrined as Goldman's shares rose from about $142, when he sold them, to their high of $235.92 in October 2007.

Henry Merritt Paulson Jr. was officially nominated for Treasury secretary on May 30, 2006. Just seven days later, the *Washington Post* featured a profile of him that opened: "In an administration with just two and a half years to go, Henry M. Paulson Jr., President Bush's nominee for Treasury secretary, may have little chance to make a mark on many economic issues."

Nothing could have played more effectively to his immediate sense of buyer's remorse—and motivated him to overcome the challenge.

———

By Wall Street standards, Paulson was something of a baffling outlier, a titan who had little interest in living a Carnegie Hill multimillionaire's life. A straight-shooting Midwesterner, he had grown up on a farm outside Chicago and had been an Eagle Scout. He and Wendy assiduously avoided the Manhattan society scene, trying to get to bed before 9:00 p.m. as often as they could, and preferred bird-watching in Central Park—Wendy led tours in the mornings for the Nature Conservancy—near their two-bedroom, twelve-hundred-square-foot apartment, a modest residence for one of the highest-paid executives on Wall Street. Paulson wore a plastic running watch, and any inclination he might have had to spend money was discouraged by Wendy, the daughter of a Marine officer whose frugality had kept him firmly grounded. One day, Paulson came home with a new cashmere coat from Bergdorf Goodman, to replace one that he had had for ten years. "Why did you buy a new coat?" Wendy asked. The next day, Paulson returned it.

And despite his prodigious fund-raising for President Bush, he hardly fit the image of a Republican hard-liner. A hard-core environmentalist whose only car was a Toyota Prius, he was the subject of a good deal of negative publicity—and the scourge of some annoyed Goldman Sachs shareholders—when in 2006 he donated 680,000 acres of land Goldman owned in the South American archipelago of Tierra del Fuego to the Wildlife Conservation Society. As it happened, his son was on the society's board of advisers. Although the irony could not be appreciated by anyone at the time, the firm had acquired the ecologically sensitive South American land as part of a portfolio of mortgage defaults.

Paulson had a long history of exceeding others' expectations. Despite his relatively modest frame—six feet one, 195 pounds—he had been an all–Ivy League tackle for Dartmouth, where his ferociousness in playing earned him the nicknames "The Hammer" and "Hammering Hank." But unlike his hard-partying teammates, he kept orange juice and ginger ale in a refrigerator at his fraternity, Sigma Alpha Epsilon, to drink during beer parties. (He met his future wife on a blind date when she was a student at Wellesley; Wendy's classmates there included Hillary Rodham, who in some ways was her rival. Wendy was president of the class of 1969; Hillary was president of the student body.) Paulson graduated Phi Beta Kappa from Dartmouth in 1968 with a major in English literature.

Paulson had first come to Washington in 1970, after graduating from Harvard Business School, and at the time he didn't even own a suit. Armed with a recommendation from one of his undergraduate professors at Dartmouth, Paulson landed a job as a staff aide to the assistant secretary of Defense and would soon display some of the skills that would later make him such an effective salesman at Goldman Sachs. In just two years he advanced to the White House, where he became assistant director of the Domestic Policy Council, then headed by John Ehrlichman, who would later be convicted of conspiracy, obstruction of justice, and perjury in the Watergate cover-up. Paulson served as a liaison with the departments of Treasury and Commerce. "Given how [Hank] moved from a low-ranking position in the Pentagon to the White House, you have to conclude he's got pretty good antenna for what's going on," recalled a friend and former Goldman executive, Kenneth Brody. "[B]ut when Watergate came, there was never a mention of Hank."

When Wendy became pregnant with their first child in 1973, Paulson, eager to earn some money, decided to leave the Nixon White House and started looking for work in the financial sector—but not if it meant living in New York. He interviewed with a number of financial firms in Chicago, and of all the offers he received, he was most attracted to two Manhattan firms with major Chicago offices: Salomon Brothers and Goldman Sachs. He decided on Goldman after Robert Rubin, a Goldman partner and future Treasury secretary, Gus Levy, a legend at the firm, and John Whitehead, among others, convinced him that he could be successful there and never have to live in Gotham. His salary: $30,000.

In January 1974, Paulson moved his family back to where he had grown up, Barrington Hills, a town of fewer than four thousand residents northwest of Chicago. Paulson bought five acres of the family farm from his father, who was a wholesale jeweler. There, up a winding road from his parents' home, he built an unpretentious wood-and-glass house, nestled among tall oak trees at the end of a half-mile driveway.

At Goldman, Paulson was given an unusual amount of responsibility for a junior investment banker. "You know, Hank, we ordinarily don't hire guys as young as you into this role but, you know, you look old," Jim Gorter, a senior partner, told him, referring to his rapidly receding hairline. Having quickly proved himself with important Midwestern clients like Sears and Caterpillar, he was soon marked as a rising star at the firm's Manhattan headquarters. In 1982 he made partner, placing him in an elite group of men and a few women who were entitled to share directly in the firm's profits. When he became co-head of investment banking and a member of the firm's management committee from Chicago, he was obliged to spend a great deal of time on the phone, which he did somewhat famously, leaving interminable messages at all hours of the day.

Only four years later, in September of 1994, however, Goldman Sachs was in turmoil. An unexpected spike in interest rates around the world had hit the firm hard, sending profits tumbling more than 60 percent during the first half of the year. Stephen Friedman, the firm's chief executive, suddenly announced he was resigning; thirty-six other Goldman partners soon left, along with their capital and connections.

To stanch the bleeding, the firm's board turned to Jon Corzine, Goldman's soft-spoken head of fixed income. The directors saw Paulson as a natural number two who would not only complement Corzine but send a signal that investment banking, Paulson's specialty, would remain as key an area as ever for Goldman. They were betting that Corzine and Paulson could form a partnership as powerful as that of Friedman and Robert Rubin, and before them, John Whitehead and John Weinberg.

There was only one problem with the plan: Neither man cared much for the other.

At a meeting at Friedman's apartment on Beekman Place, Paulson expressed resistance to the idea of working under Corzine, or even of relocating to New York, which he had doggedly avoided all these years.

Corzine, who was known to be especially persuasive in one-on-one encounters, suggested that he and Paulson take a walk.

"Hank, nothing could please me more than to work closely with you," Corzine said. "We'll work closely together. We'll really be partners." Within an hour they had reached a deal.

On arriving that year in New York, Paulson moved quickly. He was so focused on work, he never even had time to inspect the apartment Wendy wanted them to purchase before he agreed to buy it, sight unseen.

As president and chief operating officer respectively, Paulson and Corzine worked tirelessly in the fall of 1994 to address Goldman's problems, traveling around the world to meet with clients and employees. Paulson was given the unenviable task of cutting expenses by 25 percent. Their efforts paid off: Goldman Sachs turned around in 1995 and had strong profits in both 1996 and 1997. Yet the crisis convinced Corzine and some others at Goldman that the firm needed to be able to tap the public capital markets so that it could withstand shocks in the future. The solution, they believed, was an initial public offering.

But Corzine did not have a strong enough hold on the firm when, in 1996, he first made the case to its partners for why Goldman should go public. Resistance to the idea of an IPO was strong, as the bankers worried it would upend the firm's partnership and culture.

But with a big assist from Paulson, who became co-chief executive in June 1998, Corzine ultimately won the day: Goldman's initial public offering was announced for September of that year. But that summer the Russian ruble crisis erupted and Long-Term Capital Management was teetering on the brink of collapse. Goldman suffered hundreds of millions of dollars in trading losses and had to contribute $300 million as part of a Wall Street bailout of Long-Term Capital that was orchestrated by the Federal Reserve Bank of New York. A rattled Goldman withdrew its offering at the last minute.

What was known only to a small circle of Paulson's closest friends was that he was actually considering quitting the firm, tired of Corzine, New York, and all the internal politics. However, the dynamic at Goldman shifted dramatically in December 1998: Roy Zuckerberg, a big Corzine supporter, retired from Goldman's powerful executive committee, leaving it with five powerful members: Corzine, Paulson, John Thain, John Thornton, and Robert Hurst. At the same time, Goldman's board had become increasingly frustrated with Corzine, who had engaged in merger talks with Mellon Bank behind their backs.

A series of secret meetings in various apartments quickly followed and resulted in a coup worthy of imperial Rome or the Kremlin. Persuaded to stay and run the firm, Paulson and the three other committee members agreed to force Corzine's resignation. Corzine had tears in his eyes when he was told of their decision.

Paulson became sole chief executive, with Thain and Thornton as co-presidents, co-chief operating officers, and heirs presumptive. And in May 1999, shares of Goldman made their trading debut in a $3.66 billion offering.

By the spring of 2006, Paulson had stayed longer in the CEO spot than he had expected and had risen to the very top of his profession. He was awarded an $18.7 million cash bonus for the first half of the year; in 2005 he was the highest paid CEO on Wall Street, pulling in $38.3 million in total compensation. Within Goldman he had no challengers, and his hand-picked successor, Lloyd Blankfein, was patiently waiting in the wings. The bank itself was the preferred choice as adviser on the biggest mergers and acquisitions and was a leading trader of commodities and bonds. It was paid handsomely by hedge funds using its services, and it was emerging as a power in its own right in private equity.

Goldman had become the money machine that every other firm on Wall Street wanted to emulate.

———

After thirty-two years at Goldman, Paulson had a tough time adjusting to life in government. For one, he had to make many more phone calls because he could no longer blast out long voice-mail messages to staffers, as was his custom at Goldman; Treasury's voice-mail system, he was repeatedly informed, did not yet have that capacity. He was encouraged to use e-mail, but he could never get comfortable with the medium; he resorted to having one of his two assistants print out the ones sent to him through them. And he had little use for the Secret Service officers accompanying him everywhere. He knew CEOs who had security with them constantly, and he had always considered such measures the ultimate demonstration of arrogance.

Much of the Treasury staff did not know what to make of Paulson and his idiosyncracies. The staffers would go to Robert Steel, his deputy secretary and a Goldman alum, for advice on how best to interact with their quirky new boss. Steel would always tell them the same three things: "One: Hank's really smart. Really smart. He's got a photographic memory. Two: He's an incredibly hard worker, incredibly hard. The hardest you'll ever meet. And he'll expect you to work just as hard. Three: Hank has no social EQ [emotional quotient], zero, none. Don't take it personally. He has no clue. He'll go to the restroom and he'll only halfway close the door."

Early in his tenure, Paulson invited some staff members to his house, a $4.3 million home in the northwestern corner of Washington (which, in a bizarre coincidence, had once belonged to Jon Corzine). The group gathered in the living room, whose big windows looking out over the woods almost made it seem as if they were sitting in a fancy tree house. Surrounding them were photographs of birds, most of them taken by Wendy.

Paulson was intensely explaining some of his ideas to the group. Wendy, thinking it odd that her husband had forgotten to offer their guests anything to drink on such a hot summer day, interrupted the meeting to do so herself.

"No, they don't want anything to drink," Paulson said distractedly before resuming the meeting.

Some time later Wendy came out with a pitcher of cold water and glasses, but no one dared indulge in front of the boss.

Paulson had inherited a department that was in disarray. His predecessor, John Snow, the former chief of the railroad company CSX, had been marginalized, and the demoralized staff felt both neglected and underappreciated. Paulson thought he could remedy that. But what surprised him was how few employees there actually were. He had assumed that government inefficiency would guarantee that he would have to deal with thousands of bodies being underutilized. Although he now oversaw a department of 112,000, it was light on the financial side, and he knew he would have to bring in seasoned Wall Street veterans who knew what it meant to work hard.

The Goldman connection was the one factor of which Paulson had to be mindful, as impractical as that seemed to him. He knew conspiracy theories about Goldman's supposed influence over Washington bloomed anew whenever a top Goldman executive took a government job, whether it concerned Robert Rubin's becoming Treasury secretary under Clinton or even Jon Corzine's election as senator from New Jersey, despite being ousted from the firm. (Rubin, who was now at Citigroup, also reminded him before he took the job about being careful in dealing with Goldman.)

In his first few weeks on the job, as the economic clouds were gathering but no one was yet forecasting a storm, Paulson focused on improving the morale at Treasury. He visited departments that had not seen a cabinet member for years and ordered the refurbishment of the building's basement gym. Paulson was serious about physical fitness and often biked around the capital, whenever Wendy could get him off the phone.

Early on, Paulson had concerns about the markets. In his first briefing with President Bush and his economic team, at Camp David on August 17, 2006, he warned that the economy was overdue for a crisis. "When there is a lot of dry tinder out there, you never know what will light it," he said. "We have these periods every six, eight, ten years, and there are plenty of excesses."

Paulson made it clear that the administration would have to confront at least one serious problem: the subprime mortgage mess, which had already begun to have repercussions. Bear Stearns and others were deeply involved in this business, and he needed to find a way to obtain "wind down authorities" over these troubled broker-dealers. Traditional banks had the Federal Deposit Insurance Corporation, or FDIC, and the Federal Reserve effectively protecting them from going bankrupt; these agencies had a built-in transition plan that allowed them to take failing banks safely into receivership and auction them off. But the FDIC had no authority over investment banks like Goldman Sachs, Morgan Stanley, Merrill Lynch, Bear Stearns, and Lehman Brothers, and unless Paulson was given comparable power over these institutions, he said during the meeting, there could be chaos in the market.

———

On March 27, 2008, at 8:30 a.m., just three days after the "recut" Bear deal, Paulson and his lieutenants gathered for a meeting. He'd just arrived from his usual workout at Sports Club/LA in the Ritz-Carlton hotel a few blocks away. His brain trust, Bob Steel, Jim Wilkinson, David Nason, Michele Davis, Phillip Swagel, Neel Kashkari, and several others, crammed into his office on the third floor of the Treasury Building, which overlooked the White House's Rose Garden and afforded dramatic views of the Washington Monument to the south.

Paulson took a chair in the corner of the high-ceilinged space, its walls already decorated with dozens of his wife's photographs of birds and reptiles. Some staffers found seats on his blue velvet couch; others stood, leaning against his mahogany desk, with its four Bloomberg screens flickering on top.

Paulson held these meetings with his inner circle each morning at 8:30 a.m., except for every other Friday, when he had breakfast with Ben Bernanke, the chairman of the Federal Reserve. Paulson would have preferred to have the staff meetings start even earlier, but these were government workers, and he was already pushing them pretty far. Most of his senior team were being paid around $149,000 a year, though each of them could have potentially been making much more in the private sector.

As Paulson went around the room doing a postmortem on Bear, he stopped at David Nason. Nason, the thirty-eight-year-old assistant secretary for financial institutions, had joined Treasury in 2005 and was its resident policy-making brain. A Republican and free-market champion, Nason had been warning at these meetings for months about the possibility of another Bear Stearns–like run on one or more banks. He and other Treasury officials had come to recognize that Wall Street's broker-dealer model—in which banks could count on ever-dependable overnight financing by other investors—was by definition a tinderbox. Bear had taught them how quickly a bank could crumble; in an industry whose lifeblood was simply the confidence of other investors, it could wane quickly at the hint of a problem. But however perilous the overall situation, Nason remained dead set against bailouts, a concept he couldn't abide.

Instead, Nason told the group that Treasury had to concentrate its efforts on two fronts: obtaining the authority to put an investment bank through an organized bankruptcy, one that wouldn't spook the markets, and more immediately, urging the banks to raise more money. In the previous six months, U.S. and European banks—including Citigroup, Merrill Lynch, and Morgan Stanley—had managed to bring in some $80 billion in new capital, often by selling their stakes to state-run investment funds—known as "sovereign wealth funds"—in China, Singapore, and the Persian Gulf. But it clearly wasn't enough, and the banks had already been forced to tap the investors with the deepest pockets.

With the Bear Stearns situation seemingly behind them, Paulson focused his attention this morning on what he thought would be the next trouble spot: Lehman Brothers. Investors may have been mesmerized by Erin Callan's performance at the earnings conference call, but Paulson knew better. "They may be insolvent, too," he calmly told the room. He was worried not only about how they were valuing their assets, which struck him as wildly optimistic, but about their failure to raise any capital—not a cent. Paulson suspected that Fuld had been foolishly resisting doing so because he was hesitant to dilute the firm's shares, including the more than 2 million shares he personally held.

Paulson's analysis of Lehman had been heavily colored by Goldman Sachs' commonly held view of the firm during his time there: It didn't have the same level of class or talent. While Paulson had at least once referred to Lehman as "a bunch of thugs" when he was at Goldman, he did nonetheless respect its hard-driving culture, admiring how aggressively Lehman bankers hustled. And they were loyal, almost to a fault; it was a tight-knit group that reminded him of Goldman's partnership.

Still, there was something about Fuld that made him nervous. He was a risk taker—recklessly so, in Paulson's view. "He's like a cat; he's had nine lives," he said at one staff meeting. Paulson believed that his old Goldman colleague, Bob Rubin, had unwittingly bailed out Fuld in early 1995 when, as Treasury secretary, he provided aid to Mexico during its peso crisis. Lehman had wagered a fortune on the direction of the Mexican peso without hedging that bet, and it had gotten it wrong. Paulson remembered the moment well—and told his staff about it—because of accusations at the time that Rubin had actually organized the international bailout in an effort to save Goldman Sachs.

Fairly or not, Paulson lumped Fuld in with what he saw as the rear guard on Wall Street, financiers like Ken Langone and David Komansky, the type who were habitual power lunchers at Manhattan's San Pietro restaurant and were friends of Richard Grasso, a symbol of excess. Paulson had been a member of the New York Stock Exchange's Human Resources and Compensation Committee that had approved a $190 million payday for Grasso, the NYSE chairman. Fuld had been on that committee as well; Langone had been its chairman. After the uproar over the size of Grasso's compensation package, Paulson wanted him out. In his view, Grasso hadn't been just greedy; he had been deceitful. Eliot Spitzer, the New York attorney general, then at the top of his game, soon became involved in the matter, suing both Grasso and Langone. It was in the resulting battle that Paulson came to dislike Grasso's cronies, who seemed all too ready to throw Paulson under a bus if it suited their purposes.

But as secretary of the Treasury, he was obliged to be a diplomat, and as such, needed to maintain good relationships with all the Wall Street CEOs. They would be huge assets, his eyes and ears on the markets. If he needed "deal flow," he preferred to get it directly from them, and not from some unconnected Treasury lifer whose job it was to figure these things out.

About a month after he settled into the job, in the summer of 2006, Paulson called Fuld, whom he reached playing golf with a friend in Sun Valley, where he had a home. Fuld had just teed off on the 7th hole, a par 5, dogleg left, when he heard his cell ringing. Although mobile phones weren't allowed on the course, he picked up anyway, and no one protested.

"I know this call may be a little unusual," Paulson began. "You and I have been trying to kill each other for years."

Fuld laughed, flattered by Paulson's acknowledgment of him as a worthy opponent.

"I'd like to be able to call you from time to time," Paulson continued, "to talk markets, deals, competition; to find out what your concerns are."

Fuld was pleased by the gesture and told him as much.

After that conversation they talked to each other regularly. Indeed, Paulson came to rely heavily on Fuld for market intelligence, and, in turn, shared his own views about the markets, which Fuld regarded as the official read. Almost to his surprise—given how much he had vilified the man when he was Goldman's CEO—Paulson found Fuld to be engaging and impressively hands-on. Although he still didn't completely trust him, he knew he could work with him.

But in the current market climate, the past few calls had been particularly tricky, and the next one would be especially so.

As Paulson's morning meeting came to an end, he handed out a number of assignments to his staffers, one of which was urging Neel Kashkari and Phil Swagel to hurry up and finish a draft of an apocalyptic white paper they had been working on about how the government should think about saving the financial system if it started melting down.

As everyone began to leave, the Treasury secretary stopped Bob Steel and pulled him aside to discuss the special assignment he had given to himself. "I'm going to lean on Dick," he announced.

An hour later his assistant, Christal West, had Dick Fuld on line one.

"Dick," Paulson said cheerily, "how are you?"

Fuld, who had been in his office waiting for the phone call, answered, "Holding up."

They had checked in with each other a handful of times over the past week since the Bear deal, but they hadn't discussed anything substantial. This morning's call was different. They talked about the fluctuations in the market and Lehman's stock. All the banks were suffering, but Lehman's share price was being hammered the most, down more than 40 percent for the year. More worrisome was that the shorts were smelling blood, meaning that the short position—the bet that Lehman's stock had much further to fall—was swelling, accounting for more than 9 percent of all Lehman shares. Fuld had been trying to convince Paulson to have Christopher Cox, chairman of the SEC, get the short-sellers to stop trashing his firm.

Paulson was not unsympathetic to Fuld's position, but he wanted an update on Lehman's plans to raise capital. Fuld had already been hearing from some of his top investors that this would be a wise course of action, especially while things were still relatively positive for the firm in the press.

"It would be a real show of strength," Paulson said, hoping to persuade him.

To Paulson's surprise, Fuld said he agreed and had already been think-ing about it. Some of his bondholders had been pressing him to raise money on the back of the firm's positive earnings report.

"We're thinking about reaching out to Warren Buffett," Fuld replied. That had been a carefully considered remark; Fuld knew that Paulson was a friend of the legendary Omaha investor. Although Buffett had a public disdain for investment bankers in general, for years he had used Goldman's Chicago office for some of his business, and Paulson and Buffett had become friends.

An investment by Buffett was the financial world's equivalent of a Good Housekeeping Seal of Approval. The markets would love it. "You should pitch him," Paulson said, relieved that Fuld was finally taking action in that direction.

Yes, Fuld agreed. But he had a favor to ask. "Could you say something to Warren?"

Paulson hesitated, reflecting that it probably wasn't a particularly good idea for a Treasury secretary to be brokering deals on Wall Street. The situation could only be complicated by the fact that Buffett was a Goldman client.

"Let me think about it, Dick, and get back to you," Paulson said.

On March 28, Warren Buffett, the legendary value investor, sat in his office at Berkshire Hathaway's Omaha headquarters, working at the plain wooden desk that his father had once used, waiting for Dick Fuld's call. A day earlier, the call had been arranged by Hugh "Skip" McGee, a Leh-man banker, who had reached out to David L. Sokol, chairman of Berk-shire Hathaway–owned MidAmerican Energy Holdings. (Buffett receives such pitch calls almost daily, so he regarded this one as a fairly routine matter.)

He didn't know Fuld well, having met him on only a few occasions; the last time they had been together, he had been seated between Fuld and Paul Volcker, the former chairman of the Federal Reserve, at a Treasury dinner in Washington in 2007. Wearing one of his trademark off-the-rack, no-fuss suits and tortoise-rimmed glasses, Buffett had been making the rounds when he had managed to spill a glass of red wine all over Fuld just before dessert arrived. The world's second-richest man (after Bill Gates) turned crimson as the dinner guests—a group that included Jeffrey Immelt of General Electric, Jamie Dimon of JP Morgan Chase, and former Treasury secretary Robert Rubin—looked on politely. Fuld had tried to laugh the spill off, but the wine had landed directly in his lap. The two hadn't seen each other since.

When Debbie Bosanek, Buffett's longtime assistant, announced that Dick Fuld was on the line, Buffett set down his Diet Cherry Coke and reached for the receiver.

"Warren, it's Dick. How are you? I've got Erin Callan, my CFO, on with me."

"Hi there," Buffett greeted him in his dependably affable manner.

"As I think you know, we're looking to raise some money. Our stock's been killed. It's a huge opportunity. The market doesn't understand our story," Fuld said, before launching into his sales pitch. He explained that Lehman was looking for an investment of $3 billion to $5 billion. After some back and forth, Buffett made a quick proposal: He indicated he might be interested in investing in preferred shares with a dividend of 9 percent and warrants to buy shares of Lehman at $40. Lehman's stock had closed at $37.87 that Friday.

It was an aggressive offer by the Oracle of Omaha. A 9 percent dividend was a very expensive proposition—if Buffett made a $4 billion investment, for example, he'd be due $360 million a year—but that was the cost of "renting" Buffett's name. Still, Buffett said, he needed to do some due diligence before committing to even those terms. "Let me run some numbers and I'll get back to you," he told Fuld before hanging up.

In Omaha, Buffett had already begun doing a little soul searching, uncertain if he could even bring himself to put his money into an investment bank again. In 1991 he had rescued Salomon Brothers when the storied New York investment house was on the brink, but he quickly realized then that he couldn't bear the culture of Wall Street. If he now came to Lehman's assistance, the world would be scrutinizing his participation, and he was well aware that not only would his money be on the line, but his reputation as well.

Even though Buffett had often traded in the market using hedges and derivatives, he despised the trader ethos and the lucrative paydays that enriched people he thought were neither particularly intelligent nor created much value. He always remembered how unnerved he had been after paying out $900 million in bonuses at Salomon, and was especially stunned when John Gutfreund, the firm's chairman, had demanded $35 million merely to walk away from the mess he had created. "They took the money and ran," he once said. "It was just so apparent that the whole thing was being run for the employees. The investment bankers didn't make any money, but they felt they were the aristocracy. And they hated the traders, partly because the traders made the money and therefore had more muscle." Buffett decided to hunker down that evening at his office and pick apart Lehman's 2007 annual report. After getting himself another Diet Cherry Coke, he began to read Lehman's 10-K, its annual report, when the phone rang; it was Hank Paulson. *This seems orchestrated.*

Paulson began as if it were a social call, knowing all too well that he was walking a fine line between acting as a regulator and a deal maker. Nonetheless, he quickly moved the discussion to the Lehman Brothers situation. "If you were to come in, your name alone would be very reassuring to the market," he said, careful not to push his friend too far. At the same time, in his roundabout way, he made it clear that he wasn't about to vouch for Lehman's books—after all, for years Buffett had heard him, as a top executive at Goldman, rail against other firms he thought had been too aggressive in both their investments and their bookkeeping.

After years of friendship, Buffett was familiar with Paulson's code: He was a hard-charging type, and if he wanted something badly enough, he would say so directly. He could tell now that Paulson wasn't pressing too hard. The two promised to stay in touch and then bade good night.

Buffett returned to his examination of Lehman's 10-K. Whenever he had a concern about a particular figure or issue, he noted the page number on the front of the report. Less than an hour into his reading, the cover of the report was filled with dozens of scribbled page citations. Here was an obvious red flag, for Buffett had a simple rule: He couldn't invest in a firm about which he had so many questions, even if there were purported answers. He called it a night, resolved that he was unlikely to invest.

On Saturday morning, when Fuld called back, there quickly seemed to be a problem separate and apart from Buffett's concerns. Fuld and Callan were under the impression that Buffett had asked for a 9 percent dividend and warrants "up 40"—meaning that the strike price of the warrants would be 40 percent more than their current value. Buffett, of course, thought he had articulated that the strike price of the warrants would be at $40 a share, just a couple dollars from where they were now. For a moment, they were all talking past one another as if they were Abbott and Costello performing "Who's on First?" Clearly, there had been a miscommunication, and Buffett thought it was just as well. The talks ended.

Back at his desk in New York, an annoyed Fuld told Callan that he considered Buffett's offer to be preposterously expensive and that they should seek investments from other investors.

By Monday morning, Fuld had managed to raise $4 billion of convertible preferred stock with a 7.25 percent interest rate and a 32 percent conversion premium from a group of big investment funds that already had a stake in Lehman. It was a much better deal for Lehman than what Buffett was offering, but it hardly came with the confidence an investment from him would have inspired.

Later that morning, Fuld called Buffett to inform him of the success of his fund-raising effort. Buffett congratulated him but privately wondered whether Fuld had used his name to help raise the money.

Although he never brought the subject up, Buffett found it curious that Fuld never mentioned what he imagined was an important piece of news that had crossed the tape over the weekend: "Lehman hit by $355 million fraud." Lehman had been swindled out of $355 million by two employees at Marubeni Bank in Japan, who had apparently used forged documents and imposters to carry out their crimes.

Once again it reminded Buffett of his experience at Salomon—this time when John Gutfreund and Salomon's legal team hadn't told him that the firm was involved in a massive auction bid-rigging scandal of Treasury bills, a scandal that nearly took down the firm.

You just can't trust people like that.

CHAPTER THREE

On the evening of Wednesday, April 2, 2008, an agitated Timothy F. Geithner took the escalator down to the main concourse of Washington's Reagan National Airport. He had just arrived on the US Airways shuttle from New York, and his driver, who normally waited outside of security for him, was nowhere to be found.

"Where the fuck is he?" Geithner snapped at his chief aide, Calvin Mitchell, who had flown down with him.

Geithner, the youthful president of the New York Federal Reserve, seldom exhibited stress, but he was certainly feeling it at the moment. It had been less than three weeks since he had stitched together the last-second deal that pulled Bear Stearns back from the brink of insolvency, and tomorrow morning he would have to explain his actions, and himself, to the Senate Banking Committee—and to the world—for the very first time. Everything needed to go perfectly.

"Nobody's picking up," Mitchell moaned as he punched the buttons of his cell phone, trying to reach the driver.

The Federal Reserve usually sent a special secure car for Geithner, who by now had grown accustomed to living inside the bubble of the world's largest bank. His life was planned down to the minute, which suited his punctual, fastidious, and highly programmed personality. He had flown to the capital the night before the hearing precisely out of concern that something like this—a hiccup with his driver—would happen.

On the flight down he had studied the script he had been tinkering with all week. There was one point he wanted to make absolutely clear, and he reviewed the relevant passage again and again. Bear Stearns, to his thinking, wasn't just an isolated problem, as everyone seemed to be suggesting. As unpopular as it might be to state aloud, he intended to stress the fact that Bear Stearns—with its high leverage, virtually daily reliance on funding from others simply to stay in business, and interlocking trades with hundreds of other institutions—was a symptom of a much larger problem confronting the nation's financial system.

"The most important risk is systemic: if this dynamic continues unabated, the result would be a greater probability of widespread insolvencies, severe and protracted damage to the financial system and, ultimately, to the economy as a whole," he wrote. "This is not theoretical risk, and it is not something that the market can solve on its own." He continued refining those ideas, using the tray table to take notes until just before the plane landed.

Over the course of the weekend of March 15, it had been Geithner—not his boss, Ben Bernanke, as the press had reported—who'd kept Bear from folding, constructing the $29 billion government backstop that finally persuaded a reluctant Jamie Dimon at JP Morgan to assume the firm's obligations. The guarantee protected Bear's debtholders and counterparties—the thousands of investors who traded with the firm—averting a crippling blow to the global financial system, at least that's what Geithner planned to tell the senators.

Members of the Banking Committee wouldn't necessarily see it that way and were likely to be skeptical, if not openly scornful, of Geithner at the hearing. They regarded the Bear deal as representative of a major and not necessarily welcome policy shift. He'd already been the target of stinging criticism, but given the scale of the intervention, it was only to be expected. That, however, didn't make having to listen to politicians throw around the term "moral hazard" any less galling, as if they hadn't just learned it the day before.

Unfortunately, it wasn't just a chorus of the ignorant and the uninformed who had been critical of the deal. Even friends and colleagues, like former Fed chairman Paul Volcker, were comparing the Bear rescue unfavorably to the federal government's infamous refusal to come to the assistance of a financially desperate New York City in the 1970s (enshrined in the classic New York *Daily News* headline: "Ford to City: Drop Dead"). The more knowing assessments ran along the following lines: The Federal Reserve had never before made such an enormous loan to the private sector. Why, exactly, had it been necessary to intervene in this case? After all, these weren't innocent blue-collar workers on the line; they were highly paid bankers who had taken heedless risks. Had Geithner, and by extension the American people, been taken for suckers?

Geithner did have his supporters, but they tended to be people who already had reason to be familiar with the financial industry's perilous state. Richard Fisher, Geithner's counterpart at the Dallas Fed, had sent him an e-mail: "Illegitimi non carborundum—Don't let the bastards get you down."

Much as he would have liked to, Geithner had no intention of announcing to the U.S. Senate that he had been surprised by the crisis. From his office atop the stone fortress that is the Federal Reserve Bank of New York, Geithner had for years warned that the explosive growth in credit derivatives—various forms of insurance that investors could buy to protect themselves against the default of a trading partner—could actually make them ultimately more vulnerable, not less, because of the potential for a domino effect of defaults. The boom on Wall Street could not last, he repeatedly insisted, and the necessary precautions should be taken. He had stressed these ideas time and again in speeches he had delivered, but had anyone listened? The truth was, no one outside the financial world was particularly concerned with what the president of the New York Fed had to say. It was all Greenspan, Greenspan, Greenspan before it became Bernanke, Bernanke, Bernanke.

Standing at the airport, Geithner certainly felt deflated, but for now it was mostly because his driver hadn't appeared. "You want to just take a taxi?" Mitchell asked.

Geithner, arguably the second most powerful central banker in the nation after Bernanke, stepped into the twenty-person-deep taxi line.

Patting his pockets, he looked sheepishly at Mitchell. "Do you have cash on you?"

———

If Tim Geithner's life had taken just a slightly different turn only months earlier, he might well have been CEO of Citigroup, rather than its regulator.

On November 6, 2007, as the credit crisis was first beginning to hit, Sanford "Sandy" Weill, the architect of the Citigroup empire and one of its biggest individual shareholders, scheduled a 3:30 p.m. call with Geithner. Two days earlier, after announcing a record loss, Citi's CEO, Charles O. Prince III, had been forced to resign. Weill, an old-school glad-hander who had famously recognized and cultivated the raw talent of a young Jamie Dimon, wanted to talk to Geithner about bringing him on board: "What would you think of running Citi?" Weill asked.

Geithner, four years into his tenure at the New York Federal Reserve, was intrigued but immediately sensitive to the appearance of a conflict of interest. "I'm not the right choice," he said almost reflexively.

For the following week, however, the prospect was practically all he could think about—the job, the money, the responsibilities. He talked it over with his wife, Carole, and pondered the offer as he walked their dog, Adobe, around Larchmont, a wealthy suburb about an hour from New York City. They already lived a comfortable life—he was making $398,200 a year, an enormous sum for a regulator—but compared with their neighbors along Maple Hill Drive, they were decidedly middle-of-the-pack. His tastes weren't that expensive, save for his monthly $80 haircut at Gjoko Spa & Salon, but with college coming up for his daughter, Elise, a junior in high school, and his son, Benjamin, an eighth-grader behind her, he could certainly use the money.

He finally placed a call to his old pal Robert Rubin, the former Treasury secretary and Citigroup's lead director, to make sure he hadn't made a mistake. Rubin, a longtime Geithner mentor, politely told him that he was backing Vikram Pandit for the position and encouraged him to stay in his current job. But the fact that he had been considered for a post of this magnitude was an important measure of Geithner's newly earned prominence in the financial-world firmament and a reflection of the trust he had earned within it.

For much of his time at the Fed, he had detected a certain lack of respect from Wall Street. Part of the problem was that he was not out of the central banker mold with which financial types traditionally felt comfortable. In the ninety-five-year history of the Federal Reserve, eight men had served as president of the Federal Reserve Bank of New York—and every one of them had worked on Wall Street as either a banker, a lawyer, or an economist. Geithner, in contrast, had been a career Treasury technocrat, a protégé of former secretaries Lawrence Summers and Robert Rubin. His authority was also somewhat compromised by the fact that, at forty-six, he still looked like a teenager and was known to enjoy an occasional day of snowboarding—and that he was given to punctuating his sentences with "fuck."

Some Washington officials, journalists, and even a few bankers were charmed by Geithner, whose wiry intensity and dry, self-deprecating wit helped create the image of him as something of a policy-making savant: Although he often appeared distracted and inattentive during meetings, he would, after everyone had said his piece, give a penetrating analysis of the entire discussion, in coherent, flowing paragraphs.

Others, however, regarded these performances as what they saw as a form of controlling shtick. Every month the New York Fed would host a lunch for Wall Street chieftains, the very people his office oversaw, and every month Geithner would slouch in his seat, shuffling his feet, sipping a Diet Coke, and saying precisely nothing. He was as Delphic as Greenspan, one of his heroes, but he didn't have the gravitas to pull it off, certainly not to an audience of major Wall Street players.

———

"He's twelve years old!"

Such was the reaction of a nonplussed Peter G. Peterson, the former Lehman Brothers chief executive and co-founder of the private-equity firm Blackstone Group, upon first meeting Geithner in January 2003. Peterson had been leading the search for a replacement for William McDonough, who was retiring after a decade at the helm of the New York Fed. McDonough, a prepossessing former banker with First National Bank of Chicago, had become best known for summoning the chief executives of fourteen investment and commercial banks in September 1998 to arrange a $3.65 billion private-sector bailout of the imploding hedge fund Long-Term Capital Management.

Peterson had been having trouble with the search; none of his top choices was interested. Making his way down the candidates list, he came upon the unfamiliar name of Timothy Geithner and arranged to see him. At the interview, however, he was put off by Geithner's soft-spokenness, which can border on mumbling, as well as by his slight, youthful appearance.

Larry Summers, who had recommended Geithner, tried to assuage Peterson's concerns. He told him that Geithner was much tougher than he appeared and "was the only person who ever worked with me who'd walk into my office and say to me, 'Larry, on this one, you're full of shit.'"

That directness was the product of a childhood spent constantly adapting to new people and new circumstances. Geithner had had an army brat childhood, moving from country to country as his father, Peter Geithner, a specialist in international development, took on a series of wide-ranging assignments, first for the United States Agency for International Development and then for the Ford Foundation. By the time Tim was in high school, he had lived in Rhodesia (now Zimbabwe), India, and Thailand. The Geithner family was steeped in public service. His mother's father, Charles Moore, was a speechwriter and adviser to President Eisenhower, while his uncle, Jonathan Moore, worked in the State Department.

Following in the steps of his father, grandfather, and uncle, Tim Geithner went to Dartmouth College, where he majored in government and Asian studies. In the early 1980s, the Dartmouth campus was a major battleground of the culture wars, which were inflamed by the emergence of a right-wing campus newspaper, *The Dartmouth Review*. The paper, which produced prominent conservative writers such as Dinesh D'Souza and Laura Ingraham, published a number of incendiary stories, including one that featured a list of the members of the college's Gay Students Association, and another a column against affirmative action written in what was purported to be "black English." Taking the bait, liberal Dartmouth students waged protests against the paper. Geithner played conciliator, persuading the protesters to channel their outrage by starting a rival publication.

After college, Geithner attended the Johns Hopkins School of Advanced International Studies, where he graduated with a master's degree in 1985. That same year he married his Dartmouth sweetheart, Carole Sonnenfeld. His father was best man at the wedding at his parents' summer home in Cape Cod.

With the help of a recommendation from the dean at Johns Hopkins, Geithner landed a job at Henry Kissinger's consulting firm, researching a book for Kissinger and making a very favorable impression on the former secretary of State. Geithner learned quickly how to operate effectively within the realm of powerful men while not becoming a mere sycophant;

he intuitively understood how to reflect back to them an acknowledgment of their own importance. With Kissinger's support, he then joined the Treasury Department and became an assistant financial attaché at the U.S. Embassy in Tokyo, where he ruled the compound's tennis courts with his fierce competitiveness. The courts were also a place he could hold informal discussions with Tokyo correspondents from major publications, diplomats, and his Japanese counterparts.

During his tour in Japan, Geithner witnessed firsthand the spectacular inflation and crushing deflation of his host's great bubble economy. It was through his work there that he came to the attention of Larry Summers, then the Treasury under secretary, who began promoting him to bigger and bigger responsibilities. During the Asian financial and Russian ruble crises of 1997 and 1998, Geithner played a behind-the-scenes role as part of what *Time* magazine called "The Committee to Save the World," helping to arrange more than $100 billion of bailouts for developing countries. When aid packages were proposed, Geithner was automatically summoned into Summers's office. In this respect Geithner was lucky; he happened to be a specialist in a part of the world that had suddenly become critical. He had also honed the diplomatic skills he had first displayed at Dartmouth, often mediating disputes between Summers, who tended to advocate aggressive intervention, and Rubin, who was more cautious.

When the South Korean economy almost collapsed in the fall of 1997, Geithner helped shape the U.S. response. On Thanksgiving Day, Geithner called Summers at his home and calmly laid out the reasons the United States had to help stabilize the situation. After much debate within the Clinton administration, the plan that emerged—to supply Seoul with billions of dollars on top of a $35 billion package from the International Monetary Fund and other international institutions—bore a close resemblance to Geithner's original proposal. The following year, Geithner was promoted to Treasury under secretary for international affairs.

Geithner remained close to Summers, whom he used to play elaborate practical jokes on. More than once, when Summers was out giving a speech, Geithner would rewrite the wire news article about the presentation, purposely misquoting him. When Summers would return to the Treasury building after his speech, Geithner would present Summers with the doctored news report as if it were the real thing, and then just watch

Summers blow up, threatening to call the reporter and demand a correction until Geithner let him in on the joke. The two men became so close that for years they, and other Treasury colleagues, went to a tennis academy in Florida run by Nick Bollettieri, who coached Andre Agassi and Boris Becker. Geithner, with his six-pack abs, had a game that matched his policy-making prowess. "Tim's controlled, consistent, with very good ground strokes," Lee Sachs, a former Treasury official, said.

When Clinton left office, Geithner joined the International Monetary Fund, and it was from there that he was recruited to the New York Fed. Despite having served a Democratic administration, Geithner was sold on the job by Peterson, a well-connected Republican.

The presidency of the New York Fed is the second most prominent job in the nation's central banking system, and it carries enormous responsibilities. The New York bank is the government's eyes and ears in the nation's financial capital, in addition to being responsible for managing much of the Treasury's debt. Of the twelve district banks in the Federal Reserve System, the New York Fed is the only one whose president is a permanent member of the committee that sets interest rates. Owing to the relatively high cost of living in New York, the annual salary of the New York Fed president is double that of the Federal Reserve chairman.

His idiosyncrasies notwithstanding, Geithner gradually grew into his job at the New York Fed, distinguishing himself as a thoughtful consensus builder. He also worked diligently to fill in gaps in his own knowledge, educating himself on the derivatives markets and eventually becoming something of a skeptic on the notion of risk dispersion. To his way of thinking, the spreading of risk could actually exacerbate the consequences of otherwise isolated problems—a view not shared by his original boss at the Fed, Alan Greenspan.

"These changes appear to have made the financial system able to absorb more easily a broader array of shocks, but they have not eliminated risk," he said in a speech in 2006. "They have not ended the tendency of markets to occasional periods of mania and panic. They have not eliminated the possibility of failure of a major financial intermediary. And they cannot fully insulate the broader financial system from the effects of such a failure."

Geithner understood that the Wall Street boom would eventually falter, and he knew from his experience in Japan that it was not likely to end well. Of course, he had no way of knowing precisely how or when that would happen, and no amount of studying or preparation could have equipped him to deal with the events that began in early March 2008.

————

Matthew Scogin poked his head into Robert Steel's corner office at the Treasury Department. "Are you ready for another round of Murder Board?"

Steel sighed as he looked at his senior adviser but knew it was for the best. "Okay. Yeah, let's do it."

Hank Paulson had been scheduled to testify before the Banking Committee with Geithner, Bernanke, and Cox, chairman of the Securities and Exchange Commission, that morning of April 3, with Alan Schwartz of Bear Stearns and Jamie Dimon of JP Morgan to appear later. But Paulson was on an official trip to China that could not be postponed, so his deputy, Steel, would be there in his place.

Like Geithner, Steel was largely unknown outside the financial world, and he viewed his testimony before the Senate Banking Committee as presenting an opportunity, of sorts. His staff had been trying to help him prepare the traditional Washington way: by playing round after round of "Murder Board." The game involved staff members taking on the roles of particular lawmakers and then grilling Steel with the questions the politicians were likely to ask. The exercise was also designed to help make certain that Steel would be as lucid and articulate under fire as he could be.

A seasoned and assured public speaker, Steel had appeared before congressional committees, but the stakes hadn't been nearly as high. In addition to tough questions about what had come to be known as "Bear Weekend," he knew another subject was likely to arise: Fannie Mae and Freddie Mac, the so-called government-sponsored enterprises that bought up mortgages. The GSEs, which were blamed for inflating the housing bubble, had been political and ideological hot buttons for decades, but never more so than at that moment.

With Bear Stearns' failure, the senators might even begin connecting the dots. One of the first causalities of the credit crunch was two Bear

Stearns hedge funds that had invested heavily in securities backed by sub-prime mortgages. It was those mortgages that were now undermining confidence in the housing market—a market that Fannie and Freddie dominated, underwriting more than 40 percent of all mortgages, most of which were quickly losing value. That, in turn, was infecting bank lending everywhere. "Their securities move like water among all of the financial institutions," Paulson had said of Fannie and Freddie.

Quick-witted and handsome, Steel was actually a much better communicator than Paulson and would often upstage his boss, who couldn't help stammering even at routine Treasury meetings. The two men had known each other since 1976, when Steel went to work at the Chicago office of Goldman Sachs after graduating from Duke University. Like Paulson, Steel came from a modest background, growing up near the campus of Duke University. His father serviced jukeboxes and later sold life insurance; his mother worked part time at a Duke psychiatry lab. At Goldman, Steel was an ambitious banker and rising star; he moved to London in 1986 to start the equity capital markets group there and help the firm gain a foothold in Europe.

But four years earlier, Steel—now worth more than $100 million as a result of being a partner during Goldman's IPO—had decided to retire, having worked in various senior positions but not being next in line to lead the firm. Though he always planned a triumphant return to the private sector, he wanted time to pursue public service, like many other Goldman alums. After establishing his public-sector bona fides, including a position as a senior fellow at the John F. Kennedy School of Government at Harvard, he accepted Paulson's invitation to join him at Treasury as under secretary for domestic finance on October 10, 2006.

Now, as he entered the conference room with Scogin for one last round of Murder Board, he knew he had to be on his game. Treasury colleagues David Nason, chief of staff Jim Wilkinson, and Michele Davis, assistant secretary for public affairs and director of policy planning, were already seated with a small group across the table.

The burning question they all knew would be asked: What role had the government played in the negotiations that had led to the original $2-a-share price for Bear Stearns? None of the Treasury staffers had a clue as to what the other witnesses—JP Morgan's Jamie Dimon and Bear's Alan Schwartz—were going to say about what had actually occurred when they testified later in the day.

Steel knew that Paulson had pushed for a lower price to send the powerful message that shareholders should not profit from a government rescue. But no one at Treasury had ever confirmed that, and for Paulson's and everyone else's sakes, it would be best not to acknowledge what had really happened: On Sunday afternoon, March 16, Paulson had called Dimon and told him, "I think this should be done at a very low price."

Steel knew he had to dodge that issue at the hearing. It was imperative, as Davis and others had stressed during Murder Board sessions and at other meetings, that he avoid getting drawn into a debate over whether $2 was the right price—or $10, for that matter. The key idea he had to focus on was Paulson's overall concern that, because taxpayer money was involved, shareholders should not be rewarded. And more important, they encouraged Steel to remain adamant that Treasury had not negotiated the deal for Bear. If anything, he should deflect the question onto the Fed, which was the only government agency that legally could be party to such a transaction.

Before the role playing began, Nason briefed Steel on a key development. He recounted some recent conversations he had had with the staff of Senator Richard Shelby, the ranking Republican on the Senate Banking Committee. "Shelby's going to be difficult," Nason warned.

That was an understatement. Shelby was deeply unhappy with Paulson's performance, not only because of the Bear Stearns bailout, but in response to another recent Paulson project: a provision in Bush's economic stimulus package, introduced just days after the bailout, that raised the ceiling on the amount of mortgages that Fannie Mae and Freddie Mac could buy. For days Shelby had not returned the secretary's phone calls, until Paulson finally barked at his staff, "Doesn't he know I am the secretary of the Treasury?"

They also knew they had to be wary of Senator Jim Bunning, well known as a "markets know best" purist. "Senator Jim Bunning, Republican. Kentucky," Steel replied jokingly when a picture of Bunning was held up during Murder Board. "Everything we're doing? Yes, it's all bullshit. We're socialists. Thank you, Senator."

The Murder Board preparations continued until minutes before Steel left for the hearing. The key objective now was to protect Steel, and the Treasury Department, from any last-minute surprises. Staffers carefully checked that morning's newspapers to make certain there was no new revelation about Bear Stearns or some harsh opinion from a columnist that a senator might quote that morning. Happily, there was nothing.

Steel made the short trip from Treasury to Capitol Hill in a Treasury car with his aides. The hearing room in the Dirksen Senate Office Building was already buzzing with activity, as camera crews set up their equipment and photographers tested the light. As Steel took his seat, he noticed that Alan Schwartz of Bear Stearns had already arrived, even though he was not scheduled to testify until that afternoon, and greeted him. To Steel's immediate left was Geithner; to his right, Cox; and next to Cox, Bernanke. Seated in a single row were a group of men who, more than anyone else in the world, were being entrusted with solving its financial problems.

"Was this a justified rescue to prevent a systemic collapse of financial markets," asked Senator Christopher Dodd, the Connecticut Democrat and chairman of the committee, "or a $30 billion taxpayer bailout, as some have called it, for a Wall Street firm while people on Main Street struggle to pay their mortgages?"

The fireworks started almost immediately. Committee members were sharply critical of the regulators' oversight of financial firms. More important, they questioned whether funding a takeover of Bear Stearns had created a dangerous precedent that would only encourage other firms to make risky bets, secure in the knowledge that the downside would be borne by the taxpayer.

Bernanke hastened to explain the government's position: "What we had in mind here was the protection of the American financial system and the protection of the American economy. I believe that if the American people understand that we were trying to protect the economy and not to protect anybody on Wall Street, they would better appreciate why we took the action we did."

Then came the question Steel had prepped for: Had it been the Treasury secretary who determined the $2-a-share price?

"Well, sir, the secretary of the Treasury and other members of Treasury were active participants during this ninety-six hours, as you describe," he replied. "There were lots of discussions back and forth.

"Also, in any combination of this type, there are multiple terms and conditions. I think the perspective of Treasury was really twofold. One was the idea that Chairman Bernanke suggested: that a combination into safe hands would be constructive for the overall marketplace; and, number two, since there were federal funds or the government's money involved, that that be taken into account. And Secretary Paulson offered perspective on that.

"There was a view that the price should not be very high or should be toward the low end and that it should be—given the government's involvement, that that was the perspective. But with regard to the specifics, the actual deal was negotiated—transaction was negotiated between the Federal Reserve Bank of New York and the two parties."

For the most part, the Fed, the Treasury, and the SEC held their own against the Banking Committee's interrogation. But they did so largely by defending the Bear bailout as a once-in-a-lifetime act of extreme desperation, not as the expression of a nascent policy. Under the circumstances, it was a reasonable response to a run on a very large bank whose demise would disrupt the entire financial system.

Those circumstances, Geithner told the committee, were not unlike those of 1907, or the Great Depression, and he went on to draw a straight line between panic on Wall Street and the economic health of the country: "Absent a forceful policy response, the consequences would be lower incomes for working families; higher borrowing costs for housing, education, and the expenses of everyday life; lower value of retirement savings; and rising unemployment."

So they'd done what they had to do for the good of the entire country, if not the world, as Steel explained. And thanks to their efforts, he confidently told the lawmakers, the hole in the dike had been plugged.

———

Jamie Dimon was searching for a metaphor.

As he sat in a conference room down the hall from Senator Charles Schumer's office watching the morning's proceedings on C-SPAN, he strategized with his communications chief and trusted confidant, Joseph Evangelisti. How could he best account for the low price he had paid for Bear without looking as if he had been given a gift, courtesy of taxpayers?

"The average person has to understand that we took a huge risk," Evangelisti instructed him as they reviewed various approaches. "We've got to explain it in plain English."

Unlike Steel, Dimon had not engaged in any Murder Board role playing in his own Park Avenue office. Instead, he chose to do some last-minute preparation in the conference room, which had been lent to him by a Senate staffer so he wouldn't have to wait in the gallery.

Dimon came up with a simple, clear line that he thought explained the acquisition of Bear Stearns succinctly: "Buying a house is not the same as buying a house on fire." That would do it; everyone would understand that.

The message he sought to convey was straightforward: Although Fed and Treasury officials may have deserved scrutiny for their actions, he hadn't done anything out of the ordinary. It wasn't his job to protect the interests of the U.S. taxpayer, only those of his shareholders. If anything, he was a little concerned that the Bear deal presented more problems for them than it was worth.

Despite his public show of humility, Dimon was well aware of what a coup the deal had been for him. From the perspective of the financial media, at least, the Bear acquisition was viewed as a home run. They had always had a bit of an obsession with him and tended to paint him as a glorified penny pincher, an executive who would cancel the office's newspaper subscriptions to cut costs—not a real financial visionary. Now, with JP Morgan leapfrogging to the very top of the banking business, Dimon was being regarded as something akin to the reincarnation of John Pierpont Morgan, the nineteenth-century financier who helped ease the Panic of 1907.

Dimon, the *New York Times* said, "has suddenly become the most talked about—and arguably the most powerful—banker in the world today." For the *Wall Street Journal* he was "quickly becoming Wall Street's banker of last resort." *Barron's* opted for a simple "All hail Jamie Dimon!"

With all the adulation he had been receiving, Dimon had become almost giddy at the prospect of speaking at today's hearing. While most

CEOs dread being hauled in front of Congress—Alan D. Schwartz of Bear Stearns had spent days reviewing his testimony with his high-powered Washington lawyer, Robert S. Bennett—Dimon considered his first chance to testify in front of Congress to be a signal honor.

The night before the hearing, he called his parents to make sure they would watch it on TV.

———

Jamie Dimon's success is not an enormous surprise, as he is a third-generation banker. His grandfather had immigrated to New York from Smyrna, Turkey, changed his name from Papademetriou to Dimon, and found work as a stockbroker, which at the time was hardly considered a glamorous job. Jamie's father, Theodore—who met his mother, Themis, playing spin-the-bottle when they were twelve years old—was also a broker, and a very successful one. Theodore had done so well that he was able to move his family from Queens to an apartment on Park Avenue, where he raised Jamie and his brothers, Peter and Ted. One day, when Jamie was nine years old, his father asked his sons what they wanted to be when they grew up. Peter, the eldest, said he hoped to become a doctor. Ted, Jamie's twin, said he didn't know. But Jamie knew and announced self-assuredly, "I want to be rich."

After attending the Browning School on Manhattan's Upper East Side, Jamie studied psychology and economics at Tufts University; later, at Harvard Business School, he developed a reputation—as much for his arrogance as for his intelligence. Just a few weeks into the fall semester of his first year there, the professor in an introductory class on operations was going through a case study on supply chain management at a cranberry cooperative. Midway through Dimon stood up and interrupted him with, "I think you're wrong!" As the startled professor looked on, Dimon walked to the front of the class and wrote the solution to the supply problem on the blackboard. Dimon was right, the professor sheepishly acknowledged.

After a summer working at Goldman Sachs, Dimon sought career advice from the portly, cigar-chomping, serial deal maker named Sandy Weill. Jamie's family had become close to the Weills in the mid-1970s, after Sandy's brokerage firm acquired Shearson Hammill, where Dimon's father was a top broker. While at Tufts, Dimon had even written a paper on the

Hayden Stone takeover of Shearson, which his mother showed to Weill, who was impressed with its analysis.

"Can I show it to people here?" Weill asked Dimon.

"Absolutely," Dimon replied. "Can I have a summer job?" Weill was happy to oblige.

After graduating from Harvard Business School, Dimon received offers from Goldman Sachs, Morgan Stanley, and Lehman Brothers. Weill invited Dimon to his Upper East Side apartment and made his own offer: a position as his assistant at American Express, where Weill was now a top executive after having sold Shearson for nearly $1 billion. "I won't pay you as much," Weill told the twenty-five-year-old, "but you're going to learn a lot and we're going to have a lot of fun." Dimon was sold.

Weill and Dimon's tenure at the company turned out to be brief. Although he once boasted that "the Jews are going to take over American Express!" Weill still found himself thwarted by the WASP hierarchy, unable to cut deals on his own. Increasingly frozen out by his colleagues and the board, he quit as president of American Express in 1985; Dimon, whose talents had been noticed by CEO James Robinson, was asked to stay. Dimon was at a point in his life where many in the same position might have opted for security; his wife had just given birth to their first child. But he decided to stick with Weill, even though Weill hadn't yet settled on his next project and had taken space in a small office. As the months wore on and Dimon found himself watching Weill sleep off his martini lunches on their office couch, he wondered if he had made a bad bet. Weill couldn't seem to get anything off the ground, and Dimon had asked himself whether his mentor had played his last hand.

Then, in the wake of Weill's failed takeover of Bank of America, two executives at Commercial Credit, a subprime lender based in Baltimore, pitched him and Dimon on buying the company from its parent. Weill put up $6 million of his money to do the deal (Dimon invested $425,000), and the company was spun off, with Weill in charge. Dimon set himself up as the operations man, obsessively cutting costs. A lean-and-mean Commercial Credit became the cornerstone of a new financial empire, one that Weill and Dimon built through more than one hundred acquisitions. In 1988 the pair got their return ticket to Wall Street with the $1.65 billion acquisition of Primerica, the parent of the brokerage firm Smith Barney.

A $1.2 billion purchase of Shearson from American Express followed in 1993.

Dimon's reputation rose alongside Weill's. They were a team: Weill, the strategist and deal maker; Dimon, more than twenty years his junior, the numbers cruncher and operations whiz. They had moved beyond mentor and protégé to something more like a long-married combative couple. In the Midtown Manhattan offices of Primerica, the chairman and the chief financial officer would argue ferociously, their voices booming down the corridors. In meetings Dimon would roll his eyes whenever he thought Sandy had said something foolish.

"You're a fucking asshole!" Weill would yell at him.

"No, you're the fucking asshole!" Dimon would shout back.

By 1996, after a $4 billion deal for Travelers, the company needed someone to run the combined asset-management operations. Weill was quietly pushing Dimon to promote his daughter, Jessica Bibliowicz, then thirty-seven, who was running Smith Barney's mutual fund business. Dimon and Bibliowicz had known each other since they were teenagers, but she wasn't considered a top-flight manager, and he had reservations about entrusting her with so powerful a job. A top executive took Dimon aside. "Promote her," he warned Dimon. "You're killing yourself if you don't." Dimon, however, was not persuaded and told Weill and others that she wasn't ready for the job; they had better, more experienced executives in line.

The following year Bibliowicz announced that she was leaving the company. She didn't blame Dimon for her decision but tried to emphasize the positive aspects of her departure, telling her father: "Now we can be father and daughter again." But Weill was furious, and the relationship between him and Dimon would never be repaired, with tensions flaring with increasing frequency as the company continued its rapid expansion. Travelers acquired Salomon in 1997, and Weill made Deryck Maughan, a Briton who had helped steer Salomon Brothers through a Treasury bond scandal, the co-chief executive of Salomon Smith Barney, along with Dimon. This new power-sharing arrangement, although logical, greatly displeased Dimon.

A more injurious slight came after the $83 billion merger with Citicorp, the deal that rewrote the rules of the U.S. financial system as the last

Depression-era barriers between commercial and investment banking—
passed as the Glass-Steagall Act of 1933—were removed by a bill introduced by Republican senator Phil Gramm of Texas and Republican
congressman Jim Leach of Iowa. Dimon had worked tirelessly to bring
the deal to completion, yet when the time came to split the eighteen board
seats of the merged company between Travelers and Citicorp, he found
himself left out. He was made president of the company, but had only one
direct report, the chief financial officer, Heidi Miller.

The untenable situation finally came to a head a few days after the new
Citigroup reported a disappointing third quarter, the result of a summer
of turmoil as Russia defaulted and the hedge fund Long-Term Capital
Management nearly collapsed. That weekend had been set aside for a four-
day conference for executives at the West Virginia resort of Greenbrier,
capped by a black-tie dinner and dance. Around midnight a number of
couples were trading partners on the dance floor. Steve Black, one of
Dimon's closest allies at Smith Barney, approached the Maughans and
offered to dance with Maughan's wife, a gesture that was intended as
something of an olive branch, given the clashing factions within the company. But Deryck Maughan did not reciprocate, leaving Black's wife standing alone on the dance floor. A furious Black stomped off to confront
Maughan.

"It's bad enough how you treat me," he shouted. "But you're not going
to treat my wife like that!" On the verge of hitting him, Black threatened,
"I will drop you where you stand."

Dimon attempted to intervene, tracking down Maughan as he was
about to leave the ballroom. "I want to ask you a simple question. Either
you intended to snub Blackie's wife or you didn't. Which is it?"

Maughan said nothing and turned to walk away. Incensed, Dimon
grabbed him and spun him around, popping a button off his jacket in the
process.

"Don't you ever turn your back on me while I'm talking!" he shouted.

When Weill learned of the incident, he judged it inappropriate. A week
later, he and his co-CEO, John Reed, summoned Dimon to the corporate
compound in Armonk, New York, where they asked him to resign.

It proved to be both the worst and best thing that ever happened to
Dimon. Just as Weill had done after leaving American Express, he took

his time finding a new job, turning down a number of suitors—including, reportedly, the Internet retailer Amazon. Dimon knew little else outside of banking, and he waited for an opportunity in his field, finally accepting the top job at Bank One, a second-tier, hodgepodge operation based in Chicago. It was the launchpad he had been looking for, and he set out to streamline its operations and repair its balance sheet, to the point where he could engineer a deal with JP Morgan in 2004 that would put him in line to succeed William Harrison as CEO.

Once the proudest of Wall Street institutions, JP Morgan had fallen into the middle of the pack as its competitors had begun to outdo it. Dimon brought in his own team of expense cutters and integration experts and went to work. Salaries for the bank's managers were slashed. Gyms were ordered closed. Phone lines were ripped out of bathrooms. Daily fresh flowers were eliminated. Executives visibly tensed when Dimon pulled out of his breast pocket a handwritten piece of paper that served as his daily to-do list. One side was an inventory of matters that he needed to address that day; the other was for what he called "people who owe me stuff."

By 2008 JP Morgan Chase was being hailed as just about everything that Citigroup—the bank Dimon helped build—was not. Unlike Citi, JP Morgan had used scale to its advantage, rooting out redundancies and cross-selling mortages to checking account customers and vice versa. Dimon, who was paranoid by his very nature, understood the intricacies of virtually every aspect of banking (unlike many of his CEO peers) and also reduced risk; profits were literally squeezed out of each part of the company. Most important, as the credit crisis began to spread, Dimon showed himself to be infinitely more prudent than his competitors. The bank used less leverage to boost returns and didn't engage in anywhere near the same amount of off-balance-sheet gimmickry. So while other banks began to stumble severely after the market for subprime mortgages imploded, JP Morgan stayed strong and steady. Indeed, a month before the panic erupted over Bear Stearns, Dimon boasted of his firm's "fortress balance sheet" at an investors' conference. "A fortress balance sheet is [sic] also a lot of liquidity and that we can really stress it," he said, adding that it "puts us in very good stead for the future.

"I don't know if there are going to be opportunities. In my experience,

it's been environments like this that do create them, but they don't necessarily create them right away."

An opportunity came sooner than he expected.

———

On Thursday, March 13, Dimon, his wife, and their three daughters were
celebrating his fifty-second birthday over dinner at the Greek restaurant
Avra on East Forty-eighth Street. Dimon's cell phone, the one he used
only for family members and company emergencies, rang early in the
meal, around 6:00 p.m. Annoyed, Dimon took the call.

"Jamie, we have a serious problem," said Gary Parr, a banker at Lazard
who was representing Bear Stearns. "Can you talk with Alan?"

Dimon, in shock, stepped out onto the sidewalk. Rumors had been
swirling about Bear for weeks, but the call meant things were more serious than he had realized. Within minutes, Alan Schwartz, the CEO of
Bear Stearns, called back and told him the firm had run out of cash and
needed help.

"How much?" a startled Dimon asked, trying to remain calm.

"It could be as much as $30 billion."

Dimon whistled faintly in the night air—that was too much, far too
much. Still, he offered to help Schwartz out, if he could. He immediately
hung up and called Geithner. JP Morgan couldn't come up with that much
cash so quickly, Dimon told Geithner, but he was willing to be part of a
solution.

The following day, Friday, March 14, the Federal Reserve funneled a
loan through JP Morgan to Bear Stearns that would end its immediate
liquidity concerns and give the firm twenty-eight days to work out a long-
term deal for itself. Neither the Fed nor the Treasury, however, was willing to let the situation remain unsettled for that length of time, and over
the weekend, they urged Dimon to do a takeover. After a team of three
hundred people from JP Morgan installed themselves in Bear's office, they
brought their findings to Dimon and his executives.

By Sunday morning, Dimon had seen enough. He told Geithner that
JP Morgan was going to pull out; the problems with Bear's balance sheet
ran so deep as to be practically unknowable. Geithner, however, would
not accept his withdrawal and pressed him for terms that would make the

deal palatable. They finally arrived at an agreement for a $30 billion loan against Bear's dubious collateral, leaving JP Morgan on the hook for the first $1 billion in losses.

———

These final negotiations, not surprisingly, were of intense interest to the Senate Banking Committee. Had JP Morgan, realizing the leverage it had, driven an excessively hard bargain with the government, at taxpayer expense?

Dimon, looking almost regal with his silver hair and immaculately pressed white cuffs peeking out from his suit jacket, sounded neither apologetic nor defensive as he described the events leading up to the Bear deal. "This wasn't a negotiating posture," he stated calmly. "It was the plain truth." In Dimon's telling, the truth of the matter was clear—he and Geithner were the good guys who had saved the day, and against considerable odds. "One thing I can say with confidence," he told the committee members. "If the private and public parties before you today had not acted in a remarkable collaboration to prevent the fall of Bear Stearns, we would all be facing a far more dire set of challenges."

In the end, the day's testimony produced no smoking guns, no legendary exchanges, no heroic moments. But it introduced to the American public a cast of characters it would come to know very well over the next six months, and it provided a rare glimpse into the small circle of players that sits atop the world of high finance, wobbly though it may have been at the time. The senators were a long way from being able to make up their minds about the Bear deal—how necessary had it really been? And had it really fixed a problem, or merely postponed a greater reckoning?

Of all the members of the Banking Committee, Bunning, with his strong free-markets bias, was the most critical—and perhaps the most prescient. "I am very troubled by the failure of Bear Stearns," he said, "and I do not like the idea of the Fed getting involved in a bailout of that company. . . . That is socialism, at least that's what I was taught.

"And what's going to happen," he added ominously, "if a Merrill or a Lehman or someone like that is next?"

CHAPTER FOUR

O n the oppressively humid evening of Friday, April 11, 2008, Dick Fuld strode up the steps of the Treasury Building, passing the ten-foot-tall bronze statue of Alexander Hamilton that looms over the south entrance. He had come at the personal invitation of Hank Paulson for a private dinner to mark the end of a G7 summit and the beginning of the annual spring meetings of the International Monetary Fund and the World Bank. The guest list featured a group of the most influential economic policy makers and thinkers, including ten Wall Street CEOs and a number of the world's leading finance ministers and central bankers, including Jean-Claude Trichet, president of the European Central Bank.

Fuld was feeling fairly optimistic—certainly less despairing than he had been earlier. Lehman's announcement two weeks before that it would raise $4 billion had stabilized the stock, at least for the moment. The entire market was rallying, buoyed by comments from Lloyd Blankfein, CEO of Goldman Sachs, who had emphatically declared at his firm's annual meeting that the worst of the credit crisis was likely over. "We're closer to the end than the beginning," he said.

That was not to say that the gloom in the financial community had completely lifted. Just that morning Fuld had attended a contentious meeting in downtown Manhattan with Tim Geithner at the New York Fed, imploring him to do something about the short-sellers, who he was convinced were just catching their breath. Erik Sirri, the head of the SEC's Division of Trading and Markets, repeatedly pressed Fuld for proof of any illegal activity, pleading, "Just give me something, a name, anything." Fuld, who considered Sirri—a former Harvard Business School professor—to be a free-market zealot with no real-world experience, told him he had nothing concrete. He just knew what he knew.

Tonight, as Fuld was ushered across the checkered squares of black and white marble of the Treasury hallways, he tried to clear his mind and prepared to enjoy himself.

The dinner was being held in the Treasury Cash Room, so named because until the mid-1970s, it was where the public went to exchange U.S. government notes and bonds for cash. Opened in 1869, the room was intended to foster confidence in the new federal paper currency—the "greenback"—that had been introduced during the Civil War. Today, nearly a century and a half later, that confidence was in short supply.

Fuld had been looking forward to the dinner all week, eager for a chance to talk with Paulson face-to-face. Over the past few weeks, they had spoken several times by phone, but given all that was at stake, meeting in person was essential. It would give Fuld a chance to impress upon the secretary the seriousness of his efforts and to gauge where Lehman really stood with Washington.

Amid the procession of financiers slowly filing into the Cash Room, Fuld noticed an old friend in the corner, John Mack, CEO of Morgan Stanley, one of the few people in the room who understood exactly what Fuld was going through. Of all the CEOs on the Street, Fuld felt closest to Mack; they were the longest-running leaders of the major firms, and they would occasionally dine together with their spouses.

There were also a number of other men in the room whom Fuld stopped to shake hands with but didn't know well—though little did he suspect they would soon become major figures in his life. One was an American banker named Bob Diamond, who ran Barclays Capital, the investment banking arm of the British financial behemoth. Fuld had spoken with him a handful of times, usually seeking donations for his favorite charities. Diamond was polite but noticeably cool as Fuld greeted him, perhaps because Fuld had once invited him over for a casual coffee, unaware that he was based in London, not New York—a little slight that Diamond had never forgotten. Fuld also briefly paid his respects to Diamond's regulators, Alistair Darling, the head of Britain's Treasury, and Mervyn King, the governor of the Bank of England. High finance was in general a very small world, though at this particular moment, none of them realized just how small it had become.

As he made his way through the crowd, Fuld kept an eye out for

Paulson, whom he hoped to buttonhole before the dinner began. But it was Paulson, wearing a blue suit that seemed one size too big for him, who spotted Fuld first. "You guys are really working hard over there," Paulson told him, grasping his hand. "The capital raise was the right thing to do."

"Thanks," Fuld said. "We're trying."

Paulson also expressed his gratitude for the "thoughtful" dialogue that had been initiated among Tom Russo, Lehman's general counsel, and Rick Rieder, who ran Lehman's global principal strategies group, with Paulson's deputy, Bob Steel, and Senator Judd Gregg. Russo had been advocating a plan in which the government would create a special facility—what Russo called a "good bank" proposal—to help provide additional liquidity to Wall Street firms by creating a backstop for their most toxic assets, but he had met resistance. It would simply look too much like another bailout, and Washington wasn't ready for that—not yet.

"I am worried about a lot of things," Paulson now told Fuld, singling out a new IMF report estimating that mortgage- and real estate–related write-downs could total $945 billion in the next two years. He said he was also anxious about the staggering amount of leverage—the amount of debt to equity—that investment banks were still using to juice their returns. That only added enormous risk to the system, he complained.

The numbers in that area were indeed worrisome. Lehman Brothers was leveraged 30.7 to 1; Merrill Lynch was only slightly better, at 26.9 to 1. Paulson knew intuitively that Wall Street's leverage problem could not end well. He also knew that the firms would never rein themselves in; they were all blindly chasing one another. He always reminded himself of a remarkably telling question that Charles Prince, the CEO of Citigroup, had asked him the year before at a similar dinner: "Isn't there something you can do to order us not to take all of these risks?"

Paulson was worried not just about Lehman; he knew Merrill too was awash in bad assets, and mentioned the challenges that Merrill's new CEO, John Thain (who had been Paulson's number two at Goldman), was facing with his own balance sheet. But leverage and Merrill's problems weren't Fuld's primary concern at the moment; he was still irked by the short-sellers and once again pressed Paulson to do something about them. If they could be contained, it would give Lehman and the other firms a chance to find their footing and get their balance sheets in order. But if the shorts were allowed to keep hammering away, the overall situation was only going to get a lot uglier.

As a former CEO himself, Paulson could understand Fuld's frustration. Short-sellers cared only about their own profits and gave little thought to their impact on the system. "I'm sympathetic," Paulson said. "If there are bad actors, we'll put them out of business."

But Paulson was also concerned that Fuld was using the short-sellers as an excuse to avoid addressing the genuine problems at Lehman. "You know, the capital raise, as good as it was, is just one thing," Paulson told him. "It's not going to end there." He reminded him that the pool of potential buyers for Lehman was not a large one.

"Look, Dick," he continued. "There aren't a lot of people out there saying, 'I have to have an investment banking franchise.' You have to start thinking about your options."

It was a not-so-subtle hint to start thinking about selling the entire firm. Although the conversation agitated Fuld slightly, they'd had similar discussions before, so he took Paulson's advice in stride.

The group took their seats, and as each of the speakers rose to talk, the perilous state of the economy became ever clearer. The credit crisis wasn't just a U.S. problem; it had spread globally. Mario Draghi, Italy's central bank governor and a former partner at Goldman Sachs, spoke candidly of his worries about global money-market funds. Jean-Claude Trichet told the audience that they needed to come up with common requirements for capital ratios—the amount of money a firm needed to keep on hand compared to the amount it could lend—and, more important, leverage and liquidity standards, which he thought were much more telling indicators of a firm's ability to withstand a "run on the bank."

Mr. King, the governor of the Bank of England, offered perhaps the harshest assessment. "You are all bright people, but you failed. Risk management is hard," he declared. "So the lesson is, we can't let you get as big as you were and do the damage that you've done or get as complex as you were."

That night, after Fuld had finally found his car and driver outside the Treasury Building, he thumbed out an e-mail on his BlackBerry to Russo. "Just finished the Paulson dinner," Fuld wrote at 9:52 p.m.

A few takeaways//

1-we have huge brand with treasury

2-loved our capital raise

3-really appreciate u + Reiders work onm [*sic*] ideas

4-they want to kill the bad HFnds [hedge funds]+ heavily regulate the rest

5-they want all G7 countries to embrace

Mtm stnds [Mark-to-market standards]

Cap stnds

Lev + liquidity stnds

6-HP [Hank Paulson] has a worried view of ML [Merrill Lynch]

All in all worthwhile.

Dick

———

On the following Tuesday, April 15, Neel Kashkari and Phillip Swagel hurried down past the guard house of the Treasury Building to where Hank Paulson and Bob Steel were waiting for them in the secretary's black Suburban. The group was due at the Federal Reserve in Foggy Bottom at 3:00 p.m.—in ten minutes—and was running late.

The two men made something of an odd couple. Kashkari, dark with a bald dome, still dressed like the investment banker he had recently been, while Swagel, pale with dark hair and glasses, looked more like a wonky government official. A former academic, he had kept fit and seemed younger than his thirty-four-year-old colleague, even though he was eight years older.

Paulson had invited his young advisers to a meeting with Ben Bernanke so that they could present a confidential memo that the two of them had authored—a memo that had far-reaching implications for the nation's increasingly unsteady financial system.

At Paulson's request, they had done nothing less than to formulate a plan for what to do in the event of a total financial meltdown, outlining the steps that the Treasury Department might have to take and the new powers it would require to stave off another Great Depression. They had given the proposal the provocative title "Break the Glass: Bank Recapitalization Plan." Like a fire alarm enclosed in glass, it was intended to be used only in an emergency, though with each passing day, it appeared more and more likely that the proposal was no mere drill.

———

As the Suburban raced to Bernanke's office, Kashkari, who was unflappable by nature, remained calm. After a brief stint as a satellite engineer, he had gone to work as an investment banker for Goldman Sachs in San Francisco, where no one had ever needed to tell him that he was good at his job. He loved meeting with clients and putting his salesmanship to the test; like Paulson, he was an aggressive, get-it-done guy. And like Paulson, he occasionally ruffled feathers with his shoot-first-and-ask-questions-later approach, though few ever doubted his intellectual firepower.

Kashkari had always wanted to work in government, and though he'd met Paulson only once previously, he left him a congratulatory voice mail when Paulson was named Treasury secretary. To his surprise, Paulson responded the next day: "Thanks. I'd love for you to join me at Treasury."

Kashkari immediately booked a flight to Washington, during which he carefully rehearsed the pitch he would make to Paulson. They met at the Old Executive Office Building, where Paulson was camped out until the Senate could confirm him, and Kashkari had scarcely begun his presentation when he noticed a distracted, slightly irritated look come over Paulson's face. Kashkari stopped in midsentence.

"Look, here is what I'm trying to do here," Paulson told him. "I want to put together a small team that will be working on policy issues, all kinds of issues, really, just doing whatever it takes to get things done. How does that sound?"

An astonished Kashkari realized, *He's offering me a job!*

As the two men shook hands on the deal, Paulson suddenly remembered an important detail and asked, "Oh, yeah, there's just one other thing. Are you a Republican?" As luck would have it, he was. Paulson saw him out and directed him to the White House Personnel Office a few blocks away. Kashkari was soon on the team, and now he was about to lead the biggest sales pitch of his career—to the single most influential person in the entire world's economy.

———

Four words had dogged Ben Bernanke from the moment he assumed the job of chairman of the Federal Reserve on February 1, 2006: "Hard Act to Follow." It was, perhaps, an inevitable epithet for the man whom the renowned *Washington Post* investigative reporter Bob Woodward had also dubbed "The Maestro"—Alan Greenspan, who was to monetary policy what Warren Buffett is to investing. Greenspan had overseen the Federal Reserve during a period of unprecedented prosperity, a spectacular bull market that had begun during the Reagan administration and had run for over twenty years. Not that anyone outside the economics profession had a clue what Greenspan was doing or even saying most of the time. His obfuscation in public pronouncements was legendary, which only added to his mystique as a great intellect.

Bernanke, by contrast, had been a college professor for most of his career, and at the time of his appointment to replace the then-eighty-year-old Greenspan, his area of specialization—the Great Depression and what the Federal Reserve had done wrong in the 1920s and 1930s—seemed quaint. Trying to identify the causes of the Great Depression may be the Holy Grail of macroeconomics, but to the larger public, it seemed to have little practical application in a key government position. Any economic crisis of that magnitude seemed safely in the past.

By the summer of 2007, however, America's second Gilded Age had come shockingly to an end, and Greenspan's reputation lay in tatters. His faith that the market was self-correcting suddenly seemed fatally short-sighted; his cryptic remarks were judged in hindsight as the confused ramblings of a misguided ideologue.

As a scholar of the Depression, Bernanke was cut from a different cloth, though he shared Greenspan's belief in the free market. In his analysis of the crisis, Bernanke advanced the views of the economists Milton Friedman and Anna J. Schwartz, whose *A Monetary History of the United States, 1867–1960* (first published in 1963) had argued that the Federal Reserve had caused the Great Depression by not immediately flushing the system with cheap cash to stimulate the economy. And subsequent efforts proved too little, too late. Under Herbert Hoover, the Fed had done exactly the opposite: tightening the money supply and choking off the economy.

Bernanke's entrenched views led many observers to be optimistic that he would be an independent Fed chairman, one who would not let politics prevent him from doing what he thought was the right thing. The credit crisis proved to be his first real test, but to what degree would his understanding of economic missteps eighty years earlier help him grapple with the current crisis? This was not history; this was happening in real time.

———

Ben Shalom Bernanke was born in 1953 and grew up in Dillon, South Carolina, a small town permeated by the stench of tobacco warehouses. As an eleven-year-old, he traveled to Washington to compete in the national spelling championship in 1965, falling in the second round when he misspelled "Edelweiss." From that day forward he would wonder what might have been had the movie *The Sound of Music,* which featured a well-known song with that word for a title, only made its way to tiny Dillon.

The Bernankes were observant Jews in a conservative Christian evangelical town just emerging from the segregation era. His grandfather Jonas Bernanke, an Austrian immigrant who moved to Dillon in the early 1940s, owned the local drugstore, which Ben's father helped him run; his mother was a teacher. As a young man, Ben waited tables six days a week at South of Border, a tourist stop off Interstate 95.

In high school, Bernanke taught himself calculus because his school did not offer a class in the subject. As a junior, he achieved a near-perfect score on the SATs (1590), and the following year he was offered a National Merit Scholarship to Harvard. Graduating with a degree in economics summa cum laude, he was accepted to the prestigious graduate program in economics at the Massachusetts Institute of Technology. There he wrote a dense dissertation about the business cycle, dedicating it to his parents and to his wife, Anna Friedmann, a Wellesley College student whom he married the weekend after she graduated in 1978.

The young couple moved to California, where Bernanke taught at Stanford's business school and his wife entered the university's master's program in Spanish. Six years later, Bernanke was granted a tenured position in the economics department at Princeton. He was thirty-one and a rising star, admired for "econometrics" research that used statistical techniques and computer models to analyze economic problems.

Bernanke also demonstrated political skills as his intellectual reputation grew. As chairman of the Princeton economics department, he proved effective at mediating disputes and handling big egos. He also created a series of new programs and recruited promising young economists such as Paul Krugman (who happened to be his ideological opposite). Six years later Bernanke was recruited to succeed Greenspan.

Up until early August 2007, Bernanke had been enjoying his tenure at the Fed, so much so that he and Anna had planned to take a vacation that month and drive to Charlotte, North Carolina, and then on to Myrtle Beach, South Carolina, to spend time with friends and family. Before heading south, he had to see to one final business matter: the Federal Open Market Committee, the Fed's powerful policy-making panel, which among its other responsibilities sets interest rates, was scheduled to meet on August 7. On that day, Bernanke and his colleagues acknowledged for the first time in recent memory the presence of "downside risks to growth," but decided nonetheless to keep the Fed's benchmark interest rate unchanged at 5.25 percent for the ninth consecutive meeting. Rather than try to boost economic activity by lowering rates, the committee decided to stand pat. "The committee's predominant policy concern remains the risk that inflation will fail to moderate as expected," the Fed announced in a subsequent statement.

That, however, was not what Wall Street wanted to hear, for concerns about the sputtering economy had investors clamoring for a rate cut. Four days earlier financial commentator Jim Cramer had exploded on an afternoon segment of CNBC, declaring that the Fed was "asleep" for not taking aggressive action. "They're nuts! They know nothing!" he bellowed.

What the Fed's policy makers recognized but didn't acknowledge publicly was that credit markets were beginning to suffer as the air had begun gradually seeping out of the housing bubble. Cheap credit had been the economy's rocket fuel, encouraging consumers to pile on debt—whether to pay for second homes, new cars, home renovations, or vacations. It had also sparked a deal-making frenzy the likes of which had never been seen: Leveraged buyouts got larger and larger as private-equity firms funded takeovers with mountains of loans; as a result, transactions became ever riskier.

Traditionally conservative institutional investors, such as endowments and pension funds, came under pressure to chase higher returns by investing in hedge funds and private-equity funds. The Fed resisted calls to cut interest rates, which would only have thrown gasoline onto the fire.

Two days later, however, the world changed. Early on the morning of August 9, in the first major indication that the financial world was in serious peril, France's biggest bank, BNP Paribas, announced that it was halting investors from withdrawing their money from three money market funds with assets of some $2 billion. The problem? The market for certain assets, especially those backed by American mortgage loans, had essentially dried up, making it difficult to determine what they were actually worth. "The complete evaporation of liquidity in certain market segments of the U.S. securitization market has made it impossible to value certain assets fairly, regardless of their quality or credit rating," the bank explained.

It was a chilling sign that traders were now treating mortgage-related assets as radioactive—unfit to buy at any price. The European Central Bank responded quickly, pumping nearly 95 billion euros, or $130 billion, into euro money markets—a bigger cash infusion than the one that had followed the September 11 attacks. Meanwhile, in the United States, Countrywide Financial, the nation's biggest mortgage lender, warned that "unprecedented disruptions" in the markets threatened its financial condition.

The rates that banks were charging to lend money to one another quickly spiked in response, far surpassing the central bank's official rates. To Bernanke what was happening was obvious: It was a panic. Banks and investors, fearful of being contaminated by these toxic assets, were hoarding cash and refusing to make loans of almost any kind. It wasn't clear which banks had the most subprime exposure, so banks were assumed guilty until proven innocent. It had all the hallmarks of the early 1930s— confidence in the global financial system was rapidly eroding, and liquidity was evaporating. The famous nineteenth-century dictum of Walter Bagehot came to mind: "Every banker knows that if he has to prove that he is worthy of credit, however good may be his arguments, in fact his credit is gone."

After Bernanke told his wife their trip had to be canceled, he summoned his advisers to his office; those who were away called in. Fed officials began working the phones, trying to find out what was happening in the markets and who might need help. Bernanke was in his office every morning by 7:00 a.m.

Only two days later came the next shock. It was becoming a daily scramble for the Fed to keep up with the dramatically changing conditions. The following day Bernanke held a conference call with Fed policy makers to discuss lowering the discount rate. (A symbolic figure in normal times, the discount rate is what the Fed charges banks that borrow directly from it.) In the end, the Fed issued a statement announcing that it was providing liquidity by allowing banks to pledge an expanded set of collateral in exchange for cash—although not on the scale that the Europeans had—to help the markets function as normally as possible. It also again reminded the banks that the "discount window" was available. Less than a week later, Bernanke, faced with continued turmoil in the markets, reversed his earlier decision and went ahead with a half-point cut in the discount rate, to 4.75 percent, and hinted that cuts in the benchmark rate—the Fed's most powerful tool for stimulating the economy—might be coming as well. Despite these reassurances, markets remained tense and volatile.

By now it was clear even to Bernanke that he had failed to gauge the severity of the situation. As late as June 5, he had declared in a speech that "at this point, the troubles in the subprime sector seem unlikely to seriously spill over to the broader economy or the financial system." The housing problem, he had thought, was limited to the increase in subprime loans to borrowers with poor credit. Although the subprime market had mushroomed to $2 trillion, it was still just a fraction of the overall $14 trillion U.S. mortgage market.

But that analysis did not take into account a number of other critical factors, such as the fact that the link between the housing market and the financial system was further complicated by the growing use of exotic derivatives. Securities whose income and value came from a pool of residential mortgages were being amalgamated, sliced up, and reconfigured again, and soon became the underpinnings of new investment products marketed as collateralized debt obligations (CDOs).

The way that firms like a JP Morgan or a Lehman Brothers now operated bore little resemblance to the way banks had traditionally done business. No longer would a bank simply make a loan and keep it on its books. Now lending was about origination—establishing the first link in a chain of securitization that spread risk of the loan among dozens if not hundreds and thousands of parties. Although securitization supposedly reduced risk and increased liquidity, what it meant in reality was that many institutions and investors were now interconnected, for better and for worse. A municipal pension fund in Norway might have subprime mortgages from California in its portfolio and not even realize it. Making matters worse, many financial firms had borrowed heavily against these securities, using what is known as leverage to amplify their returns. This only increased the pain when they began to lose value.

Regulators around the world were having trouble understanding how the pieces all fit together. Greenspan would later admit that even he hadn't comprehended exactly what was happening. "I've got some fairly heavy background in mathematics," he stated two years after he stepped down from the Fed. "But some of the complexities of some of the instruments that were going into CDOs bewilders me. I didn't understand what they were doing or how they actually got the types of returns out of the mezzanines and the various tranches of the CDO that they did. And I figured if I didn't understand it and I had access to a couple hundred PhDs, how the rest of the world is going to understand it sort of bewildered me."

He was not alone. Even the CEOs of the firms that sold these products had no better comprehension of it all.

————

The door of the chairman's office swung open, and Bernanke warmly greeted the group from Treasury. Like Swagel, he still had the halting manner of an academic, but for an economist, he was unusually adept at small talk. He showed Paulson and his team into his office, where they settled around a small coffee table. Beside the expected Bloomberg terminal, Bernanke had a Washington Nationals cap prominently displayed on his desk.

After a few minutes of chat, Swagel reached into a folder and gingerly handed Bernanke the ten-page outline of the "Break the Glass" paper. Kashkari glanced at his colleagues for reassurance and then began to speak.

"I think we all understand the political calculus here, the limits of what we can legally do. How do you get the authority to prevent a collapse?"

Bernanke nodded in agreement, and Kashkari continued. "So, as you know, we in Treasury, in consultation with staffers at the Fed, have been exploring a set of options for the last few months, and I think we have come up with the basic framework. This is meant to be something that if we're ever on the verge of mayhem, we can pull off the shelf in the event of an emergency and present to Congress and say, 'Here is our plan.'"

Kashkari looked over at Bernanke, who, having been intently studying the text, had immediately zeroed in on the key of the plan: "Treasury purchases $500 billion from financial institutions via an auction mechanism. Determining what prices to pay for heterogeneous securities would be a key challenge. Treasury would compensate bidder with newly issued Treasury securities, rather than cash. Such an asset-swap would eliminate the need for sterilization by the Fed. Treasury would hire private asset managers to manage the portfolios to maximize value for taxpayers and unwind the positions over time (potentially up to 10 years)."

Bernanke, weighing his words carefully, asked how they had come up with the $500 billion figure.

"We are talking a ballpark estimate of, what, say, $1 trillion in toxic assets?" explained Kashkari. "But we wouldn't have to buy all of the bad stuff to make a meaningful dent. So, let's say half. But maybe it's more like $600 billion."

As Bernanke continued to study their paper, Kashkari and Swagel took a second to savor the moment: They were briefing the keeper of The Temple—as the Federal Reserve is often called—on what might be a historic bailout of the banking system. Government intervention on this scale hadn't been contemplated in at least fifty years; the savings and loan rescue of the late 1980s was a minor blip by comparison.

If the "Break the Glass" plan did get past Congress—a problem they'd concern themselves with later—they had already detailed how Treasury would designate the New York Fed to run the auctions of Wall Street's toxic assets. Together they would solicit qualified investors in the private sector to manage the assets purchased by the government. The New York Fed would then hold the first of ten weekly auctions, buying $50 billion worth of mortgage-related assets. The auctions would, it was hoped, fetch the best possible price for the government. Ten selected asset managers would each manage $50 billion for up to ten years.

Kashkari knew the proposal was very complicated but argued it was worth the risk, as the way things were heading, there was little chance of a "soft landing." Drastic action was required. "The bill would need to give Treasury temporary authorization to buy the securities, as well as the funding," he said, "and it would need to raise the debt ceiling, because we only have room for about $400 billion under the current ceiling.

"But because we would be tapping the private sector so heavily, the program would require little in the way of government overhead: no significant hiring by Treasury, for example," he continued. "But also we need to be mindful of the optics. Only public financial institutions would be eligible. No hedge funds or foreign banks."

Then Kashkari summarized what he and his colleagues at Treasury viewed as the pros and cons of their proposal. The first and most important point was that if the government acted, banks would continue lending—but not, it was hoped, in the irresponsible way that gave rise to the crisis in the first place. The primary argument against the proposal was that, to the extent that the plan worked, it would create "moral hazard." In other words, the people who made the reckless bets that initially caused the problems would be spared any financial pain.

The two Treasury officials next presented the alternative approaches, of which they had identified four:

The government sells insurance to banks to protect them from any further drop in the value of their toxic assets.
The Federal Reserve issues non-recourse loans to banks, as it did in the JP Morgan takeover of Bear Stearns.
The Federal Housing Authority refinances loans individually.
Treasury directly invests in the banks.

As he listened, Bernanke stroked his beard and occasionally offered a knowing smile. The meeting ended with no resolution except to take the plan and put it on the shelf until—or unless—it was needed, but Kashkari was gratified that the chairman took it so well—much better, in fact, than his own boss, Hank Paulson, had when Kashkari first decided to test him on the subject of intervening in the financial markets.

Everyone in Paulson's inner circle at Treasury had heard about when

Kashkari barged into his office late one evening in March, finding the secretary in an unusually good mood, chatting with his chief of staff, Jim Wilkinson.

"Hank, I want to talk about bailouts," Kashkari interrupted.

"What are you talking about? Get out of here," Paulson said, annoyed.

"Look, we keep talking about how do we get the political will to get the authority we need to really take action, right? Well, we have to have some record that shows we tried. The next president is going to come in and say, 'Here are the steps that should have been taken, but the previous administration was unwilling or unable to take them, blah, blah, blah.' You know what that means? The next president is going to bring the hostages home. Obama! *Obama is going to bring the hostages home!*"

Paulson erupted in laughter at the notion that Obama would somehow ride this crisis the way Ronald Reagan rode the Iranian hostage standoff in the late 1970s. He pointed at Kashkari.

"Ha, ha. Obama is going to bring the hostages home," Paulson said. "Oh, yeah? Get the fuck out of here."

———

A London sky of gray-pink clouds was just beginning to darken on an evening in April when the phone rang for Bob Diamond, the chief executive of Barclays Capital. Diamond had been contentedly honing his putting skills in his office in the bank's corporate enclave in Canary Wharf, the booming financial district in East London along the river Thames, and a dozen golf balls were strewn about the hole he had cut into the carpet. The office's walls were lined with Boston Red Sox mementos, which had been hung there not merely to torture visitors from New York City—of which there were many—but because Diamond, a native New Englander, was also a die-hard Sox fan.

He disliked having his precious few minutes of downtime interrupted, but in this instance he was happy to put down his putter and take the call. It was his friend Bob Steel, whom he had just seen briefly on his recent trip to Washington for the dinner party at the Treasury Building.

The two had become close after they joined the board of Barclays at the same time in 2005. They came from different parts of the country and different parts of the business—Steel, from Durham, North Carolina, was in Goldman equities; Diamond, from Springfield, Massachusetts, was a former bond trading executive for Morgan Stanley and Credit Suisse. But they recognized similar qualities in each other: Each came from middle-class families and had worked his way through college.

The arc of their careers more recently had been nearly identical: Both Steel and Diamond, as Yankees in Queen Elizabeth's court, had made quite a splash in London. For Steel, success had come with starting Goldman's European equities trading operation, a feat Hank Paulson, his former boss, always remembered. For his part, Diamond had transformed a small investment bank with some 3,000 employees into a major London powerhouse that currently had a payroll of 15,000. Barclays Capital now accounted for about a quarter of the bank's profits.

The two had remained friends after Steel quit the Barclays board to follow Paulson to Treasury, to the point that each had always been able to count on the other to pick up the phone if he called, whatever the reason.

"Listen, one of my jobs here is to brainstorm," Steel said somewhat stiffly after greeting Diamond, "and, ah, sort of sketch out various scenario plans. In that capacity, I have a question for you."

Steel's uncharacteristically distant tone surprised Diamond, who asked, "Is this official business, Bob?"

"No, no. Look, I'm not calling on behalf of anyone," he assured him. "The markets have calmed down a bit now, but I am trying to figure out that if things do get worse, and we get to a certain level, if, ah, things can happen."

"All right, shoot."

Steel took a deep breath and then asked his question: "Is there a price at which you'd be interested in Lehman? And if so, what would you need from us?"

Diamond was momentarily speechless; Treasury, he realized, was clearly trying to formulate strategic solutions in the event that Lehman found itself in a Bear Stearns–like situation. From long acquaintance he knew Steel to be a no-nonsense pragmatist, not someone who idly floated trial balloons.

"I'm going to have to think about that because I don't have an answer," Diamond said carefully.

2

"Yes, but do think about it," Steel said.

"Never say never," Diamond answered, and both men laughed. Diamond had always trotted out that line when reporters pressed him about possible acquisitions, though this was the first time that Steel had been on the receiving end of it.

Steel was well aware of Barclays Capital's desire to increase its presence in the United States, an ambition that Diamond practically wore on the sleeve of his Savile Row suits. While he had built, from the ground up, a major investment bank that had been a London phenomenon, he had always yearned to be a major player on Wall Street. His restless pursuit of that goal explained why Diamond had so abruptly left Morgan Stanley for Credit Suisse First Boston in 1992, taking much of the repo trading desk with him and inciting the wrath of John Mack. Four years later, Diamond left for BZW, whose remnants were the foundation for Barclays Capital.

Lehman was a logical merger candidate if Diamond—and, of course, his boss and the board in London—wanted Barclays to become an overnight investment banking powerhouse in New York. But he knew it would be an expensive purchase so long as Dick Fuld was running it. Still, an opportunity like this hardly came up often.

What the rest of Wall Street didn't know at the time was that Barclays had been contemplating another purchase: Diamond had been in conversation with UBS about buying its investment banking franchise and was planning to fly to Zurich later that week for further meetings. He now shared this information with Steel but cautioned him that the talks with UBS were very preliminary, and the last thing Diamond needed was word of them leaking out. As was always a possibility, the deal might not go anywhere.

Lehman, in any case, was in a different league altogether. It wouldn't be easy selling an acquisition of this magnitude to his board, who were still feeling gun shy after losing an expensive bidding war for Dutch bank ABN AMRO months earlier. But Lehman was the fourth biggest investment house in the United States. If Lehman could be had for a major discount, he'd have to consider the prospect seriously, wouldn't he?

"Yes," Diamond said to Steel, "it's definitely something to think about."

CHAPTER FIVE

Surprisingly soft-spoken when not on the air, Jim Cramer, CNBC's blustery market guru, politely told the security guard standing outside Lehman Brothers' headquarters on Seventh Avenue and Fiftieth Street that he was expected for a breakfast meeting with Dick Fuld. He was ushered through the revolving door, past Lehman's bomb-sniffing Labrador, Bella, and to the reception desk, where he made his way through the familiar security procedures. Looking rumpled as usual, he was received in the waiting area of the thirty-second floor as ceremoniously as if he were a major client who had arrived to negotiate a billion-dollar deal. Erin Callan, the CFO, was present, as was Gerald Donini, the head of global equities and a neighbor of Cramer's in Summit, New Jersey.

Fuld, who was still zealously conducting his jihad against the short-sellers, had personally invited Cramer for the meeting. By now he had come to realize that he needed an ally in his struggle against the shorts, but so far, nobody had been willing to join the battle. Not Cox. Not Geithner. And not Paulson, despite their recent conversation at Treasury. But maybe Cramer, with his huge television audience and connections deep within the hedge fund world, could somehow help sway the debate and talk up Lehman's stock price.

Fuld had known Cramer for a decade. After Long-Term Capital Management blew up in 1998, word spread that Lehman had huge exposure to the fund and might be the next to go down. Fuld had received a major public boost from Cramer, then a new face at CNBC, when he declared on television that all Lehman needed to do was buy back its own shares to halt the downward spiral and squeeze the shorts. The following morning, Fuld, who had never met Cramer, called him at his office and told him, "I bid thirty-one dollars for one million shares of Lehman." Shares of the company steadied soon afterward.

If Wall Street had indeed been taking on some aspects of a Shakespearean tragedy, Cramer would likely serve as the comic relief. Voluble and wild-eyed, he spoke in his TV appearances so quickly that it often seemed as if his head might explode from the sheer effort of communicating his ideas. But for all his carnival-barker antics, people on Wall Street knew Cramer was no fool. He had managed a hedge fund and founded TheStreet .com, an early and influential investing Web site, and had a keen understanding of how the market worked.

Fuld and Cramer had come to respect each other as no-nonsense street fighters, despite their pronounced differences in character. Cramer, a media star, was solidly Harvard, had once worked at Goldman, and counted as one of his best friends Eliot Spitzer, the bane of Wall Street. Fuld, for his part, tended to despise Ivy Leaguers, liked to think of himself as the anti-Goldman, and had never been much of a communicator. Still, he appreciated the fact that Cramer had always been an honest broker, willing to speak his mind, however unpopular his opinions might be.

After one of Lehman's wait staff had taken food orders for the group, Fuld walked an attentive Cramer through his talking points. Lehman, Fuld said, was working hard to reduce the firm's leverage and restore confidence among investors. Though they had raised $4 billion in new capital in the first quarter, Fuld was convinced that a "cabal of shorts" was preventing the stock price from being properly reflected. The franchise was undervalued.

Cramer nodded his head energetically. "Look," he said, "I think there is definitely a problem with the shorts—they're leaning all over you."

Fuld was gratified to see that he had a receptive audience. As he was well aware, his short-seller predicament touched on an obscure issue near and dear to Cramer: the uptick rule—a regulation that had been introduced by the Securities and Exchange Commission in 1938 to prevent investors from continually shorting a stock that was falling. (In other words, before a stock could be shorted, the price had to rise, indicating that there were active buyers for it in the market. Theoretically, the rule would prevent stocks from spiraling straight downward, with short-sellers jumping on for the ride.) But in 2007 the commission had abolished the rule, and to critics like Cramer, its decision had been influenced by free-market ideologues who were eager to remove even the most benign speed bumps from the system. Ever since, Cramer had been warning anyone who'd listen that without this check, hedge funds were free to blitzkrieg good companies and drive down their stock.

But until the current crisis, few had been willing to listen to his admonitions. Because their hedge fund clients wanted the rule eliminated, Wall Street firms were happy to accede—right up until the time that they themselves became the target of short-sellers and had to run for cover.

"You can be a great ally to me on this uptick rule crusade," Cramer said.

Fuld contemplated his guest's enthusiasm as he silently weighed the advantages and disadvantages of lending his firm's name to the cable news star's crusade. Cramer was probably right about the rule's removal hurting Lehman, but Fuld also knew that his firm's own arbitrage desk had hedge fund clients who were selling short, and they made the firm a great deal of money. He certainly didn't want to alienate them, and at the same time, he recognized that there was a legitimate debate about the issue. And however protective the restrictions may have been intended to be, Fuld knew perfectly well that investors could get around them by using options and derivatives.

Donini, skeptical that the uptick rule was Lehman's biggest problem, interjected on behalf of Fuld. "What are you trying to accomplish, Jim?" he asked.

"The shorts are destroying great companies," Cramer replied. "They destroyed Bear Stearns, and they're trying to destroy Lehman," he said, perhaps trying to play to Fuld's ego. "I want to stop that."

"If you're trying to accomplish that," Donini replied, "and you believe that shorts are causing the problem, then I don't believe the uptick rule is the way to do it." Donini explained to Cramer that he felt the real problem in the marketplace was "naked shorting." Normally, when investors sell shares short, the investor first borrows the shares from a broker, sells them, and then hopes they drop in value so the investor can buy them at a lower price, replace the borrowed shares, and pocket the difference as a profit.

But in naked shorting—which is illegal—the investor never borrows the underlying shares, potentially allowing them to manipulate the market.

Cramer was intrigued but also visibly taken aback by Donini's answer. He had been invited to the meeting, had offered to help, and now his offer was being rejected. He tried changing the subject back to Lehman's troubles. "Well, why don't you give me ammo so that I can tell a positive story?" he suggested.

Sensing the tension rising in the room, Callan interjected, speaking up for the first time. "We just bought this unbelievable portfolio from Peloton, and it's immediately accretive," she said, cheerfully offering what she considered a bit of good news.

But Cramer could barely conceal a frown, for he knew a good deal about Peloton. Based in London, the hedge fund had been started by Ron Beller, a former Goldman executive whose wife was a policy adviser to Prime Minister Gordon Brown. It had once been among the top-performing hedge funds in the world but had faltered, selling its assets in a virtual fire sale. "Geez," Cramer answered with as much tact as he could muster, "I'm surprised to hear it's any good, given the fact that they were levered thirty to one with what I hear is a lot of bad stuff."

"No," Fuld said enthusiastically, "we got this for a song."

Cramer did not look convinced. "One of the things I'm really unclear about is that, if you talk to Goldman, Goldman's radically trying to deleverage, and what you're saying is, 'I'm gonna deleverage,' but you actually are increasing your leverage."

Fuld, who didn't appreciate the tone of the observation, responded, "What we're doing is, we're buying really important portfolios that we think are worth a lot more and we're trading out of ones that are worth less."

Callan said that Lehman was quickly deleveraging its own balance sheet. She also said, "There are assets on the books that we have a high degree of confidence are undervalued." She spent the next ten minutes telling Cramer about the firm's residential real estate assets in California and Florida, two of the hardest hit markets, suggesting she expected them to rebound soon.

Having come to the conclusion that any alliance with Cramer could only be problematic, Fuld quickly changed the subject and began pumping Cramer for information. "So, what are you hearing out there? Who's coming after us?"

Fuld said that he had become convinced that two of the nation's most powerful financiers, Steven A. Cohen at SAC Capital Advisors in Greenwich, Connecticut, and Kenneth C. Griffin of Citadel Investment Group in Chicago, were largely responsible for both the short raid and rumormongering, though he didn't say their names aloud.

"They are liars!" Fuld said adamantly of the shorts. "I think it's pretty safe for you to go out and say they're liars."

Cramer, while sympathetic, made it clear that he wasn't prepared to go out on a limb and back Lehman's stock unless he had more information. "I can say that people could be skeptical of the rumors," he offered, and then added, "why don't you go to government? If you think this is so bad and you think that there's a real bear raid and people are lying about it, why don't you go tell the SEC?"

But Fuld, growing increasingly agitated, only repeated, "Why don't you just give me the names of people telling you negative things about us?"

Cramer was flushed. "Look, there *isn't* anybody. I do my own work, and my own work makes me feel that you're taking down a lot of crap and you're not selling a lot of crap, and that therefore you really need cash."

Fuld didn't like being challenged.

"I can just categorically dismiss that. We've been completely transparent. We don't need cash, we have tons of cash. Our balance sheet has never been this good," he asserted.

But Cramer was still skeptical: "If that's the case, why aren't you finding some way to be able to translate that cash into a higher stock price, buying some of your bonds?"

Fuld scoffed as he brought the meeting to an end.

"I'm on the board of the Federal Reserve of New York," Fuld told Cramer. "Why would I be lying to you? They see *everything*."

―――――――

It was mid-May and David Einhorn had a speech to write.

Einhorn, a hedge fund manager controlling over $6 billion of assets, was preparing to speak at the Ira W. Sohn Investment Research Conference, where each year a thousand or so people pay as much as $3,250 each to hear prominent investors tout, or thrash, stocks. The attendees get to absorb a few usually well-thought-out investment ideas while knowing that their entrance fee is going to a good cause—the Tomorrow's Children Fund, a cancer charity.

Einhorn, a thirty-nine-year-old who looked at least a decade younger, was sitting in his office a block from Grand Central Terminal, pondering what he would say. With only seven analysts and a handful of support staff, his firm, Greenlight Capital, was as peacefully quiet as a relaxation spa. No one was barking trade orders into a telephone; no one was high-fiving a colleague.

Greenlight was known for its patient, cerebral approach to investing. "We start by asking why a security is likely to be misvalued in the market," Einhorn once said. "Once we have a theory, we analyze the security to determine if it is, in fact, cheap or overvalued. In order to invest, we need to understand why the opportunity exists and believe we have a sizable analytical edge over the person on the other side of the trade." Unlike most funds, Greenlight did not use leverage, or borrowed money, to boost its bets.

Einhorn's analysts spent their days studying 10-Ks in conference areas with wonky names like "The Nonrecurring Room," a reference to the accounting term for any gain or loss not likely to occur again—a categorization sometimes used by companies to beef up their statements. For Einhorn, it was a red flag, and one that he used to spot businesses he could short. Among the companies he had identified from recent research was Lehman Brothers, which he thought might be an ideal topic for his speech. While questioning Lehman's solidity may have become the most popular recent topic of Wall Street gossip, Einhorn had been quietly worried about the firm since the previous summer.

On Thursday, August 9, 2007, seven months before Bear went down, Einhorn had rolled out of bed in Rye, New York, a few hours before dawn to read reports and write e-mails. The headlines that day struck him as very odd. All that summer, the implosion in subprime mortgages had been reverberating through the credit markets, and two Bear Stearns hedge funds that had large positions of mortgage-backed securities had already collapsed.

Now BNP Paribas, the major French bank, had announced that it was stopping investors from withdrawing their money from three money market funds.

Like Bernanke, he stopped everything he was doing that weekend to try to better understand what was really happening. "These people are workers in France, they've got a money market account that they're earning no money on. Their only goal is to have that money available to them whenever they want it; that's what a money market account is. You can't freeze the money market," he told his team.

Einhorn e-mailed some of his top analysts to assign a special project: "We're going to do something we don't usually do, research-wise," he announced. Instead of the usual painstaking investigation into a company or a particular idea, they were going to conduct—on both Saturday and Sunday—a crash investigation of financial companies that had big exposure to the world of securitized debt. He knew that this was where the problem had started, but what concerned him now was trying to understand where it might end. Any banks that held investments with falling real estate values—which had likely been packaged up neatly as part of securitized products that he suspected some firms didn't even realize they owned—could be in danger. The project was code named "The Credit Basket."

By Sunday night, his team had come up with a list of twenty-five companies for Greenlight to short, including Lehman Brothers, a firm that he had actually already taken a very small short position in just a week earlier on a hunch that its stock—then at $64.80 a share—was too high.

Over the next several weeks, names were removed from the credit basket as Greenlight closed out some short positions and focused its capital on a handful of firms, Lehman still among them.

As these banks began reporting their quarterly results in September, Einhorn paid close attention and became especially concerned by some of the things he heard in Lehman's September 18 conference call on its third-quarter earnings.

For one, like others on Wall Street at the time, the Lehman executive on the call, Chris O'Meara, the chief financial officer, seemed overly optimistic. "It is early, and we don't give guidance on future periods, but as I mentioned, I think the worst of this credit correction is behind us," O'Meara announced to the analysts.

More important, Einhorn thought Lehman was not being forthcoming about a dubious accounting maneuver that had enabled it to record revenue when the value of its own debt fell, arguing that theoretically it could buy that debt back at a lower price and pocket the difference. Other Wall Street firms had also adopted the practice, but Lehman seemed cagier about it than the others, unwilling to put a precise number on the gain.

"This is crazy accounting. I don't know why they put it in," Einhorn told his staff. "It means that the day before you go bankrupt is the most profitable day in the history of your company, because you'll say all the debt was worthless. You get to call it revenue. And literally they pay bonuses off this, which drives me nuts."

Six months later, Einhorn had listened intently to Lehman's earnings call on March 18, 2008, and was baffled to hear Erin Callan offering an equally confident prognosis. It was, in fact, the emergence of Callan as Lehman's chief defender that had galvanized his thinking. How could a tax lawyer, who had not worked in the finance department and who had been chief financial officer for only six months, understand these complicated assessments? On what basis could she be so certain that they were valuing the firm's assets properly?

He had suspected that Callan might be in over her head—or the firm was exaggerating its figures—ever since he had had the opportunity to speak directly to her and some of her colleagues back in November 2007. Lehman, having heard that Einhorn was critical of the firm, set up a conference call with him and made some of its top people available to him in hopes of assuaging his concerns.

But something about the call unnerved him. He had repeatedly asked how often the firm marked—or revalued—certain illiquid assets, like real estate. As a concept, mark-to-market is simple to understand, but it is a burden to deal with on a daily basis. In the past, most banks had rarely if ever bothered putting a dollar amount on illiquid investments, such as real estate or mortgages, that they planned to keep. Most banks valued their illiquid investments simply at the price they paid for them, rather than venture to estimate what they might be worth on any given day. If they later sold them for more than they paid for them, they made a profit; if they sold them for less, they recorded a loss. But in 2007 that straightforward equation changed when a new accounting rule, FAS 157, was enacted.

Now if a bank owned an illiquid asset—the property on which its head-quarters was located, for example—it had to account for that asset in the same way as it would a stock. If the market went up for those assets in general, it would have to record that new value in its books and "write it up," as the traders put it. And if it fell? In that case, it was supposed to "write it down." Of course, no one ever wanted to write down the value of his assets. While it may have been an interesting theoretical exercise—the gains and losses are not actually "realized" until the asset is sold—mark-to-market had a practical impact: A firm that had a huge write-down has less value.

What Einhorn now wanted to know was whether Lehman reassessed the value of its illiquid assets—including some $9 billion in mortgages—every day, every week, or every quarter.

To him it was a crucial question, because as values of virtually all assets continued to fall, he wanted to understand how vigilant the firm was being in reflecting those declines on its balance sheet. O'Meara suggested the firm marked the assets daily, but when the controller was brought onto the call, he indicated that the firm marked those assets on only a quarterly basis. Callan had been on the phone for the entire conversation and must have heard the contradictory answers but never stepped in to acknowledge the inconsistency. Einhorn himself didn't remark on the discrepancy, but he counted it as one more point against the firm.

By late April, he had already begun speaking his mind publicly about the problems he saw at Lehman, suggesting during a presentation to investors that "from a balance sheet and business mix perspective, Lehman is not that materially different from Bear Stearns."

That comment had gone largely unnoticed in the market, but it did raise the ire of Lehman. Einhorn set up another call with Lehman, and again, Callan tried to answer his questions and to turn his view of the company around. But despite her outward affability, he felt she was obfuscating.

Now, as he began preparing for his major upcoming speech in late May 2008, it was that conversation with Callan that confirmed for him that he needed to make Lehman the focus of his presentation. He decided to follow up with Callan one last time, sending her an e-mail to inform her that he planned to cite their earlier conversation in his talk at the Ira W. Sohn Investment Research Conference.

She responded immediately, skipping the niceties: "I can only feel that you set me up, and you will now cherry-pick what you like out of the conversation to suit your thesis," she wrote back.

Einhorn was accustomed to companies turning hostile—anyone who wanted to be loved in the financial industry had no business selling shares short. He fired a tough e-mail right back: "I completely reject the notion that I have been disingenuous with you in any way. You had no reason to expect that our discussion was confidential in any way." And then he finished writing his speech.

———

Einhorn stood in the wings of the Frederick P. Rose Hall in the Time Warner Center on May 21, waiting his turn to speak.

He had been scheduled to take the stage at 4:05 p.m., just after the markets closed—timing that had been carefully planned by the organizers of the conference. Given his stature within the industry and what he was about to say—and considering the firepower of the investors in the audience—he could easily rattle the markets, especially Lehman's shares.

As investor events go—and there are many—this was one that genuinely mattered. The hedge fund industry is famously reclusive, but today the key players in the field were in attendance, the auditorium packed with industry titans such as Carl Icahn, Bill Miller, and Bill Ackman. By some estimates, the guests in the audience that day had more than $500 billion under management.

From the stage's corner, Einhorn watched as his warm-up act, Richard S. Pzena, a successful value investor, was apparently finishing his speech, having run over his time allotment as he offered his big investment idea to the audience.

"Buy stock in Citigroup," he instructed, suggesting that, at $21.06 a share, its closing price that afternoon, it was a screaming buy. "This is classic value. There is lots of stress," he said. "When we come out of this, the upside is huge!"

If an investor had actually heeded that advice, he would have lost an enormous amount of money. But the audience applauded politely as it waited for the main event.

Beyond speaking about Lehman, Einhorn viewed his appearance today as an opportunity to promote his new book, *Fooling Some of the People All of the Time*, which stemmed from an earlier speech he had delivered at this very conference in 2002—a speech that had landed him in trouble with the feds. In it he had raised questions about the accounting methods used by a company called Allied Capital, a Washington-based private-equity firm that specialized in midsize companies. On the day after he criticized the firm, shares of Allied plunged nearly 11 percent, and Einhorn, at age thirty-three, immediately became an investing hero—and a villain to those he bet against.

After that talk, which happened to be the first public address he'd ever given, he had actually expected regulators to look into his accusations of fraud at Allied. Instead, the Securities and Exchange Commission started investigating *him* and whether he was trying to manipulate the market with his comments. For its part, Allied fought back. A private investigator working for the company obtained Einhorn's phone records through a frowned-upon and potentially illegal approach known as pretexting—that is, pretending to be someone else in order to obtain privileged information about another person.

Einhorn's battle with Allied had been going on for six years, but today, patient as ever, he would use his bully pulpit to take on a much larger opponent.

———

Einhorn finally placed his notes on the podium. As he surveyed the crowd, he noticed the glow of dozens of BlackBerrys in the first few rows alone. Investors were taking notes and shooting them back to their offices as quickly as possible.

The markets may have been closed for the day, but in the trading business, a valuable piece of information was worth its weight in gold no matter what the time. There was always a way to make money somewhere.

Einhorn opened his remarks in his slightly nasal Midwestern monotone by recounting the entire Allied story and tying that back to Lehman Brothers.

"One of the key issues I raised about Allied six years ago was its improper use of fair-value accounting, as it had been unwilling to take write-downs on investments that failed in the last recession," he told the audience. "That issue has returned on a much larger scale in the current credit crisis."

What he was saying was that Lehman hadn't owned up to its losses last quarter, and the losses this time were bound to be much bigger.

After laying out his provocative thesis, Einhorn related an anecdote:

"Recently, we had the CEO of a financial institution in our office. His firm held some mortgage bonds on its books at cost. The CEO gave me the usual story: The bonds are still rated triple A, they don't believe that they will have any permanent loss, and there is no liquid market to value these bonds.

"I responded, 'Liar! Liar! Pants on fire!' and proceeded to say that there was a liquid market for these bonds and they were probably worth sixty to seventy percent of face value at the time, and that only time will tell whether there will be a permanent loss.

"He surprised me by saying that I was right. He observed that if he said otherwise, the accountants would make them write the bonds down."

From there Einhorn segued back to Lehman Brothers and made it clear that he felt the evidence suggested the firm was inflating the value of its real estate assets, that it was unwilling to recognize the true extent of its losses for fear of sending its stock plummeting.

He recounted how he had listened intently to Callan's performance during her by now famous earnings call the day after the Bear Stearns fire sale.

"On the conference call that day, Lehman CFO Erin Callan used the word 'great' fourteen times; 'challenging' six times; 'strong' twenty-four times, and 'tough' once. She used the word 'incredibly' eight times," he noted.

"I would use 'incredible' in a different way to describe the report."

After that rhetorical flourish, he recounted how he had decided to call her. With a projection screen displaying the relevant figures behind him, he told how he had questioned Callan about the fact that Lehman had taken only a $200 million write-down on $6.5 billion worth of the especially toxic asset known as collateralized debt obligations in the first quarter—even though the pool of CDOs included $1.6 billion of instruments that were below investment grade.

"Ms. Callan said she understood my point and would have to get back to me," Einhorn relayed. "In a follow-up e-mail, Ms. Callan declined to provide an explanation for the modest write-down and instead stated that, based on current price action, Lehman 'would expect to recognize further losses' in the second quarter. Why wasn't there a bigger mark[down] in the first quarter?"

Einhorn explained that he had also been troubled by a discrepancy of $1.1 billion in how Lehman accounted for its so-called Level 3 assets—assets for which there are no markets and whose value is traced only by a firm's internal models—between its earnings conference call and its quarterly filing with the SEC several weeks later.

"I asked Lehman, 'My point-blank question is: Did you write up the Level 3 assets by over a billion dollars sometime between the press release and the filing of the 10-Q?' They responded, 'No, absolutely not!' However, they could not provide another plausible explanation."

Clearing his throat audibly, Einhorn ended his speech with a warning.

"My hope is that Mr. Cox and Mr. Bernanke and Mr. Paulson will pay heed to the risks to the financial system that Lehman is creating and that they will guide Lehman toward a recapitalization and recognition of its losses—hopefully before federal taxpayer assistance is required.

"For the last several weeks, Lehman has been complaining about short-sellers. Academic research and our experience indicate that when management teams do that, it is a sign that management is attempting to distract investors from serious problems."

———

Within minutes of Einhorn's leaving the stage, news of his speech had been broadcast throughout financial circles. Lehman was in for some serious pain when the market opened the following day; the shares would fall as much as 5 percent.

As Einhorn headed up Broadway to attend a book party being thrown for him at the restaurant Shun Lee West, he leafed through the program of the conference he had just left and saw something that made him smile ruefully.

Lehman Brothers had been one of the Patron Sponsors of the conference, having paid $25,000 so that the world could hear him publicly undermine the firm's credibility.

CHAPTER SIX

"Who talked?" Dick Fuld demanded, scarcely able to control his fury and looking as if he might leap across the table and strangle someone.

Lehman's executive committee—the firm's top managers—were arrayed around a conference room table on Tuesday, June 3, awkwardly sitting in absolute silence.

Fuld held a copy of that day's *Wall Street Journal* in his hand. There, on the front page, was what he described to them as "the greatest betrayal of my career." He had practically choked that morning when he read the headline—"Losses Push Lehman to Weigh Raising New Capital"—with the story adding the damning details: "Wall Street executives estimate it is likely to be $3 billion to $4 billion. They said Lehman would probably announce the capital raising in conjunction with its quarterly results."

There it was, the morning's news, the secret plan he had been working on for the past month to counter the critics and demonstrate strength, exposed for the entire world to read. He had been working frantically to shore up the firm, and now, he thought, the leak put all that effort in jeopardy.

Fuld had spoken to the reporter Susanne Craig on and off the record many times over the last few months. But he'd certainly never breathed a word of this. Fuld could only take solace in the fact that she didn't have all the facts of his plan just yet: Lehman was in discussions with the Korea Development Bank, a state-owned policy bank in South Korea. The talks, which were being orchestrated by Kunho Cho, Lehman's top executive in Seoul, could lead to a major cash infusion of more than $4 billion. Still, Fuld knew that the only way Craig could have learned that the firm was considering seeking new capital was if someone in the know—someone at the table in the conference room that morning, in fact—had leaked the story.

Coming on the heels of David Einhorn's campaign against the firm—Lehman's stock had fallen 22.6 percent since his speech in May—it was yet another public relations disaster. Fuld knew perfectly well that bankers were occasionally prone to being loose-lipped about their clients, but this concerned the firm he had given his entire life to and was about its very survival. The breach of loyalty stung him deeply.

Already that morning rumors were circulating that Lehman was so desperate for liquidity that it had tapped the Federal Reserve's discount window. That was untrue, but Lehman's stock was pummeled anyway, falling 15 percent.

For the past two weeks Fuld had been forced to respond to such rumors on an almost daily basis, as Einhorn's comments had taken on enough credibility to sow seeds of doubt about Lehman's own. To Fuld's thinking, that was precisely Einhorn's objective. Fuld's co-chief administrative officer, Scott Freidheim, had been in touch with nearly half the public relations flacks in the city, desperately attempting to formulate a counterattack against Einhorn and the shorts. "How does this guy have any credibility coming after us?" Freidheim asked Joele Frank and Steve Frankel, two crisis specialists. "We can't go tit for tat with everyone who makes a claim," he'd said to another PR executive, Steven Lipin. In the meantime, the firm had established a clear script for all discussions with the media: There would be no more winging it; they couldn't afford any mistakes.

Fuld thought Craig's coverage had crossed the line, even if it was a legitimate scoop. To him, in his fit of rage, it was as if she had knowingly set out to undermine the firm, just like Einhorn. The article made Lehman seem like a collection of petty high school cliques, a gossip mill. He had always considered her one of only a handful of trustworthy reporters. The week before she'd even asked to sit in on one of Lehman's management meetings, a request he thought was ludicrous, but he'd declined the request politely. "I'd like to be helpful," he explained. "But I can't allow that."

When Craig phoned Fuld that afternoon to follow up on her story, he lit into her mercilessly. "You pose as a responsible journalist but you're just like the rest of them!" he said. "Your seat at the table has been removed," he shouted, then slammed down the receiver. There would be a new rule in effect at Lehman, he subsequently decreed: Nobody, not even the PR department, was allowed to speak to the *Wall Street Journal* ever again.

When he learned of Fuld's diktat, Andrew Gowers, Lehman's head of communications, was beside himself. "I don't understand how on earth this policy is supposed to help us communicate in the middle of all this if we're going to shut out the biggest financial paper in the country," he complained to Freidheim.

"I don't know," Freidheim replied with a shrug. "It's between Dick and the paper."

———

Scott Freidheim knew who the leaker was, or so he believed.

At forty-two years old, Freidheim was the youngest member of Fuld's inner circle. The son of the former CEO of Chiquita, he was the ideal Fuld operative: a get-it-done loyalist with a killer instinct. As the firm's co-chief administrative officer, he wasn't so much a banker as he was a highly paid strategist. To Fuld's detractors, he was one of the chairman's pets, a know-nothing protector of the throne who shielded Fuld from any number of ugly truths. Freidheim was an executive in the Joe Gregory mold: He owned an enormous home in Greenwich and a constantly rotating fleet of cars; he had recently bought the "mobile office" once owned by one of his friends, hedge fund mogul Eddie Lampert—a black GMC Denali outfitted with Internet access that he had chauffeur him to Manhattan each day. "Isn't this awesome!" he once announced excitedly when he showed off the vehicle to colleagues as it blasted the theme song to *Mission: Impossible*.

After the tense meeting with Fuld about the *Journal* story, Freidheim was determined to find the leaker for his boss. He had in fact sensed that something was amiss the night before, after he'd had a flurry of confusing phone calls with Craig and with Lehman's spokesperson, Kerrie Cohen. He had been frustrated because he couldn't get a straight answer about the coming story.

Early the next morning, Erin Callan had dropped by his office, which she rarely did, and innocently asked about the story, "Do you think it will make the stock go up?"

With that it became clear to Freidheim that the leak had been her idea. Like a growing group of executives up and down the organization, Freidheim had come to the conclusion that Callan was in the wrong job, and he had grown tired of her perky self-assurance. She performed for the media as though she were on some kind of reality show. She might have pulled off the earnings call back in March, but now he questioned Gregory's decision to put her in the job, referring to her as a "diversity hire." He couldn't believe she had gone off and talked to Einhorn before his speech without first consulting anyone—he'd been trying to put that fire out for a week now. And he had been furious back in April when Craig, in another *Journal* story, had crowned her "Lehman's straight shooter," as if the rest of them were a pack of untrustworthy liars. Callan just didn't know where the line was drawn. She kept a model of a private jet on her desk and revealed details about her personal shopper to the press, blithely unaware of the resentment it inspired. The worst was when she framed a photograph of herself getting out of a limousine, from a gushy profile in the Condé Nast *Portfolio* magazine that pronounced her "The Most Powerful Woman on Wall Street," and hung it on her office wall; Gregory had had to tell her to take it down.

Freidheim, now on the warpath, called security and ordered the company's phone records searched. He soon discovered what he regarded as all the proof he needed: Callan had indeed spoken to Craig the day before. Whether that meant she had actually informed the reporter about the capital raise plans was yet to be determined. Had she revealed that the Koreans were a potential suitor? Freidheim did not know, but the phone record gave him an excuse to talk to Fuld about her.

When Freidheim arrived at Fuld's office, he found Gregory there and proceeded to present his findings to both men. He concluded by saying that he wanted to approach Callan about the call himself, and added, "We can't rule out firing her."

Gregory, her mentor, was aghast at the accusation. Nobody was getting fired, and as far as he was concerned, nobody was even going to mention the matter to Callan. "She has too much on her plate," Gregory insisted, and Fuld nodded his agreement. He simply could not afford to lose his CFO, not in the current climate, and not even if she had done the unthinkable and leaked the information.

In his heart, Fuld knew that his Korean gambit was a Hail Mary pass. Lehman's own banking operation in Seoul was effectively a mirage; it had never produced any business significant enough even to warrant Fuld's attention. He had also been warned repeatedly by just about everyone in the office that there were some serious doubts about the players involved. The whole success of the effort hinged on two individuals: Kunho, a well-connected banker with impeccable manners who, as far as anybody could tell, was simply unable to close any deal; and Min Euoo Sung, a former Lehman Brothers banker based in South Korea who had left the firm and had managed to snag a prestigious new appointment as the head of the Korea Development Bank. While Fuld had always liked Min—years earlier, when Min was working for Woori Financial Group, he had brought Lehman in on a joint $8.4 billion purchase of a troubled loan portfolio—some of Min's other colleagues at Lehman were stunned by the appointment, as were a number of KDB's staff, who, having judged his credentials inadequate, had tried unsuccessfully to stop it.

Min, however, was undeterred; he had grandiose visions. At a dinner with his new colleagues, he sang a song called "Leopard in Mt. Kilimanjaro" as an expression of his desire to be a powerful force in the world of finance. The Lehman situation presented the first major opportunity to achieve that goal. Before he had even formally started his job, Min had approached his friend Kunho about doing a deal. Kunho had in turn brought Jesse Bhattal, the debonair head of Lehman's Asia-Pacific operations, based in Tokyo, into the talks, and the idea started to gain momentum.

What choice did Fuld have but to play this situation out? In less than a week, on June 9, the firm would be announcing its first quarterly loss—a staggering $2.8 billion—since American Express spun it off. The stock was already down 18 percent in three days. Fuld had to find capital, and at this point, he would try any avenue he could. He had been pressing his old friend Hank Greenberg, the former chairman of AIG, to put money into the company, as well as trying to get an investment from General Electric, but he couldn't be certain that either would come through.

Certainly, Fuld did have some reason to believe that a constructive agreement might be negotiated with the Koreans. The Monday before the Lehman team had left for Asia, David Goldfarb, Fuld's chief strategy officer, had raised his boss's expectations.

"Korea situation sounds promising," Goldfarb wrote in an e-mail that he also sent to Gregory. "They really are looking to restructure and open up financial services and seem to want anchor event to initiate the effort, which could be us. I still prefer a Hank [Greenberg] or GE solution, but if that is not there, we could make this strategically based as well.

"Between Kunho and ES's [Min's] relationship it feels this could become real. If we did raise $5 billion, I like the idea of aggressively going into the market and spending 2 of the 5 in buying back lots of stock (and hurting Einhorn bad!!). Lots to do on this, been speaking to Jesse and Kunho. Sounds like the Koreans are serious on this and are looking to do something aggressive. Could be interesting timing for them, to get some attention away from faster growth Asian economies. Could be interesting, but as we know these thing often don't go further then the rhetoric."

On June 1 a small team of Lehman bankers had headed to New Jersey's Teterboro Airport and set off for Korea in the firm's Gulfstream. The senior person aboard, Tom Russo, Lehman's chief legal officer, had little deal-making experience, but as one of Fuld's confidants, he could serve as a trusted pair of eyes and ears. Mark Shafir, the firm's head of global mergers and acquisitions (and the brother of Robert Shafir, whom Gregory had unceremoniously forced to quit), was the lead deal banker, along with Brad Whitman, a talented acquisitions expert who had spent most of his career merging the nation's far-flung telecommunications firms into a handful of powerful players. Completing the group were Larry Wieseneck, the firm's head of global finance, and lawyer Jay Clayton of Sullivan & Cromwell. They would meet Kunho and Bhattal when they got there.

With a stop for refueling in Anchorage, the jet made the trip in nineteen hours, and on arrival the exhausted Lehman contingent took a fleet of cars to their hotel on the outskirts of Seoul. The Shilla was a peculiar place with a lobby that looked like a spaceship, but at least it had a bar.

The first meeting in Seoul involved only lower-level officials of KDB and Hana Financial, which was also considering an investment. Shafir and Whitman could tell immediately that this was not a deal that was likely to happen. Neither Korean firm had brought along lawyers or hired its own U.S. advisers. And Min, who had not yet officially started as chief executive of KDB, could not even take part in the talks.

"This is bullshit," Wieseneck exclaimed after the initial session ended, having served little purpose other than to make introductions. Even as the talks progressed, the Lehman team could hardly tell to whom they were speaking. At one point Russo engaged in what he thought was a productive exchange with an individual who turned out to be an outside accountant. "Relying on Kunho is like bottom of the ninth, two outs, in the World Series," Shafir complained to his American colleagues the first night in the bar, "and you send up a guy to the plate who hasn't gotten a hit all year."

Lehman had wanted to start discussions at $40 a share, but by the end of the first day the stock was at $30. Nobody—not even this group of deal-hungry Koreans—was going to pay a 33 percent premium. The whole affair became increasingly unreal.

No food was served at the meetings, so the Lehman bankers were starving by the time they got back to their hotel, where the meals were generally dreadful. The only palatable item they could find on the menu was tuna, which most of them ate every day of their stay.

But neither the subpar accommodations nor the Koreans' erratic behavior could dent Russo's enthusiasm: He was going to make this happen. "They're going to do this deal," he told his colleagues, supported by Kunho and Bhattal. "They're going to put in $10 billion. They're going to make their balance sheet available for loans."

No, they aren't, thought Shafir. *They aren't going to do anything of the kind.*

Sitting on a hotel room bed crowded around the speakerphone, the group called Fuld back in New York, with Russo leading the conversation. "Dick, I'm feeling very good about it," Russo enthused. "I think we have a 70 percent chance of getting something done with these guys."

Fuld's delight at the news, however, was short-lived. The group returned to New York empty-handed on June 5; efforts to come up with even a rudimentary term sheet had completely failed. The Koreans had obviously been deterred by Lehman's cratering stock and simply may not have had the wherewithal to bring about such a major piece of business. Even Russo had lost confidence. "We're not going to get a deal with these yoyos," he told Fuld.

Moments after hearing the news, Fuld, frustrated as ever, screamed down the hall at Steven Berkenfeld, a member of the firm's executive committee.

"Were you the one who said you can't trust the Koreans?" he asked.

"I don't think I phrased it that way," Berkenfeld said.

"Yes, you did," Fuld said. "And you were right."

The Korean deal wouldn't go away quietly, though. A few days later, Min called Fuld and insisted he still wanted to get something done. Fuld figured the only way it was remotely possible was if the Koreans hired a real adviser. So he called up Joseph Perella, the mergers and acquisitions guru who had recently started a new firm, Perella Weinberg Partners.

"Listen, I've got something for you," Fuld told Perella. "You're going to get a call from ES. Do you know him? He used to work for me."

Fuld was explicit about what he needed out of the deal. "We're trading at about $25. Our book value is $32. We need a premium, so we'd take $35 to $40."

Perella, who assigned the project to his colleague Gary Barancik, didn't think the odds were good. KDB was a national institution with what seemed to him to be a local charter. They had no business branching out with a risky international deal. "It's like the Long Island energy utility trying to buy something in Russia," he told Barancik.

But they promised to do the best they could.

———

Fuld was also dealing with another problem: a potential whistle-blower.

One of Lehman's employees, Matthew Lee, a senior vice president in the finance division whom Fuld scarcely even knew existed, had just weeks earlier sent a letter to the company's senior management in which he claimed to have uncovered a series of accounting and management problems at the firm.

Fuld's inner circle dutifully forwarded the letter to the firm's auditors and the board, but weren't overly concerned by it. To them, Lee had always been something of a troublemaker. Because they had recently demoted him and were planning to fire him, they viewed the letter as more of an extortion attempt by a disgruntled employee looking for a severance agreement than anything they should worry about.

However, during a meeting with the firm's auditors, Ernst & Young, Lee raised a serious red flag about one of the firm's practices that was also quietly being questioned in other parts of company: an accounting trick known as Repo 105.

What the public did not know—nor did some of Lehman's top executives, including Fuld—was that Lehman had been artificially lowering its quarterly leverage ratio by using an accounting sleight of hand. At the end of every quarter, Lehman's government securities business would "sell" securities to a counterparty in exchange for cash, which they'd use to pay down debt. But days after the quarter ended, Lehman would turn around and take the securities back onto their balance sheet and return the cash.

Instead of accounting for these deals in the traditional manner as "repurchase agreements" or "repos," in which the firm would lend securities in exchange for cash, classifying them as "sales" had the effect of making the firm's leverage look lower in than it really was: Lehman had managed to move $49 billion off of its books in the first quarter of 2008 and $50 billion in the second quarter.

Within certain parts of the firm, Repo 105 was an open secret. In early June Michael McGarvey, a finance controller, sent an e-mail to his colleague Jormen Vallecillo explaining the accounting practice as "basically window dressing. We are calling repos true sales based on legal technicalities." Vallecillo replied, "I see . . . so it is legally doable but doesn't look good when we actually do it?"

Lehman's London-based law firm, Linklaters, had blessed the practice, but that didn't keep other senior executives from being anxious about it. Back in April Hyung Lee, global cohead of fixed income, e-mailed Bart McDade, "Not sure you are familiar with Repo 105," he began. McDade shot back, "I am very aware. . . . It is another drug we r on." In early June McDade issued an edict that the firm would cut its use of Repo 105 by half.

Lee, as expected, was dismissed and was paid $300,000 in cash to leave the firm. As part of his severance agreement, he agreed "not to make any remarks now or at any time in the future to any third party, such as a client, a competitor, or the media, that could be detrimental or adverse in any way to Lehman."

With Lee gone, Fuld and the firm had bigger things to agonize about, or so they thought.

Skip McGee, a forty-eight-year-old Texan, commuted to New York every week from Houston to run Lehman's investment banking operations. He'd board a private plane using the firm's NetJets account every Sunday evening around 7:30, land in New York around midnight, and take a car to his rental on the Upper West Side. Come Thursday night he'd be on a first-class flight back to Houston on Continental.

McGee, a classic, old-school, back-slapping banker, was clearly ambitious. After graduating summa cum laude from Princeton and getting a law degree, he had spent nearly two decades at Lehman, first as a banker for wildcatters in the oil patch of his backyard and then moving up the ranks until he became the head of the entire investment banking division and joined Fuld's vaunted executive committee.

For some time, McGee and his team had been having deep misgivings about the way the firm was being managed. His unit, which advised corporate clients on mergers and stock offerings, had its best year ever in 2007, bringing in $3.9 billion in revenue, and yet the firm's stock, which was used to pay a large portion of everyone's bonuses, was being decimated by anxiety about what was happening on the other side of the house—namely, the firm's investments in real estate assets. Even worse, the constant rumors and headlines about Lehman's health were beginning to affect his team's ability to sign up new clients, who were reasonably worried about hiring them. It had gotten so bad that some clients had asked to include a "key man" provision in their engagement letters that would guarantee that the banker assigned to them would continue working with them if Lehman was sold or went bankrupt.

McGee had expressed his anxiety to Fuld a month earlier when he asked to be given control over the firm's capital-raising efforts, which up until that point were being overseen primarily by management on the thirty-first floor, who he felt were not professional deal makers. "You have an investment banking division that does this for a living," McGee told Fuld. "This is crazy. I should leave if you don't trust the investment bank to do this." Fuld agreed, and McGee's "troops"—Shafir and Whitman—had been included in the Korean junket.

But since that conversation, the firm's situation had only worsened. They all knew that the announcement of the next big quarterly loss was only going to exacerbate the situation. Resentment was boiling up through the ranks, and it was no longer directed exclusively at Erin Callan, who, the bankers had concluded, was merely a symptom of a bigger problem.

The person they had now come to believe was responsible for many of Lehman's troubles—the risky bets on corporate real estate, the constant reshuffling of executives into jobs they were ill equipped to handle—was Joe Gregory, the firm's president and Fuld's closest associate. McGee and Gregory had never gotten along very well to begin with; each was too headstrong for the other. And in recent months, Gregory had been discussing ways to push McGee aside, by assigning him to a new commodity trading business back in Houston, the prospect of which left McGee lukewarm.

The Sunday before preannouncing the earnings report, June 8, as everyone worked over the numbers on the thirty-first floor, McGee, in a golf shirt and khakis, slipped into Fuld's office to review the investment bank's earnings and projections. But just as McGee had finished his summary and was getting ready to leave, he said, "When we get through this, we need to have a serious conversation."

"What about?" Fuld asked.

"About a change in senior management," McGee blurted out.

"What?" Fuld said, distracted now from the numbers before him.

"Well, I guess we're having that conversation now then," McGee said, getting up to shut the door. Gregory's office was just a few feet away.

When he took his seat again, he told Fuld precisely what he had meant: "You need to move on Joe."

Fuld was dumbstruck. "Joe Gregory is off the table," he said, raising his voice. "He's been my partner for twenty-five years. It's not fair. I couldn't look at myself in the mirror."

"Whether it is fair or not, you need to do something about Joe," McGee replied. "You've not been well served by your COO. He's in over his head. He's not minding the store. He's made some horrible personnel decisions, and he's not watching your back on risk."

Reminding McGee that, as a member of the executive committee, he was responsible for making key decisions along with everyone else, Fuld said, "The entire executive committee *is* the risk committee."

McGee, realizing that he was not getting his point across, stated carefully, "You're a wonderful leader, but when the books are written, your

Achilles' heel will be that you have a blind spot for weak people who are sycophants."

Fuld barely heard the last part of McGee's comment, as he had been thinking about Gregory. "I'm not doing it," he finally said, ending the discussion.

McGee left the office, fairly certain that Gregory's job was safer than his own.

———

After McGee departed, Fuld sat in his office, stunned; he couldn't conceive of the firm without Gregory. But nothing that was happening was making any sense. The firm he had rebuilt with his own two hands was falling apart everywhere he looked.

Over at Neuberger Berman, Lehman's asset-management arm, executives were in open revolt, trying to disentangle themselves from the mess at headquarters. Lehman had bought Neuberger in 2003, and as long as times were good, it had been a useful, relatively trouble-free contributor to the firm's bottom line. But when Lehman stock started its swan dive, Neuberger employees panicked. They had become accustomed to the steady income generated by managing rich people's money, but that was now in jeopardy, as a good portion of their bonuses were paid in stock.

A week earlier, on June 3, Judith Vale, who ran a $15 billion small-cap fund for Neuberger, fired off an e-mail to the Lehman executive committee (with the exception of Fuld), demanding that top Lehman managers forgo bonuses and make preparations to spin off Neuberger.

"Morale at NB is at a dangerously low level, largely because Lehman stock is a significant portion of our compensation, and as such, our comp is not tied to anything within our control," Vale wrote. "Many believe that a substantial portion of the problems at Lehman are structural rather than merely cyclical in nature. The 'old' Neuberger franchise (which resides at 605 Third) is largely intact. However, this is a people business, and the continuing health of the franchise is dependent on retaining key producers and support personnel. Don't slam bonuses of key producers and support personnel at NB because of management mistakes made elsewhere."

George H. Walker IV, the head of Lehman's investment management division and a cousin of President Bush, immediately sought to blunt Vale's criticism.

"Sorry, team," Walker wrote in an e-mail to everyone who'd received Vale's missive. "The compensation issue she raises . . . is a particular issue for a small handful of people at Neuberger and hardly worth the EC's [executive committee] time now. I'm embarrassed and I apologize."

The correspondence was forwarded to Fuld, who wrote in reply, "Don't worry—they are only people who think about their own pockets." *Did anyone in the firm still have any loyalty?*

———

Although Joe Gregory's title was still chief operations officer, in the opinion of many Lehman executives, he had spun off into the ether years earlier. Few seemed to flaunt their personal wealth as much as he did. The helicopter commute was just the start of it. He and his wife, Niki, bought a house in Bridgehampton for some $19 million, and even though it was completely decorated, they had it redone top to bottom with their own designer. He drove a Bentley and encouraged his wife to take shopping trips to Los Angeles via a private plane. But despite an extravagant lifestyle that was estimated to cost in excess of $15 million a year, he kept most of his net worth tied up in Lehman stock. To gain access to cash, he had pledged 751,000 Lehman shares in a margin account as of January 2008, which, based on where the shares were trading, would've allowed him to borrow roughly $40 million.

It wasn't Gregory's spending habits that people inside Lehman found objectionable, though. He had a lot of money, and he obviously wasn't the only one who liked to throw it around. What did seem somewhat odd was his portfolio of responsibilities. Even in his prime Gregory had never brought in big deals or made many hugely successful trades himself. His job was to be Fuld's unquestioning confidant, and as long as he was that, everything else was up to him. He loved being the in-house philosopher-king, an evangelist on the subject of workplace diversity and a devotee of the theories described in Malcolm Gladwell's bestseller *Blink*. He gave out copies of the book and had even hired the author to lecture employees on trusting their instincts when making difficult decisions. In an industry based on analyzing raw data, Gregory was defiantly a gut man.

He was also an advocate of the Myers-Briggs Type Indicator, which used Jungian psychological principles to identify people as having one of sixteen distinct personality types. (A typical question was, "Do you prefer to focus on the outer world or on your own inner world?") Gregory used Myers-Briggs results to help make personnel decisions. It was his conviction that individual expertise was overrated; if you had smart, talented people, you could plug them into any role, as sheer native talent and brains trumped experience. Gregory seemed to revel in moving people around, playing chess with their careers.

His greatest experiment to date had been naming Erin Callan to be the chief financial officer. He and Callan eventually became so inseparable in the office that many were convinced, though it was never substantiated, that the two were linked romantically. Around the time she was promoted to CFO, Callan separated from her husband, Michael Thompson, a former Lehman vice president who'd left the firm.

Gregory loved being a mentor to younger executives like Callan, and he was fully cognizant of his role in Fuld's hierarchy: If there was a difficult conversation to have, he considered it his responsibility to handle it. In this regard, Gregory and Fuld were total opposites. While Fuld had a gruff, tough-guy exterior, he had soft spots; he could be quite sentimental and tended to struggle when faced with difficult decisions, especially those concerning personnel. Gregory, in contrast, was much more gregarious, a leader given to championing underlings and setting lofty goals for the firm. He gave generously to charities, especially those involving breast cancer, which Niki had survived, and he had spent a full year working to establish a mentoring program between Lehman and historically black Spelman College of Atlanta, a rare effort on Wall Street.

But when it came to judging the loyalty of Lehman employees, Gregory could be ruthless, given to angry, impetuous decisions. In the summer of 2006, Fuld had hosted a retreat for senior Lehman executives at his vacation home in Sun Valley, Idaho. Alex Kirk, who ran the global credit products group and had previously struck Gregory as a disloyal troublemaker, was due to make a presentation but was unable to make the trip because of an illness. Feeling better, Kirk decided to make the presentation via video feed, and when Gregory saw how well Kirk looked on the video, he was incensed. Kirk was clearly not sick, Gregory was convinced, and his failure to show up in person was nothing less than a personal insult to

Fuld. "I want him fired," he yelled. Kirk's allies at the firm had to appeal to Bart McDade, Lehman's head of equities, to intervene with Gregory and calm him down. Cooler heads eventually prevailed.

———

The Lehman deal maker who had prospered most under Fuld and Gregory was Mark Walsh, a socially timid workaholic who ran Lehman's real estate operations. An Irish American native of Yonkers, New York, Walsh made his mark in the early 1990s when he bought commercial mortgages from Resolution Trust Corporation, the outfit established by the federal government to clean up the savings and loan debacle, and packaged them into securities. A lawyer by training, Walsh seemed immune to risk, which impressed Fuld and Gregory to no end. They gave Walsh free rein, and he used it to ram through deals much more quickly than the competition. After the developer Aby Rosen closed the $375 million acquisition of the Seagram Building in only four weeks, Walsh bragged to friends about how swiftly he had been able to execute the deal.

Each success bred hunger for more, leading to monstrous deals like Lehman's partnership with SunCal Companies. A land speculator that bought property primarily outside Los Angeles, SunCal secured approvals for residential development and then sold them to home builders at a hefty markup. Lehman pumped $2 billion into what appeared to be its can't-fail transactions. Walsh had virtually unlimited use of Lehman's balance sheet and used it to turn the firm into an all-in, unhedged play on the U.S. real estate market, a giant REIT (real estate investment trust) with a little investment bank attached—a strategy that worked extraordinarily well right up until the moment that it didn't.

At the very height of the market, Walsh concluded his last great deal, a joint transaction with Bank of America, committing $17.1 billion in debt plus $4.6 billion in bridge equity to finance the purchase of Archstone-Smith, a collection of premium apartment complexes and other high-end real estate. The properties were excellent, but the price was sky-high, based on projections that rents could be hiked substantially. Almost immediately, the proposition started to look dubious, especially when the credit markets seized up. But given a chance to back out of the deal, Fuld declined. The firm had made a commitment and it was going to stick with it. Gregory made a circuit to rally the troops. "This is going to be temporary," he told Lehman colleagues. "We're going to fight through this."

———

As both Gregory and Fuld were fixed-income traders at heart, they weren't entirely up to speed on how dramatically that world had changed since the 1980s. Both had started in commercial paper, probably the sleepiest, least risky part of the firm's business. Fixed-income trading was nothing like Fuld and Gregory knew in their day: Banks were creating increasingly complex products many levels removed from the underlying asset. This entailed a much greater degree of risk, a reality that neither totally grasped and showed remarkably little interest in learning more about. While the firm did employ a well-regarded chief risk officer, Madelyn Antoncic, who had a PhD in economics and had worked at Goldman Sachs, her input was virtually nil. She was often asked to leave the room when issues concerning risk came up at executive committee meetings, and in late 2007, she was removed from the committee altogether.

In the presence of the trading executives, Gregory always tried to make an impression with his market savvy, to such a degree that it became a running joke. Traders eventually came to consider his tips as contrary indicators; if Gregory declared that a rally in oil prices had much further to go, for example, they'd short oil.

In recent years, though, a growing contingent of Lehman executives had begun to view Gregory as a menace. He just didn't know enough about what was going on, they thought. The firm was making bigger bets than it would ever be good for and nobody in the executive office seemed to understand or care. To criticize the firm's direction was to be branded a traitor and tossed out the door.

Among those who tried to sound the alarm was Michael Gelband, who had been Lehman's head of fixed-income trading for two years and had known Gregory for two decades. In late 2006, in a discussion with Fuld about his bonus, Gelband remarked that the good times were about to hit a rough patch, for which the firm was not well positioned. "We're going to have to change a lot of things," he warned. Fuld, looking unhappy, said little in reply.

The fixed-income guys had been spending a lot of time talking about the train wreck that awaited the U.S. economy. In February 2007, Larry McCarthy, Lehman's top distressed-debt trader, had delivered a presentation to his group in which he laid out a dire scenario. "There will be a domino effect," he said. "And the very next domino to fall sideways will be the commercial banks, who will swiftly become scared and start deleveraging, causing consumer borrowing to contract, which will push out the credit spreads. The present situation, where no one thinks there is any risk whatsoever, in anything, cannot possibly last."

McCarthy went on to conclude that "many people today believe that globalization has somehow killed off the natural business cycles of the past. They're wrong. Globalization did not change anything, and the current risks in the Lehman balance sheet put us in a dangerous situation. Because they're too high, and we're too vulnerable. We don't have the firepower to withstand a serious turnaround."

Around that same time, Gregory invited Gelband to lunch "just to talk." The two men had never seen eye-to-eye, and Gelband suspected another agenda. They met in the executive dining room on the thirty-second floor, and after chatting for a while, the conversation took a hard shift.

"You know," Gregory said firmly, "we've got to do things a little differently around here. *You* have to be more aggressive."

"Aggressive?" Gelband asked.

"Toward risk. You're holding back, and we're missing deals."

To Gelband's thinking, Lehman had in fact been pushing through a number of deals that didn't make much sense. They were piling up too much leverage, taking on too much risk, and getting into businesses in which they lacked expertise. At times there appeared to be no strategy whatsoever guiding the firm. Why had Lehman paid nearly $100 million for Grange Securities, an insignificant Australian brokerage? Earlier there had been discussions about becoming a player in commodities. Had there been a sound reason for acquiring Eagle Energy, a marketer of natural gas and electricity started by Charles Watson, other than the fact that Watson had been a longtime Lehman client, as well as an old pal of Skip McGee? Meanwhile, the firm seemed willing to finance buyouts indiscriminately; loans to private-equity firms were piling up on the books. Some would get securitized and sold, but the pipeline was clogging up.

None of that seemed to bother Gregory; the deals that did concern him were the ones that Lehman had failed to get a piece of, like the blockbuster $5.4 billion acquisition of Stuyvesant Town and Peter Cooper Village, a sprawling complex of more than 11,200 apartments on the East Side of Manhattan. Lehman had joined forces with Stephen Ross's Related Companies, the developer of the Time Warner Center, to bid on the project, but lost out to Tishman Speyer and Larry Fink's BlackRock Realty Advisors. Adding insult to injury was the fact that Lehman considered Tishman, which it had helped buy the MetLife Building for $1.7 billion in 2005, one of its closest clients.

Because the real estate division technically reported to fixed income, Gregory held Gelband responsible for the missed opportunity on Stuyvesant Town. "We're going to need to make some changes," he said, implying that Gelband should let a couple of heads roll on his staff.

The following day, Gelband took the elevator up to see Gregory, who was in a meeting. Gelband barged in and said, "Joe, you said you wanted to make some changes? Well, the change is me."

"What are you talking about?" Gregory asked.

"Me. I'm done. I'm leaving the firm."

"I am very disappointed" was Dick Fuld's characterization of his personal reaction to Lehman's second-quarter earnings in a report released at 6:30 a.m., Monday, June 9. The loss was $2.8 billion, or $5.12 a share. A conference call was scheduled at 10:00 a.m. to discuss the result, but by then the blood sport was already well under way on CNBC.

"Dick Fuld is Lehman. Lehman is Dick Fuld," said George Ball of Sanders Morris Harris Group. "You've got a management that wears the corporate logo on its heart. . . . It's got to hurt enormously."

Fuld and Gregory were watching the coverage in Fuld's office when David Einhorn of Greenlight Capital appeared on the screen.

"Are you saying 'I told you so' this morning?" the CNBC interviewer asked him.

"Well, it does seem that a lot of the things I've raised over the last while seem to have been borne out by today's news," he said, apparently trying to sound as humble as possible, under the circumstances.

Einhorn discussed his concerns about the extent of SunCal and Archstone's write-downs, and why they hadn't come sooner, and then delivered a strongly worded admonition: "It's time to dispense with the ad-hominem attacks and get down to an analysis of what's really going on with this business."

———

That afternoon, Charlie Gasparino, a tenacious reporter on CNBC, began hectoring Kerrie Cohen, Lehman's spokesperson, to confirm a tip he had received that Gregory and Callan were about to be fired. Off the record, Cohen dismissed his tip as a useless rumor.

But Gasparino, still skeptical, pressed her to go to her boss, Freidheim. "I've got it that Joe and Erin are leaving the firm," he said. "Unless you go on record, I'm going with it."

When Gasparino threatens to go on the air with market-moving information—a reporting tactic for extracting information from sources—most executives, however much they might resent it, try to comply. Freidheim didn't think any personnel changes were imminent, but before he officially denied it, he marched into Fuld's office.

"I'm going to have to use my name," Freidheim told Fuld, making it clear that his own credibility was on the line. "I have to know if you're even thinking about it."

"No," Fuld replied, "it's not under consideration."

"Well, I'm going to have to talk to Joe," Freidheim said, "because I need to know he's not thinking about it, either. I'm not using my name unless I know it can't happen."

"Absolutely not," Gregory stated when Freidheim put the question to him. "You can tell Gasparino you talked to me, and the answer is no."

Keeping the lid on Gasparino was a relatively easy task compared to that of containing the pressure building within the firm. Bankers and traders were alternately restless, nervous, and angry.

Late that afternoon, Skip McGee forwarded an e-mail to Fuld from Benoît D'Angelin, once his longtime counterpart—the former co-head of investment banking—in Lehman's London office; he had left the firm to start a hedge fund. McGee was clearly trying to send Fuld a not-so-subtle hint.

> Many, many bankers have been calling me in the last few days. The mood has become truly awful . . . and for the first time I am really worried that all the hard work we have put in

over the last 6–7 years could unravel very quickly. In my view two things need to happen very quickly.

1. Some senior managers have to be much less arrogant and internally admit that some major mistakes have been made. Can't continue to say "We are great and the market doesn't understand."

2. Some changes at senior management need to happen very soon. People are not and WILL not understand that nobody pays for that mess and that it is "business as usual."

Fuld read the note somberly and wrote back to McGee with a promise that he'd have lunch with the top investment bankers to give them a chance to air their grievances.

What Fuld did not know was that a palace revolt was already in the offing. The week before a group of fifteen traders had gone to dinner at the private Links Club, on East Sixty-second Street, right off Madison. The purpose of the dinner was to discuss how Fuld could be pressured into firing Joe Gregory. If Fuld wouldn't do it, they agreed, they'd threaten to resign en masse.

Jeff Weiss, the head of financial services banking, was not at the dinner, nor was Gerald Donini, but both were patched in for the key discussions on speakerphone. Weiss advised against a confrontation. "Dick is not gonna react well," he said. "You're not going to get him to move by trying to corner him. Slow down. Things are moving in the right direction. Let this thing out over the next couple of days."

At the executive committee meeting the following morning, Fuld looked exhausted, like a boxer gone one round too far. The fight had not gone out of him, but he knew that he had to try another approach. To keep the firm together, he was going to have to be more conciliatory.

"There's a lot of unrest," he acknowledged. "We haven't been together. We made some mistakes." Then he suggested they go around the table and get everyone's take on the question: How do we restore confidence?

Everyone was in attendance—Joe Gregory, Tom Russo, Skip McGee, Bart McDade, Steven Berkenfeld, and a handful by phone. Everyone except Erin Callan, who was still making calls to investors.

Fuld pointedly asked Skip McGee to go first. "Morale has never been worse," McGee told the committee. "We have to admit publicly we made some mistakes. We continue to spin like we've done nothing wrong. We're better than this."

McGee paused and then added quietly: "We need to make a senior management change."

"What do you mean?" Fuld snapped.

"We need to hold ourselves accountable—that's what the market wants, and that's what our troops want."

While McGee did not mention Gregory by name, everyone at the table understood whom he was talking about. Indeed, just a month earlier, at another executive committee meeting, Gregory had actually offered to resign. "If there's a bullet to be taken, I'll be the one to take the bullet," he said stoically. At the time everyone had dismissed the comment as a rhetorical flourish, an easy thing to propose when there was little chance of its happening.

Fuld continued around the table. As each executive took his turn, making various suggestions, nobody seconded McGee's call for change.

Russo, looking at McGee the entire time, chose to make a statement about the importance of teamwork, a sentiment that was then taken up by Gregory. "We've got to stop all the Monday-morning quarterbacking," he insisted. "We're all in this together. We've made a lot of decisions over the years—*all together*. Some have been better than others, but we can work through this *together*."

As the others spoke, McGee, his BlackBerry hidden under the table, typed a two-word message to his colleague Jeff Weiss: "I'm dead."

Returning to his office, McGee called his wife, Susie, in Houston, and told her bluntly, "I may be out of here by the end of the week."

———

That afternoon the thirty-first floor had become a gossip mill, a collection of various cliques assembling and reassembling to try to divine what might happen next. Even though Erin Callan had missed the executive meeting, she had certainly heard about what had transpired there. She was convinced that it was she, not Gregory, who might be on the firing line, and if she had to step down as CFO, she hoped to be able to keep a job of some sort at the firm. So she sent Fuld a two-sentence e-mail without a subject line: "Just to be clear I am very willing to be part of the accountability of management. Think I have become so closely tied with the performance and the public face of the firm that it may be helpful to put someone else in my role."

He didn't reply.

———

By the time Fuld met with the investment bankers for lunch on Wednesday, June 11, in the wood-paneled private dining room on the thirty-second floor, Lehman's stock price had fallen another 21 percent. This was McGee's show, Fuld knew, and that meant he was going to get tested.

He was right. It was five on one. McGee, Ros Stephenson, Mark Shafir, Jeffrey Weiss, and Paul Parker. They jumped at the chance to tell their boss why he needed to make management changes. *The real estate investments were killing the firm. Good people had been let go, while novices, like Erin Callan, had been promoted to positions out of their depth. Joe Gregory had become distracted and knew nothing about risk. If there was a single problem, he was it.*

"Look, the answer is, somebody's gotta pay," Mark Shafir said.

"Joe's been with me for thirty years," Fuld shot back. "He's great at what he does, he has a great career, he's done so much for this place. You're asking me to throw him over the side just because we have one bad quarter?"

"It's not just a bad quarter," McGee replied. "It's more deep-seated than that."

Fuld paused and looked down at the food that he had not touched. "Are you telling me that you want me to—"

"No, no!" the bankers cried out. They certainly did not want his resignation; his departure would be a death knell for the firm. But the status quo could not continue; Fuld had to break out of the inner circle that was buffering him from the firm and get more involved with its operations.

Fuld was willing to accept that criticism. "I get that, that's the feedback I've been getting," he said. "I'm going to do it. I will do the right thing." Still, he would not commit to firing Gregory.

"What are you going to say when you leave this meeting?" he asked the bankers.

"That the guy doesn't get it," said Weiss, laying it right out on the table.

"I got it," Fuld replied.

As the bankers rose from the table and headed back to the elevator bank, no one was quite certain what Fuld intended to do. It seemed unlikely that he was going to fire Gregory; nothing he'd said indicated that he was ready to take that drastic a step. Still, McGee and the bankers were relieved to have finally had an audience with Fuld and said their piece.

———

While that lunch had been going on, Gregory was stirring downstairs in his office. He knew the rumors—he could see the sentiment quickly building up against him. Fuld had made enough comments about the morale problem inside the building for him to understand that he was under fire. He wasn't blind to the snippy comments and office rumor mill about him. Indeed, if there was one thing Gregory focused on—what he called "culture"—he could now see it fraying.

His own power, he knew, had started eroding months earlier. Fuld had increasingly leaned on Bart McDade, the firm's head of equities and one of the most popular guys at the firm—honest, disciplined, and bright, maybe too much for his own good. Indeed, following Bear Stearns' near-failure, Fuld had made McDade his de facto "risk guy."

McDade had long been a fixed-income man, successfully running that division, only to be shunted over to the less profitable equities desk in 2005 in what many in the firm viewed as a classic Joe Gregory disposal of a potential rival. Or maybe, as others saw it, that decision had just been Joe being Joe, playing a hunch that a talent like McDade could be utilized wherever the need was greatest.

Though McDade was too polite to have ever said anything in front of the executive committee, he had spoken privately to Gregory about Gregory's role at Lehman, making some not so subtle comments about "doing the right thing for the firm." And while not as forceful as McGee, McDade had made it clear to Fuld that Gregory had lost his credibility, but by now that had become obvious to almost all the employees.

———

Minutes after Fuld returned to his office, Gregory came by.

"I think I should step down," he said uncertainly.

"What's going on here?" Fuld said, waving him away. "Go back in your office. I get 51 percent of the vote, and that's not happening."

Five minutes later, Fuld came to speak with Gregory, who was now talking to Russo, discussing what he had just told Fuld.

Gregory said that he was convinced the market wanted the firm to take action. "They want heads," he insisted. "Heads have to roll. And it can't be you," Gregory told Fuld. "I have to do it."

"It's not your call," Fuld told him. "This is a disease, every firm has it. It's not your fault."

Russo, who hadn't said anything up until now, chimed in. "Dick, I think Joe's right." Under the circumstances, this was best for the firm.

As Fuld began to resign himself to what everyone had come to regard as inevitable, he fought back tears, muttering, "I don't like it, I don't like it, I don't like it."

———

Erin Callan was in her office when Gregory came in to break the news. He was leaving, he said, out of loyalty to the firm. And as her mentor, he had one last request: He asked her to step down as well, arguing that while his departure might affect morale internally, her brand name was the one that mattered to Wall Street. "We should do it together," he said.

Though she had sent the e-mail to Fuld, Callan felt stricken, unable to believe it had come to this.

Minutes later, she went to see Fuld. "I lost credibility with our investors and I think I have to step down," she said, her voice quivering.

Again Fuld felt overwhelmed, the tears rising to his eyes. But he had been here before. He could go on. Left alone in his office, he started to put the new pieces in place. He called Jeff Weiss.

"I'm listening," he told Weiss.

"Uh, okay," Weiss replied, not entirely certain what Fuld was driving at.

"I'm listening," Fuld repeated, as if to suggest that Weiss's comments at lunch were being heeded.

"Do I have to tell you how I feel about Bart McDade?" Weiss said, essentially endorsing him for Gregory's job.

"No," Fuld said, "you do not."

———

That night, McGee was dining with a college friend at Maloney & Porcelli, a steak house on Fiftieth Street, when his mobile phone rang. It was Fuld. McGee stepped outside under the restaurant's green awning to take the call.

"Okay. I just want you to know that I heard you," Fuld said, "and I've got the ball."

"What?" McGee asked.

Fuld didn't answer.

"I may be a dumbass from Texas," McGee said, "but can you be a bit more explicit?"

"I heard you," Fuld said, "I've got the ball."

He told McGee to be at a special executive committee board meeting the following morning at 8:00 sharp.

Now McGee understood.

———

On Thursday morning, Kerrie Cohen began receiving voice mails from Charlie Gasparino at 6:00.

"Hey, Kerrie. You better call me back right now, because this is a problem. . . . [Y]ou guys specifically denied something that I heard, and now it sounds to me like it's true. So you better call me back now! Now means now. I better not get scooped on this—you're going to have a huge credibility problem, and so will Lehman. So call me now." Twenty minutes later, he followed up: "I better get a call back from you before this hits the tape. I am not kidding!"

Cohen had in fact been called in at 5:30 a.m. to work with Scott Freidheim on drafting the press release announcing Gregory's resignation and Callan's decision to step down; Callan had worked a deal with Fuld to remain at the firm in another role. Though it was not detailed in the release, Gregory would also be staying on, allowed by Fuld to remain on the Lehman payroll as an out-of-the-way consultant, so that he could continue to qualify for his pension and deferred compensation. Gregory's career was over, but his old friend never did quite pull the trigger on him. In the press statement, Fuld said of Gregory, "Joe has been my partner for thirty years and has been a driving force behind where we are today and what we have achieved as a firm. This has been one of the most difficult decisions either of us has ever had to make."

Freidheim also helped prepare a note to the staff from Fuld. "Our credibility has eroded," Fuld said. "The current market environment is forcing us to take a number of measures to regain the confidence of all our constituents."

For a change, that morning, the newspapers had nothing new on Lehman.

When Fuld arrived in the office, Freidheim handed him a draft of the press release to review, and then they started the executive committee meeting. Fuld looked distraught.

"This is the hardest thing I've ever done," he said as he went on to describe Gregory's role as a friend and business partner. "Joe is taking one for the team."

"I always said that if anyone should take a bullet, it should be me," Gregory said. "Let's not let this be wasted."

As Fuld again looked as if he were about to well up, Gregory grabbed his hand and said quietly, "It's okay."

"Do you want to say anything?" Fuld asked Callan.

"No, no," she replied, wiping away a tear.

Announcing that he planned to name Bart McDade as Gregory's successor, Fuld said, "He's the best operator we have."

But this was no time to celebrate McDade's appointment. As the meeting came to an end, Fuld gave Gregory one final, heartfelt hug and then watched as he slowly left the conference room.

On the afternoon of June 11, Greg Fleming, the disarmingly youthful-looking forty-five-year-old president of Merrill Lynch, was meeting with clients at the firm's headquarters when his secretary quietly slipped him a note marked "Urgent." Larry Fink, chief executive of the investment management behemoth BlackRock, was on the line and needed to talk.

Fleming couldn't imagine what might be important enough to justify the interruption, but given the commotion in the market, he agreed to take the call. Rumors that morning claimed that BlackRock might be a candidate to buy Lehman Brothers; Fink had only encouraged the specu-lation by appearing on CNBC earlier that day and declaring: "Lehman is not a Bear Stearns situation. Lehman Brothers is adequately structured in terms of avoiding a liquidity crisis."

The two executives were close—Fink, a fifty-five-year-old financier, had lent Fleming and his banking team office space after the September 11 attacks drove Merrill employees out of their downtown headquarters—and their two firms were now partners, as Fleming had helped broker a 2006 deal to merge Merrill's $539 billion asset-management business with BlackRock in exchange for a stake of nearly 50 percent in the firm. The deal had vaulted BlackRock, long known as a bond house, into the $1 trillion–asset club and had established Fink, who had helped create the mortgage-backed security market in the 1980s, as an even more influential power broker on Wall Street.

"What the fuck is going on?" Fink, nearly breathless with anger, screamed into the phone as soon as Fleming greeted him. "Just tell me what the fuck is going on! How could he do this? How could he do this to *me*?"

"Larry, Larry," Fleming tried to calm him, "what are you talking about?"

"*Thain!*" Fink bellowed, referring to John Thain, Merrill Lynch's chief executive. "CNBC says he's putting BlackRock on the block. What the fuck is he thinking?"

"Larry, I know nothing about it," Fleming replied, genuinely baffled. "When did he say this?"

"In a speech! Today he announces to the whole world that the stake is up for sale. What fucking idiot does that?" Fink shouted, still at the same pitch of fury.

"I didn't know John was giving a speech, but—"

"We have a lockup, Greg! You know that; John knows. He has to ask my permission. He hasn't called me—nothing! He has no fucking right to sell BlackRock!"

"Larry, I know we have a lockup agreement. Just take a deep breath and listen," Fleming urged him.

"Think about it," Fink continued. "What seller announces to the world he's selling? Just think about the stupidity of this."

"As far as I know, no one at Merrill wants to change the relationship we have with you," Fleming replied. "BlackRock is a strategically critical asset for us. Let me find John, find out what happened, and the three of us will talk this out," he promised, and ended the conversation.

The only speaking engagement of Thain's of which Fleming was aware had taken place the previous day, at a conference hosted by the *Wall Street Journal*; in it, he had made no notable mention of BlackRock. Indeed, Fleming had been impressed with Thain's objective assessment of the state of the industry during his talk. "Everyone is shrinking their balance sheet. There was too much leverage in the system, too much credit, for too long," Thain had said, assuming the role of the industry elder statesman. "We all have concerns about what we read in the papers."

Fleming called Thain's office but was told that he was away. Fleming knew that Merrill's balance sheet had continued to deteriorate—it was loaded with subprime loans the company had been unable to get rid of, and it likely needed to raise more money. But Fleming didn't expect that Thain would actually want to sell BlackRock, which many considered Merrill's most solid asset. Announcing a sale would only put more pressure on Merrill.

Like Lehman Brothers, Merrill had been struggling with its own crisis of confidence. For the past several months, Thain had repeatedly told investors that the firm had marked—or valued—its assets conservatively and wouldn't need to raise additional capital. But investors had been skeptical, knocking Merrill's shares down 32 percent for the year.

Thain, Paulson's former number two at Goldman Sachs, had been brought in to run Merrill just seven months earlier to help restore some semblance of order after the firm reported its biggest loss in history and ousted its chief executive, Stan O'Neal. At the time, Larry Fink actually thought he was the top candidate for the job, only to find out by reading the *New York Post*'s Web site that he had lost out to Thain. His own job interview was supposed to have been later that week, which might explain some of his frustration with Thain.

An ultra-straitlaced executive who was sometimes referred to as "I-Robot," Thain had appealed to Merrill's board because of his newly minted reputation as a turnaround artist. After rising rapidly through the ranks at Goldman, he left to overhaul the New York Stock Exchange after the extravagant compensation package for its CEO, Richard Grasso, caused an outrage. Fink, ironically, had led the exchange's search committee that selected him. At the NYSE, Thain (who, perhaps not surprisingly, took a post-Grasso $16 million pay cut) unleashed a radical transformation, shaking the world's largest stock exchange out of its clubby, anachronistic ways. He cut perks—shutting the wood-paneled Luncheon Club and firing the exchange's barber—and turned the exchange into a for-profit, publicly traded company. He took on the powerful, entrenched constituency of floor traders and specialists, who protested in vain as Thain dragged them into the electronic trading age.

Thain, who had grown up in Antioch, Illinois, a small town just west of Lake Michigan, had always been considered a talented problem solver. In his junior year at the Massachusetts Institute of Technology, when he interned at Procter & Gamble, he made a simple but highly significant observation of an assembly line he was supervising. The workers were making Ivory soap, and whenever technical problems forced the line to come to a halt, they would wait for it to start up again before getting back to work. The college boy persuaded the workers that there was no reason to stop—they could keep making soap and stack the boxes on the side until the line came back on. That way their bonuses, which were based on production, would not be affected. Thain won them over, especially after he pitched in and stacked boxes himself.

While his public image as a callous technocrat may not have been entirely fair, Thain did have his weaknesses. With an engineering background, he could come across as a purely linear thinker who sometimes seemed remarkably tone deaf. "When he made conversation, he would explain the things in detail to almost the point that I didn't know what the hell he was talking about," Steve Vazquez, one of his peers from high school, said. At a meeting at Goldman in 1999, Thain told a roomful of bankers and lawyers, "Would it hurt you to suck up to me once in a while?" He thought he was being funny; others couldn't tell.

The incident that had so enraged Fink turned out to be just another example of his tin ear, as Fleming ultimately discovered. Thain had been taking part in a conference call with Deutsche Bank investors when Michael Mayo, the analyst running the call, asked him, "So, I think you said before that you're comfortable with BlackRock and Bloomberg. Is that still the case? Under what circumstances would you say it doesn't make sense to have those investments anymore?"

Thain, reasonably enough, took the question to be a hypothetical. Of course Merrill needed to look at all its assets and figure out which ones could be turned into cold, hard cash, he said; in this environment, any investment bank needed to do that. "At the end of last year when we were looking to raise capital, we looked at various options, which included selling common, selling converts," Thain replied. "But also included using some of the valuable assets that we have on our balance sheet, like Bloomberg and BlackRock.

"And if we were to raise more capital, we would continue that process of evaluating what alternatives we had and what made the most sense for us to do from a capital efficiency point of view."

Thain's answer might have made plenty of sense to himself, but having heard him repeatedly say, "We have plenty of capital going forward," investors took it as a not-so-subtle hint, and the damage was done. Within seventy-two hours, Merrill was being described "as the most vulnerable brokerage after Lehman."

———

For a single day John Thain had the job that he had wanted for his entire career: to be the CEO of Goldman Sachs. That day, unfortunately, was September 11, 2001. As the company's actual CEO—Hank Paulson—was on a plane headed to Hong Kong when the attacks took place, Thain, the firm's co-president, was the most senior executive at 85 Broad Street, Goldman's headquarters, and somebody had to take control. (His other co-president, John Thornton, was in Washington, D.C., for a meeting at the Brookings Institution.)

Thain had always been certain that his destiny was to run Goldman himself one day. Over the Christmas holiday of 1998, he had taken part in—perhaps even instigated—the palace coup that forced Jon Corzine out and put Hank Paulson in charge of Goldman. At Robert Hurst's Fifth Avenue apartment, Thain and Thornton had agreed to support Paulson. But they thought they had received an informal promise in exchange: Paulson said he planned to be the CEO for only two years as a transition until he could move back to Chicago, and then they expected the job to be bequeathed to them. With Corzine off skiing in Telluride, Colorado, they made their pact.

For Thain, a longtime lieutenant and friend of Corzine, it was a heart-wrenching decision, but backing Paulson—whom he genuinely believed would make a better leader than Corzine—enabled him to advance his own career. As the person closest to Corzine on the executive committee, Thain was the one to have to break the news to him, and he was forced to watch as his boss fought back tears. Goldman partners, many just back from vacation, received a terse e-mail from Paulson and Corzine on the morning of January 11, 1999: "Jon has decided to relinquish the CEO title."

But after two years passed, Paulson showed no interest in stepping aside as he realized how much work he still had to accomplish and was unsure about whether his successors were up to the task. Thain, like any senior Goldman partner, had become outrageously wealthy, accumulating several hundred million dollars in stock from the IPO, but he realized that his boss wasn't going anywhere soon, and his dream of running Goldman would remain just that. Thain and Paulson got along well, but there was now an underlying tension. Thain resented the fact that Paulson hadn't stuck to what he thought was their agreement, while for his part, Paulson questioned whether Thain, whom he respected as a talented financier, had the sound judgment to be CEO. He was also bothered by Thain's un-Goldman-like displays of wealth. Though Thain was in many ways under-stated—he never appeared in the society pages, for example—he bought a ten-acre property in Rye and owned five BMWs. Paulson was also irked by Thain's vacation rituals: While normally a hard worker, Thain was always determined to take a two-week trip to Vail at Christmastime, a week over Easter, and then another two weeks in the summer. For a per-petual worker like Paulson, it was a tough pill to swallow. By 2003 it was clear to both Thain and Thornton that Paulson wasn't going anywhere. Thornton, who by then had grown frustrated he had not been elevated, decided to leave. Soon after his departure, he took Thain out to dinner.

"You can't rely on Hank's previous words," Thornton said. "If I were you, I'd be getting out of here."

Only several months later, Paulson appointed a former commodities trader named Lloyd Blankfein to be co-president with Thain. The ascen-sion of Blankfein, who was building his own power base at the firm, not just politically but through sheer profits, as he oversaw business that accounted for 80 percent of Goldman's earnings, was a sure sign to Thain to begin looking for an exit.

Paulson was speechless when Thain marched into his office to tell him he was leaving to become CEO of the New York Stock Exchange. Thain subsequently went on to deserved success in the position.

Four years later, with the credit crisis deepening in the fall of 2007, several large banks started taking huge losses and firing their CEOs. Thain was a natural candidate for firms looking for an upgrade. (Indeed, he had been considered for the position not just at Merrill Lynch but also at Citi-group, along with Tim Geithner.) He debated with himself—and with his wife, Carmen—about whether he would take the Merrill job if it was offered to him. He had done his own due diligence on the firm's books and was satisfied that, despite the roughly $90 billion in shaky loans and derivatives on its balance sheet, it was manageable. But more than that, he saw it as an opportunity to be a CEO of a major brokerage firm—to get the job he had never landed at Goldman. Given his contacts and reputation, he also saw Merrill as a platform from which he could beat Goldman at its own game. He judged the effort to be at least a five-year project; he told Merrill's board it would take him two years to fix the balance sheet and another three to take the firm to the next level. He eventually accepted the position and was paid a $15 million signing bonus and a $750,000 annual salary. The board also granted him options that would amount to another $72 million if he could bring Merrill's shares above $100; they rose 1.6 percent to $57.86 on the news that Thain would come on board but still had a long way to go for that bonus to kick in.

As soon as he arrived, he moved quickly to shore up Merrill's capital base, hoping to move a step ahead of the problem. His frame of reference was the end of Drexel Burnham Lambert, Michael Milken's firm, which had filed for bankruptcy in 1990. "The demise of Drexel was really a liquidity problem," he said at one of the firm's Wednesday-morning risk-committee meetings, explaining how the firm didn't have enough cash on hand. "Liquidity is the most important thing." In December and January, Merrill raised $12.8 billion from the sovereign wealth funds Temasek Holdings of Singapore and the Kuwait Investment Authority, among other investors.

At the same time, he went about dismantling the O'Neal empire. When he first arrived, he noticed that the security guards at Merrill's headquarters just across from Ground Zero always kept an entire elevator bank open exclusively for him. Thain walked over to one of the other elevators, and the moment he entered, all the employees shuffled out. "What's the matter, why are you getting off?" he asked. "We can't ride the elevator with you," the employees told him. "That's crazy, get back in here," he said, as he instructed security to open up the elevator bank for everyone. He also went about slashing costs by selling one of the firm's G-4 planes and a helicopter. No target was too small: The freshly cut flowers that were costing the firm some $200,000 a year were replaced with silk ones.

At the same time—in a paradox that was not lost on his staff—Thain began spending serious money on talent. In late April, with the approval of Merrill's board, he hired an old friend from Goldman, Thomas K. Montag, as his head of trading and sales. To lure him away, the firm agreed to a signing bonus of $39.4 million, even though Montag wouldn't begin work until August. In May, Thain would hire Peter Kraus, another Goldman man, whom he guaranteed a $25 million golden parachute.

And then there was his office. He and his wife had decided it was badly in need of a renovation. O'Neal's white Formica furniture didn't match the rest of the Merrill decor, and an adjacent conference room had been turned into O'Neal's personal gym, complete with an exercise bike and weights. Thain hired celebrity interior decorator Michael S. Smith (whose clients included Steven Spielberg and Dustin Hoffman) to renovate his office, the adjoining conference space, and the reception area, including repainting, carpentry, and electrical work. Thain didn't pay much attention to the details, focusing mainly on the fact that Smith had happily brought over his favorite desk from his old office at the NYSE. But Smith billed the firm $800,000 for his services and submitted an itemized list of goods that included an $87,000 area rug, a $68,000 credenza, and a $35,115 commode. The executives in the billing department who cut the checks, however, were so aghast at such profligacy that they made copies of the receipts, which they would later use against him.

For all Thain's efforts to improve morale, he seemed to be achieving precisely the opposite. On the trading floor, "39.4"—a sly reference to Montag's bonus—became a popular way to punctuate a sentence instead of using an expletive. While Merrill executives praised Thain for his prescient efforts to raise capital, there were grumblings that, as a manager, he was either too much of a micromanager or more likely the opposite, too detached. When he hired a new chief of staff, May Lee, he neglected to mention it to certain of the firm's top inner circle. On her first day on the job, she took her seat at an executive committee meeting with all of them. Robert McCann, who ran the firm's brokerage business, walked into the room, noticed the stranger, and looked at Thain quizzically. "Oh, I probably should have told you," Thain said matter-of-factly, "this is my new chief of staff."

He also rankled some executive committee members with his grandiose media appearances, in which he cast himself as the great savior of Merrill. He brought in Margaret Tutwiler, a former State Department spokeswoman in G. H. W. Bush's administration, to run communications. Within the firm some thought he might be angling for the Treasury secretary post if John McCain, the Republican front-runner, was victorious.

By that June 11, when Larry Fink made his enraged call about Black-Rock, it had become clear that the capital that Merrill Lynch had raised from Temasek and KIA, the sovereign wealth funds, back in December, was still insufficient—and that those deals were proving to be much more expensive than they appeared at the time. Under their terms, the investors were entitled to additional payouts to compensate for any dilution in their holdings if Merrill issued new shares at a lower stock price. Merrill's stock price, meanwhile, had slid steeply. To add $1 billion in new capital, the firm might actually have to raise an amount nearly three times that to compensate the 2007 investors. Thain could also see that the second quarter was shaping up to be worse than the first, though he didn't know how bad it would ultimately be.

Merrill's problems were by now becoming evident to others on Wall Street, feeding a perception that Thain did not have a solid grasp on the firm. As the banking analyst Mayo told Thain on the conference call that got him in trouble with Fink: "It's kind of 'Raise as you go' is the perception, as you have the losses, you raise more capital. Maybe it's more of a perception of the industry, if you disagree. At what point do you say let's just get far ahead of anything that could come our way?"

"I don't agree with the way you characterized it," Thain replied. "We raised $12.8 billion of new capital at the end of the year, we only lost $8.6 billion. We raised almost 50 percent extra and so we did raise more than we lost. The same actually was true at the end of the first quarter, we raised $2.7 billion, versus the $2 billion we lost. So we have been raising extra."

But that would not be enough.

———

Several weeks after Merrill's board had named Thain CEO, he was faced with an especially delicate task. Placing a call to his predecessor, Stan O'Neal (who had just negotiated an exit package for himself totaling $161.5 million), Thain asked if they might get together. Hoping to keep their meeting out of the newspapers, the two decided on breakfast in Midtown at the office of O'Neal's lawyer.

After a few pleasantries, O'Neal stared levelly at Thain and asked, "So, why do you want to talk to me?"

Thain knew that if there was one person in the world who could explain what had gone wrong at Merrill Lynch, why it had loaded up on $27.2 billion of subprime and other risky investments—what, in other words, had gone wrong on Wall Street—it was O'Neal.

"Well, as you know, I'm new, and you were the CEO for five years," Thain said carefully. "I'd like to get your take, any insight on what happened here. Who everybody is, and all that. It would be very helpful to me and to Merrill."

O'Neal was silent for a moment, picking at his fruit plate, and then looked up at Thain. "I'm sorry," he said. "I don't think I'm the right person to answer that question."

———

O'Neal was out of a different mold than most of Merrill's top executives, not least of all because he was African American—quite a change from the succession of white Irish Catholics who had headed the firm in the past. His was, by any measure, an amazing success story. O'Neal, whose grandfather had been born a slave, had spent much of his childhood in a wood-frame house with no indoor plumbing on a farm in eastern Alabama. When Stan was twelve, his father moved the family to a housing project in Atlanta, where he soon found a job at a nearby General Motors assembly plant. GM became Stan O'Neal's ticket out of poverty. After high school he enrolled at the General Motors Institute (now known as Kettering University), an engineering college, on a work-study scholarship that involved his working six weeks on the assembly line in Flint, Michigan, followed by six weeks in the classroom. With GM's support he attended Harvard Business School, graduating in 1978. After a period working in GM's treasury department in New York, he was persuaded in 1986 by a former GM treasurer, then at Merrill Lynch, to join the brokerage firm on its junk bond desk. Through hard work and support from powerful mentors, O'Neal rose rapidly through the ranks. He eventually came to oversee the junk bond unit, which rose to the top of the Wall Street rankings known as league tables. In 1997 he was named a co-head of the institutional client business; the following year, chief financial officer; and in 2002, CEO.

The firm for which O'Neal was now responsible had been founded in 1914 by Charles Merrill, a stocky Floridian known to his friends as "Good Time Charlie," whose mission was "Bringing Wall Street to Main Street."

Merrill set up brokerage branches in nearly one hundred cities across the nation, connected to the home office by Teletype. He helped democratize and demystify the stock market by using promotions, like giving away shares in a contest sponsored by Wheaties. More than the mutual fund giant Fidelity or any bank, Merrill Lynch, with its bull logo, became identified with the new investing class that emerged in the decades after World War II. The percentage of Americans who owned stock—whether directly or indirectly, through mutual funds and retirement plans—more than doubled from 1983 to 1999, by which point nearly half the country were investors in the market. Merrill Lynch was "Bullish on America" (an advertising slogan it first used in 1971), and America was just as bullish on Merrill Lynch.

By 2000, however, the "thundering herd" had become the "phlegmatic herd"—a bit too fat and complacent. The firm had gone on a shopping binge in the 1990s, accelerating its global expansion and swelling its workforce to 72,000 (compared to the 62,700 of its closest rival, Morgan Stanley). Meanwhile, its traditional power base, the retail brokerage business, was being undercut by the rise of discount online brokerage firms like E*Trade and Ameritrade. And because much of Merrill Lynch's investment banking business was predicated on volume, not profits, the dot-com crash in the stock market the previous year had left Merrill vulnerable, exposing its high costs and thin margins.

The man tasked with shrinking Merrill back to a manageable size was O'Neal. Although colleagues had urged him to proceed slowly, especially in light of the trauma of 9/11, in which Merrill had lost three of its employees, O'Neal plowed ahead with little regard for the effects of downsizing on the firm's morale and culture. Within a year, Merrill's workforce had been cut by an astonishing 25 percent, a loss of more than 15,000 jobs.

"I think this is a great firm—but greatness is not an entitlement," O'Neal remarked at the time. "There are some things about our culture I don't want to change . . . but I don't like maternalism or paternalism in a corporate setting, as the name Mother Merrill implies."

The management turnover that accompanied his ascension was likewise startling: Even before he officially became chief executive in December 2002, almost half of the nineteen members of the firm's executive committee were gone. It became clear that O'Neal would force out anyone whom he had any reason to distrust. "Ruthless," O'Neal would tell associates, "isn't always that bad."

If a colleague dared stand up to him, O'Neal was famous for fighting back. When Peter Kelly, a top Merrill Lynch lawyer, challenged him about an investment, O'Neal called security to have him physically removed from his office. Some employees began referring to O'Neal's top-management team as "the Taliban" and calling O'Neal "Mullah Omar."

As well as by vigorous cost cutting, O'Neal had plans to make Merrill great again through redirecting the firm into riskier but more lucrative strategies. O'Neal's model for this approach was Goldman, which had begun aggressively making bets using its own account rather than simply trading on behalf of its clients. He zealously tracked Goldman's quarterly numbers, and he would hound his associates about performance. As it happened, O'Neal lived in the same building as Lloyd Blankfein, a daily reminder of exactly whom he was chasing. Blankfein and his wife had come to jokingly refer to O'Neal as "Doppler Stan," because whenever they'd run into him in the lobby, O'Neal would always keep moving, often walking in circles, they thought, to avoid having a conversation.

O'Neal did force through a transformation of Merrill that, in its first few years, resulted in a bonanza. In 2006, Merrill Lynch made $7.5 billion from trading its own money and that of its clients, compared with $2.6 billion in 2002. Almost overnight, it became a major player in the booming business of private equity.

O'Neal also ramped up the firm's use of leverage, particularly in mortgage securitization. He saw how firms like Lehman were minting money on investments tied to mortgages, and he wanted some of that action for Merrill. In 2003 he lured Christopher Ricciardi, a thirty-four-year-old star in mortgage securitization, from Credit Suisse. Merrill was an also-ran in the market for collateralized debt obligations, which were often built with tranches from mortgage-backed securities. In just two years Merrill became the biggest CDO issuer on Wall Street.

Creating and selling CDOs generated lucrative fees for Merrill, just as it had for other banks. But even this wasn't enough. Merrill sought to be a full-line producer: issuing mortgages, packaging them into securities, and then slicing and dicing them to CDOs. The firm began buying up mortgage servicers and commercial real estate firms, more than thirty in all, and in December 2006, it acquired one of the biggest subprime mort-gage lenders in the nation, First Franklin, for $1.3 billion.

But just as Merrill began moving deeper into mortgages, the housing market started to show its first signs of distress. By late 2005, with prices peaking, American International Group, one of the biggest insurers of CDOs through credit default swaps, stopped insuring securities with any subprime tranches. Ricciardi, meanwhile, having built Merrill into a CDO powerhouse, left Merrill in February 2006 to head a boutique investment firm, Cohen Brothers. With his departure, Dow Kim, a Merrill executive, sought to rally those who stayed behind on the CDO front. Merrill, he promised, would maintain its ranking as the top CDO issuer, doing "what-ever it takes." One deal Kim put together was something he called Costa Bella—a $500 million CDO, for which Merrill received a $5 million fee.

But Jeffrey Kronthal, a Merrill executive who had helped recruit Ric-ciardi to Merrill, had been growing increasingly concerned that a storm was threatening not just extravagant projects like Costa Bella, but the entire CDO market, and he began to urge caution. He insisted the firm maintain a $3 billion ceiling on CDOs with subprime tranches. Kronthal's wariness put him directly in the path of O'Neal's ambition to be the mort-gage leader on Wall Street—a situation that was clearly untenable. In July 2006, Kronthal, one of its most able managers of risk, was out, replaced by thirty-nine-year-old executive Osman Semerci, who worked in Merrill's London office. Semerci was a derivatives salesman, not a trader, and had had no experience in the American mortgage market.

Despite its ongoing management turmoil, Merrill Lynch kept ratchet-ing up the volume of its mortgage securitization and CDO business. By the end of 2006, however, the market for subprime mortgages was per-ceptibly unraveling—prices were falling, and delinquencies were rising. Even after it should have recognized an obvious danger signal when it was no longer able to hedge its bets with insurance from AIG, Merrill churned out nearly $44 billion worth of CDOs that year, three times the total of the previous year.

If they were worried, however, Merrill's top executives didn't show it, for they had powerful incentive to stay the course. Huge bonuses were triggered by the $700 million in fees generated by creating and trading the CDOs, despite the fact that not all of them were sold. (Accounting rules allowed banks to treat a securitization as a sale under certain conditions.) In 2006, Kim took home $37 million; Semerci, more than $20 million; O'Neal, $46 million.

In 2007, Merrill kept its foot firmly on the gas pedal, underwriting more than $30 billion worth of CDOs in the first seven months of the year alone. With his bets paying off so incredibly well, though, O'Neal had overlooked one critical factor—he hadn't made any preparations for an inevitable downturn, having never paid much attention to risk management until it was too late. Merrill did have a department for market risk and another for credit risk, though neither reported directly to O'Neal; they were the responsibility of Jeffrey N. Edwards, the chief financial officer, and of Ahmass Fakahany, the chief administrative officer, a former Exxon financial analyst and an O'Neal favorite.

Before long, however, the fault lines started to show. Kim, who oversaw the mortgage division, announced in May that he was leaving the firm to start a hedge fund. Responding to doubts voiced by some of their colleagues that the firm's strategy could be sustained, Semerci and Dale Lattanzio became defensive. On July 21, at a meeting of the board, they insisted that the firm's CDO exposure was nearly fully hedged; in a worst-case scenario, they maintained, the firm's loss would amount to only $77 million. O'Neal stood up and praised the work of the two executives.

But not everyone agreed with that optimistic assessment. "Who the fuck are they kidding? Are you fucking kidding me with this?" Peter Kelly, Merrill's outspoken lawyer, asked Edwards after the meeting. "How is the board walking away without shitting their pants?"

As market conditions worsened, it became clear that the metrics they were using had no grounding in reality. Two weeks after the July board meeting, Fleming and Fakahany sent a letter to Merrill's directors, briefing them on the firm's deteriorating positions.

O'Neal, meanwhile, became withdrawn and brooding, and began to lose himself in golf, playing thirteen rounds, often on weekdays and almost always alone, at storied clubs like Shinnecock Hills in Southampton.

Merrill's CDO portfolio continued to plummet through August and September. In early October, the firm projected a quarterly loss of roughly $5 billion. Two weeks later, that figure had ballooned to $7.9 billion. Desperate, O'Neal sent an overture to Wachovia about a merger. On Sunday,

October 21, he had dinner with Merrill's board, and in discussing options to solidify the firm's balance sheet, he mentioned he'd talked to Wachovia. Somewhat prophetically, he told them of the market turmoil. "If this lasts for a long period, we and every other firm that relies on short-term over-night and term repo funding will have a problem." But the board did not focus on that last point. They were furious he had engaged in unauthorized merger talks. "But my job is to think about options," he protested. Two days later the board met without him and agreed to force him out. Few were sympathetic. A former co-worker told the *New Yorker:* "I wouldn't hire Stan to wash windows. What he did to Merrill Lynch was absolutely criminal."

———

One morning in late June, New York's mayor, Michael Bloomberg, left his brownstone apartment on Seventy-ninth Street, hopped into the back of his black Suburban, and headed to Midtown for a breakfast date. With his security detail waiting outside, Bloomberg, wearing his usual American flag lapel pin, strolled into New York Luncheonette, a tiny diner on Fiftieth Street across from a parking lot, and greeted John Thain. The restaurant was one of Bloomberg's favorites; he had recently brought a long-shot presidential hopeful, Barack Obama, there.

Although Bloomberg didn't know Thain very well personally, he had had a long and fruitful association with Merrill Lynch, which had supported his eponymous financial-data company since its inception. Bloomberg, who had been a partner at Salomon Brothers, the bond-trading powerhouse, and was in charge of the firm's information systems, started his terminal business in 1981; Merrill, which helped finance it, was the first customer to buy one of his machines, which delivered real-time financial data for traders. In 1985, Merrill acquired 30 percent of Bloomberg LP for $30 million, though it later reduced its stake by a third.

When Michael Bloomberg became mayor of New York, he placed his 68 percent stake of the company into a blind trust and stepped away from managing it—even if, in reality, it was closer to a half-step, especially when it came to critical company matters—like the one John Thain was about to broach. Thain, desperate for more capital and sufficiently convinced after the Larry Fink debacle that he should try to keep the firm's BlackRock stake, wanted Bloomberg to buy back Merrill's 20 percent holdings in his company. If the mayor declined to make the purchase, however, it was unclear whether Merrill would have the right to sell its share on the open market. The contract had been written in 1986 and they both knew it was murky.

Tucked away in a corner booth, the two men sipped coffee and chatted amiably. As former bond traders and ski enthusiasts, they hit it off surprisingly well.

"We'd probably be looking to do this over the summer," Thain said, trying to remain somewhat noncommittal so as not to convey any sense of panic. Within half an hour, they had an agreement to move forward.

It was the lifeline he had been hoping for, and as soon as he bid the mayor farewell, Thain raced back to the office to tell Fleming to start work on the project immediately.

CHAPTER EIGHT

J amie Dimon's 10:00 a.m. meeting was running long.

"Tell Bob I'll be there in a minute," he told Kathy, his assistant.

Robert "Bob" Willumstad and Dimon both had once been part of Sandy Weill's team of financial empire builders. At different points in time, each had been considered Weill's heir apparent at the behemoth Citigroup they had all helped create, though ultimately, neither would be given a chance to assume its leadership. The two had remained close in the decade since Dimon had been forced out.

A tall, white-haired executive who could have been the archetype of the Manhattan banker, Willumstad sat patiently on this early June day in the waiting room on the eighth floor of JP Morgan in the old Union Carbide offices. A glass cabinet displayed replicas of two wood-handled pistols with a resonant history: They had been used by Aaron Burr and Alexander Hamilton in the 1804 duel that killed Hamilton, the first U.S. secretary of the Treasury.

Like Dimon, Willumstad had been outmaneuvered by Weill and, after leaving Citi in July 2005, went on to start a private-equity fund, Brysam Global Partners, which made investments in consumer finance businesses in Latin America and Russia. His partner, Marge Magner, was another Citigroup exile. Under Dimon, JP Morgan had become the largest investor in Willumstad's fund, whose offices were just across Park Avenue from JP Morgan's own headquarters. While under his and Magner's direction, Brysam had become a profitable firm. Willumstad held another, much more important position: He was the chairman of the board of American International Group, AIG, the giant insurer, which was the reason for his visit to Dimon this day.

"I've been thinking about something and could use your advice," Willumstad, a soft-spoken man, said to Dimon after he had finally been ushered into his office. He revealed that the AIG board had just asked him if he'd be interested in becoming CEO; the current CEO, Martin Sullivan, would likely be fired within the week. As chairman, Willumstad himself would be responsible for paying a visit to AIG's headquarters the following day to warn Sullivan that his job was in jeopardy.

"I like what I'm doing," he said earnestly. "No one's looking over my shoulder."

"Except for me!" Dimon, one of his biggest financial backers, countered with a laugh.

Willumstad explained that he had been pondering accepting the top position over the past several months, ever since the credit crisis had engulfed AIG, and it had become increasingly clear that he might be given an opportunity to run the company. That prospect had left him painfully conflicted: While he had always wanted to be a CEO, he was sixty-two and now had the time to pursue outside interests, like auto racing.

A third-generation son of Norwegian immigrants, Willumstad came from a working-class background, growing up in Bay Ridge, Brooklyn, and then on Long Island. By the mid-1980s, he was rising through the executive ranks of Chemical Bank. As a favor to a former boss, Robert Lipp, he flew down to Baltimore to see what Weill and his right-hand man, Dimon, were up to at Commercial Credit, a subprime lender they were running. The drive and entrepreneurial energy of the Weill-Dimon team was strikingly different from the stuffy bureaucracy of Chemical and every other firm he'd seen in the New York banking industry.

The two offered Willumstad a job, which he accepted, though he couldn't help but feel a bit of buyer's remorse when, on his first day on the job, he met seventy-five Commercial Credit branch managers at a conference in Boca Raton and realized he had never seen so many middle-aged men in polyester leisure suits. Willumstad survived that shock—as well as the golf and the drinking—and eventually grew comfortable at the firm. In 1998 he helped lead a blitzkrieg of acquisitions that shocked the financial establishment: Primerica, Shearson, Travelers, and the biggest of all financial mergers, Citicorp. For a brief time the three of them had towered over a financial industry that had an abundance of towering figures; four years after Dimon departed Citi following a bitter falling-out with Weill, Willumstad assumed his old job of president, which proved to be as far as he would rise in the company.

For a good half hour, Willumstad and Dimon discussed the pros and cons of the AIG position. As chairman of the company, Willumstad knew better than most how deep the company's problems ran; solving them would be an unimaginably huge challenge. Its parlous state kept bringing him back to the same decision: "I should take the job on an interim basis," he said firmly.

Dimon shook his head. "Bullshit," he said. "Either you want to do the job or you don't."

"I know," Willumstad conceded. "I know."

"You're confusing the issues here," Dimon insisted. "First of all, interim CEO is a very complex and difficult thing, and as an interim CEO, it will be exactly the same job as the permanent CEO. If I were the board, I wouldn't allow it, and if it were me, I wouldn't do it. It's like cutting your own balls off."

"Zarb thinks it's all or nothing, too," Willumstad said, referring to Frank Zarb, AIG's former chairman. "He doesn't want to have three CEOs in three years with a fourth one coming in."

"You know, if you do things well, it's still going to take you two years at a minimum," Dimon said about the prospects of turning things around, leaning forward and punching the air to underscore his points. "The question is, do you want to get back in the saddle or not? If you are going back in the saddle, remember how hard the saddle is."

Willumstad nodded in agreement. But he had one other concern. "I don't like both the public appearance of it and that it looks like I'm going to throw Martin out and put myself in," he said, but Dimon assured him that that was not a serious issue.

The board wanted Willumstad to take the job; his wife, Carol, thought he should—she had always believed that he had been robbed of the CEO job at Citi—and now Dimon was adding his vote.

———

The next day Willumstad took a black Town Car to AIG's offices at 70 Pine Street. Upon taking a seat in Martin Sullivan's office, he delivered his message without any equivocation: "Listen, Martin, the board is going to meet on Sunday, and whether or not you continue in this job is the topic of discussion."

Sullivan merely sighed and said, "The board doesn't fully appreciate how difficult this market is. When I took over, I had to clean up the mess with our regulators, and I can lead us out of these troubles."

"Yes, Martin," Willumstad acknowledged, "but you have to look at what has happened over the last few months. The feeling among directors is that someone has to be accountable. . . . Look, there are three possible outcomes of the board meeting. I could be coming back to you and saying that the board fully supports you, or the board thinks you should go. The other possibility is that the board says, 'You have to do the following things in an X period of time or else you're out.'"

Sullivan looked down at the floor. "And what do you think the likely outcome will be?"

"There's a strong sentiment to make a change, but who knows?" Willumstad replied with a shrug. "You put twelve people in a room, and anything could happen."

On Sunday, June 15, the board of AIG met in the office of Richard Beattie, the chairman of the board's outside law firm, Simpson Thacher & Bartlett. Sullivan was on the agenda, but he had chosen not to attend. After a brief discussion, the board decided to remove Sullivan and install Willumstad in his place.

———

The company over which Willumstad had now been assigned stewardship was one of the most peculiar success stories in American business. American International Group began as American Asiatic Underwriters in a small office in Shanghai in 1919. Nearly half a century later, it had operations throughout Asia, Europe, the Middle East, and the Americas, but with its modest market value of $300 million and about $1 billion worth of insurance policies, the privately owned firm was hardly a juggernaut.

By 2008, however, the word "modest" was seldom used in connection with AIG. In only a few decades it had grown into one of the world's largest financial companies, with a market value of just under $80 billion (even after a steep slide in its share price earlier that year) and more than $1 trillion worth of assets on its books. That phenomenal expansion was primarily the result of the cunning and drive of one man: Maurice Raymond Greenberg, known to friends as "Hank," after the Detroit Tigers slugger Hank Greenberg, and referred to within the company simply as "MRG."

Greenberg had had a hardscrabble upbringing worthy of a Dickens hero. His father, Jacob Greenberg, who drove a cab and owned a candy store on the Lower East Side of Manhattan, died during the Great Depression when Hank was only seven years old. After his mother married her second husband, a dairy farmer, the family moved to upstate New York, where Hank would wake before dawn most mornings to help milk the cows. When he was seventeen, he faked his birth date to join the army. Two years later, Greenberg was among the troops who landed on Omaha Beach on D-day. He was in the unit that liberated the Dachau concentration camp and, after returning to the United States for law school, he returned to the military to fight in the Korean War, in which he was awarded the Bronze Star.

Returning to New York after Korea, Greenberg talked his way into a job as a $75-a-week insurance underwriting trainee with Continental Casualty, where he quickly rose to become the firm's assistant vice president in charge of accident and health insurance. In 1960, Cornelius Vander Starr, the founder of what would become AIG, recruited Greenberg to join his company.

A onetime soda-fountain operator in Fort Bragg, California, C. V. Starr was one of the prototypical restless Americans of the early twentieth century, the kind who made their names as wildcatters, inventors, and entrepreneurs. After trying his hand at real estate, he entered the insurance business and at the age of twenty-seven sailed to Shanghai to sell policies. There he discovered a market that was dominated by British insurance companies, but they sold only to Western firms and expatriates; Starr built his business selling policies to the Chinese themselves. Forced out of China after the communist takeover in 1948, Starr expanded elsewhere in Asia. With the help of a friend in the military by the name of General Douglas MacArthur, commander of the occupying force in Japan after the war, Starr secured a deal to provide insurance to the American military for several years. Before the country opened up its insurance market to foreign underwriters, AIG Japan would become the company's largest overseas property-casualty business.

By 1968, Starr was seventy-six and ailing, and with an oxygen tank and vials of pills never far from his side, he turned to Greenberg to crack the American market, naming him president and Gordon B. Tweedy chairman. Greenberg wasted no time in making it clear who was going to be taking the lead. At a meeting soon after his appointment, he and Tweedy were on opposite sides of an argument when Tweedy stood up and began loudly pressing his point. "Sit down, Gordon, and shut up," Greenberg told him. "I'm in charge now." Starr, whose bronze bust still greets visitors to AIG's art deco headquarters, died that December. The following year, AIG went public, and Greenberg became CEO. (Tweedy left soon afterward.)

Under Greenberg, AIG grew rapidly and became increasingly profitable through expansion and acquisitions, doing business in 130 countries and diversifying into aircraft leasing and life insurance. Greenberg himself became the very model of an imperial CEO—adored by shareholders, feared by employees, and a cipher to everyone outside the company. Despite his slight build, he had an intimidating presence. He drove himself relentlessly, eating nothing but fish and steamed vegetables every day for lunch, and regularly working out on a StairMaster or playing tennis. He showed little affection for anyone, with the exception of his wife, Corinne, and his Maltese, Snowball. Within AIG he was famous for his short fuse and his ceaseless drive to know everything that was happening inside the company—*his* company. He was rumored to have hired former CIA agents, and security men seemed to be posted everywhere at headquarters.

To the outside world the biggest AIG drama was Greenberg's attempt to secure a dynasty; what he created, instead, was a blood feud among insurance royalty.

Jeffrey Greenberg, his son, a graduate of Brown and Georgetown Law, had been groomed to succeed Hank. But in 1995, after a series of clashes with his father, Jeffrey left AIG, where he had worked for seventeen years. Two weeks earlier, his younger brother, Evan, had been promoted to executive vice president, his third promotion in less than sixteen months, establishing him as a rival to Jeffrey. With the departure of his brother, Evan, a former hippie who for many years had shown no interest in following his father into the business, was clearly the heir apparent. Yet Evan soon ran afoul of a patriarch who could not surrender any power and, like

Jeffrey before him, bolted the company. Jeffrey would go on to become chief executive of Marsh & McLennan, the biggest insurance broker in the world, while Evan became CEO of Ace Ltd., one of the world's largest reinsurers.

Ultimately it was clashes with regulators, not family members, that led to the downfall of Hank Greenberg. Headstrong and combative as ever, Greenberg simply picked the wrong time to take a stand against the feds. After the collapse of Enron and a procession of corporate scandals that dominated the front pages at the start of the new century, regulators and prosecutors became emboldened to come down hard on companies that were proving to be uncooperative. In 2003, AIG agreed to pay $10 million to settle a lawsuit brought by the Securities and Exchange Commission that accused the company of helping an Indiana cell phone distributor hide $11.9 million in losses. The settlement figure was relatively high, as the SEC acknowledged at the time, because AIG had attempted to withhold key documents and initially gave investigators an explanation that was later contradicted by those documents.

The following year, after yet another long tussle with federal investigators, AIG agreed to pay $126 million to settle criminal and civil charges that it had allowed PNC Financial Services to shift $762 million in bad loans off its books. As part of that settlement, a unit of AIG was placed under a deferred prosecution agreement, meaning that the Justice Department would drop the criminal charges after thirteen months if the company abided by the terms of the settlement. (After the indictment of the giant accounting firm Arthur Andersen had led to its collapse, the government preferred the softer cudgel of deferred prosecution agreements as a kind of probation—an approach that had previously been more common in narcotics cases.)

It was the AIG unit that had been placed on probation for thirteen months—AIG Financial Products Corp., or FP for short—that became Ground Zero for the financial shenanigans that would nearly destroy the company.

———

FP had been created in 1987, the product of a remarkable deal between Greenberg and Howard Sosin, a finance scholar from Bell Labs who became known as the "Dr. Strangelove of Derivatives." A great deal of money can be made from derivatives, which are, in simplest terms, financial instruments that are based on some underlying asset, such as residential mortgages, to weather conditions. Like the bomb that ended the film *Dr. Strangelove*, derivatives could, and did, blow up; Warren Buffett called them weapons of mass destruction.

Sosin had been at Drexel Burnham Lambert, Michael Milken's ill-fated junk bond operation, but left before that Beverly Hills–based powerhouse folded amid an epoch-defining scandal that drove it into bankruptcy in 1990. Seeking a partner with deeper pockets and a higher credit rating, Sosin fled to AIG in 1987 with a team of thirteen Drexel employees, including a thirty-two-year-old named Joseph Cassano.

Working from a windowless room on Third Avenue in Manhattan, Sosin's small, highly leveraged unit operated almost like a hedge fund. The early days at the firm were awkward: The wrong rental furniture arrived at the office, and employees had to make do for a while sitting on children's chairs and working on tiny tables—generating almost immediately, nevertheless, the same immensely profitable returns as they had at Drexel. As was the practice with some hedge funds, the traders got to keep some 38 percent of the profits, with the parent company getting the rest.

The key to the success of the business was AIG's triple-A credit rating from Standard & Poor's. With it the fund's cost of capital was significantly lower than that of just about any other firm, enabling it to take more risk at a lower cost. Greenberg had always recognized how valuable the triple-A rating had been to him and guarded it carefully. "You guys up at FP ever do anything to my Triple-A rating, and I'm coming after you with a pitchfork," he warned them.

But Sosin chafed under the short management leash that had been placed on the unit and in 1994 left along with the other founders after a falling-out with Greenberg.

(Long before Sosin's departure, however, Greenberg, infatuated with the profit machine that FP had become, had formed a "shadow group" to study Sosin's business model in case he ever decided to leave. Greenberg had PricewaterhouseCoopers build a covert computer system to track Sosin's trades, so they could later be reverse engineered.) After much persuasion from Greenberg, Cassano agreed to stay on and was promoted to chief operating officer.

A Brooklyn native and the son of a police officer, Cassano was known for his organizational skills, not his acumen in finance, unlike most of the talent Sosin had brought with him—"quants," quantitative analysts, with PhDs who created the complex trading programs that defined the unit.

In late 1997, the so-called Asian flu became a pandemic, and after Thailand's currency crashed, setting off a financial chain reaction, Cassano began looking for some safe-haven investments. It was during that search that he met with some bankers from JP Morgan who were pitching a new kind of credit derivative product called the broad index secured trust offering—an unwieldy name—that was known by its more felicitous acronym, BISTRO. With banks and the rest of the world economy taking hits in the Asian financial crisis, JP Morgan was looking for a way to reduce its risk from bad loans.

With BISTROs, a bank took a basket of hundreds of corporate loans on its books, calculated the risk of the loans defaulting, and then tried to minimize its exposure by creating a special-purpose vehicle and selling slices of it to investors. It was a seamless, if ominous, strategy. These bond-like investments were called insurance: JP Morgan was protected from the risk of the loans going bad, and investors were paid premiums for taking on the risk.

Ultimately, Cassano passed on buying BISTROs from JP Morgan, but he was intrigued enough that he ordered his own quants to dissect it. Building computer models based on years of historical data on corporate bonds, they concluded that this new device—a credit default swap—seemed foolproof. The odds of a wave of defaults occurring simultaneously were remote, short of another Great Depression. So, absent a catastrophe of that magnitude, the holders of the swap could expect to receive millions of dollars in premiums a year. It was like free money.

Cassano, who became head of the unit in 2001, pushed AIG into the business of writing credit default swaps. By early 2005, it was such a big player in the area that even Cassano had begun to wonder how it had happened so quickly. "How could we possibly be doing so many deals?" he asked his top marketing executive, Alan Frost, during a conference call with the unit's office in Wilton, Connecticut.

"Dealers know we can close and close quickly," Frost answered. "That's why we're the go-to."

Even as the bubble was inflating, Cassano and others at AIG expressed little concern. When in August of 2007 credit markets began seizing up, Cassano was telling investors, "It is hard for us, without being flippant, to even see a scenario within any kind of realm of reason that would see us losing $1 in any of those transactions." His boss, Martin Sullivan, concurred. "That's why I am sleeping a little bit easier at night."

———

The pyramidlike structure of a collateralized debt obligation is a beautiful thing—if you are fascinated by the intricacies of financial engineering. A banker creates a CDO by assembling pieces of debt according to their credit ratings and their yields. The mistake made by AIG and others who were lured by them was believing that the ones with the higher credit ratings were such a sure bet that the companies did not bother to set aside much capital against them in the unlikely event that the CDO would generate losses.

Buoyed by their earnings, AIG executives stubbornly clung to the belief that their firm was invulnerable. They thought they'd dodged a bullet when, toward the end of 2005, they stopped underwriting insurance on CDOs that had pieces tied to subprime mortgage-backed securities. That decision enabled them to avoid the most toxic CDOs, issued over the following two years. The biggest reason, though, for the confidence within the firm was the unusual nature of AIG itself. It was not an investment bank at the mercy of the short-term financing market. It had very little debt and some $40 billion in cash on hand. With a balance sheet of more than $1 trillion, it was simply too big to fail.

Speaking to investors at the Metropolitan Club in Manhattan in December 2007, Sullivan boasted that AIG was one of the five largest businesses in the world. His company, he stressed, "does not rely on asset-backed commercial paper or the securitization markets responding, and importantly, we have the ability to hold devalued investments to recovery. That's very important."

He did acknowledge that AIG had a large exposure to underwriting a certain financial product whose future even then seemed dubious: tranches of credit derivatives known as super-seniors. "But because this business is carefully underwritten and structured with very high attachment points to the multiples of expected losses, we believe the probability that it will sustain an economic loss is close to zero."

By that point in time, however, how AIG saw itself and how everyone had come to view it were rapidly diverging. The clients who bought super-seniors insured by AIG might still be making their payments, but on paper they saw their values falling. Market confidence in CDOs had collapsed; the credit-rating agencies were lowering their rankings on tens of billions of dollars' worth of CDOs, even those that had triple-A ratings.

In 2007 one of its biggest clients, Goldman Sachs, demanded that AIG put up billions of dollars more in collateral as required under its swaps contracts. AIG disclosed the existence of the collateral dispute in November. At the December conference, Charles Gates, a longtime insurance analyst for Credit Suisse, asked pointedly what it meant that "your assessment of certain super-senior credit default swaps and the related collateral . . . differs significantly from your counterparties."

"It means the market's a little screwed up," Cassano said, playing on his Brooklyn roots. "How are you, Charlie? Seriously, that is what it means. The market is—and I don't mean to make light of this—actually just so everybody is aware—the section that Charlie was reading from was a section that dealt with collateral call disputes that we have had with other counterparts in this transaction. It goes to some of the things that James [Bridgwater, who did the modeling at AIG Financial Partners] and I talked about, about the opacity in this market and the inability to see what valuations are."

The dispute with Goldman had become an irritant to Cassano. Another counterparty, Merrill Lynch, had also been seeking more collateral but wasn't being as aggressive about it as Goldman. Cassano seemed almost proud of his ability to get these firms to back off. "We have, from time to time, gotten collateral calls from people," he said on December 5, 2007. "Then we say to them: 'Well, we don't agree with your numbers.' And they go, 'Oh.' And they go away."

At a board meeting that fall, Cassano bristled when questioned about the Goldman collateral issue. "Everyone thinks Goldman is so fucking smart," he railed. "Just because Goldman says this is the right valuation, you shouldn't assume it's correct just because Goldman said it. My brother works at Goldman, and he's an idiot!"

Even before Willumstad had been given the position of CEO, he had been consumed by FP. Problems at the unit had been simmering at AIG since Greenberg had been forced to resign in 2005 as the result of another major accounting scandal. New York attorney general Eliot Spitzer had even threatened to bring criminal charges against him after launching an investigation into a transaction between AIG and a subsidiary of General Re, an insurer owned by Warren Buffett, that inflated AIG's cash reserves by $500 million.

In late January of 2008, Willumstad had been sitting in his corner office at Brysam Global Partners when he noticed something startling in a monthly report issued to AIG board members: The FP group had insured some $500 billion in assets, including more than $61 billion in subprime mortgages—most of that for European banks. That piece of business was actually a very clever bit of financial engineering on FP's part. To meet regulatory requirements, banks could not exceed a certain level of debt, relative to their capital. The beauty of AIG's insurance—for a short time, at least—was that it enabled banks to step up their leverage without raising new money because they had insurance.

Willumstad did the math and was appalled: With mortgage defaults rapidly mounting, AIG could soon be forced to pay out astronomical sums of money.

He immediately contacted PricewaterhouseCoopers, AIG's outside auditor, and ordered them to come to his office for a secret meeting the following day to review exactly what was happening at the troubled unit. No one bothered to tell Sullivan, who was still CEO, about the gathering.

By early February, the auditor had instructed AIG to revalue every last one of its credit default swaps in light of recent market setbacks. Days later the company embarrassingly disclosed that it had found a "material weakness"—a rather innocuous euphemism for a host of problems—in its accounting methods. At the same time, a humiliated AIG had to revise its estimate of losses in November and December, an adjustment that raised the figure from $1 billion to more than $5 billion.

Willumstad was vacationing at his ski house in Vail, Colorado, when he finally called Martin Sullivan to deliver the order to fire Joe Cassano.

"You have to take some action on him," Willumstad said.

A startled Sullivan responded that, even if the firm had to restate its earnings, it wasn't anything to worry about: They were only paper losses. "Well, you know, we're not going to lose any money," he said calmly.

It was now Willumstad's turn to be taken aback. "That's not the issue," he said "We're about to report a multibillion-dollar loss, a material weakness! You have the auditors saying that Cassano has not been as open and forthcoming as he could be."

Sullivan acknowledged the controversy surrounding Cassano, but was it really necessary that he be fired?

"Two very high-profile CEOs have just been fired for less," Willumstad reminded him. Charles Prince of Citigroup and Stan O'Neal of Merrill Lynch had both been ousted in the fall of 2007 after overseeing comparably large write-downs. "You can't not take some action both publicly as well as to send a message to the rest of the organization."

Finally, Sullivan relented but made one last pitch for Cassano. "We should keep him on as a consultant," Sullivan recommended.

"Why?" Willumstad asked, as perturbed as he was baffled by the suggestion.

Sullivan maintained that FP was a complicated business and that he didn't have the resources to manage it without some help, at least initially.

In exasperation Willumstad said, "Take a step back. Just think about it for a minute, both from an internal as well as an external point of view. The guy's not good enough to run the company, but you're saying you're going to need to keep him around?"

Sullivan then appealed to Willumstad's sense of competitiveness. If the firm kept Cassano on the payroll, he wouldn't be able to jump to a rival firm—which, leaving aside his questionable business schemes, might still be valuable to the company. "If I keep him on a consulting contract, he'll have a noncompete and he won't go someplace else and steal all our people."

On that issue Willumstad finally relented. He was a pragmatist, and consultants were easily gotten rid of.

"Okay," he agreed, "but you have to figure out how to manage that if you want to keep consulting with him. And you can't let him stay actively engaged in the business. That's just insanity."

Cassano did remain on a consulting contract, at the rate of $1 million a month, but Sullivan and others continued to worry about the defection of their staff. With Cassano shunted aside and the FP group already reporting a $5 billion loss, there was constant speculation that FP's top producers would quickly depart. William Dooley, who replaced Cassano, went to Sullivan with a request: "We need to put together a retention program or we're going to lose the team."

Sullivan appreciated the scope of the problem. Because AIG's employees were paid a percentage of profits—and the firm had just recorded such a huge loss—"the likelihood of these guys getting paid out anything is zero going forward," as he told the compensation committee. "It's not like it's a bad quarter; they can't make it back next quarter or next year." For most FP employees it would make more sense to start over elsewhere than to stay in place, he told the board. (In a way, ironically enough, FP's compensation package better aligned the interests of the employees with shareholders than most traders on Wall Street, who were paid based on the performance of their own book rather than on the profits of the entire firm.)

In early March, AIG's board, after requiring Sullivan to redraft the proposed retention program more than once, approved a plan that would pay out $165 million in 2009 and $235 million in 2010. At the time, it hardly seemed like a decision that anyone outside AIG would care about—let alone give rise to the political nightmare that would result in censure, death threats, and a mad scramble on Capitol Hill to undo the bonuses.

In May, AIG reported dismal results for the first quarter, a $9.1 billion write-down on credit derivatives and a $7.8 billion loss—its largest ever. Standard & Poor's responded by cutting its rating on the company by one notch, to AA minus. Four days later, on May 12, the *Wall Street Journal* reported that management at one of AIG's most profitable units, the aircraft-leasing business International Lease Finance Corp., was pushing for a split from the parent company through either a sale or a spin-off.

Hank Greenberg, meanwhile, who had just turned eighty-three years old, was urging AIG to postpone its annual meeting, pointing to the poor quarterly performance and the effort to raise $7.5 billion in capital. "I am as concerned as millions of other investors as I watch the deterioration of a great company," Greenberg wrote in a letter made public. "The company is in crisis."

In private, other large AIG shareholders had also begun campaigning for changes. Two days before the annual meeting on May 14, 2008, a fax arrived at Willumstad's office at Brysam—a letter from Eli Broad, a former AIG director who had sold his giant annuities business, SunAmerica, to AIG in 1998 for $18 billion in stock, and a close business associate of Greenberg's. Joining Broad in the missive were two influential fund managers, Bill Miller of Legg Mason Capital Management and Shelby Davis of Davis Selected Advisers. The group, which controlled roughly 4 percent of AIG's shares, wanted a meeting to discuss "steps that can be taken to improve senior management and restore credibility."

On the following evening, Willumstad and another AIG director, Morris Offit, went to Broad's apartment at the Sherry-Netherland hotel on Fifth Avenue to meet with the three investors. Joining them was Chris Davis, Shelby's son, a portfolio manager at his firm. Sitting in his expansive living room, with dramatic views of Central Park and the city skyline, Broad quickly launched into a list of complaints about Sullivan and the company's performance.

After hearing him out briefly, Willumstad interrupted him. "Listen, before you go too far, I just have to be very clear. We are in the middle of raising capital, so I cannot disclose to you anything we haven't told everyone else. We're happy to listen and to try to answer any questions." From then on the evening was awkward and uncomfortable for all parties involved, as Willumstad and Offit could say little more than that the board understood their concerns. "You're not telling us anything we don't know," he acknowledged.

Even in the face of mounting shareholder pressure to have him removed, Sullivan appeared to be in good spirits before the annual meeting that morning. He worked the conference room on the eighth floor of the AIG tower, shaking hands and greeting shareholders. He chatted amiably with one investor about a 2–0 win by soccer's Manchester United over Wigan Athletic the previous Sunday, which enabled the team to nip Chelsea for the league championship on the last day of the season. The victory was a feather in Sullivan's and AIG's caps: The company had paid Manchester

United $100 million to have its logo on the players' shirts for four seasons. Apart from that, there was little else to mollify disgruntled shareholders. The headline in the *Wall Street Journal* the next day observed trenchantly: "AIG Offers Empathy, Little Else."

Despite Willumstad and Offit's assurances about the company's efforts to increase its liquidity, the decision to try to raise new capital only led to further clashes. JP Morgan and Citigroup were spearheading the push for AIG to take additional write-downs and to disclose them. By this time, AIG had been hit by calls for an additional $10 billion in new collateral on the swaps it had sold to Goldman and others. The JP Morgan bankers knew what was being said on Wall Street and they knew how considerably others' valuations disagreed with AIG's own. To the bankers, the finance executives at AIG were amateurs. Not a single one impressed them—not Sullivan, not Steven J. Bensinger, the firm's CFO.

The contempt was mutual; AIG executives were dismayed by the arrogance of the JP Morgan team. They and the bankers at Citi had been entrusted with one of the biggest capital-raising efforts ever and were being paid handsomely for their services: more than $80 million for each bank. Their high-handedness in piously informing AIG how its assets should be valued achieved little but to provoke the insurers to dig in their heels.

JP Morgan persisted in asking AIG for a disclosure. On a Sunday afternoon conference call about the capital effort, Sullivan himself came on the line, sounding less cheerful than usual. "Look, we are going to put our pencils down right now. I think either you need to get on board with us or we will have to move on without you."

The JP Morgan bankers hung up and discussed their options. Steve Black, who had dialed in from South Carolina, was deputized to call Sullivan back. "Okay, you want us to put our pencils down. We will. But then we are not going to participate in the capital raise, and when people ask us why we're dropping out, we will have to tell them that we had a disagreement, that there are different views on the potential losses on some of your assets."

In the face of that threat, AIG had no choice but to cave; raising the money was critical, and it could not afford to have a battle with its main banker become public. AIG executives were further irritated when the dispute over valuations was disclosed and JP Morgan did not want to have its name attached to it; the filing refers to "another national financial services firm."

———

At a large conference table at Simpson Thacher, just moments after AIG's directors voted Willumstad the new CEO, he addressed the board.

He stressed that one of the first things that needed to be done was to make peace with Greenberg. He was AIG's largest shareholder, controlling 12 percent of the company, and his various battles with the firm were a costly distraction. "He'll be linked to the company forever anyway," Willumstad added.

After the board meeting, Willumstad returned to his apartment on the Upper East Side. He dialed Hank Greenberg's number with some trepidation; Greenberg never made anything easy. It took some time to get him on the phone.

"Hank? Hi, this is Bob Willumstad. I wanted to let you know that the board has just met and decided to replace Martin—"

"Good riddance," Greenberg muttered.

"—and a release is going to go out tomorrow announcing that I am the new CEO."

There was a moment of painful silence. "Well, congratulations, Bob," Greenberg finally said, almost faintly. "It was good of you to call and let me know."

"Look, Hank. I know that there have been a lot of issues between you and the company. But I'm willing to make a fresh start and see if there's some way we can't resolve these issues."

"I am willing to listen," Greenberg replied. "I do want to help the company with its problems."

The two men agreed to have dinner together that week. As he hung up the phone, Willumstad was further convinced that settling with Greenberg had been a necessary step. It would even help the stock price. But Greenberg was a hard-ass negotiator, and any deal would take time and patience.

The problem was, Willumstad wasn't at all sure just how much time he had.

CHAPTER NINE

O n Friday, June 27, 2008, Lloyd Blankfein, exhausted after a nine-hour flight to Russia, took a stroll around the square outside his hotel in St. Petersburg. He had just arrived in the city on a Gulfstream, along with his wife, Laura, and Gary D. Cohn, Goldman's president and chief operating officer. A history buff, Blankfein had finished David Fromkin's *A Peace to End All Peace: The Fall of the Ottoman Empire and the Creation of the Modern Middle East* during the flight.

The other members of the Goldman board weren't due to land for several hours, so Blankfein had some time to himself. It was a pleasantly warm afternoon, so he decided to take in the sights. Towering above him across the square, the gold dome of St. Isaac's Cathedral was radiant against the overcast sky. That night the Goldman board and their spouses would be treated to a private tour of the State Hermitage Museum, which was housed in six buildings of the former imperial palace along the Neva River.

If all around him the financial world was in a state of chaos, Blankfein had reason to feel contented about Goldman on the eve of its board meeting. The firm was once again proving itself to be the best on Wall Street, weathering—so far, at least—the toughest market anyone could remember.

And what better place to be gathering than in Russia? What China was to manufacturing, Russia was to commodities, and commodities were king at the moment. Oil, most crucially, was going for $140 a barrel, and Russia was pumping out millions of barrels a day. For a moment, it could make anyone forget about the problems back in the United States.

Every year the board of Goldman took a four-day working trip abroad, and since being handed the reins of the firm from Hank Paulson two years earlier, Blankfein had insisted that they meet in one of the new emerging economic giants, one of the BRIC nations: Brazil, Russia, India, or China. It seemed only appropriate: It had been one of Goldman's economists who had coined the appellation for those four economies, to which the world's wealth and power were now shifting. To Blankfein it was a matter of walking the talk.

St. Petersburg was only the first part of the trip, where they'd be given an update on the firm's finances and have a strategy-review session; it would be followed by two days in Moscow. Goldman's chief of staff, John F. W. Rogers, had used his pull to set up the board meeting with Russia's tough prime minister, Vladimir Putin, whose anticapitalist ideology made it clear that he would be no patsy to the United States.

As Blankfein ambled back to the Hotel Astoria, past the massive equestrian monument to Nicholas I, he pondered his fears: *What if oil prices were to slide, say, to $70 a barrel? What then? And what about Goldman itself?* Despite his proven success, Blankfein admitted to being "paranoid," as he often described himself.

Being in Russia did bring back some anxious memories. It was here in 1998 that things went very wrong for Goldman when the Kremlin caught the world unawares by suddenly defaulting on the nation's debt, sending markets around the world into a tailspin. They called it a contagion: Soon afterward, Long-Term Capital Management was struck.

The chain of events caused Wall Street firms to rack up enormous trading losses, and the damage at Goldman was eventually so severe that it had to push back its plans to go public.

As the current market troubles unfolded, Goldman was being mercifully spared the kinds of hits that Lehman, Merrill, Citi, and even Morgan Stanley were taking. His team was smart, but Blankfein knew that luck had played a big role in their accomplishments. "I really think we are a little better," he had said, "but I think it's *only* a little better."

Certainly, Goldman had its share of toxic assets, it was highly leveraged, and it faced the same funding shortfalls caused by the seized-up markets as did its rivals. To its credit, though, it had steered clear of the most noxious of those assets—the securities built entirely on the creaky foundation of subprime mortgages.

Michael Swenson and Josh Birnbaum, two Goldman mortgage traders—along with the firm's chief financial officer, David Viniar—had been instrumental in making the opposite wager: They had bet against something called the ABX Index, which was essentially a basket of derivatives tied to subprime securities. Had they not done so, things could have turned out differently for Goldman, and for Blankfein.

Blankfein couldn't help but notice all the Mercedes clogging the streets as he walked back to his hotel room. And that was only the most visible conspicuous consumption taking place. Flush from their profits not only from gas and oil but from iron, nickel, and a host of other increasingly valuable commodities, Russia's so-called oligarchs were buying up supersized yachts, Picassos, and English soccer teams. Ten years ago, Russia could not pay its debts; today it was a fast-growing, $1.3 trillion economy.

Goldman's own complicated history with Russia dated back much earlier than its stunning default. Franklin Delano Roosevelt once offered to make Sidney Weinberg, Goldman's legendary leader, ambassador to the Soviet Union. "I don't speak Russian," Weinberg replied in turning down the president. "Who the hell could I talk to over there?"

After the collapse of the Soviet Union, Goldman was among the first Western banks to try to crack its market, and three years after the fall of the Berlin Wall, Boris Yeltsin's new government named the firm its banking adviser.

Profits proved to be elusive, however, and Goldman pulled out of the country in 1994 but would eventually return. By 1998 it had helped the Russian government sell $1.25 billion in bonds; when, two months later, after the default, the bonds proved to be virtually worthless, the firm again withdrew. Now it was back for a third try, and Blankfein was determined to get it right this time.

———

The next morning, at 8:00, the Goldman board began its session in a conference room on the ground floor of the Hotel Astoria, which had been in operation since 1912 and was named after John Jacob Astor IV. Legend had it that Adolf Hitler had planned to hold his victory celebration there the moment he forced the city to surrender, and was so confident in his triumph that he had had invitations printed in advance.

Blankfein, dressed in a blazer and khakis, gave the board an overview of the company's performance. As board meetings go, it had been unexceptional.

But it was the following session that was perhaps the critical one. The speaker was Tim O'Neill, a longtime Goldmanite, who was virtually unknown outside the firm. But as the firm's senior strategy officer, he was a major player within the firm. His predecessors included Peter Kraus and Eric Mindich, both of whom were considered Goldman superstars, and O'Neill definitely had Blankfein's ear.

Board members had received a briefing book three weeks earlier and understood why this session was so vital: In it O'Neill would outline survival plans for the firm. He was effectively serving as the office's fire marshal. Nothing was burning, but it was his responsibility to identify all the emergency exits.

The issue facing them was this: Unlike a traditional commercial bank, Goldman didn't have its own deposits, which by definition were more stable. Instead, like all broker-dealers, it relied at least in part on the short-term repo market—repurchase agreements that enabled firms to use financial securities as collateral to borrow funds. While Goldman tended to have longer term debt agreements—avoiding being reliant on overnight funding like that of Lehman, for example—it still was susceptible to the vagaries of the market.

That arrangement was something of a double-edged sword. It could bet its own money utilizing enormous amounts of leverage—putting up $1, for example, and using $30 of debt, a practice common in the industry. Bank holding companies like JP Morgan Chase, which were regulated by the Federal Reserve, faced far more restrictions when it came to debt-fueled bets on the market. The downside was that if confidence in the firm waned, that money would quickly evaporate.

Blankfein sat nodding in approval as O'Neill made his case. What had happened to Bear, he explained, was not just a one-off event. The independent broker-dealer was considered a dinosaur well before the current crisis had begun. Blankfein himself had watched Salomon Smith Barney be absorbed by Citigroup, and even Morgan Stanley merge with Dean Witter. Now, with Bear gone and Lehman seemingly headed in that direction, Blankfein had good reason to be worried.

———

Blankfein's own rise to the top at Goldman underscored for him just how fast things could change: A decade earlier he had been the short, fat, bearded guy who wore tube socks to the firm's golf outings. Today he was the head of the smartest and most profitable firm on Wall Street.

In one sense the arc of his career was classic Goldman Sachs. Like the firm's founders and its longtime leader Sidney Weinberg, Blankfein was the son of working-class Jewish parents. Born in the Bronx, he grew up in Linden Houses, a project in East New York, one of the poorest neighborhoods in Brooklyn. In public housing you could hear neighbors' conversations through the walls and smell what they were making for dinner. His father was a postal clerk, sorting mail; his mother was a receptionist.

As a teenager Blankfein sold soda during New York Yankees games. He graduated as valedictorian of his class at Thomas Jefferson High School in 1971, and at the age of sixteen, with the help of scholarships and financial aid, he attended Harvard, the first member of his family to go to college. His perseverance revealed itself in other ways. Because he was then dating a Wellesley student from Kansas City, he took a summer job at Hallmark to be near her. The relationship, however, did not last.

After college came Harvard Law School, and after graduating in 1978, he joined the law firm of Donovan, Leisure, Newton & Irvine. For several years he practically lived on an airplane flying between New York and Los Angeles. On the rare weekends he found time to relax, he would drive out to Las Vegas with a colleague to play blackjack. They once left their boss a memo: "If we don't show up Monday it's because we've hit the jackpot."

By now Blankfein had started on the track toward becoming a partner at the firm, but in 1981 he had what he termed a "prelife crisis." He decided that he wasn't meant to be a corporate tax lawyer and applied for jobs at Goldman, Morgan Stanley, and Dean Witter. He was rejected by all three firms but a few months later got his foot in the door at Goldman.

A headhunter sought him out for a job at J. Aron & Company, a little-known commodities trading firm that was looking for law school graduates who could solve complex problems and then explain to clients precisely what they had done. When he told his fiancée, Laura, who was also a corporate lawyer, with the New York firm of Phillips, Nizer, Benjamin,

Krim & Ballon, that he was taking a job as a salesman of gold coins and bars, she cried.

Several months later, Blankfein became a Goldman employee when the firm acquired J. Aron in late October 1981.

After the oil shocks and inflation spikes of the 1970s, Goldman was determined to expand into commodities trading. J. Aron gave the firm a powerful gold and metals trading business and an international presence, with a significant London operation. But while Goldman was disciplined and subdued, J. Aron was wild and loud. When Goldman ultimately moved the trading operations of J. Aron into 85 Broad Street, its immaculately groomed executives were stunned to see traders with their ties wrenched loose and their sleeves rolled up, who shouted out prices and insults alike. When angered, they pounded their desks with their fists and threw their phones. This was not the Goldman way. And while Goldman prided itself on its culture and its calculated hierarchy, J. Aron had no use for formalities. After joining, when Blankfein asked what his own title was, he was told: "You can call yourself contessa, if you want."

Goldman's Mark Winkelman was given the task of taming this unruly crowd. The Dutch Winkelman was one of Goldman's first foreign partners, known for his analytical brilliance; he was one of the first executives on Wall Street to recognize the importance of technology for trading, as computers became smaller and more powerful. Winkelman first noticed Blankfein when he saw the short salesman wrestle the phone away from a trader who was trying to yell at a client who had cost him money.

He shielded his protégé from a wave of job cuts at J. Aron that came the following year, the first widespread layoffs at Goldman. Blankfein was fortunate in other respects as well. Goldman had decided to make a major push into trading bonds, commodities, and currencies, and to take on larger risks. The firm had been a pioneer in commercial paper and a leader in municipal finance, but remained an also-ran in fixed income, compared with Salomon Brothers and others. Winkelman and Jon Corzine overhauled that part of the business and recruited talent from Salomon.

Impressed by Blankfein's well-honed diplomacy and his obvious intelligence, Winkelman placed him in charge of six salesmen in currency trading and, later, the entire unit.

Robert Rubin, who then ran fixed income with Stephen Friedman, was opposed to the move.

"We've never seen it work to put salespeople in charge of trading in other areas of the firm," Rubin told Winkelman. "Are you pretty sure of your analysis?"

"Really appreciate your experience, Bob, but I think he'll do all right," Winkelman responded. "Lloyd's driven, and he is a very smart guy with a very inquiring mind, so I have some confidence."

The young lawyer soon demonstrated his trading prowess by structuring a trade that allowed a Muslim client to obey the Koran's proscriptions against interest payments. At the time, the complex $100 million deal, which involved hedging Standard & Poor's 500 contracts, was the biggest Goldman had ever done.

Blankfein was also a serious reader, taking stacks of history books with him when he went on vacation. Never flashy or self-promoting, he was an almost ideal embodiment of the culture at Goldman, where no one ever said, "I did this trade," but rather, "We did this trade."

Winkelman was crushed when he was passed over for Corzine and Hank Paulson in the top jobs at Goldman in 1994. Blankfein, who was made partner in 1988, was one of four executives named to take over Winkelman's responsibilities. Winkelman left the firm.

By 1998, as co-head of fixed income, currency, and commodities, Blankfein was running one of the most profitable businesses at the firm, but he was not seen as an obvious candidate for the top job.

Eventually, Paulson was won over by Blankfein's raw intellect and made him his co-president, prompting John Thain to leave the firm. For his part, Blankfein shaved his beard, lost fifty pounds, and quit smoking. When Paulson was nominated as Treasury secretary in May 2006, he announced that he had selected Blankfein as his replacement.

———

For as long as Blankfein could remember, Goldman had been thinking that it might need a partner. In 1999, during Paulson's stewardship, he had held secret merger talks with JP Morgan, soon after the firm had gone public. Those discussions ended abruptly when Paulson came home to his apartment one day and had an epiphany: "Legally, we would be buying Morgan, but JP Morgan was so much bigger than Goldman Sachs that in reality *they* would be taking *us* over, and they would bury us," he later recalled. "I also knew that somehow we'd figure out how to do everything they could do."

During the Clinton administration's first term, Congress was working on the legislation that would repeal the Glass-Steagall Act of 1933, tearing down the walls dividing banks, brokers, and other financial businesses. At the time, lobbyists for Goldman actually persuaded the committee writing the bill—which became the Gramm-Leach-Bliley Act of 1999—to include a minor amendment they had sought in the event that they ever wanted to become a bank holding company. That provision allowed any bank that owned a physical power plant to continue to own it as a bank holding company. Of course, Goldman was the only bank that owned a power business.

———

Blankfein reflected on this history as O'Neill finished his presentation with a series of questions: Do we need to become a commercial bank? What does it mean if we become a commercial bank? How can we use deposits? How do we build a deposit base?

Blankfein was quick to speak up afterward to encourage discussion. "Deposits provide funding only for certain activities," he reminded the group.

Gary Cohn tried to explain the situation in greater detail, saying that they wouldn't be allowed to make bets with all of the deposits and advising them that they would "have to go out and buy some mortgages or go into the credit card business or originate mortgages." These were businesses in which Goldman had no experience, and entering them would mean changing the company in a fundamental way.

Sitting beneath twenty-foot-high chandeliers in the conference room, the directors and executives batted around a number of different ideas—developing an Internet bank, growing the firm's private-wealth-management business. After an hour of debating alternatives, O'Neill shifted the discussion in another direction by proposing a different alternative: buy an insurance company.

Insurance might have seemed, at first glance, an even more radical departure for Goldman than becoming a commercial bank. But Blankfein made the case that the two industries were more similar than dissimilar.

Insurers use premiums from ordinary customers, just as bankers use deposits from customers, to make investments. It was no accident that Warren Buffett was a big player in the industry; he used the float of premiums from his insurance companies to finance his other businesses. Similarly, what was known in insurance parlance as "actuarial risk" was not unlike Goldman's own risk-management principles.

Goldman could not buy just any insurer, however; it would have to be a company large enough to put more than a dent in Goldman's already hefty balance sheet. The top name on O'Neill's list was AIG, American International Group, which by some measures was the biggest insurance company in the world. The stock price of AIG had recently been decimated, so it might even be economical. Doing a deal with AIG had not, in fact, been a new idea; a possible merger had been talked about in hushed whispers at 85 Broad Street for years. Previous leaders of Goldman, John Whitehead and John Weinberg, both of whom were friends of Hank Greenberg, had suggested to him that the companies should perhaps do a deal some day.

Everyone in the group had a view about AIG. Rajat K. Gupta, senior partner emeritus of McKinsey & Company, was intrigued, as was John H. Bryan, the former CEO of Sara Lee and one of Paulson's closest friends.

Bill George, the former head of Medtronic, the medical technology giant, appeared a bit more hesitant, and Gary Cohn said frankly that the idea made him nervous. They all looked to one particular board member for direction: Edward Liddy.

As the chief executive of Allstate, the major auto and home insurer, Liddy was the one person in the room with actual experience in the insurance business. Some five years earlier Liddy had even tried to sell his firm to AIG, and Greenberg had dismissively rejected his pitch. "I think you ought to keep it," Greenberg told him.

Whenever the subject of insurance had come up at previous board meetings, Liddy had been unenthusiastic. "It's a totally different game," he had warned. His view on the matter hadn't changed, no matter how much of a bargain AIG may have seemed. "It isn't worth getting entangled with AIG," he insisted.

The morning session ended without any decisions being made about AIG, but the insurer came up again after lunch for an entirely different reason. AIG traded through Goldman as well as other Wall Street firms, and like many other companies would put up securities as collateral. There was just one problem: AIG was claiming that its securities were worth a good deal more than Goldman thought they were. Although Goldman's auditor was looking into the matter, there was another snag: the auditor, PricewaterhouseCoopers, also worked for AIG.

In a videoconference presentation from New York, a PWC executive updated the board on its dispute with AIG over how it was valuing or, in Wall Street parlance, "marking to market," its portfolio. Goldman executives considered AIG was "marking to make-believe," as Blankfein told the board.

Strangely, however, no one in the room in St. Petersburg made the critical connection; no one raised the collateral dispute as evidence of a potential fatal flaw in Goldman's consideration to merge with AIG—that the company itself was in serious trouble and had resorted to overvaluing its securities as a stopgap. Instead, the afternoon session proceeded with upbraiding PricewaterhouseCoopers: "How does it work inside PWC if you as a firm represent two institutions where you're looking at exactly the same collateral and there's a clear dispute in terms of valuation?" Jon Winkelried, Goldman's co-president, pointedly asked.

It was the second time PWC had been criticized during a Goldman board meeting. Goldman's board had first learned of the collateral dispute with AIG in November 2007. At the time, the sum involved was more than $1.5 billion. Nervously, Goldman started buying up protection in the form of credit default swaps—insurance—against the possibility that AIG would fail. Given that no one at the time seriously thought that would ever happen, the insurance was relatively cheap: For $150 million, Goldman could insure some $2.5 billion worth of debt.

The Goldman board ended its day in St. Petersburg in a more leisurely manner. With the northern sky still light well after 10:00 p.m., the thirteen directors and their spouses rode gondolas along the city's storied canals.

On Sunday, the board flew down to Moscow for the second part of the meeting, gathering at the Ritz-Carlton, on the edge of Red Square. Mikhail Gorbachev was the speaker at their dinner that evening. Power in Russia was still very much in the hands of Vladimir Putin, even though Dmitry Medvedev had recently been elected to succeed him. Many foreign investors feared that Russia's commitment to open and free markets was quickly fading, particularly in light of the power grabs in the energy industry.

Gorbachev, who had initiated the changes that led to the end of communist rule, struck several Goldman directors as oddly deferential to the Kremlin. "Russia is now realizing its potential as a democratic state, opening itself up to new ideas and outside investment."

Some directors joked that if the last hotel wasn't bugged, this one certainly must be.

In a strange coincidence, late that afternoon another key figure in American finance arrived in Moscow. Treasury secretary Henry Paulson had come there on a stop on a five-day European tour that would later take him to Berlin, Frankfurt, and then London.

He had been on the road a great deal that month—visiting the Persian Gulf states; attending the Group of Eight meeting of finance ministers in Osaka, Japan; and now passing through Europe and Russia. The highlight of his trip, he hoped, would be London, where he had been preparing to give what he believed would be an important speech at Chatham House, an international affairs research group, in St. James's Square. Crafted with the help of his lieutenant David Nason, the talk would herald a proposed overhaul of financial regulation. As he continued to be concerned about firms like Lehman, he knew he needed to call for new tools to deal with troubled institutions. He wanted to get ahead of the problems while things still seemed stable.

On the flight over he had reviewed the speech, making last-minute changes, knowing that he'd have little time to do so once he arrived in Moscow. "To address the perception that some institutions are too big to fail, we must improve the tools at our disposal for facilitating the orderly failure of a large, complex financial institution," he planned to say. "As former Federal Reserve chairman Greenspan often noted, the real issue is not that an institution is too big or too interconnected to fail, but that it is too big or interconnected to liquidate quickly. Today our tools are limited."

It was a risky gambit to announce to the world that the government lacked the authority to prevent a major failure—such a sentiment could undermine confidence in the markets even further—but he also knew that it needed to be said, and even more so, that the situation needed to be fixed.

On Sunday night, Paulson had dinner with Finance Minister Alexei Kudrin in the Oval Dining Room at Spaso House, the residence of the American ambassador in Moscow. On Monday he had scheduled a busy day, including half a dozen meetings, a radio interview, and private sessions with Medvedev and Putin. Paulson had earlier told reporters that he wanted to discuss with the Russians "best practices" for huge state-owned investment funds known as sovereign wealth funds, which were primarily associated with wealthy Middle East nations.

But before he ended his evening on Saturday, he had one last meeting after dinner. Just days earlier, when Paulson learned that Goldman's board would be in Moscow at the same time as him, he had Jim Wilkinson organize a meeting with them. Nothing formal, purely social—for old times' sake.

For fuck's sake! Wilkinson thought. He and Treasury had had enough trouble trying to fend off all the Goldman Sachs conspiracy theories constantly being bandied about in Washington and on Wall Street. A private meeting with its board? *In Moscow?*

For the nearly two years that Paulson had been Treasury secretary he had not met privately with the board of any company, except for briefly dropping by a cocktail party that Larry Fink's BlackRock was holding for its directors at the Emirates Palace Hotel in Abu Dhabi in June.

Anxious about the prospect of such a meeting, Wilkinson called to get approval from Treasury's general counsel. Bob Hoyt, who wasn't enamored of the "optics" of such a meeting, said that as long as it remained a "social event," it wouldn't run afoul of the ethics guidelines.

Still, Wilkinson had told Rogers, "Let's keep this quiet," as the two coordinated the details. They agreed that Goldman's directors would join him in his hotel suite following their dinner with Gorbachev. Paulson would not record the "social event" on his official calendar.

That evening, the Goldman party boarded a bus to take them the dozen or so blocks to the Moscow Marriott Grand Hotel on Tverskaya Street. Some felt as if they were taking part in a spy thriller, what with the security detail and the grandeur of downtown Moscow. The directors walked through the bright lobby with its large fountain and were escorted upstairs to the Treasury secretary's rooms.

"Come on in," a buoyant Paulson said as he greeted everyone, shaking hands and giving bear hugs to some.

For the next hour, Paulson regaled his old friends with stories about his time in Treasury and his prognostications about the economy. They questioned him about the possibility of another bank blowing up, like Lehman, and he talked about the need for the government to have the power to wind down troubled firms, offering a preview of his upcoming speech. "Nonetheless," he told them, "my own view is that we have tough times ahead of us, but based upon history, I think we may come out of this by year's end."

It was that comment that Blankfein recalled the following day to a director over breakfast. "I don't know why he'd say that," Blankfein said quizzically. "It can only get worse."

CHAPTER TEN

One afternoon in late June, Dick Fuld stepped into the bustling lobby of the Hilton Hotel on Sixth Avenue at Fifty-third Street. He was late, which made him even more anxious about the meeting he was about to attend. Within days of Bart McDade's being named Lehman's new president, he had made a startling demand of Fuld: He wanted to rehire Michael Gelband and Alex Kirk, the two senior traders Joe Gregory had fired. The men, whom Gregory used to call the "naysayers," were among the most vocal opponents of the firm's escalation of risk over the years.

"We need these guys," McDade had told Fuld, regarding his decision. "They already know the positions," referring to Lehman's portfolio of toxic assets, which they still hoped to sell. And McDade said that both of them had the support of "the troops on the trading floor," which was critical in restoring confidence.

McDade hadn't given Fuld much choice in the matter. And, given that Fuld had just handed McDade authority over the day-to-day operations of the firm, he felt he had to go along with his wishes for the good of the firm, as embarrassing as it might be to have his own judgment challenged so publicly. Before he did, however, he told McDade, "Look, you're not hiring either guy back until I talk to them."

Now Fuld was on his way to a face-to-face with Gelband, whom he hadn't seen in over a year.

The tension was palpable as they both took seats in a dark meeting room. "We need to clear the air," Fuld said, acknowledging that there was still some unfinished business to resolve. "Let's understand: You're coming back. I want to fucking hear from you."

Gelband, a broad six-footer with a closely shaved head, didn't appreciate

Fuld's aggressive tone and had no patience for bullying or bluffing. As far as he was concerned, he was doing Fuld a favor by returning amid the turmoil. Indeed, ironically enough, before agreeing to come back to Lehman he had been recruited to take Joe Cassano's job at AIG.

"How's that, Dick?" he asked.

"The last time we talked, okay, not the last time, but when you were at the firm and you and I talked about your bonus, I got the sense that you were unhappy with it, and that pissed me off, because you made a shitload of money in 06," Fuld said, pouring himself a glass of water.

Gelband thought this was an unusual way to begin a meeting that he believed had been intended as something of a reconciliation. They had had a frank discussion about his bonus the year that he left, when he had earned more than $25 million, but he didn't remember having complained about it too vociferously. "That's interesting, because I didn't have a problem with my bonus," Gelband said. "In fact, I was completely fine with it."

"Well, that's not what Joe told me," Fuld said.

For a moment they set aside their differences and talked about the firm, reminiscing about the better times and reviewing Lehman's prospects. It was clear the company would have to unwind its positions as quickly as possible and try to get the best possible price for them. Gelband said he would have to conduct an inventory of the assets to get a sense of their value. Fuld also told him that it was his intention to raise additional capital.

"There is just one thing you need to understand," Gelband said as the meeting was coming to a close. "The one reason I am coming back is because of Bart."

As Fuld knew, Gelband had been a longtime friend of McDade's; they had been classmates at the University of Michigan Business School, and it was McDade who had helped Gelband get his initial job interview at Lehman. "Well, yes, Bart is going to be running the day-to-day business," Fuld said, trying to sound nonchalant, "but I hope it has something to do with me as well."

Gelband looked at him quizzically and replied, "No, no. This has to do with Bart."

———

On the Fourth of July weekend, Hank and Wendy Paulson were walking along the beach on Little St. Simons Island when they spotted a loggerhead sea turtle laying its eggs in the sand. For nature lovers like the Paulsons, it was an extraordinary moment, and they stopped to marvel at the sight. Paulson had flown down to the tiny island, just off of Georgia's coast and some sixty miles south of Savannah, to relax with his wife after what had seemed like a whirlwind of travel and work. The island, a sanctuary for unusual birds and reptiles, is where he liked to go to clear his head; he liked it so much that the Paulsons bought up three quarters of the ten-thousand-acre property starting in 2003 for $32.65 million.

The European trip had been a success. His speech in London about the need to build a safety net for investment banks in order to prevent a failure from reverberating throughout the system had attracted a great deal of notice, and at the reception afterward at 10 Downing Street, Gordon Brown, the prime minister, congratulated him "for thinking ahead and getting out in front of the problem."

Still, as Paulson walked the shore, he was finding it difficult to unwind. He continued to have deep misgivings about the economy in the near term and had stated as much on his trip: "The U.S. economy is . . . facing a trio of headwinds: high energy prices, capital markets turmoil, and a continuing housing correction." Apart from his general systemic concerns, though, Paulson's immediate worry was Lehman Brothers. He had spoken to Fuld from his cabin on the island earlier in the day, and it was becoming clearer to him that the firm was unlikely to find a buyer. Most of the large sovereign wealth funds in the Middle East and Asia had been stung by investments they had made in other U.S. banks back in December and wouldn't be likely to invest in Lehman, at least not in the present. Paulson feared that Fuld could soon run out of options.

However much these concerns preoccupied Paulson, he kept them to himself; he never discussed business with Wendy. The topic of Lehman was off-limits within the family for another reason: Hank's younger brother, Richard Paulson, worked as a fixed-income salesman in Lehman's Chicago office. They purposely avoided discussing the matter whenever they spoke, but he knew that if Lehman were to fail, his brother could lose his job.

Paulson was also grappling with another potential setback: He might be losing his deputy, Bob Steel, who was on the short list to run Wachovia, the giant Charlotte-based bank that had just ousted its CEO after reporting a $708 million loss tied to the housing market. Paulson and Steel had talked about the prospect in June, when things were calmer, and Paulson had even encouraged him to pursue the position. But now it looked as if it was actually going to happen, leaving Paulson with a big hole to fill. The timing could not have been worse: Steel's jurisdiction included Fannie Mae and Freddie Mac—the government-sponsored enterprises (GSE) that had been the engine of the real estate boom and were now coming undone.

By the time Paulson had flown back home on a private chartered jet to Dulles Airport on Monday afternoon, his worst fears were being realized. The financial markets were in a meltdown, but for reasons Paulson could not quite put his finger on. Freddie tumbled as much as 30 percent on Monday, before recovering to end down 17.9 percent. Fannie shares slid 16.2 percent, to their lowest level since 1992. Other financial stocks were suffering as well; Lehman shares closed down more than 8 percent. As he tried to absorb all that, Steel announced that he had gotten the job, and it would be announced publicly on Tuesday.

At home that night in his living room, Paulson paged through the piles of faxes that had been sent to him by his assistant at Treasury. One of them was the report that had set off the panic: Bruce Harting, an analyst at Lehman Brothers, wrote that revised accounting rules might require Fannie and Freddie to raise an additional $75 billion in combined new capital. The report revived all the fears about the two mortgage giants, reminding investors of how thin a cushion they had if the housing slump deepened. If confidence was eroding in the government-sponsored enterprises— businesses that the market believed had the implicit backing of taxpayers— the entire U.S. economy could be threatened.

Paulson could see that unease about Fannie and Freddie was growing. On CNBC's *Squawk Box* that Tuesday morning, James B. Lockhart III, chairman of the Office of Federal Housing Enterprise Oversight, which regulated Fannie and Freddie, tried to calm the markets: "Both of these companies are adequately capitalized," he said. "Both of these companies are managing through these issues and have tested management teams."

Paulson had a one-word judgment of that assessment that he later shared with his staff: "Bullshit."

For months Paulson and his team had been discussing ways to unwind

Fannie and Freddie should a real crisis hit—he considered their situation far more important to the long-term health of the economy than Lehman's or the other investment banks'. But he knew it was all too easy to get bogged down in the political fighting over the controversial companies that had made home ownership a near right during the boom. With its critics insisting that Fannie and Freddie were neck-deep in the subprime mess, Paulson had a year earlier called the debate over Fannie and Freddie "the closest thing I've seen to a holy war."

While shares of the companies recovered on Tuesday from the Monday sell-off, both were still trading below $20, and there were other indications of nervousness. Credit default swaps on the debt sold by Fannie and Freddie—essentially, insurance—were trading at levels reserved for companies with credit ratings five levels below their own triple-A ratings, the highest a company could have. Those ratings were, in fact, more a reflection of the government's implicit backing than the companies' own fundamentals.

As Paulson and his staff prepared for a congressional hearing two days hence to discuss the fates of Fannie and Freddie, Steel stuck his head into the conference room next to his office.

"Okay, Hank. I'm taking off."

Paulson glanced up for a moment. "Okay, Bob. I'll see you later."

"No, no," said Steel. "I mean, this is it. I'm *leaving*."

Finally realizing that Steel was bidding his farewells to the staff, Paulson got up to see his deputy off.

As they walked down the hall, Paulson joked, "You're getting out just in time."

———

Virtually from the moment that Congress created Fannie Mae (originally the Federal National Mortgage Association) in 1938, it was politically divisive. A product of the housing slump of the Great Depression and Franklin Delano Roosevelt's New Deal, the company was formed to buy loans from banks, savings banks, and other lenders in order to promote home lending by reducing lenders' risk and to increase the amount of capital available for housing. Republicans saw Fannie as a mere sinecure for their political opponents. In 1968, with a federal budget burdened by the costs of both the Vietnam War and the Great Society, Lyndon Johnson began the process of privatizing Fannie. As a sop to its critics, a rival company, the Federal Home Loan Mortgage Corporation, or Freddie Mac, was created in 1970.

Fannie and Freddie played the political game even more fiercely than their opponents, spending millions of dollars on armies of lobbyists on Capitol Hill. Each company was a revolving door for the powerful in Washington—both Republican and Democrat. Newt Gingrich and Ralph Reed, among others, worked as consultants for Fannie or Freddie; Rahm Emanuel was a board member of Freddie.

By the 1990s, Fannie's chief executive could boast, without much exaggeration, that "we are the equivalent of a Federal Reserve system for housing." At their pinnacle the two mortgage giants—neither of them an originator of loans—owned or guaranteed some 55 percent of the $11 trillion U.S. mortgage market. Beginning in the 1980s, the two companies also became important conduits for the business of mortgage-backed securities. Wall Street loved the fees it collected from securitizing all kinds of debt, from car loans to credit card receivables, and Fannie's and Freddie's portfolios of mortgages were the biggest honeypot around.

But in 1999, under pressure from the Clinton administration, Fannie and Freddie began underwriting subprime mortgages. The move was presented in the press as a way to put homes within the reach of countless Americans, but providing loans to people who wouldn't ordinarily qualify for them was an inherently risky business, as telegraphed by the *New York Times* the day the program was announced:

"In moving, even tentatively, into this new area of lending, Fannie Mae is taking on significantly more risk, which may not pose any difficulties during flush economic times. But the government-subsidized corporation may run into trouble in an economic downturn, prompting a government rescue similar to that of the savings and loan industry in the 1980s."

The success of the two companies in both the financial and political arena inevitably fostered a culture of arrogance. "[We] always won, we took no prisoners and we faced little organized political opposition," Daniel Mudd, then the president of Fannie Mae, wrote in a 2004 memo to his boss. That overconfidence led both companies eventually to move into derivatives and to employ aggressive accounting measures. They were later found by regulators to have manipulated their earnings, and both were forced to restate years of results. The CEOs of both companies were ousted.

Fannie and Freddie were still reeling from the accounting scandals when in March 2008, just days after the rescue of Bear Stearns, the Bush administration lowered the amount of capital the two companies were required to have as a cushion against losses. In exchange, the companies pledged to help bolster the economy by stepping up their purchases of mortgages.

But by that Wednesday, July 10, 2008, with investors unloading the stocks in droves, it was all coming undone. That afternoon William Poole, the former president of the Federal Reserve Bank of St. Louis, said unambiguously, "Congress ought to recognize that these firms are insolvent, that it is allowing these firms to continue to exist as bastions of privilege, financed by the taxpayer."

———

"Unfuckingbelievable!" Dick Fuld exclaimed to Scott Freidheim as he sank deeper into his office chair.

Lehman's stock had opened Thursday morning down 12 percent, to an eight-year low, in response to a rumor that Pacific Investment Management Company, the world's biggest bond fund, had stopped trading with the firm. Another piece of speculation was swirling that SAC Capital Advisors, Steven Cohen's firm, was also no longer trading with Lehman.

"I know it's not true, you know it's not true," Fuld said to Freidheim. "You've got to call these guys and get them to put out a statement."

It had been an excruciating week. With the continued market jitters over Fannie and Freddie—the result of Lehman's own analyst's report, no less—investors were also taking it out on the firm. Fuld couldn't understand it; Lehman had taken its lumps in its previous quarter and raised new capital. Its balance sheet, he thought, was in better shape than it had been in a long time, reflecting Lehman's decision to deleverage its investments—that is, reduce the amount of debt it used to make those investments.

To Fuld, it was the shorts who kept driving down the stock price, spreading false information about Lehman's health. Fuld had been told by several people that the "whisper campaign" against the firm was emanating from one place: Goldman Sachs. It made Fuld sick. His son, Richie, worked at Goldman as a telecommunications banker.

He decided the time had come to call Lloyd Blankfein personally.

"You're not going to like this conversation," Fuld began. He said he had been hearing "a lot of noise" about Goldman's spreading misinformation. "I don't know that you're not ordering this," he said menacingly, as if trying to intimidate Blankfein into admitting it.

Blankfein, offended that Fuld would even attempt to bully him, said he knew nothing about the rumors and ended the call.

These conversations became almost daily occurrences. Days later, Fuld heard rumors that Credit Suisse was spreading rumors about Lehman. He jumped on the phone to Paul Calello, CEO of Credit Suisse's investment bank. "I feel like I'm playing whack-a-mole," Fuld told Calello.

The constant stream of bad news was not only affecting Lehman's stock but was hampering Fuld's efforts to raise more capital. Skip McGee's investment banking team had been reaching out to at least a dozen prospects—Royal Bank of Canada, HSBC, and General Electric among them—but was coming up empty. The only suitor with any real interest continued to be the Korea Development Bank's Min Euoo Sung, and though many executives on the thirty-first floor still had doubts about him, Fuld had directed the bankers to keep working on the Koreans. Indeed, he was even thinking about taking a trip to Asia himself to see Min in person to try to seal a deal.

Then it struck him: What about his old friend John Mack at Morgan Stanley, the second-largest investment bank in the country after Goldman Sachs? The firm had had an ugly second quarter, reporting a 57 percent decline in earnings from a year earlier, but it still had enough cash and buoyancy in its stock price to be able to make a deal.

Fuld and Mack had come up on Wall Street together, with Mack joining Smith Barney's training program in 1968 before moving to Morgan Stanley in 1972, when it had just 350 employees. Like Fuld, Mack had begun his career in bond sales and trading. And again like Fuld, he had quickly made a name for himself. He was an effective salesman and someone who could be both charming and physically intimidating. Mack would stride through the trading floor and, seeing a chance to make big profits, would yell, "There's blood in the water, let's go kill someone!" Coming across a trader reading the *Wall Street Journal* at 8:00 a.m., he was known for saying: "I see that again, and you're fired." But, again like Fuld, he was also fiercely loyal to his people, once physically barring entry to the trading floor by upper management when he was still a trader.

Fuld called Morgan Stanley in New York and was transferred to Paris, where Mack was visiting with clients in the firm's ornate headquarters, a former hotel on the rue de Monceau.

After some mutual disparagement of the markets, the rumors, and the pressure on Fannie and Freddie, Fuld asked candidly: "Can't we try to do something together?"

Mack had suspected the reason for Fuld's call, and while he didn't believe there was much chance that he'd be interested in such a prospect, he was willing to hear Fuld out. There might at least be some assets that he would be interested in; he doubted he would want to buy the entire firm. Mack told him he would be flying back to New York on Friday and suggested they see each other on Saturday.

Fuld, clearly anxious to set up the meeting, said, "We'll come over to your offices."

"No, no, that makes no sense. What if someone sees you coming into the building?" Mack asked. "We're not going to do that. Come to my house, we'll all meet at my house."

———

A harried Hank Paulson walked into room 2128 of the Rayburn House Office Building and took his seat. Today's House Financial Services Committee hearing was scheduled to discuss "financial market regulatory restructuring," but it was really just about Fannie and Freddie. Paulson also wanted to start laying the groundwork for obtaining authority from Congress to wind down these government-sponsored enterprises—if it became necessary, which he didn't anticipate. Paulson had visited Barney Frank, the chairman of the hearing, earlier in the week and had been encouraged "to ask for what you need." Frank had pledged to support him.

Now, as Paulson appeared before the committee with Ben Bernanke beside him, he made his case: "We're going to need broader emergency authorities too—for the resolution or wind-down of complex financial institutions that don't have federal deposit insurance," he explained. "But that's where we need to get. That's what we've got to drive toward."

Representative Dennis Moore, a Democrat from northeast Kansas, asked, "Do you still believe the GSEs pose a systemic risk to the economy?" Paulson replied: "I would say, Congressman, in today's world I don't think it is helpful to speculate about any financial institution and systemic risk. I'm dealing with the here and now."

But by the time the market closed that day, the "here and now" had grown even worse, with more than $3.5 billion in the combined market value of Fannie and Freddie wiped out. Concerns were mounting about Fannie's and Freddie's debts and the rocky state of the mortgage-backed securities that the agencies had guaranteed. The markets were testing Washington's resolve. How much chaos would the government tolerate before it stepped in?

Although Paulson hadn't believed he would require in the immediate future the authorities that he had discussed that morning, the overall economic situation was beginning to become alarming. He called Josh Bolten at the White House to sound him out about pressing Congress for the authority he wanted; Bolten was encouraging. He also wanted Alan Greenspan's advice, and after some confusion about tracking down Greenspan's home phone number, Paulson and a half dozen staff members huddled over the Polycom on his desk to hear the former Fed chairman's faint voice through the speaker.

Rattling off reams of housing data, Greenspan described how he considered the crisis in the markets to be a once-in-a-hundred-year event and how the government might have to take some extraordinary measures to stabilize it. The former Fed chairman had long been a critic of Fannie and Freddie but now realized that they needed to be shored up. He did have one suggestion about the housing crisis, but it was a rhetorical flourish befitting his supply-and-demand mind-set: He suggested that there was too much housing supply and that the only real way to really fix the problem would be for the government to buy up vacant homes and burn them.

After the call, Paulson, with a laugh, told his staff: "That's not a bad idea. But we're not going to buy up all the housing supply and destroy it."

———

As Paulson took a seat in the small conference room next to his office to begin breakfast with Ben Bernanke, he was flushed and scarcely able to eat. "This is a real problem," he said.

The front page of the *New York Times* had reported that morning that senior administration officials were "considering a plan to have the government take over one or both of the companies and place them in a conservatorship if their problems worsen."

Someone had leaked the story about Fannie and Freddie.

Paulson, guzzling a can of Diet Coke as his oatmeal grew cold, couldn't fathom why a member of the administration would be so foolish as to disclose the plans they had been considering. Whoever it had been, the leak was bound to undermine confidence even further, and Paulson was furious.

It had already been a long morning for Paulson, and it showed in his eyes. He had briefed the president in the Oval Office at 7:10 a.m.; had a conference call with Tim Geithner at 7:40 a.m.; checked in with Larry Fink of BlackRock to get his thoughts on what to do about Fannie and Freddie at 8:00 a.m.; and even squeezed in time to reach out to Dick Fuld five minutes later.

Soon after the stock market opened, Treasury staffers Jim Wilkinson and Neel Kashkari barged into the room, interrupting Paulson and Bernanke's breakfast to tell them that the stocks of both Fannie and Freddie were sinking like a stone, down about 22 percent, and suggesting that Paulson put out a statement to calm the markets. Just as he had feared, the story in the *Times* had created a panic, with nobody certain what the implications of the government getting involved with Fannie and Freddie could possibly mean. Investors were recalling Paulson's decision to press for the $2-a-share deal for Bear Stearns and asking themselves, *Would that be the model?*

Paulson agreed he needed to tamp down all the anxiety. By 10:30 a.m. Treasury issued a statement under Paulson's name, stating: "Today our primary focus is supporting Fannie Mae and Freddie Mac in their current form as they carry out their important mission." By using the phrase "in their current form," Paulson was trying to send a signal that he had no

plans to nationalize the companies, even though he knew he might ultimately have to seek the power to do so.

Still miffed by the leak, Paulson walked over to the White House as
President Bush was preparing to go over to the Department of Energy on
Independence Avenue for a briefing on oil and the energy markets. "Can
I ride over with you, sir?" Paulson asked, and on the short trip there briefed
Bush on the Fannie and Freddie situation. Bush, who had been a critic of
the GSEs for years, was supportive of Paulson's plan. As the motorcade
arrived at their destination, Paulson suggested that when the president
spoke to the press that afternoon he needed to tread carefully, fearful of
spooking the markets even more. "Emphasize how committed we are to
the stability of these organizations," Paulson told him.

Although Freddie's stock price would plunge as much as 51 percent that
day, falling to as low as $3.89, and Fannie shares sank by as much as 49
percent, they managed to pare back their losses, with Freddie ending the
session down only 3.1 percent and Fannie down 22 percent. Paulson, meanwhile, began calling congressional leaders to determine what it would
take to get Treasury the authority to put capital into Fannie or Freddie or
to backstop their debt.

Just as the market closed, Paulson had a call with Sheila Bair, the chairwoman of the Federal Deposit Insurance Corporation, who shared further
dismaying news of the intense pressures in the mortgage market: The
FDIC was about to seize IndyMac Bancorp, a mortgage lender, marking
the fifth FDIC-insured bank failure that year and the biggest since the
savings and loan debacle.

Recognizing that Fannie and Freddie could soon spin out of control,
Paulson summoned his brain trust to his office at 4:15 p.m. and told them
to get ready to work throughout the weekend on a way to stabilize the GSEs.
His plan was simple: He wanted to ask for the authority to put money into
Fannie and Freddie, in the hopes that he'd never actually have to use it.

"I want," he instructed, "to announce a plan before the Asian markets
open Sunday night."

On Saturday morning, Fuld pulled up to John Mack's Tudor mansion in
Rye, New York. Despite the beautiful weather, he was tense about the

upcoming meeting. *God help me,* he thought, *if this leaks.* He could already imagine the headlines.

"Dick, good morning," Mack said amiably as he greeted Fuld at the front door. Mack's wife, Christy, stepped out to say hello as well.

The Morgan Stanley management team had arrived and were socializing in Mack's dining room. There was Walid Chammah and James Gorman, the firm's co-presidents; Paul Taubman, the firm's head of investment banking; and Mitch Petrick, head of corporate credit and principal investments. *They have probably been strategizing for hours,* Fuld thought.

McDade showed up next, dressed in a golf shirt and khakis. McGee was running late.

On a table in the den, Christy had put out plates of wraps that she had ordered from the local deli and said, "Everything is all set for you guys." As the group took their seats on sofas around a coffee table, an awkward silence followed; no one knew exactly how to begin.

Fuld looked at Mack as if to say, *It's your house, you start.* Mack imperturbably glared back, *You asked for the meeting. It's your show.*

"Well, I'll kick it off," Fuld finally said. "I'm not even sure why we're here, but let's give it a shot."

"Maybe there's nothing to do," Mack said in frustration as he noticed the discomfort around the room.

"No, no, no," Fuld hurriedly interjected. "We should talk."

Fuld began by discussing Neuberger Berman, Lehman's asset-management business and one of its crown jewels, as an asset that he would be prepared to sell. He also suggested that Morgan might buy Lehman's headquarters on Seventh Avenue—the same building that had been Morgan Stanley's until Philip Purcell, the firm's former CEO, sold it to Lehman after 9/11. The irony would be rich.

"Well," said Mack, not entirely sure what Fuld was proposing, "there are ways we can, you know, there are ways we can work together." He wanted to segue the conversation to Lehman's internal numbers, because even if nothing were going to come of the meeting, it would be helpful to Morgan Stanley to get at least a peek at what was going on inside the firm. The Morgan team began to throw out a barrage of questions: *How are things marked? Were you able to sell them inside your marks? How much business has left the firm?* McDade ended up doing more of the talking than his boss as he tried to answer them.

McGee, whose driver had gotten lost, finally arrived in the middle of the meeting, and Fuld gave him an anxious glare.

When Fuld's cell phone started ringing, he excused himself and retreated to the kitchen, leaving the Morgan Stanley side perplexed: *Was Lehman working on another deal at the same time?*

What they didn't know was that the caller was Paulson, at his Treasury office, checking on Fuld and updating him on his plans to propose a bill about Fannie and Freddie. Fuld was happy to hear that Paulson was seeking to stabilize the GSEs—he knew such a measure could help him as well.

When Fuld returned to the living room, he unexpectedly broke into the conversation, saying, "You know, with all these rumors going around about Lehman, I would hope that you won't try to poach any of my people."

The Morgan Stanley executives were taken aback.

Chammah, a Lebanese-born banker who spent most of his time running Morgan's operations from London, retorted: "If you recall, you weren't shy about building your European operation off of our talent."

The meeting ended with no agreement and what seemed like no incentive to keep talking.

"What the fuck was that all about?" Mack asked after the Lehman executives departed. "Was he offering to merge with us?"

"This is delusional," Gorman said. Taubman had other worries. Maybe they were being used to help Lehman goose its stock price? "We're playing with fire here," he warned them. "If I were their guys, I'd want to put my own spin on this."

———

Fuld, discouraged but undeterred, drove from Mack's house to Lehman's headquarters in Manhattan, racing down the Henry Hudson Parkway. He had scheduled a call with Tim Geithner for that Saturday afternoon. His outside lawyer, Rodgin Cohen, chairman of Sullivan & Cromwell, had recently suggested a new idea to help stabilize the firm: to voluntarily turn itself into a bank holding company. The move, Cohen had explained to Fuld, "would give Lehman access to the discount window indefinitely, just like Citigroup or JP Morgan have." That, in turn, could take some of the pressure off investors worried about the firm's future. It would also mean that Lehman would become regulated by the Federal Reserve of New York, which would have to sign off on the plan.

Cohen, a sixty-four-year-old mild-mannered mandarin from West Virginia, was one of the most influential and yet least well-known people on Wall Street. While soft-spoken and small in physical stature, he had the ear of virtually all the banking CEOs and regulators in the country, having been involved in nearly every major banking transaction of the last three decades. Geithner often relied on him to understand the Federal Reserve's own powers.

For the past several months, Cohen had been speaking with Fuld almost daily, trying to help him formulate a plan. He was very familiar with bank failures and wanted to make sure Lehman would not become one of them. Cohen had spent many days in the summer of 1984 in a hot, windowless room in Chicago, trying to work out a rescue of Continental Illinois National Bank and Trust. "We have a new kind of bank," Stewart McKinney, U.S. representative from Connecticut, announced that year. "It is called 'too big to fail.' TBTF, and it is a wonderful bank." The $4.5 billion government rescue plan that emerged was shaped in large part by Cohen. Cohen, who had also advised the board of Bear Stearns in its takeover by JP Morgan, had organized the call with Geithner's office.

Pacing back and forth in his hotel room in Philadelphia before the wedding of his niece that night, Cohen joined the call between Lehman and the Federal Reserve of New York.

"We're giving serious consideration to becoming a bank holding company," Fuld started out by saying. "We think it would put us in a much better place." He suggested that Lehman could use a small industrial bank it owned in Utah to take deposits to comply with the necessary regulations.

Geithner, who was joined on the call by his general counsel, Tom Baxter, was apprehensive that Fuld might be moving too hastily. "Have you considered all the implications?" he asked.

Baxter, who had cut short a trip to Martha's Vineyard to participate, walked through some of the requirements, which would transform Lehman's aggressive culture, minimizing risk and making it a more staid institution, in league with traditional banks.

Regardless of the technical issues that would have to be faced, Geithner said, "I'm a little worried you could be seen as acting in desperation," and the signal that Lehman would send to the markets with such a move.

Fuld ended his call deflated. He had worked his way through a checklist of every alternative he could think of, and nothing was sticking. He and McDade had even begun working up a plan to consider shrinking Lehman Brothers into a hedge fund with a boutique bank attached and trying to take the firm private, outside the glare of public investors. But he'd need to raise cash from someone even to do that.

Later that evening, Fuld called Cohen, finding his lawyer in the waiting room of a hospital, attending to a cousin who had become ill at the wedding. It was time to consider a different kind of deal, he told Cohen. "Can you reach out to Bank of America?"

Selling Lehman had always been anathema to Fuld—"As long as I am alive this firm will never be sold," he had said proudly in 2007. "And if it is sold after I die, I will reach back from the grave and prevent it." He had, however, longed to make a big acquisition. For a brief moment he came close to buying Lazard—so close that he had even settled on calling the firm Lehman Lazard—a purchase that might have been his crowning achievement, turning his scrappy bond-trading operation into a white-shoe firm with a global reputation. Fuld had held a meeting in his then-office at the World Financial Center on September 10, 2001, with William R. Loomis and Steve Golub of Lazard. They left the meeting with plans to continue their discussions. Then, of course, came 9/11.

Bruce Wasserstein, who later took over Lazard, tried to resurrect the discussions, but Fuld became so outraged by the price Wasserstein said he wanted—$6 billion to $7 billion—that their conversation quickly devolved.

"Clearly we don't see value the same way," Fuld derisively told him. To Fuld, Wasserstein, who had been branded "Bid-em up Bruce," had just lived up to his name. "There's just no way I could pay that."

———

Still standing in the emergency waiting room of the hospital, Rodgin Cohen found Greg Curl, Bank of America's top deal banker, on his cell phone in Charlotte, where the bank was based. Curl, a sixty-year-old former naval intelligence officer who drives a pickup truck, had always been a bit of an enigma to Wall Street. He had helped orchestrate nearly every deal Bank of America had made over the past decade, but even within the bank he kept to himself and was generally considered a tough read.

Cohen, who had dealt with Curl over the years but had never been able to take an accurate assessment of him, trod carefully, explaining that he was calling on behalf of Lehman Brothers.

"Do you have any interest in doing a deal? Of all the institutions we've been considering, you'd be the best fit," Cohen said, promising that he could get Fuld on the phone if Curl was curious enough to have a conversation.

Curl, though intrigued to be getting a call on a Saturday night, was noncommittal; he could tell they must be desperate. "Hmm . . . let me talk to the boss," he said. "I'll call you right back."

The boss was Ken Lewis, the silver-haired CEO of Bank of America, a hard-charging banker from Walnut Grove, Mississippi, who was on a mission to beat Wall Street at its own game. (When he was a child, two boys once ganged up on him; his mother, catching sight of the scrap, came out of the house and said, "Okay, you can fight him, but you're going to have to do it one at a time.")

A half hour later, Curl called back to say he'd hear them out, and Cohen set up a three-way call with Fuld through the switchboard at Sullivan & Cromwell.

After some brief introductions—the men had never met before—Fuld began with his pitch.

"We can be your investment banking arm," Fuld explained, the idea being for Bank of America to take a minority position in Lehman Brothers and for the two to merge their investment banking groups. He invited Curl to meet with him in person to discuss the proposal further.

Curl, sufficiently intrigued, said he would fly up from Charlotte to New York on Sunday. While Fuld thought it odd that he wasn't negotiating directly with Ken Lewis, there was a compelling reason for Curl to travel alone: Lewis could legitimately deny that he had ever spoken with Fuld, should the discussion leak.

Before signing off, Curl made certain to underscore his greatest anxiety: "We want to be absolutely sure this is confidential."

At midmorning on Sunday, David Nason and Kevin Fromer were sitting on the couch in Nason's office at Treasury, going over a draft of the proposal to petition Congress for the authority to inject money into Fannie and Freddie in the case of an emergency. The office was littered with sandwich wrappers and bags from nearby Corner Bakery Café. Most of the staff had been working since early Saturday morning and had gone home only to grab a few hours of sleep. The proposal had to be ready by 7:00 p.m.

Suddenly, Paulson walked into the office with a look of horror on his face and, holding up a page of the draft, bellowed, "What the fuck is *this*? 'Emergency authority on a temporary basis?' *Temporary?*" he said, almost shouting. "We are not going to ask for temporary authority!"

The draft provided for emergency authority for a period of eighteen months, the rationale for which Fromer, who was Treasury's liaison to lawmakers, leaned forward and attempted to explain. "Look, you can't ask Congress for permanent—"

Paulson rarely allowed himself to show his anger, but he now made no attempt to restrain it as he paced the room.

"First of all, this is my judgment to make, not yours," he said. "Secondly, this is a half measure. I am not leaving my successor with the same shit that I've got. We are going to fix these problems. I am not pushing this crap down the road."

Nason's cell phone rang. "Tim!" he shouted, checking the caller ID, before realizing he was interrupting Paulson's soliloquy. Tim Geithner had been calling for updates nearly every hour.

Nason and Fromer tried again to calm Paulson down. They reiterated that it would be much more palatable politically to say that they were asking for temporary powers rather than permanent ones. And, as Fromer told him, "It's a distinction without a difference," explaining that during the period they had the authority, they could still make decisions that would be permanent.

Paulson, starting to recognize the value of the political calculus, relented. He told them to keep working on it and walked out as abruptly as he'd walked in.

———

Greg Curl, dressed in a blazer and slacks, arrived at Sullivan & Cromwell's Midtown offices in the Seagram Building on Sunday afternoon, having flown up to New York from Charlotte that morning on one of the firm's five private jets.

Taking a seat in the empty reception area, he waited for Fuld and Cohen to appear, uncertain about how fruitful the meeting could possibly be. While "The Boss" may have wanted to conquer the commercial banking world, he had an aversion to the fast-money investment banking business. "No, we wouldn't use our *petty cash* to buy an investment bank," he'd dryly said just a month earlier. Almost a year before, his own investment banking business, long considered an also-ran, showed a stunning 93 percent plunge in profit in its third quarter. At the time, Lewis had remarked that he "had had about all the fun he could stand in investment banking right now."

Curl was soon escorted to a conference room, where he paid careful attention as Fuld walked him through his idea in greater detail. He wanted to sell a stake of up to a third of Lehman Brothers to Bank of America and merge their investment banking operations under the Lehman umbrella.

As Curl listened, he was dumbfounded, though characteristically gave no sign of what he was thinking. Far from the plea for help he had been expecting, the pitch he was hearing struck him as a reverse takeover: Bank of America would be paying Fuld to run its investment banking franchise for it.

Fuld also suggested that any investment would "boost our stock price" overnight, creating even more value for Bank of America. He rationalized that buying a stake in Lehman—as opposed to buying the entire firm— would provide incentive for the firm's savvy bankers to stay in their jobs. "You're not going to be able to keep these people if they can't see a financial upside," he argued, making a relevant point about most full-bank mergers—namely, that the talent usually cashes out and leaves.

Curl nodded appreciatively throughout the presentation, before finally stating that the boss—Lewis—would be interested in entertaining the prospect of a deal only if he had a clear path to taking control of the firm in a reasonable amount of time.

Cohen, interjecting on behalf of Fuld, suggested that they should think about a time frame of two to three years, depending on how successful the investment was.

That was more along the lines of what Curl wanted to hear. He told them he was intrigued, but that he and Lewis had often disagreed about whether they should acquire an investment bank or continue buying up other commercial banks. "I don't like the retail business," Curl confided, "because of the susceptibility of litigation and attorneys general and regulators.

"I'd prefer a deal with you," he continued, "but to be honest, Ken would probably prefer to buy Merrill or Morgan."

Fuld was confused. *What was Curl signaling?*

"So do you think we have something here?" Fuld asked.

"I don't know," Curl said. "I need to talk to the boss. It's obviously his decision."

———

By late afternoon, Paulson, unshaven and wearing jeans, was pacing the halls and pestering his staff with so many questions about the Fannie and Freddie proposal that his chief of staff, Jim Wilkinson, finally took him aside and said forcefully, "You've got to get out of our hair and let us do our jobs."

To blow off steam, Paulson decided to take a quick bike ride around the near-empty Washington streets. He couldn't stop thinking about the plan and what it might mean to his legacy: He, a Republican, a man of the markets, was going to ask for authority to invest U.S. taxpayer money in the two institutions that were perhaps most responsible for the housing boom and bust. On the other hand, after decades of political infighting over these two entities, he would have the opportunity to undo them. But would he actually need to use the authority that he was asking for? Would simply having the authority be enough to calm the markets? As he pedaled his bike, he hoped that would be the case.

When Paulson returned, Michele Davis, his communications chief, was trying to figure out where he could physically announce the proposal. "We can't have reporters and camera crews in the building," she said. "We could have you go outside on the steps." Nason, walking over to a window, warned that the forecast called for a thunderstorm.

"I don't know what to do," she said, trying to figure out if they had a podium they could bring outdoors. "But you have to go home and change clothes," she told Paulson, pointing at his rumpled jeans. "You can't go out there like that."

At 6:00 p.m., cleanly shaven and now dressed in a blue suit, Paulson walked out onto the Treasury's steps to a podium that had been hauled downstairs from the fourth floor and addressed the swarm of reporters who had assembled hastily.

"Fannie Mae and Freddie Mac play a central role in our housing finance system and must continue to do so in their current form as shareholder-owned companies," Paulson said, reading a statement. "Their support for the housing market is particularly important as we work through the current housing correction.

"GSE debt is held by financial institutions around the world. Its continued strength is important to maintaining confidence and stability in our financial system and our financial markets. Therefore we must take steps to address the current situation as we move to a stronger regulatory structure.

"To ensure the GSEs have access to sufficient capital to continue to serve their mission, the plan includes temporary authority for Treasury to purchase equity in either of the two GSEs if needed."

Minutes after he finished, thunder rumbled in the distance. Soon the skies opened up.

———

Paulson could tell the hearing on Tuesday morning was going to be hostile the moment he took his seat to the right of Bernanke and Cox. His announcement on the Treasury steps had done little to shore up confidence. In fact, it seemed to be undermining it even further, creating confusion in the marketplace about what this new "authority" he was seeking really meant. Freddie ended down 8.3 percent, to $7.11, while Fannie lost 5 percent, falling to $9.73 on Monday. He knew he needed to start spinning fast, as much for Congress as for the markets.

"Our proposal," he explained to the Senate Banking Committee, "was not prompted by any sudden deterioration in conditions at Fannie Mae or Freddie Mac. . . . At the same time, recent developments convinced policy makers and GSEs that steps are needed to respond to market concerns and increase confidence by providing assurances of access to liquidity and capital on a temporary basis if necessary."

As he was barraged with questions, Paulson emphasized the "temporary" nature of the authority he was seeking, hoping to win over the congressmen. "It is very intuitive," he said, "that if you've got a squirt gun in your pocket, you may have to take it out. If you have got a bazooka, and people know you've got it, you may not have to take it out."

Some panel members, however, were not buying that justification.

"When I picked up my newspaper yesterday, I thought I woke up in France," said Senator Jim Bunning, the Kentucky Republican. "But no, it turned out it was socialism here in the United States of America. The Treasury secretary is now asking for a blank check to buy as much Fannie and Freddie debt or equity as he wants. The Fed purchase of Bear Stearns' assets was amateur socialism compared to this. . . . Given what the Fed and Treasury did with Bear Stearns, and given what we are talking about here today, I have to wonder what the next government intervention into the private enterprise will be? More importantly, where does it all stop?"

Clearly frustrated by what he was hearing, Paulson struggled to articulate his defense. "I think our idea is that, that by having the government provide an unspecified backstop, the odds are very low that it will be used and the cost to the taxpayers will be minimized."

"Do you think we can believe exactly what you're saying, Secretary Paulson?" Bunning replied patronizingly.

"I believe everything I say and that I've been around markets for a long time—" Paulson began to reply before Bunning cut him off.

"Where is the money going to come from if you have to put it up?" Bunning asked.

"Well, obviously, it will come from the government, but I would say—"

"Who is the government?" Bunning asked indignantly.

"The taxpayer," Paulson acknowledged.

"Secretary Paulson, I know you're very sincere in your proposal," Bunning continued. "But come January, you will be gone, and the rest of us will be sitting at these tables—or at least most of us—and we all have to be responsible to the taxpayer for what we have done."

———

A socialist. Mr. Bailout. Hank Paulson believed he was fighting the good fight, a critical fight to save the economic system, but for his efforts he was being branded as little less than an enemy of the people, if not an enemy to the American way of life. He couldn't understand why no one could see how bad the situation had really become. That afternoon another faction had joined the group of antagonists: The hedge funds were furious with him for having convinced Christopher Cox at the SEC to begin cracking down on improper short selling in the shares of Fannie and Freddie, as well as seventeen other financial firms, including Lehman.

With Bob Steel gone, he felt he had been left on his own to confront the biggest challenge of his tenure. He valued his staff, whom he regarded as a remarkably intelligent group, but questioned whether he had enough firepower to wage what he could see was quickly becoming a heated war. That afternoon he left a message for Dan Jester, a forty-three-year-old retired Goldman Sachs banker who had been the firm's deputy CFO and was now living in Austin, Texas, managing money, mostly his own. Paulson had depended heavily on Jester, a long-haired "human calculator," when he was the firm's CEO, and he hoped he might be able to convince Jester to come out of retirement to help him work on the GSEs.

The night before, feeling somewhat desperate, he had also placed a call from home to Ken Wilson, an old friend from Dartmouth whom he had persuaded to leave Lazard for Goldman a decade earlier. As head of the financial institutions group, Wilson was Goldman's top adviser to other banks and respected as an éminence grise throughout the industry. Paulson so respected his judgment that he had put Wilson in an office near his own on the thirtieth floor of 85 Broad Street.

"Ken, I really need help around here. I need some adults," Paulson said when he reached him. "Bob Steel is gone. I'd like you to think about coming down here and joining my team." Wilson, Paulson proposed, would be a "classic dollar-a-year man," meaning that he would come on board as a "special adviser" for the nominal salary of $1 for the final six months of the administration. He suggested that Wilson take a leave from Goldman.

Wilson, who at sixty-one had already been considering retiring from the firm, said that he would think about it.

"I could use your help," Paulson repeated earnestly. "I have lots of issues, um, lots of problems."

———

Given all the gyrations in Lehman's stock price and the nonstop rumors about its long-term viability, Fuld had scheduled a board meeting in July to update the firm's directors on the progress he had been making on both fronts.

Lehman's board was a strange mix of both the financially sophisticated and the truly naive; most had been old friends of Fuld's or had been clients of the firm. They included Roger S. Berlind, a seventy-five-year-old theater producer, and Marsha Johnson Evans, sixty-one, a former navy rear admiral and head of the Red Cross; until two years earlier, the eighty-three-year-old actress and socialite Dina Merrill had also been a member. Among the more experienced were Henry Kaufman, then eighty-one, who was a former chief economist at Salomon Brothers; John Akers, a former chief executive of IBM; and Sir Christopher Gent, sixty, former head of Vodafone PLC. Of the ten outside directors, four were over seventy-four years old.

For this meeting, Fuld had invited a guest to give a presentation. Gary Parr, a banker at Lazard, had been speaking with Fuld recently and suggested he could try to help the board if the directors needed independent advice.

The tall, bearded Parr was one of the most prominent of the bankers specializing in the financial services industry, having worked on many of the capital-raising efforts that companies like Morgan Stanley and Citigroup pursued in late 2007. Fuld may not have trusted Parr's boss, Bruce Wasserstein, but he respected Parr.

Parr was asked by one of the directors to offer some perspective on how bad the market really was. An assured speaker, Parr launched into his regular skeptical boardroom speech.

"It's tough out there," he said forebodingly. "Having been through Bear Stearns and MBIA"—two former clients—"there are some lessons we've learned." Trying to make certain that Lehman's directors understood the gravity of the situation they were facing, he told them, "Liquidity can change faster than you can imagine," suggesting they should not think Bear Stearns was a once-in-a-lifetime event. "Rating agencies are dangerous," he went on. "Wherever you think you stand with the rating agencies, it's worse. . . . And let me tell you, it's difficult to raise money in this environment because asset prices are hard for outside investors to under—"

"Okay, Gary," Fuld said, impatiently cutting him off in midsentence. "That's enough."

An awkward silence fell over the room for a moment. Some directors thought Fuld had become upset with the negative direction Parr had taken; others believed that he had rightly quieted him for shamelessly plugging his services. Within ten minutes, Parr had left the meeting.

An hour later, back in his office at Lazard in Rockefeller Center, Parr was informed by his secretary that Dick Fuld was on the phone.

"Goddamit, Gary!" Fuld screamed when Parr picked up the receiver, half expecting an apology. "What the hell are you doing trying to scare my board and advertising yourself to them like that? I should fire you!"

For a moment Parr didn't respond. Frustrated that Lehman hadn't yet signed an engagement letter, Parr snidely fired back, "Dick, that might be difficult because you haven't hired us yet." Then, collecting himself, he said, "I'm sorry. I didn't mean to go down a path you didn't want me to go."

"You'll never do that again," Fuld said, and the phone went dead.

The next day, Fuld—perhaps fearing that he was beginning to become unwound—realized that berating Parr had been a mistake; the stress was beginning to get to him. In his mind he had cut off Parr for running an advertisement for Lazard, not for suggesting the firm was imperiled. But the damage had been done. He called Parr back, hoping to mend the relationship and to invite him for another meeting.

"Have you recovered from the phone call?" Fuld asked contritely.

———

Ken Wilson was standing in line at Westchester County Airport at 6:45 on the morning of Thursday, July 17, on his way to Montana to start a vacation and do some fly-fishing, when his cell phone rang.

"Kenny, we really need you," President Bush told him. "It's time for you to do something for your country." Wilson and the president knew each other from Harvard Business School, but Wilson knew this call had not been the president's idea. This was classic Paulson; he must be really hurting. If Paulson wanted something, he would keep going until he got it, even if it meant enlisting the highest authorities.

That weekend, Wilson, after talking it over with his colleagues at Goldman, called Paulson. "I'll do it."

———

On the evening of July 21, Paulson arrived for a dinner in his honor at the New York Fed, organized by Tim Geithner as an opportunity for the secretary to get together with Wall Street leaders—Jamie Dimon, Lloyd Blankfein, and John Mack among them.

The dinner would be the second gathering of Wall Street heavyweights he'd attended that day. He had earlier been to a private luncheon in his honor at the offices of Eric Mindich, a former protégé at Goldman Sachs who now ran a hedge fund called Eton Park Capital, where he pressed his case for the pending GSE legislation. Paulson was feeling slightly better about the overall situation, as both Wilson and Jester had agreed to join Treasury, and the prospects for the legislation's passing were improving. And as he mingled among his former colleagues, he congratulated John Thain of Merrill, who days earlier had sold the firm's stake in Bloomberg for $4.5 billion.

What still had Paulson worried, however, was Lehman, and particularly a secret meeting that had been scheduled for after the dinner: He and Geithner had helped orchestrate a private meeting between Dick Fuld and the boss, Ken Lewis, in a conference room at the NY Fed. Fuld had been ringing Paulson for the past two weeks about Bank of America, trying to get Paulson to make a call on behalf of Lehman.

"I think it's a hard sell, but I think the only way you're going to do it is go to him directly," Paulson had told Fuld. "I'm not going to call Ken Lewis and tell him to buy Lehman Brothers."

As the dinner was ending, Paulson walked over to Lewis and said affably, "Those were some good earnings," reaching out to clasp Lewis's hand and giving him a knowing look about the upcoming meeting. Although earlier that day Bank of America had reported a 41 percent slide in second-quarter earnings, the results were far better than what Wall Street analysts had expected. That positive surprise followed a series of stronger-than-expected earnings from Citigroup, JP Morgan Chase, and Wells Fargo, all of which were at least temporarily buoying the market.

When Paulson turned to leave and other executives started to get up and mill around, Geithner approached Lewis and, leaning close to him, whispered, "I believe you have a meeting with Dick."

"Yeah, I do," Lewis replied.

Geithner gave him directions to a side room where they could speak in private. Geithner had apparently already given Fuld the same instructions, because Lewis noticed him across the room looking back at them like a nervous date. Seeing Fuld start to walk in one direction, Lewis headed in the other; with half of Wall Street looking on, the last thing either of them needed was to have word of their meeting get out.

The two men eventually doubled back and found the room, but when Lewis arrived, Fuld was in the midst of a heated argument with a Fed staff member. It was only the second time the men had ever met, and the sharp tone of his hectoring startled Lewis.

For about twenty minutes Fuld explained how he pictured a deal might work, reiterating the proposal he had made to Curl a week earlier. Fuld said he'd want at least $25 a share; Lehman's shares had closed that day at $18.32. Lewis thought the number was far too high and couldn't see the strategic rationale. Unless he could buy the firm for next to nothing, the deal wasn't worth it to him. But he held his tongue.

Two days later, Lewis called Fuld back.

"I don't think this is going to work for us," Lewis said as diplomatically as he could, while leaving open the possibility that they could discuss the matter again.

Fuld was beside himself as he called Paulson at 12:35 p.m. to relay the bad news. Now all he was left with was the possibility of the Koreans, and he pressed Paulson to make a call to them on his behalf—a request that Paulson, having already interceded with Buffett and Bank of America, was now resisting.

"I'm not going to pick up the phone and call the Koreans," Paulson told him. "If you want to scare someone, call them up and tell them I said they should buy Lehman Brothers," he said, explaining that his involvement would only heighten suspicion about the firm's prospects.

"Dick, if they call me and want to ask questions, I'll do what I can to be constructive."

It was just the latest bad piece of news of a very long day. That night, Bart McDade forwarded Fuld an e-mail from a trader with more speculation about where the negative rumors were coming from. "It is clear that GS [Goldman Sachs] is driving the bus on the hedge funds kabal [*sic*] and greatly influencing the downside momentum, LEH and others. Thought it was worth passing on."

Fuld replied: "Should we be too surprised? Remember this, though—I will."

CHAPTER ELEVEN

Robert Willumstad could feel the perspiration begin to soak through his undershirt as he strode along Pearl Street at 9:15 a.m. on Tuesday, July 29, in Manhattan's financial district. Although the humidity was oppressive that summer morning, he was also anxious about his upcoming appointment with Tim Geithner at the Federal Reserve Bank of New York.

Since accepting the position of CEO at AIG just over a month earlier, he had been working long hours to try to get a handle on the company's myriad problems. With the exception of a weekend trip to Vail over July Fourth to visit his daughter, he had been at the office seven days a week. When he began the job he had announced plans "to conduct a thorough strategic and operational review of AIG's businesses" and "to complete the process in the next sixty to ninety days and to hold an in-depth investor meeting shortly after Labor Day to lay it all out for you."

As Willumstad started his investigation, his head of strategy, Brian T. Schreiber, pulled him aside and shared a startling discovery he had made: "It could actually be a liquidity problem, not a capital problem." In other words, even though this massive insurance conglomerate had hundreds of billions of dollars' worth of securities and collateral, given the credit crisis, it could find itself struggling to sell them fast enough or at high enough prices to meet its obligations. The situation could become even worse if one of the ratings agencies, like Moody's or Standard & Poor's, were to downgrade the firm's debt, which could trigger covenants in its debt agreements to post even more collateral.

"You scared the shit out of me last night," Willumstad told Schreiber the following day, after spending the night contemplating the firm's liquidity issues. The problem would soon be further compounded, Willumstad realized, with the firm scheduled to report a $5.4 billion loss in its second quarter.

On this muggy July day, Willumstad was on his way to see Geithner, whom he had only met for the first time a month earlier, to sound him out about getting some help if the markets turned against him. The Federal Reserve Bank of New York did not regulate AIG, or any insurance company for that matter, but Willumstad figured that between AIG's securities-lending business and its financial products unit, Geithner might take an interest in his problems. Even more he hoped that Geithner appreciated how closely AIG was interconnected with the rest of Wall Street, having written insurance policies worth hundreds of billions of dollars that the brokerage firms relied on as a hedge against other trades. Like it or not, their health depended on AIG's health.

"No reason to panic, no reason to believe anything bad is going to happen," Willumstad said after Geithner had greeted him with his usual firm, athletic handshake and invited him back into his office. "But we've got this securities lending program. . . ."

He explained that AIG lent out high-grade securities like treasuries in exchange for cash. Normally it would have been a safe business, but because the company had invested that cash in subprime mortgages that had lost enormous value, no one could peg their exact price, which made them nearly impossible to sell. If AIG's counterparties—the firms on the other side of the trade—should all demand their cash back at the same time, Willumstad said, he could run into a serious problem.

"You've made the Fed window available to the broker-dealers," he continued. "What's the likelihood, if AIG had a crisis, that we could come to the Fed for liquidity? We've got billions, hundreds of billions of dollars of securities, marketable collateral."

"Well, we've never done that before," Geithner replied briskly, meaning that the Federal Reserve had never made a loan available to an insurance company, and he seemed none too swayed by Willumstad's argument.

"I can appreciate that," Willumstad replied. "You never did it for brokers before either, but obviously there's some room here." After Bear Stearns' near-death experience, the Fed had decided to open the discount window to brokerage firms like Goldman Sachs, Morgan Stanley, Merrill Lynch, and Lehman.

"Yes," Geithner acknowledged, but said that it would require the approval of the entire Fed board and, he added pointedly, "I would only recommend it if I thought I was making a good credit decision."

He then delivered to Willumstad the same warning that he had given to Fuld the month before when Fuld had sought bank holding company status for Lehman.

"I think the problem is it's going to exacerbate what you're trying to avoid," he said. "When it would get disclosed, that would cause concern among the counterparties. It would exacerbate anything we had."

Willumstad could see he wasn't getting anywhere with his argument as Geithner rose to indicate that he had to get to his next meeting, saying only, "Keep me informed."

———

On July 29 Lehman's Gulfstream circled over the airport in Anchorage, Alaska, preparing for its approach to land to refuel. Aboard was Dick Fuld, heading back from Hong Kong, where he and a small Lehman team had met with Min Euoo Sung of the Korea Development Bank.

Fuld was in uncharacteristically good spirits that day, confident that he was finally getting closer to a deal. He had had a productive conversation with KDB, and both sides had agreed to continue talking. It would still be a "long putt," he knew, but KDB had become his best hope. Min had indicated that he would be interested in buying a majority stake in Lehman. He knew Min was still anxious about Lehman's real estate portfolio—the toxic assets weighing it—but Min also seemed to be upbeat about the prospect of making KDB a major player on the world stage. There hadn't been much discussion about price at the meeting at the Grand Hyatt in downtown Hong Kong, but Fuld was confident that a deal might finally be at hand.

Fuld was also pleased with himself for having kept the talks out of the press. He had been so concerned about leaks this time around that he had instructed the team he took with him to the meetings—Bart McDade, Skip McGee, Brad Whitman, Jesse Bhattal, and Kunho Cho—not to answer their phones. McGee had gone so far as to mislead his staff back in New York by leaving a voice mail for Mark Shafir, who had gone on the earlier trip to South Korea, telling him that he had flown to China to visit with clients. Fuld had organized the meeting in Hong Kong, as opposed to the more likely Seoul, partly so that if anyone was tracking the firm's plane, its destination would lead to less speculation.

On the return trip the Lehman team watched *The Bank Job*, a British heist movie, on the plane's large screen. Fuld had already seen it and made the case for an action film instead, but McDade, who was increasingly taking control of the firm, won out.

As they taxied to the refueling station, Fuld's good mood suddenly vanished: The maintenance crew had discovered an oil leak. As the pilot tried to coordinate a repair, the Lehman team ate lunch on the plane as it sat on the tarmac. But after an hour, it was uncertain whether that damage could be repaired.

McDade started calling his secretary to see if they could book a commercial flight home.

"When's the last time you flew commercial?" McDade ribbed Fuld, who was plainly not amused.

———

On August 6, 2008, a team of bankers from Morgan Stanley arrived at the Treasury building and was escorted up to a conference room across from Paulson's office for what they all knew would be an unusual meeting. Looking for help with Fannie Mae and Freddie Mac, Paulson had called John Mack a week earlier to hire his firm as an adviser to the government. Paulson would have chosen Goldman were it not for the obvious public relations problem that would almost assuredly ensue in the media. He also briefly considered hiring Merrill Lynch, but Morgan Stanley seemed the best option.

Mack had originally been reluctant even to take the assignment, for the cost of serving as Treasury's adviser on Fannie Mae and Freddie Mac was that the firm could not conduct any business with the mortgage giants for the next six months, and therefore stood to lose out on tens of millions of dollars in fees. "How can we tell our shareholders we're walking away from this kind of money? I'm going to get asked about why I did that," he told his team.

But after some soul-searching, Mack decided working for the government was the patriotic thing to do. Morgan Stanley would receive a token payment of $95,000, which would barely cover the cost of their secretaries' overtime.

Just a week earlier the Senate had passed, and President Bush had signed into law, an act that gave Treasury the temporary authority to backstop Fannie and Freddie. Now the question that faced Paulson was: What to do with that authority?

He recognized that he had created an odd dilemma: Investors now assumed the government was planning to step in. That would make it even harder for Fannie and Freddie to raise capital on their own, as investors worried that a government intervention would mean they would get wiped out. Any sort of investment by the government increasingly seemed as if it could become a self-fulfilling prophecy. "Either investors are going to be massively diluted, given the amount of equity they are going to need, or [Freddie and Fannie] are going to be nationalized," Dan Alpert, managing director of Westwood Capital LLC, had told Reuters that morning. "Without a larger equity capital base, they are going to be incapable of surviving."

In a Treasury conference room, Anthony Ryan, assistant secretary for financial markets, briefed the bankers on the department's work to date on the GSEs. Attending from Morgan Stanley were Robert Scully, fifty-eight, the firm's co-president, who had worked on the government's bailout of Chrysler nearly three decades earlier; Ruth Porat, fifty, the head of its financial institutions banking group; and Daniel A. Simkowitz, the forty-three-year-old vice chairman of global capital markets.

Ten minutes into Ryan's presentation, Paulson walked in, looking slightly distracted. "Everyone's going to scrutinize what we do," he told the group as he tried to inspire and scare them simultaneously. "I'm going to work you to the bone. But I'm confident of this: It will be the most meaningful assignment of your career."

Scully pressed Paulson to explain his rationale for the assignment. "Just tell us what you're really looking to do here," he said. "Do you want to kick the can down the road?"

"No," said Paulson, shaking his head. "I want to address the issue. I don't want to leave the problem unsolved." He was adamant that the project not become another bureaucratic exercise in producing PowerPoint presentations that would just get filed away. "I, ah, we have three objectives: market stability, mortgage availability, taxpayer protection."

Scully was still skeptical, certain there had to be some political calculus involved. And, with Freddie's reported loss of $821 million that morning, doing nothing no longer seemed a viable option.

"Are there any policy options that are off the table or, alternatively, are there any stakes you have in the ground in terms of starting points and approaches to this problem that you'd like us to think about?" Scully probed.

"No, you have a clean sheet of paper," Paulson said. "All options are on the table; I'm willing to consider *everything*."

A young child's squeal a few doors down suddenly halted the discussion. It was Paulson's granddaughter, Willa, who was visiting that day and waiting in a small conference room across from his office. Paulson was about to catch a flight with his family to attend the Olympic Games in Beijing. It was, however, a working vacation—he had a busy set of meetings with Chinese officials—and as they all knew, he would be attached to his cell phone.

He apologized to the group for cutting the meeting short.

"I'll be back in ten days," he told them. "I want a lot of progress."

––––––

In the first week of August, Min Euoo Sung arrived in Manhattan from Seoul to continue talks with Lehman Brothers. The parties were still far from signing a final agreement, but they were inching closer to nailing down at least the outlines of one.

On that Monday, McDade, who remained skeptical that a deal would come to pass, walked over to Sullivan & Cromwell's Midtown offices with his colleagues to begin formal negotiations. "They are never going to have the balls to do this," Mark Shafir said as he headed up Park Avenue with McDade and Skip McGee. Kunho Cho and Jesse Bhattal of Lehman, who were closest to Min, had flown over from Asia to help shepherd a deal. McGee had urged Fuld to stay at the office, despite his insistence on coming to the meeting. "Chill out," McGee had told him. "You're the CEO. You have to be the 'missing man'"—Wall Street parlance for the handy excuse they could use when they closed in on the final terms of the deal but wanted to push for slightly better ones: They'd simply say they still needed approval from the CEO.

McDade also had become increasingly anxious that Fuld's fragile state wouldn't help the negotiations. McDade was beginning to fear that Fuld suspected him of attempting to take over the firm. Often when he was in conversation with Gelband and Kirk, his protégés, Fuld would emerge seeming apprehensive, as if imagining they were plotting his ouster. Fuld's paranoia was only further encouraged when McDade refused to inhabit Joe Gregory's old office directly next to Fuld's, citing its "bad karma"; instead, he took an office farther down the hall, where it was harder for Fuld to monitor him.

In truth, McDade was increasingly in control of Lehman. He was in the process of putting together a document called "The Gameplan," a detailed examination of the firm's finances and a vision for a way forward. It included a half dozen possible scenarios, most of which included some variation on dividing Lehman in two: a "good bank" that they'd keep and a "bad bank" that they'd spin off, thereby ridding themselves, at least on paper, of their worst real estate assets. The plan would enable Lehman to make a fresh start, unencumbered by assets that continued to fall in value. McDade also had pressed Fuld to put Neuberger Berman and the firm's investment management business up for sale, and an auction was already under way among a series of private-equity firms.

While the rumors about Lehman may have continued unabated, the leaks coming out of the company appeared to be shrinking in volume. A few weeks after McDade was appointed president, McGee gave him a T-shirt with the inscription: "A Person Familiar with the Situation" —a wry reference to how the financial press generically referred to its sources. McGee had told him, "Give it to Scott!" a not-so-subtle dig at Scott Freidheim, who managed much of the firm's media strategy.

The first meeting that morning at Sullivan & Cromwell was to allow the Koreans an opportunity to review Lehman's commercial real estate assets. Mark Walsh, the architect of the firm's foray into the commercial real estate market, gave a presentation to the group. But Min quickly found Walsh unprepared and pulled aside Kunho to tell him as much. "I need to understand this better," he told him in Korean. "I feel very uncomfortable with the valuations."

It quickly became clear that Min wanted nothing to do with Lehman's commercial real estate holdings. For at least an hour it looked like the talks could collapse. But that afternoon the two sides started working on a new structure: Min said he was interested in buying a majority stake in Lehman, but only if it were to spin off its commercial and residential real estate assets into a separate company so that KDB's investment couldn't be impacted. The discussions seemed to be going well, except for the fact that Fuld kept calling McDade's and McGee's cell phones every twenty minutes to ask for an update.

By the next morning, at 11:00, Min said he had received authorization for Korean regulators to make an initial offer. He said he was prepared to pay 1.25 times Lehman's "book value"—or the value at which Lehman held its assets on its balance sheet. The deal, which was still subject to a discussion about the firm's true book value and would have included Lehman spinning off the real estate business, meant that KDB was valuing Lehman somewhere between $20 and $25 a share, a premium over its current share price, which had closed the day before at $15.57.

Whether Min was posturing—as some of the Lehman bankers suspected—remained an open question, but McDade, McGee, and the rest of the Lehman team said they were inclined to accept his offer. However, McDade said he wanted to retreat back to the firm's headquarters to discuss it with Fuld first. They agreed that both sides would return at 7:00 p.m. in hopes of reaching at least an agreement in principle.

When both sides reconvened several hours later, a surprise guest arrived: Fuld. The goal for the Lehman team was to press Min to sign a letter of intent ahead of the final agreement, even if it meant it would take several more weeks to hammer out the details. That gesture, everyone agreed, would take some pressure off Lehman's stock.

Fuld took a seat alongside McDade, McGee, and Kunho, an inexplicable scowl on his face. Across from them at the table were Min, his banker, Gary Barancik of Perella Weinberg Partners and his lawyer, Victor I. Lewkow of Cleary Gottlieb Steen & Hamilton.

"Look, we hear you. We understand what you want to do," McDade said, referring to Min's plan to acquire a controlling stake in Lehman after it spun off the real estate assets. "Let's start—"

Fuld interjected. "I think you're making a big mistake," he told Min. "You're going to miss a great opportunity. There's a lot of value in these real estate assets," pressing Min to buy at least some of them. As the conversation continued, Fuld suggested that Min's plan to pay 1.25 times book value was "too low," instead recommending they negotiate on the basis of 1.5 times book value.

McDade and McGee couldn't believe what they were witnessing. They had spent the past two days orchestrating a deal based on spinning off the real estate assets, and now Fuld was trying to retrade on their work. Worse, a look of horror crossed Min's face. Min pulled Barancik aside and whispered, "I'm not comfortable with this," and in response, Barancik spoke up on behalf of KDB. He said they would only negotiate on the basis of 1.25 times the book value valuation, and then, as his aggravation mounted, started questioning Lehman's accounting. "I don't believe that you've taken all the write-downs," he said, reiterating why they weren't interested in the real estate assets.

"Okay," Fuld said, his frustration showing. "What do you think our real estate portfolio *should* be marked at?"

Before Barancik could answer, McDade piped up. "Well, we have a term sheet," he interjected, trying to steer the conversation back in a more productive direction. "Why don't we look at that?"

"Look, I just think we need to take a break," Barancik said, sensing the tension could topple the talks.

As they stepped into the hallway, Fuld, having misread Min's mood, approached him and again started promoting the idea of selling him the real estate.

McGee, who was standing behind Min and could see this conversation was only antagonizing him, tried to signal Fuld , slicing his finger across his throat to urge him to stop badgering the Korean.

Finally managing to break free of Fuld, Min took Barancik to a small room to study the term sheet—which was more a list of broad principles than a formal agreement. As they reviewed it, Min nodded at each bullet point until he reached the final one, which stipulated that KDB would provide credit to Lehman to help support it. To Min that was an instant red flag. Was Lehman seeking an open-ended credit line, hoping to leverage KDB's balance sheet to bolster its own standing?

Min, looking pained, grabbed Kunho Cho, his friend when they worked at Lehman together, and asked to talk with him privately. Even before Min spoke a word, Cho could tell it wasn't going to be good.

"There is a serious credibility problem here," he said in Korean. "All of this time we have negotiated in good faith consistently, and we were moving toward the goal we all wanted, and now, all of sudden, it's a new picture."

Clearly frustrated, Min continued, "Look, it's not about 1.25 versus 1.5 times book, or a $2 billion versus a $4 billion credit line. It's none of that. It's the way you conducted the meeting. I just feel uncomfortable about the way this whole thing has been conducted by Lehman senior management. I cannot continue on this basis."

Cho, who had helped persuade Min to fly to New York for the meeting, was devastated.

When Min returned to the main conference room he looked apologetically at Fuld, and then at the rest of the bankers assembled around the table. "I'd like to thank you all, but I don't think we have a structure that works," he said, and got up to leave. "Gary Barancik can continue the dialogue."

A dolorous look came over Fuld's face. "So, you mean, that's it?" he asked, raising his voice. "You're just going back to Korea?"

———

Steve Shafran was at a gas station in Sun Valley, Idaho, one brisk morning in August when Hank Paulson called. Shafran, one of Paulson's special advisers at Treasury, was on vacation. "Give me an update on Lehman," Paulson instructed.

Shafran, who turned off the engine of his fifteen-year-old Land Rover, recognizing that this might take some time, had been assigned by Paulson earlier in the summer to a special project: to act as a coordinator between the SEC and the Federal Reserve to begin contingency planning for a Lehman Brothers bankruptcy. The original assignment had actually been to ascertain systemic risk in the banking system and to make sure the various government agencies were talking to one another, but it had soon morphed into focusing almost exclusively on Lehman.

It was by its very nature a secret undertaking, given that he wasn't allowed to let anyone—least of all Lehman Brothers—know that the government was even thinking about the possibility, no matter how improbable it might be. If the stock market caught even a whiff of it, Lehman's shares would plunge. But Paulson, who had been speaking to Fuld almost

every day, had become convinced that Lehman was going to face a struggle in its attempts to raise capital, and they needed to prepare for the very
worst.

Indeed, Paulson had become so frustrated with Fuld's various plans that
he had assigned Ken Wilson to be Fuld's personal liaison. "I'm going to tell
Dick that he's talking to you," Paulson told Wilson. "It's just a waste of time.
I'll talk with him when he's got something really important to say to me."

Paulson wasn't the only one worried about Lehman. Shafran's assignment followed a series of e-mail exchanges within the Federal Reserve
back in June between Bernanke and his colleague, Donald Kohn, the Fed's
vice chairman. Kohn had written to Bernkane to say that he had spent
time "thinking about options" for Lehman "in the event the slow erosion
of confidence turns into a rout and liquidity fled quickly. None are good,
given the lack of interest by a purchaser." He followed up with second
e-mail: "One of the hedge fund types on Cape Cod told me that his colleagues think Lehman can't survive—the question is when and how they
go out of buinsess not whether."

For Shafran, dealing with other government agencies was something
of a novelty. He had moved himself and his children to Washington only
a year earlier, after his wife of twenty-four years, Janet, was killed in a plane
accident. They had been living in Sun Valley, where he had gone after retiring from Goldman Sachs. Shafran had worked at the firm for fifteen years,
serving as Paulson's point person in Hong Kong, helping him in his efforts
to gain entrée to China. He had come to Washington to start over.

For Shafran the Lehman project was even more awkward than it would
be for other Treasury staffers because he was a casual friend of Fuld's.
They knew each other from Sun Valley, where Shafran had become a city
councilman in Ketchum and Fuld owned ninety-seven acres in the area
(worth some $27 million), with a main home on a private road across the
Big Wood River and a cabin on the shore of Pettit Lake, right near Shafran's.
They played golf together at the Valley Club and socialized occasionally.
Shafran liked Fuld and admired his intensity.

But now, as Shafran was sitting in the gas station parking lot on the
phone, he gave Paulson a progress report. He said he had held some conference calls with the Fed and SEC, and while they thought it was impossible to truly estimate the systemic risk, he felt that they were finally at

least paying attention to the challenge. "They are on it," he said. "I'm comfortable." He explained that they had identified four risks within Lehman: its repo book, or portfolio of repurchase agreements; its derivative book; its broker dealer; and its illiquid assets, such as real estate and private equity investment.

Paulson knew he couldn't do much for Lehman himself. Treasury itself did not have any powers to regulate Lehman, so it would be left to the other agencies to help manage a failure. But that made him anxious.

Earlier in the summer, David Nason had held a meeting with the SEC and told Paulson they were not on top of the situation. With streams of spreadsheets of Lehman's derivative positions splayed before them in the Grant conference room, he had questioned Michael A. Macchiaroli, an associate director at the SEC, about what they would do if Lehman failed.

"There are a lot of positions," Macchiaroli said. "I'm not sure what we'd do with the positions, but we'd try to net them out, and we'd go in there, and SIPC would come in," he added, referring to Securities Investor Protection Corporation, which acts in a quasi-FDIC capacity but on a much smaller scale.

"That can't be the answer," Nason replied. "That would be a mess."

"The problem is that half their book is the U.K.," Macchiaroli said, explaining that many of Lehman's trades went through its unit in London.

"And their counterparties are outside the United States, and we don't have jurisdiction over them." In the event of a disaster, all the SEC could do was try to maintain Lehman's U.S. broker-dealer unit, but the holding company and all of its international subsidiaries would have to file for bankruptcy.

There were no good answers. Nason had raised the possibility that they might have no choice in an emergency but to go to Congress and seek permission to guarantee all of Lehman's trades.

But as quickly as he raised the idea, he shot himself down.

"To guarantee all the obligations of the holding company, we would have to ask Congress to use taxpayer money to guarantee obligations that are outside the U.S.," he announced to the room. "How the hell would we ask for that?"

———

Across a sweeping meadow from the Jackson Lake Lodge, the towering white peaks of the Tetons offered a majestic view, but one that no longer took Ben Bernanke's breath away the way it once had. As he walked its trails on August 22 he recalled that it was here, at the Federal Reserve Bank of Kansas City's summer symposium in the Grand Teton National Park, that he had first made his name nearly a decade ago. For the next three days, however, he could expect little more than criticism, questioning of his actions over the past year, and questions about what role the government should play with respect to Fannie and Freddie. In the summer of 1999, when the mania for Internet stocks was in full bloom, Bernanke and Mark Gertler, an economist at New York University, had presented a paper at Jackson Hole that contended that bubbles of that sort need not be a huge concern of the central bank. Pointing to steps taken by the Federal Reserve in the 1920s to pop a stock's bubble that only created problems when an economic downturn took hold, Bernanke and Gertler argued that the central bank should restrict itself to its primary responsibility: trying to keep inflation stabilized. Rising asset prices should only be a concern for the Fed when they fed inflation. "A bubble, once 'pricked,' can easily degenerate into a panic," they argued in a presentation that had been the talk of the conference and had attracted the favorable notice of Alan Greenspan.

A year ago Jackson Hole had been a more trying experience for Bernanke. As the credit crisis escalated that summer, Bernanke and a core group of advisers—Geithner; Warsh; Donald Kohn, the Fed vice chairman; Bill Dudley, the New York Fed's markets desk chief; and Brian Madigan, director of the division of monetary affairs—huddled inside the Jackson Lake Lodge, trying to figure out how the Fed should respond to the credit crisis.

The group roughed out a two-pronged approach that some would later call "the Bernanke Doctrine." The first part involved using the best-known weapon in the Fed's arsenal: cutting interest rates. To address the crisis of confidence in the markets, the policy makers wanted to offer support, but not at the expense of encouraging recklessness in the future. In his address at the 2007 conference, Bernanke had said, "It is not the responsibility of the Federal Reserve—nor would it be appropriate—to protect lenders and investors from the consequences of their financial decisions." Yet his very next sentence—"But developments in financial markets can have broad economic effects felt by many outside the markets, and the Federal Reserve must take those effects into account when determining policy"—bolstered what had been perceived as the central bank's policy since the hasty, Fed-organized, Wall Street–financed bailout of the hedge fund Long-Term Capital Management in 1998: If those consequences were serious enough to impact the entire financial system, the Fed might indeed have broader obligations that might require intervention. It was precisely this view that influenced his thinking in protecting Bear Stearns.

By this year's conference the Bernanke Doctrine had come under attack. As Bernanke, looking exhausted, sat slumped at a long table in the lodge's wood-paneled conference room, speaker after speaker stood up to criticize the Fed's approach to the financial crisis as essentially ad hoc and ineffective, and as promoting moral hazard. Only Alan Blinder, once a Fed vice chairman and a former Princeton colleague of Bernanke's, defended the Fed. Blinder told this tale:

> One day a little Dutch boy was walking home when he noticed a small leak in the dike that protected the people in the surrounding town. He started to stick his finger in the hole. But then he remembered the moral hazard lesson he had learned in school. . . . "The companies that built this dike did a terrible job," the boy said. "They don't deserve a bailout, and doing so would just encourage more shoddy construction. Besides, the foolish people who live here should never have built their homes on a floodplain." So the boy continued on his way home. Before he arrived, the dike burst and everyone for miles around drowned—including the little Dutch boy.
>
> Perhaps you've heard the Fed's alternative version of this story. In this kinder, gentler version, the little Dutch boy, somewhat desperate and worried about the horrors of the flood, stuck his finger in the dike and held it there until help arrived. It was painful and not guaranteed to work—and the little boy would rather have been doing other things. But he did it anyway. And all the people who lived behind the dike were saved from the error of their ways.

The previous day, Bernanke, in his address to the symposium, had made a plea to move beyond a finger-in-the-dike strategy by urging Congress to create a "statutory resolution regime for nonbanks."

"A stronger infrastructure would help to reduce systemic risk," Bernanke noted.

> It would also mitigate moral hazard and the problem of "too big to fail" by reducing the range of circumstances in which systemic stability concerns might be expected by markets to prompt government intervention.
>
> A statutory resolution regime for nonbanks, besides reducing uncertainty, would also limit moral hazard by allowing the government to resolve failing firms in a way that is orderly but also wipes out equity holders and haircuts some creditors, analogous to what happens when a commercial bank fails.

Bernanke did not mention Fannie or Freddie, but their fate was on the minds of many at Jackson Hole. That Friday Moody's cut its ratings on the preferred shares of both companies to just below the level of noninvestment grade, or junk. Expectations increased that Treasury would have to pull the trigger and put capital in Fannie and Freddie.

Jackson Hole also had, of course, long been a popular destination for the very wealthy. James Wolfensohn, the former Schroder's and Salomon Brothers banker who became president of the World Bank, was one of Jackson Hole's celebrity residents, and during the 2008 symposium he held a dinner at his home. In addition to Bernanke the guest list included two former Treasury officials, Larry Summers and Roger Altman, as well as Austan Goolsbee, an economic adviser to Barack Obama, who was about to be officially nominated as the Democratic candidate for president.

That night Wolfensohn posed two questions to his guests: Would the credit crisis be a chapter or a footnote in the history books? As he went around the table and surveyed opinions, everyone agreed that it would probably be a footnote.

Then, Wolfensohn asked: "Is it more likely that we'll have another Great Depression? Or will it be more of a lost decade, like Japan's?" The consensus answer among the dinner guests to that question was that the U.S. economy would probably have a prolonged, Japan-like slump. Bernanke, however, surprising the table, said that neither scenario was a real possibility. "We've learned so much from the Great Depression and Japan that we won't have either," he said assuredly.

———

"We've made a decision," Paulson announced to his team and advisers in a conference room at Treasury the last week of August about the fate of Fannie and Freddie. "They can't survive. We have to fix this if we are going to fix the mortgage market."

Upon his return to Washington from Beijing, Paulson had spent a day listening to presentations from Morgan Stanley and others and had decided that they had no choice but to take action, especially as he watched the shares of both companies continue to slide. To Paulson, unless he solved Fannie and Freddie, the entire economy would be in jeopardy.

Morgan Stanley had spent the past three weeks working on what was internally called "Project Foundation." Some forty employees had been assigned to the task, working nights and weekends. "It's easier in jail," complained Jimmy Page, an associate. "At least you get three meals a day and conjugal visits."

The firm had undertaken a loan-by-loan analysis of the portfolios of the two mortgage giants, shipping reams of mortgage data from Fannie and Freddie off to India, where some thirteen hundred employees in Morgan's analytic center went through the numbers on every single loan—nearly half the mortgages in the entire United States.

The Morgan Stanley bankers had also conducted a series of phone calls with investors to get a better sense of the market's expectations. The outcome was, as Dan Simkowitz described it to the Treasury team: "The market cares what the Paulsons think. John Paulson and Hank Paulson. They want to know what John Paulson thinks is enough and they want to know what Hank Paulson is going to do." (John Paulson was the most successful hedge fund investor of the past two years, having shorted subprime before anyone else, making some $15 billion for his investors and personally taking home more than $3.7 billion.)

The Morgan Stanley bankers estimated that the two mortgage companies would need some $50 billion in a cash infusion, just to meet their capital requirement, which should be equal to 2.5 percent of their assets; banks, at a minimum, had to have at least 4 percent. With the housing market deteriorating it was clear that the GSEs' thin capital cushion was in danger.

Worse, Paulson had heard rumors when he was in China that Russia had approached some Chinese officials to suggest that both countries start selling large amounts of Freddie and Fannie debt to force the United States to prop them up. Jamie Dimon had separately called him and encouraged him to take decisive action.

Paulson led a discussion around the table at Treasury about whether it made sense to put Fannie and Freddie in Chapter 11 bankruptcy protection or whether conservatorship—in which the companies would still be publicly traded with the government as a trustee exercising control—was the better option.

Ken Wilson was a bit anxious about pursuing what Paulson was describing as a "hostile takeover" without more professional guidance. "Hank, there is no fucking way we can pursue these kinds of alternatives without getting a first-rate law firm," Wilson told him.

"Okay," Paulson agreed. "So what do you think?"

"Let me call Ed Herlihy at Wachtell and see if he'll do it," Wilson said. "The idea of putting these guys in Chapter 11 is a joke. These are still privately owned entities with obligations to shareholders and bondholders. It's going to get ugly."

Wilson had a compelling reason for having recommended Herlihy: He had been involved in some of the biggest takeover battles in corporate America. Earlier in the year he had helped advise JP Morgan Chase in its acquisition of Bear Stearns. His firm—Wachtell, Lipton, Rosen & Katz—was synonymous with corporate warfare. One of its founding partners, Martin Lipton, had devised among the most famous of antitakeover defenses, the "poison pill." If Treasury was planning a government-led hostile takeover—the first in history—then Herlihy was certainly the lawyer they wanted.

They began their battle plans on the weekend of August 23. Herlihy and a team of Wachtell, Lipton lawyers came to Washington on a half dozen different Delta and US Airways shuttles in order not to arouse suspicion. Paulson walked them through the game plan, assisted by Dan Jester, the lanky Texan who had joined Treasury less than a month earlier. The hope was that like megamergers that are often completed over the course of a single three-day weekend to protect against a leak impacting the stock market, they could take Fannie and Freddie over during the Labor Day holiday, which was the following weekend.

The lawyers and the Treasury officials spent several hours debating possible tactics, relevant statutes, and the structures of each of the companies. Jester and Jeremiah Norton, another staffer at Treasury, outlined a plan to put capital into Fannie and Freddie, and an actual mechanism to take control of them, via the purchase of preferred stock and warrants.

But Paulson soon realized that the Labor Day target was going to be impossible. One of the lawyers had noticed that Fannie's and Freddie's regulator from the Federal Housing Finance Agency, James Lockhart, had written letters to both companies over the summer saying that they were considered adequately capitalized. "You've got to be kidding me," Paulson replied when he heard about the letters. Treasury could face resistance from the GSEs' supporters in Congress and from the companies themselves if the government were to reverse itself apparently arbitrarily. The companies' claims that they were well capitalized and the regulator's endorsement would both have to be challenged.

"That's intangibles and all the stuff that I would call bullshit capital," Paulson complained.

"We need to reconstruct the record," Jester announced about the Federal Housing Finance Agency letters.

"Right, right," Herlihy chimed in. "We need new letters that are pretty bad—or at least accurate."

The Federal Reserve was then asked to provide examiners, and they would spend the next two weeks going through the books, desperately trying to document the capital inadequacies at Fannie and Freddie.

As the Treasury team went around the table, one issue kept getting raised about pushing forward with a takeover: What if the boards of the two companies resisted?

"Look, trust me," Paulson said. "You don't believe me, but I know boards, and they're going to acquiesce. When we get done talking with them, they'll acquiesce."

On the morning of Tuesday, August 26, Paulson walked over to the White House and was escorted downstairs to the basement of the West Wing, where he was given a seat in the five-thousand-square-foot Situation Room. At 9:30 President Bush was beamed onto one of the large screens from his ranch in Crawford, Texas, for a secured videoconference with Paulson. After some brief pleasantries, Paulson laid out his plan to mount the equivalent of a financial invasion on Fannie and Freddie. Bush told him he could proceed with the preparations.

As Labor Day weekend approached, the Treasury team and its advisers started to plot the actual details of the dual takeover. They knew they would have to move quickly, with military precision, and in secrecy before the GSEs could start rallying their supporters in Congress. They wrote scripts specifying exactly what they would tell the companies and their boards. They wanted to make certain that there could be no compromises, no delays. Internally, Treasury officials talked about offering Fannie and Freddie two doors: "Door 1, you cooperate; Door 2, we're doing it anyway."

———

On Thursday morning, August 28, Bob Willumstad and AIG's head of strategy, Brian Schreiber, walked into JP Morgan's headquarters at 270 Park Avenue and, escorted by a security guard, were taken by private elevator to the firm's executive floor, where they had an appointment with Jamie Dimon.

Passing through the main glass doors into a wood-paneled reception area, Willumstad and Schreiber took in the newly renovated offices on the forty-eighth floor. As the two men sat waiting, Willumstad knew his associate was silently irate. Schreiber had been working throughout August on various plans to raise capital and extend the company's credit lines to avoid facing a cash crunch if the market were to worsen. As part of his efforts he had held a bakeoff among a number of banks and had been unimpressed with JP Morgan's pitch—and he was still smarting from the firm's aggressive attitude when they raised capital for AIG in the spring. He had hoped to use Citigroup and Deutsche Bank, but Willumstad had insisted that they consider JP Morgan. The way things were playing out, if things really did get much worse, Willumstad figured he'd rather be dealing with an ally in Dimon, even if his colleague felt otherwise.

The AIG executives were escorted to Dimon's office, which actually consists of an office with a desk, a sitting room, and a conference room. In the conference area Dimon, Steve Black, co-head of the investment bank, Ann Kronenberg, and Tim Main took their places around a wood table with a whiteboard behind them.

After some small talk, Dimon thanked them for coming, and Main, who headed the bank's financial institutions group, launched into his pitch for why AIG should use JP Morgan. Main pointed out his group's number one ranking in the latest league underwriting tables and noted its work in helping CIT Group issue two equity offerings worth $1 billion.

"That's a dubious achievement to cite," Willumstad later commented to Schreiber, "given that shares of CIT were trading below $10 [in August 2008] when they were more than four times that a year ago." All in all, however, it was a fairly standard pitch from a Wall Street banker, the kind everyone in the room had heard dozens, if not hundreds, of times before: We're the best suited to help you, we have the most talent, the most resources; we understand your needs better than anyone else.

But then Main concluded with a not-so-subtle dig at AIG and his past experience with the company. He pointed out that JP Morgan had a lot to offer but stressed that it was important that its clients recognize their own problems and shortcomings. Many in the room, including Dimon, were taken aback.

"Forget Mr. Obnoxious," Dimon said, cutting Main off. But the damage had been done, and the AIG executives were clearly upset, Willumstad finding the performance annoying while Schreiber thought it was offensive. After a few minutes they shrugged the comment off and resumed their talks with Dimon directly, as an embarrassed Main slumped in his chair.

"Jamie, one of my concerns here is that there's a higher probability now that we're going to get downgraded," Willumstad explained. "The rating agencies promised me they would wait until the end of September, but then the Goldman report came out and they got nervous," he said, referring to an analyst report issued by Goldman Sachs raising questions about the firm. The report was so influential that Willumstad had received a call from Ken Wilson and Tony Ryan at Treasury to check up on the company.

"Maybe you should just take the downgrade. It's not the end of the world," Dimon suggested.

"No, this is not just a downgrade," Willumstad insisted. As the company had warned in an SEC filing several weeks earlier, a downgrade would be very expensive. If either Standard & Poor's or Moody's lowered its rating by one notch, AIG would be required to post $10.5 billion in additional collateral; if *both* agencies lowered their ratings, the damage would soar to $13.3 billion. As part of its contract to sell credit default swaps, AIG was required to maintain certain credit ratings—or add new collateral to compensate—as insurance against its potential inability to pay out any claims on the swaps. AIG was now a AA-minus company, and it was facing a tab that was growing quickly. Its executives were estimating that the firm could soon be hit with demands for as much as $18 billion in additional collateral.

Left unspoken was the fact that if AIG could not come up with the cash, bankruptcy was the only alternative.

As Dimon saw it, this was a short-term liquidity problem. "You have a lot of collateral, you know, you have a trillion-dollar balance sheet, you have plenty of securities," he told them. Yes, it could get much worse, but for now, it was just a temporary annoyance.

"We do," Willumstad agreed, "but it's not that simple. Most of the collateral is in the regulated insurance companies."

By midyear AIG had $78 billion more in assets than it had in liabilities. But most of those assets were held by its seventy-one state-regulated insurance subsidiaries, which could not be sold easily by the parent company. There is no federal regulation or supervision of the insurance business. Instead, state insurance commissioners and superintendents have substantial powers to regulate and restrict an insurer's asset sales. The responsibility of the state regulator at all times is to protect the policyholder. There was virtually no possibility that AIG would be able to raise cash quickly by selling some of these assets.

Now Dimon finally understood the scope of the problem, as did everyone else in the room.

Just as they were walking out, Dimon pulled Willumstad aside. "Listen, you don't have the luxury of time," he told him. "If it's not us, get someone else, but you need to get on this."

The next day, Willumstad followed up on the meeting.

"Jamie, this is only going to work if there is chemistry on both sides," Willumstad began. "With all due respect, I know you guys have a lot of confidence in Tim Main, but the reality is, you saw what I saw."

Dimon knew exactly what Willumstad was about to say and interrupted him with, "Steve Black will handle it."

"Good," Willumstad replied.

"You got to plan on packing your clothes and coming up," Ken Wilson told Herb Allison, the former Merrill Lynch and TIAA-CREF executive whom he located on a beach in the Virgin Islands on Thursday night and let in on the big secret: The government planned to take over Fannie and Freddie that coming weekend, September 6.

It wasn't just a social call, however; Wilson had phoned Allison to hire him as the CEO of Fannie. After all, if they were going to take over the company, they wanted to install their own management.

"Look, Ken," Allison told him. "I would like to. For reasons of public service, I'm interested in this job. I want to help you guys, and so you have to let me know what to do. I don't have any clothes. All I have is shorts and flip-flops." Wilson promised to buy him some clothes when he arrived in Washington.

Paulson had decided to execute the takeover plan earlier in the week after a visit by Richard Syron, the chief executive of Freddie Mac. Syron, whom Paulson detested, told him that he had gone to Goldman Sachs' headquarters to pitch potential investors but several days of meetings proved to be in vain: No one was willing to make a significant investment in the company. Paulson's conversation with Dan Mudd, Fannie Mae's CEO, whom Paulson liked better, still wasn't inspiring.

And so on the night of Thursday, September 4, Treasury began its battle plan.

Like clockwork, the chief executives of Fannie and Freddie were instructed to attend meetings on Friday afternoon with Paulson and Bernanke at the offices of the Federal Housing Finance Agency. Mudd's meeting would start at 3:00; Syron's at 4:00. They were each advised to bring their lead director, but told nothing else. Paulson figured that by the time any of this could leak, the markets would be closed and he'd have forty-eight hours to execute his plan.

That afternoon, dark rain clouds massed over the capital as Tropical Storm Hanna approached. In an upstairs conference room Bernanke took a seat on one side of James Lockhart while Paulson took his place on the other. At each meeting, James Lockhart began by telling the Fannie and Freddie executives and their lawyers that their companies faced such potentially great losses that they could not function and fulfill their mission. The FHFA, he said, reading from his prepared script, was acting "rather than letting these conditions fester."

The businesses would be put into conservatorship, he explained, and while they would still be private companies with their shares listed, control over them would be in the hands of the FHFA. Existing management would be replaced. There would be no golden parachutes.

"I want to be fair, open, and honest," Paulson told them. "We'd like your cooperation. We want you to consent." But then he added, "We have the grounds to do this on an involuntary basis, and we will go that course if needed." Syron capitulated quickly, calling his board and breaking the bad news to them.

————

Fannie's CEO, Daniel Mudd, wasn't so easy. He and his lawyers retreated to Sullivan & Cromwell's Washington office. The attorneys were furious, and Rodgin Cohen, usually an entirely self-possessed man, called Ken Wilson at Treasury directly and shouted, "Ken, what is going on here? This is bullshit!"

When Fannie executives began calling around for support from lawmakers on the Hill they discovered that Paulson and Treasury had already secretly lobbied them on the wisdom of a takeover. For Democrats, the pitch was that the step had to be taken to keep the system of mortgage financing functioning, while for Republicans the emphasis was on the systemic risk that Fannie and Freddie posed.

Fannie's advisers summoned all the members of the board to Washington for a meeting at the FHFA the following day. Treasury had made it clear that it wanted only board members present—the only outside banker Fannie invited was Gary Parr of Lazard, who, separately, had returned to advising Lehman as well.

At noon on Saturday the lawyers—Beth Wilkinson, Rodgin Cohen, and Robert Joffe of Cravath, Swaine & Moore, who were advising Fannie's board—accompanied the entire thirteen-member board, who crowded into the same small room at FHFA as had been used the day before when Treasury presented its terms: It would acquire $1 billion of new preferred senior shares in each company, which would give it 79.9 percent of the common shares of each. The government would contribute as much as $200 billion into both companies if necessary. The terms were nonnegotiable.

The meeting ended quickly, and the Fannie directors left to deliberate. Wilkinson realized that she would have to cancel a birthday dinner she had planned for her husband, David Gregory of NBC News. Late that Saturday night the board of Fannie Mae finally voted to give its assent. Paulson was awoken at 10:30 that night by a call from Barack Obama, the Democratic presidential candidate. Earlier that day, on a campaign stop in Indiana, Obama had said about the Fannie and Freddie situation that "any action we take must be focused not on the whims of lobbyists and special interests worried about their bonuses and hourly fees, but on whether it will strengthen our economy and help struggling homeowners." Obama and Paulson spoke for nearly an hour.

After the takeover was announced on Sunday, there was palpable relief among the Treasury staffers who had been working on it for weeks. They had accomplished something that they were convinced would go a long way toward stabilizing the financial system. The markets would steady now that a major source of uncertainty had been removed. They had hit a home run.

Paulson, however, still had one pressing concern: Lehman Brothers.

Ken Wilson, with a free afternoon on his hands for the first time since he had started working for Paulson, left Treasury and walked to his apartment, and then to a pub in Georgetown to have dinner while watching a football game.

That night he checked his voice mail to find several messages from Dick Fuld.

When he returned the call, Fuld told him how thrilled he was about the Fannie and Freddie news, hoping it would calm the markets. But he was distraught over the lack of deals available to him. The Korean situation seemed doomed. Bank of America was nowhere. Fuld said that the firm was planning to pursue a good bank–bad bank strategy, in which he hoped to spin off the firm's toxic real estate assets into a separate company. Stephen Schwarzman, the co-founder of Blackstone Group and a former Lehman banker, had just had a blunt conversation with Fuld. "Dick, this is like cancer. You've got to lop off the bad stuff. You need to get back to the old Lehman," he told him.

Wilson, getting nervous that the spin-off plan wouldn't be enough, told

Fuld, "You have to really think about doing what's right for the firm," trying politely to suggest that he needed to sell the firm without actually using the word.

"What do you mean?" Fuld asked.

"If your stock price continues to slide, something might come out of the woodwork here with a price that doesn't look that compelling. But you might have to take it to keep the organization intact."

"What do you mean, low price?"

"It could be low single digits."

"No fuckin' way," Fuld said heatedly. "Bear Stearns got $10 a share, there's *no* fuckin' way I will sell this firm for less!"

CHAPTER TWELVE

The news started crossing the tape late Monday night, and by 2:00 a.m., it had been picked up by every wire service in the world: The Korea Development Bank was no longer a bidder for Lehman. "Eyes on Lehman Rescue as Korea Lifeline Drifts," the Reuters headline screamed.

Jun Kwang-woo, chairman of the Financial Services Commission in Korea, had held a briefing with reporters in Seoul that night and all but proclaimed that the summer-long talks with Lehman were dead: "Considering financial market conditions domestically and abroad, KDB should approach buying into Lehman at this point of time very carefully."

Dick Fuld, alone in his office on Tuesday morning, sat staring at his computer screens, fixated in an unmitigated rage. To Fuld the talks had long since ended. KDB had returned briefly with an offer of $6.40 a share, though Fuld didn't think they were serious. But to the public, which had heard about a rumored deal, the news would come as a shock. Shares of Lehman dropped precipitously from virtually the moment the stock market opened.

The timing of the report was especially embarrassing to Fuld in that it had come while Lehman was in the midst of holding its high-profile annual banking conference at the Hilton Hotel in Midtown Manhattan, just two blocks away from his headquarters. A CNBC van was parked out front to cover the second day of the event; Bob Steel, now of Wachovia, and Larry Fink, of BlackRock, were set to present that morning; Bob Diamond of Barclays Capital had spoken at the conference the day before.

Bart McDade walked into Fuld's office just after the market's open, but before he could say anything, Fuld started shouting and pointing to the TV. "Here we go again," Fuld said. "Perception trumping reality once more." McDade politely turned his attention to the screen.

CNBC's headline warned: "Time Running Out for Lehman." David

Faber, the network's seasoned reporter, elaborated on that theme, pointing out, "They need to do an awful lot between now and next Friday [*sic*], when the company reports earnings." But then he added, somewhat prophetically: "Can they actually report the losses that are anticipated on Friday [*sic*] and simply say we're continuing to review strategic alternatives? Perhaps they can, and perhaps they will have to. But there are certainly a lot of questions."

As it happened, McDade had come to speak to Fuld about precisely the subject that Faber had raised. McDade told Fuld he thought they should preannounce earnings before the scheduled earnings call next Thursday—maybe as early as the next day. "We have to settle things down," he told Fuld.

Fuld, nodding in agreement, said, "We've got to act fast so this financial tsunami doesn't wash us away."

McDade's overture to Fuld was, at least in part, Kabuki theater, for at this juncture, asking Fuld's permission was simply a courtesy. McDade had already told Ian Lowitt, Lehman's CFO, to get the numbers ready. He was also thinking of announcing the SpinCo plan—the good bank–bad bank plan—at the same time.

Although McDade didn't require Fuld's blessing to release the numbers—he and his cohorts had already stripped Fuld of any real authority—he did need Fuld's cooperation in leading the earnings call. For better or worse, he was still the public face of the firm, and his presence would be a key factor in helping to calm the markets.

Given the complexities of their current situation, however, McDade was worried about Fuld's emotional state. "I don't know if he can do it. He's under an enormous amount of stress," McDade told Gelband before he went to see Fuld. From a public relations point of view, however, they had few alternatives, and McDade knew Fuld would want to lead the earnings call. Fuld wouldn't have it any other way.

———

Hank Paulson looked dispirited Tuesday morning as he walked into the main conference room across from his office in the Treasury Building, his team of advisers in tow: Tony Ryan, Jeremiah Norton, Jim Wilkinson, Jeb Mason, and Bob Hoyt. Their 10:00 a.m. meeting with Jamie Dimon and JP Morgan Chase's operating committee had been set up weeks earlier as part of a series of all-day meetings the firm had scheduled to establish better relations with the government. That strategy had been devised by Rick Lazio, a former Republican representative from New York, whom Dimon had hired as executive vice president of global government relations and public policy. Internally, JP Morgan's operating committee trips to Washington were jokingly referred to as "OC/DC." With the financial system teetering, Dimon knew that there would be calls for tighter federal regulation of Wall Street and wanted to make certain that he had shaken all the right hands well in advance.

"Thanks for coming down here," Paulson said somewhat sheepishly as he opened up the meeting. He was, in fact, still preoccupied with reaction to the takeover of Fannie and Freddie just forty-eight hours earlier. He believed that he had made exactly the right moves in orchestrating the affair, but investors hadn't seemed to agree. Far from stabilizing them, as he thought they might, the markets seemed to be on the verge of tanking again.

Perhaps most grating of all was the reaction from Congress. He was particularly upset with Senator Dodd, whom he had personally briefed on Sunday, soon after the announcement. Dodd, he thought, had tacitly signaled his support, but the following day had publicly mocked him, quipping that his request for temporary powers—which Paulson had clearly indicated that he didn't intend to utilize—was merely a big ruse. "[A]ll he wanted was the bazooka, he didn't want to use it," Dodd wryly observed to reporters in a conference call on Monday.

"We certainly accepted him at his word that that was all that was going to be necessary," Dodd said. "Fool me once, your fault. Fool me twice, my fault." And then Dodd openly raised the question that until then had only been whispered around Washington: "Is this action going to produce the desired results, or are there other actions being contemplated?"

Senator Jim Bunning, who had sparred with Paulson over the summer, going as far as to brand him a Socialist, was even more pointed: "Secretary Paulson knew more than he was telling us during his appearance before the Banking Committee. He knew that Fannie and Freddie were in an irreversible state of damage. He knew all along he was going to have to use this authority despite what he was telling Congress and the American people at the time."

Paulson had allotted less than an hour to the JP Morgan meeting, even though he knew how important it was to Dimon. "I've been trying to encourage opening up the lines of communication between Wall Street and Capitol Hill," he now told the bankers, explaining that when he ran Goldman, he hadn't "appreciated how important it was to establish the right relationships in Washington."

"Trying to get things done here ain't as easy as it seems," he said, his audience laughing at the clear reference to the nationalization of Fannie and Freddie.

He asked Dimon what he thought of the move. Dimon, who had encouraged Paulson to pursue the conservatorship, responded positively but diplomatically: "It was the right thing to do. We could see just how big the problem was becoming over the weekend," and added that it had become clear that certain Fannie and Freddie bonds wouldn't roll on Monday. Dimon tactfully avoided mentioning the fact that the stock market didn't seem to be steadying.

"If you guys believe that, share it," Paulson said before they got up to leave. "I could use the help. No one around here wants to listen to my analysis."

———

After that singular plea for help from the Treasury secretary, JP Morgan's top executives splintered into smaller groups to make several obligatory courtesy drop-bys on the Hill to their federal overseers. Charlie Scharf, head of the firm's consumer business, and Michael Cavanagh, its new CFO, went to see Sheila Bair, head of the FDIC; Steve Black paid a visit to James Lockhart; and later in the day, there was a meeting scheduled with Barney Frank for several members of the team.

But the most important of the visits was Dimon's, with the Federal Reserve's Ben Bernanke. Dimon brought Barry Zubrow, the firm's chief risk officer, along with him. Zubrow, a relative newcomer to JP Morgan, was quickly becoming one of its key executives. A former banker at Goldman Sachs, where he had worked for more than twenty-five years, he was a close friend of Jon Corzine, the deposed Goldman boss who had gone on to become governor of New Jersey. If anyone at JP Morgan understood the risks in the market as well as Dimon, it was Zubrow.

As Dimon and Zubrow entered the Federal Reserve's Eccles Building on Constitution Avenue, Zubrow sneaked a quick look at his BlackBerry before passing through the security X-ray machine. He was alarmed at what he saw: Lehman's stock had plunged 38 percent, dipping to about $8.50 a share.

———

In Lower Manhattan's financial district, Robert Willumstad, AIG's CEO, sat on the thirteenth floor of the Federal Reserve Bank of New York waiting to meet with Tim Geithner. With the markets in turmoil, he had returned to see Geithner to press him again to consider making the discount window available to his company. While Geithner may have spurned his abstract request last month, this time Willumstad had come with a more detailed proposal to turn AIG into the equivalent of a primary dealer like Goldman Sachs or Morgan Stanley—or Lehman Brothers. "It's going to be a few minutes. He's on the phone," Geithner's assistant told him.

"No problem, I have time," Willumstad replied.

Five minutes passed, then ten. Willumstad looked at his watch, trying to keep from getting annoyed. The meeting had been scheduled to start at 11:15.

After about fifteen minutes, one of Geithner's staffers, clearly embarrassed, came to speak with him. "I don't want to hide the ball on you," he said. "He's on the phone with Mr. Fuld," he revealed with a knowing smile, as if to indicate that Willumstad might be waiting a while longer. "He's up to his eyeballs in Lehman."

Finally, a half hour later, Geithner appeared and greeted Willumstad. Geithner was clearly overwhelmed, his eyes darting around his office as he nervously twisted a pen between his fingers. He had also just flown back from an international banking conference in Basel, Switzerland.

After some pleasantries, Willumstad explained the purpose of his request for this meeting: He wanted to change—no, very much needed to *have*—AIG's role in the finance sector codified. He said that he wanted AIG to be anointed a primary dealer, which would give it access to the emergency provision enacted after Bear Stearns' sale, and thus enable it to tap the same extremely low rates for loans available only to the government and other primary dealers.

Geithner stared poker-faced at Willumstad and asked why AIG FP deserved access to the Fed window, which, as Willumstad was well aware, was reserved for only the neediest of financial institutions, of which there were now far more than usual.

Willumstad made his case again, this time with a litany of figures to back up his argument: AIG was as important to the financial system as any other primary dealer—with $89 billion in assets, it was actually larger than some of those dealers—and should therefore be granted the same kind of license. And he mentioned that AIG FP owned $188 billion worth of government bonds. But most of all, he told Geithner, AIG had sold what was known as CDS protection—essentially unregulated insurance for investors—to all of the major Wall Street firms.

"Since I've been here, we've never issued any new primary dealer licenses, and I'm not even sure what the process is," Geithner said. "Let me talk to my guys and find out." Before Willumstad turned to leave, however, Geithner posed the question that really concerned him, the one that had been occupying his thoughts all morning: "Is this a critical or emergency situation?"

Willumstad, fortunately, had been prepared to address this very topic. In meetings with AIG's lawyers and advisers, including Rodgin Cohen at Sullivan & Cromwell and Anthony M. Santomero, the former president of the Federal Reserve Bank of Philadelphia, he had been guided on how to field the question with the advice, "Tread carefully." If he acknowledged that AIG had a true liquidity crisis, Geithner would almost certainly reject its petition to become a primary dealer, denying the company access to the low-priced funds it so badly needed.

"Well, you know, let me just say that it would be very beneficial to AIG," Willumstad carefully replied.

He left Geithner with two documents. One was a fact sheet that listed all the attributes of AIG FP and argued why it should be given the status of a primary dealer. The other—a bombshell that Willumstad was confident would draw Geithner's attention—was a report on AIG's counterparty exposure around the world, which included "$2.7 trillion of notional derivative exposures, with 12,000 individual contracts." About halfway down the page, in bold, was the detail that Willumstad hoped would strike Geithner as startling: "$1 trillion of exposures concentrated with 12 major financial institutions." You didn't have to be a Harvard MBA to instantly comprehend the significance of that figure: If AIG went under, it could take the entire financial system along with it.

Geithner, his mind still consumed with Lehman, glanced at the document cursorily and then put it away.

———

At Treasury, Dan Jester, Paulson's special assistant, had just returned to his office when his assistant announced something surprising: David Viniar, Goldman Sachs' chief financial officer, was on the telephone.

Any call from Goldman would mean an awkward conversation for Jester, given that he used to work there. Unlike Paulson, Jester hadn't been required to sell all his Goldman Sachs stock when he took the job in Washington. And, unlike Paulson, who had had to run the congressional gauntlet before joining Treasury, Jester, as a special assistant to the secretary, didn't require that official confirmation. Although Viniar had been a longtime friend and colleague from their days together at Goldman, he surely wanted to talk business. With the markets going wild, it was no time for social calls. After a short pause, Jester picked up the phone, and Viniar, after quickly greeting him, got right to the point.

"Could we be helpful on Lehman?"

While the question itself was carefully phrased, Viniar's timing was curious: Jester had just learned from Geithner that Lehman was likely to preannounce a $3.9 billion loss on Wednesday. Fuld had given the government a private heads-up—and less than an hour later, here was Goldman, sniffing around.

Anxious about running afoul of the rules, Jester stepped gingerly around the issue. But he did learn just enough to determine that Viniar was serious about its offer of assistance. Viniar told him that Goldman would be interested in buying some of Lehman's most toxic assets; of course, it was clear that Goldman would only do so if it could buy the assets on the cheap. Viniar asked if Treasury could be helpful in arranging an entrée.

As soon as they hung up the phone, Jester reported the call to Robert Hoyt, Treasury's general counsel. With all the conspiracy theories circulating about Goldman and the government, any leaks about the call could be explosive; he needed to cover his ass.

Now it was time to tell Paulson.

At the Lehman tower, Alex Kirk sprinted down the hall to McDade's office. "Something strange is going on," he said, catching his breath. "I just got off the phone with Pete Briger."

Briger, the president of Fortress Partners, a giant hedge fund and private-equity firm, was well wired into the rumor mill, a carryover from his days as a Goldman Sachs partner. He was calling, Kirk recounted, with what sounded like an ominous proposal.

"I know you're really loyal to Bart and to Lehman Brothers, and I would never make this call in any other circumstance," Briger had told Kirk. "But if you happen to be taken over this weekend by another financial institution, and you're not sure whether you want to go work at that financial institution as opposed to Lehman Brothers, I really want you to come talk to me."

Kirk, taken aback, managed to reply, "I'm flattered," his mind racing all the while. "I hope that actually doesn't happen," he continued. "I didn't even think you liked me."

"I was talking to Wes about you the other day," Briger said, referring to Wesley R. Edens, Fortress's CEO, "and I said—you know, not that I don't like you, but I was saying to Wes—'I would much rather have partners that are really, really smart motherfuckers than guys that I like.'"

Kirk laughed as he related the conversation to McDade, repeating the punchline twice.

But it wasn't Briger's backhanded compliment that was the odd part; it was his timing, which could hardly have been coincidental; Kirk was convinced that it was the result of a leak. "Why the hell is he calling me now?" Kirk asked McDade, throwing his hands in the air. Lehman wasn't in merger talks with anyone, at least not yet.

Then, after McDade stared at him without answering, Kirk answered his own question: "I guarantee they know something that we don't."

Jamie Dimon and Barry Zubrow sat in the Anteroom of the Federal Reserve waiting for Chairman Bernanke and his colleagues to appear. Their meeting was scheduled to run from 11:15 a.m. to 11:45 a.m.—which meant that the two JP Morgan officers would have to speak quickly in order to tell the Keeper of the Secrets of the Temple everything they had planned to in the half hour they had been allotted.

Overlooking Constitution Avenue, the Anteroom, despite its name, is a capacious space with thirty-foot-high ceilings standing just off the boardroom, where the nation's main fiscal policies are hammered out, and steps from Bernanke's office.

Looking around as he sat waiting, Dimon studied the portraits of all the former Fed chairmen, including Marriner S. Eccles, who was appointed the first chairman of the Board of Governors of the Federal Reserve System in 1934, when he noticed the conspicuous omission of Alan Greenspan among them. "Maybe that's appropriate," he joked, given what had been transpiring in the economy. (Greenspan's portrait had, in fact, not yet been completed.)

Bernanke finally arrived and took his seat. He, too, had just been privately briefed that Lehman might preannounce a staggering loss the following day but had decided that he would keep that news to himself during his meeting with the JP Morgan executives.

Dimon informed Bernanke that they had just come from a visit with Paulson at Treasury, and the conversation turned to the blowback he had been facing for orchestrating the Fannie Mae and Freddie Mac takeover. "The negative publicity is really getting to him," Bernanke acknowledged of Paulson, who had spoken to him yesterday morning and gotten an earful about the press coverage.

Dimon then launched into his semiprepared remarks, glancing down occasionally at a paper on which he had scribbled some notes during the car ride over.

"There's a broad lack of confidence out there," he said. "We're hearing it from our clients, our customers; we're seeing it in our prime brokerage." He pointed out that despite the fact that the turmoil was, temporarily and perversely, helping JP Morgan's business—since customers trusted it as one of the most solid banks—it was bad for everyone else and ultimately would be bad for his firm, too.

This, of course, was hardly news to Bernanke, who sat politely nodding in his best professorial manner.

Dimon then told the chairman—who had been joined by late-arriving Kevin Warsh, one of the Fed governors—that he was particularly worried about Lehman Brothers. He praised the decision to nationalize Fannie and Freddie, but noted the move had not helped calm the markets. "There's confusion about the role government will play going forward," he said, looking for the answer to the question on everyone's mind: Would the Fed back additional bailouts?

Bernanke, however, wasn't prepared to show his hand, and as the meeting came to an end would say only, "We're working on a number of initiatives. We're just trying to stay ahead of this thing."

———

At Lehman, the air on the thirty-first floor seemed to only grow thicker as the day advanced. To some of his colleagues, Fuld looked as if he were having trouble breathing. He had been debating all weekend about whether to call Bank of America, and Treasury's Ken Wilson had phoned him at least three times that morning to press that case. "You gotta make the call," Wilson instructed him. Wilson knew Bank of America well; during his stint at Goldman, he had been its banker for more than a decade. It's a good strategic fit," Wilson urged. What Wilson hadn't told Fuld was that he had already worked over Greg Curl of Bank of America to tee up the phone call. During an earlier conversation, Wilson had informed Fuld that the only way a deal was going to take place was if he was willing to take price off the table as a bargaining point. That was an indirect way of warning Fuld that he didn't have much negotiating power—or time.

———

Rodgin Cohen, who has a bad back, was standing at the computer in his corner office on the thirtieth floor of Sullivan & Cromwell's offices overlooking the New York Harbor when the phone rang. It was Dick Fuld, giving him the instructions to call Bank of America's Curl. Cohen scribbled out a script for himself as Fuld was speaking; the stakes on this one were too high to do a presentation off the top of his head.

"Got it. I'll call you back after I've talked to him."

Cohen studied his script one final time and got Curl on the line. "Look," he said amiably, "the world has moved a lot. We'd like to reengage."

"O . . . kay," Curl said slowly, making it clear that, while he agreed to listen to Cohen's pitch on behalf of his client, he remained wary.

"We have two priorities. Preserving Lehman's brand and reputation and doing well by the Lehman people," Cohen said.

Then, checking the next sentence in the script, he paused for effect.

"You will notice price is not a priority," he said, "but there is, of course, a price at which we could not do a transaction."

"We could be interested," Curl replied cautiously. "Let me talk to the boss and call you back."

"Greg, we'd be looking to do something quickly," Cohen told him.

"Got it."

Dimon and Zubrow hopped out of their black Town Car in front of 601 Pennsylvania Avenue, a six-story modern limestone building northwest of the White House that serves as JP Morgan's Washington headquarters. It was here that all of the government-relations people worked, so a constant stream of Gucci-clad lobbyists was a familiar sight.

By the time Dimon and Zubrow arrived most members of the operating committee had already finished their morning meetings and were eating lunch in a conference room on the second floor. Sandwiches and sodas were being passed around as Cavanagh was recounting how his conversation with Sheila Bair had gone and Black was regaling the group with anecdotes from his encounter with James Lockhart.

As the conversation inevitably turned to Lehman and its falling stock price, Dimon told the group about their discussion with Bernanke. "I think he gets it," Dimon said, but when a banker asked if the Fed was likely to bail out Lehman, Dimon's reply was unequivocal: "Not going to happen."

Black had long been bearish on Lehman. At an internal leadership forum at JP Morgan in January 2007, he had predicted: "Dick Fuld will end up selling that company when he has to sell instead of when he should have sold it." Reminding the group of his earlier prognostication, he announced: "I *told* you they would be fucked!"

The mood grew more somber, however, as they all realized what an upheaval of that order would mean to them. If Lehman went down—and the government elected not to intervene—JP Morgan itself could suffer colossal losses. Zubrow informed the group that John Hogan, chief risk officer for JP Morgan's investment bank, had sought more than $5 billion in collateral from Lehman the week before, and again during the weekend, but had received nothing as of yet. Zubrow had also been to see Lehman's

CFO, Ian Lowitt, and put him on notice that JP Morgan was worried about them.

Black suggested that they call Fuld and demand that he send the collateral immediately. Just as important, the group decided that they should probably broaden the collateral agreement so that they'd be able to ask for even more money if other parts of Lehman's business were to falter.

Everyone agreed that this was the best course of action, so Black and Zubrow slowly rose from their seats and left the conference room. Their faces told the story: It was not going to be a pleasant conversation.

Black dialed Fuld on the speakerphone and when the connection was made immediately explained their plight: "We got, you know, $6 to $10 billion worth of intraday exposure to you, and we don't have enough collateral," Black said. He reminded him that JP Morgan had asked for $5 billion the week before.

"We understand that that's a tough ask for you guys," he continued, "so let's spend some time on how we might solve our issue without creating a major issue for you." In the back of Black's mind he knew he was being far too generous; he could easily have said, *If you don't, we'll shut you down tomorrow morning, which we have every right to do.*

Initially, it seemed as if Fuld had understood the veiled threat. "Let me get my guys, and we'll take a look at it," he said resignedly. Fuld proceeded to conference Lowitt into the call and calmly explained the situation to him. The four men discussed a handful of options that would enable Lehman to provide the collateral. Perhaps Lehman could move all its cash over to JP Morgan and just leave it on deposit, so it wouldn't count against the firm's capital?

Fuld tried to turn the call around, using it as an opportunity to ask Black if JP Morgan might be willing to offer Lehman some amount of cash, perhaps in the form of a loan that could be converted into Lehman stock. After all, Dimon had always told Fuld to call if he needed anything.

"We're getting ready to preannounce tomorrow," Fuld told Black. "Maybe we need to hold that up for a day if you guys seriously think Jamie would consider doing a convert and taking a piece of us."

To the JP Morgan bankers, it was a ludicrous suggestion, like someone's asking the repo man if he had any spare change.

Black looked at Zubrow as if to say, *Fuld has lost it,* and replied carefully, "I don't have any ideas, any brilliant ideas off the top of my head, but if you're telling me you're at that point where you would consider . . . that you're at the point where it's really getting difficult, then let us still talk and come back and see if there's anything we can do."

Five minutes later, after a quick and sober discussion with his colleagues, Black was back on the phone with Fuld.

"Dick, there's nothing that anybody's gonna . . . there's nothing we can do, and frankly, there's nothing anybody's gonna do other than what might be in their own self-interest," Black explained. "I'm sorry to say this, but my suggestion is to call the Fed and see if they might try and put together a Long-Term Capital–type proposal, and herd all the cats into one room."

There was a pause at the other end of the line, and then Fuld said icily, "That would be terrible for our shareholders."

Black could hardly keep from laughing. "No one is going to give a shit about your shareholders," he replied.

Stilling his frustration, Fuld tried to reengage Black. "I just talked to Vikram," he announced. "Citi is sending a bunch of guys over to meet with our capital markets guys, and some of our management team, to see if there is some type of a capital market solution that we could announce at the same time that we're pronouncing earnings."

Citi? Was Fuld joking? "OK," Black said guardedly. "We can send over some of our guys."

Black immediately called Doug Braunstein, head of JP Morgan's investment banking practice: "I'd like you to go and John [Hogan] to go," he told him after explaining the situation. "I have no idea what they want. The fact that Citi has an idea probably means it doesn't work," he said with a chuckle. "But see what is up and see what they're talking about."

Hank Paulson had his eyes fixed on his Bloomberg terminal as he watched Lehman's share price carefully. It was 2:05 p.m., and the stock was down 36 percent, to $9, its lowest level since 1998.

He had just gotten off the phone with Fuld, who had called with an update on his approach to Bank of America. Paulson was pleased to hear Fuld was now taking this seriously but afraid it was all too late.

On Paulson's television that moment, tuned to CNBC, the speculation among the network's commentators was illuminating.

"The stock is coming down at the rate it's coming down because a number of people believe strongly that the company is headed for bankruptcy," explained Dick Bove, a veteran banking analyst at Ladenburg Thalmann. "I think that that belief is what is driving the short selling."

Erin Burnett, the anchor of *Street Signs,* countered: "But if people are still using the company as a counterparty, trusting the company, isn't that a significant statement?"

"The key thing you have to understand is it's not in anyone's interest for Lehman to fail," replied Bove, who, oddly enough, had a buy on the stock and a $20 price target. "It's not in the interest of its competitors—Goldman Sachs, Morgan, Citigroup, JP Morgan—because if Lehman were to fail, then the pressure moves to Merrill Lynch and then it moves to who knows who else?

"It's also, you know, not in the interest of the U.S. government for Lehman to fail," Bove stressed again. "You have to believe, although I can't tell you this is true, that Lehman has been talking to the Federal Reserve of New York, to Ben Bernanke, probably to Hank Paulson, because they don't want this company to fail."

How true. Paulson picked up the phone to call Geithner to discuss what other options they might pursue.

———

By the time the closing bell rang at the New York Stock Exchange, Lehman's shares had taken a brutal beating, ending the day at $7.79, having fallen 45 percent. McDade's secretary could hardly keep up with the calls. McDade himself had to help his new CFO, Ian Lowitt, prepare the numbers for the following day's earnings call. They'd officially decided they had to preannounce something—anything, really—as investors needed to hear from them.

McDade also had to brief Larry Wieseneck and Brad Whitman, whom he had designated to meet with JP Morgan and Citigroup executives at Simpson Thacher's Midtown offices later that day. They would ask for one or both banks to extend a credit line or perhaps to consider helping them raise capital. Finally, perhaps the trickiest task of all, he had to figure out how the firm would position its good bank–bad bank plan to investors.

The reason that was such a challenging proposition was that nobody could or would put a price on the firm's abundance of toxic assets.

If all that weren't enough to deal with, McDade had just had a baffling conversation with Fuld, who informed him that Paulson had called him directly to suggest that the firm open up its books to Goldman Sachs. The way Fuld described it, Goldman was effectively advising Treasury. Paulson was also demanding a thorough review of Lehman's confidential numbers, courtesy of Goldman Sachs.

McDade, though never much of a Goldman conspiracy theorist, found Fuld's report discomfiting, but moments later was on the phone with Harvey Schwartz, Goldman's head of capital markets. "I'm following up on Hank's request," he began.

After another perplexing conversation, McDade walked down the hall and told Alex Kirk to immediately call Schwartz at Goldman, instructing him to set up a meeting and get them to sign a confidentiality agreement.

"This is coming directly from Paulson," he explained.

At 4:30 p.m. Paulson asked Christal West, his assistant, to get Ken Lewis on the phone. Ken Wilson had just briefed Paulson on his most recent call with Fuld—his seventh of the day—about Bank of America again. Now, Wilson told Paulson that all he needed to do was to make the case directly to its CEO. Paulson and Lewis did not know each other well, and the only real time they had spent together was a lunch in Charlotte several years back, when Paulson was still at Goldman. Ken Wilson had brought Paulson down to meet Lewis then to demonstrate Goldman's loyalty to their acquisitive client.

"I've got Lewis on the line," West finally called out to Paulson, who picked up the receiver.

"Ken," he began gravely, "I'm calling about Lehman Brothers," and after pausing said, "I'd like you to take another look at it."

The receiver was silent for a few seconds. Lewis agreed to consider it, but added: "I don't know how much it will do for us strategically." He made it clear, however, that the price would have to be right. "If there's a good financial deal there, I could see doing it."

Lewis's biggest concern about a potential deal, as he told Paulson, was Fuld, who Lewis worried would be unrealistic about his asking price.

He recounted to Paulson how badly their meeting had gone back in July.

"This is out of Dick's hands," Paulson assured him. It was a powerful statement that could be interpreted only one way: *You can negotiate directly with me.*

By 7:30 p.m., the conference room on the thirtieth floor of Simpson Thacher was packed with executives from JP Morgan and Citigroup, who were milling about impatiently. "This is going to be a waste of two hours of our time," John Hogan of JP Morgan whispered to his colleague, Doug Braunstein, who just smiled wryly.

Larry Wieseneck greeted Gary Shedlin—co-head of global financial institutions M&A of Citigroup and one of his closest friends and regular golf partners at Crestmont, their club in New Jersey—then assessed the crowd. Realizing that he wasn't even certain who everyone was, he passed around a piece of paper asking them all to sign in. If he was going to share confidential information with them, he wanted to know precisely with whom he'd be dealing.

Wieseneck was particularly worried about the imbalance of people from JP Morgan's risk department, compared to the deal-making bankers he had expected would be coming to help them think through their options. "These are all risk guys," he told his colleague Brad Whitman, as the two chatted in the corner, plotting strategy. *This was supposed to be a meeting on how to save Lehman,* he thought, *not a due diligence session for JP Morgan to figure out the extent of its exposure if Lehman fails.*

Apologizing for the delay, Wieseneck announced to the room that they were waiting for Skip McGee, Lehman's head of investment banking, to arrive.

"We've got a lot of people here," Braunstein, who had brought his whole team along, complained. "We can't wait here all night."

As tension in the room continued to rise, Whitman finally received an e-mail from McGee, who told him to go ahead and begin, as it was unlikely that he would be able to make it at all.

After calling the group to order, Wieseneck walked it through Lehman's plan to spin off its real estate assets as a "bad bank." Everyone agreed the plan was a good one, but there was general concern that it might have come too late, given that it would take months to put into effect. And Lehman would need to infuse the entity with at least a modicum of capital to prevent it from toppling immediately.

Wieseneck then opened up the meeting to questions, and almost immediately became annoyed by the sheer volume of them posed by the JP Morgan bankers—most of which had nothing to do with helping Lehman raise capital. "How big is the book? What assumptions are you using around the models?" Hogan asked. "It sounds like you probably need some capital to make this whole thing work." The Lehman representatives didn't have any answers, suggesting that he get in touch with their CFO.

To Wieseneck it was obvious that what the queries were really about was determining Lehman's liquidity position: whether counterparties were trading with it and the status of its cash position. These were all legitimate concerns that any prudent investor might have, but in this case, Wieseneck and Whitman suspected that they were intended more as a means to protect JP Morgan. Shedlin's questions, in contrast, were directed at various possible structures of deals that could help Lehman, but he was getting drowned out by the other bankers around the table.

The one point on which bankers from both sides agreed was that Lehman should not announce its SpinCo plan unless it could identify the exact "hole" that it needed to fill—that is, how big a capital infusion was necessary. "You don't know how much money you're going to need," Hogan told them. "By going out and announcing this, you'd only add uncertainty to the market," he warned. "You'd get crushed."

Shedlin was even blunter. "Look, we think it's very dangerous for you guys to lay out a strategy with a SpinCo where people basically will conclude that you guys still have a very significant capital hole," he said. "Going out with a story that suggests you have a big capital hole and no solution to raising it is only gonna put you at the mercy of the market even more."

As the meeting broke up, two messages were clear as day to Wieseneck and Whitman. The first: *Forget about announcing the plan, but if you feel you must do so, be very careful about talking about raising new capital and don't get pinned down to a specific number.*

It was the other, however, that made them appreciate the true depth of their predicament: *You're on your own.* None of the banks volunteered to offer any new credit lines.

As soon as Braunstein and Hogan left the building and crossed Lexington Avenue, they called Jamie Dimon and Steve Black.

"Here's the story," Hogan said, virtually shouting into his cell phone. "I think these guys are fucked." They proceeded to walk Dimon and Black through all of the details of what Lehman was preparing to announce the following day.

"We have to go back and tie everything up and line up all of our contingent risks," Hogan insisted. "I don't want to take a hickey on this."

From the Bank of America headquarters in Charlotte, North Carolina, Greg Curl dialed Treasury's Ken Wilson, who was still in his office, frantically fielding calls. Wilson had been expecting to hear from Curl, notifying him that he was getting on a plane to New York to begin his due diligence on Lehman.

Curl, however, was phoning with very different news. "We're having an issue with the Richmond Fed," he explained. Jeff Lacker, the president of the Federal Reserve of Richmond, Bank of America's regulator, had been concerned about the bank's health and had been putting pressure on it to raise new capital ever since it had closed its acquisition of Countrywide in July. As the official overseer of banks in Virginia, Maryland, North Carolina, South Carolina, the District of Columbia, and part of West Virginia, the Richmond Fed wielded considerable power through its regulation of capital reserves.

"They've been screwing around," Curl complained to Wilson, who was hearing of this for the first time. Curl told him that at the time that Bank of America was considering acquiring Countrywide back in January—a purchase that the government had quietly encouraged to help keep that firm from imploding—the Fed had quietly promised to relax its capital requirements if it proceeded with the deal. Or at least that's what Ken Lewis thought.

Now, two months after the Countrywide acquisition had been completed, Lacker was threatening to force the bank to slash its dividend. Bank of America had not disclosed the conversations, hoping they'd be able to resolve the matter before the news ever leaked. The bank had been working the phones that afternoon with the Richmond Fed to try to figure out where the bank now stood with Lacker, but it was having little luck. "We're going to need your help," he told Wilson. "Otherwise, we can't move forward."

Wilson recognized the gambit all too clearly: Bank of America was using the Lehman situation as a bargaining chip. The bank would help Lehman, but only if the government would do it a favor in return. Lewis, through Curl, was playing hardball.

Wilson promised to look into the matter and then immediately called Paulson. "You're not going to believe this . . ."

———

At 10:00 p.m., a frustrated Bart McDade was still holding court in the boardroom on the thirty-first floor at Lehman Brothers. He had just learned that Bank of America wasn't coming up to New York in the morning, though he didn't yet understand exactly why. "We're playing against the clock," he railed.

Hours earlier, McDade had implored Fuld to go home and get some sleep before tomorrow's earnings call, for which he needed to be in his best form. Since Fuld left, he had been reviewing various drafts of the press release. What should they say? What *could* they say? How should they say it?

McDade had just finished coaching Lowitt, his CFO, through his part of the presentation when Wieseneck and Whitman returned from their meeting with JP Morgan and Citigroup.

Before joining everyone in the boardroom, they huddled with Jerry Donini and Matt Johnson, along with a half dozen other bankers. Whitman described the entire meeting to them. "It was unbelievable," he concluded his account, shaking his head. "It was like a JP Morgan risk convention!"

The group then joined McDade in the conference room, where, after Wieseneck and Donini walked the group through the SpinCo plan, Wieseneck shared the advice that JP Morgan and Citigroup had given them earlier. "We've got to be careful how we message if we intend to raise capital or not," Donini warned.

It was about 1:30 a.m. before everyone finally packed it in. A small fleet of black Town Cars lined Seventh Avenue in front of the building to whisk the bankers home. They'd need to be back at the office only five hours later, giving them time for perhaps a brief nap and a shower, before a day that they suspected would determine the course of their futures.

CHAPTER THIRTEEN

The day's papers for Wednesday, September 10, 2008, were strewn everywhere in Dick Fuld's office, where a sleep-deprived Bart McDade and Alex Kirk had arrived at 6:30 a.m. for last-minute preparations for the looming conference call, scheduled to begin in only three and a half hours. The news was not good.

The lead of the *New York Times* read: "Only days after the Bush administration assumed control of the nation's two largest mortgage finance companies, Wall Street was gripped by fears that another big financial institution, the investment bank Lehman Brothers, might founder—and that this time, the government might not come to the rescue."

Several paragraphs down came the quote that succinctly stated the threat that now faced them: "Some may worry that Treasury has taken on so much taxpayer burden they don't have any remaining capacity to take on the burdens of Lehman," said David Trone, an analyst at Fox-Pitt Kelton.

The *Wall Street Journal* noted the differences between what had taken place during the final days of Bear Stearns and what was now occurring at Lehman. For one thing, Lehman could borrow from the Federal Reserve.

It wasn't just the stock investors who were nervous; Fuld and McDade had already begun receiving reports from the trading floor that morning indicating that more hedge funds were pulling their money out of Lehman. A sign of just how desperate the situation had become was that GLG Partners of London—whose largest shareholder, with a 13.7 percent stake, was Lehman—reduced the amount of business it conducted with the firm.

As they were making yet another pass through the earnings call script,

Kirk's cell phone rang. It was Harvey Schwartz from Goldman Sachs, phoning about the confidentiality agreement that Kirk was preparing. Before Schwartz began to discuss that matter, however, he said that he had something important to tell Kirk: "For the avoidance of doubt, Goldman Sachs does not have a client. We are doing this as principal."

For a moment Kirk paused, gradually processing what Schwartz had just said.

"Really?" he asked, trying to keep the shock out of his voice. *Goldman is the buyer?*

"Yes," Schwartz replied calmly.

"Okay. I have to call you back," Kirk said, nervously ending the conversation, and then almost shouted to Fuld and McDade, "Guys, they don't have a client!"

"What do you mean?" Fuld asked, looking up bleary-eyed from his notes.

"They're doing this for themselves. For Goldman. That's what he told me."

For the next few minutes the three men frantically brainstormed about their course of action. McDade, reasonably, was concerned about sharing information with a direct competitor: How much did they really want to divulge? At the same time, he felt they couldn't take a stand against a plan that he believed had originated with Paulson.

Kirk was even more apprehensive. "Why are we letting Goldman Sachs in here? Haven't you read *When Genius Failed*? The reference was to Roger Lowenstein's bestselling book about the Long-Term Capital Management crisis. In it Goldman Sachs is depicted in one scene as trying to take advantage of the disaster by using its offer of assistance as a way to get inside Long-Term Capital's books and download all its positions into a laptop—a charge Goldman fervently denied.

"They will rape us," Kirk cautioned.

McDade, turning back to his preparations for the fast-approaching call, made his position clear: "We were told by Hank Paulson to let them in the door. We're going to let them in the door."

Twenty-seven floors below, Lehman traders gathered for a preview of SpinCo, the "bad-bank" spin-off that would be discussed an hour later during the earnings call. McDade had appointed Tom Humphrey and Eric Felder to explain what investors were about to hear.

After learning the details of the plan, the traders were unusually quiet, and the silence was broken only when Mohammed Grimeh, global head of emerging markets, stood up with a horrified look on his face.

"That's it? That's fucking *it*?" he asked. "Well, what the hell have those fucking idiots up on thirty-one been working on for the past two months? *This?* You have to be kidding me. If this is all we have, we're toast!"

In the time it had taken Humphrey and Felder to describe SpinCo, Grimeh had already seen through it—had seen exactly what JP Morgan and Citigroup saw the night before, and what he feared the market would see as well.

"All we've done is to take a dollar out of our right pocket and put it in our left. The heavy debt load would make it insolvent before it started," he said, backed by a growing chorus of angry muttering from the disconcerted bankers.

———

Gregory J. Fleming, Merrill Lynch's president and chief operating officer, had one eye on CNBC as he jogged on a treadmill at the health club at the Ritz-Carlton hotel in downtown Dallas. He had spent the day before with clients in Houston and had scheduled a town hall session here with Merrill employees before hopping on a flight back to New York.

As he leaned into his jog, CNBC reported that Lehman Brothers had just announced its earnings ahead of its conference call. The firm, the reporter elaborated, had also described its extraordinary spin-off plans in its press release. When Fleming returned to his room, he got a colleague to send him the announcement, which included an important headline buried at the bottom: "The firm remains committed to examining all strategic alternatives to maximize shareholder value," which meant that it was open to just about anything. He knew the company had been quietly shopping pieces of itself, but that statement effectively made it official, at least to those paying attention. Lehman, the entire firm, was up for sale.

From his days as a merger banker focusing on financial services, he knew that if Lehman was on the auction block, Bank of America would be the likely buyer. But if Lehman was sold to Bank of America, the implications for his own firm, Merrill Lynch, would be enormous. He had long believed that Bank of America was the natural buyer for Merrill; at a Merrill board meeting just a month earlier, Bank of America had been listed in a presentation as just one of a handful of compatible merger partners.

Fleming began trying to figure out whom he knew who might be working on a deal with Bank of America. Ed Herlihy of Wachtell, a longtime friend and one of the legal deans of banking M&A, immediately came to mind. Herlihy had worked on nearly every deal Bank of America had orchestrated over the past decade.

"This is getting ugly," Fleming told Herlihy when he reached him on his cell. "How are my friends in Charlotte?"

Herlihy could see where this conversation was heading and took steps to deflect it immediately. "Let's not go there, Greg," he replied.

"Just tell me. If you're thinking about Lehman, you have to tell me. We could be interested in talking at some point. You and I both know that would be a much better deal."

Herlihy, clearly uncomfortable, said, "We've been down this road before. We're not going to do anything unless we're invited in. If you are serious, now would be a good time to get moving on that."

That was all the confirmation Fleming needed to be convinced that Bank of America was indeed bidding for Lehman.

Fleming had one more call to make before his first meeting that morning. He wouldn't contact John Thain just yet—Thain, he suspected, wouldn't be interested at this point, for whenever Fleming had tried previously to discuss contingency plans to sell the bank, he had been dismissive. Instead he phoned Peter Kelly, Merrill's deal lawyer, and recounted his conversation with Herlihy.

"Look, you have to make sure Bank of America is there for us," Kelly instructed him after the two had discussed the ramifications. "You have to convince John."

"That's a high bar," Fleming said. They both knew that he and Thain had a fundamentally antagonistic relationship.

"I know," Kelly said, "but that's why you get paid the big bucks." Before hanging up, he made one last point: They might have to go over Thain's head. "If you can't convince John—and I know this is subversive behavior, but this is in the interest of the shareholders—you need to reach out to the board."

The conference room on the thirty-first floor of Lehman Brothers was more crowded than usual for an earnings call, but what was typically a fairly routine affair had lately begun to be perceived as something more akin to an impeachment trial. Lehman was taking the situation seriously enough to have stocked the room with additional lawyers. Lehman technicians, meanwhile, were scrambling to ensure that the conference call and Webcast would go off without a major hitch. The firm had ordered hundreds of extra phone lines to keep up with the demand. The press release issued that morning forecast a third-quarter loss of $3.9 billion—the firm's biggest ever.

Fuld strode in assuredly, as if nothing was out of the ordinary. Everyone in the room, however, knew that for years he had always let his chief financial officer handle these calls, as he had never been truly comfortable participating in them. As he took his seat at the head of the table, Fuld looked around the room with his trademark disarming glare, trying to settle in with his script and papers. He knew what the stakes were. Moments earlier he had taken a quick glance at the Bloomberg terminal to see if U.S. stock index futures might be higher on the hopes that he, Dick Fuld, would be able to ease fears about Lehman. But overnight, Asian stocks had slid, and Europe was even lower. There was a lot riding on what he would say today; millions of dollars would either be made or lost on exchanges the world over depending on how his presentation was received.

Shaun Butler, the head of investor relations, looked over at her boss. "Are you ready?"

"Yeah," answered Fuld, faintly growling.

As the call was engaged, he slowly lowered his head and launched into his script, intoning deliberately: "In light of these last two days, this morning we prereleased our quarterly results. We are also announcing several important financial and operating changes that amount to a significant repositioning of the firm, including aggressively reducing our exposure to both commercial real estate and residential real estate assets.

"These will accomplish a substantial de-risking of our balance sheet and reinforce the emphasis on our client-focused businesses. They are also meant to mitigate the potential for future write-downs, and to allow the firm to return to profitability and strengthen our ability to earn appropriate risk-unadjusted equity returns."

The executive summary: Lehman Brothers will be just fine. We appreciate your concern, but we have the situation under control.

"This firm has a history [of facing adversity] and delivering," he continued. "We have a long track record of pulling together when times are tough and then taking advantage of global opportunities. . . . We are on the right track to put these last two quarters behind us."

Fuld now handed off to his CFO, Lowitt, who, in his clipped South African accent, outlined what Lehman billed as its "key strategic initiatives." The firm would seek to sell a 55 percent stake in its money-management business, which included Neuberger Berman, and it would spin off much of its commercial real estate holdings—otherwise known as "the bad stuff."

Shifting as much as $30 billion of Lehman's commercial real estate holdings, including its investments in Archstone-Smith, the owner of 360 high-end apartment buildings, and SunCal, a property developer, was no small undertaking. One thing that would be changing immediately was how Lehman valued its real estate assets.

Lowitt continued: "The real estate held-for-sale portfolio, consisting of assets across the capital structure, is booked at lower of cost or market as we take write-downs on this book, but do not reflect market value gains until a sale event occurs. REI Global"—the new entity's infelicitous acronym—"will account for its assets on a held-to-maturity basis and will be able to manage the assets without the pressure of marked-to-market volatility. REI Global will not be forced to sell assets below what it believes to be their intrinsic value."

On the surface the spin-off appeared to be a clean, elegant solution. It removed the troubled assets from Lehman's balance sheet, leaving a stronger firm, just as Fuld had indicated that it would. But what was left unsaid was precisely what had concerned the bankers at the meeting with JP Morgan and Citi the night before: The new company would likely need to be funded. Where was Lehman going to come up with the money to accomplish that when it needed to retain as much capital as possible?

Less than half a mile away, in his office near Grand Central Terminal, David Einhorn huddled with his team of analysts listening to the Lehman earnings call on a speakerphone. He could not believe what he was hearing. *They were still trying to avoid writing this garbage—the toxic stuff—down. What did they hope to accomplish?* It was clear to him that the assets in question were worth much less than what Lehman was claiming.

"There's an admission right in the press release that they're not writing these things down!" Einhorn told his analysts. He zeroed in on a sentence in the company's statement: "'REI Global will be able to manage the assets without the pressure of marked-to-market volatility.'" Instead, Lehman maintained, by spinning off the real estate assets they'd be able "to 'account for its assets on a held-to-maturity basis.'"

In other words, as Einhorn continued to rail, "they can keep making up the numbers however they want."

———

Downtown, Steven Shafran and a team of staffers at the New York Federal Reserve Building were also listening to the call, some of them also in a state of utter disbelief. Shafran, the special assistant from Treasury, had flown to New York the night before at Paulson's urging to help coordinate communication among the Treasury, the Fed, and the SEC in the event that Lehman's situation quickly deteriorated. He and most of the Fed team had already been given a preview of the plan the night before by Lehman but hearing it presented live proved to be a completely different experience. A former investment banker at Goldman, Shafran shook his head in exasperation and announced, "This isn't going to work."

As the investor call went on, Shafran observed to the staffers, "What's really amazing about this is that these guys are investment bankers who get paid by large corporations for tough advice in tough situations. You know the old saying about how a doctor should never treat himself? It feels like one of those situations."

———

About halfway into the question-and-answer portion of the call, Michael Mayo, the prominent analyst with Deutsche Bank, addressed the capitalization issue with blunt directness: "To the extent you might need $7 billion to capitalize that entity," his voice boomed over the speakerphone, "and you'll get $3 billion with the spin of part of IMD [the more viable investment management division], how would you get the other $4 billion?"

Lowitt paused as he recalled the explicit instructions, given the conversation the firm had had the night before with the JP Morgan and Citigroup bankers: *Don't get pinned down talking about any specific numbers. You will be crushed.* He was now being asked the one question that he didn't want to answer.

"Well, we don't feel that we need to raise that extra amount to cover the $7 billion," he replied, trying to sound confident about the firm's capital position, "because you will have less sort of leverageable equity in core Lehman than in, you know, where you are at the end of this quarter."

In other words, the plan was essentially an accounting gimmick: Lehman would be smaller and less leveraged as a result of the spin-off, and would therefore need less capital.

Mayo responded that he had his doubts about Lehman's plan, but in adherence to Wall Street protocol, he left it at that. This was not the place for a showdown.

For a few moments it almost appeared as if Fuld would be able to claim victory: Shares of Lehman Brothers opened that morning up 17.4 percent. The rise might give him the breathing room he needed.

———

Across the Atlantic a group of senior executives from Barclays in London were likewise intently listening in on the call, taking meticulous notes as they sat in a conference room at the firm's headquarters, known as "The Bungalow," in Canary Wharf. They had registered for the call under an assumed name. Bob Diamond, Barclays Capital's CEO, had been mulling buying Lehman for months, ever since he had received the call from Bob Steel, when he was still at Treasury in April. In June, Diamond had broached the idea with Barclays' board, which had been discussing possible expansion plans in the United States. The group ultimately decided against pursuing Lehman—unless, as John Varley, the firm's chairman, put it, "the firm could be bought at a distressed price." Diamond had in turn communicated that message directly back to Steel.

But the timing now seemed ripe for a deal. "I'm surprised, given how shaky this is, that I actually haven't had a call from Treasury, because it knows that we would be willing to do this at a distressed price, and it's not that far off," Diamond had told Varley only a day earlier. Diamond had been in the middle of giving a recruiting presentation at Wharton, the elite business school at the University of Pennsylvania, on Tuesday, when his cell phone vibrated. Seeing that it was Varley, he abruptly stopped his presentation and walked off the stage. "If we're going to meet with the board, we're going to meet with the board tomorrow," Varley told him. Diamond found one of the only three direct overnight flights to Heathrow from Philadelphia.

He took the last-minute overnight return flight to London to resolicit support to buy Lehman. He would have to win over Varley and the board—and do so quickly.

Varley was a model of the conservative Englishman and had married into one of the bank's founding Quaker families. Soft-spoken and courtly, he wore suspenders every day, listed table tennis and fishing as his hobbies, and had far less tolerance for risk than Diamond. Whatever his own professional predilections, however, Varley had always given Diamond a long leash, even if he did maintain a quiet uneasiness with his colleague's appetite for deal making.

The two men had long had a complicated relationship, having both vied for the top job in 2003. Although Varley won the position, Diamond was paid nearly six times what Varley, his superior, made. (In 2007, Diamond earned $42 million to Varley's $8.4 million.) For years, Diamond had avoided taking a seat on the Barclays' board to avoid disclosure of his compensation agreement, which would have landed him squarely in the pages of the British tabloids as a "Fat Cat." Despite his title, Diamond was to many the de facto CEO. In 2006 a Dresdner Kleinwort analyst wrote a report provocatively titled "Bob Diamond 3, John Varley 0."

As soon as the Lehman call came to an end, the Barclays executives discovered they were in agreement: They'd make a play for the firm. But only—Varley reiterated the point—if they could get it for a song.

Diamond went back to his office and phoned Bob Steel at his new number at Wachovia. "Remember our conversation about Lehman?" he asked.

"Of course," Steel answered.

"Well, we're now interested."

———

Lehman's stock may have temporarily stabilized after the earnings call, but only hours later Fuld was faced with a new problem: Moody's Investors Service announced that it was preparing to place Lehman's credit rating on review, warning that if the firm did not soon enter into "a strategic transaction with a stronger financial partner," it would cut its rating.

Fuld decided to call John Mack, CEO of Morgan Stanley; he needed options. And, unlike his relationships with Ken Lewis and Lloyd Blankfein, he actually trusted Mack.

"Listen, I really need to do something," Fuld told him. "Let's do something together."

Mack had always genuinely liked Fuld and was concerned by the stress he could now hear in his voice. But he had no interest in entering into a deal and wondered if Fuld was deluding himself by even making the call.

"Dick, I want to help, but it just doesn't make any sense. We've talked about this before," Mack said, reminding him of the meeting they had had at his house over the summer. "There's so much overlap."

After getting off the phone, however, Mack continued to think about the possibility of a deal with Lehman and found that he was intrigued. His initial impulse about its unfeasibility may have been correct when Lehman's stock was trading at $40 a share, but given its current price, a deal might well be financially attractive.

"I've been thinking," he said, after calling Fuld back. "I agree with you. We should talk."

After Fuld thanked him for reconsidering, Mack paused a moment and then said firmly, "Dick, I'm a very straightforward guy. I really like you, but let's be clear, this is not a merger of equals. Only one person can run this. We have to get that up front now."

After an awkward silence, Fuld finally responded, "I wasn't thinking that way," and then, after another brief hesitation, added, "Let me think about it. I'll call you back."

Twenty minutes later Fuld was back on the phone.

"Look, you're right," he said, the toll that recent days had taken shading his voice. "I want to do the right thing. Let's see what can be done."

Fuld suggested that they set up a meeting between the senior managements of both firms, without Fuld or Mack present; let them be the ones to decide if it was a good or bad idea.

The gathering was arranged for that night at the apartment of Walid Chammah, Morgan Stanley's co-president.

———

Bob Diamond drummed his fingers on the desk as he waited on hold for Tony Ryan at Treasury, whom Bob Steel had suggested he call. "Tony," Diamond began, "do you recall the conversation I had with Steel?"

For a moment, Ryan was confused.

"Which?" he asked, trying to act as if he knew what Diamond was talking about.

"On Lehman."

"Oh, yes, yes."

"I wanted to call you because I thought it would be worthwhile for me to talk to Hank. If not, no big thing, but my sense is that we should have a conversation."

Ryan said he'd get Paulson to contact him as soon as he could.

An hour later Diamond's secretary informed him that Tim Geithner was on the line. "What can I do to help this along?" he asked.

Diamond explained that he was very interested in buying Lehman, if it could be had at a distressed price.

"Why don't you call Fuld?" Geithner asked.

"You don't understand," Diamond said. "I am not trying to be provocative here." He told Geithner about their experience trying to buy ABN AMRO—how the deal had fallen apart and how big an embarrassment it had been for the firm. "We don't want to be seen as dabbling around," Diamond said. "It would be inappropriate."

To Geithner, such unnecessary delicacy seemed characteristically British, even if Diamond was an American, and he just listened.

"We need to be seen, to be invited by you and shepherded by you," Diamond insisted. "You guys asked me if there was a price at which we'd be interested and you asked me, if so, 'What do you need?' That doesn't mean I'm gonna call Fuld. That's completely different."

Geithner, growing frustrated with his equivocation, asked again, "Why can't you just call Fuld? Why can't you do it?"

"I'm not going to ask a guy if I can buy him, you know, at a distressed price," Diamond said. "It only works if you guys are looking to arrange a deal. If you're not, fine, no hard feelings, we're okay."

However much Barclays may have wished to avoid giving the impression that they might be taking advantage of someone else's misfortune, it was, of course, precisely what they were seeking to do.

———

Ben Bernanke was finding it hard to focus as he sat in a meeting Wednesday afternoon with the local board of the Federal Reserve. Despite the chaos on Wall Street, he had continued making his regular visits to the Fed's regional offices, and this particular trip had brought him to its St. Louis branch, located in a squat limestone building on North Broadway in the city's downtown.

The Lehman crisis, however, was never far away. He had already been on the phone with Tim Geithner and Hank Paulson twice about it, once at 8:30 a.m. and again at 1:00 p.m., with another conversation scheduled for 6:00 p.m.

On the last call, Geithner and Paulson had informed Bernanke of their latest headache: Bank of America's demand to have its capital ratio relaxed. "They are pissed off bigtime because they thought when they closed on Countrywide, they closed like big boys," Paulson explained.

Geithner argued that they needed to get Bank of America to New York by whatever means necessary so that they could begin their due diligence; he was concerned that they were losing critical time.

Paulson asked Bernanke to call Ken Lewis himself and see if he could smooth the situation over, stressing again, "We need to get them a glide path."

From a temporary office at the St. Louis Fed, Bernanke dialed Lewis.

"You really ought to come look at Lehman," Bernanke urged him, still slightly uncomfortable about his new role as deal maker. "We'll work with you on capital relief and anything you might need."

Lewis thanked him for the call and said he planned to send his men up to New York to start discussions with Lehman.

Believing he had solved that problem, Bernanke returned to the reason for his trip to St. Louis: to visit with the staffers and spend more time with the St. Louis branch's new president, James Bullard. Bullard had taken over in April from William Poole, one of the more outspoken Fed presidents, who, as it happened, was in Washington that day giving a speech about the Fed's bailouts. Given the ongoing speculation in the market about the need for a government rescue of Lehman, Poole's comments had been attracting an inordinate amount of attention.

"Unless I've missed something, the Fed and Treasury have been silent about who might have access to Fed resources, except to say that Fannie and Freddie would have access," Poole said during his speech.

"The Fed said no to New York City in 1975 and no to Chrysler in 1979," he reminded his audience, but "with the Bear Stearns precedent, it will not be so easy to say no next time.

"What I anticipate is that we will not know the limits to Fed lending until the Fed says no to a large, influential firm seeking help."

———

Ken Lewis was leaning hard on the Fed. No sooner had he gotten off the phone with Bernanke than he placed a call to Tim Geithner. Lewis explained that he had had an encouraging call with Mr. Bernanke, but he still couldn't send his team up to New York until the credit situation was officially settled.

"We're working to help you on this," Geithner said, politely but firmly.

Lewis, however, was beyond accepting such assurances. "We've been dicked around on this for too long," he complained. "If you want us to get involved in Lehman, we're going to need something in writing."

Geithner, taken aback at being presented with such an ultimatum, replied, "You've heard what the chairman said he would do. If you don't believe the word of the chairman of the Federal Reserve, we have a larger problem."

Realizing that Geithner would not budge on the issue, Lewis finally backed down and agreed to send a team of executives up to begin due diligence that Thursday morning.

———

As Wednesday wore on, Fuld tirelessly continued to work the phones—his call log was a list of virtually every major Wall Street and Washington player—while keeping a watchful eye on the markets for any further signs of panic.

The news, it was becoming ever clearer, was grim: After holding up for most of the day, Lehman's shares sank in the last hour of trading, ending at $7.25 a share, a 6.9 percent decline. Lehman's CDS had also blown out, rising by 135 basis points, to 610, which meant that the cost of buying insurance against its going bankrupt had just risen to $610,000 a year to protect $10 million of bonds. Investors were effectively betting that the situation was only going to worsen. Any hope that the SpinCo plan was going to turn Lehman's fortunes around was quickly vanishing.

Nor were the results of Fuld's phone blitz encouraging. Earlier in the day he had had a tough conversation with Lloyd Blankfein, who had called to express his frustration that Lehman had ended discussions with Goldman. Alex Kirk and Mark Walsh had held a two-hour-long meeting with Harvey Schwartz of Goldman and his team at a Midtown law firm that morning, but both Kirk and Walsh were skittish about opening up all their books to Goldman and quickly had shut down the talks.

Fuld had also spoken to Paulson, who had tried to convince him of the merits of a deal with Barclays. But Fuld was uneasy with that prospect, he explained: With Bank of America already in the hunt, he didn't want to do anything to jeopardize a deal with them.

"Dick," Paulson patiently reminded him, "Ken Lewis has turned you down multiple times; the other guys have expressed an interest. We need to pursue both of these options."

Fuld, however, seemed more interested in returning to the topic that had so long obsessed him: denouncing the short-sellers who, he told Paulson, "are going to ruin this firm." He spent ten minutes again imploring Paulson to call Christopher Cox at the SEC to press him to instate a short-selling ban, to announce an investigation—anything that would give him an opportunity to recover. By late afternoon, Fuld was channeling Steven Berkenfeld, a Lehman managing director, whose office was just down the hallway, using his favorite catchphrase about the raids on Lehman's stock: "Short and distort!"

———

In London, Bob Diamond of Barclays was waiting in the bar of Fifty, a private club on St. James St., just off of Piccadilly. He had invited Jeremy Isaacs, the former head of Lehman's European operations, for drinks. If there was anyone who could give him an accurate insider view of Lehman, if there was anyone who knew the numbers and culture, it was Isaacs, who had officially announced his plans to "retire" from the firm just four days earlier.

Isaacs had left when it became clear that McDade was ascending. In truth, he probably ought not to have come to this drinks engagement, as he was in the midst of negotiating a $5 million severance agreement with Lehman that would literally be approved the following day. As part of the arrangement he agreed he would not "engage in detrimental activity" or "disparage the firm," and would "keep company information confidential."

Tonight he would come as close as he could to breaking every provision in that document with the intention of helping Lehman survive.

———

Walid Chammah's apartment is one of only three town houses on Manhattan's Upper East Side with its own doorman. The beaux arts limestone structure just off Fifth Avenue contains only nine apartments. Tucked away a safe distance from Midtown and the banker riffraff on Park Avenue, it was the perfect place to hold a secret meeting to discuss a merger between Lehman and Morgan Stanley. Chammah's wife and children were in London, where he was normally based, so the group had the place to themselves.

By 9:00 p.m., Chammah; James Gorman, Morgan Stanley's other co-president; and the rest of the Morgan Stanley team were milling around his kitchen, waiting for Bart McDade and the Lehman contingent to appear. "Let's at least go through the motions," Chammah instructed his colleagues, "but acknowledge that this meeting wouldn't likely lead to anything."

When McDade finally arrived with Skip McGee, Mark Shafir, Alex Kirk, and several others, the strain of the day was evident from their drawn and pale faces.

Gorman had known McDade from when they were both directors on the board of SIFMA, the Securities Industry and Financial Markets Association. Only a week earlier they had had a tense conversation about Morgan Stanley's exploiting Lehman's turmoil by recruiting away its talent, including the firm's best private-wealth advisers. Outraged, McDade had called Gorman and told him, "You have to back off. We got really big problems here, and this is killing us." Ultimately, Gorman stopped the recruiting effort, and the two were seasoned enough professionals to have moved on.

Chammah poured a bottle of Tenuta dell'Ornellaia 2001, a $180-a-bottle Bordeaux blend, in an effort to settle the mood while keeping things proceeding. Everyone quickly took a seat in the living room.

McDade told the group that being there tonight all felt a bit déjà vu; only a few months earlier nearly every person in the room had met to discuss the very same topic. Only now—an observation he left unspoken—Lehman was desperate. He then began to explain that Lehman was exploring various options for raising capital: selling assets, or perhaps selling the entire firm. In case that wasn't clear enough, he indicated that if Morgan Stanley was interested in buying the company, he wouldn't press them on terms. He then added that "social issues" shouldn't hold up a potential deal—code for the question of who would run the combined businesses. McDade had effectively just given up Fuld.

"If you want any of us involved, we'll be involved; if you don't want us, we don't have to be. It's not about us anymore," he said.

Shafir told the men that a deal "might feel like a stretch," but he thought there was an opportunity to remove a good deal of cost from both firms, which was, after all, the baseline logic behind any corporate merger.

Despite Shafir's optimistic spin on a potential deal, Chammah was well aware that an agreement of this magnitude would result in a bloodbath, with probably hundreds if not thousands of layoffs. He also knew that the upside in any merger could prove elusive.

Then, for a good hour, the bankers went over the numbers and the various assets that Lehman owned to determine if there was anything among its holdings that Morgan Stanley might want. But as the discussion went on and papers were passed back and forth, it became clear there was no common ground. Chammah then acknowledged that he didn't think Morgan's board could move quickly enough to be of any real assistance to Lehman in any case—a signal that everyone in the room recognized meant that he believed that Lehman Brothers was simply too far gone.

Soon after McDade's team left, Gorman looked solemnly at his group, as if to remind them, *It could be us,* but said only, "We just watched guys who are staring into the abyss."

Longtime friends Dick Fuld (*left*), Lehman's CEO, and Joe Gregory (*right*), Lehman president, during boom times.

Erin Callan, Lehman's onetime CFO, posing for a photograph printed in the *Wall Street Journal* that triggered jealousy and resentment within the firm.

Hank Paulson, Treasury secretary, who logged countless hours on his Motorola Razr cell phone during the financial meltdown. The phone is now part of the Smithsonian's archives.

Warren Buffett (*right*), the world's wealthiest investor, and his friend and former banker Hank Paulson (*left*). Behind the scenes, Buffett was a key adviser to Paulson and he considered aiding Lehman and AIG. He ended up buying a stake in Goldman Sachs.

Timothy Geithner (*right*), president of the Federal Reserve Bank of New York, talking to Kevin Warsh (*left*), a Federal Reserve governor. Both men secretly tried to orchestrate mergers for Goldman Sachs and Morgan Stanley.

Bob Steel, the under secretary for domestic finance at Treasury who headed the nation's efforts to reform Fannie Mae and Freddie Mac before leaving government to become the CEO of Wachovia.

Jamie Dimon (*left*), CEO of JP Morgan Chase, and Lloyd Blankfein (*right*), CEO of Goldman Sachs. Amid the crisis, Blankfein called Dimon, accusing his firm of spreading misinformation about Goldman.

Paulson and his staff (*from left*): Jim Wilkinson, Michele Davis, Neel Kashkari, Bob Hoyt, Kevin Fromer, and Tony Ryan.

Paulson with some of his inner circle (*from left*): Dan Jester, Jeremiah Norton, and David Nason.

David Einhorn, a hedge-fund manager who shorted shares of Lehman Brothers and publicly questioned the firm's accounting.

Min Euoo Sung, CEO of the Korean Development Bank, who held negotiations to buy Lehman Brothers throughout the summer of 2008, but ultimately passed.

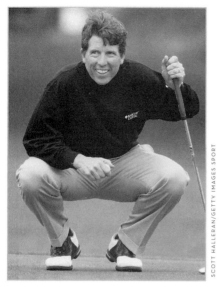

Bob Diamond, CEO of Barclays Capital, who sought to buy Lehman Brothers until withdrawing his bid at the eleventh hour; he bought the remnants of Lehman out of bankruptcy.

Rodgin Cohen, chairman of Sullivan & Cromwell, was a ubiquitous consigliere throughout the crisis. His clients included Lehman Brothers, AIG, Goldman Sachs, Wachovia, and Mitsubishi, among others.

Lehman's executive committee in Sun Valley, Idaho (clockwise from top): Tom Russo, Jeremy Isaacs, Bart McDade, Ted Janulis, David Goldfarb, Stephen Lessing, Jesse Bhattal, George Walker, Skip McGee, Joe Gregory, and Dick Fuld.

Robert Willumstad (*left*), CEO of AIG, and the firm's former CEO, Martin Sullivan (*right*). Willumstad broke the news to Sullivan that he was being ousted.

Joseph Cassano, former head of AIG's financial products unit, was dubbed the Man Who Crashed the World.

Goldman Sachs' top executives (*from left*): Gary Cohn, co-president; Lloyd Blankfein, CEO; John Winkelried, co-president.

Chris Flowers, a banker and financier, played roles as both an adviser to the Bank of America and as a potential investor to AIG. A former Goldman man, he long feuded with Paulson.

Steve Black, JP Morgan's president, as he went to the Fed the weekend of September 13. Days before Lehman's collapse, he called Fuld to ask for more collateral.

Douglas Braunstein, head of JP Morgan's investment bank, was asked to advise during its final weekend with AIG.

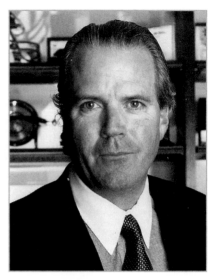

John Hogan, JP Morgan's chief risk officer, told Dimon after a meeting with Lehman, "I don't want to take a hickey on this."

Dimon asked Jimmy Lee, vice chairman at JP Morgan, to head up a government-organized private-sector rescue of AIG.

Paulson (*left*) had a pivotal conversation with Alistair Darling (*right*), chancellor of the Exchequer of Britain, on Sunday, September 14, about Barclays' bid for Lehman. That conversation, in which Darling expressed reservations about the deal, occurred fourteen hours before Lehman filed for bankruptcy.

John Thain (*left*), Merrill's CEO, and Ken Lewis (*right*), Bank of America's CEO, after they agreed to merge. Lewis fired Thain months later.

Greg Fleming, Merrill's president, who pushed John Thain to sell the firm over the weekend

Peter Kraus, outside the Fed the weekend of September 13, had joined Merrill Lynch only a little more than a week before he was negotiating to sell the firm to Bank of America.

Ed Herlihy, the Wachtell Lipton lawyer behind the Bank of America–Merrill Lynch deal; the rescue of Fannie and Freddie; and Morgan Stanley's stake sale to Mitsubishi

Paulson and his closest staff members in his office as they were developing TARP, the afternoon of September 18, 2008

Ken Wilson, a former Goldman banker, joined Treasury in the summer of 2008 to help Paulson manage through the crisis, playing a key role in various deals among bank CEOs.

Calendar

Start	End	Category	Description
16 8:00 PM	8:05 PM		Call from FED Chairman Bernanke and Tim Geithner
8:05 PM	8:25 PM		Call from Senator Barack Obama - (b) (6)
8:25 PM	8:35 PM		Call to Senator Barack Obama
8:35 PM	8:45 PM		Call to Keith Hennessey
17 7:10 AM	7:20 AM		Call from the President
7:20 AM	7:40 AM		Call from Tim Geithner
7:40 AM	7:45 AM		Call to Jaime Dimon, JP Morgan, left word
7:45 AM	7:50 AM		Call from Sheila Bair, FDIC
7:50 AM	8:00 AM		Call to Tim Geithner
8:15 AM	8:20 AM		Call to Dick Fuld, Lehman Brothers
8:20 AM	8:30 AM		Call to Jamie Dimon, JP Morgan
8:30 AM	8:35 AM		Call to SEC Chairman Chris Cox
8:35 AM	8:50 AM		Staff Meeting, Secretary's Large Conference Room
8:50 AM	9:05 AM		Call to Congressman Steny Hoyer, left word
9:05 AM	9:10 AM		Call to FED Chairman Ben Bernanke, left word
9:10 AM	9:15 AM		Call to Lloyd Blankfein, Goldman Sachs
9:15 AM	9:20 AM		Call to SEC Chairman Chris Cox
9:20 AM	9:30 AM		Phone Call with Russian Finance Minister Kudrin
9:30 AM	9:50 AM		Drop by Ken's Meeting with Richard Davis, President and CEO USB and Andy Cecere, CFO and Vice Chairman, Ken Wilson's Office
9:50 AM	10:05 AM		Call to FED Chairman Ben Bernanke, left word
10:05 AM	10:10 AM		Call to Tim Geithner, left word
10:10 AM	10:20 AM		Call to SEC Chairman Cox
10:20 AM	10:25 AM		Call to Tim Geithner
10:25 AM	10:30 AM		Call to Senator Richard Shelby, left word
10:30 AM	10:35 AM		Call to Senator Chris Dodd, left word
10:35 AM	10:40 AM		Call to Congressman Barney Frank, left word
10:40 AM	10:45 AM		Call to Congressman Spencer Bachus
10:45 AM	10:50 AM		Call to Congressman John Boehner
10:50 AM	10:55 AM		Call to Josh Bolten
10:55 AM	11:00 AM		Call to Congressman Barney Frank
11:00 AM	11:05 AM		Call to Ed Herlihy
11:05 AM	11:15 AM		Call to Congressman John Boehner
11:30 AM	12:00 PM		Phone Interview with Greg Ip, The Economist
12:05 PM	12:10 PM		Call to Josh Bolten
12:10 PM	12:15 PM		Call to SEC Chairman Chris Cox
12:15 PM	12:20 PM		Call to Lloyd Blankfein, Call to Tim Geithner
12:20 PM	12:25 PM		Call to FED Chairman Bernanke
12:25 PM	12:30 PM		Call from John Thain
12:30 PM	12:40 PM		Call to FED Chairman Bernanke
12:40 PM	12:50 PM		Call to Senator Chris Dodd
12:50 PM	12:55 PM		Call to FED Chairman Bernanke
12:55 PM	1:00 PM		Economic Principals Lunch, Ward Room, White House
1:00 PM	1:05 PM		Call to SEC Chairman Chris Cox
1:05 PM	1:10 PM		Call to John Mack, Morgan Stanley
1:10 PM	1:15 PM		Call to Tim Geithner
1:15 PM	1:20 PM		Call to Senator Richard Shelby

Paulson's calendar and call log illustrates the frantic scramble. During the heart of the crisis, on September 17, 2008, sixty-nine phone calls and meetings were recorded between 7:10 a.m. and 8:55 p.m. This document does not reflect calls on his cell phone or home phone.

Bob Scully (*above left*) and Ruth Porat (*above right*) of Morgan Stanley advised the government about its rescue of Fannie and Freddie as well as of AIG. *Right:* Colm Kelleher, Morgan Stanley's CFO.

John Mack (*left*), Morgan Stanley's CEO, and Vikram Pandit (*right*), Citigroup's CEO. The two men talked about merging.

Walid Chammah (*left*) and James Gorman (*right*), Morgan Stanley's co-presidents

The night before announcing the $700 billion TARP plan, Paulson and Bernanke brief key congressional leaders, including Rahm Emanuel, Barney Frank, Nancy Pelosi, Christopher Dodd, and Mitch McConnell, among others.

Left to right: Ben Bernanke, chairman of the Federal Reserve; President Bush; Christopher Cox, chairman of the SEC; and Hank Paulson head to the Rose Garden to announce TARP.

A 002059 **The Bank of Tokyo-Mitsubishi UFJ, Ltd.**

HEAD OFFICE TOKYO OCTOBER 13, 2008 REF. NO. *CO/- 3452850*

USD $9,000,000,000.00***********

PAY AGAINST THIS
CHECK TO THE ORDER OF MORGAN STANLEY*************************************

USD $9,000,000,000.00
TO

BANK OF TOKYO MITSUBISHI UFJ LTD
NEW YORK

The Bank of Tokyo-Mitsubishi UFJ, Ltd.
HEAD OFFICE TOKYO

AUTHORIZED SIGNATURE

Because it was a holiday in Japan, rather than wire the money, Mitsubishi UFJ presented Morgan Stanley with a $9 billion check for its investment in the firm.

THE WHITE HOUSE

WASHINGTON

September 17, 2008

MEMORANDUM FOR HENRY M. PAULSON, JR.
SECRETARY, U.S. DEPARTMENT OF THE
TREASURY

FROM   FRED F. FIELDING
                        COUNSEL TO THE PRESIDENT

SUBJECT   WAIVER UNDER 18 U.S.C. § 208(b)(1)

This memorandum provides a waiver, pursuant to 18 U.S.C. § 208(b)(1), that will allow you to participate in your position as Secretary of the United States Department of the Treasury, in particular matters affecting certain disqualifying financial interests in a defined benefit pension plan through your former employer, the Goldman Sachs Group, Inc. This waiver is based on disclosure of your financial interests and consideration of the nature and circumstances of the particular matters in which you may be involved as Secretary. Given the size of your overall investment portfolio, your financial interests in the matters covered by this waiver are not so substantial as to be likely to affect the integrity of your services to the Government.

Executive Branch employees are prohibited by 18 U.S.C. § 208(a) from participating personally and substantially in an official capacity in any particular matter that has a direct and predictable effect on either their financial interests or the interests of certain other persons whose interests are imputed to them. With the exception of your financial interest in the defined benefit pension plan for which this waiver is being issued, you may not participate personally and substantially in any particular matter that will have a direct and predicable effect on your financial interests or those of anyone whose interests are imputed to you, unless you first obtain a written waiver, pursuant to 18 U.S.C. § 208(b)(1), or qualify for a regulatory exemption, pursuant to 18 U.S.C. § 208(b)(2).

The term "particular matter" includes only matters that involve deliberation, decision, or action that is focused on the interests of specific persons, or a discrete and identifiable class of persons. The term may include matters that do not involve formal parties and may extend to legislation or policy making that is narrowly focused on the interests of a discrete and identifiable class of persons.

In your position as Secretary of the United States Department of the Treasury, you are responsible for serving the American people and strengthening national security by managing the U.S. Government's finances effectively, promoting economic growth and stability, and ensuring the safety, soundness, and security of the United States and international financial systems.

Paulson sought and received a "waiver" of his previously signed ethics agreement so he could participate in discussions about saving Goldman Sachs, his former employer.

Dick Fuld, confronted by an angry mob of citizens, after he told a congressional hearing, "This is a pain that will stay with me for the rest of my life."

After the crisis subsided, Robert Kindler, vice chairman of Morgan Stanley, had this license plate made as a joke and a reminder that, as he put it, "no one is too big to fail."

Shortly after sunrise, Greg Curl walked across the plaza of the Seagram Building, the thirty-eight-story masterpiece of architectural modernism and a Park Avenue landmark. He entered the lobby, checked his watch, and waited for his go-to adviser to arrive.

Curl, Bank of America's point man for a possible Lehman Brothers deal, had flown from Charlotte to New York with a team of over one hundred executives on Wednesday night to begin their diligence at Sullivan & Cromwell's Midtown conference center. To assist them Curl had enlisted Chris Flowers, a private-equity investor whose specialty was the arcana of the banking industry. The two made for an odd couple, given that Curl was a Bank of America veteran with a low profile and had few Wall Street connections, while Flowers was a fast-talking, and often profane, former Goldman Sachs banker whose daring deals often landed him in the headlines.

But as Curl had considered what to do about Lehman, his first thought was that he wanted Flowers at his side. Flowers could read a balance sheet in less than thirty seconds and was bold enough to offer an articulate and well-reasoned judgment of it. He had left Goldman in the late 1990s and started his own private-equity firm to invest in banks, a business in which he had done very well indeed, personally pocketing some $540 million from an investment in Shinsei Bank in Japan. He was regularly listed as one of the wealthiest men in America, and when he purchased a town house on the Upper East Side for $53 million, it set a record for Manhattan real estate.

Curl trusted very few bankers, but Flowers was an exception. He particularly admired Flowers's dispassionate, no-bullshit approach to deal making—and to life. In 2007, just before the credit crisis hit, they had bid together on Sallie Mae, the student-loan company. They soon realized the deal was a mistake, and for the rest of the year, they worked together to try to undo it. Curl hadn't held the Sallie Mae investment against Flowers, largely because Flowers was ultimately able to get them out of it by invoking an escape hatch in the merger agreement, with ensuing legal fireworks.

Flowers could be useful for more than just providing advice, as Curl knew that he might be eager to invest in Lehman alongside Bank of America. Curl thought that he might even be willing to take Lehman's riskiest assets.

When he had sought out Flowers just twenty-four hours earlier, Curl had found him in Tokyo, where Flowers had been in the middle of a board meeting of Shinsei. "You'll want to look at Lehman Brothers, and we want to look at it in partnership with you," Curl told him. "Can you get back to New York for this purpose?" Flowers hardly needed persuading and quickly arranged for a car to the airport to make the fourteen-hour flight back to Manhattan.

When Flowers arrived, clearly wearing the jetlag on his face, he had brought along Jacob Goldfield, a fellow Goldman alum. (Goldfield happened to be the banker depicted in Roger Lowenstein's *When Genius Failed* as surreptitiously downloading all of Long-Term Capital Management's information into a laptop during Goldman's attempt to assist the beleaguered firm; it was Goldfield whom Alex Kirk of Lehman had mentioned in his nervous comment to Fuld about providing information to Goldman Sachs a day earlier.)

Goldfield also knew Lehman well—he had helped Hank Greenberg examine the firm back in the spring when Greenberg was part of a group of investors who bought $6 billion of common and preferred shares.

On the flight over, Flowers had studied Lehman's second-quarter report from the day before and had focused on what he knew was going to be the big discussion point: the value of Lehman's real estate assets. Could they possibly be worth $25 to $30 billion?

Curl, Flowers, and Goldfield set up operations in a conference room that Sullivan & Cromwell provided, laid out with coffee and pastries.

This was going to be a long day.

———

With twenty-four hours to mull over Lehman's SpinCo plan, Wall Street analysts turned against it—and the firm—en masse. They blasted out skeptical e-mails to clients on Thursday morning, adding to the weight that was already dragging down Lehman's shares. The stock price had ended the previous day down 7 percent at $7.25; it was about to sink even lower.

"Management did not successfully put to rest the issues that had been pressuring the stock," William Tanona, an analyst at Goldman Sachs, declared in his e-mail.

Michael Mayo, an analyst who had kept a buy rating on Lehman shares since April 2007, sent out an even bleaker prognosis, given his concerns about the possible fallout as credit-rating firms grew more bearish about Lehman: "The change in rating agency posture is an unexpected negative that may create a distressed sale situation." In other words, a fire sale could be next. His buy rating was summarily removed.

Guy Moszkowski of Merrill Lynch was also grim on the subject of Lehman's sale prospects, writing that the firm could be forced to accept a "take-under"—Wall Street parlance for a takeover at a price below where a company's shares are trading.

Even analysts who believed that Lehman was basically sound were beginning to see that it had become a matter of perception trumping fundamentals: Lehman's tumbling stock price inflamed the market's fears, creating a self-fulfilling prophecy that was forcing Lehman to find a buyer, and fast.

As Wall Street analysts seemed poised to write the epitaph for Dick Fuld's firm, the only person to come to his public defense was John Mack, the man who Fuld had hoped would be his merger partner. Mack was quoted in the *Times* that morning as saying, "He is as feisty as ever, but there is no question this is wearing on him, as it would wear on anyone."

In private, however, Mack had just delivered shattering news in a phone call to Fuld: He didn't believe there was a good reason for Morgan Stanley to move forward with the talks.

However, there were still signs of life. Tim Geithner confirmed to Fuld that Barclays was indeed interested in bidding for the company, even though they had not contacted Fuld directly, and gave him Diamond's phone number in London.

"He knows you'll be calling," Geithner assured him.

"I understand I'm supposed to call you," Fuld said when he later reached Diamond.

Diamond, however, was clearly flustered, as he thought he had been explicit with Geithner that he *didn't* want to talk directly with Fuld about a deal. A deal would have to be brokered by the U.S. government.

"I think we should talk," Fuld said, trying to engage with him.

"I don't see an opportunity for us here," Diamond answered.

Fuld couldn't understand what was going on. *He had been told by Geithner to make this contact, and now Diamond was telling him that he wasn't interested?*

Unwilling to force the issue, he ended the conversation and called back Geithner.

"I just got off the phone with Bob Diamond," he told Geithner heatedly. "He says he's not interested. I thought you said he wanted to talk to us?"

"Yes, he does," Geithner insisted. "You should call him back."

Five minutes later, he tried Diamond again.

"I just told you that we're not interested," Diamond repeated.

Fuld, by now feeling as if he were part of some kind of charade, again phoned Geithner. "I don't know what's going on here. I've called him twice, and both times he says he doesn't want to talk to me. You tell me he's interested. He says he's not."

Geithner promised he'd reach out to Diamond and urged Fuld to try him one last time.

On his final attempt, Diamond was suddenly willing to talk.

"We're going to be flying over tonight," Diamond said. "I'll have a team ready to go by Friday morning."

With that sentence, it was official: Barclays and Bank of America were now in competition.

———

What Fuld hadn't been aware of was that for the entire morning, Diamond and his team had already been in contact with Geithner and Paulson and had come to an agreement that Barclays would examine Lehman's books as soon as possible. Fuld's role in any rescue effort was becoming a polite formality.

Before he left for New York that night, Diamond had hoped to receive some assurances that his trip would be worthwhile. On his call with Paulson, Diamond had specifically asked if Barclays could be the exclusive bidder for Lehman. He had read the news about Bank of America's interest, and he knew firsthand that it could be a formidable rival—and a potential spoiler.

A year earlier, Bank of America had jumped into the takeover battle for the Dutch bank ABN AMRO, a duel that pitted Barclays against a group that included the Royal Bank of Scotland. By agreeing to buy Chicago's LaSalle Bank from ABN for $21 billion, Bank of America had effectively snatched the crown jewel of the deal, which the RBS group was particularly coveting and whose absence from the portfolio made it more difficult to outbid Barclays. In the end, Barclays lost the bidding war for ABN, but Bank of America still got LaSalle. The failed deal was a blow for Diamond and his expansionist dreams, and he had always believed that Bank of America had hugely overpaid for the property.

"If BofA is going to be there, don't embarrass us," Diamond told Paulson. "Don't get us to do a deal and have BofA top us."

"You can't have an exclusive," Paulson responded. "But let me tell you, you're in a strong position, and I'll make sure you're not embarrassed."

Before the call ended, Diamond wanted to make another thing clear: He was looking for a "Jamie" deal—in other words, he might come looking for some form of government help.

Paulson stated firmly that no assistance from the government would be forthcoming, but added, "We'll figure out how to get you help."

———

As Tom Russo burst into Dick Fuld's office, the glum look on his face got Fuld's immediate attention, which was fairly remarkable, considering the general somberness on the thirty-first floor.

"What?" Fuld barked.

"I just got off the phone with Tom Baxter," Russo said, referring to the general counsel of the Federal Reserve of New York. "He said that Geithner wants you to resign from the board of the NY Fed." Russo paused to allow Fuld to take that news in before adding, "That given our position, it's too complicated, too many conflicts."

Geithner's request should not have come as a shock, for if there was even the possibility that the government was going to have to put up money as part of a deal to find Lehman a buyer, the last thing he would have wanted was to be seen as helping a member of his own board, an insider. The slightest appearance of favoritism could prove disastrous.

Fuld, even so, took the message as a personal slight and stared morosely down at the table. For a moment it looked as if he might cry, but he steadied himself and whispered, "I can't believe this."

Together Fuld and Russo dictated a resignation letter addressed to Stephen Friedman, chairman of the board of directors:

Dear Steve,

It is with deep regret that I hereby tender my resignation as a member of the Board of Directors of the Federal Reserve Bank of New York. In light of my current business situation at Lehman Brothers, I unfortunately do not have the time to devote to Board matters and, therefore, feel it is in the best interests of the Board that I resign, effective immediately. I have very much enjoyed my time on the Board and have enormous respect for both the Board and the institution. Thank you.

Sincerely,

With a restrained but heavy sigh, Fuld added his signature, scribbling a huge "D" in place above "Dick."

———

At 70 Pine Street the pressure was building as Bob Willumstad paced his office ahead of a crucial meeting that morning with the credit-rating agency, which had been making menacing noises about downgrades. He had just gotten off the phone with Geithner to follow up on their meeting about turning AIG into a broker-dealer, and to apply a little additional pressure. "We're a little busy right now with Lehman," Geithner apologized. "But let's talk again tomorrow morning."

It was only 10:30 a.m., but the marketplace was already sensing the nervousness that Willumstad had been trying his best to conceal all week. The cost to insure the debt of AIG had jumped by 15 percent to 612 basis points, the highest level in its history. That meant that it would cost investors $612,000 to insure $10 million of AIG's debt every year for the next five years. With Lehman clearly desperate to raise money, investors were betting AIG was soon going to face the same struggle. It might also have to pay out astronomical amounts to investors who were loading up on insurance to protect themselves from a potential Lehman default.

To make matters worse, Hank Greenberg, being deposed that day by the New York State attorney general about previous questionable accounting practices at AIG, badgered Willumstad at every chance. "What the hell are you people waiting for?" he demanded, wanting to know why efforts to shore up the company hadn't been moving more quickly.

Amid all the other pressures, Willumstad was still pressing to settle the long-running lawsuit that Greenberg had brought against the firm after he had been ousted. He had been counting on Greenberg's helping the firm raise some capital by leveraging his relationships in Asia, where he had built AIG into a powerhouse that dominated the tricky and semitransparent Japanese and Chinese markets. He told Greenberg he'd have his lawyer, Jamie Gamble, at Simpson Thacher, set up a meeting with Greenberg's lawyer, David Boies, to try to come up with a settlement Greenberg could live with.

Perhaps the most pressing problem weighing on Willumstad was the result of a conversation he had had with Jamie Dimon earlier in the week. "We seem to be not getting enough done," Willumstad had told him, urging him to help raise capital or lend the firm the money himself.

"Well, you know, you got a bigger problem than we had anticipated," Dimon replied. "Our models show you're running out of money next week."

It was then that Willumstad accepted the fact that JP Morgan might well not be willing to provide any further funds. AIG's treasurer, Robert Gender, had already warned him that that might be the case, but Willumstad hadn't fully believed him. "JP Morgan's always tough," he reminded Gender. "Citi will do anything you ask them to do; they just say yes." But the prudent Gender only acidly replied, "Quite frankly, we can use some of the discipline that JP Morgan is pushing on us."

Dimon had been encouraging Willumstad to just come up with a plan, even if it wasn't perfect. "It doesn't have to be in place," Dimon told him. "You just have to tell the markets what you're going to do and then go and do it. If you need to raise capital, tell them you need to raise capital."

A lot of good that did Lehman yesterday, Willumstad thought.

Finally, the time came for the dreaded meeting with Moody's. Steve Black from JP Morgan had come downtown to lend some credibility to the affair and to help answer questions about AIG's plans to raise capital. It was one thing for Willumstad to state that he had every intention of raising capital and quite another entirely to have the president of JP Morgan affirm that he intended to support the company in that effort. The stakes were high: If the agency cut AIG's credit rating by even one notch, it could trigger a collateral call of $10.5 billion. If Standard & Poor's followed suit, which was likely—"the blind leading the blind," Willumstad said of them—the figure would rise to $13.3 billion. Should that happen, and AIG be unable to come up with the extra capital, it would be a virtual death sentence.

No more than fifteen minutes into the meeting, the Moody's analyst made it clear that the agency would downgrade AIG by at least one notch and possibly two. By Willumstad's calculations, if they did so on Monday, the company would have at least three days before it would have to post the collateral. That meant he had until Wednesday, or at the latest, Thursday, to come up with an astronomical amount of money.

JP Morgan's Black feared they had even less time; by his count, Tuesday morning would be their deadline. After the meeting, he pulled Willumstad aside and warned him, "You guys are going to get downgraded, so you better start figuring out now what to do."

Willumstad nodded. "We need to prepare for that. I totally agree with that."

Black left the building even more down on the company than when he had arrived. *Nobody,* he thought, *is moving nearly as fast as he needs to.*

In the General Motors Building, which occupies an entire block on Fifth Avenue and Fifty-ninth Street, Harvey Miller, the legendary bankruptcy lawyer at Weil, Gotshal & Manges, got up from his desk and began pacing. As he made a circuit of his office, he gazed at the miniature Texaco trucks and Eastern Airlines jets that dotted his bookshelves, mementos of two of his most famous cases.

At seventy-five, Miller was considered the dean of bankruptcy law, and he billed clients nearly $1,000 an hour for his services. Besides Texaco and Eastern, he had been involved in the bankruptcies of Sunbeam, Drexel Burnham Lambert, and Enron, and was also among the lawyers who'd represented the city of New York during its financial crisis in the 1970s.

Always reassuringly calm, he was also known for his deftly tailored suits, his love of opera, and his ability to speak in long, eloquent paragraphs. He had grown up in the Gravesend neighborhood of Brooklyn, the son of a wood-flooring salesman, and was the first in his family to receive an education beyond high school, attending Brooklyn College. After a stint in the army, he went to Columbia Law.

At that time, bankruptcy was one of the few areas of corporate finance that smaller, predominantly Jewish law firms dominated in the still-WASP-dominated industry. In 1963 Miller joined the small bankruptcy shop Seligson & Morris; six years later, Ira Millstein, the governance guru, recruited Miller to start a bankruptcy and restructuring practice at Weil Gotshal.

Earlier that afternoon, the firm's chairman, Stephen J. Dannhauser, had phoned him and posed a startling question: Would the firm be available to do some preliminary work on Lehman—just in case? Miller said he understood; he had been reading the financial press. Lehman was a very important client—the firm's biggest, in fact, and the source of more than $40 million in fees annually. He knew the company very well.

Dannhauser had received a call from Steven Berkenfeld, a Lehman managing director, who told him they should get their ducks in order if things didn't go well in the next seventy-two hours. Before Berkenfeld ended the call, he insisted that Dannhauser keep their conversation confidential—Berkenfeld hadn't even told Fuld that he was contacting Weil Gotshal.

As a bankruptcy lawyer, Miller was well accustomed to engaging in these delicate pas de deux with clients. "Bankruptcy," he once said, "is like dancing with an eight-hundred-pound gorilla. You dance as long as the gorilla wants to dance."

Just a few hours later, however, Miller received another call from the embattled bank.

"I'm Tom Russo, the chief legal officer of Lehman Brothers," the voice on the other end of the line bellowed. "Are you working on Lehman?"

Miller, who did not know Russo, was taken aback. "Well, yes, as it happens."

Russo had no interest in discussing any details but wanted to deliver a message: "You know you can't talk about this to *anybody*. It's a very tense situation. We can't have any rumors coming out."

Miller was about to assure him that he appreciated the urgency of the matter when Russo asked anxiously, "How many people do you have working on it?"

"Ah, maybe four," Miller told him. "It's ah, preliminary at this point."

"Yes, preliminary," Russo insisted. "Don't add any more people. We've got to keep it contained."

Russo ended the call, leaving a baffled Miller to wonder precisely what was going on.

———

With his team over at Sullivan & Cromwell working with Bank of America, Dick Fuld decided to call Ken Lewis in Charlotte. After all, if they were going to do a deal, he figured that they should start talking CEO to CEO.

When Fuld reached Lewis, he launched into a heartfelt soliloquy about working together and how excited he was about the merger, marrying Lehman Brothers' top-flight investment banking franchise with Bank of America's massive commercial bank. The resources of the combined entity, he suggested, could match those of JP Morgan and Citigroup, finally making Bank of America a true financial supermarket.

Lewis listened patiently, not exactly certain how to respond. In his mind he wasn't negotiating with Fuld; he was negotiating with the government. Whatever Fuld had to say was, frankly, irrelevant.

Before ending the call, Fuld, feeling confident, said: "You and I both know we're doing this deal. Glad we're partners."

———

BlackRock was in the middle of a two-day board meeting at its headquarters on Fiftieth Street, just off Madison Avenue, when the markets closed for the day. As a part owner of BlackRock, Merrill has two seats on BlackRock's board, and John Thain and Greg Fleming, who were attending that day, quickly consulted their BlackBerrys to check the closing prices. Merrill's shares had fallen 16.6 percent to $19.43, the most of any investment bank that day besides Lehman, whose shares had tumbled 42 percent, to $4.22. If Lehman was in this much trouble, the general thinking seemed to be going, Merrill could well be next.

During a break in the meeting, Fleming stepped outside to make a phone call. He had been thinking all day about the conversation he had had with Herlihy about the possibility of a deal with Bank of America. He had yet to approach Thain about it, waiting for just the right opportunity to present itself.

He had, however, spoken privately with John Finnegan, a Merrill board member with whom he was close. Finnegan, who, like Fleming, tended to be nervous by nature, had worried that Thain would have little interest in selling the firm; he had, after all, only been named CEO ten months earlier.

The person Fleming needed to contact now was Rodgin Cohen, also a close friend and, he knew, Lehman's lawyer. Fleming was eager to get a reading on how the talks with Bank of America were going and how desperate the situation had become for Lehman—and, consequently, for Merrill.

When Cohen, who had been in a conference room with the Lehman team meeting with Bank of America, stepped out to take the call, Fleming greeted him casually, as if this were merely a social communication. After the obligatory pleasantries, he offhandedly remarked on Merrill's stock price decline and then told Cohen, "We're thinking about our options. I don't know how much runway we have."

But Cohen was quickly on to Fleming; he knew Merrill was in no position to buy Lehman. And, being a student of the M&A business, he knew Fleming probably wanted to do a deal with Bank of America, thwarting Lehman's own efforts.

"There's not much I can say," Cohen told him.

Abandoning any attempt to conceal his motives, Fleming confided in Cohen, "We've got to do a deal. The numbers are looking too risky. If Lehman goes, we'll be next."

Cohen didn't know how to respond, other than to excuse himself as quickly as possible. For now, at least, he would keep the conversation confidential.

———

When Steve Black got back to his office at JP Morgan from AIG, he described the meeting to Dimon as "a fucking nightmare." He asked Tim Main to call Brian Schreiber to get an update on AIG's latest forecast and to see if Schreiber had signed the engagement letter—essentially a specification of JP Morgan's terms for trying to put AIG back together again.

Main told Black that the document had not yet been signed but that he would call that afternoon to check on its status. "Can we schedule my weekly beating at two p.m.?" he asked, only half joking. His relationship with the AIG folks remained as frosty as ever.

When Main finally got through to Schreiber, he asked without any preamble, "So, where are you on the engagement letter?"

Schreiber had always believed that the terms of the engagement letter were excessive. Not only was JP Morgan asking for a $10 million fee, but the bank was also demanding that it be guaranteed work on any big AIG assignment over the next two years.

"Where are you on the repo commitment?" Schreiber retorted indignantly.

Main, who was already angry about rumors he'd heard that Schreiber had also been talking to Blackstone and Deutsche Bank, finally lost his temper. "Are you fucking *kidding*? You think we're going to lend you money?" he barked. But he was just getting warmed up. "You're running a shitty process. Your company is *fucked*! You're working with other bankers that you're not telling us about. You're carving it all up."

"Don't scream at me," Schreiber replied coldly. "I'm not going to take this from you. I've got to talk to Bob."

Five minutes later Schreiber was angrily recounting the conversation to Willumstad, who in turn called Black to demand an explanation for Main's behavior.

Instead of offering an apology, though, Black exploded at him as well. "There's no sense of urgency down there; you guys don't have anything close to the information that you need to be trying to make decisions," Black said. "Every time we ask for something, you drag your feet. We sent an engagement letter three weeks ago, and Brian is still dickin' around with signing it.

"We'll do whatever you want us to do," Black finally said wearily. "But if this is the way it's going to go, then you might as well . . . we should probably resign. You should get somebody else. This has gotten to a poisonous point, and the people that work for you don't get the position that you guys are in."

"If you were that upset about it, why didn't you just call me?" Willumstad asked.

When the call came in from Ken Lewis late Thursday afternoon, Paulson knew what he was about to hear.

"We've looked at it and we can't do it—we can't do it without government assistance," Lewis said levelly. "We just can't do it because we can't get there." Like many of Lehman's critics at the time, including the anxious shareholders who were flooding the market with sell orders, Lewis said that the valuations that Lehman had placed on its assets were far too high. Buying them could expose Bank of America to huge risks.

Given that Bob Diamond of Barclays had already come to him, hat in hand, looking for a government assist in a Lehman deal, Paulson had fully expected Lewis would do the same.

But Paulson still wasn't prepared to resort to drawing on federal money—at least not yet. It was politically unpalatable, especially with the Fannie and Freddie bailouts still making headlines. And if this was going to become a negotiation, Paulson didn't want to show all his cards so early on.

He knew, however, that he needed to keep Bank of America in the hunt, so he offered, "Okay, if you need help on assets, you tell us what you need help on, and we will come up with a way to get there."

Lewis, nonplussed, replied, "I thought you said there would be no public money."

"I will work on this," Paulson promised. "We will get the private sector to get involved."

Private-sector involvement was a concept that Paulson and Geithner had been discussing all day—the assembly of a consortium of banks to help subsidize a sale of Lehman, if Bank of America or Barclays refused to do the deal on its own. But neither Paulson nor Geithner had completely fleshed out the idea yet, and even in the best of times, herding bankers was a feat far from easy.

Lewis paused, not at all pleased with what Paulson seemed to be suggesting. He didn't want to get involved in a quasi-public-private rescue; he wanted a Jamie deal. And he knew full well that his rivals were unlikely to want to foot the bill so he could buy Lehman for a song.

Lewis nonetheless agreed that he would keep examining Lehman with an eye toward making a bid. With so much at stake, he assumed he would ultimately get some sort of assistance—whatever form it might take.

———

On Thursday afternoon, David Boies, Hank Greenberg's lawyer, arrived at the offices of Simpson Thacher to meet with AIG's lawyers: Dick Beattie, the chairman of the firm; and Jamie Gamble. Only a small circle knew about the meeting or what it was intended to accomplish. After four years of public battles, AIG was about to reach a settlement with Greenberg, one that would bring him back into the company fold. Willumstad had instructed Beattie and Gamble to get in a room with Boies and hammer out a deal once and for all.

Given the tumult in the market, Willumstad was eager to announce that Greenberg was returning to AIG as its chairman emeritus. The news would certainly come as a shock, but Willumstad was hoping the settlement might buy them some time and goodwill from investors, many of whom were still Greenberg loyalists.

Willumstad also knew that Greenberg was fervent about helping AIG raise capital, and given Greenberg's deep relationships with wealthy investors in Asia and the Middle East, he could prove to be an asset.

They still had to work out the details, but they had come to an agreement in principle that would resolve the dispute. AIG would turn over $15 million worth of artwork, papers, and property that Greenberg believed was his and AIG would pay for Greenberg to defend himself in the dozens of shareholder lawsuits that had been brought against him. In return, Greenberg would turn over somewhere between 25 to 50 million AIG shares that had been held by Starr International in a trust and had been at the center of the dispute. In total, the settlement would cost Greenberg as much as $860 million based on AIG's share price that day, but it would end AIG's $4.3 billion lawsuit against him and would reinstall him within the company that he loved so dearly.

With the basics of the settlement agreed, Boies, wearing a blue blazer and casual black Merrell shoes, thanked the other men and suggested that they try to memorialize the arrangement by getting Willumstad and Greenberg in the same room to wrap it up the following week.

"Call me this weekend," Boies said to them as he turned to leave.

———

Paolo Tonucci, Lehman's global treasurer, looked horror-stricken as he set down his cell phone. "I've got to talk to you right now!" he said quietly to Bart McDade and Rodgin Cohen. "We've got a real problem."

Everything had been going smoothly at Sullivan & Cromwell's Midtown offices, where they had been helping Bank of America with its due diligence, but now, as Tonucci revealed, "JP Morgan is pulling another $5 billion in collateral from us! I just got off the phone with Jane Byers Russo [head of JP Morgan's broker-dealer unit]. She says that we need to wire it by tomorrow. And she might pull another $10 billion by the weekend."

"*What?*" Cohen asked, clearly dismayed by the demands. "This sounds unbelievable. I don't understand this. I know everyone's in panic mode, but this is too much."

Tonucci shared the news with his boss, Ian Lowitt, Lehman's CFO, and the rest of the room.

"This is bullshit," McGee yelled out, breaking an awkward silence.

Tonucci and Lowitt called Fuld to tell him the news and to set up a conference call with Jamie Dimon. "Listen, we need you to send us the collateral," Dimon told the group when he finally clicked into the call, saying it was a fair request to make given Lehman's deteriorating position. Fuld calmly told Dimon he'd have his team work on it. Tonucci, however, whispered to the Lehman team, "Does Dick not understand? It's almost operationally impossible for us to do that." Dimon, too, worried that Fuld might be treating the matter far too casually. "Are you taking notes?" Dimon snapped. When the call ended, McDade was apoplectic. "We have to call the Fed," he said. "Jamie can't just do this."

Cohen, who had had the most experience of any of them with Fed matters, wasn't so sure. "I'm quite sure Jamie has been there before us," he told them. "Jamie's tough. He wouldn't have done this without the tacit approval of the Fed."

For the next ten minutes the room was a cacophony of different conversations taking place simultaneously, all on the common theme of *They're trying to put us out of business!* Finally they decided that the best step to take was to call Tim Geithner.

When Cohen reached Geithner and put him on speakerphone, he quickly explained the situation to him. Geithner appeared unconcerned, as if he had been expecting their call. McGee shot a nervous glance at McDade, as if to say, *We're fucked.* "I cannot advise a bank not to protect itself," Geithner said unperturbedly.

Cohen, politely hoping to get Geithner to realize that he believed JP

Morgan was doing this to undermine its rival, asked, "Do they need that protection?"

"I'm not in a position to judge that," Geithner answered.

———

At 6:00 p.m. Paulson joined a strategy call with Geithner, Bernanke, and Cox. He felt they were about to go into crisis mode and feared another Bear Stearns–like weekend. This time, however, he was determined that it end differently. He believed they needed to prepare what he called a "LTCM-like solution"—in other words, he was committed to the idea of encouraging firms in the private sector to band together and put their own money up to somehow save Lehman Brothers. Geithner was supporting the concept, and apparently some Wall Street chiefs were as well. Geithner had received calls from both John Thain of Merrill Lynch and Vikram Pandit of Citigroup earlier in the day suggesting just such a solution.

Paulson was also deeply concerned about the apparent lack of resolve of both Bank of America and Barclays to "cross the finish line." He had come to feel that Bank of America was merely going through the motions and was anxious that Barclays wasn't especially serious about coming to an agreement either. "Listen, the thing about these Brits is that they always talk and they never close," he told them. He also had a particular instinct about Barclays' chairman, John Varley, whom he remembered from his Goldman days as a waffler. "Let me tell you," Paulson said, "Varley is a weak man."

Perhaps most important, Paulson stressed, was that they couldn't afford the political liability of putting up government money for Lehman as they had for Bear Stearns. "I can't be Mr. Bailout," he insisted. He had been getting calls from politicians all week suggesting as much. Senator Dodd had called earlier to tell Paulson, "Fuld is a friend. Try to help, but don't bail Lehman out." Given that everyone on the conference call had already lived through the backlash of the Bear deal, they hardly needed convincing about not wanting to repeat it.

Still, Geithner was a bit hesitant about taking such a severe stance in public, but only because, as he explained, "we don't want to scare people away. We need as many bidders in this as possible."

Nonetheless, he quickly fell in line, and the four men made a pact:

Unless something miraculous happened, they would plan to place calls to the CEOs of the major Wall Street houses late on Friday and have them all come down to the NY Fed, where they'd press them to come up with a private solution.

In the meantime, Paulson instructed them, the message should be clear: *No bailouts.*

———

Brian Schreiber, removing his thick-framed glasses to rub his eyes, could see from his examination of AIG's daily cash tally that the firm could soon be out of money if it didn't start selling assets quickly. He nervously began working through the list of people whom he could call whose companies would be capable of providing assistance almost immediately.

The first name that occurred to him was Chris Flowers. His fund had several billion dollars available to buy financial-services assets, and as a former financial-services banker he understood the insurance business well enough that he could move instantly if he was interested. They had also worked together before; Flowers had sought to partner with the firm to buy some smaller insurance companies in the past.

Schreiber tracked down Flowers over at Sullivan & Cromwell, still doing diligence on Lehman's books.

"We have a huge problem," Schreiber told him. "We're going to run out of cash shortly, um, and, you know, we only have, you know, one or two shots to get this right."

"Well, I'm in the middle of Lehman here," Flowers replied. "I'm working with BofA."

"Is there any way you could come down here tomorrow?" Schreiber persisted.

"We'll come take a look," he said somewhat noncommittally, uncertain whether he'd be finished with Lehman by then, and then added, "I see this is really important."

———

After ending his conference call with Geithner and Bernanke, Paulson summoned Michele Davis, his head of communications, to his office.

"So, I talked to Lewis and Diamond. They're, of course, all saying that they want government money," he told her. "And we've got Pelosi and everybody else all over us," he added, referring to rumblings that the

Speaker of the House had made expressing her disapproval of any more bailouts.

Davis had brought with her a handful of articles that had already been published by the major papers on the Internet, and it was clear that a possible bailout would be the primary focus of the following day's news cycle.

A Dow Jones article published at 7:03 p.m., just minutes earlier, opened: "With a beleaguered Lehman Brothers Holdings Inc. likely to be sold, one key issue is what a backstop from the Federal Reserve, if it materialized, would look like."

"You cannot have this in tomorrow's headlines, tomorrow's newspapers saying this," Davis said, shaking her head. "Everyone is going to think, *Oh, Hank is coming with his checkbook.* That is not the way you want to start this negotiation." As a former staffer herself, she was also aware of the Bush administration's stand on the matter, and knew how politically problematic it would be if the possibility of a bailout of a major Wall Street firm were even being entertained.

Although the subject was left unspoken, both she and Paulson knew another reason a Lehman bailout could quickly become a public relations nightmare: Bush's brother, Jeb, the former governor of Florida, worked as an adviser to Lehman's private-equity business. Bush's cousin, George H. Walker IV, was on the firm's executive committee. And then there was Paulson's brother, Richard. The press, needless to say, would have a field day.

"We should make some calls," she urged him, subtly suggesting they begin leaking to the press word that the government wouldn't be pursuing any bailout of Lehman.

Paulson mulled over his dilemma. He had always opted to be cautious with the press and hated the very idea of leaking as a tactic. But he trusted Davis's instincts, and in any case, he preferred not to get his own hands dirty in the matter.

"Do what we need to do," he told her. "Just, you know, don't have it be me on the record."

———

As soon as Paulson awoke on Friday, he began poring through the morning papers, looking for evidence of Davis's handiwork. The message was supposed to have been made clear: *Read Our Lips: No More Bailouts.*

0

The mood in Washington was not hard to discern: There was no desire whatsoever for any further Wall Street rescues. All punditry could talk about was moral hazard, as if it were some sort of emerging disease that had just reached pandemic proportions. Bail out Lehman, the thinking went, and you will make bailouts the default solution at a time when no firm seems safe.

And what could be more satisfying than having your decision—the buck stopped there, thank you very much—manifested on the front pages of the country's leading publications? Paulson first turned expectantly to the newspaper of financial record, the *Wall Street Journal*, and was sorely disappointed. The A1 article about the financial crisis merely tiptoed around the issue without ever being forceful enough about it, he thought as he read the piece. As close as the reporter got to explaining his position was this sentence: "Federal officials currently aren't expected to structure a bailout along the lines of the Bear transaction or this past weekend's rescue of mortgage giants Fannie Mae and Freddie Mac."

The *New York Times* was even worse: "But while the Treasury Department and Fed were working to broker an orderly sale of Lehman, it was unclear whether the Fed would stand behind any deal, particularly after the Bush administration took control of the nation's two largest mortgage finance companies only days ago."

No, that doesn't quite capture what they have been trying to convey, Paulson thought.

He turned to the *Journal*'s editorial page, where the air was typically more rarefied, and was able to take solace, as conservatives so often had, in its hyperintellectual and at times harsh right-wing opinions. The typically unsigned editorial was called "Lehman's Fate," and its position was right out of Paulson's playbook.

"At least in the Bear case," the *Journal* editorial read, "there was some legitimate fear of systemic risk. The Federal Reserve's discount window hadn't yet been opened to investment banks, and so there was some chance of a larger liquidity panic.

"That's far less likely with Lehman. The discount window is now wide open to Merrill Lynch and Morgan Stanley, among others, and federal regulators have had months to inspect the value of Lehman's assets and its various counterparties. If the feds step in to save Lehman after Bear and Fannie Mae, we will no longer have exceptions forged in a crisis. We will have a new de facto federal policy of underwriting Wall Street that will encourage even more reckless risk taking."

Yes, yes, all true, Paulson thought as he finished the editorial. Still, it didn't go far enough. He needed somehow to make it clear to all the banks that there would be no handouts, no more "Jamie Deals." And he needed to do so in a way that would leave no room for misunderstanding.

When he arrived at the office Paulson walked down the hall into Michele Davis's office and asked sullenly, "What do we do?"

"I'd rather say today that we don't want to use our money and on Sunday night have to explain why we were backed into a corner," Davis told him. "You want me to call Liesman?" she asked.

Liesman was Steve Liesman, CNBC's economics reporter, known popularly as "The Professor." Davis had a good relationship with him and had successfully leaked other information to him; Paulson considered him both intelligent and sympathetic to their cause. He could get the word out quickly and accurately.

Yes, the Professor, Paulson smiled. *He'll know what to do with this.*

———

As Ed Herlihy sat in his office working on Bank of America's bid, he kept his TV on mute, until at around 9:15 a.m. he saw the headline crawl across the bottom of CNBC's screen—"Breaking News: Source: There will be no government money in the resolution of LEH situation"—and quickly turned up the volume to hear what Steve Liesman was telling David Faber, the network's mergers reporter.

"Let me start here with a comment that I just got from a person familiar with Paulson, State Secretary Treasurer [*sic*] Hank Paulson," Liesman explained. "He's saying there will be no government money in the resolution of this situation."

Herlihy turned the volume even higher.

"They're saying there are two things that make the Lehman deal different," Liesman continued. "The market's been aware and had time to prepare for over six months, and the second is the PDCF, that is, the access of the investment banks to the Fed's emergency window that exists now, to allow for an orderly process."

It was a lot to take in, and the Professor turned the floor over to his colleague. "David, what do you think of that?"

"An interesting gamble," Faber replied. "Would the government be willing to say, 'Hey, you're on your own?' There's divided opinion in terms of what the ultimate risk will be to the creditors, to everybody involved in the credit default swap market where Lehman certainly is a counterparty on many trades."

Liesman added: "I'm sure the Federal Reserve is looking for a situation where it can say, 'There is moral hazard out there. You will take a hit if you did not pay attention for the last six months.'"

Herlihy couldn't believe what he was hearing and ran into the conference room across the way where an army of bankers and Bank of America executives was mulling over documents.

"Did you just see what they just said on CNBC?" Herlihy asked Curl, almost out of breath. Curl not only hadn't, but seemed slightly annoyed that he'd even been asked the question.

"Look, guys, we got a real problem here," Herlihy insisted, after noticing he wasn't getting much of a reaction from anyone in the room.

After Herlihy recounted the details of the Liesman interview, Curl only rolled his eyes. *Why was Herlihy taking the CNBC report so seriously?* To him, the channel was a professional rumor mill.

"It's coming from Treasury," Herlihy stressed again. "That's Paulson. They're trying to send us a message!"

Herlihy was media-savvy enough to know how the game worked: When he had been at Treasury just a week earlier during the takeover of Fannie-Freddie, he had watched the department deftly leak news out to the public through its favorite reporter, Liesman.

The room turned sour, as even Curl acknowledged that Herlihy had a point.

"How serious do you think they are?" Curl asked.

———

Before heading back uptown for the second day of the BlackRock board meeting, John Thain decided to hold a conference call with his own board. With the markets gyrating and rumors flying, he wanted to make it clear publicly that Merrill was solid. Already there was a news report that morning quoting Malcolm Polley, chief investment officer at Stewart Capital Advisors, saying, "I think the market's telling you that if Lehman is going to go away, Merrill is probably the next victim."

Thain first briefed the board on recent market swings, which showed no sign of stopping. One look at the futures made it clear that stocks were likely to sink at the opening bell. With Merrill down 16 percent the previous day, things were only going to get worse.

The discussion quickly turned to Lehman. Thain told the board what he knew, which wasn't too different from what had been reported in the papers, except that Thain was getting his information directly from Geithner: Bank of America and Barclays were both vying to buy Lehman.

John Finnegan, a chief executive of the insurer Chubb, sounded worried. "Lehman is going down, and the shorts are coming after us next," he told Thain. "Tell me how this story is going to end differently."

Thain, frustrated by the remark, had never liked being challenged. "We are not Lehman," he said, his eyes flashing behind his glasses, and then repeated for emphasis, *"We're not Lehman."*

Regaining his usual composure, Thain calmly rehearsed the virtues of Merrill. "We have a wealth-management business that's going to have value no matter what," he told the board. "And we own half of BlackRock, which would also have value no matter what—so our stock's not going to zero."

———

Fuld was growing restless. It was 9:30 a.m., Lehman's stock opened down 9 percent to $3.84, and he hadn't heard from Diamond in over twelve hours.

"So where are we?" Fuld asked Diamond when he finally reached him.

"I've literally just gotten the okay from my board that we can pursue this," said Diamond, who had arrived in New York from London after midnight the night before. "We've just begun doing diligence with your public filings."

Before he continued, however, Diamond decided that he needed to be blunt with Fuld. "To be honest," he said stiffly, "this is a horrible situation for you, because we're only going to be interested if the price is quite distressed."

Fuld, leaning back in his desk chair, looked at Russo, who had taken a seat across the desk for the call. He understood.

"You and I should talk, because you should know exactly what my ideas are, what my plans are," Diamond said. He suggested meeting at noon at the Racquet and Tennis Club, a members-only establishment on Park Avenue and Fifty-second Street, where they would be able to get a private meeting room.

"No, no, no. You don't understand. I can't walk out of here," Fuld insisted. "There's photographers all over the place. Why don't you come over here? We can sneak you in the back. I'll send my car for you."

"AIG Shares Fall 20 Percent on Mortgage Woes" proclaimed the Reuters headline at 10:14 a.m.

Catherine Seifert, a Standard & Poor's analyst, had just released a research note saying that the stock was falling on "concerns about AIG's ability to shed its troubled mortgage-related assets, and we expect the shares to remain volatile as investors await news from the company."

As he followed these stories with increasing alarm, Bob Willumstad decided to call Jamie Dimon. He was increasingly frustrated with the JP Morgan team and needed assurances.

"Jamie, we're going to get downgraded," he told him. "You need to help me figure out how to get $18 billion. There's no plan for the end of September anymore," he added, referring to his plan to announce the results of his firmwide review and a new strategy at the end of the month. He stopped to let that sink in and then continued, "You know, if you guys can't help us, tell me now, but we've got to do *something* this weekend. We hired you guys to do this," he said, his voice rising ever so slightly. "Listen, just tell me if you can't, just tell me now."

"Look, we want to make this work," Dimon said, sounding a contrite note. "Give me five minutes and I'll call you back."

When he phoned back he apologized on behalf of the firm and said that he would take Black off the case; his other lieutenant, Doug Braunstein, who ran the firm's investment banking practice, would now be in charge. Braunstein, a no-nonsense deal maker, had been entrusted with some of the firm's biggest transactions after working his way up the ranks, initially at First Boston in the 1980s, and then at Chase. He helped negotiate the firm's acquisition of JP Morgan, its purchase of Bank One (bringing Dimon with it), and then the Bear Stearns deal. "We're going to send Braunstein down with the team, and we're going to see what we can do about raising capital for you over the weekend." Dimon promised him that he'd keep "the trains on the tracks."

As he ended the conversation with Dimon, another call came in—Tim Geithner, who was finally getting back to Willumstad.

"So, where are we?" Geithner asked.

"We're working on a capital raise," Willumstad explained. "And we're talking to some bidders for assets that may come in this weekend. We expect to have some more information later in the day."

"We're going to send over some of our market guys this morning to help," Geithner told him in a tone that made it clear that this was not an offer but an order. "Keep me posted," Geithner said before hanging up.

The conversation had lasted no more than thirty seconds.

By now Hank Paulson had become so agitated by the problems at Lehman that he scarcely noticed his assistant, Christal West, trying to get his attention. Alistair Darling, the chancellor of the Exchequer of Britain, was on the line.

Paulson had gotten to know Darling over the past two years, and though they had visited each other on both sides of the Atlantic, they had not grown close. Paulson considered Darling more a politician than a businessman, and he had nothing like the experience that Paulson himself had had in financial markets. But he respected Darling's judgment and admired the quick and decisive action he had taken a year earlier when Northern Rock, one of Britain's biggest mortgage lenders, was on the brink of failing. Darling has prevented a run on the bank by authorizing the Bank of England to lend Northern Rock billions of dollars to guarantee its deposits. That incident had been an early wake-up call for Paulson.

Darling, who had just ended a daylong meeting in Nice with other European finance ministers, made a bit of chitchat and, after an awkward pause, said that he was calling about Barclays. "You should know that we have serious concerns about this deal," he told Paulson sternly.

Paulson tried to assuage him, explaining that there was another bidder,

Bank of America, involved in the matter as well. He also spoke about the systemic importance of Lehman Brothers to the global economy and stressed how a deal between Barclays and Lehman would turn Barclays into an international giant with the might of Wall Street behind it. Paulson explained that he was trying to put together an industry consortium to aid a bid by either Barclays or Bank of America.

Nonetheless, with characteristic British understatement, Darling continued to express apprehension about any potential purchase and said adamantly, "Barclays shouldn't take on any more risk than they could possibly manage."

Paulson, confidently dismissing his concerns, promised him he'd keep him updated throughout the weekend.

———

Bob Diamond arrived at Lehman's headquarters in Fuld's Mercedes and was taken through the back entrance, avoiding the battalion of cameras stationed out front. Hoping to keep any of Lehman's staff from seeing the visitor, the firm's security team shuttled him up in the building's freight elevator and hurriedly led him to Fuld's office.

Fuld offered him a cup of coffee, and between Fuld's anxiety and Diamond's not having slept, they both looked like hell.

Diamond was clearly in a rush to get to Simpson Thacher, where his team of bankers had just begun diligence, and he wanted to dig into the numbers himself. He walked Fuld through the day's plan and then discussed the various synergies and overlaps between the two firms.

In the middle of Diamond's presentation, Fuld interrupted him and told him there was something he wanted to get off his chest. An almost frightening intensity came over him as he began to speak.

"Look into the whites of my eyes," he said. "There isn't enough room for both of us at the top here. We both know that." He paused and stared at Diamond intently. "I'm willing to step aside to make this work for the firm."

For Fuld, it was the biggest concession he could offer: to give up the firm he loved.

For Diamond, the moment was somewhat baffling. He had never imagined Fuld would stay; he didn't want him to.

"If there's a way for me to help with a transition, help with clients, you know, I will do that," Fuld offered.

"I've always heard you were a good man," Diamond told Fuld consolingly. "Now you've proven that."

———

After a twenty-minute crawl through traffic on the FDR Drive, Chris Flowers finally arrived at AIG's offices just before noon. He was led to a meeting room where Willumstad, Schreiber, Steven J. Bensinger (the firm's CFO), and a team of others were waiting. Schreiber immediately passed around a one-page summary of the firm's cash outflows that was set up like a calendar: Each day from Friday through the next Wednesday was marked with various scenarios, depending on the outcome of Moody's decision about its credit rating. If the executives hadn't yet come to appreciate the full extent of the quandary in which they now found themselves, Schreiber's document put it into stark relief. By next Wednesday, the calendar indicated, the parent company would be negative $5 billion, with the shortfall each successive day only growing worse.

Flowers's eyes widened as he studied the numbers. "You guys have a real problem here."

"Yes. But we should be okay if we can make the capital raise work," Willumstad said.

"Have you guys thought about Chapter 11?" Flowers blurted out. It was as if he had touched the third rail.

"Why are you using words like that?" Bensinger asked, clearly upset.

"Um, I can assure you," Flowers told him, "that if you don't pay people $5 billion on Wednesday, they're going to be really, *really* upset, so you can call it whatever you want, but they are not going to be happy if you don't pay them on Wednesday."

Just then Jamie Dimon called back and was patched into the conference room's speakerphone.

Schreiber described the potential cash-flow problems and their plans to fix them. "I've begun putting together a process for the weekend," he said, explaining how they'd reach out to possible suitors beginning that afternoon. He also walked through the company's various divisions and the amount of cash that each had on hand.

Before Schreiber could continue with his inventory, Dimon cut him off. "You're a smart guy but you're running a fucked-up process." The worst-case scenario that Schreiber was describing wasn't anywhere near bad enough, Dimon insisted, and scoffed, "You guys have no idea what you're doing. This is amateurish, it's pathetic."

Even worse, Dimon didn't think that they had an accurate read of their financial data. As far as he could tell, Schreiber was simply reading off a sheet of siloed information that had never been aggregated and analyzed in one piece.

"You guys need to get a handle on the numbers," he said. "The real numbers. You need to sit down with those numbers and figure out the size of the real hole, not the made-up hole. How big is the securities lending? You have to go contract by contract, like bottoms-up, real work. Then you need to make a list of who can help you fill it. This isn't like, you know, you're going to be late on your credit card bill."

Willumstad just stared at the speakerphone in silence. He knew this routine well from their days with Sandy Weill: This was Jamie the hothead. *Better to shrug it off*, Willumstad thought. The worst part of Dimon's tirade, he knew, was that he might be right.

As the AIG team awkwardly attempted to get the conversation back on a less hostile footing, Flowers suggested they call Warren Buffett. He didn't know Buffett well, and the last time they had spoken, Flowers had tried to get him interested in buying Bear Stearns during that fateful weekend in March. In times of crisis—when a big check had to be written almost immediately—Buffett was the obvious man to turn to.

"Warren!" Flowers said enthusiastically, after reaching Buffett, as if they were best friends. He reminded him of their past dealing and then immediately explained the purpose of his call. He was staring at a piece of paper, he said, that showed that AIG would soon run out of money. He told Buffett that the spreadsheet was so basic, and so poorly done, that "I might have used it to track my grocery bill."

Hearing that Buffett was amused by the comment, Flowers continued, "They're a bunch of morons!" and paused meaningfully before saying, "but there's a lot of value here." He explained that he was looking for Buffett to invest $10 billion of capital in AIG; he hoped, in fact, that they could make an investment together.

Buffett, however, wasn't especially interested in getting mixed up in such a mess. "You know, I don't have as much money as I used to," he said with a laugh. "I'm kind of low on cash." He also wasn't exactly sure he wanted to step into a battle between Hank Greenberg and Eli Broad, who were both waging war against the company. The only thing he might be willing to take a look at, he told Flowers, was AIG's property and casualty business.

"Listen, there might be a real opportunity here," Flowers agreed. "Let me get Willumstad to at least call you."

Flowers returned to the room and told them Buffett was an unlikely candidate but urged Willumstad to contact him.

Willumstad, who had never met Buffett, called and began his pitch, but before he could get very far into it, Buffett stopped him.

"I've looked over the 10-K," he said. "The company is too complicated. I don't have enough confidence to do that. Look, nothing is going to work with us, so don't waste your time. You've got plenty to do."

But then he held out one glimmer of hope. "If you wanted to sell some assets that I might have some interest in . . . but I don't know."

Willumstad thanked him for his time and consideration and slammed the phone down in frustration.

———

By midday, rumors were now rampant at Lehman Brothers that the board might be about to fire Fuld. With the stock trading down another 9.7 percent to $3.71 a share, the possibility was being discussed openly not only throughout the office but in the media as well.

By now the anger was also becoming increasingly palpable on the trading floor among the firm's staff. Lehman's employees were unique on Wall Street in that they owned a quarter of the company's shares. For all the complaints about Wall Street being short-term oriented, most Lehman employees had a five-year vesting period, which meant huge sums of their own wealth were tied up in the firm without the ability to sell their shares. And as of Friday, those shares had lost 93 percent of their value since January 31; $10 billion had disappeared. (Fuld, who owned 1.4 percent of the company—some 10.9 million shares—had lost $649.2 million.) To make matters worse, in a cruel irony, Lehman employees were sent a memorandum that morning saying that the unrestricted shares that they did own outright, they could not sell; it was the standard blackout notice they received around earnings every quarter preventing them from selling shares for several weeks.

Reports of Fuld's possible ouster reached new heights when word spread that morning that John D. Macomber, one of Lehman's board members and the former CEO of the chemical giant Celanese Corporation, had arrived at the building and was headed for the thirty-first floor. Almost a dozen people were milling about Fuld's corner office when they saw Macomber, who was eighty years old, hobbling down the hallway toward them. Several began to leave as Macomber got to the door, expecting they would soon be asked to excuse themselves.

"Stay," Macomber ordered them.

Fuld, looking haggard, greeted Macomber with a handshake. He didn't think he was getting fired, but he could sense the nervousness in the room.

"I want to talk to you," Macomber said, and though for a moment some of the bankers thought he indeed intended to tell Fuld that his services were no longer required, he instead launched, to everyone's surprise, into a rousing speech to rally the troops.

"I want everyone in the room to know that *I* know that you guys have done a good job," he said. "This was just bad luck. We're one hundred percent behind *all* of you."

Fuld's board, it seemed, was still loyally Fuld's board.

———

Rodgin Cohen was still over at Sullivan & Cromwell's Midtown offices trying to coax Bank of America into buying Lehman. But he could tell something had gone wrong; Greg Curl's body language had changed, and the BofA team seemed as if it had slowed down, as if it had already decided against bidding.

Cohen, who was one of the few lawyers in the city who had direct access to Tim Geithner, dialed his office to report his suspicions that the government's hard line against offering any help had scared Bank of America away.

"I don't think this deal can get done without government assistance," Cohen stressed to Geithner. "They may be bluffing us, and they may be bluffing you. But we can't afford to call that bluff."

Geithner, who had expressed similar worries to Paulson the day before but had been told to stand down, was succinct in his response: "You can't count on government assistance."

———

At about 2:20 p.m., just as Lehman's shares fell another 6 percent to $3.59, Hank Paulson, visibly frazzled, ran downstairs and out of the Treasury Building to head to the airport. Dan Jester, Jim Wilkinson, and Paulson's assistant, Christal West, jumped in his Suburban with him. Christopher Cox was planning to meet them at the airplane.

On a call just hours earlier, he and Geithner had officially determined that *something* needed to be done about Lehman.

If they really were going to convene all the CEOs on Wall Street and try to urge them to come up with a private-market solution, now was the time to do it. Otherwise, by Monday, Lehman would be unsalvageable. "We have the weekend," he reminded them.

They settled on setting up a meeting at 6:00 p.m. at the New York Fed. Geithner's office wouldn't start calling all the CEOs until just past 4:00 p.m., after the market had closed. The last thing they could afford was for news of the meeting to leak.

Paulson, who usually made the trip to New York on US Airways, which offered a government discount—Wendy had always given him grief about flying in a private jet—arranged to charter a plane to New York, using his NetJets account. He couldn't afford to be delayed; the matter at hand was too important, and the weather was atrocious. If anything, he was worried the plane wouldn't even be able to take off.

As they sped toward Dulles to catch the flight, Paulson, almost inaudibly, said, "God help us."

CHAPTER FOURTEEN

Lloyd Blankfein was milling about the greenroom at the Hilton Hotel on Fifty-third Street at Sixth Avenue, waiting to make a speech at the Service Nation Summit, an annual conference coordinated by a coalition of nonprofits that promotes volunteerism in America. Dressed in his customary blue suit and pressed white shirt and blue tie, he had come to give one of the keynote addresses—following Governor Arnold Schwarzenegger and preceding Hillary Clinton—to discuss Goldman's 10,000 Women nonprofit program, which fostered business and management education for women in developing and emerging economies.

Clinton, who had been at the other side of the greenroom returning phone calls, now strolled over to him and politely asked if she might speak before him; she had to get to a dinner, she explained. Blankfein was a big fan; he had given her some $4,600 in donations and had endorsed her in the Democratic primaries over Barack Obama. Since he had no pressing business himself, Blankfein gladly agreed to the switch.

Two minutes later, however, Blankfein's cell phone rang. "We got a call from the Fed. There's a meeting at six p.m. for all the bank CEOs," his assistant told him, sounding simultaneously excited and nervous. "Paulson, Geithner, and Cox are supposed to be there."

This is it, Blankfein thought. *The big one.* Paulson was going to have "the families" meet to try to save Lehman.

Blankfein looked at his watch. It was already getting close to 5:00 p.m., Schwarzenegger was still chattering away, and he had just given his spot away to Clinton.

He tried to reach Gary Cohn, Goldman's co-president, to find out what was going on but didn't get an answer—Cohn was likely still on the shuttle back from D.C. after testifying at a hearing for the Committee on Energy and Natural Resources.

Blankfein sheepishly walked over to Clinton. "Remember I told you that you could go ahead of me?" he asked. "Well, I have an emergency. I just got a call that I have to go to the Fed."

Clinton looked at him as if she didn't understand what he was saying.

Embarrassed, he tried to explain: "They usually don't call me up when it's something really pleasant, since they've done this a total of never."

She half smiled sympathetically and let him speak first.

———

Jamie Dimon could hardly believe his bad luck. He was supposed to be home by 7:00 p.m. to have dinner with his daughter Julia's boyfriend's parents, whom he and his wife were meeting for the first time. Julia, his eldest daughter, had been begging her father all week to be on his best behavior and to make a good impression. And now the Fed was calling an all-hands-on-deck meeting of Wall Street's top brass.

Dimon called his wife, Judy, who was well accustomed to receiving calls like this from her husband. "Geithner's called us down to the Fed," Dimon told her. "I don't know how long it'll go. I'll try to get there as soon as I can."

Dimon hung up the phone and hurried down the hallway to tell Steve Black the news. Black had just confirmed his plans to play in a tournament at the Golf Club of Purchase in Westchester, teeing off the next morning at 7:00.

"We're going down to the Fed," Dimon told him.

"You've got to be fucking kidding me," he replied.

Black immediately called the Purchase club back. "Sorry," he said with a weary sigh, "I was only kidding. Take me out."

———

Brian Moynihan, Bank of America's president of global corporate and investment banking, was reviewing some of Lehman's asset valuations at Sullivan & Cromwell's Midtown offices when Ken Lewis phoned from Charlotte.

"We got a call from Geithner's office," Lewis told him. "You have to go down to the Fed. They're going to do a meeting to figure out what to do about this whole situation."

Moynihan rushed downstairs, bolted without an umbrella through the revolving doors and into the pouring rain, and commandeered one of Sullivan & Cromwell's Town Cars to take him down to the New York Federal Reserve.

Just as the car was making its way into Park Avenue traffic and he dried himself off, Moynihan's cell phone rang again.

"There's been some crossed wires, Mr. Moynihan," one of Tim Geithner's assistants told him. "I know we had invited your firm to this meeting—"

"Yes, I'm on my way down right now," he assured her.

After a brief pause she said, "Given your bank's role in the merger discussions, we believe it would be inappropriate for you to attend the meeting."

Moynihan had gotten no farther than eight blocks before turning around and calling Lewis to tell him the news.

———

John Mack and Colm Kelleher, Morgan Stanley's chief financial officer, were sitting in the backseat of Mack's Audi, having hurried to the car just ten minutes earlier after Mack's secretary had instructed them to get down to the Fed as soon as possible. "This must be Lehman," Kelleher had said as they rushed out.

Not only was the rain pelting the roof furiously, but they were now sitting in bumper-to-bumper traffic on the West Side Highway, still miles away from their destination.

"We're not fucking moving," Mack said, repeatedly checking his watch.

"We're never going to get there," Kelleher agreed.

Mack's driver, John, a former police officer, noticed the bicycle lane running alongside the highway—a project of the Bloomberg administration to encourage walking and cycling.

"Boss, that bike lane on the right, where does it go?" John asked, craning his neck back at them.

Mack's face lit up. "It goes all the way down to the Battery."

"Fuck it!" the driver said as he found a break in the street divider and inched the car onto the bike lane, speeding down it.

———

Hank Paulson's Cessna Citation X touched down on runway 1-19 at New Jersey's Teterboro Airport at 4:40 p.m. The pilot, navigating through a torrential downpour and fifty-mile-an-hour winds, threw the switch on the flaps and taxied to the main gate, where the Secret Service was waiting in two black Chevrolet Suburbans.

Now, as they inched their way through the Holland Tunnel toward Manhattan in rush-hour traffic, Paulson took a call from Greg Curl of Bank of America and Chris Flowers, the firm's banker, who had completed their assessment of the Lehman numbers.

"We're going to need the government to help to make this work," Curl told Paulson bluntly and then launched into a series of proposed deal terms, conditions that would have to be met in order for this transaction to take place.

Paulson listened patiently, even if he had a hard time understanding why Curl felt he had the upper hand to the point that he could dictate the conditions. But, as Paulson himself liked to say, "You only need two girls at the dance to call it an auction," and under the circumstances, he needed BofA to be one of them. If he could just keep Bank of America around long enough to close a deal with Barclays, he'd have succeeded. Paulson handed his cell phone over to Dan Jester (who had, ironically, worked for Flowers at Goldman in the financial services group in the 1990s), who took notes.

Curl told Jester that Bank of America would agree to the deal only if the government was willing to take $40 billion of losses on Lehman's assets. "We've been through the books, and they're a mess," Curl explained, referring to Lehman's bountiful toxic assets. Bank of America, he said, would be willing to split the first $1 billion of losses with the government, but after that, the next $40 billion, the government would have to guarantee. In exchange, Curl told him, the bank would give the government warrants (the option to buy shares at a later date) for Bank of America, with a strike price of $45 a share. (BofA shares closed that day at $33.74.) Jester mouthed the figures to Paulson as Curl relayed them. Both men shook their heads, knowing full well that under these terms a deal was never going to happen.

As the Suburban made its way through downtown Manhattan, Paulson called Geithner to strategize. It was already past 6:00 p.m., when the meeting was set to begin; they figured they would let the CEOs stir for a bit until Paulson arrived, just to let them know they meant business.

Thirty-three Liberty Street, the New York Federal Reserve Building, is an imposing, fortresslike sanctuary of old-fashioned, traditional finance. In 1927 Margaret Law, a critic for *Architecture* magazine, wrote that the three-year-old building had "a quality which, for lack of a better word, I can best describe as epic." Deep below the limestone and sandstone building, which was modeled after the Strozzi Palace of Florence, lies a three-level vault built into the bedrock of Manhattan, fifty feet below sea level. It holds more than $60 billion of gold. Real hard assets, with real value.

If Lehman's fate was going to be resolved—if Wall Street was going to be saved—the matter would be decided at 33 Liberty Street. While modern finance may have allowed investors to zip money across continents in milliseconds, the New York Federal Reserve stood as one of the last bastions of tangible values.

As John Thain's black GMC Yukon pulled up to the building, he couldn't help but recall the last time he had come there, as a partner at Goldman, in response to another such cataclysmic event, the rescue of Long-Term Capital Management in 1998. For three straight days, he had worked around the clock to come up with a solution.

And had they not saved Long-Term Capital, the next domino back in 1998 was clearly Lehman Brothers, which was suffering from a similar crisis of confidence.

The irony of the situation was rich. Ten years earlier, on a Saturday morning just past 7:30 a.m., Thain had run into Fuld in the Fed hallways and asked, "How's it going?"

"Not so well," Fuld had said. "People are spreading nasty rumors."

"I can't imagine that," Thain had replied, trying to be polite, but knowing full well that the rumors were everywhere.

"When I find out who it is," Fuld had said furiously, "I'm going to reach down his throat and tear out his heart."

They were back where they started.

The meeting of "the families" did not begin until 6:45 p.m., when Paulson, Geithner, and Cox finally emerged, briskly walking down a long hall on the first floor, almost as if they were marching in a formation, toward a conference room in the south corner of the building overlooking Liberty and Williams streets.

The CEOs had all been milling about, tapping away on their BlackBerrys, and pouring themselves cups of ice water to cool themselves from the miasma of humidity that hung in the building. If there had been any question about the subject of this gathering, it was readily apparent before Paulson ever said a word: Conspicuous by his absence was the longest-running member of their tribe, Dick Fuld.

"Thanks for coming down here on such short notice," Paulson began.

He explained that Lehman Brothers was in a "precarious position" and told the group, "We're going to need to find a solution before the weekend is out."

And then to make it perfectly clear what the parameters of that solution were going to be, he stated flatly: "It's not going to be government money; you're going to have to figure this out."

"We've got two buyers that are each going to need help in my judgment," he continued. He did not mention Bank of America or Barclays by name, but everyone knew who the players were—the names had crossed the tape twenty-four hours earlier. He revealed to the men arrayed around the table that each bidder had already indicated to him that it would not buy Lehman Brothers unless the government—or someone—consented to finance at least part of the deal.

"There's no consensus for the government to get involved; there is no will to do this in Congress," he said, stammering and stuttering at one point about how Nancy Pelosi had been all over him about bailouts. "You will need to come up with a private-market solution. You have a responsibility to the marketplace.

"I know it's unpleasant to help a competitor do a deal, but it's not going to be as unpleasant as it will be if Lehman goes," Paulson stressed. "You need to do this."

For many in the room, the idea of coming to the assistance of a rival was more than unpleasant: It was anathema. What made the situation even worse was that the competitors they were being asked to aid were Bank of America and Barclays, the ultimate outsiders. Ken Lewis, Bank of America's CEO, had disparaged them every chance he got, and they all viewed Barclays as a wannabe, a second-tier player trying to break into the big leagues. *How was helping these firms going to do anything other than hurt everyone assembled in the room?*

Lehman wasn't attracting much sympathy either. "Dick is in no condition to make any decisions," Paulson announced, with a tinge of derision, explaining why Fuld wasn't present. "He is in denial," Paulson continued, before calling him "distant" and "dysfunctional."

It was now Geithner's turn to speak. As one of his assistants passed around copies of a document charting Lehman Brothers' balances, he said sternly, "If you don't find a solution, it's only going to make the situation worse for everybody here." The problem was evident: Lehman had virtually no cash left. If there was no solution by Monday, the risk was that investors would demand what little money was left and put the firm out of business within minutes of the opening bell. That in turn would put the financial system as a whole at risk, as counterparties—investors on the other side of a trade with Lehman— wouldn't be able to settle their trades, creating a cascading problem that could soon turn into a catastrophe. As sophisticated as the world's markets have become, the glue that holds the entire arrangement together remains old-fashioned trust. Once that vanishes, things can unravel very quickly.

Both Blankfein and Dimon countered that they believed that the risk inherent in a Lehman bankruptcy was being overstated, at least from their respective firms' points of view. They had already told Paulson privately that they had reduced most of their risk to Lehman Brothers, and Blankfein didn't mind now bringing that fact up in front of the group. "We've all seen this coming from miles," he told the room.

Geithner, taking their opinions in without responding, instructed the bankers to break up into three working groups. The first would value Lehman's toxic assets, the portion of the business that it had announced it would spin off into the company called SpinCo. The bankers in the room quickly renamed it ShitCo, offering a bit of much-needed comic relief.

The second group, Geithner continued, would look at developing a structure for the banks to invest in Lehman. And finally, there was what he had described in private meetings earlier that day as the "lights-out scenario": If Lehman was forced to file for bankruptcy, he wanted all the banks that traded with it to see if they could contain the damage in advance by trading around Lehman to "net down their positions."

In case there was any confusion, Geithner reiterated Paulson's decree: "There is no political will for a federal bailout." As he spoke those words, a subway train passed underneath the room, rumbling ominously as if to underscore his point.

Christopher Cox, as impeccably dressed and coiffed as ever, made a brief statement, telling everyone in the room that they were "great Americans" and impressing upon them "the patriotic duty they were undertaking."

Most of the bankers in the room rolled their eyes at the sentiment, as they regarded Cox as a lightweight and would later describe him as "cryogenically frozen."

The conversation quickly turned to both the philosophical and the practical as the bankers talked over one another.

"I assume we are going to talk about AIG?" Vikram Pandit of Citigroup asked, as the room grew quiet.

Geithner shot him a harsh look. "Let's focus on Lehman," he said firmly, trying to avoid losing control of the meeting.

"You can't deal with Lehman in isolation," Pandit persisted. "We can't find ourselves back here next weekend."

Dimon jumped in. "We're there at AIG, our team is there," he said, explaining that JP Morgan was advising the insurer, and suggesting that they were working to find a solution.

"You know, Jamie," Pandit replied brusquely, "we've got a team there, too, and I don't think it's as under control as you think."

Pandit and Dimon continued to trade barbs, and the mounting tension began to remind many in the room of a conference call that Geithner had coordinated among the big-bank CEOs the night that JP Morgan acquired Bear Stearns. "Stop being such a jerk," Dimon had yelled at Pandit then when he questioned him about Citi's exposure to Bear, now that he had bought the firm.

Geithner insisted that the Fed had AIG under control and again attempted to move the conversation along. What remained unacknowledged was that JP Morgan and Citigroup, as advisers to AIG, were the only parties in the room that had any true appreciation for the depth of the problems that the firm faced.

Thain, whose bank was likely the next to fall, as everyone in the room understood all too well, remained notably silent during the exchanges.

Before ordering the roomful of bankers to get their teams together and be back at the Fed by 9:00 the next morning, Paulson made one last pitch that to many in the room sounded more like a threat: "This is about our capital markets, our country. We will remember anyone who is not seen as helpful."

The room emptied as the bankers left, expressionless and mute, dumbstruck at the magnitude of the work that lay before them.

———

John Mack pulled out his cell phone the moment he left the New York Fed Building to report back to the office.

"Guys, it's going to be a long night," he told his lieutenants, James Gorman, Walid Chammah, and Paul Taubman, and ordered them to prepare for Lehman to go under. "We're going to need lots of bodies this weekend." The Morgan Stanley bankers had two related tasks: self-preservation and helping the Fed. They'd once again have to review the extent of their exposure to Lehman, looking through their derivatives book and also examining their clients' exposures to Lehman. Investment banking, meanwhile, should start looking through Lehman's client list to see whom they could pick off. A board call would have to be arranged to keep everyone updated. Another team would have to run numbers on Lehman's asset values. They would finally get a chance to see Lehman's finances; if nothing else, it could prove to be an interesting education.

Mack directed his driver to his favorite Italian restaurant, San Pietro, to pick up some food for the team, who would need to be fortified for the sleepless night they all faced. Everyone would have to start acting like a first-year analyst.

———

Upon leaving the meeting, John Thain, who had been joined at the meeting by his colleague Peter Kraus, immediately phoned Peter Kelly, the firm's deal lawyer, and told him to be at the Fed on Saturday. He followed up with a call to Greg Fleming as his Yukon made its way up the Merritt Parkway; he had planned to have dinner with his wife and two friends and was already an hour late. "It's a food fight down here," Thain told Fleming. "It looks like Lehman isn't getting saved."

As he related, with surprise, how Paulson had refused to offer any government help, he knew how Fleming was going to respond.

"We have to start thinking about ourselves. We have to think about our options," Fleming said. "Really, John. We're going to run out of time."

Thain, still noncommittal, said only, "Let's go get some sleep, and we'll talk in the morning."

When Thain finally arrived for his dinner engagement at Rebecca's restaurant in Greenwich, he saw Steve Black of JP Morgan, who had been on his cell phone for the past half hour with the firm's management team, standing out front, still talking. As it happened, he was in the middle of a conversation speculating about what might happen to Merrill Lynch.

Black, who was aghast to see Thain—*His company is next! What's he doing here?*—nonchalantly greeted him with, "Great minds think alike."

"Yeah, but I was supposed to meet another couple and my wife, and they've been sitting here for the last two hours," Thain replied.

"At least I called," Black said with a laugh.

As Thain went inside, Black returned to the conference call. "You're never going to believe who I just ran into . . ."

———

At Lehman's headquarters, a stunned and livid Dick Fuld had just gotten off the phone with Bart McDade, who had the unenviable task of informing the CEO that a meeting had been held down at the Fed about his company, and that he hadn't been invited.

Rodgin Cohen had been notified by the Fed to instruct McDade to bring a team down to the Fed on Saturday morning—and had explicitly warned him not to bring Fuld, explaining, "The Fed doesn't want him down there."

Trying to soften the blow, McDade prevaricated: He told Fuld that there would be a lot of grunt work to do downtown, and that his time would be better spent manning the office so that he could remain in constant contact with the regulators and his CEO brethren. What he didn't relay to Fuld, of course, was that they would all be together at the Fed in person.

As he ended the call with McDade, Fuld had another reason to be furious when he realized that he hadn't heard back from Ken Lewis all day, and it was already past 9:00 p.m. Bank of America's diligence teams over at Sullivan & Cromwell had left hours earlier, and from what he had heard, their body language suggested they weren't leaving just for the night.

"I can't believe that goddamn son of a bitch won't return my call," Fuld complained to Russo. Fuld had phoned him at least a half dozen times, sometimes not leaving a voice mail for fear of seeming desperate. He thought Lewis had practically shook his hand over the phone just twenty-four hours earlier; where the hell had he gone?

Enough was enough. Fuld swallowed his pride and dialed Lewis's home in Charlotte.

Lewis's wife, Donna, picked up in the kitchen.

"Is Ken there?" Fuld asked.

"Who is it?"

"Dick Fuld."

There was a long pause as Donna looked over at her husband, who was sitting in the living room. When she mouthed *Fuld is on the line,* Lewis shook his finger, signaling to her to duck the call.

Donna felt uncomfortable, but she had had plenty of experience in dodging unwanted callers for her husband.

"You really have to stop calling," she said sympathetically to Fuld. "Ken isn't coming to the phone."

Crestfallen, Fuld replied, "I'm really sorry to have bothered you."

Fuld placed the phone down and put both hands on his head.

"So, I'm the schmuck," he shouted at nobody in particular.

———

Harvey Miller, Lehman's bankruptcy lawyer, walked into Weil Gotshal's conference room just down the hall from his office and told the associates to go home and have dinner. It was getting late, and he hadn't heard anything new from anyone at Lehman. *This is just a fire drill,* he thought. *Lehman Brothers isn't going to have to file.*

Miller hopped into a cab to his apartment on Fifth Avenue. As he opened the door, his cell phone rang. James Bromley, a lawyer with Cleary Gottlieb Steen & Hamilton, which was advising the New York Fed, asked almost matter-of-factly, "Harvey, are there any plans for a bankruptcy?"

Miller was taken aback. "It's not the objective; it's not in the forecast," he replied decisively. "There certainly isn't any intensive work being done on it. I'm at home. I can tell you that right now the company really believes it's going to get a deal."

"Are you sure?" Bromley persisted.

Miller related how the New York Fed had not seemed very worried during a presentation by one of his associates earlier that day.

Bromley, uncertain what to make of this news, muttered, "Err, maybe we should meet again tomorrow morning," and hung up.

As Miller headed into the living room, he said to his wife, Ruth, bewilderedly, "I just got the strangest call . . ."

Back at AIG, Willumstad was still searching for a quick fix. He and Braunstein decided to try Warren Buffett one last time. Perhaps they could sell him some assets—anything, really—that he might want in his portfolio. Buffett had already left the office, but his assistant patched the call through to his home, the same home he had purchased in 1958 for $31,500.

"You said you'd be interested in assets. Anything in particular?" Willumstad asked, after greeting him and explaining the purpose of his call.

Buffett, reticent, offered, "Well, we could be interested in the auto business."

"Would you be interested in taking all of the U.S. property and casualty business?" Willumstad suggested. That was a major piece of the company, representing $40 billion in annual revenue.

"What's it worth?" Buffett asked.

"We'd say $25 billion; you'd probably say $20 billion," Willumstad replied. "What information do you need to do that?"

When Buffett told him to send what he could, Willumstad said, "Okay. Give us an hour and we'll get a package of material together. Where can we e-mail it?"

Buffett let out a loud laugh and informed him that he didn't use e-mail.

"Can I fax it to you?" Willumstad asked.

"I don't have a fax machine here," Buffett said, still chuckling. "Why don't you fax it to the office. I'll go get in my car and drive back down to the office and pick it up."

An hour later, Buffett was back on the phone, politely rejecting the proposal: "It's too big a deal; $25 billion is too big." Willumstad never thought he'd hear Buffett call any prospective deal too big.

"I'd have to use all my cash and can't do anything to jeopardize Berkshire's triple-A rating," Buffett explained. For a moment, he alluded to the possibility of raising the money, but then acknowledged that he "didn't want to have that kind of debt on my balance sheet."

"Okay, thanks a lot," Willumstad said. "But, by the way, if there's any-thing else in the pool that you're interested in, let us know."

———

Merrill's Greg Fleming was tossing and turning in bed that night, so much so that his wife, Melissa, finally insisted that he tell her what was bother-ing him. "It's Friday night, and you're not sleeping," she mumbled. Wide awake, he turned to her. "This is a different kind of Friday night. The next week or so in this industry is going be epic."

After nodding off briefly, Fleming finally rose at 4:30 a.m., his mind racing. He recalled his conversation of the night before with John Finnegan, his closest confidant on Merrill's board. Finnegan was clearly as anxious as Fleming about the firm's mounting problems, and they agreed they had to persuade Thain to seek a deal with Ken Lewis.

"You've got to push this, Greg," Finnegan urged him. "There's a way to get this done."

Fleming had had essentially the same conversation with Peter Kelly. "You just need to get the imprimatur of John" to approach Bank of Amer-ica, Kelly had told him. "We've got to start getting things going. If the meeting tomorrow morning doesn't go right, we have thirty-six hours to put a trade together."

It was coming up on 6:30 on Saturday morning when Fleming finally decided it was late enough to phone Thain's home. Thain was just leaving and returned the call five minutes later from the backseat of his SUV.

"I've been thinking about this," Fleming said resolutely. "We have to call Ken Lewis."

Thain, taken aback, had spent much of the night thinking about whether such a deal made sense—and had come to the opposite conclusion, at least for the time being. Merrill might want to try to raise some money over the weekend by selling a small stake in the firm to raise market confidence, but there was no reason to sell the entire company immediately, he told Fleming. As he had always warned his troops before entering talks, "Once you initiate, you're in motion." Negotiations could quickly spiral beyond your control.

"They are our best partner," he said dejectedly of Bank of America. "Where are we going to be if we lose them?"

As his SUV barreled down the FDR Drive, Thain promised to consider the issue further, but for now, he needed to focus on the meetings ahead of him.

———

Jamie Dimon's black Lexus pulled away from the curb of his Park Avenue apartment to head down to the Fed just before 8:00 a.m. Dimon, who sat in the backseat returning e-mails on his BlackBerry, had just gotten off a conference call with his management team. He had dropped a bombshell on them, telling them to prepare for the bankruptcies of Lehman Brothers, Merrill Lynch, AIG, Morgan Stanley, and even Goldman Sachs. He knew he might have been overstating the case, but he figured they needed to be prepared. Dimon was anxious—fearful, really. He was the Man Who Knew Too Much. As the "clearing bank" for both Lehman and Merrill—all trades for those firms passed through JP Morgan—he could see how quickly their businesses were crumbling. And as the adviser to AIG, well, that had been a nightmare for weeks. He probably knew more than Paulson.

He just hoped he was wrong.

———

Pacing in his kitchen, Fleming decided to try one last time to impress upon Thain that talking to Bank of America wasn't just a good plan, it was perhaps the only way to save Merrill Lynch. If Bank of America bought Lehman instead, Merrill faced an onslaught of unimaginable proportions. The math was clear: If Lehman was swallowed up, there would be a run on the next biggest broker-dealer—and that was his firm. Merrill Lynch, perhaps the most iconic investment bank in the nation, was on the brink of ruin.

Thain picked up Fleming's call just as his SUV was winding down Maiden Lane and about to enter the underground parking lot at the Fed Building. A half dozen photographers had already camped out and were snapping away.

"This is our time to move," Fleming insisted. "We don't even necessarily have to do the deal, but we should at least examine it now, and we should see if we can put it together.

"We should use the weekend to do that," Fleming pressed on, before Thain could interrupt him. "We shouldn't try to do this potentially under duress next week."

As a longtime deal maker, Fleming certainly knew how valuable even a weekend could be. The biggest deals on Wall Street had always been finalized when the markets were closed on Saturday and Sunday, so that the details could be refined without worrying that a leak could quickly affect stock prices and potentially scuttle an agreement.

Thain still counseled patience. "If Lehman doesn't make it, if they file for Chapter 11, Bank of America will still be there," he told Fleming. But he assured him: "I hear you loud and clear. I'm keeping an open mind, and if we need to make the call, we'll make the call."

That was all Fleming needed to hear. He was making progress.

———

By 8:00 a.m., the grand lobby of the New York Federal Reserve was teeming with bankers and lawyers. They had gathered not far from a giant bronze statue of young Sophocles, his outstretched arm holding a tortoiseshell-and-horn lyre. The statue was a symbol of victory after the Battle of Salamis, a clash that saved Greece and perhaps Western civilization from the East. On this day the bankers assembled at the Fed had their own historic battle to wage, with stakes that were in some ways just as high: They were trying to save themselves from their own worst excesses, and, in the process, save Western capitalism from financial catastrophe.

An hour later the group shuffled into the same boardroom at the end of the corridor where they had sat, mostly shell-shocked, the night before.

By morning they had settled on the working groups: Citi, Merrill, and Morgan Stanley were put in charge of analyzing Lehman's balance sheet and liquidity issues; Goldman Sachs, Credit Suisse, and Deutsche Bank were assigned to study Lehman's real estate assets and determine the size of the hole. Goldman had had a jump start as a result of its mini–diligence session earlier in the week, and both Vikram Pandit and Gary Shedlin of Citigroup were so nervous that Goldman would try to buy the assets themselves on the cheap that they attached themselves to their group.

"As you know, the government's not doing this, you're on your own, figure it out, make it happen," Geithner said. "I'm going to come back in two hours; you guys better figure out a solution and get this thing done."

His tone struck many in the room as patronizing if not ridiculous. "This is fucking nuts," Pandit said to John Mack; it was as if they had all been handed a test without the customary number 2 pencils.

Lloyd Blankfein raised a question: "Tim, I understand what you want to do, but how do *I* get in the other room?" In other words, he wanted to know how he could become a buyer subsidized by his competitors. Blankfein wasn't serious—he had no interest in buying Lehman, but he was clearly trying to make a point. *Why are we helping our competition?*

Geithner deflected the question and left the room, followed by the bankers, who were simultaneously daunted and deflated.

Thain, Peter Kraus, and Peter Kelly of Merrill found a corner to talk in.

"So, what do you think?" Kelly asked.

"Lehman's not going to make it," Thain said.

"Then we're not going to make it either," Kelly replied calmly.

"We have to start thinking about options," Kraus said.

Thain nodded in agreement. *Maybe Fleming was right after all.*

Thain dialed Fleming and, after telling him about the conversation, said: "Set up the meeting with Lewis."

———

Upstairs, on the seventh floor of the Fed, Lehman's Bart McDade and Alex Kirk felt a little bit like mail-order brides as they waited to meet the bankers from the firms that they hoped would save them. This, they knew, would be the ultimate "road show."

They had brought binders of materials, including what were perhaps the two most important documents, known as decks. One described the spin-off that Lehman referred to as REI Global; the other was labeled "Commercial Real Estate Business Overview"—in other words, the worst of the worst holdings, the toxic assets that no one knew precisely how to value and that everyone was nonetheless certain that Lehman was overvaluing.

Even now Lehman seemed to be in denial: The decks revealed that it had marked down the value of its commercial real estate assets by an average of only 15 percent. Most Wall Street bankers had already assumed the reduction would be far greater.

"Okay, let's just make sure you and I agree exactly on all of these issues and how they're financed," McDade said to Kirk. They reviewed each line in order: how the balance sheet was broken down by liabilities, their derivatives, receivables, payables, repo lines, and long-term debt.

If they were confused about any given detail, McDade phoned Ian

Lowitt, who was a veritable financial encyclopedia. "*He* should be the one down here," McDade blurted during one of his explanations of an especially obtuse passage.

As they completed their preparations, Steve Shafran, Hank Paulson's top lieutenant, phoned and instructed the two men to go and meet their possible saviors. A security guard escorted them downstairs to the main dining room, where several dozen bankers waited. Wall Street's most elite firms were effectively about to go shopping in the equivalent of a government-sponsored Turkish bazaar.

The Lehman executives were seated at a table in the farthest corner of the huge room, where everyone stopped to look—to gawk, in fact. "Do you know what this is like?" Kirk asked McDade when they were finally settled. "We're the kid with the dunce cap in the corner!"

McDade let out a big laugh just as a group of bankers they did not know from Credit Suisse wandered over, flashing wide grins, and started eyeing them. "What's going on?" one of them asked. Kirk rolled his eyes in a way that clearly indicated, *Please, do not mess with us.* "What the fuck do you *think* is going on?" he replied. Before things could get too ugly, the cream of Wall Street suddenly appeared: Vikram Pandit, John Mack, John Thain, and Peter Kraus came over to the table and got down to business. Mack, who had met McDade at his home over the summer when they had considered merging, struck a sympathetic note: "Oh, God, I feel awful for you guys. This is just terrible." Thain sat quietly, sipping a coffee, with every reason to think, *This could be me.* McDade pulled out his documents and began walking them through the numbers. As Kraus began to question some of the assumptions, Pandit stopped him. "Okay, okay," he said, impatiently waving his hand in the air. "You have a homework assignment," he told the Lehman bankers. "Give me a full business plan on how you would run this thing, so we can consider whether we're going to finance it. You have two hours to complete it."

Five minutes later a security guard came over to McDade and Kirk and told them, "We're going to take you up to another floor so you can work." The Fed had hoped to provide them with an actual conference room, but because there wasn't any space available, they were escorted to the Fed's medical center, where a makeshift office had been prepared. It was, if nothing else, all too apt a metaphor, as the Lehman executives immediately realized. Kirk looked at the defibrillator on the wall and deadpanned, "Well, this is appropriate. We're clearly the heart attack victim."

————

Greg Curl and Joe Price of Bank of America were on their way downtown with their lawyer, Ed Herlihy, for a 10:00 a.m. meeting with Paulson and Geithner. They had by now resolved not to pursue a deal with Lehman; Curl had already sent some of his people back to Charlotte.

Before they arrived, Herlihy's cell rang; he could see from the caller ID that it was Fleming. For a moment, he hesitated answering.

Before they had left, the group had discussed what to do if Fleming called again. Chris Flowers had advised Curl, "Let's not waste another fucking minute on this until John Thain himself calls Ken Lewis and says the words out of his own mouth: 'I want to do this deal.' Otherwise, it's just a bunch of bullshit."

Exasperated, Herlihy finally answered the phone.

"We're going to make this happen," Fleming said excitedly. "John says we should set it up."

Herlihy had heard this before and had grown tired of the routine.

"Greg, I've said it once and I'll say it again: We're not doing this without being invited in. I'm actually in the car with Greg Curl now. I'll put him on. He'll tell you we're serious about that."

"Listen, we're interested," Curl said after being handed the phone. "But we do need to hear from Thain directly on this."

"Okay, okay," Fleming told him. "I'll call you back."

For all their interest in acquiring Merrill Lynch, Curl, Price, and Herlihy had reason to be wary of Fleming's overtures. The three men knew something that no one else knew, a bizarre turn of events that had never leaked out—*and thank god for that,* they thought to themselves, for it would have left them the laughingstocks of Wall Street.

Ken Lewis had, in fact, already been through this dance with Merrill Lynch a year ago almost to the week with Stan O'Neal. No one outside of O'Neal and a handful of BofA executives even knew the talks had taken place, and not even Merrill's or Bank of America's board had been informed of them.

On the last Sunday of September, O'Neal had driven down to Manhattan from his weekend home in Westchester to meet with Lewis at his plush corporate apartment in the new Time Warner Center. The meeting had been set up by Herlihy, who had acted as an intermediary. O'Neal showed up alone, though—Lewis had brought Curl with him.

As a precondition of the meeting, O'Neal had indicated that he wanted $90 a share for Merrill Lynch, a substantial premium over its then stock price of slightly more than $70 a share. Lewis and Curl got right down to business, handing O'Neal a bound presentation of what a combination of Bank of America and Merrill would look like from a numbers and operational standpoint. As Lewis went through the proposal and was ready to start a discussion, O'Neal jumped out of his chair, excusing himself to go to the bathroom. After what felt like twenty minutes, as Lewis and Curl waited anxiously for him to return, they wavered between concern for O'Neal's health and frustration that he seemed to have vanished.

Finally, O'Neal returned, as if nothing unusual had occurred. Lewis shrugged it off and continued going through the presentation. As he continued, O'Neal stopped him.

"Look, if we're going to do a deal, it's going to have to be at a reasonable premium," O'Neal said, raising the price he wanted for the firm to $100 a share. "I've done some subsequent analysis and thought about it more," he said, explaining how he justified the higher price by a sum-of-the-parts analysis of Merrill's asset management, retail, and investment banking businesses.

The number took Lewis aback. At first he almost ended the conversation. But then he allowed that he would continue the talks, but suggested if O'Neal wanted more money, "it would require more cuts."

"How much cost reduction do you have baked into the numbers that you have?" O'Neal asked.

Lewis's presentation projected $6 billion in cuts over two years.

To O'Neal that was a huge number, even for someone who had been famous for his own cost cutting. And if he wanted $100 a share, it would be even more.

O'Neal asked, "So, how would you see me fitting into this?"

"Well, you'd be part of the management team, but I haven't really thought about a structure," Lewis told him.

That answer clearly was unsatisfactory. If they were going to have to reduce costs by as much as Lewis was saying, O'Neal said, he'd want to be the president of the firm so that at least somebody would be looking out for the Merrill employees. Lewis now became angry. "So, what you're sayin' is, you want me to sell out my management team to get this deal done for your benefit?"

For a moment O'Neal only stared down at his feet, until finally saying, "I appreciate you spending the time. I appreciate the presentation and the thought that went into it. I've always thought that, on paper, that if Merrill were to do a strategic merger you are the most compelling partner." As he turned to the door, O'Neal said, "I'll think about everything you said."

Lewis never heard from him again.

What he didn't know was that the next day O'Neal confided in Alberto Cribiore, a Merrill board member, that he had gone to see Lewis, and told him about the meeting. Cribiore, always a good proxy for the rest of the board, was clearly not receptive to the merger idea, quickly brushing it aside.

In his heavy Italian accent, Cribiore said, "But Stan, Ken Lewis is an asshole!"

———

The sixteenth floor of AIG was already a beehive of activity, with hundreds of bankers and lawyers roaming the floors, darting into the various rooms that had been set up to perform due diligence on different AIG assets up for sale.

Before the high-end tire kickers arrived, Douglas Braunstein of JP Morgan, fresh off a conference call with Dimon, pulled Bob Willumstad aside to confide, "You need to think about more than the $20 or $30 billion we were talking about before, because Lehman could go bankrupt this weekend.

"The market's going to be bad," Braunstein warned. "We should probably be thinking about $40 billion."

Willumstad was flabbergasted; the challenge he faced had almost immediately doubled in size.

A minute later, Sir Deryck Maughan, the former head of Salomon Brothers, emerged from an elevator. Maughan—who was working for KKR, one of the bidders in the AIG fire sale—and Willumstad had known each other well but hadn't been in touch for years. The last time they had seen each other was in 2004, when Maughan was being fired by Charles Prince, literally in Willumstad's presence. It was Maughan, too, who had snubbed Steve Black's wife on the dance floor more than a decade ago, resulting in a confrontation with Dimon, and his eventual ousting by Sandy Weill.

And now, on a weekend when the entire financial system hung in the balance, Willumstad, Dimon, and Black were all looking to Maughan for help. *Ah,* Willumstad thought as he greeted Maughan with a wide smile, *life is rich with irony.*

A few minutes earlier David Bonderman of Texas Pacific Group, one of the wealthiest private-equity moguls in the nation, had arrived with his own team. Bonderman, who was known for turnarounds, thanks to successful projects like fixing Continental Airlines, had also become increasingly leery of financial companies. He had acquired a $1.35 billion stake in Washington Mutual in April 2008 and watched his investment lose virtually all of its value in less than half a year.

Willumstad was becoming increasingly anxious that all these bidders were there to suck AIG dry.

Perhaps sensing Willumstad's anxiety, Dr. Paul Achleitner, a board member of the insurance giant Allianz who had cut short his vacation in Majorca, Spain, to fly in for the diligence session, approached him.

"Can I see you privately?" he asked.

"Sure," Willumstad replied.

Achleitner had been invited to the diligence session by Chris Flowers, who had chartered a plane to fetch Achleitner and bring him across the Atlantic.

Willumstad and Achleitner found a quiet corner.

"I want you to know that I'm not here with all these vultures," Achleitner said, pointing at the scrum of private-equity investors swirling about. "I'm here as Allianz. If we're going to invest, we might invest alongside them, but we're going to make our own decision."

"Thank you, I appreciate that," Willumstad said, before returning to the vultures.

Willumstad and the AIG team were quickly having a difficult time keeping track of everyone in the growing crowd and, as the weekend wore on, whom they actually represented.

When Christopher A. Cole from Goldman Sachs appeared with a small army of bankers, John Studzinski, AIG's banker from Blackstone, became alarmed. Goldman? Who invited them?

"Who are you working for?" Studzinski asked Cole. At first Cole seemed oddly reticent to say. "Well," he said, "we have several clients here." Studzinski just stared at him, hoping to hear more. As they spoke, Richard Friedman, who ran Goldman Sachs' private investment business, walked by, which did not go unnoticed by everyone else in the room. Was Goldman actually there for itself? "We're here," Cole started speaking again, "working with Allianz, Axa, and Goldman Sachs Capital Partners." It was all so confusing and conflicted.

Skeptical about the answers he was getting, and perhaps a bit paranoid, Studzinski raced up to the senior security guard on the eighteenth floor, Nathan T. Harrison. "Listen," he told him, "I want you to watch all these people like a hawk. If you see anything untoward, anything at all—people walking around the wrong floors, whatever—come find me immediately."

———

Without a minute to spare the Bank of America team, which included Greg Curl, Joe Price, and Ed Herlihy, marched into the Fed building for their 10:30 a.m. meeting with Paulson and Geithner. Christopher Flowers had raced over on foot from AIG, two blocks away.

As they waited in a conference room outside Geithner's office, Curl recounted to the group how Fuld had been phoning Lewis's home all night.

"Dick . . . what an asshole!" Flowers said dismissively.

As Paulson, Geithner, and Dan Jester entered the room, the mood quickly turned chilly. Paulson hated Flowers, and the antipathy was mutual. They had been feuding for years, ever since Paulson passed over Flowers for the top job of running Goldman's investment banking division back when the firm was planning to go public. Flowers—who was given to telling his peers that Paulson was an "idiot"—quickly left the firm. Paulson told him that his decision to quit, coming as it did at the critical time of the IPO, was a "disgrace." Flowers was bought out of the partnership ahead of the offering, but when the IPO was canceled, he made overtures about trying to return to the firm. That conversation had ended in a near-shouting match.

Trying to break the tension, Geithner now asked, "So what's the latest?"

Curl indicated in no uncertain terms that BofA was no longer interested in buying Lehman Brothers unless the government was prepared to help even more than they had asked for the day before. He said that they had identified at least $70 billion in problem assets that Bank of America would need guaranteed—the figure had grown from the $40 billion of a day earlier—and that it might be even larger. Given that, they were going to put their pencils down unless Paulson was willing to "step up."

Curl also said that he was concerned that Fuld was still seeking a premium for the stock. "We think that's bullshit," Flowers remarked.

"You know, no one cares what they think. Don't worry about what they think," Paulson told them. "At this point, it doesn't matter what Dick Fuld thinks."

In the middle of the meeting, Herlihy's cell phone began ringing, and he saw that it was Fleming. After ignoring his first two calls, Herlihy whispered to Curl that it was Fleming and excused himself from the meeting.

"What's up?" Herlihy asked impatiently.

"Okay. He'll do the meeting at two thirty p.m.!" Fleming exclaimed.

"Well, can you get Thain to call Lewis?" Herlihy asked.

"Not now," Fleming said. "Thain can't speak to him because he's in a meeting with Paulson."

Herlihy rolled his eyes. "No, he's not, Greg. *I'm* in a meeting at the Fed with Paulson. I just stepped out of the room and can see him. He's down the hall from me."

Herlihy was growing increasingly concerned that Fleming didn't have Thain's blessing, and repeated, "Listen, this isn't going to work. He's got to call. If I can step out to take your call, he can step out and call Lewis."

"He's going to be there, I promise. I'm not risking my reputation by having Lewis fly up here and go to an empty meeting," Fleming insisted.

"He's got to make the call," Herlihy insisted again.

———

By the time Herlihy stepped back into the room, it was clear that the meeting was winding down, and while the government was still refusing to become involved, Paulson was trying to keep Bank of America from dropping out altogether.

As everyone stood up to leave, Chris Flowers pulled Paulson aside and said, "I've got to talk to you about AIG." He paused to make certain they weren't being overheard and continued, "I've been over there working with them, and it's just remarkable what we found." He took out the same piece of paper that had been handed out the day before, showing the firm's cash outflows and how by Wednesday it would be out of money.

"Here's how big the hole is," Flowers said, pointing to the negative $5 billion cash balance coming due that next week. "AIG is just totally out of control. They're incompetent!" Flowers offered to come back to the Fed with Willumstad to go over the numbers in more detail, and while Paulson was shocked at the numbers, he tried not to give Flowers the satisfaction of knowing how unnerved he was.

When Flowers walked out of the meeting and rejoined the Bank of America team in the hallway, he smugly told them, "They're not on top of it."

———

As Paulson, Geithner, and Jester reassembled in Geithner's office, Jester stressed that they had to somehow keep Bank of America "warm" so that it remained in the auction. And if Bank of America had dropped out, it had to be kept quiet—especially from Barclays.

Paulson, however, was focused on the AIG document that he had just seen, doing the math in his head. "It's much worse than I thought," he finally said. "These guys are in *deep* doo-doo."

Geithner reached Willumstad on speakerphone and told him that they had just met with Chris Flowers, who had walked them through the numbers.

"He's looking at buying some assets, putting together a deal," Willumstad responded, and for a moment the confused government officials all looked at one another: Wasn't Flowers advising AIG? But then Jester smiled knowingly at Paulson. This was classic Flowers, playing both sides. It quickly became evident to everyone that Flowers was likely trying to tee up a deal for his buyout shop with government assistance. "He's frankly a troublemaker," Paulson exclaimed. "He doesn't want to save this country!"

The discussion returned to the numbers, and Willumstad explained that they had teams of bidders at his office and were hoping to sell enough assets over the weekend to cover the pending shortfall.

Geithner suggested Willumstad come over later that day to review the firm's books so that they could get a better handle on what its plans were.

"Okay," Willumstad said. With a laugh, he added, "I won't be bringing Flowers."

———

Downstairs the CEOs were now summoned from the dining room to the conference room to deliver a progress report to Paulson and Geithner.

Each of the groups offered up what they had accomplished, which amounted to very little. Part of the problem was that there was still huge disagreement over what Lehman's assets were actually worth, especially its notorious commercial real estate assets. While Lehman had been valuing that portfolio at $41 billion, consisting of $32.6 billion in loans and $8.4 billion in investments, everyone knew it was worth far less. But how much less?

One set of estimates making the rounds was a spreadsheet called "Blue Writedowns" that cut the estimated value of Lehman's commercial real estate loans by about one quarter, to less than $24 billion. Others thought the situation was much worse. A handwritten sheet with more estimations making the rounds had the numbers "17–20"—less than half the estimated value.

The story was much the same with residential mortgages, which Lehman had estimated at $17.2 billion. While the Blue spreadsheet placed the value at about $14 billion, others in the room put the real value at closer to $9.2 billion, or roughly half.

But Pandit had another issue to raise: He wanted to talk again about AIG. And then he added: "What about Merrill?"

It made for an awkward moment, as John Thain was only seats away.

"You guys get this done for me, and I'll make sure I can take care of AIG and Merrill," Paulson replied. "I'm a little uncomfortable talking about Merrill Lynch with John in the room."

———

Harvey Miller, Lehman's bankruptcy lawyer, had just had a terrible meeting with representatives of the New York Fed. He couldn't answer any of their questions, and frankly, he was embarrassed at having continually to resort to the same answer: "We don't have access to information. Everybody at Lehman is either working on Bank of America or Barclays." After they left, Miller complained to his colleague, Lori Fife, "That was bullshit."

Miller had dealt with tough clients before—bankruptcy was always a parlous transaction—but he had never been shut out like this. When he called Steve Berkenfeld, Lehman's general counsel, to complain, Berkenfeld tried to explain why the information had not been as forthcoming as he had hoped. "The problem is that many of our financial team have gone downtown to give an update to the Fed."

"I see," replied Miller frostily. "And what is the latest with Barclays?"

"We're still hopeful, but there's not much new to report at this moment."

"And with BofA?"

Berkenfeld paused before answering. "They've gone radio silent."

That didn't sound very encouraging to Miller, who had developed a keen ear for detecting a tone that indicated the end was near. His team of lawyers had been operating on the assumption that the bankruptcy work was a contingency; no one was expecting Lehman to have to make a filing immediately. But as the clouds over the firm grew darker, Miller decided to move forward. He told Fife that if Lehman were to need to file for bankruptcy, it would take them at least two weeks to get the paperwork in order. They might as well begin now.

Just after noon he sent out an e-mail to a handful of colleagues with an apocalyptic subject line: "Urgent. Code name: Equinox. Have desperate need for help on an emergency situation."

———

Thain was in the middle of a conversation strategizing with Peter Kraus when Fleming called.

"I've set it up," Fleming told him excitedly. "You'll meet with Lewis this afternoon."

Thain knew that the meeting was a good idea, but there was one complication: "Paulson's not going to like this," he warned Fleming. A merger, he thought, would be a death sentence for Lehman, as he'd have stolen Lehman's sole potential savior. He didn't know that Bank of America had dropped its bid for Lehman.

"Paulson's constituency is the taxpayer," Fleming responded. "Ours is Merrill Lynch shareholders. Paulson has the ability to step in. We're going to have to listen to him, but we don't have to anticipate that. He may not like it, but unless he tells us we can't do it, if we think this is in the best interest of Merrill Lynch shareholders, we need to do it."

Thain still hesitated, wanting to make certain that he wasn't putting the company into play.

"I've set the meeting for two thirty p.m.," Fleming pressed, and then carefully added, "But you have to call Ken first."

"Why?" Thain asked, perplexed at the request.

"Because he wants to hear your voice," Fleming answered.

"What do you mean?"

"I don't know, just tell him the weather is nice in New York and you're looking forward to seeing him."

"I don't understand why I need to make the call," Thain persisted.

"John, you *just have* to call him."

"You're getting on my nerves," Thain said, annoyance straining his voice.

"You know what? That's probably going to happen again this weekend," Fleming said, raising his own voice to his boss for the first time. "But call the guy. He's not going to fly until you call him."

"Okay," Thain agreed. They decided that they'd meet at Merrill's Midtown office in thirty minutes to plan for the meeting.

Soon after Thain hung up with Fleming, John Mack walked over to him.

"We should talk," Mack said quietly. He didn't have to elaborate—the phrase was accepted code for *We should talk about doing a deal together.*

"You're right," Thain said, and they agreed to organize a meeting later that day. *It was becoming a busy day.*

On the fourth floor of the Fed, Bob Diamond of Barclays was tapping his foot impatiently.

For most of the morning, it seemed to him that Lehman and the government were exclusively focused on Bank of America. He had come to suspect that he was being used, that he was the government's stalking horse so that they could coax out a higher bid for Lehman from Bank of America.

But then, just past 2:00 p.m., Diamond had an indication that his bid might be taken seriously when someone at the Fed taped a piece of paper on Barclays' conference room door that said "Bidder." The Fed's kitchen staff had also finally shown up with food. All small gestures, but encouraging signals, nonetheless.

Still, Diamond knew he had a big problem to deal with before a Lehman deal could take place—a problem that he had yet to share with Paulson or anyone in the U.S. government. His general counsel in London, Mark Harding, had informed him on an internal conference call that morning that if Barclays were to announce plans to acquire Lehman, the deal would require a shareholder vote—a vote that might take as long as thirty to sixty days to complete. That meant that it would be critical that Barclays find a way to guarantee Lehman's trading from the time they signed the deal until it was approved by its shareholders—or the acquisition would be worthless. Without the guarantee, Lehman's trading partners would stop doing business with it, swiftly draining its resources and destroying any value for Barclays. This was about confidence: Counterparties needed to know that there was someone standing behind Lehman in the same way that JP Morgan had stepped up to the plate for Bear Stearns and guaranteed all of its trades even before the deal closed. The problem was that legally Barclays could not guarantee any more than about $3.5 billion of Lehman's trades without seeking permission from shareholders first, a process that could take as long as completing the deal.

Paulson and Geithner had repeatedly told Diamond in no uncertain terms that the U.S. government was not going to help, but he hadn't been able to determine if that was just a negotiating stance. As for the British government, there was no mystery there to him: It was perfectly clear that it wouldn't get involved.

What Barclays needed was a partner—a big, rich one—and it was a matter that Diamond knew he had to discuss with his brain trust, which was led by Archibald Cox Jr., Barclays Capital's chairman (and the son of the Watergate prosecutor), Rich Ricci, the firm's COO, and Jerry del Missier, Barclays Capital's co-president. Diamond had also hired his own outside adviser, Michael Klein, a smart former senior banker at Citigroup. Klein had resigned from Citigroup months earlier rather than be marginalized by Pandit's new team, but he was still a hot commodity. To keep him from going to work for a competitor, Citigroup had agreed to pay him out $28 million in deferred compensation that he would have lost by leaving. In exchange, he had to stay "on the beach" for an entire year. Diamond, convinced he needed Klein on his side, had called Pandit earlier in the week to get his on the beach status temporarily suspended so that he could work for Barclays on an emergency basis.

As they began brainstorming about the trading-guarantee problem, Klein asked aloud, "Who could possibly do this?"

"This is the kind of thing that, a year ago, you'd go to AIG, and they would have wrapped this for you, right?" del Missier asked.

That clearly was no longer possible, and Klein offered, "What about Buffett?" "Yeah, but Buffett only does deals if it's a fantastic deal for Buffett," del Missier pointed out.

Klein had done some deals with the Omaha Oracle when he was at Citigroup and had all his phone numbers. He called and found Buffett at the Fairmont Hotel Macdonald in Edmonton, Alberta, as he and his second wife, Astrid Menks, were about to leave for a gala, unbeknownst to them, as the surprise guests.

Klein put him on speakerphone with Diamond and his team. Del Missier began to explain to Buffett why the guarantee was so important. "If Lehman trades dollars for yen with somebody, that bank needs to know that Lehman is going to deliver the dollars before they deliver the yen," he told Buffett. "If there are worries that they're going to be able to settle that trade, the whole thing is going to unravel."

Buffett understood what was at stake but couldn't fathom guaranteeing Lehman's books for up to two months. But wanting to be polite, he suggested, "If you fax me something written out about it, when I get back, I'll be glad to read it."

As he shut his cell phone and strolled to his car on the way to the gala, Buffett remembered the last time he had received a call like this. What a mess that turned out to be. In 1998, the week before the rescue of Long-Term Capital, Jon Corzine of Goldman Sachs called asking if he'd consider joining a group interested in buying the giant, troubled hedge fund. Buffett was about to leave on a trip to Alaska with Bill and Melinda Gates, so he asked Corzine to send him some information on that deal. Then he ended up spending a day trying in vain to get his satellite phone to connect while he viewed grizzly bears in Pack Creek. He tried to orchestrate a deal

between himself, Goldman, and AIG, but failed. It was a big waste of time
and energy. Maybe he had to stop being so polite to these Wall Street
boys.

———

Downstairs at the New York Fed, the CEOs and their underlings had all
begun milling around the lunch buffet tables. Despite the grave assignment they'd been given, there was little they could actually accomplish
on the spot. Not only did they not have computers with them, but the
people with any real expertise in analyzing balance sheets and assets were
either with the Lehman team upstairs or back at their offices, poring over
volumes of spreadsheets.

In one corner a number of executives, trying to pass the time, were
doing vicious imitations of Paulson, Geithner, and Cox. "Ahhhh, ummm,
ahhhh, ummm," one banker muttered, adopting Paulson's stammer.
"Work harder, get smarter!" another shouted, mocking Geithner's Boy
Scoutish exhortations. A third did his best impression of Christopher Cox,
whom they were all convinced had little understanding of high finance:
"Two plus two? Um—could I have a calculator?" In another corner, Colm
Kelleher, Morgan's CFO, had begun playing BrickBreaker on his Black-
Berry, and soon an unofficial tournament was under way, with everyone
competitively comparing scores.

After lunch, they were all summoned back into the main conference
room, where John Thain's absence did not go unnoticed.

If there was one topic besides Lehman's future on the minds of the
CEOs, it was the fate of their own firms. What would Lehman's bankruptcy mean for them? Was Merrill really next? What about Morgan Stanley or Goldman Sachs? And what about JP Morgan or Citigroup? While
commercial banks like JP Morgan had large, stable deposit bases, they still
funded part of their business the same way the broker-dealers did: by
regularly rolling over short-term commercial paper contracts that had
become subject to the same erosion of confidence that had brought down
Bear Stearns—and now Lehman Brothers. To them the waning trust only
suggested the nefarious handiwork of short-sellers.

At one point, John Mack questioned the whole idea of bailouts and
ruminated aloud about whether they should just let Merrill fail, too, even
though seated just a few places away from him was Peter Kraus, who was

standing in for John Thain. The question quickly quieted the room. Some thought he was gaming all of them—maybe he wanted to buy Merrill on the cheap? What they didn't know was that he had approached Thain just hours earlier and had set a meeting for that evening.

Dimon looked at Mack dumbfounded. "If we do that," he said caustically, "how many hours do you think it would be before Fidelity would call you up and tell you it was no longer willing to roll your paper?"

———

When Thain finally did call Ken Lewis, the conversation was brief and to the point—merely a discussion of the logistics of their meeting. Thain was concerned enough to get the details correct that he called Lewis back a second time to confirm which entrance of the Time Warner Center he ought to use.

Before driving over to Lewis's apartment, Thain met with Fleming at the firm's Midtown offices to strategize. He made it clear to Fleming that the discussions were purely exploratory—and that he wanted to sell only a small stake in the firm, maybe up to 20 percent.

"He's not going to go for that," Fleming warned. "Lewis is going to say that he wants to buy the whole company."

Thain opened the car door himself, making a beeline to the entrance. Ducking under the extended steel-and-glass awning, with its One Central Park address, he rushed solo up the South Tower to Lewis's apartment.

Lewis greeted Thain warmly in a room with striking views but one that revealed its status as a corporate apartment by the virtual absence of artwork or furniture.

"Given all the events that were going on," Thain said, once they settled themselves, "I am concerned about the impact on the market and on Merrill if Lehman were to go bankrupt." He paused for a few seconds and then said bluntly: "I'd like to explore whether you'd have an interest in buying a 9.9 percent stake in the company and providing a large liquidity facility."

"Well, I'm not really very interested in buying 9.9 percent of the company," Lewis shot right back just as directly. "But I am interested in buying all the company."

"I didn't come here to sell the entire company," Thain replied with a slight grin on his face, having not expected Lewis to be so aggressive.

"That's what I'm interested in," Lewis repeated firmly.

Thain nervously tried to forge a compromise. "Are you willing to go down two tracks, explore a 9.9 percent sale and explore a 100 percent sale?"

"Yes," Lewis agreed, "but remember that I said to you, I'm not really interested in 9.9 percent, I'm really interested in a full merger."

Lewis and Thain spent the next half hour reviewing the various mixes of businesses, the strategic rationale for a merger, and assembling some due diligence teams. Lewis suggested they reconvene with "the two Gregs"— Greg Curl and Greg Fleming—at 5:00 p.m.

"I can't do it then," Thain told Lewis.

Strange, Lewis thought. Thain showed up wanting to do a deal and now he couldn't meet in two hours? Did he have somewhere better to be? Was he in talks with someone else?

As he was about to leave, Thain stopped and raised a final point: "I have to tell Hank about these conversations," he explained, "because I'm worried that if Hank finds out about them, he's going to think that I screwed up the Lehman deal."

"Well, look, you know," Lewis answered, "I would prefer the Merrill deal. You can tell Hank that we're having these discussions, because we're not going to pursue Lehman without government assistance."

In the end, the men would separately brief Paulson, who, as it happened, was thrilled to hear the news. As far as he was concerned, Barclays was about to buy Lehman, and now Bank of America was talking about acquiring Merrill. It was all coming together.

———

"I got voice mail again," a frustrated Fuld told Tom Russo. "Nobody's picking up his goddamn phone!"

He could not locate anyone he needed—Paulson, Geithner, Cox, Lewis. Even Bart McDade, his own employee, was unreachable. They were all down at the NY Fed, but no one was taking his call or calling him back.

Fuld wanted an update. He had been in his office all of Saturday, dressed in a blue suit and starched white shirt as if it were a typical work day, but hadn't heard a word about Bank of America or Barclays.

When the phone did ring, it was Rodgin Cohen, who, calling from the

NY Fed, said, "Yeah, we've got a problem. I think Merrill and BofA are talking."

"What do you mean?" Fuld barked.

Cohen explained that he had just left a meeting with Geithner at which he tried to persuade him again that government assistance was necessary to avoid the collapse of the entire banking system. As Cohen recounted it, he had told Geithner: "If you don't help, Merrill will be gone by Monday."

Geithner's response—"We're working on a solution for Merrill"—had been purposefully vague, but both Cohen and Fuld knew exactly what it meant. It also explained Bank of America's silence. They both hadn't forgotten Greg Curl's comment to them over the summer about how Lewis had always wanted to buy Merrill. And it explained the odd phone call Cohen had received from Merrill's Fleming earlier in the week, casting about for information.

"I can't even believe this," Fuld said, sinking deeper into his chair.

___

During some downtime at the NY Fed, Gary Cohn and David Viniar of Goldman Sachs greeted their former colleague Peter Kraus, who was now a week into his new job at Merrill.

"Peter, come for a walk," Cohn suggested, and all three men stepped out the front door onto Liberty Street.

"So, what's going on?" Cohn asked after they had gone a short way, hinting that he knew that Merrill was under enormous pressure—perhaps more so than anyone in the room.

"We just have a liquidity problem," Kraus said. "JP Morgan just upped our intraday margin lines by $10 billion." He paused. "We're fine, we're totally fine."

"Peter, should we be looking at you guys?" Cohn asked.

Kraus looked down before answering. "Yes." Any deal with Goldman would not just shore up Merrill's teetering financial position but also would be seen as a vote of confidence by the smartest guys in the room.

"Why didn't you say something?" Cohn asked. "We've been friends forever. We've been sitting next to each other for a day and a half."

As they strolled around the block, Kraus said that it would be worth having a meeting. He said that Merrill would be looking for a credit line to get over the hump of their liquidity crisis in exchange for selling a small stake in the company, probably under 10 percent. It was nearly the same arrangement that Thain had originally been seeking from Lewis.

They agreed to meet the following morning at Goldman Sachs' offices.

The instructions were specific: Don't use the main entrance of the New York Federal Reserve on Liberty Street; use instead the employee entrance on Maiden Lane and show your driver's license to the security guards. Your name will be on a list; an escort will be waiting for you.

Bob Willumstad of AIG and his advisers, Doug Braunstein of JP Morgan, Jamie Gamble of Simpson Thacher, and Michael Wiseman of Sullivan & Cromwell walked over from AIG's headquarters to meet with Paulson and Geithner, strolling past the photographers and reporters, who, to the bankers' relief, didn't recognize them.

"Where do you stand on the capital raise?" Geithner asked without preamble.

Willumstad said that he believed that they were making progress. A half dozen bidders were still at the building, including Flowers, KKR, and Allianz.

But, Willumstad said, the bigger news—the good news—was that he had persuaded Eric R. Dinallo, superintendent of the New York State Insurance Department, to release some $20 billion in collateral from AIG's regulated insurance entities, which would help it meet its capital requirement. Dinallo had made the agreement contingent on AIG's raising another $20 billion to fill the hole. Willumstad intimated that he thought he had another $5 billion loan commitment coming from Ajit Jain, who ran Berkshire Hathaway's reinsurance business. That left him with a $15 billion gap, but he told the regulators that the company had assets up for sale that were worth more than $25 billion.

With that, Paulson and Geithner rose and abruptly left the meeting. They had heard all they needed to; progress was being made.

The doorman opened the cast-iron and glass doors to allow Thain, Kraus, and their colleague Tom Montag into the lobby of Walid

Chammah's apartment building. It was the second secret merger meeting to take place there in one week. Thain was a little worried about being spotted: Among others, Larry Fink of BlackRock lived at the same address.

Mack, Chammah, and Gorman were waiting for them in Chammah's living room.

Gorman, who had run Merrill Lynch's private client business for five years before joining Morgan Stanley, was immediately struck by the fact that no one in the group representing Merrill had been with the company for more than ten months. The firm Gorman helped to build, and where his brother, Nick, still worked, was going to be sold out from under it by bankers with no sense of the firm's heritage.

Thain opened the discussion by indicating that he was looking to do a deal. "With what's going on with Lehman," he said, "we recognize this is the right time to look at our options."

Kraus began to go over the numbers, flipping through the pages of a book he had brought along with him. For someone who had only a few days on the job, Chammah and Gorman thought, he seemed to know his stuff. (Kraus had, in fact, stayed up till 3:00 a.m. earlier that week poring over the firm's balance sheet.)

But the gaps in his knowledge soon became apparent. When Gorman started asking him about Merrill's retail business—the part of the company in which Morgan Stanley was most interested—neither Thain, Kraus, nor Montag knew the numbers.

Still, Mack said he was interested and asked what the next step was. "We have a board meeting scheduled for Monday night," he explained, "and Tuesday we could probably start diligence and take a look then. It's obviously intriguing but this is complicated."

Thain gave Kraus an anxious glance and then turned to Mack: "No, no. You don't understand. We would need to have a decision before Asia opens."

Gorman was confused: "What do you mean by 'decision'?"

"We're looking to have a signed deal by then," Thain said calmly.

"We can keep talking," Mack answered, shocked by the request, "but I don't know that that's physically possible."

After they saw themselves out of the apartment, Thain looked at Kraus and said, "Well, it's pretty clear that they don't have the same sense of urgency that we do."

———

Greg Curl of Bank of America was already at Wachtell, Lipton when Greg Fleming of Merrill Lynch arrived. While he waited, Curl had been on the telephone trying to undo his decision from four hours earlier: He had sent more than a hundred bankers back to Charlotte, assuming they were no longer needed, because as far as he had been concerned, the Lehman deal was dead. Now, with the possibility of a deal with Merrill, he needed them on the next plane back to New York. He recognized that the situation was almost comical and had assigned several people to coordinate looking into chartering flights, because the three remaining direct US Airways flights to New York that night were already full.

Curl invited Fleming into one of the law firm's conference rooms that he had commandeered, grabbing a handful of cookies from the catering cart that was parked there. He quickly asked him for his assessment of where he thought they were in terms of pursuing a deal.

"I'm thinking we announce Monday morning," Fleming said.

"That's very quick," Curl replied, taken aback by the timetable.

"You know the company really well," Fleming answered. He was one of the few people who were aware that Merrill's former CEO Stanley O'Neal had talked to Lewis about a merger, though he didn't know all the details. "I know all the work you've already done. I'll open up everything. Just tell me what you need."

For the next half hour they drew up a process that would enable Bank of America to examine Merrill's books within literally twenty-four hours. Curl, who dusted off the work he had done a year ago for the talks with O'Neal, said he was going to bring Chris Flowers in to advise him, as Flowers had recently looked into buying some of Merrill's toxic assets over the summer (assets that were ultimately sold to Lone Star National Bank), so he would have a head start. Bank of America already even had a code name for the deal: "Project Alpha."

Before the meeting broke, the issue of price was raised. Fleming boldly declared that he was looking for "something with a three-handle," by which he meant $30 a share or more, which represented a 76 percent premium over Merrill's share price of $17.05 on Friday. It was a shockingly high number, especially in the context of the greatest financial crisis of the firm's history, but Fleming felt he had no choice: Merrill had just sold $8.55 billion of convertible stock a month earlier to big investors like Singapore's state-owned Temasek, at $22.50 a share. He needed to get them a reasonable premium.

For most bankers, a number that high would have stopped the talks in their tracks, but Curl understood the rationale behind the price that Fleming was seeking. Fleming argued that Merrill's shares were temporarily depressed and that he needed a price that reflected a "normalized basis." Just a year and a half ago, he reminded him, Merrill's shares were trading at more than $80.

Curl had a strong view about takeovers: You never want to overpay, but if you believe in the business, you're better off paying more to guarantee you own it than to lose it to a competitor.

"Okay," Curl said, not committing to Fleming's number, but clearly indicating that he wasn't going to reject it altogether. "We've got a lot to do."

The weather was beautiful for a late Saturday-night dinner on the patio of San Pietros, the southern Italian restaurant on East Fifty-fourth Street off Madison Avenue. During the week the restaurant plays host to Wall Street bigwigs over lunch: Joseph Perella of Perella Weinberg, the dean of the M&A banking business, has a table there; other regulars include Larry Fink, chief executive of BlackRock; Richard A. Grasso, the former chairman of the New York Stock Exchange; Ronald O. Perelman, the chairman of Revlon; and David H. Komansky, the former chief executive of Merrill Lynch; and even former president Bill Clinton and his pal Vernon Jordan.

Tonight Mack and Morgan Stanley's management took a quiet table outside. For Chammah it was an opportunity to unwind and smoke a cigar. It had been a draining twenty-four hours.

Gerardo Bruno, a big personality from southern Italy who owns the restaurant with his three brothers, showed the group to their table. Mack took his blazer off and threw it over the back of his chair. Soon, Paul Taubman, Colm Kelleher, and Gary Lynch met them there. There was a lot to talk about.

After ordering a bottle of Barbaresco they launched into a postmortem of the grueling day, specifically the last crazy hour with Merrill Lynch, with Mack recounting the meeting with Thain for the benefit of those who hadn't been in the room with him.

"And then he says, 'Can you do it in twenty-four hours?'" Mack reported as the table erupted in laughter.

"No fucking way," Colm Kelleher said.

Once the laughter died down, Mack raised the biggest question before them: Given the scope of the crisis now enveloping the industry, did they need to do a deal?

Chammah spoke up first. "Listen, there are not too many dancing partners out there that we want to dance with. If there's ever going to be a time to talk, now's probably the time."

Gorman stepped in and explained that Merrill Lynch, given their conversation just an hour ago with Thain, was likely to merge with Bank of America, perhaps within the next twenty-four hours. That meant that Bank of America would be taken off the table as a merger partner. Gorman was still shaking his head over the audacity of Thain, Kraus, and Montag's attempt to sell Merrill, a firm they had only recently joined and hardly knew.

"We could call Lewis," Gorman suggested.

Mack had always thought that Bank of America could be a natural merger partner for Morgan Stanley; indeed, before the crisis, he had often half joked with friends that it was his "exit strategy." When his stock price was higher, he had often thought a deal with Bank of America would be one triumphant way of demonstrating that he had restored Morgan Stanley, the firm he loved, to its former glory. Strategically, they were a perfect fit: Bank of America was an outstanding commercial and retail bank, but its investment side was weak. Morgan Stanley had the opposite configuration: It was a superior investment bank but had few stable deposits. Perhaps the best part of the merger would be that Mack, born near Charlotte, where Bank of America was based, could retire there with his family as the new, combined bank's chairman.

But tonight, Mack understood, it wasn't meant to be. "If Merrill goes to BofA, what do you think about Wachovia?" he asked as plates of Timballo di Baccala con Patate, Fave e Pomodoro arrived at the table.

For the next two hours, they debated the merits of reaching out to Wachovia, also based in Charlotte; JP Morgan Chase; or HSBC. They could call China Investment Corporation, the nation's largest sovereign wealth fund, Kelleher suggested, while Paul Taubman mentioned Mitsubishi.

Whomever they might select, Mack was adamant on one point: "We shouldn't be rushed into anything." While it might be ugly out there, he reminded everyone of the obvious: They were Morgan Stanley, the global financial juggernaut. The firm's market value was still more than $50 billion as of that Friday—a lot less than a month earlier but hardly a joke. And they had $180 billion in the bank.

Kelleher, the bank's CFO, had been diligently building up liquidity for months, in the event of just such a situation in which they now found themselves. There was no way there could be a run on Morgan Stanley; they had too much credibility in the market. At the same time, he recognized that if Lehman was sold to Barclays, and Merrill was sold to Bank of America, his firm would be in the hot seat.

Chammah, taking a sip of wine, said soberly, "We could be up next."

———

It was after 8:00 p.m., and Jamie Dimon, who was starving, made his way up to the executive dining room on the forty-ninth floor of JP Morgan's headquarters. The operating committee had been working flat out for the entire day, calculating the firm's exposure to Lehman, Merrill, Morgan Stanley, Goldman, and, of course, AIG, and the dining staff had been called in to work overtime to feed everyone. Tonight was tacos, and though the food may not have been as good as what the Fed offered downtown, it was better than Dimon had remembered. It was also the first time he'd eaten dinner in the recently renovated partners' dining room.

In the middle of his meal, Dimon stood up and began pacing back and forth in front of the floor-to-ceiling windows, surveying the cityscape. From his vantage point he could see all of Manhattan in every direction. The sun had just crested below the Empire State Building a half hour earlier, and a fog hung over the city.

Dimon was mulling over the day's events, realizing how bad it was out there. "They want Wall Street to pay," he told the room of bankers relaxing after their late dinners, hoping to get them to appreciate the political pressure Paulson was facing. "They think we're overpaid assholes. There's no politician, no president, who is going to sign off on a bailout." Then, channeling the populist anger, he asked, "Why *would* you try to bail out people whose sole job it is to make money?"

"We just hit the iceberg," Dimon bellowed to his men, as if he were standing upon the deck of the *Titanic.* "The boat is filling with water, and the music is still playing. There aren't enough lifeboats," he said with a wry smile. "Someone is going to die."

"So you might as well enjoy the champagne and caviar!"

With that, he returned to his table and took a final bite of taco.

———

At the Fed, Barclays, against all odds, appeared to be making progress. Earlier that day, Michael Klein, Diamond's adviser, had come up with a structure for the deal with which they were all happy. Diamond wasn't interested in Lehman's real estate assets; what he wanted was the "good bank"—Lehman minus its troubled property holdings.

Klein's plan was simple: Barclays would buy "good" Lehman, and the rival banks across the hall at the Fed would help finance the "bad bank's" debt. That struck Diamond as a "clean" deal he could easily sell to his board back in London and to the British regulators, who he knew were still a bit skittish about the transaction. All in, it would cost $3.5 billion, which would be used to help support the "bad bank."

Past midnight, the Barclays team decamped from their conference room, planning to leave. But as they marched downstairs, they were pulled aside into another conference room and asked to explain their plan to the rival bankers who were still at the Fed. This would be a tricky maneuver: They were, in effect, being asked to sell their bitterest rivals in the industry to subsidize their bid.

Despite the hour, a group of bankers from Goldman, Citi, Credit Suisse, and other firms were still lingering about. Klein proceeded to explain, in the most delicate way possible, Barclays' plan, which everyone in the room instantly realized meant that an industry consortium would have to come up with some $33 billion to finance ShitCo, or as Klein kept describing it to people, "RemainderCo." For the other banks, this would be less an investment in Lehman or Barclays than it would be in themselves, hoping to stave off the impact of a Lehman failure.

The way Klein explained it, the consortium would own the equivalent of an alternative investment management firm like Fortress Investment or Blackstone Group, owning Lehman's real estate and private-equity assets.

The idea was not received with enthusiasm. Gary Shedlin of Citigroup, a former colleague of Klein's, was the first to raise red flags, perhaps because an undercurrent of tension still existed between him and Klein stemming from clashes during their time together at Citi.

"How much equity do you need to raise to do the deal?" Shedlin asked.

"Why is that important?" Klein responded, seemingly confused about its relevance. "Why do you need to know that?"

"You're making an offer for this company," Shedlin snapped back, "and we've got to know how you're going to finance it."

Archie Cox of Barclays, frustrated by the questioning, replied icily, "We will not have to raise any incremental capital as part of this transaction."

Klein, realizing that the bankers didn't understand the structure of the deal, explained it again. Barclays wasn't going to be investing in Lehman's "bad bank" alongside the consortium; it was only buying Lehman's "good bank."

The bankers around the table looked at one another, as his explanation set in. They really were being asked to subsidize a competitor. Barclays would have no stake in Lehman's worst assets, which they were being asked to take on.

After Shedlin calmed down, the group, while not happy about the proposal, agreed that it might be the best of many bad options. They set about hammering out a term sheet. As unbelievable as it seemed to all the bleary-eyed bankers in the room, they were inching toward a possible deal.

———

"We've got a big problem. I mean, *fucking* big," Douglas Braunstein of JP Morgan announced to his team at AIG just past midnight.

The lights were still ablaze where a battalion of bankers, hunched over laptops and spreadsheets, had just discovered a new hole in AIG's finances. Its securities lending business had lost $20 billion more than anyone had recorded.

"We're not trying to solve for $40 billion anymore," Braunstein shouted. "We need $60 billion!"

AIG was such a sprawling mess, and its computer systems so bizarrely antiquated, that no one conducting diligence had until that moment discovered that its securities lending business had been losing money at a rapid clip for the past two weeks. As the JP Morgan bankers dug deeper, they found that AIG had been engaged in a dubious practice: They had been issuing long-term mortgages and financing them with short-term paper. As a result, every time the underlying asset, the mortgages, lost value—which had happened every day of the previous week—they needed to pony up more promissory notes.

"This is unbelievable," Mark Feldman, one of the JP Morgan bankers, said as he stormed out of the room in search of Brian Schreiber of AIG.

When he finally tracked Schreiber down, he told him, "We need you to sign the engagement letter. This is getting ridiculous. We've been here all weekend."

Dimon and Steve Black had ordered Feldman to get the engagement letter signed or leave and take everyone with him. After all, as Black reminded him, JP Morgan had no indemnification if they didn't have a signed engagement letter, leaving them with exposure to lawsuits; and perhaps more important, they wanted to make sure they got paid for their time and efforts. Black told him to blame his boss in the event of any complaints.

Schreiber, who'd been given signing authority by Willumstad, was nevertheless annoyed. His unit at AIG had taken to calling the junior JP Morgan team "The Hitler Youth," but how could Feldman actually pressure him to sign such a document at a time like this? The entire firm was teetering, and his banker was asking for his fee?

At first, Schreiber tried to suggest that the firm's counsel might have to be responsible for any signature, but Feldman was having none of it.

Schreiber finally erupted. "I can't sign this! My board won't sign this letter. This is disgusting. It's offensive. It's vulgar. I just can't justify signing this!" he shouted.

Feldman, who had called Schreiber "a fucking imbecile" to his face at least once, had now also reached his limit. "If you don't sign this letter this minute, I'm going to have every fucking JP Morgan banker pack up and leave right this second!"

At that Schreiber relented and, irately pulling out his pen, signed it.

At 3:00 on Sunday morning, more than two hundred bankers and lawyers from Bank of America and Merrill Lynch were on their second round of pizza delivery at Wachtell, Lipton, and they were still sprinting to complete their diligence.

Greg Fleming, who had been awake for almost twenty-four hours, had booked a room at the Mandarin Oriental, so that he wouldn't have to drive back to Rye.

He was gathering his belongings and about to call it a night when Peter Kelly, Merrill's deal lawyer, entered the conference room.

"I've got news," Fleming told him. He enthusiastically explained that he had already broached the issue of price with Curl and had reason to believe that Bank of America might be willing to pay as much as $30 a share.

For a moment Kelly thought Fleming had to be joking.

"I can't believe they're going pay us $30," Kelly told him. "Greg, this trade is never going to happen. It doesn't make any sense. We're on our knees here."

"I'm telling you," Fleming insisted. "I think they're going to get there."

"You're getting gamed right now and you don't know it!" Kelly snapped, trying to talk some sense into his friend at this late hour. "You need to wake up and figure out how you're getting gamed, because there's no way they're doing a $30 trade! They're going to lead us to the altar and they're going to renegotiate it at $3, or they're just going to let us go."

"Don't doubt me, Pete," Fleming insisted. "The trade is going to happen."

CHAPTER FIFTEEN

At around 8:00 the next morning, Sunday, September 14, Wall Street's groggy CEOs trudged back to the NY Fed.

Lloyd Blankfein and Greg Palm, Goldman's general counsel, each of whom had had roughly four hours of sleep, entered the building together.

"I don't think I can take another day of this," Palm said wearily.

Blankfein laughed. "You're getting out of a Mercedes to go to the New York Federal Reserve—you're not getting out of a Higgins boat on Omaha Beach! Keep things in perspective." Blankfein was making a not-so-subtle reference to John Whitehead, one of Goldman's former CEOs and a company patriarch, who had written a book titled *A Life in Leadership: From D-Day to Ground Zero*, which Blankfein had made required reading at the firm.

A Fed staffer announced to all the CEOs that Paulson, Geithner, and Cox would soon be coming downstairs. When Jamie Dimon, dressed in tight blue jeans, black loafers, and a shirt showing off his muscles, wandered into the room, Colm Kelleher whispered to John Mack, "He's in pretty good shape for his age."

Paulson and Geithner appeared and announced that they had good news, which everyone in the room already seemed to know. Overnight, Barclays had put together a proposal to buy Lehman and was prepared to move ahead. The only stumbling block that remained was getting all the other banks to contribute enough money—some $33 billion—to finance Lehman's "bad bank." After instructing the group to finish working out all the details, Geithner abruptly left the room.

A document titled "Certain Deal Issues" was now circulated, identifying some of the more difficult questions the bankers would have to consider. Would the two parts of a split-up Lehman each have enough funding after the deal closed? And could Lehman's bad bank be made "bankruptcy remote"—in other words, legally sealed off so that creditors couldn't go after the healthy part later?

It was then that Dimon decided to play the role of John Pierpont Morgan, who helped rescue the nation following the Panic of 1907.

"Okay, let's make this really simple," he announced. "How many of you would kick in $1 billion—I don't care what form it takes—to stop Lehman from going down?"

It was the question on everyone's mind but the one that no one had dared to ask. It was the same question that Herbert Allison, then of Merrill Lynch, had posed a decade earlier in the same building when at stake was saving Long-Term Capital Management. Dimon, then at Citigroup, had had a seat at the table for that one, too. The only difference between then and now was that Allison had asked how many banks could put up $250 million; even factoring in inflation, $1 billion a bank was a steep request.

At the time, Jimmy Cayne, Bear's chairman, had refused to take part. "What the fuck are you doing?" Merrill's CEO, David Komansky, screamed at him.

Cayne shouted back: "When did we become partners?"

Everyone in the room today was well aware of that famous exchange between the two Wall Street kingpins.

Blankfein told the room that while he wasn't convinced that Lehman actually posed a systemic risk, there was a larger issue of all the banks' reputations and public perception to consider. "Bear Stearns did a lot of good things over the last decade, but the only thing they're remembered for is, they didn't step up when the industry needed them to."

What went unspoken but was surely on the minds of many of the bankers in the room was the role that Dick Fuld had played in the rescue of LTCM. When it came time for him to contribute his $250 million share, he explained that he couldn't afford to do so. Given the pressure on his firm—and the rumors then that Lehman was about to go out of business—he had contributed only $100 million.

Now, with a dozen banks represented around the table, Dimon kicked off the fund-raising effort.

"I'm in," he said. One by one the bankers began to indicate what they might be willing to ante up as well. When the tally was added up, they were close to saving Lehman—or so they thought.

———

Peter Kraus and Peter Kelly of Merrill Lynch arrived at Goldman Sachs' headquarters just after 8:00 a.m., rode the elevator up to the thirtieth floor, strode through the glass doors, and slipped into the virtually empty executive suite on their own. Kraus, having worked at Goldman for twenty-two years, knew his way around the place.

Gary Cohn and David Viniar of Goldman greeted them and escorted them to a conference room. Before the meeting, Cohn had privately told Viniar that if Goldman were to buy a stake in Merrill, the price was going to be a lowball one. "I'm going to be low single digits," he asserted, a far cry from the $30 a share that Fleming had been hoping to get out of Bank of America. (Cohn didn't say so at the time, but he was thinking the entire firm's value might be just several billion dollars; Merrill's market capitalization on Friday had been $26.1 billion.)

Kraus brought with him the same deck, or presentation, that he had taken to Morgan Stanley. He told the Goldman bankers that Merrill was looking to sell a 9.9 percent stake in the firm and also looking for a $20 billion credit facility.

Before the negotiating even began, Cohn, always blunt, told them: "I'm going to write down your mortgage portfolios to a place where I think they click." In other words, he was going to value Merrill's toxic assets at next to nothing.

"I know the way you think," Kraus replied. "You *could* put a positive number on it," he said, hoping that Cohn and Viniar would at least assign some value to the portfolio.

Just as Kraus began digging deeper into Merrill's balance sheet, Kelly, the only non-Goldman-connected man in the room, stopped him. He was clearly anxious about providing Goldman with too much information. Kraus may have trusted his former colleagues, but Kelly was more circumspect. To him, the odds of pulling off a deal with Goldman were low, and given Cohn's comments, if a deal did come together, Merrill would be sold for a song.

"Guys, nothing personal, but let's just lay low here," Kelly said. "If you want to do due diligence, let us talk to John and let's figure out what we want to do."

That was acceptable to Cohn and Viniar, who, in any case, had to get back to the NY Fed. They agreed they'd resume the talks once Kraus and Kelly could get their information in order.

As the meeting was breaking up, Kelly called Fleming to give him a progress report. He said that he and Kraus had made their pitch, but he acknowledged that simply getting a credit line in exchange for 9.9 percent might not be enough to save the firm.

"That's not going to fill the gap if Lehman goes," he told Fleming.

———

"It looks like we may have the outlines of a deal around the financing!" Steve Shafran, a senior adviser at Treasury, announced to Bart McDade and the Lehman team at the NY Fed. Brandishing a huge smile, Shafran told the Lehman bankers that the CEOs downstairs were close to agreeing to funding the spin-off of Lehman's real estate assets.

The men felt as if an unimaginable burden had been lifted almost instantaneously from them. And McDade excitedly tapped out a message on his BlackBerry to Michael Gelband, who was at Simpson Thacher's offices.

Standing in a conference room uptown, Gelband read McDade's message and shouted, "We got it!" he said, a broad grin spreading across his face as he let out a sigh of relief.

———

Hector Sants, the deputy head of Britain's Financial Services Authority, was driving along the A30 from Cornwall on the southwestern tip of England back to London on Sunday afternoon with his cell phone clutched precariously between his ear and his shoulder.

Sants had been on the phone for most of the weekend with his boss, Sir Callum McCarthy, head of the FSA and a former Barclays banker himself. McCarthy, at sixty-four years old, had only six days remaining in his tenure in the post and was scheduled to step down that Friday.

Sants and McCarthy had spent hours trying to assess the state of affairs between Barclays and Lehman. Sants had been in contact several times with Varley that day, but McCarthy's efforts to contact Geithner, his counterpart in the United States, were proving more difficult. They had spoken briefly on Saturday, but he had heard nothing since.

"He hasn't called me back," McCarthy grumbled. "You can't get hold of any of these people."

They had no idea what Barclays' Diamond had—or had not—communicated to the U.S. government about what conditions had to be met to receive their blessing back in Britain. Indeed, McCarthy was nervous that Diamond, an American who had never become part of Britain's gentlemen's club, may have been a bit reckless in the negotiations, like any aggressive Wall Streeter. Both men were especially concerned that Diamond, in his zeal to sign a deal, might not have fully explained the requirements that the British regulators would ask for before approving it. To them, buying Lehman could put the bank and the British financial system as a whole in jeopardy. Varley, who was supportive of pursuing Lehman but clearly less enthusiastic than Diamond, had assured Sants during a call on Friday that Barclays' board would only pursue the deal if it could receive adequate help from the U.S. government or another source. "I would not recommend a transaction to my board unless I'm satisfied both in terms of the quality of the assets we're purchasing and in respect to the funding positions," Varley had said.

McCarthy and Sants also faced another looming problem, one that, in the grand scheme of things, may have seemed minor but was nonetheless important at that very moment: The London Clearing House (LCH, Clearnet), which clears many of the derivative counterparty trades across Europe, was scheduled to migrate its entire energy futures business—worth over 100 billion pounds—to a completely new computer system that weekend. They had instructed the London Clearing House on Saturday to hold off on proceeding with the upgrade until they knew more about the fate of Lehman and Barclays, but were now being badgered for a final answer, as dozens of technicians had been engaged to handle the switch-over.

"We shouldn't allow this to drag on," Sants said to McCarthy, hoping they could get an answer back to the London Clearing House. "We ought to try to contact Geithner and just make our position very clear."

They scripted out what McCarthy would say: "We feel as the regulator [sic], in the best interest of the global financial system, that it's important you understand—we hope Barclays has already made this clear to you, but in the event Barclays has not made this clear to you—that we need the appropriate funding assurances both on the trading side and with regards to the asset issues if we're going to allow this to go forward."

McCarthy said he would try Geithner one last time.

————

On the thirteenth floor of the NY Fed, Hilda Williams, Geithner's assistant, told him that Callum McCarthy was on the phone. Geithner finally took the call, explaining, brusque as ever, that he had been in back-to-back meetings trying to get a deal together for Lehman and apologizing for not returning his call sooner.

McCarthy stopped him, saying that he was very concerned that he didn't know anything about the deal being contemplated. He had a list of questions that he needed answered.

"The capital requirements and, in particular, the transaction risk between the time of taking on the risk and the completion of the transaction leaves a very big open-ended exposure," McCarthy said, keying in on his biggest problems with the deal. He explained that the FSA still needed to determine whether Barclays was properly capitalized enough to take on the risk of buying Lehman. And, he said, even if it was—which he suggested was a possibility—Barclays still would need to find a way to guarantee Lehman's trades until the deal was completed. "I'm very doubtful Barclays can ever get to a position to fulfill the requirements, and it is far from clear that they will be able to do so," he said.

Geithner had no idea that the FSA would take such an aggressive position and asked McCarthy directly whether the authority was formally saying it wouldn't approve the deal.

"It is completely impossible for us to take a view on whether these risks are risks that we would accept," McCarthy replied, unless "you bring a proposal forward." But, he added, since it was so late in the day—about 3:30 p.m. in London—the chances were remote they'd be able to come to a conclusion within the next several hours.

McCarthy went on to present another problem: He said that Barclays could not guarantee Lehman's trading obligations without a shareholder vote, which was a UK "listing requirement" for all publicly traded firms in Britain. However, not only was there insufficient time for such a vote, but he said that he wasn't authorized to waive the vote requirement—only the government could do that.

Geithner explained that, based on his conversations with Barclays, he thought the British government had already indicated it would be supportive of the transaction.

"I have no indication that that is the case at all," McCarthy said firmly, and then expressed anxiety, as Darling had to Paulson on Friday, about Barclays' own health and that of the rest of the market.

"Look," Geithner said impatiently, "we're going to have to decide in the next half hour what we do. Time is running out."

"Good luck," McCarthy said curtly.

Geithner ended the call and rushed into Paulson's office, where the secretary and Chris Cox were speaking, and recounted the conversation.

"I asked him if he was saying no," Geithner said, "and he kept saying that he wasn't saying no." But clearly, Geithner complained, that's exactly what he was saying.

Paulson was beside himself. "I can't believe this is happening now."

After a brief discussion of strategy, Paulson ordered Cox, who was the only regulator in the room with legal authority over Lehman Brothers, to call McCarthy. Cox, Paulson thought to himself with a sense of annoyance, was supposed to have prewired these very regulatory issues. "I don't want to be left here holding Herman," the Treasury secretary said, glancing at his zipper in case the joke wasn't clear.

Cox reached McCarthy on his cell phone in the living room of his two-story home in Blackheath, across the Thames River. After the FSA head patiently reiterated the problems that the Barclays deal faced, Cox suggested they could try to work around them, adding, "You seem to be very unsympathetic to this."

"No," retorted McCarthy coldly, "I'm trying to establish the facts of life so that you understand them and approach this with some realism."

"You're being very negative," Cox insisted.

"Look, you should understand, one of the great problems for us at this end is not actually being properly kept in the loop of what you're up to," McCarthy complained, growing increasingly agitated. "You must understand, we're hearing things late in the day," he said, ticking off a list of requirements that Barclays would need to meet. "We could have told you earlier which ones would run into problems and which ones wouldn't."

Five minutes later Cox returned to Paulson and Geithner, notepad in hand, deathly pale.

"They're not going to do it," he said. "This is a total reversal. They never said a word to us about this before!"

Tom Baxter, the NY Fed general counsel, who had just walked in, couldn't believe what he was hearing. "We've come this far, the money's on the table," he said in disbelief. "Didn't they know this when they took the plane over here?"

"I'll call Darling," Paulson said.

––––––

In Edinburgh, Scotland, Alistair Darling, Prime Minister Gordon Brown's Chancellor of the Exchequer, was preparing to head to London for the workweek, as he did every Sunday.

It was about 4:00 p.m. local time, and Darling had been on the phone for much of the day with John Varley of Barclays, officials at the FSA, and Prime Minister Brown himself, trying to decide whether the U.K. government should approve the deal with Barclays.

Darling had deep misgivings about the transaction, especially after he had learned from one of his staffers that Bank of America had dropped out of the bidding. Was Barclays going to be left buying leftovers? He had read all the coverage of the deal in the papers that morning, including an editorial in the Sunday *Telegraph*:

> Free things can still make expensive purchases. Investors should only get behind Diamond if he can prove two things: that he is retaining the kind of discipline that has been sadly lacking from the world's leading banks in recent times; and that Lehman, as transparently as it is possible to prove, is a genuine bargain.

Darling thought it was impossible that Barclays could have done a deep enough examination of Lehman's books to be satisfied that the bank wouldn't be exposed to extreme markdowns of Lehman's assets in the future. Even worse, Darling had other problems on his mind: HBOS, the United Kingdom's biggest mortgage bank, was struggling; he also knew that Lloyds was interested in buying them. Between Barclays, Lloyds, and HBOS, the entire British banking system, he thought, was at risk.

As all these concerns ran through his mind, he answered the phone call from Hank Paulson.

"Alistair," Paulson said gravely. "We've just had a distressing conversation with the FSA."

Darling explained that he understood that they had been in touch and that there seemed to be numerous unanswered questions. "I have no objection in principle to the deal," Darling said. "But you're asking the government to take on a huge risk. We need to be sure what it is that we are taking on and what the U.S. government is willing to do. The questions we are asking are not unreasonable."

"We're at the end of the line here," Paulson said, surprised at Darling's position, and pressing him again about whether he was prepared to lift the requirement for a shareholder vote.

"If this were to go ahead, you know, what would the U.S. government be doing? What are you offering?" Darling asked in return.

Paulson reiterated that he was hoping the private consortium was coming together, but now Darling shifted the conversation and began peppering Paulson with questions about the United States' contingency plans for Lehman's bankruptcy. "Well, if Lehman is going into administration, we need to know because it will have implications over here," Darling said before ending the call.

———

"He's not going to do it," Paulson told Geithner in amazement. "He said he didn't want to 'import our cancer.'"

For the next two minutes in Geithner's office, a half dozen excited voices were speaking at once, until he finally quieted the group and asked, raising his voice for the first time the entire weekend, "Why didn't we know this earlier? This is fucking crazy."

Paulson began to wonder aloud if President Bush should call Gordon Brown personally, but almost before finishing the question, he answered it himself. "There's no chance," he said, explaining that he thought that Darling had implied he had already spoken to Gordon Brown about the situation. "He was so far away from, ah, wanting Barclays to do anything," he remarked of Darling.

"Okay. Let's go to Plan B," Geithner said after a moment's reflection.

In case it wasn't clear what all of this meant, Shafran of Treasury spelled it out in simple terms in a text message to his colleagues: "We lost the patient."

They agreed to assemble downstairs to relate the news to the bankers so that they could begin preparing for Lehman's bankruptcy. Plan B was simple: Regulators would press the banks to unwind trading positions they had with Lehman and with one another in a way that minimized the impact on the markets.

And then there was the next critical issue to address, Geithner said: "We have to deal with Merrill."

As they got up to leave, Paulson, clearly depressed, remarked drily: "If you're going to ride the pony, sometimes you have to step in the shit."

———

A NY Federal Reserve security guard who had been searching for Bart McDade and Rodgin Cohen eventually found them on the first floor. "Secretary Paulson would like to see you," he announced before escorting them to Geithner's waiting room.

Cohen was already uneasy, for while McDade had been sending out enthusiastic e-mails about the near-consummation of the deal, Cohen had overheard a number of government officials who seemed to be more circumspect about its prospects. McDade now also sensed that something was amiss and sent a message to Gelband while he was waiting, telling him, "There might be a holdup."

The door to Geithner's office opened and out walked Geithner, Paulson, and Cox, all looking alarmingly dour.

"We got the banks to agree to fund, but the U.K. government has said no," Paulson announced.

"Why? Who?" Cohen asked, incredulous.

"It came from Downing Street. They don't want U.S. problems infecting the U.K. system," Paulson said.

While McDade just stood mutely in shock, Cohen, who was famous for his equanimity, virtually shouted, "I cannot believe this! You have to do something!"

"Look," Paulson said sternly, "I'm not going to cajole them and I'm not going to threaten them."

Cohen was not finished.

"I know a lever we can pull with the U.K. government," Cohen offered. "I have a friend I can call."

Paulson just stared at him, shaking his head. "You're wasting your time. The decision was made at the highest levels."

Cohen walked to a corner and dialed Callum McCarthy directly. They had known each other for years; Cohen had been Barclays' lawyer in the 1990s when McCarthy worked there. But the look on Cohen's face as he explained the situation told the story unequivocally: McCarthy was clearly not able to help his friend.

"You've really got this wrong if you don't think this is going to infect you," Cohen told McCarthy, nearly begging him to reverse his decision. "By *not* doing the deal, it's going to infect you."

———

Downstairs, Paulson, Geithner, and Cox entered the main conference room where the CEOs were still trying to coordinate funding of Lehman's real estate assets. The mood in the room had been noticeably upbeat as they continued to make progress.

"Those of you who do not want to assist a Barclays deal can breathe a sigh of relief," Paulson announced, somewhat awkwardly, and a number of bankers in the room did not understand what he was trying to convey until he formally announced that the deal was dead. "The British are not allowing for this type of guarantee; they can't get it done by tonight; they need a shareholder vote."

"But we have the money!" Jamie Dimon said.

"Isn't this our closest ally in the world?" one of the bankers asked.

"Guys, trust me," Paulson said. "I know how to be a tough guy. I've done everything I can. There is no deal."

The general opinion in the room was that they had been blindsided; Paulson merely shook his head and declared that the British had "grin-fucked us."

Geithner steered the conversation to the necessity of setting up contingency plans. He said that Lehman's holding company would file for bankruptcy that day. He also indicated that the government would open up an emergency trading session in the afternoon for all of the biggest banks to unwind positions with the firm.

Finally, Geithner broached the idea of creating a revolving credit facility, which would effectively serve to help the next bank in trouble. The proposal was for a $100 billion emergency fund, with each bank in the room putting up $10 billion: $7 billion funded and $3 billion unfunded. Any one bank could withdraw up to $35 billion from it in the case of an emergency.

At the end of the meeting, Paulson and Geithner pulled Thain aside and quietly told him, "We've got to talk to you."

———

"John, you see where we are with Lehman Brothers," Paulson told Thain once they had seated themselves in a conference room. "You've got to do something here. We don't have the authority it's going to take if you're looking for the government to save you."

"I'm working on it," Thain said solemnly. "I'm trying to save myself."

Thain explained that he was working on two parallel paths: one to sell a small stake in the firm to Goldman Sachs, and the other to sell the entire firm to Bank of America. He said that he had had coffee with Ken Lewis that morning and that Bank of America was much farther along, but that he expected Goldman could move quickly, too.

Geithner had heard enough; he had to brief Bernanke, so he got up and left.

Paulson could tell that Thain might be leaning toward the Goldman investment option—he knew Thain wanted to remain CEO of Merrill—but instructed him to push forward on the deal with Bank of America.

"John, you have to get this done," he urged. "If you don't find a buyer by this weekend, heaven help you and heaven help our country."

———

So far, Paulson had been trying to show no sense of fear among his colleagues and CEOs, but, in truth, the moment was beginning to overwhelm him. He was getting increasingly anxious that the market could end up toppling.

Paulson stepped out of a meeting room and found a quiet corner to call his wife Wendy on his cell phone. His voice immediately betrayed his own panic. "What if the system collapses?" he confided in her. "Everybody is looking to me, and I don't have the answers. I'm really scared."

Wendy tried to allay his fears with encouragement and prayer. She immediately began reciting Timothy 1:7—"For God hath not given us the spirit of fear, but of power, and of love, and of a sound mind."

"I understand it's not going through," Bart McDade told Bob Diamond when he reached him at his desk at Barclays' headquarters.

"What do you mean?" Diamond replied, completely taken aback. "I haven't heard that."

"It's off. The government says it's not happening," McDade told him, and recounted Paulson's discussion with the British regulators.

Diamond immediately got off the phone and called Tim Geithner's office.

"I just heard," Diamond said, exasperated. "What happened?"

"You should talk to Hank," Geithner told him.

When he finally managed to reach Paulson, he said, somewhat curtly, "I want to tell you that it was really difficult for me to get a call from someone else well after you did this." He paused, trying to keep his voice level. "And what I've been told you said is very much against what I think the facts are, and I think I deserve an explanation."

When he hung up after hearing Paulson's account of the communications, Diamond was in turn deflated, furious, and embarrassed. He was livid with Paulson and dismayed by the British government. How could they have led him so far only to quash the plan at the last moment?

At 12:23 p.m., Diamond tapped out a message on his BlackBerry to Bob Steel, who had been trying to set the deal up for six months:

Couldn't have gone more poorly, very frustrating. Little England.

Bart McDade, Alex Kirk, and Mark Shafir walked in silence through the underground garage at the NY Fed and piled into McDade's black Audi A8 to drive back to Lehman headquarters. For at least five minutes nobody said a word as they all just tried to comprehend what had just happened. They had all come to accept that they were out of options.

As they drove up the West Side Highway, McDade dialed Fuld on the speakerphone.

"Dick, you've got to sit down," he began.

"I've got bad news. Horrible news, actually," he said. "Supposedly the FSA turned the deal down. It's not happening."

"What do you mean 'not happening'?" Fuld bellowed into the phone.

"Paulson said it's over. The U.K. government won't allow Barclays to do the deal. Nobody's saving us."

Fuld, too, was speechless.

———

Across town, Greg Fleming of Merrill Lynch and Greg Curl of Bank of America were getting closer to formulating their own agreement, as lawyers began to draft the outlines of a deal document. The combined company would be based in Charlotte but would have a major presence in New York; the brokerage business would continue to use the iconic Merrill Lynch name and its familiar bull logo.

Fleming was working through some of the details when he took a call from Peter Kraus, who was on his way back to Goldman Sachs. He told Fleming that he needed part of the diligence team sent over to meet him there.

"I'm not sending anybody anywhere," Fleming replied. "We've got a good deal in hand and we're going to finish it."

Fleming was worried that Kraus, who he felt had been unhelpful from the day he had arrived at Merrill just over a week earlier, was trying to undermine the agreement with Bank of America and that he was more interested in a deal with his old pals at Goldman. Fleming was also concerned that if Bank of America officials discovered that Merrill was talking to Goldman, they would simply walk.

"We need as many options as we can get," Kraus told him. "You're the president of the company, it's your call, but you're making a big mistake."

"Well, it is my call," Fleming agreed, "and I just made it."

———

"John, we have to talk," said Dick Fuld, almost begging, when he reached John Mack on his cell phone at the New York Fed. "There's a way to make a deal work. Let's set something up." Mack was clearly devastated for his friend, but there was no way to do what he was asking. "I'm sorry, Dick," he said sympathetically. "I'm really sorry."

When he got off the phone, he strolled over to a group of bankers that included Jamie Dimon and recounted the conversation, lamenting Lehman's fate.

Dimon furrowed his brow.

"I just had the most surreal conversation with a guy at Lehman," Dimon said. "He seems to be in denial."

Mack just shook his head. "This is bizarre."

———

Over at AIG, Chris Flowers, taking a break from working with Bank of America, had stationed himself at one of the secretarial desks in the hallway, waiting to meet with Willumstad. Accompanying him was Dr. Paul Achleitner of Allianz; together they had prepared an offer for the company.

When they were invited into a conference room, they found Willumstad there with Schreiber and a group of his advisers, including Doug Braunstein from JP Morgan, Michael Wiseman from Sullivan & Cromwell, and several others.

"We have an offer," Flowers announced, producing a one-page term sheet that he handed to Willumstad.

Flowers, who hadn't yet heard about the additional $20 billion hole that JP Morgan's bankers had discovered, explained that he had put together a deal that valued AIG at $40 billion. (The company's actual market value on Friday had been about $31 billion.) Given the company's problems, he asserted, it was the best estimate he could come up with quickly.

He then spelled out the rough terms: His own firm and Allianz would put up about $10 billion of equity—$5 billion each—and they planned to raise $20 billion from banks; they would also sell $10 billion of assets. The investment they'd be making would be directly in AIG's regulated subsidiaries, but they'd gain control of the parent company. That condition was a move to protect Flowers and Allianz: If the parent company were to falter, they'd still own the subsidiaries. Finally, Flowers said they would have to be able to convince the Federal Reserve to turn AIG into a broker-dealer, so that it had the same access to the discount window that investment banks like Goldman Sachs and Morgan Stanley had.

Before ending his presentation, Flowers added that he had one other term that hadn't been noted on the deal memo: "Bob, we would replace you as CEO."

The silence that greeted the offer reflected the fact that Willumstad and his advisers thought the bid had to be a joke—not because Flowers had the audacity to tell Willumstad that he would be fired, but because the deal was also filled with potential pitfalls; Flowers was putting up scarcely any of his own money, and he hadn't lined up 80 percent of the funds needed to do the deal. They also thought the price ludicrously low. In their minds the company was worth at least twice that.

"That's fine," Willumstad said calmly. "We have an obligation, we'll take it to the board, but I have to tell you, you know, you've got contingencies in here that none of us can agree to," he said, referring to the need for Flowers to still receive bank financing. "Thank you," Willumstad said and stood, trying to get them to leave as quickly as possible. As soon as Flowers departed the room, Achleitner closed the door and took his seat again.

"I don't approve of what he just did," Achleitner said, almost whispering.

"Well, you read the letter before you came," Willumstad said, his temper in check.

"No, no, no, that's not how we do business," Achleitner said apologetically.

"Okay. Whatever," Willumstad responded. "Thank you very much."

When the entire group had finally left, Willumstad turned to Schreiber and whispered, "Don't let those guys back in the building!"

———

For a brief moment Dick Fuld allowed himself to smile. Ian Lowitt, Lehman's CFO, had just gotten word that the Federal Reserve was planning to open the discount window even wider, a move that would enable broker-dealers like Lehman to pledge even more of their assets—including some of their most toxic assets—as collateral in exchange for cash.

"Okay, here we go!" Fuld said, believing they might be able to hang on a bit longer as they sorted out their options.

"This is great, great news," Lowitt said, already tallying in his head the tens of billions of dollars of real estate assets he thought they might be able to pledge to the Fed. "We have enough collateral!"

———

"Lehman's got to file immediately," Paulson, leaning back in his chair, instructed Geithner and Cox. He made it clear that he didn't want Lehman adding to the uncertainty in the marketplace by dragging the situation out any longer.

Paulson had another reason for insisting that Lehman file: If the Fed was going to open its discount window even wider to the remaining broker-dealers, he didn't intend that Lehman be granted that access; doing so would represent another opportunity for moral hazard.

Cox said that he wanted to hold a press conference to announce the bankruptcy. As the sole regulator with formal authority over the firm, he felt he needed to communicate the news to the public before it crept out on its own and panic ensued.

He summoned Calvin Mitchell, the head of communications for the NY Fed, and Jim Wilkinson, Paulson's chief of staff, into his temporary office and asked when a conference could be scheduled.

"Well, can't you do it at the SEC office somewhere? Isn't that more appropriate?" Mitchell asked, clearly uncomfortable about arranging a media event in the middle of such chaos.

"It's easier to do it here; no one is there," Cox insisted. "The journalists are here," pointing out the window at the scrum of press lined up on Liberty Street.

"Okay, so, we could do it on this floor," Mitchell said. "Or, if we do it on the main floor, we have a podium we can bring down."

Cox liked the idea of holding the press conference downstairs and added, "That's a good backdrop."

As they began discussing the substance of what Cox would say at the conference about Lehman's bankruptcy, Erik Sirri, the SEC's head of markets and trading, pointed out a slight problem with the plan.

"We can't announce this," Sirri said. "We can't say a company has filed for bankruptcy until they decide to file. And that's a decision for Lehman's board."

———

Just after 1:00 p.m., Stephen Berkenfeld of Lehman called Stephen Dannhauser of Weil Gotshal, the firm's bankruptcy lawyer, frantically explaining that a group of Lehman executives—led by Bart McDade—had just been ordered to appear at the New York Fed. "You'd better get down there," he urged, and said nothing further.

Seconds later, Dannhauser grabbed three senior partners—Harvey

Miller, Thomas Roberts, and Lori Fife—and dashed to the street to find a cab. As the four sat sweating in gridlocked traffic, Roberts took a call from a partner back at the Weil Gotshal office who told him that Citigroup had just asked about the firm's availability to represent it as a creditor in a Lehman bankruptcy.

"That doesn't make any sense," Roberts told the partner. "We're on our way to discuss a deal with Barclays."

An hour after leaving the General Motors Building, the cab finally approached the New York Federal Reserve Building. News camera crews were still camped outside, watched over by uniformed Fed security. As the lawyers finally entered the building, they encountered Vikram Pandit of Citigroup hurrying out, looking as if he was late for another appointment.

Bart McDade and other Lehman representatives had already arrived upstairs and were sitting across from several rows of government officials and lawyers. Baxter, the general counsel for the New York Fed, was clearly running the meeting, as were lawyers from Cleary Gottlieb, representing the Securities and Exchange Commission.

McDade was just then telling Baxter, "You don't understand the consequences. You don't understand what is going to happen!"

Baxter, on noticing the arrival of the Weil Gotshal team, politely stopped the conversation to explain what was going on. "Harvey, we have had a great deal of deliberations and we've been thinking about this a lot, and it's clear now that there isn't going to be a Barclays transaction. We've come to the conclusion that Lehman has to go into bankruptcy."

Incredulous, Miller leaned forward until he was inches from Baxter. "Why? Why is bankruptcy necessary?" Miller demanded. "Can you explain, can you please elaborate on this?"

"Well, I'm not sure it's really necessary, given all the circumstances," Baxter responded, sheepishly. "But, ah, there's not going to be any kind of bailout, so we think it's appropriate that Lehman go into bankruptcy."

Miller looked at his colleagues. "I'm sorry, Tom, but we don't understand."

Alan Beller, a lawyer at Cleary Gottlieb, cut in peremptorily. "You need to do this, and it should be done before midnight tonight. We have a program to calm the markets."

Miller raised his voice. "Oh, you have a program to calm the markets, do you? Could you possibly tell me what that program is?"

"No, it's not necessary for your decision making," Baxter shot back.

"Tom," Miller persisted, "this makes no sense. Yesterday, no one from the Fed was talking to us about bankruptcy, and now we have to have a filing ready before midnight. And what is the magic of midnight? The only way we could ever file, and it won't be by midnight, is with a skinny Chapter 11 petition. What will that accomplish?"

"Well, we have our program," Baxter repeated.

Miller stood up, his six-foot-two frame looming over the other lawyers.

"What," he slowly bellowed, "is this *program?*"

Baxter just stared uneasily, offering no immediate answer.

"If Lehman goes into bankruptcy, totally unprepared, there's going to be Armageddon," Miller warned. "I've been a trustee of broker-dealers, little cases, and the effect of their bankruptcies on the market was significant. Here, you want to take one of the largest financial companies, one of the biggest issuers of commercial paper, and put it in bankruptcy in a situation where this has never happened before. What you're going to do now is take liquidity out of the market. The markets are going to collapse." Miller waved his finger and repeated, "This will be Armageddon!"

Baxter looked at the SEC lawyers, and, considering for a moment, finally said, "Okay, I'll tell you what we're going to do, we're going to caucus."

"This is insane," Miller said to Roberts as soon as the Lehman team was alone in the conference room. "They're telling us to fucking file. The government is telling us to *file.*"

"I don't even know what to say," Roberts replied. "This has got to be illegal."

About a half hour later, Baxter and the other government lawyers returned to the room, and the meeting resumed. "Well," Baxter announced, "we've considered everything you said, and it hasn't changed our position. We are convinced that Lehman has to go into bankruptcy, but what we are prepared to do is keep the Fed window open for Lehman so that the broker-dealer can continue operating the business."

Baxter was making the case for compromise, that there could be a way for an orderly winding down of Lehman. The Fed would loan money to Lehman's broker-dealer unit, but not indefinitely, only as part of a bankruptcy.

Sandra C. Krieger, executive vice president at the NY Fed, asked, "How much cash are you going to need us to provide you tomorrow to fund yourself on Monday night?"

"It's impossible to know the answer to that," Kirk told her.

"Well, that seems highly irresponsible!" she replied edgily.

"Really?" Kirk said, growing angry. "You want to tell me on the $50 billion of trades selling tomorrow how many of our counterparties are going to send us the money when we file for bankruptcy?"

Seeing that the conversation was quickly devolving, Miller jumped in and asked again why this measure was necessary.

"We've listened to your comments and we have concluded that our decision is correct, and we don't have to discuss this any further," Baxter said.

Miller still persisted. "You are asking this company to make a very momentous decision. It is entitled to all the information it can get."

"You're not going to get that information," Baxter replied.

Alan Beller interrupted to say, "Look, we will have a series of releases that we are fairly confident will calm the markets tomorrow."

"I'm sorry," Miller responded sardonically, "you're talking to me about *press releases*?"

At that the meeting was brought to a close.

———

Greg Fleming saw Peter Kelly in the hallway at Wachtell Lipton and gave him a big bear hug. As he did, he whispered into Kelly's ear: "It's done. Twenty-nine dollars. You owe me a beer," he said with a big smile.

Fleming had just gotten off the phone with Thain, who had given him the green light to go ahead with the deal at $29 a share.

After an afternoon of haggling with Greg Curl, Fleming had persuaded him not only to accept the agreement but to fund Merrill's bonus pool, up to the amount paid out in 2007. Nobody would get an employment contract, including Fleming and Thain—a point that Curl admired. To ensure that the deal would be completed, Fleming had convinced Curl to agree to a virtually airtight MAC agreement—meaning that even if Merrill's business continued to deteriorate, Bank of America couldn't later wiggle out of the transaction by claiming a "material adverse change" had occurred.

By Curl's thinking, as he explained to Ken Lewis before agreeing to the price, "We might be able to get it for cheaper later, but if we don't do the deal today, we could lose the opportunity entirely." For Curl, a journeyman dealmaker, this was his crowning achievement.

Bank of America scheduled a board call for 5:00 p.m., while Merrill set up a board meeting at the St. Regis hotel at 6:00 p.m. to approve the deal. In a matter of hours, Merrill Lynch, with a history of nearly one hundred years as one of the most storied names on Wall Street, would be sold to Bank of America for the biggest premium in the history of banking mergers. It was, as one newspaper later put it, as if Wal-Mart were buying Tiffany's.

At the NY Fed the banks had just finished trying to unwind their Lehman positions, an effort that had not gone particularly well. The Fed had passed out a memo to the CEOs earlier in the day explaining the program, which would be an extraordinary two-hour trading session in New York and London, during which firms that had opposing trades with Lehman tried to pair up and cut out the middleman.

The process was based on the assumption that Lehman was going under: "All trades conducted will be done on a contingency basis, contingent on the filing of bankruptcy of the Lehman parent," the Fed memo said. "Trades will 'knock in' if the Lehman Brothers Holding Inc. files for bankruptcy before 9am ET on Monday." The memo was intentionally never distributed to anyone at Lehman.

However neatly laid out the Fed proposal might have been, the various banks struggled to find matching trades that could remove Lehman from the picture. When frustrated traders left their desks at 4:00 p.m. in New York, many of them faced as much exposure to Lehman as they had on Friday afternoon.

"The extraordinary trading session held today to facilitate a partial unwind of these positions saw very little trading—perhaps $1 billion total—but at much wider spread levels for corporate bonds," Bill Gross, head of PIMCO, told reporters that afternoon. "It appears that Lehman will file for bankruptcy and the risk of an immediate tsunami is related to the unwind of derivative and swap-related positions worldwide in the dealer, hedge fund, and buy-side universe."

Word was also starting to spread that Merrill was about to be sold to Bank of America, a rumor that Gross, one of the nation's most respected investors, said that he heavily discounted. "To some extent, the rumored bid for Merrill by Bank of America lends some confidence to all markets, although I am skeptical that BofA would pay such a premium on such short notice," he said.

Ruth Porat, a Morgan Stanley banker who was present at the Fed, also doubted the speculation, especially the price. She called Jonathan Pruzan, Morgan Stanley's banking industry expert, to tell him the latest buzz.

"The rumor is $29 a share, and it's going to get announced in the morning," she told him. "I can't believe it, because they didn't have time to do due diligence. It's an absurd price."

Without missing a beat, Pruzan replied, "Then it's absolutely Ken. It's true. That's what Ken does."

———

"Are you getting all this?"

Gary Lynch, the chief legal officer of Morgan Stanley, was barking into the phone as Paul Calello, the chief executive of Credit Suisse's investment bank, paced nearby. With no access to a computer at the New York Fed, Lynch was in the process of dictating the text of an important press release to Jeanmarie McFadden, a Morgan Stanley spokeswoman, who was typing frantically to keep up.

The plan was to let the markets know that while Lehman might fail, Wall Street banks were cooperating to keep the whole financial system from imploding.

The release would open: "Today, a group of global commercial and investment banks initiated a series of actions to help enhance liquidity and mitigate the unprecedented volatility and other challenges affecting global equity and debt markets."

It would go on to say that the world's biggest financial institutions were creating a $100 billion borrowing facility for themselves—over and above what the Federal Reserve was providing through its Primary Dealer Credit Facility. Any one bank would be able to borrow up to $35 billion from the pool.

So far, ten banks were lined up to provide $7 billion each, for a total of $70 billion. The individual banks were a Who's Who of the global financial system: Goldman Sachs, Merrill Lynch, Morgan Stanley, Bank of America, Citigroup, JP Morgan, Bank of New York, UBS, Credit Suisse, Deutsche Bank, and Barclays. In normal times, many of them were the fiercest of rivals.

The press release ended by stating assuredly that "the industry is doing everything it can to provide additional liquidity and assurance to our capital markets and banking system."

———

Panic was starting to build within the Lehman ranks. George H. Walker IV, head of the firm's investment management unit, sat in his office at 399 Park Avenue, scrambling to find a way to save the division. He had received bids for it on Friday from two separate private-equity firms, Bain Capital and TPG, and was in the middle of trying to bring them together when he received a telephone call from Eric Felder, one of McDade's traders.

Felder was talking so fast that it sounded as if he were hyperventilating.

"You have to call your cousin," he insisted. "If there was ever a time to call the president, now is the time."

Walker, a second cousin to President Bush, was hesitant about using his family connections.

"I don't know," he said.

"You've got to do it, George," Felder said to him. "The whole fucking firm is going down. Someone's got to stop this!"

He placed the call but ended up leaving a message with the White House operators. The call would go unreturned.

———

With bankruptcy seemingly less than hours away, a new problem suddenly confronted Steven Berkenfeld, Lehman's managing director: $18.5 million in unpaid bills from Weil Gotshal, the law firm he had hired to work on the bankruptcy filing. The debt, which was for previous legal work, was minuscule compared to the billions of dollars Lehman owed all over Wall Street. But it would prevent Weil and Harvey Miller from representing Lehman in Chapter 11. Since Weil was officially a creditor of Lehman, it would constitute a conflict of interest that a judge could use to throw Weil off the assignment.

To Berkenfeld, it was critical that Weil be involved in the case. After all, its lawyers knew the firm the best, and Lehman's filing was due in almost record time. For Stephen Dannhauser, Weil's chairman, the assignment was also of paramount importance: Judging from the size and complexity of the Lehman filing, which promised to be even bigger than Enron's, the fees were likely to be well over $100 million.

Dannhauser had instructed Berkenfeld to pay Weil immediately, in advance of the bankruptcy, with cash sent by wire directly into the law firm's accounts. Even this approach had risks: Being on the receiving end of such a payment could result in a law firm's being disqualified from a case.

Still, with all of the pressure Lehman was under, Berkenfeld made the effort.

Because it was Sunday, there was only one place that the firm had cash available to wire—JP Morgan—and Berkenfeld had accordingly called over and made the request.

But now Dannhauser had called to say that the transfer hadn't gone through: JP Morgan had frozen Lehman's account, a decision that, Dannhauser was told, "came from the top."

Berkenfeld immediately dialed JP Morgan's general counsel, Stephen Cutler, and furiously demanded what it meant that the decision had "come from the top."

"Look, I don't know what that means," Berkenfeld said, his voice rising. "I don't know if that's Jamie Dimon or someone outside of the firm. But one day, we'll take your deposition and find out what happened."

Cutler agreed he would try to make the payment.

———

When Bob Diamond got back to his room at the Carlyle Hotel, tired and deflated, he had a surprise waiting for him. His wife, Jennifer, and daughter, Nellie, a sophomore at Princeton, were there. Nellie, who had been scanning the news wires on her laptop, gasped when she read that the deal her father had been trying to broker had fallen apart and headed for New York.

They decided to go for dinner at the Smith & Wollensky steak house. Just as they were approaching the restaurant Diamond's cell phone rang. He looked down at the caller ID and saw that it was McDade.

"I can't answer it," he told his daughter, who was puzzled by his unchar-acteristic timidity. "I can't do it anymore."

"Dad, answer your phone!" she insisted.

Reluctantly, he took the call.

"I've got a question," McDade said immediately when he picked up. "If we go into bankruptcy, would you consider taking the U.S. broker-dealer out of bankruptcy?"

Diamond whispered to Jennifer and Nellie, "I have to take this for a second."

As the women entered the restaurant, he asked, "Is that what's going to happen? Is this going to be Chapter 11?"

"We don't know for sure," McDade replied, "but if it goes into Chapter 11, if that's the result, would you consider taking the U.S. broker-dealer?"

"Bart," Diamond told him, "that's exactly the part we want. So abso-lutely. We would consider it. But I have to tell you, I know nothing about bankruptcy law and I don't know where to start. I have to talk to my board, I have to talk to John, but I'm pretty sure our answer would be yes."

"Why don't we do this," Diamond continued. "I'll get up early and get my team together, and we'll meet you at five a.m. But leave me an e-mail if you haven't declared bankruptcy. You get your team, and we'll get our team."

———

Bob Willumstad, with his advisers from JP Morgan, returned to the Fed on Sunday night to offer the latest update.

After Paulson, Geithner, and Jester took their seats around a conference table, Willumstad told the group somberly, "We're in the same place, actually maybe a worse place than before." He explained that the hole had since grown to $60 billion and detailed what they considered to be the "shenanigans" of Chris Flowers's bid, to everyone's amusement.

Jester, taking notes, started to grill Willumstad and Doug Braunstein about the numbers. Jester didn't understand why they kept talking in ranges; he wanted to know how much money AIG needed to the last decimal point.

Braunstein sighed. "I can't give you an exact figure. It's difficult to get clear numbers," he said, describing the antiquated systems at AIG.

It was clear to everyone in the room that AIG was now, as Willumstad expressed it, "in a bind"—though no one had as yet spoken of bankruptcy.

Willumstad suggested, again, that the Federal Reserve loan AIG just enough money to avoid being downgraded by the ratings agencies.

Geithner, again, said that that was out of the question. Given that Lehman was being left to die, Willumstad knew that Geithner's refusal was serious. Still, he persisted.

"I'm proposing a transaction, not a bailout," Willumstad said. "If we just get the Fed's backing in exchange for collateral, I give you my word I'll sell every asset needed to pay you back."

Paulson repeated with exasperation that it wasn't going to happen.

Once the AIG team had left, Geithner told Paulson that they needed to start thinking about what they could do to rescue the company—perhaps via another private consortium?

"I don't know, I don't know," Paulson said wearily. He was still preoccupied with the fates of Lehman Brothers and Merrill Lynch, and now he was supposed to find a solution for AIG?

Jim Wilkinson, Paulson's chief of staff, trying to keep his boss's spirits up, marveled, "This would be extremely interesting from an analytical perspective if it wasn't happening to us."

Neither Treasury nor the Federal Reserve had oversight over AIG, but if it was going to fall to someone, it would be Geithner, who seemed closest to the situation. But before Paulson washed his hands of the situation, Geithner asked him if he could "borrow" the services of Dan Jester, who had proved to be quite helpful over the weekend working through many of the practical issues around Lehman and Merrill. As a former deputy CFO of Goldman, Jester understood financial services companies better than virtually all of them, Paulson said. And he was one of the few people among them who appreciated the complexities of the problem that lay ahead of them: When he was at Goldman, one of his clients back in the 1990s was none other than AIG.

———

As the evening wore on, Jamie Dimon, now back at JP Morgan's headquarters, rang Doug Braunstein for an update on AIG.

"It's not good," Braunstein told him, referring to AIG's growing hole as a "snowball."

Dimon understood that AIG might have immediate problems because of a "liquidity crisis," but he continued to believe that there was enormous value in its underlying business. For a moment, he started to daydream. "Maybe we should be taking a look at it. There's got to be value there. Got to be."

"What do you mean? *For us?*" Braunstein asked in disbelief.

"Yeah," Dimon replied.

"No, no, no," Braunstein insisted, trying to talk Dimon out of it. "They don't seem to have a handle on their own numbers."

"I don't know," Dimon mused, still unconvinced that AIG could really be worthless. "It could be a good idea."

———

Paulson checked his watch and saw that it was past 7:00 p.m., which meant the Asian markets were opening, and Lehman still hadn't filed for bankruptcy.

"Has Cox talked to them yet?" he barked at his chief of staff, Jim Wilkinson.

Wilkinson said that he had been trying to get Cox to call Lehman directly, but that he had been resistant.

"He hasn't done shit," Wilkinson said dismissively. "I went in there and repeated what you said, and it's like he's frozen. Like a fucking deer in the headlights."

Cox, for whom Paulson had had very little respect to begin with, was proving how over his head he really was. Paulson had assigned him the task of coordinating Lehman's filing by, well, *now*. "This guy is useless," he said, throwing his hands in the air and heading over to Cox's temporary office himself.

After barging in and slamming the door, Paulson shouted, "What the hell are you doing? Why haven't you called them?"

Cox, who was clearly reticent about using his position in government to direct a company to file for bankruptcy, sheepishly offered that he wasn't certain if it was appropriate for him to make such a call.

"You guys are like the gang that can't shoot straight!" Paulson bellowed. "This is your fucking *job*. You have to make the phone call."

The Lehman board had already begun its meeting when the bankruptcy lawyers from Weil Gotshal, towing wheeled suitcases stuffed with documents, finally arrived. Speaking in a subdued voice, McDade gave the directors a detailed account of what had happened at the New York Fed. He was answering their questions when Fuld's assistant came in and handed a slip of paper to her boss, who began to slump in his chair as he read it.

"Hold on a minute—sorry, Bart," he blurted. "Chris Cox is calling and he wants to address us."

The board members looked at one another, their surprise etched in their expressions. No one could recall a time when the chairman of the SEC had asked to address a corporate board. One director questioned whether they should even take the call, but he was overruled. What did they have to lose? The lawyers, however, cautioned that if there were any questions, only the directors themselves should speak.

Fuld leaned in toward the speakerphone and said in a weary voice, "Ah, Chris, this is Dick Fuld. We got your message, and, ah, the board is in session here, everyone is here, all the directors and the firm's counsel."

A Lehman bankruptcy, Cox argued deliberately, stiffly, as if he were reading off a script, would help calm the market. It would be in the best interests of the nation, he said. He then introduced Tom Baxter, general counsel of the Federal Reserve of New York, who told the directors that the Fed and the SEC were in agreement that Lehman should file for bankruptcy.

One of Lehman's outside directors, Thomas Cruikshank, who had led the oil services company Halliburton through the 1980s oil bust before anointing Dick Cheney his successor as CEO, was the first to speak.

"Why is it so important," he asked, with a slight air of umbrage, "for Lehman to be in bankruptcy?"

Cox repeated that the markets were in turmoil and that the government had taken everything into consideration. Others followed up with variations of that same query, but Cox and Baxter stayed on message. The directors grew increasingly and visibly frustrated by the vagueness of the two men's answers.

Finally, Cruikshank stated point-blank: "Let me see if I understand this. Are you directing us to put Lehman into bankruptcy?"

For several moments there was silence on the other end. Then Cox said, "Ah, give us a few moments, and we will get right to you."

After one of the lawyers reached over the table and pushed the mute button on the speakerphone, the Lehman directors erupted with questions. Is the SEC telling us to file? Is the Fed? *What the hell is going on here?* To the best of anyone's knowledge, the government had never ordered a private firm to declare bankruptcy, essentially hanging the Going Out of Business sign on the door itself.

Ten minutes later, Cox, clearing his throat, got back on the line. "The decision on whether to file for bankruptcy protection is one that the board needs to make. It is not the government's decision," Cox said in the same steady, methodical tones. "But we believe that in your earlier meetings with the Fed, it was made quite clear what the preference of the government is. . . ."

John Akers, the former chief executive of IBM, interrupted. "So you're not actually directing us?"

"I'm not saying anything more than what I just said," Cox replied before ending the conversation.

The directors looked around at one another dumbfounded as Fuld sat impassively, his head buried in his hands.

Tom Russo, Lehman's chief legal officer, stood and outlined the board's responsibilities under securities laws. As he spoke, some directors talked quietly among themselves. *Bankruptcy seems inevitable. Do we file now? Next week?*

The government, they all knew, had plenty of leverage. If they did not do what Cox wanted, who knew what the consequences could be? The Fed, which had agreed to lend money to Lehman's broker-dealer unit to allow it to fund trades, could just as easily close it and force Lehman into liquidation. There was a motion to vote on filing for bankruptcy.

Henry Kaufman, an eighty-one-year-old former Salomon Brothers economist who headed the Lehman board's risk-management committee, haltingly stood up to speak. Known as "Dr. Doom" for his downbeat outlooks in the 1970s, Kaufman had been sharply critical of the Fed earlier in the year, accusing the central bank of "providing only tepid oversight of commercial banking." Now he again took aim at the government for pushing Lehman into bankruptcy.

"This is a day of disgrace! How could the government have allowed this to happen?" Kaufman thundered. "Where were the regulators?" He went on for another five minutes without stopping, and when he finally slumped into his seat the other directors could only look on in sadness.

As midnight approached, the resolution to file was put to a vote and passed. Some of the directors had tears in their eyes. Fuld looked up and said, "Well, I guess this is good-bye."

One of the bankruptcy lawyers, Lori Fife, laughed. "Oh, no. You're not going anyplace," she said. "The board will be playing a pivotal role going forward."

Miller elaborated on her point: "You're going to have to decide what to do with these assets. So it's not good-bye. We're going to be seeing each other for a while."

Fuld looked at the lawyers for a moment, dazed. "Oh, really?" he said softly, and then slowly walked out of the room, alone.

———

Warren Buffett, just back in Omaha from Edmonton, had received word of Lehman's pending bankruptcy before he arrived at the Happy Hollow Country Club for a late dinner with Sergey Brin, the co-founder of Google, and his wife, Anne.

"You may have saved me a lot of money," he said to the Brins with a laugh in the grand dining room. "If it wasn't for getting here on time, I might have bought something."

———

Mayor Michael Bloomberg, who had been on the phone with Paulson, called Kevin Sheekey, his deputy mayor for government affairs, from his brownstone. "I think we have to cancel our trip to California," he told Sheekey, who was already packing his bags for a high-profile event with Governor Arnold Schwarzenegger that he had been planning for months.

"The world is about to end tomorrow," Bloomberg explained, without a hint of sarcasm.

"Are you sure you want to be in New York for that?" Sheekey deadpanned.

———

Peter G. Peterson, co-founder of the private-equity firm the Blackstone Group and the CEO of Lehman in the 1970s before being ousted by Glucksman, was watching television with his wife, Joan Ganz Cooney, when she passed him the phone. It was a *New York Times* reporter asking him to comment on the day's events.

After pausing for a moment to take it all in, he said: "My goodness. I've been in the business thirty-five years, and these are the most extraordinary events I've ever seen."

———

Christian Lawless, a senior vice president in Lehman's European mortgage operation in London, still at the office, e-mailed his clients Sunday night with a final sign-off:

> Words cannot express the sadness in the franchise that has been destroyed over the last few weeks, but I wanted to assure you that we will reappear in one form or another, stronger than ever.

———

At Wachtell Lipton, Ken Lewis, of Bank of America, had a wry smile on his face. "Wow!" he exclaimed.

The deal with Merrill had been concluded—both boards had approved it—and he was waiting to share a champagne toast.

But reaching the deal was not what he now found so amusing. Out of the blue, Stan O'Neal, Merrill's former CEO, had sent an e-mail message to Herlihy that he read aloud: "I deeply regret my inability to convince the Merrill board a year ago," O'Neal wrote, referring to their secret talks last September. Then he followed up: "While I would expect the answer is no, I would offer my advice and counsel to Ken Lewis Re: Merrill."

That e-mail was perhaps the only moment of levity in an atmosphere that had grown increasingly sour. Lewis had grown frustrated waiting around for the lawyers to finish with the deal documents so that he could sign them.

Lewis himself hadn't gotten involved in the specific details, but the merger agreement contained a handful of "side letters" and separate agreements covering compensation that seemed to be taking some extra time for the lawyers to hammer out. Fleming had convinced Curl to agree to pay as much as $5.8 billion in "incentive compensation," which was considered an unusual arrangement, given that that was the amount Merrill had paid out a year earlier, before the market downturn. But both Curl and Fleming felt the sum was necessary to make certain they could retain the firm's employees.

———

It was growing late, and the Federal Reserve was still trying to get a reading of where the Bank of America–Merrill deal stood. The Federal Reserve Bank of Richmond, which had been overruled by Bernanke and Geithner earlier in the week about Bank of America's capital ratios, was particularly concerned.

At 9:49 p.m., Lisa A. White, assistant vice president at the Federal Reserve Bank of Richmond, concluded a conversation with Amy Brinkley, Bank of America's chief risk officer. White immediately sent out an e-mail to her colleagues titled "BAC Update":

> Just got off the phone with Amy Brinkley. She says that a deal with Merrill is solidified except for a few legal details that need to be worked out. Both boards have approved the deal, and once the legal issues are finalized, they will make an announcement . . . .

> Amy indicated that BAC management feels a much higher level of comfort with Merrill than it did with Lehman, specifically with the value of the franchise and the marks on the assets. While Amy acknowledged that it may look to the outside world as if BAC is paying a bit of a premium for Merrill, BAC's estimates of Merrill's asset values indicate they are getting the firm at a 30–50% discount. Chris Flowers, the prominent private equity guru, has done extensive due diligence on Merrill over the past few months for potential equity investors, and I got the impression that BAC is at least partially relying on this work.

> Will pass along more details as we get them.

———

After Chris Flowers left AIG, heading for a walk around Trinity Church at the intersection of Broadway and Wall Street, he decided to check in with Jamie Dimon, hoping to get some insight about the status of his bid for AIG, which he had left with Willumstad in the afternoon.

"What are you hearing?" Flowers asked. "Willumstad hasn't told us shit."

"You know, I think you pissed them off," Dimon told him.

"Okay. I don't know why, but I guess we did," he said, and hung up.

As he walked back to 70 Pine Street, he took a moment to marvel at the huge takeover of Merrill on which he had just worked. With all the time he had been spending on AIG, it seemed almost like an afterthought. In the end, he hadn't gotten a piece of the Merrill deal, but that hardly mattered. During the weekend's insanity, his firm and Fox-Pitt Kelton, a boutique investment bank, had each been paid to write BofA a "fairness opinion."

A fairness opinion is usually touted as an independent, unconflicted seal of approval for a deal. But on Wall Street, they are often seen as little more than paid rubber stamps. In this case the situation was even more complicated, not only because Flowers himself had considered taking part in the Merrill deal, but because Flowers's firm also owned Fox-Pitt Kelton.

For their troubles, Flowers and Fox-Pitt would earn a combined $20 million in fees, $15 million of which was contingent on the conclusion of the deal. Not bad for less than a week's work.

Ruth Porat of Morgan Stanley had gone over to the apartment of a friend, a Lehman executive, to console her. Just as they were pouring a glass of wine to commiserate, she took a call from Dan Jester, her pal from Treasury, with whom she had just worked for over a month on Fannie and Freddie.

"I need your help," he told her. "You're not going to believe this, but we think AIG may go into bankruptcy this week. I'm wondering if we can reconvene the team to focus on AIG." In this case, the assignment would be to work on behalf of the Federal Reserve. He told her that he'd like Morgan Stanley to pull a team together and be down at the Fed in the morning.

"Hold on, hold on," Porat said in disbelief. "You're calling me on a Sunday night saying that we just spent the entire weekend on Lehman and now we have this? How the fuck did we spend the past forty-eight hours on the wrong thing?"

The drive home was excruciating; Fuld sat in the backseat feeling paralyzed. Gone was the bluster, the gusto, the fight. He was still angry, but really, he was just sad. For once, it was completely quiet except for the hum of the engine and the tires rolling down the highway. He had stopped looking at his BlackBerry.

By the time his Mercedes rolled into his driveway, it was 2:00 a.m. His wife, Kathy, was waiting up for him in bed. He slowly walked into his bedroom, still in a state of shock. He hadn't slept in days; his tie was undone and his shirt wrinkled. He sat down on the bed.

"It's over," he said mournfully. "It's really over."

Looking on solemnly, she said nothing as she watched his eyes well up. "The Fed turned against us."

"You did everything you could," she assured him, rubbing his hand.

"It's over," he repeated. "It's really over."

CHAPTER SIXTEEN

A t 7:10 a.m. on Monday, September 15, Hank Paulson was sitting at the edge of his bed in a suite at the Waldorf Astoria, the day's newspapers spread out before him. He had gotten very little sleep, worrying about how the markets would react to the previous day's news—and about whether AIG would be the next domino to fall.

The headline on the front page of the *Wall Street Journal*—spanning all six columns and running to two lines, in double the normal point size—told the story: CRISIS ON WALL STREET AS LEHMAN TOTTERS, MERRILL IS SOLD AND AIG SEEKS TO RAISE CASH. The *Journal* had gone to press before Lehman formally filed for bankruptcy protection at exactly 1:45 that morning in the Southern District of New York.

Paulson was just finishing dressing when he received a call from President George W. Bush.

Paulson had spoken to the president the night before but only briefly. This would be his first opportunity to explain fully where things stood with the economy and to strategize with him about the administration's message to the American people.

His voice more hoarse than usual, Paulson began by telling Bush that Lehman's bankruptcy filing was official. "I'm sure some in Congress are going to be happy about this, but I'm not sure they should be," he added, acknowledging the political pressure that had been brought to bear against another bailout.

Paulson said he was cautiously optimistic that investors would be able to accept the news but warned him that there could be further pressure on the financial system. Jim Awad, managing director of Zephyr Management, was quoted in that morning's *Wall Street Journal* as saying, "Everybody's prepared this time—it's different from Bear Stearns. There could be a brief relief rally. You won't get a 1,000-point shock drop because we're all ready for it. But a grueling, long bear market will resume."

Although the U.S. markets wouldn't open for another three and a half hours, Paulson told Bush that the Asian and European markets were down only slightly, and while the Dow Jones futures were off, it was only by approximately 3 percent.

Paulson then recounted the specific details of the weekend, blaming the British government for misleading them. "We were out of options," Paulson told Bush, who was sympathetic.

But the president wasn't concerned about what might have been. He told Paulson that he was unhappy about the bankruptcy, but that allowing Lehman Brothers to fail would send a strong signal to the market that his administration wasn't in the business of bailing out Wall Street firms any longer.

As they spoke, the first clues that the market wasn't going to take the news especially well began appearing. Alan Ruskin, a banking analyst at RBS Greenwich Capital, had sent out a note to his clients early that morning trying to divine the meaning of Lehman's bankruptcy:

"At the time of writing it seems the US Treasury has decided to teach us ALL a lesson, that they will not backstop every deal in the wave of financial sector consolidation that is upon us," he wrote. "Their motivation is part fiscal and part moral hazard. I suspect more the latter. Presumably the most important reason to teach Wall Street this lesson, is that they will change their behavior, and not take the decisions that are reliant on a public bail-out. For many, but not all, this is an impossible lesson to learn in the middle of the worst financial storm since the Great Depression."

Paulson walked Bush through the Fed's plan to keep Lehman's broker-dealer functioning so that it could complete its trades with other banks. "We're hoping that over the next couple of days, they can unwind this thing in an organized way," he said.

While Paulson was clearly more disturbed than the president about Lehman's bankruptcy, he expressed his elation about Bank of America's decision to buy Merrill Lynch, a sign, he suggested, "of strength" in the market that might "mitigate" the possibility of panic.

Paulson also warned him for the first time that "AIG could be a problem" but assured him that Geithner and the Fed were planning to rally the troops and help raise capital for the firm later that day.

"Thanks for your hard work," the president told him. "Let's hope things settle down."

———

Doug Braunstein of JP Morgan was leaving his apartment on Manhattan's Upper East Side at about 7:00 a.m. to head down to AIG when he received a call from Jamie Dimon.

"New plan," Dimon told him. "Geithner wants us to work with them to do a huge capital raise for AIG. There's going to be a meeting down at the Fed at eleven a.m." Braunstein, blocking his ear against the noise of Manhattan traffic, protested, "We can't raise this kind of money."

Dimon promised that he'd have some help. "The government is inviting us and Goldman to make this happen."

A look of horror came over Braunstein's face as he asked, raising his voice, "Where the hell did Goldman Sachs come from? Don't they have a conflict? I mean, look at their exposure to AIG. They're a huge counterparty."

Dimon dismissed his concerns. "The U.S. government is telling us to do this," he repeated.

Braunstein persisted. "But—"

"Stop it," Dimon insisted, annoyed that his top banker was challenging him. "This isn't about us versus them," he said. "We've been asked to help fix this situation."

Once Braunstein got to the office, he, Dimon, and Black huddled to come up with a game plan about how to handle the Fed's unusual request. They decided to enlist the help of James B. Lee Jr., the firm's vice chairman.

Dimon hurried down the hall to give Jimmy Lee his marching orders. Lee, a classic suspender-wearing banker with a Golden Rolodex, had also arrived early to help manage the aftermath of Lehman's collapse and had just gotten off the phone with one of his big clients, Rupert Murdoch. Sitting at a desk flanked by four computer screens, with a giant flat-screen television tuned to CNBC's *Squawk Box* and his own private news ticker on the wall modeled after the Zipper in Times Square, Lee spun around in his chair.

"I have a job for you," Dimon barked, standing in the doorway. "I want you to go down to the Fed."

"To do what?" Lee asked in disbelief. After all, he had a busy day ahead of him, and he was expecting the market to be a disaster.

"I want you to run the AIG deal," Dimon told him. "Geithner called. He wants us to find a private-market solution for AIG. It's a big hole. This could be the mother of all loans."

If there was one banker in the city who understood the world of debt and how to raise money in a pinch, it was Jimmy Lee. He was perhaps JP Morgan's most senior deal maker, a mogul unto himself with his own banquette at the Four Seasons at lunch. His power derived, in part, from the fact that he was a virtual ATM for corporate America, writing massive checks to finance some of the biggest deals in history. Dimon told him he was hoping that Lee could structure a deal to loan AIG enough money to keep operating and sign up a dozen other big financial players to follow him.

With that tall order delivered, Dimon disappeared, and Steven Black followed him into Lee's office to give him a five-minute briefing and a folder of AIG materials heavier than a phone book. Describing AIG as a "fucking nightmare client," Black described how dire the situation was becoming. "You can carry the ball from here," Black said with a wry smile, happy to have AIG in someone else's lap.

Lee was informed that he was expected at AIG for a meeting immediately and then he had to get over to the Federal Reserve Building by 11:00 a.m.

Lee met Braunstein and Mark Feldman in front of JP Morgan's headquarters on Park Avenue, where Lee's driver, Dennis Sullivan, a retired police officer who had shuttled him from his home in Darien, Connecticut, to Manhattan every day for more than twenty years, was waiting with his black Range Rover. Braunstein and Lee jumped in the back so that Braunstein could continue briefing him.

"C'mon. We've got to get downtown," Lee instructed Sullivan. "No bullshit. We have to be down there like yesterday."

———

John Mack looked tired as he rose to a podium and began to address his top lieutenants. It had been a long weekend, he told the managers squeezed into Morgan Stanley's main conference room. During two and a half days of meetings at the New York Fed, he said he subsisted on "nothing but wrap sandwiches" and fruit that had "been out a little too long.

"I am energized and you ought to be energized, too," Mack said encouragingly. He acknowledged that the market had come under tremendous pressure after Lehman's "lost weekend"—United States stock index futures and bank shares in Europe were already tumbling—but the good news for them was that Morgan Stanley had survived.

Mack proceeded to summarize the discussions about Lehman and Merrill that had taken place at the New York Fed over the weekend, calling Lehman's demise "very unfortunate."

"I mean, I wish I could come in here and say, you know, this is a great opportunity, kick back, we're going to do great, all of the competitors have basically been eliminated. I'm not going to say that," he allowed. "What I want to say is: Kick it up. Work harder. Think about what has happened this year. And what has happened is that all of a sudden, three of our competitors are no longer in business."

Mack added: "I understand that all of you, and not just all of you here, but I think in the industry, are shaken. You should be shaken. But that doesn't mean that we crawl back in and we shake. . . .

"We're here to do business, to serve our clients, to take market share. Just think about this: Every 1 percent in equity market share we gain is a billion dollars in revenues. . . .

"I think that once this turmoil abates, and it will settle down, the opportunities going forward are unbelievable. Now I am a positive guy but I am not a Pollyanna, and I believe with all my heart that this firm and our competitor, Goldman, have unique opportunities now. And I am sorry that we got to these unique opportunities the way we did. I don't want my competitors out of business, I just want to beat them."

His chief financial officer, Colm Kelleher, chimed in to punctuate that point: "There is Darwinism here. . . . Weak people are being taken out. Strong people, I believe, are going to do very, very well."

Over at Lehman Brothers, the thirty-second-floor conference center was a beehive of activity, with hundreds of dazed people streaming in and out—bankruptcy lawyers, restructuring experts, outside consultants.

Fuld, who had been escorted upstairs by Lehman's security detail for fear that employees might actually attack him, wandered in and out of the conference rooms in shock. He had already placed a call that morning to Geithner, pleading with him to undo the bankruptcy filing, as if it had all been just a bad dream.

Down on Lehman Brothers' massive trading floor, the mood was grim. The staff wasn't just devastated, they were angry. And while that anger was at first directed toward the government, it had quickly shifted to management. A Wall of Shame had been erected on the south side of the building containing, among other exhibits, photos of Fuld and Gregory with the caption, "Dumb and Dumber."

With Lehman's holding company now officially in bankruptcy, Barclays' Bob Diamond arrived with a team to pick over the assets it wanted and leave the worst ones behind. To Diamond, it was the perfect opportunity to obtain only Lehman's choicest parts at a bargain price and with the blessing of a judge. Barclays was mainly interested in Lehman's U.S. broker-dealer and its buildings, and this time around both the FSA and the British government had given him their support. Another plus: There was no need for a shareholder vote.

Bart McDade had assembled a team to begin negotiations with Barclays. He believed there was a chance that he could save the ten thousand jobs that were likely to disappear, even if shareholders themselves had already been wiped out by the bankruptcy. Before that meeting began, however, Alex Kirk pulled McDade aside. Kirk, emotionally drained from the past week, was becoming increasingly suspicious that Barclays had dropped its bid twenty-four hours earlier only so that it could buy the business for even less today. He was outraged, as were many of the traders on the third floor.

"Either Barclays was duped or they were part of the charade," he told McDade. "I have no interest in working for a company that's either the dupe or is part of this charade. And I have no interest in working for a highly leveraged financial institution with regulators who behave like I just saw. So I'm out on this whole thing."

McDade was disappointed but sympathetic. "I get it, I understand, you do whatever you want," he told Kirk but asked if he would stay at least through the week to help manage the trading floor as they tried to arrange a deal. Kirk reluctantly agreed.

McDade then assigned Skip McGee and Mark Shafir to find a way to execute a deal with Barclays.

In the corner conference room, meanwhile, Harvey Miller was holding court with Barclays' management arrayed around the table. Jay Clayton of Sullivan & Cromwell, who had previously been Lehman's lawyer with his colleague Rodgin Cohen, had been hired by Barclays that morning. "I think I'm switching from shirts to skins," he said awkwardly as he sat down next to the Barclays team.

Miller was trying to sort out how quickly they could sell the company, aware that in a business based on the confidence and trust of its trading partners, every second the firm remained on its own, it was losing value.

Michael Klein, Barclays' adviser, announced, "We are only doing this deal if we're not bringing any liabilities with us."

"What do you mean by that?" Miller asked.

"Well, we're not going to buy any of these assets unless it is an absolutely 'clean deal,'" he explained.

Barclays' Archie Cox jumped in and added, "And we have to close tomorrow."

Miller shot a black stare at him. "Well, if that's the case, we should just discontinue this right now. Generally, a sale of even perishable assets takes twenty-one to thirty days."

"We can't wait that long," Cox insisted. "By that time the business will be gone."

"The only thing I can think of right now is you get the court to accelerate the time lines," Miller offered. "We get an agreement in principle with the Securities Investor Protection Corporation, and it will commence a separate proceeding to coincide with this sale. But that's never been done before."

"Can you do that?" Cox asked.

"Until we try, we won't know," Miller replied.

———

Timothy Geithner was sitting at his desk at the NY Fed with Jamie Dimon on the speakerphone, waiting to be conferenced in with Lloyd Blankfein, who was just returning from the firm's Monday-morning internal meeting.

It had been Geithner who had decided the night before, after consulting briefly with Paulson, to pair JP Morgan and Goldman to help AIG. By his logic, JP Morgan knew AIG inside out as a result of having worked for it for the past six months and could get everyone up to speed quickly on the depth of its problems. Goldman, he thought, could help value the assets and syndicate the loans. "They're freakin' smart!" he liked to tell his staff. He knew that Goldman had advised AIG in the past and had spent the weekend looking to buy assets themselves, so they were aware of what was going on.

"Lloyd, I'm on with Jamie," Geithner said when Blankfein finally came to the phone. He explained that he was hoping to find a private-market solution for AIG and wanted Goldman to help them.

"JP Morgan's coming down here," Geithner told him. "Can you get a team together and come over here?"

"Okay," Blankfein said. "What time?"

"Can you be here by eleven a.m.?"

"We'll be there," Blankfein replied, even though it was already past 10:15.

Blankfein immediately went to work organizing a small army of the firm's top bankers: Jon "Winks" Winkelried, the co-president; David Solomon, the co-head of investment banking; Richard Friedman, who ran the principal investment area; and Chris Cole, who had spent the weekend over at AIG. They all met downstairs to walk over to the Fed.

Chris Flowers, after the relatively uneventful press conference of Bank of America and Merrill Lynch that morning, headed down to Goldman Sachs with Paul Achleitner of Allianz. They had made an appointment to see Chris Cole as something of a postmortem and a discussion to determine if they could team up to make another run at some AIG assets. After waiting in a conference room for Cole for nearly a half hour, Flowers and Achleitner, both frustrated, went downstairs to get some food.

Standing at the back side of 85 Broad Street, they saw Blankfein and Cole at least thirty yards ahead of them intently marching down William Street toward the Fed with Goldman's entire senior team.

"They're fucking standing us up!" Flowers said.

———

When the JP Morgan bankers Lee, Braunstein, and Feldman arrived at AIG, they found the building practically empty, which struck the men as odd, given that the firm was squarely in the middle of a life-or-death crisis.

To Willumstad, who came to greet them, their arrival meant that his already frosty relationship with JP Morgan had just taken another turn for the worse: Were they still his adviser? Or were they now working for the government? Or were they working for themselves?

Before beginning the meeting, Braunstein had a private conversation with Willumstad. "The government asked us to do this. Are you okay with that?"

"Of course," Willumstad replied.

When they returned to the conference room, Lee, in a hurry to get over to the Fed, fired off a half dozen questions in rapid succession. "How firm a grip do you have on your cash? Where are the ratings agencies on this? What kind of credit lines do you have?"

Willumstad was tentative with his answers. The numbers kept getting worse, he said. And with Lehman's failure, and the markets likely to swoon, the value of AIG's assets was likely to tumble further, giving them even less collateral to post.

To Lee, it was abundantly clear that the company—and Willumstad—didn't have a firm grip on its finances, exactly as Black had told him.

Just before the bankers left for the Fed, Willumstad, trying to maintain an air of calm, said encouragingly, "I think we still have some time."

As the JP Morgan contingent began briskly walking over to the Fed, Lee said, shaking his head: "Whenever someone says they have time, there's never enough. And when they say they need money, the number is always too low." He paused before declaring, "They won't last the week."

———

After spending an arduous weekend in the NY Fed's lobby, many of the same members of the band of bankers and lawyers now disconcertingly found themselves reassembled there.

One of the key new figures in attendance was Eric R. Dinallo, the superintendent of the New York State Insurance Department. Earlier that morning, he had formally agreed to allow AIG to use some of its regulated insurance company assets—up to $20 billion—as collateral to help stabilize the company. Dinallo had been driving up to Governor Paterson's office—he had been slated to stand behind the governor during a press conference to announce the plan—when Geithner called and told him he should be at this meeting instead.

As they milled about waiting for the meeting to begin, Blankfein poured a cup of coffee for Dinallo. "I hope you represent the bookends of this financial crisis," he said, "because the last time I saw you was at the monolines, and I hope we're done with AIG." Dinallo had convened a meeting of Wall Street chiefs back in January to discuss the fate of the insurers Ambac and MBIA, which were faltering amid the credit crisis.

When Lee, Braunstein, and Feldman finally arrived, they immediately felt outgunned, as it appeared as if Goldman's entire executive thirtieth floor had cleared out and set up shop at the Fed. Bob Scully and Ruth Porat from Morgan Stanley, who had now been officially hired by the Fed to represent its interests, were also stunned by the depth of Goldman's presence. "Why is Lloyd here?" Scully whispered to Porat.

What went unspoken was the fact that all three banks, and virtually all of Wall Street, were huge counterparties to AIG. If the company were to fail, they would all face serious consequences. Therefore, there was a huge incentive to keep the insurer alive for everyone at the table.

On the surface, Goldman looked like one of AIG's biggest counterparties, but earlier that morning, Goldman's Gary Cohn had boasted internally that the firm had hedged so much of its exposure to AIG that it might actually *make* $50 million if the company collapsed. The firm's decision to buy insurance in the form of credit default swaps against AIG beginning in late 2007 was starting to seem like a smart investment. The firm had conducted what it internally called a "WOW analysis"—a worst-of-the-worst case scenario—and it was quickly coming true. Even though Goldman had hedged its direct exposure to AIG, Blankfein appreciated the larger problem: The collateral damage to its other counterparties and the rest of the market could expose the firm to untold billions in crippling losses.

The group was ushered into a conference room with Tim Geithner. Dan Jester was at his side and Jeremiah Norton from Treasury, who had flown up from Washington that morning, joined them.

As everyone took a seat, Blankfein noticed Jamie Dimon's absence. He himself had come because he assumed that Geithner had invited both of them. "Where the hell is Jamie?" Blankfein whispered to Winkelried, who just shrugged his shoulders.

"Look, we'd like to see if it's possible to find a private-sector solution," Geithner said, addressing the group. "What do we need to make this happen?"

For the next ten minutes the meeting turned into a cacophony of competing voices as the bankers tossed out their suggestions: *Can we get the rating agencies to hold off on a downgrade? Can we get other state regulators of AIG's insurance subsidiaries to allow the firm to use those assets as collateral?*

Geithner soon got up to leave, saying, "I'll leave you with Dan," and pointed to Jester, who was Hank Paulson's eyes and ears on the ground. "I want a status report as soon as you come up with a plan."

Before departing, he added one more thing: "I want to be very clear: Do not assume you can use the Fed balance sheet."

The meeting then devolved again into a half dozen side conversations until some order was restored when Braunstein walked the room through AIG's financial position, explaining how quickly it had deteriorated over the weekend. It was coming under pressure not only because of the impending ratings downgrade but also because its counterparties were making constant requests for more collateral. The comment was a not particularly subtle jab at Goldman Sachs, which itself had been battling all weekend, as it had all year, for AIG to put up more collateral. To some in the room, it seemed Blankfein picked up on the slight immediately.

"So, when *is* the money going to be paid out?" Blankfein asked, ostensibly referring to all the counterparties but to some he seemed to mean himself. One attendee scribbled a note to himself: "GS—$600 million," which was an approximation of what he thought Goldman was seeking. Even though Goldman may have been hedged against AIG, it still wanted what it thought was the appropriate amount of collateral to keep trading with the firm. Scully of Morgan Stanley interrupted with: "Is there anything you can do to put Moody's off so that we get a little breathing room for the next couple of days?"

At that point, Jimmy Lee tried to break the logjam and take control of the meeting, having quickly become convinced that they were never going to get anywhere unless they started focusing on the big picture. AIG had forty-eight hours left to live unless the bankers sitting in this room did something productive to save it.

Lee had already started listing on a notepad some of the issues that had been raised and things he needed to know:

> liquidity forecast
> valuation—business, securities
> term sheet
> participants
> legal in all

In the margins he scribbled some questions about the size of the hole— "50? 60? 70?" billion—and then drafted a mini–term sheet for a loan of this magnitude. "Maturity: 1–2 years; Collateral: Everything; Consideration: Fees, Ratcheting Spreads, Warrants."

Given the size of loan AIG would require, the fees would be mind-boggling. He might be able to charge as much as 500 basis points, or 5 percent, of the entire amount for taking on this level of risk. For a $50 billion loan, that would add up to a $2.5 billion payday in fees.

Lee had even begun assembling a list of the banks to contact to raise the credit line, virtually all of whom had exposure to AIG and were therefore also vulnerable: JPM, GS, Citi, BofA, Barclays, Deutsche, BNP, UBS, ING, HSBC, Santander. He could have come up with many more names but stopped at eleven.

"Okay, okay," Lee now said to the group and ran through the items on his list.

"I like that. That sounds right to me," Winkelried chimed in.

The group decided to start their work with a round of basic due diligence, breaking the businesses into a half dozen categories and passing out assignments among themselves.

Before they got into the specifics, Blankfein took advantage of a pause in the discussion to make a beeline for the door. Without Dimon there, this was below his pay grade.

As they all decamped from the Fed and marched back to AIG to start crunching the numbers, Lee's brain was already doing the math.

"Who is going to buy this shit?" he asked aloud to no one in particular.

———

That afternoon at 1:30 p.m., Paulson stepped out to the lectern in the White House briefing room. "Good afternoon, everyone. And I hope you all had an enjoyable weekend," he began, to some awkward laughter. "As you know, we're working through a difficult period in our financial markets right now, as we work off some of the past excesses."

He had just gotten back to Washington, rushing first to the Treasury and then across the way to the White House, to take questions from reporters. Jim Wilkinson had coached him on the flight down about how he should approach the issues. "We've got to say we've drawn a line in the sand," Wilkinson instructed him and warned him to expect to be asked about why Lehman had been allowed to fail while Bear Stearns was saved. Wilkinson presented it as an opportunity to discuss moral hazard and to make it clear that the U.S. government "is not in the business of bailouts."

Paulson himself was doubtful that this was quite the time to be dogmatic and challenged Wilkinson on the point, but the fact was, he was dead tired and could not keep his mind from drifting to AIG.

As he finished his remarks, the first question came from the press corps, and it was a softball: "Can you talk about what the federal role should be going forward? Are we likely to see any more federal involvement in rescues like you did with Fannie and Freddie and Bear Stearns?"

Paulson paused for a moment. "Well, the federal role is obviously very important because, as you've heard me say before, nothing is more important right now than the stability of our capital markets, and so I think it's important that regulators remain very vigilant."

"Should we read that as 'no more'?" the reporter screamed out.

"Don't read it as 'no more,'" Paulson replied, clearing his throat. "Read it as . . . that I think it's important for us to maintain the stability and orderliness of our financial system. Moral hazard is something that I don't take lightly."

And then came the anticipated question: "Why did you agree to support the bailout of Bear Stearns but not Lehman?"

Paulson paused to gather his thoughts carefully. "The situation in March and the situation and the facts around Bear Stearns were very, very different to the situation that we're looking at here in September, and I never once considered that it was appropriate to put taxpayer money on the line with . . . in resolving Lehman Brothers."

It was an answer that would come back to haunt him. He had parsed his words carefully. Technically, his answer was true, but he knew that if Bank of America or Barclays had decided to buy Lehman he might have used taxpayer money to support a deal, but he wasn't about to bring that up now.

As the questions poured in, Paulson grew more and more agitated. "Why is the Federal Reserve giving AIG a bridge loan?" one journalist asked.

"Let me say what is going on right now in New York has nothing to do with any bridge loan from the government. What's going on in New York is a private-sector effort again focused on dealing with an important issue that I think is important that the financial system work on right now and there's not more I can say on that."

He was about to step down when he announced, "I've got time for one more question . . . the woman in the middle there," he said, pointing to another reporter.

The journalist asked him how he handicapped the health of the banking system today.

"There are going to be some real rough spots along the road, but I believe we're making progress. And when I look at the way the markets are performing today, I think it's a testament to the way the financial industry has come together, because they're dealing with an extraordinary set of circumstances and they're dealing in a way we should all be proud of.

"Thank you very much."

———

By midafternoon, chaos reigned in the conference room on the sixteenth floor of AIG, where more than a hundred bankers and lawyers, led by Goldman Sachs and JP Morgan, had assembled to begin conducting diligence on the company. The only problem was, no one there seemed to *have* any of the company's actual numbers.

"Is there anyone who works for AIG in this room?" a voice shouted out. When no one raised a hand a wave of nervous laughter swept the room.

Finally, Brian Schreiber of AIG was summoned. Working on three hours of sleep, he looked as if he might have a breakdown right there. He took a moment to collect himself before beginning a presentation of the latest numbers. After he finished a less than inspiring performance, the core group from that morning at the Fed huddled in AIG's boardroom.

For a while it seemed as if progress was being made. Lee and Winkelried felt confident that AIG's assets were strong, at least strong enough for them to lend against. What they believed the company was experiencing was merely a liquidity crisis: If they could provide AIG with a bridge loan, they'd be home free.

The group started discussing drafting a preliminary term sheet. They'd try to raise $50 billion, in exchange for warrants for 79.9 percent of AIG. It was almost a punitive price, but given the insurer's status, it might be their only alternative to bankruptcy. Winkelried and Lee also discussed the fees they would collect, which would be split between the firms. If they sought to raise $50 billion, that would leave each firm with a $1.25 billion fee for organizing the loan.

As the group dispersed to return to the Fed to present their progress report to Geithner, Ruth Porat of Morgan Stanley, who was representing the Fed, pulled aside John Studzinski of Blackstone, who was representing AIG. They were old friends; Studzinski used to run Morgan Stanley's mergers and acquisitions practice in London.

"So, what do you think?" Porat asked.

"What do you mean?" Studzinski replied. "I can't tell from this meeting whether there's going to be a term sheet or not."

"That's not what I meant," Porat replied. "We're worried that these guys are going to try to steal the business."

———

"He was as useless as tits on a bull."

Bob Willumstad, normally a calm man, was in an uncharacteristic rage as he railed about Dan Jester of Treasury, while telling Jamie Gamble and Michael Wiseman about his and Jester's call to Moody's to try to persuade them to hold off on downgrading AIG.

Willumstad had hoped that Jester, using the authority of the government and his powers of persuasion as a former banker, would have been able to finesse the task easily.

Willumstad explained the original plan "was that the Fed was going to try to intimidate these guys to buy us some time." Instead, when Jester finally got on the phone, "he didn't want to tell them." Clearly uncomfortable with playing the heavy, Willumstad told them that Jester could only bring himself to say, "We're all here, and you know, we got a big team of people working and we need an extra day or two."

The core group of bankers who had been over at AIG now returned to the Fed, Jester having unsuccessfully tried to persuade Geithner to come to them at AIG—given that they were a group of some thirty and he was just one. Being the president of the Federal Reserve of New York had its privileges, however: They would come to him.

The hole that they needed to fill, Winkelried now reported in their summary to Geithner, was some $60 billion and "possibly more." No one knew how any solution could work without financial help from the Fed.

"There's no government money for this," Geithner told them, repeating what Paulson had said earlier that day in Washington and echoing the same sentiment he had been conveying all weekend with regard to Lehman. If they needed proof that he was serious, Lehman's bankruptcy was Exhibit A.

Geithner authorized Lee to begin making phone calls to Asia that night to see if he could begin raising some money there. JP Morgan and Goldman made it clear they still had a good deal more work ahead of them.

Late that evening, Jamie Gamble, AIG's lawyer; John Studzinski; and Brian Schreiber gathered in a conference room for a morose meal of take-out Chinese. The situation seemed hopeless. Dinallo and Governor Paterson may have bought them a day by announcing their plan to release $20 billion of collateral, but it was too little, too late. Hours earlier they had called in the bankruptcy experts, and when the markets opened on Tuesday, they planned to draw down their credit lines, a clear sign to the markets that they were in trouble. When they had suggested the move, Willumstad had told them it was akin to "lowering the lifeboats into the water because you're about to abandon ship. That's the last thing you do. Shutting the lights off on the *Titanic* before it goes down."

Schreiber still couldn't believe they were in this position and remained convinced that the Fed would ultimately come to the rescue. "At this point, it's a game of chicken," he said, with a slight air of cockiness.

"Do you think the Fed gets what's at stake?" Gamble asked.

"Are you crazy?" Studzinski replied. "Of course not. They just let Lehman fail. It's like a bad Woody Allen movie."

By 1:00 a.m., Scully and Porat of Morgan Stanley, who were still representing the Fed, decided they needed to talk privately. They hid in one of AIG's small kitchens and closed the door, so they'd be out of earshot of the Goldman and JP Morgan bankers.

"This isn't going to work," Porat said. "They aren't going to get there."

"Agreed," Scully replied. "We need a fallback plan."

They gave their assignment a code name and decided they'd head back to the Fed to alert Dan Jester.

When they opened the kitchen door, they noticed that everyone else had already left, which only seemed to confirm their worst fears: Any chance of a deal had officially ended.

When they reached the Fed, it, too, was deserted, apart from Jeremiah Norton passed out on a couch. He had originally tried to commandeer Geithner's couch but was told he had to find a napping place elsewhere.

Scully and Porat woke him, and the three of them went to deliver the bad news to Jester.

A conference call was set up for 3:00 a.m. with the Fed team and Treasury, leaving Hilda Williams, Geithner's assistant, the unenviable task of calling everyone at that ungodly hour to coordinate it.

"We've got a problem . . ." Geithner began the call.

For the first time in weeks, on Tuesday morning the editorial pages of the major newspapers were heralding Hank Paulson. They applauded his decision to not use taxpayer money to bail out Lehman Brothers. "It is oddly reassuring that the Treasury Department and Federal Reserve let Lehman Brothers fail, did not subsidize the distress sale of Merrill Lynch to Bank of America, and tried to line up loans for the American International Group, the troubled insurer, rather than making a loan themselves," the *New York Times*' lead editorial read. "Government intervention would have been seen either as a sign of extreme peril in the global financial system or of extreme weakness on the part of federal regulators."

Given the conversation he'd had with Dan Jester at 6:00 that morning, however, it was looking increasingly likely that AIG and the global financial system were now in such peril that the government would have no choice but to intervene.

Paulson had seen the panic gripping the markets in the past twenty-four hours, which was duly reflected in the headlines on every newsstand. That morning's *Washington Post* was typical of the tone of the coverage: "Stocks Plunge as Crisis Intensifies; AIG at Risk; $700 Billion in Shareholder Value Vanishes."

The Dow Jones Industrial Average had slumped 504.48 points on Monday, the biggest point decline for the index since September 17, 2001, when trading started up again after the September 11 terrorist attacks. AIG's stock had fallen 65 percent to close at $4.76.

By 7:45 a.m., Ben Bernanke was in his office preparing for the Federal Open Market Committee meeting that was due to begin forty-five minutes later in the boardroom just down the hall from his office. It was purely a matter of chance that the FOMC, the Fed's board of directors that determines monetary policy and decides whether to raise or lower interest rates, had one of its eight meetings a year scheduled for this morning.

Before his meeting began, Bernanke called Kevin Warsh and Don Kohn into his office to join him in a conference call with Tim Geithner, who instead of attending the FOMC gathering had decided he had to stay in New York to deal with AIG, sending Christine Cumming, his vice president, in his place. There was only one small problem with that decision: FOMC meetings were relatively public affairs, and Bernanke was concerned that Geithner's absence could leak to the press and cause further panic in the markets.

"There's nothing we can do about it at this point," Geithner said, eager to focus the group's attention on the larger problem at hand. He told them that he was expecting to receive a full progress update from JP Morgan and Goldman Sachs at 9:00 a.m., but cautioned that all the signals he had gotten from Dan Jester and Morgan Stanley had not been promising.

He advised them, consequently, to start thinking about a Plan B.

———

Jimmy Lee was worried he'd be late for the meeting at the NY Fed, having gotten stuck in traffic on the FDR after a quick trip back to his home in Darien to take a shower and put on some fresh clothes. While waiting he called Dimon from his cell phone. "So this is what I'm going to tell them," he said about his planned presentation to the Fed. "I'm going to have to say the numbers are just too big. We can't do it. No one can do it. The company is going down."

"If that's the answer, that's the answer," Dimon replied.

"This is my best judgment," Lee assured him.

The good news—if it could be called that—was that Lee expected he'd have to tell only Dan Jester, since Geithner would be in Washington at the FOMC meeting.

When Lee finally arrived, he found everyone had already gathered in the conference room that had become the de facto lounge for these meetings. He took a seat near his colleague, Doug Braunstein, and they all began waiting patiently for Dan Jester.

The door opened and Jester and Norton entered, followed by Geithner, who gave no explanation for his unexpected presence.

"So where are we?" he asked in his clipped, all-business manner.

Jimmy Lee consulted his yellow pad, on which he had written two notes to himself in the margins: "Deal stands little chance" and "AIG out of cash."

"We've gone through it all," Lee said. "They have $50 billion in collateral and they need $80 to $90 billion. We're short $30 to $40 billion. I don't know how we can bridge that gap."

Winkelried of Goldman then jumped in. "Let me just say there is a huge systemic risk to letting this institution fail. I don't need to tell you the number of counterparties that would be exposed."

A document generated listing AIG's biggest counterparties in order of size was passed around. The most exposed firm listed on the orange and blue sheet was ABN AMRO, which had been acquired by Royal Bank of Scotland, with $65 billion; the second largest was Calyon; Goldman Sachs was the seventh; Barclays was the eighth; and Morgan Stanley was the ninth.

Geithner studied the figures, furrowing his brow every few lines, and after setting them down said, "Okay. Here's what we're going to do." He paused, leaning forward for all to hear what he was about to say.

"I want everyone to put his cell phone away, BlackBerrys, everything. I don't want anybody communicating outside of this room. Not to your office. Not to anybody. Do you understand me? This conversation is confidential," he said. When Geithner was satisfied that everyone had complied, he posed a question for which no one in the group had been prepared: "What would it look like if we said the Fed was going to do this?"

For the past seventy-two hours the government had been insisting that it would not bail out any financial institution. Now, with that one sentence, Geithner had turned everything on its head. Even if it was just a hypothetical, the rules of engagement had evidently just changed.

Geithner continued, throwing out a series of questions. "How would this work? How would you structure the terms? How will the capital markets respond? How will the debt markets react?"

Goldman's Winkelried could not hide a slight smile. Scully of Morgan Stanley, realizing the night before that he needed a Plan B, had already roughed out a term sheet based on the numbers that JP Morgan and Goldman Sachs had put together. If it was good enough for them—and by Morgan Stanley's estimation, they were going to be stealing the company—it should be good enough for the Federal Reserve.

"Work on it," Geithner said, and then left the room.

"Braunstein isn't picking up his fucking phone," Willumstad railed after dialing his cell several times, worried that he was being kept in the dark.

John Studzinski, his adviser from Blackstone, had just heard from one of his colleagues who was down at the NY Fed that he had seen Goldman and JP Morgan executives high-fiving one another—even while another team from the two banks was still camped out at AIG, rifling through its books.

Studzinski finally managed to reach Porat by text-messaging her. However, she was purposely being vague, and would only offer, "The deal is changing. Stop sharing information with JPM and GS."

A few minutes later, Willumstad's assistant announced that Tim Geithner, whom Willumstad had frantically attempted to reach several times that morning, was on the phone.

396 | Andrew Ross Sorkin

"Hi, Tim," Willumstad said, somewhat impatiently.

"Give me a progress report," Geithner instructed, rather than offering the progress report that Willumstad had been waiting for desperately.

"I just want you to know that we're preparing for bankruptcy," Willumstad told him steadily. "I've called the backup lines. I just think you should know that."

Geithner seemed anxious and quickly cut him off with, "Don't do that."

"You have to give me a reason not to," he said, mystified by the odd reply. "I have an obligation and responsibility. I can get $15 billion and keep me going for a couple of days. I have to protect the shareholders here."

"Well, I'll tell you something confidential," Geithner finally said. "We're working on some help for you, but there's no guarantees, it has to be approved by Washington."

Willumstad, still dubious, replied, "Well, unless you can assure me that there's going to be some help, we're going to go ahead with the backup."

"You should try and undo whatever you've done," Geithner ordered and hung up.

When he got off the phone, Willumstad immediately informed his lawyers, Jamie Gamble and Michael Wiseman, and, none of them quite knowing what to do next, tried Braunstein's phone again, with no success.

"Screw it," Wiseman said. "I know we're not invited, but let's just go over there ourselves."

———

Hank Paulson was in his office at Treasury when Lloyd Blankfein called him at 9:40 a.m. in a panic. Blankfein, anxious by nature, was even more so now, and Paulson could sense it.

Blankfein told Paulson about a new problem he was seeing in the market: Hedge funds that had traded through Lehman's London unit were suddenly being cut off, sucking billions of dollars out of the market. While the Fed had kept Lehman's broker-dealer in the United States open in order to wind down the trades, Lehman's European and Asian operations were forced by law to file for bankruptcy immediately.

Blankfein explained that through an arcane process called rehypothecation, Lehman had reloaned the hedge funds' collateral to others through its London unit, and sorting out who owned what had become a logistical nightmare. To stay liquid, many hedge funds were forced to sell assets, which pushed the market even lower. Some hedge funds, fearing that Lehman was on the brink, had already dropped it as a prime broker before the bankruptcy. But for those who stuck by it, the results were painful, as was the case with Ramius Capital, whose founder, Peter A. Cohen, was once the chairman of Lehman's predecessor, Shearson Lehman. In the week before the bankruptcy he had declared on CNBC that his firm wouldn't pull its business from Lehman. Now he had to tell his investors that their money had become trapped in a mysterious bankruptcy process in London.

Pleading with his former boss to do something to calm the markets, Blankfein told Paulson that his biggest worry was that so much money was clogged up inside Lehman that investors would panic and start pulling their money out of Goldman Sachs and Morgan Stanley, too.

———

Bernanke was clearly distracted as he presided over the FOMC meeting at the Federal Reserve in Washington, passing notes back and forth with Kevin Warsh as they tried to come up with a game plan for AIG. They had agreed to another conference call with Geithner at 10:45 a.m. to get an update.

Geithner reiterated that "a private-market solution is dead" and told them, "We need to think about using our balance sheet. We need to act with force and determination," suggesting that if the Fed made a big, bold deal to backstop AIG, it could help restore confidence in the markets. He proposed using the Federal Reserve Act, Section 13, point 3, a unique provision that permitted the Fed to lend to institutions other than banks under "unusual and exigent" circumstances.

As Paulson and Bernanke both knew, AIG had effectively become a linchpin of the global financial system. Under European banking regulations, financial institutions had been allowed to meet capital requirements by entering into credit default swap agreements with AIG's financial products unit. Using the swaps, the banks had essentially wrapped AIG's triple-A credit rating around riskier assets, such as corporate loans and residential mortgages, allowing the banks to take on more leverage.

If AIG were to fail, however, those protective wrappers would vanish, forcing the banks to mark down assets and raise billions of dollars—a frightening prospect in the current markets. And the numbers were staggering: Halfway though 2008, AIG had reported more than $300 billion in credit default swaps involved in this wrapping procedure, which it politely called "regulatory capital relief."

Then, of course, there was the matter of AIG's vast insurance empire, which included about 81 million life insurance policies around the world with a face value of $1.9 trillion. While that part of the business was highly regulated and the policies generally protected, there was a risk that panicky customers would cash in their policies in droves and create instability at other major insurers.

Bernanke listened patiently as Geithner made his case, but Warsh made his reluctance known, as he had been promoting a "buying time" plan. His view was that the Fed should open its checkbook, but only for thirty days—enough time to really examine AIG seriously.

"I know it could leave us with open-ended exposure," Warsh admitted, "but let's actually figure what the hell is going on here."

Although Bernanke bluntly acknowledged, "I don't know the insurance business," Geithner continued to urge them to commit. The systemic risk was just too great, he insisted.

After hearing his arguments, Bernanke told him to develop a plan. Once he came back to them with more details, they'd formally vote on how to proceed.

"Let me just make sure I'm characterizing the support of you and the board on this accurately. . . ." Geithner then repeated what had just been said.

Michael Wiseman and Jamie Gamble passed through security at the Fed and went in search of Braunstein. They needed to understand what was happening with AIG, and if nothing was happening, they needed his team to help them plan for the bankruptcy.

Wiseman finally tracked him down in the confidential meeting that was still going on about how the Fed could backstop AIG. "Listen, we don't have a lot of time and we could use your help with some of the numbers," he told him angrily after pulling him out of the room. "But we need to know which hat you're wearing. Are you working for us, the Fed, or JP Morgan?"

"I don't think I can answer that question without talking to my lawyer," Braunstein said after a pause. Signaling that he needed a second, he dashed back into the conference room.

When he emerged a few moments later, he said stiffly to Wiseman: "I can't talk. You should contact Treasury directly."

"Okay. Thanks," Wiseman said, putting out his hand to shake it, but Braunstein only turned around and returned to his meeting.

Within seconds, an aide from the Federal Reserve appeared and informed Wiseman and Gamble that they had to leave the building.

"Did you just see that?" Wiseman asked Gamble as they were escorted to the door. "Doug wouldn't even shake my hand. What the fuck is going *on* in there?"

However resistant Hank Paulson had been to the idea of a bailout, after getting off the phone at 10:30 a.m. with Geithner, who had walked him through the latest plan, he could see where the markets were headed, and it scared him. During his time at Goldman, he had educated himself about the insurance industry, and with that background he understood how an AIG bankruptcy could very well trigger a global panic. As a regular visitor to Asia, he also knew how much business AIG did there and how many foreign governments owned its debt. Foreign governments had already been calling Treasury to express their anxiety about AIG's failing.

Jim Wilkinson asked incredulously, "Are we really going to rescue this insurance company?"

Paulson just stared at him as if to say that only a madman would just stand by and do nothing.

Ken Wilson, his special adviser, raised an issue they had yet to consider: "Hank, how the hell can we put $85 billion into this entity without new management?"—a euphemism for asking how the government could fund this amount of money without firing the current CEO and installing its own. Without a new CEO, it would seem as if the government was backing the same inept management that had created this mess.

"You're right. You've got to find me a CEO. Drop every other thing you're doing," Paulson told him. "Get me a CEO."

Wilson got back to his office and started scrolling though his computer's address book. After years as a financial institutions banker at Goldman

Sachs, he knew the top people in the industry. Before even getting to the B's, a name popped into his brain: Ed Liddy, the former CEO of Allstate and a Goldman board member. He was a perfect candidate, currently "on the beach" without a job and someone who would welcome the challenge. Liddy also knew AIG: He was the Goldman board member to whom everyone turned for advice whenever they discussed whether the firm should acquire it.

But Wilson didn't have his phone number. So he called Chris Cole at Goldman Sachs, who had been at AIG all weekend and had attended the meeting at the Fed on Monday, who gladly retrieved the number for him.

There was no time for small talk when Wilson reached Liddy, and he immediately explained why he was calling.

"Do you have time to take a call from Hank?" Wilson asked, and Liddy assented enthusiastically.

"You have to hang up," Wilson told Paulson, who was on the phone when he appeared in his boss's office door. "I've got your CEO."

———

AIG's stock had fallen below $2 a share when Willumstad's assistant stepped into his office and handed him a fax from Hank Greenberg. Willumstad had heard earlier that Greenberg was out telling the press that he planned to mount a proxy contest or a takeover of the company.

"Do I have to read it?" he asked warily, and was not surprised at what he saw:

Dear Bob,
We have been discussing for several weeks my offer to assist the company, in any way that you and the Board desired. Throughout those discussions, you have told me and David Boies that you believed my assistance was important to the company. The only concern that you have expressed to me is the fear that if I were to become an advisor to the company that I would overshadow you. I respectfully suggest to you, and to the Board, that the continuing refusal to work together to save this great company is far more important than any concern over personal positions or perceptions.

I do not know whether or not it is now too late to save AIG. However, we owe it to AIG's shareholders, creditors and our country to try.

Since you became Chairman of AIG, you and the Board have presided over the virtual destruction of shareholder value built up over 35 years. It is not my intention to try to point fingers or be critical. My only point is that under the circumstance, I am truly bewildered at the unwillingness of you and the Board to accept my help.

———

Geithner began to prepare in his office for a conference call with Bernanke. *We're going to do this,* he thought. *We're really going to do this.*

Jester and Norton were poring over all the terms. They had just learned that Ed Liddy had tentatively accepted the job of AIG's CEO and was planning to fly to New York from Chicago that night.

To draft a rescue deal on such short notice, the government needed help, preferably from someone who already understood AIG and its extraordinary circumstances. Jester knew just the man: Marshall Huebner, the co-head of insolvency and restructuring at Davis Polk & Wardwell, who was already working on AIG for JP Morgan and who happened to be just downstairs.

Meanwhile, Bob Scully of Morgan Stanley, whom Geithner had hired to advise the Fed, wanted to make sure he was aware of all the risks ahead of the call. As Scully continued to study the rapid deterioration in the markets, he became increasingly anxious about whether AIG would be able to maintain its payments on a government loan. What had looked like a steal before might still be a tough sell.

"I want to be clear that there's a real risk you may not be made whole on this loan," he warned as Geithner dialed into the conference call.

While Bernanke said that he had decided to back the deal, he nevertheless wanted to take a straw poll among the participants in the call. He was clearly anxious, asking, "Are you sure we're doing the right thing?"

But with his implicit support—and Geithner's insistence that this was the only way to avert a financial Armageddon—the vote was 5–0. There was no longer any discussion of moral hazard, and no talk of Lehman Brothers.

———

Before Wiseman and Gamble had gotten far after being escorted by security guards from the NY Fed, they were surprised to suddenly find themselves being invited back in. There had been a mix-up, they were told, and they were taken to a table in the dining room.

"This isn't the cool kids' table," Gamble remarked, looking over at another table at the other end of the enormous space, where JP Morgan and Goldman bankers were waiting.

"One thing is for certain," Wiseman said, "they are not doing a private deal. They'd never look this relaxed."

While they waited, Gamble took a call about two new issues: Insurance regulators in Texas, where AIG had a major life insurance business, were starting to panic. Even worse, JP Morgan had just pulled a line of collateral in Japan, which was AIG's largest market outside the United States. Gamble couldn't believe it: JP Morgan, AIG's adviser just twenty-four hours earlier, was now only exacerbating the problem, however prudent it might have been to do so.

Twenty minutes later, Eric Dinallo, superintendent of the New York State Insurance Department, came over to a relieved Wiseman and Gamble's table. "I can't tell you much," Dinallo said, "but don't do anything precipitous."

"Eric," a frustrated Gamble replied, "we're happy to hold tight, but our securities lending business is in trouble." Then he pointed at the JP Morgan and Goldman Sachs contingent. "The guys over there are creating this problem. Go talk to those guys."

———

"I think we're about to be out of cash!" John Studzinski announced at the teetering insurance giant's headquarters. It was nearly 1:00 p.m., and if Studzinski's math was correct, AIG was minutes away from bankruptcy.

Just then, Willumstad walked out of his office with something that hadn't been seen in some time in the building: a smile.

"They blinked," he said.

He had just gotten off the phone with Geithner, who told him about the bailout plan: The Fed would extend to AIG a $14 billion loan to keep the firm in business through the rest of the trading day. But Geithner added that AIG would have to immediately post collateral before it could receive the loan. Officially, it was called a "demand note."

While clearly relieved, Willumstad understandably wondered how they were supposed to come up with $14 billion in the next several minutes.

Then it dawned on one of them: the unofficial vaults. The bankers ran downstairs and found a room with a lock and a cluster of cabinets containing stock certificates for AIG's insurance units—tens of billions of dollars' worth, dating mostly from the Greenberg era. They began rifling through the drawers, picking through fistfuls of securities that they guessed had gone untouched for years. In an electronic age, the idea of keeping physical certificates on hand was a disconcerting but welcome throwback.

AIG's senior vice president and secretary, Kathleen Shannon, stacked the bonds up on the table and put them in a briefcase.

"I don't think it's worth you getting mugged carrying $14 billion of certificates," Michael Wiseman from Sullivan & Cromwell advised her over the phone. "We'll get Fed security to escort you over."

Ten minutes later, Shannon was carrying an inestimably valuable briefcase across Pine Street, flanked by two armed guards.

Hank Paulson hustled down the stairs and out the side exit of the Treasury building, briskly heading for the White House. He and Ben Bernanke had scheduled a meeting with President Bush to brief him on the extraordinary steps they were about to take.

After passing through security and a brief stay in a waiting room, they were escorted to the Oval Office, where Paulson delicately walked the president through the terms.

As Paulson explained the deal, however, detailing its points in Wall Street jargon, Bush clearly looked perplexed.

Bernanke jumped in and said, "Mr. President, let's step back for a minute." Donning his professorial hat, he explained how deeply entwined AIG had become in the banking system. More important, he tried to appeal to the Everyman in Bush, emphasizing how many citizens and small businesses depended on the firm. People used AIG's life insurance policies to protect their families. They used AIG's annuities to fund their retirements. AIG also provided surety bonds, a kind of guarantee for construction projects and public works.

The president then posed a question that, in its own way, went directly to the heart of the problem: "An insurance company does all this?"

This one did.

At around 4:00 p.m. that afternoon, the Fed's offer clattered through an AIG fax machine (which should have been replaced and shipped to the Smithsonian a decade earlier). An army of lawyers on AIG's eighteenth floor were anxiously awaiting it. After the three-page document finally appeared, a lawyer grabbed it and quickly made copies.

"Well, you finally get your chance to work for the federal government," Richard Beattie, the lead lawyer for the outside directors on the AIG board, told Willumstad as he scanned the terms.

"What do you mean?" asked Willumstad.

"They own you now," Beattie replied with a grin.

And they did. The Federal Reserve was providing AIG a credit line of $85 billion—which it hoped would be enough to avert catastrophe and keep it afloat. But in exchange for the loan, the government was taking a large ownership stake—79.9 percent in the form of warrants called "equity participation notes." It was similar to the proposal that JP Morgan and Goldman had been working on.

If Washington was going to take Wall Street off the hook, the government wanted to make certain that at least the old stakeholders didn't profit in any untoward fashion. "Paulson is handling this the same way he did Fannie, Freddie, and Bear Stearns—if the government steps in, the shareholders will pay for it," Cohen observed.

The Fed loan also came with a significant debt burden. AIG would have to pay at a rate based on a complex formula—the London interbank offered rate, a benchmark for short-term loans between banks, which then came to about 3 percent—plus an extra 8.5 percentage points. Based on that day's rate, the interest the company would have to pay soared to more than 11 percent, which at the time was considered usurious. The loan would be secured by all AIG's assets, and the government would have the right to veto payments of dividends to both common and preferred shareholders.

In order to pay back the government, AIG would have to sell off assets—and under the circumstances, that meant a fire sale. To AIG loyalists, the loan was proving to be less a bridge to solvency than a plank to an organized breakup.

"This is unbelievable," Willumstad said, setting aside the document.

The board of AIG was prepared to meet soon for an emergency session.

As Willumstad stood and reread the terms in a virtual state of shock, his assistant called out to say that Tim Geithner was on the phone. It was 4:40 p.m.

Willumstad followed Beattie and Cohen into his office and hit the speakerphone button.

"Can you hang on a minute?" Geithner said after greeting him. "Secretary Paulson is going to pick up."

"Okay," Willumstad said, adding, "I've got Dick Beattie and Rodgin Cohen sitting here with me."

"So, you've seen the new agreement, right?" Geithner asked after Paulson joined in. "We want to know that you are going to accept the terms. We need an answer back from you soon, because trading is going to start in Asia."

In the back of his own mind, Geithner had a nagging worry: *Were the terms too harsh?* But he was at least as concerned about potential blowback from the other direction—that Treasury would be criticized for giving AIG a sweetheart deal.

It was no coincidence, though, that the government's terms had so much in common with what the private sector had been considering. For one thing, they had used many of the same advisers. And in the current political environment, there was safety in being able to say that AIG was only getting what the market had been willing—or almost willing—to offer.

"Obviously, we have a board meeting in fifteen minutes, and I'm prepared to present it there," Willumstad said.

"Tim, it's Dick," Beattie said, jumping in. "I just want to be clear that you know that you shouldn't assume just because you stepped in that the board will approve this. We've got a fiduciary duty to our shareholders, so it is going to be complicated."

Beattie, playing hardball, had effectively implied a threat that AIG might be better off filing for Chapter 11 bankruptcy than taking the government's deal.

Geithner didn't flinch. "This is the only proposal you're going to get," he tersely replied, and then added, "There's one other condition. . . ."

Paulson, interrupting, said, "The condition is that we're going to replace you, Bob."

Beattie and Cohen looked at Willumstad in embarrassed silence.

"O . . . kay," Willumstad said. "If that's what you want."

"We're going to bring in a new CEO," Paulson said matter-of-factly. "He'll be showing up tomorrow."

Willumstad had had no illusions that a government rescue would mean anything other than his ouster, but he was stunned by the speed of events. The government had just made its offer moments ago—and it had already completed an executive search to find his successor?

"Should I still be here?" Willumstad asked, confused about how to proceed.

"Yeah, we would appreciate whatever cooperation and help you can offer," Paulson replied.

"Is it okay if I ask who it is?"

"It's Ed Liddy," Paulson said.

For a moment, Willumstad wracked his memory. "Who the hell is Ed Liddy?" Beattie whispered, but Cohen only shrugged his shoulders.

"Ed just retired recently as the CEO of Allstate," Paulson interjected, realizing they had no idea who he was.

After the call, Willumstad slumped in his chair, sighed, and then looked over at Beattie and laughed.

"Well, you're wrong," he said. "I won't be working for the federal government after all."

———

The directors of AIG were already gathered in the boardroom when Willumstad and the advisers made their entrance. Willumstad wasted no time on preliminaries.

"We are faced with two bad choices," he began. "File for bankruptcy tomorrow morning, or take the Fed's deal tonight." He explained the terms of the deal and told them that Blackstone would come in with bankruptcy advisers to discuss the merits of that route.

And then he told them his personal news.

"I'm going to be replaced," he said quietly. "Ed Liddy is going to take my place."

"Ed Liddy?" asked Virginia Rometty.

"Yeah, he's Allstate," Willumstad explained.

"I've known him for fifteen years," she said. A top executive with IBM,

Rometty had once headed the sales group for the computer company's division that catered to the insurance and financial industries. "I wouldn't have thought Ed would have been the guy."

"I know Ed Liddy!" James Orr chimed in. Orr had been chief executive of Unum, a Maine insurer that had fought off an effort by Allstate to grab market share from the company in the long-term disability category it dominated. "If we were looking for a CEO of this company, not only wouldn't he have been on the short list, he wouldn't have been on the long list!"

"Well, that's one of the decisions you'll have to digest," Willumstad said calmly, and turned the meeting over to Cohen.

Martin Feldstein, an AIG director and former economic adviser to President Ronald Reagan, couldn't believe that the government—a Republican administration—was going to be effectively buying a stake in a private business.

Rodgin Cohen, reminding the board that they had a fiduciary duty not only to shareholders but to bondholders as well, pressed for a bankruptcy.

"You should consider all these things," Beattie said. "Just because it's the Fed doesn't mean you have to accept this. You should listen to all the options."

Willumstad's assistant slipped into the room and handed him a note: *Hank Greenberg is on the phone.* He rolled his eyes, leaned over to John Studzinski, and passed him an instruction: "Would *you* please call Hank Greenberg back?"

———

Studzinski crept out of the boardroom, aware of just how awkward this call was going to be for him to make. To help smooth the way, Studzinski enlisted Pete Peterson, Blackstone's co-founder and a longtime friend of Greenberg, to join the call. At Greenberg's suggestion, AIG had invested $1.35 billion in Blackstone when the firm was flagging in the aftermath of the 1998 Russian debt crisis.

While Studzinski waited on the line, Peterson dialed Greenberg's office on Park Avenue.

"He can't talk right now," Greenberg's assistant said. "He's going on *Charlie Rose* to talk about AIG."

"You've got to be kidding me," Peterson said.

When Studzinski returned to the board meeting, he passed a note to Willumstad and relayed the news. For a moment, Willumstad smiled.

The board quickly returned to the grim subject at hand. Cohen, offering the pros and cons of the government's deal, explained the argument for a Chapter 11 bankruptcy filing, saying that the company might do better in an orderly unwinding in court rather than accept the government's take-it-or-leave-it offer.

Each of the various advisers offered their view. Studzinski said that a bankruptcy filing by a company as large and as complex as AIG would take many months to get under control and that the likelihood was that even more value would be eroded. "I just spent the last ten minutes giving you all the banking reasons to do this," Studzinski summed up. "But there's one more," he said, looking around the room.

"Isn't twenty percent of something better than one hundred percent of nothing?"

The room fell silent.

As the meeting wore on, Willumstad checked his watch, knowing that he owed Paulson and Geithner an answer quickly.

"Let's go around the table and let everybody say what you think we should do," Willumstad instructed. "To be honest with you, I urge you to vote in favor of the Fed proposal," he told them, starting off. "We have three constituents. Shareholders, customers, employees. This is not something that's friendly to the shareholders, but it will preserve the customers, keep the company afloat, and you have a better chance these people will keep their jobs."

As they made their way around the table, all the board members voted in favor of the government deal with the exception of Stephen Bollenbach, the former chief executive of Hilton Hotels. Bollenbach, who was supported by Eli Broad and other major dissident AIG shareholders, had joined the board in January. He thought that a proper judge would give shareholders a fairer deal.

Before the vote was formally tallied, Bollenbach asked a question: Was there any room to renegotiate the terms of the deal?

Willumstad and the lawyers retreated to his office to call Geithner.

"Tim, Dick and Rodge are here," Willumstad said. "It's probably appropriate to let me have Dick explain to you the directors' feelings."

Leaning in toward the speakerphone, Beattie said, "Tim, the board wants to know whether the terms can be renegotiated. They think eighty percent is outrageous."

"Terms cannot be negotiated," Geithner said firmly. "These are the only terms you're going to get."

As the three men looked at each other resignedly, Beattie continued, "We have a second question. The board wants to know whether, if the company can come up with its own financing to take the Fed's place, would that be acceptable?"

Geithner hesitated and then replied: "Nobody would be happier than I if the company, you know, would pay the Fed back."

Beattie returned to the boardroom and relayed the conversation. The deal was done.

———

Paulson and Bernanke, after finishing with the president, ran over to the Hill to brief key congressmen, who were none too pleased with the AIG bailout news. Senate majority leader Harry Reid hosted the meeting in his second-floor conference room. The gathering had been hastily organized; some congressmen were invited only twenty minutes before it began. Senator Judd Gregg of New Hampshire, the ranking Republican on the Senate Banking Committee, was supposed to be at a black-tie dinner and showed up in his tuxedo, sans tie. Barney Frank arrived late in an untucked shirt.

Paulson and Bernanke explained why they thought their decision had been a necessary one. "If we don't do this," Paulson told them, the impact of an AIG bankruptcy would "be felt across America and around the world."

Frank, concerned about the cost, looked at Bernanke. "Do you *have* $80 billion?"

With a barely concealed smile, Bernanke answered, "Well, we have $800 billion."

———

Back at JP Morgan, Jamie Dimon and Jimmy Lee were sitting in Dimon's office when the AIG press release came across the tape. "They're never going to get their money back," Lee told Dimon. "There's no way."

"I guarantee you they'll get more than $50 billion of it back," Dimon shot back, thinking that Washington had just cut itself a good deal, however bad it was from a public relations perspective. "AIG has a lot of good insurance businesses it can auction off. You'll see."

Dimon and Lee placed a $10 bet on who would turn out to be right.

Around 11:00 that night, Bob Willumstad's driver pulled up to his building on Park Avenue, just across from Lenox Hill Hospital. Dashing under its green awning, Willumstad, tired and depressed, rode up the elevator to his seventh-floor apartment. Pacing in his kitchen, he recounted the day's events to his wife, Carol.

Before turning in for bed, Willumstad checked his BlackBerry one last time. David Herzog, the company's controller and a man who had been working behind the scenes nonstop for the past weekend to keep the firm afloat, had sent him an e-mail. The time stamp was 11:54 p.m.; the subject line, "Last Steps":

Thank you for taking on this very difficult challenge. The events that unfolded tonight were set in motion long ago.

Before you leave office, I ask only one thing. Please clean the slate for Mr. Liddy. I urge the following dismissals immediately:

Schreiber

Lewis & McGinn

Nueger & Scott

Bensinger

Kelly

Kaslow

Dooley

While this may seem a bit harsh, this group of executives each have shown in their own ways a clear pattern of ineptness that contributed to the destruction of one of America's greatest companies. Please, don't make Mr. Liddy figure this out on his own.

I mean no disrespect to these individuals, but the 120,000 employees around the world deserve better, and some sense of accountability for what just happened.

We need leadership, and these individuals are simply not leaders.

Respectfully yours,

David

Willumstad, standing in the hallway in his boxer shorts, just shook his head in disbelief.

CHAPTER SEVENTEEN

When Tim Geithner began his run on Wednesday morning along the southern tip of Manhattan and up the East River just after 6:00, the sun had yet to come up. He was tired and stressed, having slept only several hours in one of the three tiny, grubby bedrooms in the New York Fed's headquarters.

As he stared at the Statue of Liberty and the first of the morning's commuter ferries from Staten Island gliding across the harbor, he tried desperately to clear his mind. For five days his brain had been trapped in a maze of numbers—huge, inconceivable, abstract numbers, ranging in the span of twenty-four hours from zero for Lehman to $85 billion for AIG. Eighty-five billion dollars was more than the annual budgets of Singapore and Taiwan combined; who could even begin to understand a figure of that size? Geithner hoped the sum was sufficient—and that the crisis would finally be over.

Those ferries, freighted with office workers, gave him pause. *This is what it is all about,* he thought to himself, *the people who rise at dawn to get in to their jobs, all of whom rely to some extent on the financial industry to help power the economy. Never mind the staggering numbers. Never mind the ruthless complexity of structured finance and derivatives, nor the million-dollar bonuses of those who made bad bets. This is what saving the financial industry is really about,* he reminded himself, *protecting ordinary people with ordinary jobs.*

But as he passed the South Street Seaport and then under the Brooklyn Bridge, he had inadvertently begun thinking about what fresh hell the day would bring. He was most anxious about the latest shocking development: A giant money market fund, Reserve Primary Fund, had broken the buck a day earlier (which meant that the value of the fund's assets had fallen to below a dollar per share—in this case, 97 cents). Money market funds were never supposed to do that; they were one of the least risky investments available, providing investors with minuscule returns in exchange for total security. But the Reserve Primary Fund had chased a higher yield—a 4.04 percent annual return, the highest in the industry—by making risky bets, including $785 million in Lehman paper. Investors had started liquidating their accounts, which in turn forced managers to impose a seven-day moratorium on redemptions. Nobody, Geithner worried, knew just how extensive the damage could end up being.

Between the money-market funds being under pressure, Geithner thought, *and billions of dollars of investors' money locked up inside the now-bankrupt Lehman Brothers, that means only one thing: the two remaining broker-dealers— Morgan Stanley and Goldman Sachs—could actually be next.*

———

The panic was already palpable in John Mack's office at Morgan Stanley's Times Square headquarters. Sitting on his sofa with his lieutenants, Chammah and Gorman, drinking coffee from paper cups, he was railing: The major news on Wednesday morning, he thought, should have been the strength of Morgan Stanley's earnings report, which he had released the afternoon before, a day early, to stem any fears of panic about the firm following the Lehman debacle. His stock had fallen 28 percent in a matter of hours on Tuesday, and he decided he needed to do something to turn it around. The quarterly earnings report had been a good one—better than that of Goldman Sachs, which had announced their earnings Tuesday morning and also had suffered, but not nearly as much. Morgan had reported $1.43 billion in profits, down a mere 3 percent from the quarter a year earlier. But the headline on the *Wall Street Journal* was gnawing at him: "Goldman, Morgan Now Stand Alone; Fight On or Fold?" And as the futures markets were already indicating, his attempt to show strength and vitality had largely failed to impress.

Apart from the new anxiety about money market funds and general nervousness about investment banks, he was facing a more serious problem than anyone on the outside realized: At the beginning of the week, Morgan Stanley had had $178 billion in the tank—money available to fund operations and to lend to their major hedge fund clients. But in the past twenty-four hours, more than $20 billion of it had been withdrawn, as hedge fund clients demanded it back, in some cases closing their prime brokerage accounts entirely.

"The money's walking out of the door," Chammah told Mack.

"Nobody gives a shit about loyalty," Mack railed. He had wanted to cut off the flow of funds, but up until now had been persuaded by Chammah to keep wiring the balances. "To put the gates up," Chammah warned, "would be a sign of weakness."

The question was, how much more could they afford to let go? "We can't do this forever," Chammah said.

While Mack was beginning to believe the hedge funds were conspiring against the firm—"This is what they did to Dick!" he roared—there was fresh evidence that some of them actually did need the cash. Funds that had accounts at Lehman's London office couldn't get at them and came begging to Morgan Stanley and Goldman.

As far as Mack was concerned, they needed to keep paying out money. He had spent years building their prime brokerage business into a major profit center—eighty-nine of the top one hundred hedge funds in the world traded through Morgan Stanley. It was essential in the midst of a crisis that the firm not display even the slightest sign of panic, or the entire franchise would be lost.

"We are confident," he said. "We cannot be weak, and we cannot be confused."

Under normal circumstances, John Mack could be unflappable. The previous day he'd even been out on the floor, as was his habit, chatting with traders and eating a slice of pizza. But in his office that morning, he was starting to come unwound. There was just too much to do, too many options to explore, too many things to worry about.

The night before, he'd received a call from his old friend Steven R. Volk, a vice chairman at Citigroup and former lawyer who years earlier had helped Mack engineer the merger with Dean Witter. Now Volk, ostensibly calling to offer congratulations on the earnings reports, quietly planted the seed of another merger—with Citi.

"Look, John, we're here for you. We're not aggressive. And if you want to do something strategically to put us together, we would like to talk to you," Volk said.

It was potentially explosive news. A merger between Morgan Stanley and Citigroup would be like combining Microsoft and Intel.

Mack, Chammah, and Gorman batted around the idea. Given the pressure on the broker-dealer model, merging with Citigroup would give it a stable base of deposits. JP Morgan and Citigroup were the only two left of the big, strong banks.

They had all heard about Bank of America's conference call on Monday regarding its deal with Merrill Lynch and couldn't ignore Ken Lewis's comments all but declaring the broker-dealer model officially dead.

"For seven years, I've said that the commercial banks would eventually own the investment banks because of funding issues," Lewis said. "I still think that. The Golden Era of investment banking is over."

Gorman, at least for the moment, was thinking that he might well be right. "Do you think we should call Citigroup back?" he asked.

Mack nodded and asked his assistant to phone Vikram Pandit's office. The two men knew each other well—Pandit, then at Morgan Stanley, had been given a big promotion by Mack in 2000—but had never been particularly close.

"Steve tells me you want to do a deal," Mack said when Pandit got on the line. "It's tough out there," Mack continued. "We're looking at our options."

"Well, we'd like to be helpful," Pandit said, "and this could be the time to do something."

But before he got too far he said, "I'll come back to you. I need to talk to my board."

The black and orange screen flickered as Hank Paulson skimmed the updates about the Reserve Primary Fund on his Bloomberg terminal. With $62.6 billion in assets, the fund was a major player, and as a result of its troubles, doubt, he could see right in front of him, was starting to spread throughout the rest of the field.

"We've got an emergency," Ken Wilson said, coming into Paulson's office and ticking off a list of panicked CEOs who had begun phoning him that morning at 6:30: Larry Fink of BlackRock, Bob Kelly of Bank of New York Mellon, Rick Waddell of Northern Trust, and Jim Cracchiolo at Ameriprise.

"They're telling me people are clamoring for redemptions. Hundreds of billions of dollars where people want out!" Wilson said. "People are concerned about anyone who has any exposure to Lehman paper."

Paulson fidgeted nervously. The Lehman-induced panic was spreading like a plague, the black death of Wall Street. The money market industry needed to be shored up. Wilson also told him that he was hearing that Morgan Stanley was coming under pressure from hedge funds seeking redemptions as well. And if Morgan Stanley were to go, Goldman, the firm where both had spent their entire careers, would likely be next in line.

"Another day, another crisis," Paulson said with a nervous laugh that betrayed an uneasy sense that he was truly beginning to panic himself.

Paulson's instinctive response had been serial deal making—the private sector's solution to systemic problems. Firms consolidated, covered one another's weaknesses.

But this situation didn't feel normal, in that respect; behind every problem lurked another problem. He may have been praised for not bailing out Lehman, but he could see now that the unintended consequences had been devastating. The confidence that had supported the financial system had been upended. No one knew the rules of engagement anymore. "They pretended they were drawing a line in the sand with Lehman Brothers, but now two days later they're doing another bailout," Nouriel Roubini, a professor at New York University's Stern School of Business, complained that morning.

And now he could understand it: commercial paper and money markets—that was his bread and butter, Goldman's specialty. The crisis was hitting close to home.

———

Across town, Kevin Warsh, a thirty-eight-year-old governor at the Federal Reserve, whose office was a few doors down from Bernanke's, was having his own worries.

He was just finishing up a conference call with Bernanke and central bankers in Europe and Asia in which they explained what they had just done with AIG. Jean-Claude Trichet, the president of the European Central Bank, had been furious with them for their decision to "let Lehman fail" and was lobbying Bernanke to go to Congress to implement a large government bailout for the entire industry, to restore confidence.

But Warsh was nervous about a different issue: Morgan Stanley, where he had worked as an M&A banker before leaving seven years earlier to become special assistant to the president for economic policy. He could tell that his former firm was quickly losing confidence in the marketplace. To him, there was an obvious solution to its problems: Morgan Stanley needed to buy a large bank with deposits. His top choice? Wachovia, a commercial bank with a large deposit base that itself was struggling. Wachovia's 2006 acquisition of Golden West, the California-based mortgage originator, was turning into a catastrophe, saddling the bank with a giant pile of bad debt that was beginning to reveal itself.

Given that no one at Treasury was allowed to talk to Bob Steel now that he had become CEO of Wachovia, worrying about that firm had become Warsh's responsibility. And he increasingly had more to worry about: as a former deal maker himself, he knew that Wachovia, too, needed a partner desperately and he just might have to play the role of matchmaker. *There is no way the bank will make it on its own,* he thought.

But like Paulson with Goldman, Warsh had his own conflict-of-interest problem with Morgan Stanley, so he sought out Scott Alvarez, the Fed's general counsel, and requested a letter clearing him to make contact with his former employer, based on an "overwhelming public interest."

Warsh contacted Steel and instructed him to call Mack in twenty minutes, which left him enough time to give Mack a heads-up.

Warsh then called Geithner and asked, "Do you want me to call John? Or do you want to call John?"

They decided to call him together.

———

Despite its terminal illness, Lehman Brothers was bustling with activity. Legions of sleep-deprived, depressed traders, lawyers, and other employees were still working the phones and doing what they had to do before closing up the shop. Fresh in their minds was the memo that Dick Fuld had sent out the previous night: "The past several months have been extraordinarily challenging, culminating in our bankruptcy filing," he wrote. "This has been very painful on all of you, both personally and financially. For this, I feel horrible." To some angry employees, it was an extraordinary understatement that called to mind Emperor Hirohito's famous surrender broadcast on August 15, 1945, when he told a stunned nation that "the war situation has developed not necessarily to Japan's advantage."

But later that day, Bart McDade, Skip McGee, and Mark Shafir, working off of four hours' sleep in three days, were able to announce a welcome bit of good news: Though it was far too late to save the entire firm, Lehman had an agreement to sell its U.S. operations for $1.75 billion. The buyer was Barclays, Lehman's onetime would-be savior, which ended up getting the part it wanted without having to acquire the whole firm. The deal would allow at least some of Lehman's ten thousand employees in the United States to keep their jobs.

As McDade, McGee, and Shafir walked the floors, some employees stood up to applaud.

———

Mack knew what Bob Steel was calling about, and he was happy to speak with him. Both men were graduates of Duke and members of the university board, and not long after Steel had taken over at Wachovia, Mack had gone down to see him in Charlotte, to pitch Morgan Stanley as an adviser. No business had come out of the meeting—the bank had Goldman to help them sort through the Golden West quagmire—but the men realized they spoke the same language and agreed to stay in touch.

"Very interesting times," Steel now said. "I imagine you've already heard from Kevin. He told me he thought we should connect."

Steel went on, intentionally keeping the discussion vague until he gauged Mack's intentions. "There might be an opportunity for us. We're thinking about a lot of things. I think this could be the right time to talk. But we'd need to move fast."

"I could see something," Mack replied, intrigued but noncommittal. "What's your timing?"

"We're moving in real time," Steel said.

Considering the meltdown in the markets, Mack thought it was at least worth talking. For Steel, a Morgan Stanley deal happened to be both commercially and personally attractive. All the tumult within the firm had left Mack without a clear successor. While he may not have wanted Mack's job immediately, their mutual friend Roy Bostock, a Morgan Stanley board member, had privately hinted to Steel that a deal between Morgan Stanley and Wachovia could present an elegant solution to Morgan's succession problems down the road. This could be Steel's big opportunity to finally run a top Wall Street firm.

After speaking with Steel, Mack called Robert Scully, his top deal maker, and told him about the conversation. Scully had his doubts; he didn't know much about Wachovia's books, but what he did know alarmed him. He agreed, however, that at this point, no options could be automatically ruled out. Besides, Wachovia had one of the biggest, most solid deposit bases in the country, an extremely attractive feature as Morgan Stanley was watching its cash fly out the door.

Scully in turn called Rob Kindler, a vice chairman, to tell him that Dave Carroll, Wachovia's head of business development, was coming to meet them on Thursday and get things started.

In the relatively straitlaced banker culture of Morgan Stanley, Kindler was an outlier—loud, indiscreetly blunt, and predisposed to threadbare old suits. In the 1990s, he had been a star lawyer at Cravath, Swaine & Moore, but he always preferred banking. He left law and originally joined JP Morgan. (A constant prankster, he soon had hats made with the slogan, "One Firm, One Team, Bribe a Leader," mocking JP Morgan's slogan of "One Firm. One Team. Be a Leader.") Despite his idiosyncrasies, when it came to deal making, his advice was highly valued. Kindler didn't initially like the notion of a Wachovia merger either, he told Scully, and took a reflexively cynical view: "Let's put this in context for a moment: Bob Steel comes from Goldman; Wachovia's investment bankers are Goldman; Paulson is obviously from Goldman. The only reason we're having this meeting with Wachovia is because Goldman won't do the deal!"

Scully had been thinking much the same thing but hadn't been willing to say so. "I don't know," he said. "Seems like a bad idea."

But Kindler couldn't help himself and soon began to wrap his brain around the possibilities of the deal. "It could be good for us," he told Scully. "It brings us a deposit base; a regional banking franchise. Let's see how it plays out."

Scully and Kindler got Jonathan Pruzan, co-head of Morgan Stanley's financial institutions practice, to start running the numbers on Wachovia. The obvious concern was its gargantuan subprime exposure, some $120 billion worth. As the Wachovia due diligence got under way, Mack got a call back from Vikram Pandit, delivering what amounted to a soft no on the merger talks. "The answer is no. The timing isn't right, but at some point we'd like to do something."

Mack clicked off, exasperated. Wachovia was nobody's idea of a dream date, but at the moment, it was the only girl at the dance.

———

"This is an economic 9/11."

There was chilling silence in Hank Paulson's office as he spoke. Nearly two dozen Treasury staffers had assembled there Wednesday morning, sitting on windowsills, on the arms of sofas, or on the edge of Paulson's desk, scribbling on legal pads. Looming over them was a portrait of Alexander Hamilton, a copy of a portrait painted in 1792, when the young nation endured its first financial panic. A Treasury associate, William Duer, who also happened to be a personal friend of Hamilton's, had used inside information to build up a huge position in government securities. When bond prices slid, Duer could not cover his debts, setting off a panic. Hamilton decided against bailing out his friend but did direct the Treasury to buy government securities, steadying the market—a long-forgotten but potentially instructive model of government intervention.

Paulson was seated in a chair in the corner, slouching, nervously tapping his stomach. He had a pained look on his face as he explained to his inner circle at Treasury that in the past four hours, the crisis had reached a new height, one he could only compare with the calamity seven years earlier, almost to the week. While no lives may have been at stake, companies with century-long histories and hundreds of thousands of jobs lay in the balance.

The entire economy, he said, was on the verge of collapsing. He had been on the phone that morning with Jamie Dimon, who had expressed his own anxiety. Paulson was no longer worried just about investment banks; he was worried about General Electric, the world's largest company and an icon of American innovation. Jeffrey Immelt, GE's CEO, had told him directly that the conglomerate's commercial paper, which it used to fund its day-to-day operations, could stop rolling. He had heard murmurs that JP Morgan had stopped lending to Citigroup; that Bank of America had stopped making loans to McDonald's franchisees; that Treasury bills were trading for under 1 percent interest, as if government-backed bonds were the only thing that investors could still trust.

Paulson knew this was *his* financial panic and perhaps was the most important moment of his tenure at Treasury, and possibly of his entire career. The night before, Bernanke and Paulson had agreed that the time had come for a systemic solution; deciding the fate of each financial firm one at a time wasn't working. It had been six months between Bear and Lehman, but if Morgan Stanley went down, probably no more than six hours would pass before Goldman did, too. The big banks would follow, and God only knew what might happen after that.

And so Paulson stood in front of his staff in search of a holistic solution, a solution that would require intervention. He still hated the idea of bailouts, but now he knew he needed to succumb to the reality of the moment.

"Nothing is breaking our way," Paulson declared. "We can't solve the problems of today; we need to think of tomorrow. We need to get ahead of this. It's deepening, moving too quickly. This is the financial equivalent of war, and we're going to need wartime powers." They needed to start thinking about what kind of program they could put together, he said, and while he wasn't sure that that approach would even be politically feasible, it had to be explored.

He told the staff that he knew and accepted that he would be subjected to an enormous amount of political flak; he had already been criticized for the bailout of AIG, with Barney Frank mockingly declaring that he was going to propose a resolution to call September 15—the day Lehman filed for bankruptcy—as "Free Market Day." "The national commitment to the free market lasted one day," Frank said. "It was Monday."

Senator Jim Bunning, Republican from Kentucky, was decrying that "once again the Fed has put the taxpayers on the hook for billions of dollars to bail out an institution that put greed ahead of responsibility." Richard Shelby, Republican from Alabama, added that he "profoundly disagrees with the decision to use taxpayer dollars to bail out a private company."

The first order of business, Paulson said, was addressing the money market crisis. Steve Shafran, a former Goldman banker, suggested that the Treasury could simply step in and guarantee the funds. "We have the authority," he said, citing the Gold Reserve Act of 1934, which set aside a fund, now totaling $50 billion, to stabilize essential markets. The key, Shafran said, was that all they needed to access it was presidential approval, bypassing Congress.

"Do it!" Paulson said, and Shafran slipped out of the room to put the process in motion.

There was, however, no such easy solution to begin stabilizing the banks. Phil Swagel, the wonky assistant secretary for economic policy, emphasized the necessity of being bold and not avoiding addressing the problems for fear of political fallout. "You don't want to be running Japan," he said.

Swagel and Neel Kashkari dusted off the ten-page "Break the Glass" paper they had prepared the previous spring: In the event of a liquidity crisis, the plan called for the government to step in and buy toxic assets directly from the lenders, thereby putting right their balance sheets and enabling them to keep extending credit. The authors knew that executing their plan would be complicated—the banks would fight furiously over the pricing of the assets—but it would keep the government's involvement in the day-to-day businesses as minimal as possible, something conservatives strongly desired.

"This is what we should do," Kashkari told Paulson. He had been involved in HOPE NOW, one of the government's early efforts at helping distressed homeowners, and had learned firsthand how difficult it would be to get the banks making new loans as long as they were carrying bad loans on their balance sheets. On the speakerphone from New York, where he still was embroiled in the AIG situation, Paulson's adviser Dan Jester argued that the purchasing of assets was too cumbersome and recommended instead that capital be injected directly into the institutions. "The more bang for your buck is to put capital in," he said, explaining that even if the market continued to fall, it would help the banks manage the downturn.

The difficulty with that approach, countered Assistant Secretary David Nason, was the specter of nationalization. If the government put money into firms, it became a de facto owner, which is precisely what most of the people in the room wanted to avoid. "Are people going to think we're going to AIG them?" he asked, already using the government's investment less than twenty-four hours earlier as a verb. Paulson had liked the "Break the Glass" idea when it had first been presented to him and was now leaning to move in that direction. AIG was a disaster they couldn't afford to repeat, and buying the assets maintained a clear border between government and the private sector. The job now was to begin preparing the outlines of legislation for Congress. They were going to need a ton of money, and they were going to need it immediately.

He assigned Kashkari and a team of staffers the task of fleshing out the idea; "Break the Glass" might have been an interesting document in theory, but it lacked details and was far from executable. He gave them twenty-four hours to fill them in.

Before ending the meeting, Paulson asked, "How much is this going to cost?"

Kashkari, who had originally estimated the expense at $500 billion back in the spring, said gravely, "It's going to be more. I don't know, maybe even double."

Dismissing everyone with a warning that their conversation had been confidential, Paulson then called Geithner to compare notes. "You cannot go out and talk about big numbers with regard to capital needs for banks without inviting a run," Geithner told him. "If you don't get the authority, I'm certain you'll spark a freaking panic. You have to be careful about not going public until you know you're going to get it."

———

By midafternoon Wednesday, Morgan Stanley's stock had fallen 42 percent. The rumors were flying: The latest gossip had the company as a trading partner with AIG, with more than $200 billion at risk. The gossip was inaccurate, but it didn't matter; hedge funds continued to seek nearly $50 billion in redemptions. Hoping to poach Morgan Stanley's hedge fund clients, Deutsche Bank was sending out fliers with the headline: "DB: A Solid Counterparty."

John Mack was meeting with his brain trust, already anticipating what had become a grim end-of-day ritual. At 2:45 p.m., hedge funds would start pulling money out of their prime brokerage accounts, asking for all the credit and margin balances. At 3:00, the Fed window would close, leaving the firm without access to additional capital until the following morning. Then, at 3:02, the spread on Morgan Stanley's credit default swaps—the cost of buying insurance against the firm's defaulting—would soar. Finally, its clearing bank, JP Morgan, would call and ask for more collateral to protect it.

"It's outrageous what's going on here," Mack almost shouted, arguing that a raid on Morgan Stanley's stock was "immoral if not illegal." Intellectually he understood the benefit that shorts provide in the market—after all, many were his own clients—but at risk now was his own survival.

Colm Kelleher, Morgan Stanley's CFO, was more fatalistic—the short-sellers couldn't be stopped, he believed, or even necessarily blamed. They were market creatures, doing what they had to do to survive. "They are cold-blooded reptiles," he told Mack. "They eat what's in front of them."

Mack had just gotten off the phone with one of his closest friends, Arthur J. Samberg, the founder of Pequot Capital Management, who had called about withdrawing some money.

"Look, if you want to take some money out, take money out," Mack told him, frustrated.

"John, I really don't *want* to do it, but my fund-to-funds accounts are saying I have too much exposure to Morgan Stanley," he said, citing the rumors about its health.

"Take your money," Mack told him, "and you can tell all your peers to take their credit balances out."

Mack believed negative speculation was purposely being spread by his rivals and repeated uncritically on CNBC. He was so furious with the "bullshit coverage" that he called to complain to Jeff Immelt, the CEO of GE, which owned CNBC as part of its NBC Universal unit.

"There's not a lot we can do about it," Immelt could only say apologetically.

Tom Nides, Mack's chief administrative officer, thought they needed to go on the offensive. Nides, a former CEO of Burson-Marsteller, the public relations giant, had been one of Mack's closest advisers for several years, his influence so great that he had persuaded the lifelong Republican to support Hillary Clinton. He now encouraged Mack to start working the phones in Washington and impress upon them the need to instate a ban against short selling. "We've got to shut down these assholes!" he told Mack.

Gary Lynch, Morgan Stanley's chief legal officer and a former enforcement chief at the SEC, volunteered to call Richard Ketchum, the head of regulation of the New York Stock Exchange, and put a bug in his ear about suspicious trading. "I'm in favor of free markets—and I'm in favor of free streets too, but when you have people walking down the streets with bats, maybe it's time for a curfew," he said.

Nides set up a series of phone calls for Mack, who also contacted Chuck Schumer and Hillary Clinton, pleading with them to call the SEC to press the case on his behalf. "This is about jobs, real people," he told them.

After speaking with Christopher Cox, the head of the SEC, however, he was in an even fouler mood. Cox, a free-market zealot, seemed to Mack to be almost intentionally ineffectual, as if that were the proper role of government regulators. There was nothing he was going to do about the shorts, or about anything at all, for that matter.

Paulson, who was next on his call list, was clearly sympathetic to Mack's cause to ban the short-sellers, but it was unclear whether he could do anything to help him. "I know it, John. I know it," he said, trying to pacify him. "But this is for Cox to decide. I'll see what I can do."

Mack then contacted his most serious rival, Lloyd Blankfein of Goldman, desperate for an ally. "These guys are taking a run at my stock, they're driving my CDS out," Mack said frantically. "Lloyd, you guys are in the same boat as I am." He then made a request of Blankfein: to appear on CNBC with him, as a show of force.

While Blankfein kept a television in his office, he was so disgusted with what he called Charlie Gasparino's "rumormongering" that he turned it off in protest. "That's not my thing," he told Mack. "I don't do TV."

As Goldman wasn't in total crisis mode, Blankfein explained, he was disinclined to join Mack in a war on the shorts until he absolutely needed to.

Making little progress, Nides had another, perhaps shrewder, angle to play. He could call Andrew Cuomo, the New York State attorney general, who badly needed a cause to resurrect his political fortunes. Nides had a hunch that he might be willing to put a scare into the shorts. It was an easy populist message to get behind: Rich hedge fund managers were betting against teetering banks amid a financial crisis. Everybody remembered what Eliot Spitzer had managed to do to Wall Street from the same platform.

When Nides reached Cuomo, he pitched on announcing an investigation of the shorts. Cuomo had voiced concerns about short-selling before, but this would be a shot across the bow. "If you do this," Nides said, "we'll come out and praise you." Nides knew Mack would be reluctant—he'd be assailing his own clients—but this was a matter of survival.

Before the market closed, Mack sent the following e-mail to the entire staff.

To: All Employees

From: John Mack

I know all of you are watching our stock price today, and so am I. After the strong earnings and $179 billion in liquidity we announced yesterday—which virtually every equity analyst highlighted in their notes this morning—there is no rational basis for the movements in our stock or credit default spreads.

What's happening out there? It's very clear to me—we're in the midst of a market controlled by fear and rumors, and short sellers are driving our stock down. You should know that the Management Committee and I are taking every step possible to stop this irresponsible action in the market. We have talked to Secretary Paulson and the Treasury. We have talked to Chairman Cox and the SEC. We also are communicating aggressively with our long-term shareholders, our counterparties and our clients. I would encourage all of you to communicate with your clients as well—and make sure they know about our strong performance and strong capital position.

"It's ridiculous that I can't deal with Goldman at a time like this!" Paulson complained to his general counsel, Bob Hoyt. He was supposed to take part in a 3:00 p.m. call with Bernanke, Geithner, and Cox to discuss Goldman Sachs and Morgan Stanley, but unless he could get a waiver, he would be unable to participate.

With Morgan Stanley on the ropes, Paulson had been growing increasingly worried about Goldman, and if Goldman were to topple, it would, he believed, represent a complete destruction of the system. He'd had enough of recusing himself. Part of him regretted signing the original ethics letter agreeing not to get involved in any matter related to Goldman for his entire tenure. At the time it had seemed a good-faith gesture to go above and beyond the typical one-year moratorium on dealing with former employers, but now, he thought, it had come back to bite him.

Geithner had raised this very issue back in March after the Bear Stearns deal. "You know, Hank, if another one of these banks goes," he said, "I don't know who would have the ability to take them over other than Goldman, and we have to do something about your waiver-recusal situation because I don't know how we can do one of these without you."

Given the extreme situation in the market, Hoyt told Paulson he thought it was only fair that he try to seek a waiver; Hoyt had, in fact, already even drafted the material needed to request one. As Paulson had sold all of his Goldman stock before he took office, Hoyt thought he could easily tell the Office of Government Ethics that Paulson had no conflict, apart from his remaining stake in Goldman's pension plan, but that constituted only a small part of his overall wealth. After he turned sixty-five years old, Goldman would pay him $10,533 a year.

Paulson appreciated that the "optics" of receiving a waiver to engage with his former employer would only feed the continuing conspiracy theories about his efforts to help Goldman, but he felt he had no other choice. And he hoped it would remain a secret: He and Hoyt discussed keeping the existence of a waiver confidential.

Hoyt reached out to Fred F. Fielding, counsel to the White House and a longtime Washington hand who knew his way around the system, and to Bernard J. Knight Jr., the DAEO, or designated agency ethics official, at Treasury, who was attending a conference in Florida with another colleague from the White House ethics office. With virtually no pushback, given the gravity of the situation, they quickly accepted Hoyt's recommendation.

"I have determined that the magnitude of the government's interest in your participation in matters that might affect or involve Goldman Sachs clearly outweighs the concern that your participation may cause a reasonable person to question the integrity of the government's programs and operations," Knight wrote in an e-mail.

Fielding's office made it official by having a copy of the formal waiver walked over to the Treasury Building. On White House letterhead, it began, "This memorandum provides a waiver. . . .

In your position as Secretary of the United States Department of the Treasury, you are responsible for serving the American people and strengthening national security by managing the U.S. Government's finances effectively, promoting economic growth and stability, and ensuring the safety, soundness, and security of the United States and international financial systems.

You currently have an interest in a defined benefit pension plan through your former employers, the Goldman Sachs Group, Inc. Your total investment in this plan represents only a small fraction of your overall investment portfolio. For this reason, your financial interest in the plan is not so substantial as to be likely to affect the integrity of your services to the Government. With this waiver, you may participate personally and substantially in the particular matters affecting this defined benefit pension plan, including the ability or willingness of the Goldman Sachs Group, Inc. to honor its obligations to you under this plan.

Unknown to the public, Paulson was now officially free to help Goldman Sachs.

———

"Stop the insanity—we need a time out" was the subject line of Glenn Schorr's e-mail. An analyst at UBS who covered the banking industry, Schorr had sent the missive to accompany his latest report to his clients on Wednesday afternoon. But by the time the market closed—with Morgan Stanley's shares plummeting 24 percent, to $21.75, after dropping to $16.08 earlier in the day, and Goldman plunging 14 percent, to $114.50, after hitting a low of $97.78—Schorr's e-mail was being forwarded all around town.

"We think investors should be focused on risk management and performance and not just whether you have retail deposits (banks go out of business, too, last we checked—and at this rate, following money fund redemptions, deposits could be around the corner). In our view, a lack of confidence and forced consolidation into firms that are 'too big to fail' can't be the final solution," he wrote. "The world should really be concerned about this because if we continue to squeeze the financial system's balance sheet and see fewer players in the business, the available credit to corporations and hedge funds will shrivel up and the cost of capital will continue to skyrocket across the board."

The e-mail eventually found its way to the Treasury Building, where Paulson was returning phone calls from a long list, trying to get a realistic view of what was taking place on Wall Street. Among the people he spoke with was Steve Schwarzman, the chairman of Blackstone Group, the private-equity giant.

"Hank, how's your day going?" Schwarzman jibed when the call was connected.

"Not well. What do you see out there?" Paulson asked.

The conversation quickly turned serious. "I have to tell you, the system's going to collapse in the next few days. I doubt you're going to be able to open the banks on Monday," Schwarzman said, deeply spooked by what he was seeing.

"People are shorting financial institutions, they're withdrawing money from brokerage firms because they don't want to be the last people in—like in Lehman—which is going to lead to the collapse of Goldman and Morgan Stanley. Everybody is just pursuing his self-interest," Schwarzman told him. "You have to do something."

"We're working on some things," Paulson said. "What do you think we should do?"

"You have to approach what you're doing from the perspective of being a sheriff in a western town where things are out of control," Schwarzman replied, "and you have to do the equivalent of just walking onto Main Street and shooting your gun up in the air a few times to establish that you're in charge because right now no one is in charge!"

Paulson just listened, trying to picture himself in that role. "What do you recommend?"

"Well, the first thing you could do is stop short-selling of financial institutions—forget whether it's effective in removing the pressure, although it might be. What will be accomplished is that you will scare the participants in the market, and they will recognize that things are going to change and they can't continue to invest in the exact same way, and that will force people to pause," Schwarzman said.

"Okay. That's not a bad idea," Paulson agreed. "We've been talking about that. I could do that. What else you got?"

"I would stop the ability of people to withdraw, you know, transfer their brokerage accounts," Schwarzman continued. "Nobody really wants to transfer their account out of Goldman or Morgan. They just feel they have to do it so they're not the last person on a sinking ship."

"I don't have the powers to do that," Paulson replied.

"You could get rid of the ability for people to write credit default swaps on financial institutions," Schwarzman offered as an alternative, "which is putting enormous pressure on financial institutions."

"I don't have the powers to do that either," Paulson protested.

Schwarzman, concerned that he wasn't getting through to Paulson, replied, "Look, you're going to have to announce something very big to rescue the system, some huge amount of money that gets utilized to address the problems of the system."

"Well, we're not ready to do that yet," Paulson told him. "We've got some ideas," he said.

"I don't think that it's relevant if you haven't fully baked everything," Schwarzman said, "You need an announcement tomorrow to stop the collapse and you've got to figure something out that will grab people's attention."

"What's wrong?" John Mack asked in alarm as his CFO, Colm Kelleher, walked into his office late Wednesday, his face ashen.

"John," Kelleher said in his staccato British inflections, "we're going to be out of money on Friday." He had been nervously watching the firm's tank—its liquid assets—shrink, the way an airline pilot might stare at the fuel gauge while circling an airport, waiting for landing clearance.

"That can't be," Mack said anxiously. "Do me a favor, go back to the financing desk, go through it again."

Every hour was bringing a new problem. The internal memo he had sent out earlier decrying short-sellers had started leaking out, and now several prominent hedge fund clients that used shorting strategies—some simply to hedge their exposures to other securities—were closing their Morgan Stanley accounts in protest.

"It's one thing to complain, but another to put out a memo blaming your clients," railed Jim Chanos, the short-seller who famously unearthed the problems at Enron. He had been a Morgan Stanley client for twenty years, but now he was making his displeasure known by pulling $1 billion from his account at the firm. Julian H. Robertson Jr., the founder of Tiger Management, one of the first and most successful hedge funds, called the firm apoplectically, though he stopped short of redeeming the money he kept with Morgan Stanley.

As annoyed as they might have been by the attack on shorts, the firm's clients were about to become a good deal angrier. Mack was reviewing draft language for the statement he would publish the following day in support of Cuomo's investigation into short selling. Though he knew full well that his language would infuriate his clients and send even more of them packing, Mack didn't believe he had a choice but to lend his support:

> Morgan Stanley applauds Attorney General Cuomo for taking strong action to root out improper short selling of financial stocks. By initiating a wide-ranging investigation of this manipulative and fraudulent conduct, Attorney General Cuomo is showing decisive leadership in trying to help stabilize the financial markets. We also support his call for the SEC to impose a temporary freeze on short selling of financial stocks, given the extreme and unprecedented movements in the market that are unsupported by the fundamentals of individual stocks.

Kelleher returned to Mack's office thirty minutes after having been sent to review the firm's balances again, slightly less shaken, but only slightly. After finding some additional money trapped in the system between trades that hadn't yet settled, he revised his prognosis: "Maybe we'll make it through early next week."

———

Paulson was hunched over his telephone, straining to hear Bernanke and Geithner on the speakerphone. It was late Wednesday, and the Treasury staff was already girding for another all-nighter.

Bernanke was making his frustration clear; he didn't believe the crisis could be solved by individual deals or some one-off solution. "We can't keep doing this," he insisted to Paulson. "Both because we at the Fed don't have the necessary resources and for reasons of democratic legitimacy, it's important that the Congress come in and take control of the situation."

Paulson agreed in theory but was concerned that Bernanke was underestimating the political calculus. "I understand that you guys don't want to be fighting this fire alone, but the worst outcome would be if I go ask, and they tell me to screw off," Paulson said. "We will then show that we're vulnerable and we don't have the armaments we need."

"There are no atheists in foxholes and no ideologues in financial crises," Bernanke, trotting out a phrase he had tried out on some Fed colleagues a day earlier, told Paulson, trying to persuade him that intervention was necessary.

Paulson agreed but said if they were going to proceed, he wanted to promote his plan to have the government buy toxic assets, a solution that he thought would be the most politically palatable, because it would be comparable to the Resolution Trust Corporation of the late 1980s. Congress created the RTC in 1989 to handle the more than $400 billion in loans and other assets held by 747 failed savings and loans as part of the S&L crisis. The RTC had been the recipient of a wide range of loans, properties, and bonds from the failed thrifts. Like the predicament Paulson currently faced, some of the assets were good but most were bad, and some, including construction and development loans, had no discernible market. The task was daunting: L. William Seidman, the RTC chairman, initially estimated that even if the agency sold $1 million of assets a day, it would take three hundred years to dispose of everything. By the time the RTC completed its job in 1995, a year ahead of its deadline, the cost to the taxpayers was nearly $200 billion (in 2008 dollars)—a much lower tab than what many had feared at the time the agency had been created.

Paulson thought the idea had merit and was buoyed by an op-ed in the *Wall Street Journal* that morning touting a similar plan by Paul A. Volcker, the former chairman of the Federal Reserve; Nicholas F. Brady, a former U.S. Treasury secretary; and Eugene A. Ludwig, a former U.S. comptroller of the currency.

"This new governmental body would be able to buy up the troubled paper at fair market values, where possible keeping people in their homes and businesses operating. Like the RTC, this mechanism should have a limited life and be run by nonpartisan professional management," they wrote. "The pathology of this crisis is that unless you get ahead of it and deal with it from strength, it devours the weakest link in the chain and then moves on to devour the next weakest link."

On Thursday morning, Tom Nides, who lived in Washington and commuted every week to New York, woke up early at the Regency Hotel and went to the gym. As he read the *New York Times* on an elliptical machine, he nearly fell off when he came upon the front-page story, which ran under the headline: "As Fears Grow, Wall St. Titans See Shares Fall."

Directly in the middle of the story was a quote, citing two people who had been briefed on merger talks between Morgan Stanley and Citigroup, saying that John Mack had told Vikram Pandit, "We need a merger or we're not going to make it."

Nides couldn't believe Mack even said that. He had been in the room for one of the calls with Pandit and it didn't go like that, he thought. Morgan Stanley, Nides knew, could not afford that sort of coverage, whether or not it was true. The more people who knew it, the truer it would become.

"Did you see this irresponsible piece of shit in the *Times*?" Nides asked when he got Mack on the phone. Mack, however, only read the *Wall Street Journal,* the *Financial Times,* and the *New York Post,* having canceled his *Times* subscription in protest after the Sulzberger family pulled its money from Morgan Stanley because one of its asset managers had decided to run a proxy contest against the *Times* ownership.

Now Mack had reason to be upset at the *Times* all over again. And he and his colleagues were furious with Pandit, who they were convinced must have leaked it.

"You didn't say this, did you?" Nides asked.

"No, no," Mack insisted. "I never said that; I definitely didn't use those words."

Nides knew he needed to challenge the veracity of the quote immediately. He was already getting calls from other news organizations.

"What fucking kind of reporter are you?" he berated one of the article's authors, Eric Dash, when he reached him on his cell phone. "You have to rescind the story!"

Mack, meanwhile, prepared to address his employees for the second time in four days, eager to offer them reassurance, especially after the *Times* story. He had invited Eugene A. Ludwig, chairman of Promontory

Financial Group and one of the authors of the editorial in the previous day's *Wall Street Journal* advocating for an RTC-like structure, to join him this morning as his adviser.

Battling a cold, his glasses slipping down his nose, Mack stood on Morgan Stanley's main trading floor, his speech piped in to its employees around the world. He spoke in a plain, unscripted manner, his North Carolina accent perhaps more pronounced than usual.

"You know you've seen the cash position, you've seen our earnings, ah, all that stuff, unlike what people said about other firms, ah, those numbers are real numbers," he told them. "We're clean, we're making money. We made a lot of money the last eight days also. But it doesn't make any difference. We deal in a market today that financial chicanery, rumor, and innuendo are much more powerful than real results."

He related a phone conversation with a "a good friend," a hedge fund manager who confided his fears about Morgan Stanley. Mack reassured the man, only to receive another call four hours later from the same fund manager about still another market rumor. "My point being, no matter what we say, there's another rumor that pops up."

Mack acknowledged that the firm was examining all its options, while expressing bewilderment at how the industry had been turned upside down.

"What I find remarkable is not too long ago, two months ago, four months ago, people said the Citibank model was broken—ah, complicated, big, global, unmanageable. And now our model's broken. Is our model—and I include Goldman Sachs—is our model broken because we are not part of a bank? Is our model broken, because we've consistently in the last three quarters delivered good earnings? Is our model broken because we could not have regulators who stepped in and took strong stands? That might be the issue here.

"I think the issues are: How do you get through chaos? This is chaos. It pains me to go on the floor and see how you guys look."

Mack then addressed the most sensitive issue for his employees—the selling of stock. According to SEC regulations, employees could sell only during certain designated periods, such as immediately following an earnings report—which meant at the present.

"I know this is a window period," Mack said, "and I know some of you are very scared—well, maybe all of us are very scared. You want to sell stock, sell your stock. I'm not going to look at it and I don't care. I'm not selling, and there, well, John, you've got a lot of it, you don't have to worry about it . . . ah, you know, I do have a lot and I do worry about it, but I really care much more about your getting peace of mind. So if you want to sell, sell. Do it."

When the time came for questions from the staff, Stephen Roach, Morgan Stanley's unfailingly bearish economist, asked a pointed question about the shorts: "Short-sellers, John. Many, if not most of them, are clients of the firm. Put yourself in the room with one of these, quote, clients, unquote. What do you say to them?"

Mack drew a deep breath. "Well, um, I've thought long and hard about that, and my gut reaction is that I'm angry and I want to tell them what I think. And I don't want to do business with you and all that other stuff. Then on my second breath, I say, you know, they have their job to do, that's what they're doing. I am not going to get pulled into that kind of discussion.

"And this is what I wanted to say, I put a note here about being angry. We can be angry, we are angry, we are upset, and we just have to deal with it. We are not here to beat up on clients and tell them how they deserted us and all of that stuff. We're here to run this firm, work with our clients as best we can. Some don't want to do business, we'll deal with that later, let them go. Let's stay focused on things that are productive. And venting and telling people what you think and calling them all the names you want to call them is not going to help us," he said, punctuating the point by adding, "I love beating the shit out of people when they screwed us. But I'm not going there. And I don't want you to go there."

———

The panic at Goldman Sachs could no longer be denied. Perhaps the greatest sign of anxiety was the fact that Gary Cohn, Goldman's co-president, who usually remained perched in his thirtieth-floor office, had relocated himself to the office of Harvey M. Schwartz, head of global securities division sales, who had a glass wall looking out to the trading floor. The door was left open; he wanted to see and hear exactly what was going on.

The Federal Reserve, along with the other central banks, had just announced plans to pump $180 billion to stimulate the financial system, but the scheme did not seem to be having any appreciable effect. Goldman's shares opened down 7.4 percent. CNBC, which was airing on flat-screen TVs hanging from the walls of Goldman's trading floor, had introduced a new "bug" on the bottom left-hand side of the screen that provocatively asked, "Is Your Money Safe?"

It was a question that Goldman clients were beginning to ask themselves. The firm's own CDS spreads had blown out in a way the firm had never seen before, indicating that investors were quickly beginning to believe the unthinkable: that Goldman, too, could falter. In two days, Goldman's stock had dropped from $133 to $108.

Every five minutes a salesman would tear into Schwartz's office with news of another hedge fund announcing its plan to move its money out of Goldman and would hand Cohn a piece of paper with the hedge fund's phone number so he could talk some sense into them. With Morgan Stanley slowing down its payouts, some investors were now testing Goldman, asking for $100 million just to see if they could afford to pay. In every case, Cohn would wire the money immediately, concerned that if he didn't, the client would abandon the firm entirely.

The good news for Goldman was that withdrawals were only slightly outpacing inflows. To some extent it had been able to capitalize on the distress of others, as hedge funds needed to execute their trades *somewhere*. When Steve Cohen of SAC Capital transferred several billion over to Goldman, traders began to whoop it up on the floor.

On the other hand, Stanley Druckenmiller, a George Soros acolyte worth more than $3.5 billion, had taken most of his money out earlier that week, concerned about the firm's solvency. If word got around that a hedge fund manager of Druckenmiller's reputation had lost confidence in Goldman, it alone could cause a run. Cohn called him and tried to convince him to return the money to the firm. "I have a long memory," Cohn, who was taking this personally, told Druckenmiller, for whom he had even hosted a charity cocktail party in Druckenmiller's honor in his own apartment. "Look, the one thing I'm doing is I'm learning who my friends are and who my enemies are, and I'm making lists."

Druckenmiller, however, was unmoved. "I don't really give a shit; it's my money," he shot back. Unlike most hedge funds, Druckenmiller's did consist primarily of his own money. "It's my livelihood," he said. "I've got to protect myself and I don't really give a shit what you have to say."

"You can do whatever you want," Cohn said in carefully measured tones. But, he added, "this will change our relationship for a long time."

———

Half an hour before David Carroll and the Wachovia team were due to arrive at Morgan Stanley, Kindler called down to Scully. Kindler was in his office, peering out his window down at the camera crews camped outside the building.

"Why are we having him meet us here, of all places?" Kindler asked. "There's reporters outside."

"Don't worry. It'll be fine," Scully, who took the precaution of sneaking Carroll in via the employee entrance on Forty-eighth Street, assured him.

Kindler's sole objective was to get his hands on Wachovia's mortgage book so that he could crack the tape—Wall Street–speak for examining the mortgages individually. That was the only way he could really understand Wachovia's real value. This was no small undertaking: The tape contained $125 billion of loans, including all manner of bespoke adjustable rates, like "pick a pay," which gave borrowers a variety of choices each month on how—and even how much—to pay. Among the options was a payment that covered only the interest on the loan.

Morgan Stanley also insisted on seeing Wachovia's business plan, but Carroll balked at that request. "Our general counsel says it's a real problem," he said.

Kindler, convinced that Wachovia was trying to hide something, called Morgan's general counsel, Gary Lynch, in a rage and told him to put the screws to his counterpart at Wachovia, Jane Sherburne.

"It's a big legal issue," she explained. "We can't give over the data without disclosing it in the merger agreement if we do the deal."

Lynch, too, was starting to suspect a problem. *Are Wachovia's numbers worse than anyone knows?* he wondered to himself. "Well, we can't do the deal without seeing the data," he told her.

Sherburne relented.

———

Lloyd Blankfein, his top shirt button undone and tie slightly askew, looked at his computer screen and saw in dismay that his stock price had dropped 22 percent to $89.29. Blankfein, who up until now had resisted pushing back against short-sellers, was becoming convinced that the pressure his stock was under was not an accident. He had just ended a call with Christopher Cox in which he had told the SEC chairman, "This is getting to be intentional. You know, you may need to do something here."

In his e-mail in-box was another message from one of his traders saying that JP Morgan was trying to steal his hedge fund clients by telling everyone that Goldman was going under. It was becoming a vicious circle.

Blankfein had been hearing these rumors for the past twenty-four hours, but he had finally had enough. He was furious. The rumormongering, he felt, had gotten out of control. And he couldn't believe JP Morgan was trashing his firm to his own clients. He could feel himself becoming as anxious as Mack had sounded when they spoke the day before.

He called Dimon. "We've got to talk," Blankfein began as he tried to calmly explain his problem. "I'm not saying you're doing it, but there are a lot of footprints here."

"Well, people may be doing something that I don't know about," Dimon replied. "But they know what I've said, which is that we're not going after our competitors in the middle of all this."

Blankfein, however, wasn't buying his explanation. "But, Jamie, if they're still doing it, you can't be telling them not to!" Trying to get his point across, Blankfein, a movie buff, started doing his own rendition of *A Few Good Men*: "Did you order the Code Red? Did you say your guys would never do anything?" Dimon just listened patiently, eager not to get Blankfein even more wound up.

"Jamie, the point is, I don't think you're telling them to do this, but if you wanted to stop them in your organization, you could scare them into not doing it," Blankfein said.

Even in its panicked state, Goldman was still Goldman, and Dimon didn't want a war. Within half an hour he had Steve Black and Bill Winters, co–chief executives of JP Morgan's investment bank, send out a company-wide e-mail:

> We do not want anyone at JP Morgan capitalizing on the irrational behavior that's going on in the market toward some of the U.S. broker-dealers. We are operating as business as usual with Morgan Stanley and Goldman Sachs as counterparties. While they are both formidable competitors, during this period, we do not want anyone approaching their clients

or employees in a predatory way. We want to do everything possible to remain supportive of their business and not do anything that would impact them negatively.

We do not believe anyone has engaged in any inappropriate behavior, but we want to underscore how important it is to be constructive during this time. What is happening to the broker-dealer model is not rational, and not good for JP Morgan, the global financial system or the country.

———

Around midday, Hank Paulson reviewed the latest term sheet that his staff had drafted overnight on the issue of dealing with toxic assets, hoping it would be acceptable to present to Congress. His inner circle had assembled in his office, pulling up chairs around a corner sofa.

"It looks much better," he said, turning the pages. "It's very simple." He paused and scanned the bleary-eyed faces in the room. "I want to reiterate that we have to get this up to the Hill quickly," he said. "We need to keep this simple, very simple. And we have to do it in a way that we encourage, ah, banks and financial institutions to want to participate. We don't want to have punitive measures with this. This is about recapitalizing our banks and financial institutions setting a price for assets."

There was just one more issue to deal with, perhaps the most important of all: the price tag.

While the toxic-asset program made sense in theory, for it actually to work, for it to be effective, Paulson knew they'd need to buy large swaths of toxic securities from the nation's largest banks. The cost was going to be enormous, and it would be perceived, both within and outside of the Washington Beltway, as another bailout.

Paulson looked to Kashkari, who sat on the sofa to his left, for guidance.

The key concern at that moment was whether spending so much money would require them to have to ask Congress to increase the debt ceiling—a political flashpoint that would require Congress to vote to raise the amount of debt the country could take on. It had just increased that amount to $10.615 trillion in July.

As the group discussed the outlines of the proposed legislation, Kashkari's view was that they ought to try to skirt the issue entirely. "I don't know if that's workable, not having a reference to the debt ceiling. Or why don't we just say it's not subject to a debt ceiling?"

"You can't do that," Paulson pointed out and then added, "I don't want to go for the debt ceiling and fail. That's the issue, and then people start focusing on it."

"I did the analysis," Phillip Swagel offered, reading from his notes. He had determined that they would need only $500 billion, but only if the situation didn't grow any worse.

To Paulson, who thought of himself as fiscally conservative, the answer was obvious. "Okay, so I think the responsible thing is to go for the debt ceiling," he said, instructing Kevin I. Fromer, assistant secretary for legislative affairs, whose job it was to work the Hill, to construct some new language.

"You can go after it but you don't have to put it in this document," Fromer replied, resisting Paulson's request. "We never go up and propose legislation to do the debt ceiling. We just simply arrive at the fact that we have to do it and literally tell Congress they have to do it. They do it because they're too scared not to do it. It's just a question of optics."

They decided that, for the time being, they wouldn't mention the debt ceiling in the document itself but would address it later, ideally when Congress had already bought into the plan and it was too late to make a change.

Before wrapping up the meeting, Paulson raised one last problem: Wachovia, he said, might falter. He was getting back-channel messages from Kevin Warsh that the bank's finances were in much worse shape than they believed. Everyone understood the significance of his statement. After all, Bob Steel, their former colleague, was its CEO.

"If Wachovia fails, I'm going to be trotting up to Congress again. So I'm hoping it happens after January!" he said to a roomful of laughs.

———

"Listen, Jamie just called me fishing around for something," Colm Kelleher told John Mack midday Thursday as he marched into his office. "He said he was calling to see if he could be of help," Kelleher added. "It was strange."

James Gorman, the firm's co-president, had just reported receiving a similar call, Mack replied, and Geithner had phoned earlier to suggest that he talk to Dimon as a possible merger partner too.

"It's clear that for him to be calling us, he wants to do a deal," Kelleher said. "Jamie is always hanging around the hoop. You know Jamie's saying, 'Let's make friends with these guys before I eat them.'"

Mack was irritated by these suggestions; he didn't particularly want to do a deal with Dimon, as he believed it would involve far too much overlap. But he decided to stop guessing what Dimon might be up to and ask him directly.

"Jamie, Geithner says I should call you," Mack said abruptly when he reached Dimon on the phone a few minutes later. "Let's get this out in the open: Do you want to do a deal?"

"No, I don't want to do a deal," Dimon said flatly, frustrated that this was the second call he had gotten that day from a competitor who was annoyed with him.

"Well, that's interesting," Mack retorted. "You're calling my CFO and you're calling my president, why would you do that?"

"I was trying to be helpful," Dimon repeated.

"If you want to be helpful, then talk to me. I don't want you calling my guys," Mack said, hanging up the phone.

———

The fiftieth floor of Goldman's fixed-income trading unit was in near meltdown by lunchtime on Thursday. No trading was taking place, and the traders themselves were glued to their terminals, staring at the GS ticker as the market continued its swoon. Goldman's stock dropped to $85.88, its lowest level in nearly six years; the Dow had fallen 150 points. "The market is trading under the assumption that every financial institution is going under," Michael Petroff, portfolio manager for Heartland Advisors, told Agence France-Presse that morning. "It's now emotional."

Jon Winkelried, Goldman's co-president, had been walking the floors, trying to calm everyone's nerves. "We could raise $5 billion in an hour if we wanted to," he told a group of traders as if to suggest nothing was amiss.

But just then, at 1:00 p.m., the market—and Goldman's stock—suddenly turned around, with Goldman rising to $87 a share, and then $89. Traders raced through their screens trying to determine what had been responsible for the lift and discovered that the Financial Services Authority in the U.K. had announced a thirty-day ban on short selling twenty-nine financial stocks, including Goldman Sachs. It was exactly what Blankfein and Mack had tried to persuade the SEC's Christopher Cox to do.

The squawk boxes on Goldman's trading floor soon crackled to attention. A young trader found a copy of "The Star-Spangled Banner" on the Internet and broadcast it over the speakers to commemorate the moment. About three dozen traders stood up from their desks, placed their hands over their hearts, and sang aloud, accompanied by rounds of high fives and cheers. The market was turning around, *and our flag was still there.*

Nine minutes later word began to spread that Paulson, too, was working on something big. "Treasury, Fed Weighing Wider Plan to Ease Crisis, Schumer Says" a Bloomberg headline read, buoying the market further.

At exactly 3:01 p.m. the market took off. Traders all over Wall Street turned up the volume when Charlie Gasparino of CNBC reported what he was hearing from his sources on Wall Street: The federal government was preparing "some sort of RTC-like plan" that would "get some or all of the toxic waste off the balance sheets of the banks and brokerages." Taking "RTC" as code for "everything's going to be all right," traders pushed stocks higher immediately. Between the time Gasparino began his report and the segment ended, the market jumped 108 points, a brief respite from the steady downward spiral.

———

At the Treasury, Paulson and Kashkari had been on a conference call with Geithner and Bernanke for the past hour, trying to decide on a path of least political resistance for shoring up the banks. Bernanke, who seemed bothered by the plan, was arguing in favor of direct capital injections, a measure that had worked in other countries.

Geithner, who had been railing about the need for "decisive action," all of a sudden started talking about the possibility of opening up the Fed window to virtually any financial institution with any kind of assets. It would be a bold act that would likely be applauded by investors.

"I don't understand, what do you mean?" Kashkari piped up. "If the Fed really wanted to interpret its authorities creatively, it could do all this without legislation?"

Paulson shot Kashkari an angry look, as it was precisely what he had been hoping that Geithner might convince Bernanke to do—and thus save Paulson a trip to Congress.

"We can't do that," Bernanke admonished Geithner.

The call had to end quickly because Paulson and Bernanke were scheduled to brief President Bush in the West Wing on their plan at 3:30 p.m., and Bernanke still needed to drive over from the Fed.

As Paulson and Kashkari began the three-minute walk across the parking lot to the White House, Paulson received a call from Nancy Pelosi.

"Mr. Secretary," she announced sternly, "we would like to meet with you tomorrow morning because of some of the chaos we see in the markets."

Knowing that he would need to start building congressional support for his plan as soon as possible, he replied, "Madam Speaker, it cannot wait until tomorrow morning. We have to come *today.*"

Upon reaching the Oval Office the Treasury officials took their places on the pair of sofas in the middle of the room. Vice President Cheney; Josh Bolten, Bush's chief of staff—and Paulson's old friend from Goldman—and several other White House staffers soon joined them, along with Bernanke and Warsh.

Paulson told Bush in no uncertain terms that the financial system was collapsing. "If we don't act boldly, Mr. President," he said, "we could be in a depression deeper than the Great Depression," an assessment with which Bernanke concurred.

Bush was struggling to wrap his mind around the precise course of events. "How," he questioned, "did we get here?"

Paulson disregarded the question, knowing that the answer would be way too long and lay in a heady mix of nearly a decade of overly lax regulation—some of which he had pushed for himself—overzealous bankers, and home owners living beyond their means. Instead he pressed ahead and told the president that he planned to seek at least $500 billion from Congress to buy toxic assets, explaining that he hoped the program would stabilize the system.

He hastened to point out the political ramifications, suggesting that buying toxic assets was overall a more palatable option than buying stakes in banks themselves.

Bush nodded in agreement but, still confounded by the $500 billion figure, asked, "Is that enough?"

"It's a lot. It will make a difference," Paulson assured him. Even if he did want to seek a higher number, Paulson told the president, "I don't think we can get more."

They all knew it was going to be a highly politicized issue, but Paulson insisted, "We absolutely need to go to Congress. Treasury doesn't have the authority."

For a moment, Paulson paused and then added, "In theory, Ben could always do it."

Paulson, unexpectedly playing politics himself, appeared to be trying to see how far he could push Bernanke, who, as far as Paulson was concerned, had virtually unlimited powers as long as he was willing to use them.

"Ben, you can do this?" President Bush asked, sensing an opportunity.

Bernanke, however, did not appreciate being put on the spot and tried to sidestep the question. "That is really fiscal policy, not monetary policy," he said in his professorial tone.

Bush understood. "We need to do what it takes to solve this problem," he agreed, but given his low approval ratings, he knew he could be of little help on the Hill. "You guys should go up," he told Paulson and Bernanke. The implication was clear: You're on your own. But he insisted that the two men sell Congress on the idea quickly.

As they left the White House, Kashkari turned to Paulson and remarked, "I couldn't believe the kind of pressure you were putting on Ben."

Paulson just smiled. "Maybe Ben will get there."

———

Lloyd Blankfein had not been mollified by the market's late turnaround, with Goldman's stock ending the day up at $108, which was still better from its low of $86.31. In his office were Gary Cohn; David Viniar, the firm's CFO; Jon Winkelried, the co-president; John Rogers; and David Solomon. He knew that until Morgan Stanley fell, Goldman was probably safe, though that was hardly a comfort.

Gary Cohn had been on the phone earlier in the day with Kevin Warsh of the Federal Reserve, brainstorming a way to get in front of the financial tsunami. Warsh threw out the idea that perhaps Goldman should be looking to merge with Citigroup, a fit that could solve major problems for both parties. Goldman could get a huge deposit base, while Citigroup would acquire a management team that investors could support.

Cohn had expressed his doubts about the suggestions. "It probably doesn't work because I could never buy their balance sheet," he explained.

"And the social issues would be enormous." The expression "social issues" was yet another Wall Street code for who would run the firm. Goldman's management didn't exactly have high regard for Pandit and his team.

"Don't worry about the social issues," Warsh told him. "We'll take care of them."

That was a not so subtle hint that if a deal was struck, Pandit might be out of a job.

But Blankfein wasn't particularly interested in either alternative. Rodgin Cohen had been encouraging Goldman to think about transforming the firm into a regulated bank holding company, which JP Morgan and Citigroup were, giving them unlimited access to the Fed's discount window. It was the same idea that Cohen had unsuccessfully pressed Geithner to consider for Lehman Brothers over the summer, and while Geithner had turned that proposal down, Cohen had become convinced that he might now rule differently given the grave state of the markets.

The notion of becoming a bank holding company had arisen at Goldman from time to time over the years, most recently at their board summer meeting in Russia, where they had discussed the necessity of holding more deposits. Blankfein appreciated that Goldman's dependence on even a modicum of short-term financing made investors, in this highly charged environment, anxious, and that a deposit base provided a more stable source of capital. Blankfein had always resisted the idea, however, because it came with a hefty price tag in the form of increased regulatory oversight. But these were extraordinary circumstances, to say the least, and the CEO sensed that the world might be moving inexorably in that direction. Given that the bank already had temporary access to the Fed discount window, and that the Fed had literally placed several staffers inside Goldman to monitor the firm, Blankfein started to believe that the prospect of a little extra government regulation didn't seem particularly onerous.

"This is only going to work if you scare the shit out of them."

That had been Jim Wilkinson's advice to Paulson before he and Bernanke left to meet with the congressional leadership at Nancy Pelosi's office that evening. By Wilkinson's reckoning, unless they could convince Congress that the world was literally going to come to an end, they would never receive approval for a $500 billion bailout package for Wall Street. Republicans would complain it was socialism; Democrats would carp about rescuing white-collar fat cats.

At a burled wood table just off Pelosi's office, two dozen congressmen gathered to meet with Paulson, Bernanke, and Christopher Cox, who had been invited more as a courtesy than anything else.

Pelosi began the meeting by welcoming them and thanking them for coming "on such short notice."

Bernanke, who was known never to exaggerate, began by saying gravely, "I spent my career as an academic studying great depressions. I can tell you from history that if we don't act in a big way, you can expect another great depression, and this time it is going to be far, far worse."

Senator Charles Schumer, sitting at the end of the table, noticeably gulped.

Paulson, with a deep sense of intensity, went on to explain the mechanics of his proposal: The government would buy the toxic assets to get them off the banks' books, which in turn would raise the value of the assets by establishing a price and make the banks healthier, which in turn would help the economy and, as Paulson repeatedly said, "help Main Street."

Barney Frank, sitting next to Bernanke, thought Paulson's reference to "Main Street" was a disingenuous ploy to line the pockets of Wall Street and provided no direct help for average Americans saddled with mortgages they can't afford, foisted on them by the big banks being rescued. "What about the home owner?" he asked. "You aren't selling this plan to a Wall Street boardroom," he said derisively. "That's right," Christopher Dodd chimed in. Richard Shelby disapprovingly characterized the proposed program as a "blank check."

Paulson said he understood their concerns. But he continued to play his "scare the shit out of them" card, insisting that it was absolutely necessary: "I don't want to think about what will happen if we don't do this." He said he hoped that Congress could pass the legislation within days and promised to get a full proposal to them literally within hours.

"If it doesn't pass, then heaven help us all," Paulson said.

Harry Reid, sitting across from Bernanke, looked at Paulson with a sense of bemusement about the prospect that Congress would pass a bill of this magnitude that quickly. "Do you know what you are asking me to do?" he said. "It takes me forty-eight hours to get the Republicans to agree to flush the toilets around here."

"Harry," Mitch McConnell (R-Kentucky), who was deeply frightened by Paulson and Bernanke's presentation, interjected, "I think we need to do this, we should try to do this, and we can do this."

———

John Mack was still at his office in Times Square when Tom Nides, his chief administrative officer, told him the good news: His sources at the SEC had confirmed that the agency was preparing to finally put in place a ban on shorting financial stocks, affecting some 799 different companies. The measure would likely be announced the following morning.

Rumors of the pending action were already moving on the wires. James Chanos, perhaps the best known of the short-sellers, who had pulled his money from Morgan Stanley because of Mack's support for the ban, was already on the warpath. "While this is all politically pleasing to the regulatory powers that be, the fact of the matter is that there has been no evidence presented of short-sellers circulating false market rumors to drive down the price of stocks," he said.

That day, Morgan Stanley's stock had fallen 46 percent, only to turn around in the last hours of trading, ending up 3.7 percent, or 80 cents. Between word of the government's intervention and the short-selling ban, Mack was hoping that he'd finally have some breathing room.

He knew, though, that beneath the surface the firm was hurting. Hedge funds continued to seek redemptions. Other banks were buying insurance against Morgan Stanley's going under, covering more than $1 billion. Within the past two days, Merrill Lynch had bought insurance covering $150 million in Morgan debt. Citigroup, Deutsche Bank, UBS, Alliance-Bernstein, and Royal Bank of Canada had all made similar moves to protect themselves from a collapse.

Mack knew that what the firm needed most was an investor to step up and take a big stake in the company to shore it up. "I don't know how this happened," he confided in Nides, searching himself. Morgan Stanley had been considered too conservative and Mack pushed the firm to take on more risk at exactly the wrong moment. And now here they were, in the perfect storm, on the cusp of insolvency.

Mack could think of only one investor who might be seriously inter-

ested in making a sizable investment in the firm: China Investment Corporation, China's first sovereign wealth fund. Wei Sun Christianson, CEO
of Morgan Stanley China and a fifty-one-year-old dynamo with close relationships throughout the government, had initiated discussions with Gao
Xiqing, president of CIC, within the past twenty-four hours. She happened
to be in Aspen at a conference with him hosted by Teddy Forstmann, the
leveraged buyout king who coined the phrase "Barbarians at the Gate" in
the late 1980s, during the bidding war for RJR Nabisco. CIC already held
a 9.9 percent stake in Morgan Stanley, and Gao indicated to Christianson
that he'd be interested in buying up to 49 percent of the firm. Gao had a
major incentive to keep Morgan Stanley alive: He had invested $5 billion
in the firm in December 2007, which was now worth half that. Another one
of his major investments, in Blackstone Group's IPO, was down more than
70 percent. If Morgan Stanley filed for bankruptcy, he might lose his job.

Mack and Nides discussed the deal, and while neither man was particularly interested, given their choices, they knew it might prove to be the
only solution. Gao, whom Mack had come to know as a fellow Duke trustee,
was planning to fly to New York Friday night to meet with them.

Earlier in the day, Mack had spoken with Paulson, who prided himself
on his extensive Chinese contacts, trying to persuade him to make a call
to the Chinese government to encourage them to pursue the deal. It was
a tad unusual to ask the government to serve as a broker, but Mack was
desperate. "The Chinese need to feel as if they are being invited in," Mack
explained. Paulson said he'd work on it and see if President Bush would
be willing to call China's president, Hu Jintao. "We need an independent
Morgan Stanley," he affirmed.

Nides, however, had a more cynical view of Paulson's desire to protect
Morgan Stanley. "He'll keep us alive," Nides told Mack, "because if he
doesn't, then Goldman will go."

CHAPTER EIGHTEEN

Hoarse and a little haggard, Paulson made his way to the podium in the press room of the Treasury Building the morning of Friday, September 19, 2008, to formally announce and clarify what he had dubbed earlier that morning the Troubled Asset Relief Program, soon known as TARP, a vast series of guarantees and outright purchases of "the illiquid assets that are weighing down our financial system and threatening our economy."

He also announced an expansive plan to guarantee all money market funds in the nation for the next year, hoping that that move would keep investors from fleeing them. But he had already gotten an earful that morning about that effort from Sheila Bair, chairwoman of the FDIC, who had called, furious she wasn't consulted and anxious that the guarantee plan would backfire and investors would perversely start moving their money out of otherwise healthy banks and into the guaranteed money market funds. Paulson just shook his head; he couldn't win.

As he stood in front of the press corps he did his best to sell the center-piece of his plan, the TARP. "The underlying weakness in our financial system today is the illiquid mortgage assets that have lost value as the housing correction has proceeded. These illiquid assets are choking off the flow of credit that is so vitally important to our economy," he explained, his tie slightly askew and looking paler and more tired than he ever had before. "When the financial system works as it should, money and capital flow to and from households and businesses to pay for home loans, school loans, and investments that create jobs. As illiquid mortgage assets block the system, the clogging of our financial markets has the potential to have significant effects on our financial system and our economy. . . .

"I am convinced that this bold approach will cost American families far less than the alternative—a continuing series of financial institution failures and frozen credit markets unable to fund economic expansion," he asserted, clearly reading from his script, having never learned how to read from a teleprompter.

Evidently confident that Washington had finally brought the financial crisis under control—between Paulson's TARP and Cox's ban on short-sellers—the stock market had risen 300 points at the open and continued to hold its ground as Paulson spoke.

Paulson had intentionally chosen not to mention how much the program would cost; after a briefing earlier that morning from Kashkari, he now feared that he might actually need more than the $500 billion he had mentioned to the president a day earlier—a great deal more. Back in his office after the speech, he met with Fromer and Kashkari and debated what the precise cost might be.

"What about $1 trillion?" Kashkari said.

"We'll get killed," Paulson said grimly.

"No way," Fromer said, incredulous at the sum. "Not going to happen. Impossible."

"Okay," Kashkari said. "How about $700 billion?"

"I don't know," Fromer said. "That's better than $1 trillion."

The numbers were, at best, guesstimates, and all three men knew it. The relevant figure would ultimately be the one that represented the most they could possibly ask from Congress without raising too many questions. Whatever that sum turned out to be, they knew they could count on Kashkari to perform some sort of mathematical voodoo to justify it: "There's around $11 trillion of residential mortgages, there's around $3 trillion of commercial mortgages, that leads to $14 trillion, roughly five percent of that is $700 billion." As he plucked numbers from thin air even Kashkari laughed at the absurdity of it all.

———

John Mack had been watching CNBC on Friday morning when he received a phone call from Lloyd Blankfein. Charlie Gasparino, still reveling in his scoop about the government's toxic asset program, was arguing that it meant that Morgan Stanley would no longer be forced to do a deal, or at least not have to move as quickly.

Mack, laughing to himself, knew better; he had to get something accomplished by the weekend or Morgan Stanley could well go the way of Lehman Brothers.

"What do you think of becoming a bank holding company?" Blankfein asked Mack when he picked up the receiver.

Mack hadn't really studied the issue and asked, "Would that help us?"

Blankfein said that Goldman had been investigating the possibility and explained to him the benefits—namely, that if they allowed themselves to be regulated by the Federal Reserve, they'd have unlimited access to the discount window and would have an easier time raising capital, among other things.

"Well, in the long run it would really help us," Mack said. "In the short run, however, I don't know if you can pull it off fast enough to help us."

"You have to hang on," Blankfein urged him, clearly still anxious about how punishing the markets had become, "because I'm thirty seconds behind you."

———

Jonathan Pruzan, the Morgan Stanley banker who had been assigned to review Wachovia's $120 billion mortgage portfolio—to crack the tape—finally had some answers. A team of Morgan bankers in New York, London, and Hong Kong had worked overnight to sift through as many mortgages as they humanly could.

"Now I know why they didn't want to give us the tape!" Pruzan announced dourly at a meeting before they headed over to Wachtell Lipton to begin diligence on Wachovia. "It shows they're expecting a nineteen percent cumulative loss."

Just a week earlier, at a public presentation at Lehman's conference, Bob Steel had estimated that figure at 12 percent. In fairness, Pruzan noted, the market had deteriorated markedly since then, and cumulative loss figures were inherently unreliable, because a bank could manipulate them up or down. Still, that big a discrepancy couldn't be explained away easily. At best, Pruzan thought, Wachovia had been foolishly optimistic.

"You've got to be fucking kidding me," Scully exclaimed. "We obviously can't do this deal."

To make it work, Morgan Stanley would have to raise some $20 billion to $24 billion of equity to capitalize the combined firm, a virtual impossibility under the current market conditions. Even so, the Morgan bankers decided not to cancel the all-day diligence session, as they figured they had nothing to lose. Morgan Stanley might well be able to take advantage of Paulson's new plan to buy toxic assets from Wachovia and, indeed, investors had already bid up Wachovia's shares that morning on precisely that expectation.

Thirty people each from Morgan Stanley and Wachovia showed up at Wachtell Lipton's Fifty-second Street offices. Wachovia, purposely not using Goldman Sachs as an adviser for this project given its rivalry with Morgan Stanley, brought a new set of advisers from Perella Weinberg Partners: Joe Perella, the legendary financier; and Peter Weinberg, a former Goldman banker who was the grandson of Sidney Weinberg, the Goldman patriarch. As Weinberg came to shake Kindler's hand, they could hardly believe they were even talking to each other under such dire circumstances. "What happened? How the fuck did we get here?" Weinberg asked aloud.

"God only knows. You can't make this shit up," Kindler said.

Within the first two hours of their work, however, something began to feel wrong to the Morgan bankers. Paulson's TARP announcement had eased the climate of fear at Wachovia—which would likely be a huge beneficiary of the program because it could sell its most toxic assets to the government—and thus the urgency of rushing into a deal. Kindler became concerned that Wachovia was just buying time while the bank worked on another deal, probably with Goldman. Surveying the room, he announced to his colleagues, "Look at us. We're the B team. This isn't going to happen."

The Wachovia team, meanwhile, had its own doubts about Morgan Stanley's commitment. If this deal was so important to it, where were its top people? David Carroll, who was leading the Wachovia team, couldn't understand why Colm Kelleher, Morgan's CFO, was not involved.

By 2:00 p.m., the Morgan Stanley team had withdrawn from Wachtell and gone back to Times Square to consult with Mack.

"These guys are clearly disengaged," Kindler told him. Scully described Wachovia's mortgage book as "a $40 to 50 billion problem. It's huge. The junior Wachovia team is not disputing our analysis."

Kelleher, who had been keeping a careful watch over the firm's dwindling cash pile, had just taken a look at Wachovia's numbers for himself and observed, "That's a shit sandwich even I can't get my big mouth around."

It became increasingly clear to everybody that the only way this deal was going to take place was if the government provided cover.

Mack, not having heard anything that soothed his nerves, had his secretary get Steel on the line. "You called us and said you wanted to go a hundred miles an hour," he reminded him, his Southern manners starting to fray, "and I'm sensing from your team that there's not the same urgency."

Steel was apologetic. "You're right," he told Mack. "We're not doing this for the next couple of days."

They agreed they'd get back in touch, but before he hung up, Steel asked Mack for a favor. "It wouldn't be helpful if it leaked out that we're not talking," he said.

———

"Fortress Goldman." Tim Geithner had written those two words on a pad on his desk after a Friday-afternoon conversation with Lloyd Blankfein, who must have uttered the phrase a dozen times. It was his way of saying he wanted Goldman to remain a stand-alone institution.

Geithner had been concerned that Blankfein didn't appreciate how perilous his situation actually was and had quizzed him about the firm's financial health. Blankfein had said he was hopeful that Goldman would weather the crisis but had acknowledged: "It depends on what happens to the rest of the world."

Geithner had also sounded Blankfein out about the bank holding company idea. While Blankfein was originally somewhat resistant, by now he had officially warmed up to it. He had become increasingly convinced that if the market knew that the Federal Reserve was behind him, it would instill confidence in investors. And after doing the math, by his estimate 95 percent of Goldman's assets could already be pledged to the Fed's discount window, so another 5 percent didn't represent that big a hurdle. Rodgin Cohen, Goldman's lawyer, had already discussed this with Geithner earlier in the day; of course, he'd have to sell Bernanke on the idea.

Blankfein, whose voice revealed to Geithner an almost panicked state, had also said that he was planning to raise capital and was certain that the firm would be able to do so from private investors. Maybe even Warren Buffett would be interested.

———

The waiter at Blue Fin had just brought several massive plates of sushi— spicy lobster rolls, pieces of yellowtail tuna, and *tobiko*—when Colm Kelleher's cell phone rang. He had gone to get a late lunch with his Morgan Stanley colleagues, including James Gorman, Walid Chammah, and Tom Nides, and the group had been chatting about their plan to meet later that night with Gao Xiqing of China Investment Corporation, who was bringing an entire team to New York. With Wachovia effectively out of the picture, the Chinese were now their sole prospect.

When Kelleher looked down at the caller ID, he saw it was a number in Japan and walked to the corner of the restaurant.

Jonathan Kindred, president of Morgan Stanley's securities business in Tokyo, greeted him and said excitedly, "This is interesting. I just got a call from Mitsubishi. They want to do the deal." Mitsubishi UFJ, Japan's biggest bank, was interested in buying a stake in Morgan Stanley.

The call had come completely unexpectedly, and totally unsolicited. Morgan Stanley's management had actually ruled out calling Mitsubishi earlier in the week after its chairman, Ryosuke Tamakoshi, said publicly at a conference that following Lehman's bankruptcy his firm would not be making any investments in the United States.

Kindred said he thought Mitsubishi was prepared to move quickly. But Kelleher, rolling his eyes, was skeptical. He had worked with other Japanese banks before and, in his experience, they had always lived up to their reputation as being slow, risk-averse, and deeply bureaucratic.

James Gorman's eyes widened when Kelleher returned to the table with Kindred's news. This could be exactly what they needed, he thought.

Kelleher only scoffed, "This is a waste of time, they're never going to do anything."

"Colm, I really feel they're going to do something," Gorman insisted. When Gorman worked at Merrill Lynch he had orchestrated a joint venture with Mitsubishi to combine their private banking and wealth-management businesses in Japan. He thought that the fact that Mitsubishi had initiated the call to express interest was an encouraging sign. "This stuff doesn't happen by accident," he said.

———

Kevin Warsh, the Fed governor, had taken the US Airways shuttle to New York late on Friday to help Geithner think through how to handle the upcoming weekend. Just as important, he would be Bernanke's eyes and ears on the ground. As he and his driver made their way through traffic from LaGuardia Airport to the New York Fed, he received a call from Rodgin Cohen, who by now was advising both Wachovia on its talks with Morgan Stanley and Goldman Sachs on its bank holding company status. He told Warsh he had an idea—a potentially big one. It wasn't a plan officially sanctioned by his clients, just a friendly suggestion from an old-timer in the business.

He suggested to Warsh that the government attempt a shotgun wedding between Goldman and Wachovia. He knew it was a long shot—the "optics," he acknowledged, would be problematic, given Paulson had worked at Goldman for thirty years and been its CEO from 1999 to 2006 and that Wachovia's CEO, Bob Steel, was a former Goldman man and Paulson's former deputy at Treasury too—but it would solve everyone's problems: Goldman would get the deposit base it had been seeking, and Wachovia would have its death sentence stayed.

Warsh listened to the proposal and, almost to his own surprise, liked it.

———

Gao Xiqing, dressed in a sporty turtleneck and blazer, arrived at Morgan Stanley with his team just after 9:00 p.m., having flown into New York with Morgan Stanley's Wei Sun Christianson on a private jet from Aspen. He had been on a panel that afternoon with Carlos Slim, the Mexican billionaire, at Ted Forstmann's gathering and had asked the moderator, Charlie Rose, to make certain the session didn't run long so that he could reach the airport in time. Given the rumors in the newspapers, everyone at the panel knew exactly where he was headed.

Gao's back was causing him so much pain that when James Gorman first went to introduce himself, he found Gao lying on the floor of a conference room on the fortieth floor, in the middle of a telephone call. Mack, ever the accommodating host, had a couch brought from the executive dining room for his guest to lie on.

Over dinner, ordered in from Mack's favorite restaurant, San Pietro—

again—they discussed a possible transaction. Alternating between standing up and lying down, Gao reiterated his interest in buying 49 percent of Morgan Stanley.

As he had told Christianson on the flight over, he now indicated that he was prepared to provide the firm with a credit line of as much as $50 billion and a nominal equity investment—no more than $5 billion, maybe less.

Mack was stunned. He had known the price that would be offered might be low, but to him this was absurdly so—it was effectively merely a loan. While it might help Morgan Stanley stay in business, Gao was clearly taking advantage of its weakened condition. To Gao, the offer presented a way to reset the price he had paid for the 10 percent stake he had acquired in Morgan Stanley in 2007, which was now worth far less. Unlike deals that other sovereign wealth funds had struck then, giving them the right to reset the value of the deal if the firms sold equity at a lower price later, CIC hadn't had the presence of mind to insist on that stipulation. For some inexplicable reason, Gao had convinced himself that the agreement did include such a provision until Morgan Stanley got him a copy to show him that it didn't.

However insulting Gao's proposal, Mack recognized that his situation was desperate. Despite the market rally, the firm had continued to bleed cash. Kelleher had given him the cash balances and they were not good—about $40 billion in the tank. A few bad days could wipe them out, and most days lately had been bad ones.

Without many other options, Mack told Gao the firm would open its books to him. Gao had hired Sullivan & Cromwell's seemingly omnipresent lawyer, Rodgin Cohen, as well as Deutsche Bank, to advise him, and both companies were already sending over teams to assist the Chinese. A sheet of paper marked "CIC" was affixed to the conference room door that would become Gao's temporary office. Mack also had a physical therapist summoned to work on his bad back.

When Mack returned to his office and huddled with Christianson and his team, they were flabbergasted; Chammah initially thought he had misheard Christianson when she presented it.

"That's a ludicrous ask," Kelleher said. "They are being unreasonable."

Gorman, trying to calm everyone down, said they should all hope it might just be an opening salvo: "They ask for the moon and then maybe they get more reasonable?"

———

It was just past midnight, and Courtroom 601 of the courthouse at One Bowling Green in Lower Manhattan was still packed with people standing shoulder to shoulder.

The occasion was the approval of the sale of Lehman Brothers to Barclays by a bankruptcy judge. While the rest of the world had already moved on to the fates of Morgan Stanley and Goldman Sachs, ten thousand Lehman employees' jobs still lay in the balance. More than 150 lawyers, including some of the most prominent bankruptcy practitioners in the nation, were present on behalf of various creditors. Chelsea Clinton was in attendance, representing the hedge fund Avenue Capital.

The proceedings had begun at 4:36 p.m., and Judge James Peck had insisted that he would reach a verdict before leaving for the night. The urgency of getting the sale approved was growing more and more evident as with each passing hour the markets chipped away at the value of Lehman's assets. Not only was the bankruptcy of Lehman, which had filed for Chapter 11 with $639 billion in assets, by far the largest in the nation's history, but an unwinding of so complex a financial institution had never before been attempted.

On this late summer evening, the courtroom was on the warm side—the windows were closed and, for lack of enough chairs, people had taken to sitting on the air vents. Lawyers from the firm representing Lehman, Weil Gotshal, carried in ice water.

Signaling to Harvey Miller of Weil Gotshal, Judge Peck said: "You may approach, if that's what you're doing. I can't really tell. Frankly, with so many people in the courtroom, whenever I see the movement this way, I get a little concerned. Mr. Miller?"

Miller, even under these circumstances dapper in a gray suit, red tie, and blue shirt, outlined the deal: Barclays would pay $1.75 billion for Lehman's North American operations. "This is a tragedy, Your Honor," Miller said of what had happened to Lehman Brothers. "And maybe we missed the RTC by a week," he added, referencing the development of the new TARP program. "That's the real tragedy, Your Honor."

"That occurred to me as well," Judge Peck said sympathetically.

Many of the lawyers for Lehman's creditors, however, were less chari-
table. They were furious about Lehman's deal with Barclays, suggesting
it was paying far too little and complaining about ambiguities in the purchase agreement. Daniel H. Golden of Akin Gump Strauss Hauer & Feld,
representing an ad hoc group of investors holding more than $9 billion of
Lehman bonds, pleaded with the court for a brief delay.

"There has simply been no credible evidence adduced at this hearing
that the price that Barclays is paying for these assets represents fair value,"
he said. "There's no other testimony or evidence that suggests the other
assets being purchased by Barclays represent fair value or an attempt to
maximize value for creditors."

Miller, taking umbrage at the mere suggestion that the deal wasn't
fair, shot back that the transaction had to be approved by the court immediately.

"I don't want to use the melting ice cube" analogy, he said, the emotion
showing on his face. But "it's already half melted, Your Honor. . . . The
things that have happened since Wednesday, make it imperative that this
sale be approved. In the interest of all of the stakeholders, including Mr.
Golden's clients, they will benefit by this, Your Honor, because if the alternative happens, there will be very little to distribute to creditors, if anything."

Nearly eight hours and three recesses into the hearing, after arguments
by dozens of lawyers, several interruptions because of static from the
speakers, and one brief aside about Judge Wapner's *The People's Court,* Judge
Peck, moved by the enormity of trying to save what was left of a more
than century-old firm, agreed to sign off on the Barclays deal.

"This is not simply approving the transaction because Mr. Miller is
putting pressure on me to do so," the judge explained. "This is not approving the transaction because I know it's the best available transaction. I have
to approve this transaction because it's the only available transaction."

With a heavy heart, he went on to offer a eulogy: "Lehman Brothers
became a victim. In effect, the only true icon to fall in the tsunami that
has befallen the credit markets. And it saddens me. I feel that I have a
responsibility to all the creditors, to all of the employees, to all of the
customers and to all of you."

It was 12:41 a.m. when Judge Peck ended the hearing. As he stepped down from the bench, the courtroom, with at least several people moved to tears, erupted in a wave of applause.

———

Tim Geithner hadn't slept well on Friday night, having decided to stay in one of the grim rooms on the twelfth floor of the Federal Reserve. By 6:00 a.m., he had returned back upstairs to his office dressed in an oxford dress shirt and sweatpants and begun puttering around the hallways in his stocking feet.

In his mind, he was already making battle plans. He had made it safely to the weekend, but he already was worried about what would happen on Monday if he didn't find a way to save Morgan Stanley and Goldman Sachs.

"John's holding on to a slim reed," Paulson had told Geithner about John Mack's perilous position on a phone call the night before. They had heard that Morgan Stanley had only about $30 to $40 billion left, but Paulson was also still anxious about Goldman Sachs, his former employer. "We've got to find a lifeline for these guys," said Paulson, and they reviewed the possible options.

On a pad that morning, Geithner started writing out various merger permutations: *Morgan Stanley and Citigroup. Morgan Stanley and JP Morgan Chase. Morgan Stanley and Mitsubishi. Morgan Stanley and CIC. Morgan Stanley and Outside Investor. Goldman Sachs and Citigroup. Goldman Sachs and Wachovia. Goldman Sachs and Outside Investor. Fortress Goldman. Fortress Morgan Stanley.*

It was the ultimate Wall Street chessboard.

———

Lloyd Blankfein arrived at his office at just past 7:00 on Saturday morning. Even though he was still pushing his "Fortress Goldman" bank holding plan, he and Gary Cohn had assigned more than a half dozen teams to start investigating different deals: HSBC, UBS, Wells Fargo, Wachovia, Citigroup, Sumitomo, and Industrial and Commercial Bank of China.

Cohn had had another conversation on Friday with Kevin Warsh of the Federal Reserve who encouraged him to keep looking at merger options, especially at Citigroup. While it had never been made public, Goldman had explored the idea of merging with Citigroup several times over the past eighteen months but had never engaged in formal talks. Cohn and

Warsh had discussed the possibility at least twice before, and even though Cohn always resisted the idea, he was intrigued.

Initially Cohn's notion was that Citi should buy Goldman; he had even established an asking price. But Warsh suggested that Cohn approach it the other way around: Goldman should be the buyer. To Cohn that made no sense given that Citi was so much bigger. But what Warsh knew—and hadn't yet shared with Cohn—was that Citigroup's balance sheet had so many holes that its value was likely a lot lower than its current stock price.

As a result, the Fed was considering three possible outcomes for Citi, code-named "NewCo," "Goldman Survivors," and "Citi Survivors."

Blankfein was reading an e-mail when John Rogers, the firm's chief of staff, arrived. Blankfein pressed a secret button under his desk to open remotely the glass door to his office. (Paulson had installed the Inspector Gadget–like device when he was Goldman's CEO.)

As he and Rogers were reviewing their own battle plans, Geithner called. In his usual impatient tone, he insisted that Blankfein immediately call Vikram Pandit, Citigroup's CEO, and begin merger discussions. Blankfein, slightly shocked at the directness of the request, agreed to place the call.

"Well, I guess you know why I'm calling," Blankfein said when he reached Pandit a few minutes later.

"No, I don't," Pandit replied, with genuine puzzlement.

There was an awkward pause on the phone. Blankfein had assumed that the Fed had prearranged the call. "Well, I'm calling you because at least some people in the world might be thinking that combining our firms would be a good idea," he said.

After another few moments of uncomfortable silence Pandit finally replied, "I want you to know I'm flattered by this call."

Blankfein now began to wonder if Pandit was putting him on. "Well, Vikram," he said briskly, "I'm not calling with any flattery towards you in mind."

Pandit hurriedly ended the call: "I'll have to talk to my board. I'll call you back."

Blankfein hung up and looked up at Rogers. "Well, that was embarrassing. He had no idea what I was talking about!" From Blankfein's perspective, he had done what he was asked to do, only to be shown up.

Blankfein phoned Geithner back immediately. "I just called Vikram," he said testily. "As I think about it, you never told me whether Vikram was expecting a call, but I inferred it. He behaved as if he wasn't expecting the call and he convinced me that he wasn't expecting the call."

Geithner had miscalculated—could Pandit not see the gift that was being handed to him? It defied all reason. But Geithner had no time to deal with anybody's injured feelings. "Okay, I'll talk to you later," he said before hanging up. Blankfein sat there, wondering what the hell had just happened.

―――――

Alan Greenspan and his wife, Andrea Mitchell, the NBC News journalist, were mingling in the crowd outside the grand ballroom at the St. Regis Aspen Resort on Saturday morning, the second day of Teddy Forstmann's weekend conference. They were all waiting for the next panel to begin, entitled "Crisis on Wall Street: What's Next?" By Wall Street standards it was a star-studded event: The panelists included Larry Summers, the former Treasury secretary; Mohamed El-Erian, CEO of PIMCO, whose book *When Markets Collide* had just been published; CNBC's conservative talk-show host Larry Kudlow; and perhaps the most intriguing, Bob Steel of Wachovia. Steel, who had considered canceling, had flown into Aspen that morning, leaving his home at 4:00 a.m. to arrive on time.

By the time the moderator, Charlie Rose, got to the Q&A portion of the panel, however, Steel was nervously checking his watch. Greenspan had entered a debate about the controversies of mark-to-market accounting, but Steel knew he had to get back to the East Coast immediately. The moment the panel ended, he tried to bolt out of the room but on the way out encountered Richard Kovacevich, the chairman of Wells Fargo, someone he thought could be a merger partner.

"I was going to call you next week," Steel told him.

"Yes, I wanted to catch up," Kovacevich replied.

"I'm running back to the airport. I'll call you," Steel promised.

Jumping into his black Jeep Wrangler on the way to the airport, he finally had a minute to check his BlackBerry and discovered that Kevin

Warsh had sent him several e-mails urging him to contact him immediately.

"Listen, I have a call for you to make," Warsh told Steel when he finally reached him. "We think you should connect with Lloyd!"

Steel, reading between the lines, was stunned: The government was trying to orchestrate a merger between Goldman Sachs and Wachovia! On its face, he knew that it could be a politically explosive deal, considering the two firms' connections to Treasury. Paulson, he imagined, must be involved somehow. But, of course, Paulson wasn't allowed to contact him directly. Steel was immediately anxious about the idea. If Goldman had really wanted to buy Wachovia, he thought, it would have done so long ago. After all, up until this week when he spoke to Mack, Goldman had been on Wachovia's payroll as its adviser, and as such, knew every aspect of its internal numbers. So, if there was a bargain to be had, then Goldman hadn't seen it. Still, Steel saw the merits in such a deal, and if it was being encouraged by the Federal Reserve, he imagined it might just happen.

"I spoke to Kevin, and he said to give you a call," Steel began when he got through to Blankfein.

This call, unlike the Citibank fiasco, *had* been prewired. "Yes, I know," Blankfein said. "We'd be interested in putting a deal together."

Steel told Blankfein he was about to step onto Wachovia's corporate jet and could be in New York by late that afternoon.

As his plane headed for the East Coast, Steel mused how a deal with Goldman would be something of a homecoming, even if it had come as a direct order from the government. Perhaps he could even wangle the chairman title.

———

Jamie Dimon had been hoping to be able to take his first day off in two weeks. That was until Geithner called him early Saturday morning and instructed him—the president of the New York Federal Reserve seldom suggested anything—to start thinking about whether he'd like to buy Morgan Stanley.

"You've got to be kidding me," Dimon replied.

No, Geithner said, he was quite serious.

"I did Bear," Dimon objected, referring to buying Bear Stearns. "I can't do this."

Geithner ignored his answer. "You'll be getting a call from John Mack," he said and hung up the phone.

Mack, who had had a similar peremptory call from Geithner, phoned Dimon five minutes later. Dimon reiterated that he didn't want to buy Morgan Stanley, which he had already told Mack earlier in the week. But Dimon was under orders to try to help Mack, so the two rivals talked about whether JP Morgan could offer Morgan Stanley a credit line that might give it some breathing room. Dimon said he'd think about it and get back to him with a decision.

As soon as he got off the phone with Mack, Dimon called Geithner. "I talked to John," he said. "We're talking about getting him a credit line."

"I don't know if that'll be enough," Geithner said, frustrated at the news. His order had not been explicit, but he hinted heavily that the Federal Reserve very much wanted the two firms to form a union and wasn't the slightest bit interested in any temporary measures.

Dimon immediately sent an e-mail to his operating committee, summoning them to the office, and within an hour, dressed in golf shirts and khakis, they had assembled in a conference room on the forty-eighth floor.

Dimon had a grimace on his face as he related the call he'd received from Geithner. Merging the "Houses of Morgan" was not a new idea but hadn't come up in any serious fashion since June 20, 1973, when Morgan Stanley, JP Morgan, Morgan Guaranty, and the British Morgan Grenfell held a top secret meeting in Bermuda, code-named "Triangle," at the Grotto Bay Hotel.

On a whiteboard Dimon used a black marker to sketch out what he had been thinking. "We can either buy them, buy part of them, or give them some type of financing."

For the next two hours they went around in circles, considering their options. What parts of Morgan Stanley could be spun off? What parts could be warehoused (the term for buying a property, keeping it relatively intact if not in fact making it healthier, and then selling it later, when the market recovered)? Maybe they could buy Morgan Stanley, Dimon suggested aloud, and then create a new tracking stock for it?

But all these scenarios wound up circling back to the same problem: What, exactly, would they be buying? The overlap between the firms was enormous. And what were Morgan Stanley's toxic assets really worth? These were all but unanswerable questions at that time.

John Hogan, JP Morgan's chief risk officer, who had attended the meeting with Lehman Brothers the previous week, stepped out of the operating committee conference room and called Colm Kelleher and Ken deRegt at Morgan Stanley.

"I don't know exactly what you guys have in mind, but under any scenario where we 'help you,' we're going to need a bunch of information," he said. "Could you go back and talk to Mack and find out exactly what it is that you're expecting, that you'd like from us in terms of this 'help'?" There was more than a little condescension in Hogan's voice, and Kelleher and deRegt picked up on it immediately.

A half hour later Kelleher got back to Hogan with an outline for a request for a $50 billion line of credit. Kelleher was hoping that if JP Morgan did come through with an offer, Dimon would not be as punitive as CIC had been.

Hogan sent an e-mail to JP Morgan's senior team with the subject line "URGENT and Confidential." In it he spelled out the plan:

> Pls plan to meet at Morgan Stanley's offices at 750 7th Ave tomorrow at 9:30am. We don't have the floor or room as yet—MS contact person is David Wong. The purpose of the meeting is for us to consider entering into a secured financing against a variety of different unencumbered assets at MS.

———

Geithner was by now seriously miffed. He had been trying to reach Pandit since eight in the morning and had just heard back from Blankfein, who had somehow actually managed to get through to Pandit again. The only problem was that Pandit had turned Goldman down, and Geithner hadn't even had a chance to speak with him.

Finally, he got through to him.

"I haven't been able to reach you for four hours," Geithner barked into the phone. "That's unacceptable on a day like today!"

Apologizing, Pandit explained that he had been talking to his team about the Goldman proposal, which they had ultimately rejected. "We're concerned about taking on Goldman," Pandit said, trying to explain his rationale for turning them down. "I don't need another trillion dollars on my balance sheet."

Geithner could only laugh to himself. "This is a bank," Pandit said. "And a bank takes deposits and a bank has a prudency culture. I cannot envision a bank taking its deposits and investing them all in hedge funds. I know that's not what Goldman is, but the perception is that they'd be taking deposits and putting them to work against a proprietary trade. That can't be right philosophically!"

Having dispensed with pushing Goldman and Citigroup together, Geithner moved on to his next idea: merging Morgan Stanley and Citigroup.

Pandit had been considering that option, too, and while he was more predisposed to merging with Morgan Stanley, he still was reluctant. "It's still not our choice to do this deal, but we could think about it," he told Geithner.

———

By 2:00 p.m., John Mack was growing concerned that the talks with CIC were going nowhere. Gao hadn't budged on what Mack was calling an "offensive" offer. He had no idea what Jamie Dimon would come up with, and he hadn't heard anything from Mitsubishi.

Downstairs, Paul Taubman, the firm's head of investment banking, was experiencing much the same panic as Mack. A disarmingly young-looking forty-eight-year-old, Taubman had worked his entire career at Morgan Stanley, rising to become one of the most trusted merger advisers in the nation, and could now only wonder if it was all going to come to an end this weekend.

Taubman and his colleague Ji-Yeun Lee were on the phone to Tokyo, where it was past midnight, with Kohei Yuki, his Morgan Stanley counterpart who was trying to coordinate talks with Mitsubishi.

"I think they've gone to bed for the night, we'll pick it up in the morning," Yuki said.

"That's not going to work," Taubman answered. "You need to call them at home and wake them up."

There was a long pause; this was certainly a breach of Japanese protocol.

"O . . . kay," he said.

"Listen, if you're a senior executive, you're not going to say, 'You know what, I'm not going to wake my boss and I'll just keep it to myself and then if it turns out that I missed the opportunity of a lifetime, how am I going to explain it to him if he wasn't awakened?'"

Twenty minutes later, Yuki was back on the phone with Taubman. "I got him." Mitsubishi was going to wake up its entire deal team and get working. In a conference room just two floors down, Morgan Stanley's board had arrived, and things had grown tense quickly. Some had flown across the country to get there; others, like Sir Howard J. Davies, had flown in from London. The only person missing was Charles E. Phillips, president of the software giant Oracle (and a former Morgan Stanley technology analyst).

Kelleher had just finished giving a presentation on the firm's finances, and it was not good. Charles Noski, a director and former chief financial officer of AT&T, asked him point-blank: "When do we run out of money?"

Kelleher paused and then said somberly, "Well, depending on what happens Monday and Tuesday, it could be as early as middle of the week."

It was a shot across the bow. If this weekend didn't go well, they'd all end up the targets of shareholder lawsuits. The independent board members, led by the lead director, C. Robert Kidder, decided they needed to hire an independent adviser and, after a short conversation, chose Roger Altman, the former deputy Treasury secretary and founder of the boutique bank Evercore Partners (and Dick Fuld's former carpool-mate). He would advise the board on whatever transactions they would be presented with and provide a modicum of cover; in the event that whatever happened over the weekend led to legal battles, at least they would look like they were trying to be responsible.

After Mack came downstairs again Gene Ludwig, Mack's outside consultant, explained the bank holding concept that they were pursuing. Ludwig said that he believed that Paulson would be motivated to protect them.

"If we go, Goldman goes," he said, stating the obvious, at least internally, by that point. But then he added a new insight that the board hadn't considered.

"And then GE will go."

———

At Goldman Sachs, two of its top bankers, David Solomon and John Weinberg, had just returned from a morning meeting in Fairfield, Connecticut. They had met with Jeffrey Immelt, General Electric's CEO, and Keith Sherin, its CFO.

Seated on Cohn's couch, Solomon recounted the meeting to him. It was a complicated, and almost comical, situation: Solomon and Weinberg had traveled to Fairfield to advise its client on coping with the financial crisis, beginning with a plan to raise capital. One of Immelt's primary concerns, however, was what would happen if its adviser, Goldman Sachs, went out of business.

General Electric was more about manufacturing than financial engineering, but roughly half of its profits in recent years had come from a finance company unit called GE Capital. Like most Wall Street firms, GE Capital relied on the short-term paper market and the confidence of investors worldwide, and Immelt was worried about how the fate of Goldman and Morgan Stanley might affect it. The meeting ended without much clarity, apart from some preliminary plans to raise capital—and an assurance to Immelt that Goldman was staying in business.

But Cohn was already thinking about Goldman's talks with Wachovia. Cohn, speaking to Kevin Warsh of the Fed, had agreed to entertain the idea, but only on the condition the Fed would provide assistance; Warsh had said they'd strongly consider it. Cohn believed him: Paulson had spoken with Blankfein and told him to take the talks seriously. "If you go into this looking for all the problems and how much help you're going to get, it's never going to happen," he said, adding, "You're in trouble and I can't help you." In the meantime, Warsh instructed Cohn to make sure they could work out the personal dynamics.

"Let's not waste our time on economics if you guys are never going to solve the social issues," he said. "If you aren't willing to accommodate them, if Bob's not willing to do whatever, this isn't going to happen."

Steel was scheduled to land at Westchester County Airport in White Plains, a suburb of the city, in only a few hours, and Cohn walked into Blankfein's office and made a suggestion.

"Lloyd, you should go pick Steel up at the airport," Cohn said, believing it would be a gracious gesture to kick off the merger talks.

Blankfein looked seriously annoyed, having never felt that he got along with Steel particularly well ever since Paulson had made them co-heads of the equities division years earlier. "Do I have to?"

"Yes," Cohn said firmly. "I would go with you but it would be awkward. You should go pick him up."

Blankfein was still resistant. "Can you go by yourself?"

"No," said Cohn, who considered Steel a friend. "I already have a very good relationship with him."

Blankfein relented. He'd head to the airport.

———

For a moment Paulson felt he could breathe a sigh of relief. His team had finished the first draft of the TARP legislation and gotten a quick sign-off from the Office of Management and Budget to begin distributing it on the Hill.

Given that he had promised the congressional leadership on Thursday night that he could get them something to work on "in hours," he figured he'd make it succinct. Paulson; Kevin Fromer, his head of legislative affairs; and Bob Hoyt, his general counsel, had rushed to draft it, and it came in at just under three pages.

After much debate, Paulson's team settled on the $700 billion figure that Kashkari had proposed the day before. If passed, it would be the largest one-time expenditure in the history of the federal government. Concerned about the potential for political interference, Hoyt had slipped several lines into the bill aimed at preventing it, as well as granting Paulson whatever powers he might need:

> Decisions by the Secretary pursuant to the authority of this Act are non-reviewable and committed to agency discretion, and may not be reviewed by any court of law or any administrative agency. The Secretary is authorized to take such actions as the Secretary deems necessary to carry out the authorities in this Act . . . without regard to any other provision of

law regarding public contracts. . . . Any funds expended for actions authorized by this Act, including the payment of administrative expenses, shall
be deemed appropriated at the time of such expenditure.

It might have been too early to expect any feedback, but Treasury staffers were already excitedly forwarding copies to one another.

And the reaction was instant: Even inside the department there were
worries that Paulson might look like he was overreaching. The three-page
bill had no oversight plan and virtually no qualifiers. Its terse length alone
was making people uneasy.

"So, have you seen the bill?" Dan Jester asked Jeremiah Norton, neither
of whom had worked on the proposal.

"I've seen the talking points," Norton replied.

"No," said Jester, "That *is* the bill!"

———

Late Saturday afternoon, Colm Kelleher and Morgan Stanley's deputy
treasurer, Dave Russo, headed down to the NY Fed with their advisers,
Ed Herlihy of Wachtell and Promontory's Gene Ludwig, to present their
application for bank holding company status.

In the thirteenth-floor reception area, two staffers approached them
and asked, "Which of you is the CFO?"

"I am," Kelleher said.

"You need to come with us by yourself."

Kelleher mockingly bade farewell to his colleagues as he was escorted
to a conference room where the New York Fed's top leadership—William
Rutledge, Bill Dudley, Terry Checki, and Christine M. Cumming—were
assembled.

"Look," Rutledge said, "if all else fails this weekend, will you agree to
become a bank holding company?"

"What does that mean?" Kelleher asked, still somewhat unsure of the
technicalities.

The benefits of a bank holding company were explained to him: Short-
term financing would be available through the Fed's discount window,
provided Morgan Stanley established a sufficient deposit base and submitted to various regulations.

"Will you get your board to agree?" they asked Kelleher.

Kelleher now understood what this meeting meant: The Federal
Reserve might be offering to save his firm. The tank might not reach
empty after all. "Of course," he replied.

———

Lloyd Blankfein, wearing slacks and a button-down shirt, was waiting in
the Westchester County Airport parking lot when Bob Steel arrived.
Always perfectly coiffed, Steel nonetheless looked as if he could use some
sleep as he walked out of the terminal. He had already been awake for
fifteen hours and his day was hardly done.

"What a birthday present!" Blankfein said to Steel brightly when he
saw him. Blankfein, who turned fifty-four that day, was still hoping to get
to a birthday dinner later that evening at Porter House New York, a steak
restaurant, with his wife, Laura.

As they drove into the city they delicately began discussing the outlines
of a deal and discussing their history together. Neither of them knew what
to make of the merger idea or, for that matter, each other.

When they reached 85 Broad Street, Steel went directly to the thirtieth
floor, where he used to spend a lot of his time. As he stepped into the
conference room, he saw Chris Cole, who had been his firm's adviser for
the past five months. Now Cole would be on the other side, trying to buy
Wachovia. Meanwhile, Steel's own lawyer, Rodgin Cohen, was also Goldman's lawyer. It had all become so confusing and rife with conflicts, but
they all agreed that if they were going to do a deal, they'd have to reach
an agreement by Monday morning.

Goldman's biggest issue was, as it had been with Morgan Stanley, trying
to determine the scope of the hole. Wachovia owned $122 billion of pay
option ARMs, which Goldman Sachs quickly felt wasn't going to be worth
much. They each agreed to put teams on it to work up the numbers; Steel
said he'd have his group fly up by morning.

Before decamping for the night, Blankfein invited Steel back to his
office. He wanted to talk about titles, perhaps the most sensitive issue for
men who often measure themselves as much by their business cards as by
their wallets.

Blankfein said he was thinking of making Steel one of three co-presidents, along with Gary Cohn and Jon Winkelried; Steel would continue
to manage Wachovia as the consumer arm of Goldman Sachs.

Steel was taken aback and slightly offended. He was already the CEO of a major bank; he'd been a vice chairman of Goldman and a deputy Treasury secretary in Washington. And now he was being asked to become one of three co-presidents?

"I'm not sure I want to be at the same level with Gary and John," he said diplomatically. "But we'll figure this out."

———

"Is Jamie trying to buy us?" Gary Lynch, Morgan's general counsel, asked Mack in the corridor outside his office.

"I don't think so," Mack said, explaining that they were simply negotiating with JP Morgan to extend a credit line to the firm. "Why do you ask?"

"Well, something strange is going on, then," Lynch replied.

Lynch related that an outside lawyer for Morgan Stanley's independent board members, Faiza J. Saeed, a partner at Cravath, had just informed him that JP Morgan had called a Cravath colleague seeking to hire her to work on a deal for Morgan Stanley. She had been a little vague, but she wanted him to clear the conflict, Lynch explained.

"Wow," Mack said.

"Yeah, this is a nice way of sending a message."

———

As dusk was setting, Hank Paulson was still in his office and had just gotten off the phone with Geithner. The news was not promising. Geithner told him that Morgan Stanley had no plan apart from what he called the "naked" bank holding company scenario. Geithner said he was uncertain whether any investor—JP Morgan, Citigroup, the Chinese, or the Japanese—would come through. And he was skeptical of the Goldman-Wachovia deal.

"We're running out of options," he told Paulson.

Paulson, who had been living on barely three hours of sleep a night for a week, was beginning to feel nauseated. Watching the financial industry crumble in front of his eyes—the world he had inhabited his entire career—was getting to him. For a moment, he felt light-headed.

From outside his office, his staff could hear him vomit.

———

Saturday night, John Mack returned to his Upper East Side apartment, still nursing a persistent cold he couldn't shake. His wife, Christy, who had driven into the city from Rye to console him, was waiting up.

He was quieter than usual, wondering yet again how he would manage to raise billions of dollars in capital in only twenty-four hours. "You know, there's a chance I could lose the firm," he said, a sense of despair in his voice.

He needed some air, he told Christy, and decided to go on a walk. As he roamed up Madison Avenue, he realized that his entire adult life, his entire professional career was on the line. He had been in battles before—his losing fight with the firm's former CEO, Philip J. Purcell, had been a notable one—but never anything like what he faced now. But this was not just about his personal survival; it was about the fifty thousand people around the globe who worked for him, and for whom he felt a keen sense of responsibility. Images of Lehman employees streaming out of their building the previous Sunday night carrying boxes of their possessions still haunted him. He needed to buck himself up. Somehow, he was going to save Morgan Stanley.

When he stepped into his living room a few minutes later, he admitted to Christy with a grateful smile, "I'd rather be doing this than reading a book in North Carolina."

———

Even before the black Suburban had come to a stop in his driveway on Saturday evening, Hank Paulson was stepping out the door, his RAZR at his ear. His Secret Service agent, Jim Langan, preferred that Paulson wait inside until Langan got out of the vehicle, but Paulson had long since abandoned such protocol.

Paulson raced inside to get on a call with Vice Premier Wang Qishan in China. For the past day, he had been trying to coordinate the call to press his case for China to pursue an investment in Morgan Stanley. Originally, he had wanted President Bush to call China's president and had spoken with Josh Bolten, the president's chief of staff, about it. But Bolten had concerns about whether it was appropriate for the president to be calling on behalf of a specific U.S. company. He suggested that, at best, the president might be able to call and speak broadly about the financial industry, finding a subtle way to be encouraging. But before such a call could be made, Paulson needed to size up China's true interest.

Paulson had scheduled the call with Wang for 9:30 p.m. He knew Wang well from his trips to China as the CEO of Goldman, and they had a comfortable rapport. He also knew it was highly unusual to be orchestrating a private market deal with another country, in this case the largest holder of U.S. debt. Before placing the call, Paulson had reached out to Stephen Hadley, assistant to the president for national security affairs, to get some guidance. The instructions: Tread carefully.

When Paulson was finally connected to Wang, he moved quickly to the topic at hand, Morgan Stanley. "We'd welcome your investment," Paulson told Wang. He also suggested that one of China's biggest banks, like ICBC, should participate, making the investment a strategic one.

Wang, however, expressed his anxiety about CIC becoming involved with Morgan Stanley, given what had happened to Lehman Brothers. "Morgan Stanley is strategically important," Paulson said, suggesting he would not let it fail.

Wang remained unimpressed, asking for a commitment that the U.S. government would guarantee any investment. Paulson, trying to avoid making an explicit promise but also trying to assuage him, said, "I can assure you that an investment in Morgan Stanley would be viewed positively."

———

Only a few hours later, Sunday morning, Paulson was back in the Suburban, where Michele Davis, his communications chief, was waiting. "You're not going to like this," she said as she pulled out a copy of the cover of the new *Newsweek,* which would appear on newsstands on Monday. Under the headline "King Henry" was a photograph of Paulson.

They were headed to an early taping of NBC's *Meet the Press* to sell his TARP proposal with his fishing buddy, Tom Brokaw, who had temporarily taken over hosting responsibilities for the political talk show after Tim Russert died. From there they would head to ABC's *This Week* and then to CBS's *Face the Nation.*

Paulson skimmed through the article. It was a flattering profile, with the exception of a quote from Governor Jon Corzine, his old nemesis from Goldman, questioning his consistency. But more important, the cover was a tacit acknowledgment of the enormous power that Paulson now wielded, not only in America, but on the world stage. President Bush had taken a backseat; Paulson had become the de facto leader of the country in this time of crisis.

The power pleased him, but he also knew that it cut both ways. He discovered just how far it cut within minutes of the red light's going on for the Brokaw interview, when the host lit into him about the lack of details in the TARP plan, the same lack of details that Treasury staffers had privately worried about the day before.

"If you were in your old job as chairman of Goldman Sachs and you took this deal to the partners," Brokaw said, "they'd send you out of the room and say, 'Come back when you've got a lot more answers,' wouldn't they?"

———

Kenneth deRegt, Morgan Stanley's chief risk officer, was trying to put the best face on his firm's finances as he prepared for the meeting with JP Morgan that morning, assembling lists of collateral that he hoped would be considered strong enough to lend against. But as he worked it began to dawn on both him and Ruth Porat, who ran the firm's financial institutions group, that an unrestricted show-and-tell session with JP Morgan bankers might be counterproductive. If all went well, Morgan Stanley would become a bank holding company that very evening—a plan that JP Morgan was unaware of—giving it access to far more liquidity. So they decided to be selective about what they would and wouldn't feature in the presentation and included only the bank's collateral that they wouldn't be able to pledge to the Fed, which represented some of the worst holdings on its books. It would be a risky move. Rather than burnishing the firm for a sale, they could unknowingly scare off a potential partner.

———

Braunstein, Hogan, and Black of JP Morgan arrived at 750 Seventh Avenue punctually at 8:45 a.m., bringing the firm's general counsel, Steven Cutler, with them. Several dozen underlings had already arrived and were waiting. The location, a nondescript office building with no signage a block west of Morgan Stanley's headquarters, was where the company typically held any meeting it wanted kept secret.

"This is highly confidential," Hogan reiterated to the team as they set up in a meeting room that Morgan Stanley had provided. Braunstein was surprised that no coffee or food was provided for his team—*Is this some kind of negotiating tactic?*—and immediately sent an associate to Dunkin' Donuts.

They all knew they were there for what could be the most historic diligence session of their lives. While Hogan had told them the meeting was about extending a line of credit to Morgan Stanley, they all knew that it could quickly turn into a full-blown merger, a transaction that would make the Bear Stearns deal look like Little League practice. War rooms were set up to review each major part of Morgan Stanley's business—prime brokerage, real estate, principal investments, and commodities.

JP Morgan's lawyers had expressed serious doubts to the team that they could pull off a deal like this in such a short compass of time. They kept referring to the problem of "perfecting security interests in less than twenty-four hours."

In fact it wouldn't take nearly that long: Within two hours, JP Morgan decided to pull the plug. They were shocked that the assets that Morgan Stanley was offering as collateral were of such low quality, surely too low for JP Morgan to lend against.

"This stuff is crap," Hogan told Steve Black, JP Morgan's president.

———

By midday, Goldman Sachs and Wachovia, which was represented by a half dozen executives whom Bob Steel had brought along, were making rapid progress toward completing a deal. Peter Weinberg, Bob Steel's adviser and a former Goldman man, had constructed the outlines of an agreement in which Goldman would pay $18.75 a share for Wachovia's shares in Goldman stock. The price represented the closing price of Wachovia's shares on Friday.

There remained, however, one serious obstacle: Goldman wanted a "Jamie" deal. The next step was to go back to Warsh at the Fed and ask whether the Fed was prepared to subsidize the deal by guaranteeing Wachovia's most toxic assets.

During a lull in the negotiations, Weinberg took a break and walked down the hall of the executive floor. As he passed a series of portraits of the firm's past chief executives, he stopped when he reached Sidney Weinberg, his grandfather. Sidney Weinberg, who became a Goldman partner in 1927, represented the epitome of the old Wall Street, a business that had been defined by personal relationships and implicit trust, not leverage and ever more complicated financial engineering. His grandfather's world had been obliterated over the past decade as firms sought to go public and began using shareholder money to place what had proved to be dangerously risky bets.

Jon Winkelried, Goldman's co-president, was passing down the hall when he saw Weinberg gazing thoughtfully at the portrait.

"The world has really been turned on its head," Winkelried said wistfully.

———

Warren Buffett was at his home in Omaha on Sunday when he received a phone call from Byron Trott, a vice chairman at Goldman Sachs. Buffett, who disliked most Wall Street bankers, adored Trott, a mild-mannered Midwesterner based in Chicago. Paulson had introduced the men years earlier, and Trott was now the only investment banker Buffett truly trusted. "He understands Berkshire far better than any investment banker with whom we have talked and—it hurts me to say this—earns his fee," Buffett wrote in Berkshire Hathaway's 2003 annual report. For Buffett, there is no more lavish praise.

Trott was calling Buffett with a proposition. For the past several weeks he had been trying in vain to persuade Buffett to make an investment in Goldman, but he had now come up with a new idea. He disclosed to Buffett that Goldman was in talks to buy Wachovia, with government assistance, and wanted to know whether Buffett might be interested in investing in a combined Goldman-Wachovia.

At first, Buffett wasn't sure he was hearing Trott correctly. Government assistance? In a Goldman deal?

"Byron, it's a waste of time," he said in his folksy way, after considering the new configuration. "By tonight the government will realize they can't provide capital to a deal that's being done by the firm of the former Treasury secretary with the company of a retired vice chairman of Goldman Sachs and former deputy Treasury secretary. There is no way. They'll all wake up and realize even if it was the best deal in the world, they can't do it."

———

John Mack had received some promising news Sunday afternoon: Mitsubishi looked like it would actually pull through and make a sizable investment in Morgan Stanley. A conference call had been arranged for Mack to speak with Mitsubishi's chief executive, Nobuo Kuroyanagi, that evening.

Just as they were going over the details, however, Paulson called.

"John, you have to do something," Paulson said sternly.

"What do you mean I have to do something?" Mack asked, his voice rising with impatience, explaining that he had just learned that the Japanese were inclined to do the deal. "You've been so supportive, you said we can get through this."

"I know," Paulson said, "but you've got to find a partner."

"I have the Japanese! Mitsubishi is going to come in," he repeated, as if Paulson hadn't heard him the first time around.

"Come on. You and I know the Japanese. They're not going to do that. They'll never move that quickly," Paulson said, suggesting that he focus more on the deal with the Chinese or JP Morgan.

"No, I do know them. And I know I don't agree with you," Mack answered angrily. He explained that Mitsubishi had had a long-term relationship with the firm; it had used Morgan Stanley as an adviser during its hostile bid for a part of Union Bank in California earlier in the year. "Japanese rarely do a hostile," Mack reminded him. "They hired us, they followed through and got it done, so they'll come through for us."

Paulson was still skeptical. "They won't do it," he said with a sigh.

"You and I disagree," Mack sputtered, agreeing to keep him updated on his progress as he hung up the phone.

———

Calling the Fed's Kevin Warsh out of a meeting to come to the phone, Gary Cohn outlined the preliminary Goldman-Wachovia terms for him. They had agreed to a deal at market—Friday's closing price of $18.75—and considering that Wachovia's stock had jumped 29 percent that day on the back of the TARP news, Cohn thought it was a generous concession.

But then he wound up for his big pitch: To complete the deal, he said, Goldman would need the government to guarantee, or ring-fence, Wachovia's entire portfolio of ARM option mortgages—all $120 billion worth.

Warsh stopped Cohn in midsentence. "We're just not prepared to do that," he said. "We can't look as if we're just writing a blank check." Warsh, who was still championing the idea of a merger, explained that they needed to think about the "optics" of the deal. He suggested that if they structured it so that Goldman would take a first loss on the deal—in the same way

that JP Morgan had agreed to accept the first $1 billion of losses at Bear
Stearns before the Federal Reserve would step in and guarantee the next
$29 billion—the government might well consider acting as a backstop.

———

As several of Wachovia's board members milled about a Goldman conference room, waiting to get some feedback on the deal from Steel, Joseph
Neubauer, the chairman and chief executive officer of ARAMARK Holdings Corporation, looked down at his cell phone, which was buzzing. It
was Paulson.

Neubauer knew Paulson well; Goldman had been ARAMARK's banker,
taking it public and private a handful of times and making Neubauer—and
the firm—millions of dollars. But Neubauer felt this was a risky call. Paulson, he thought, was not supposed to involve himself with anything related
to Wachovia or Goldman, and here he was phoning him in the midst of
perhaps the most transformative transaction either might ever pursue.
Paulson had phoned Neubauer the day before to gauge whether a deal
would ever be workable, but that had just seemed like an exploratory call.
Now they were in the heat of negotiations. Paulson justified making the
call because he wasn't speaking directly with Steel, but Neubauer worried
that in practical terms it seemed like a meaningless distinction.

"This is not just about Goldman Sachs," Paulson told him. "I'm concerned about Wachovia. Aren't you concerned?"

Paulson hadn't told Neubauer that he had received an ethics waiver to
get involved with matters relating to Goldman. Instead, he just continued
to press him to take the Goldman bid seriously, worried that Wachovia's
board did not appreciate the severity of the situation in the world economy.
"I think there should be a sense of urgency," Paulson instructed him.

When Neubauer put the phone down, he looked up at the other board
members.

"You're not going to believe this. That was Hank."

He didn't need to explain to the directors why the call was so surreal.
To many in the room, the Treasury secretary had just ordered them to
merge with Goldman.

———

At Treasury, Jim Wilkinson, Paulson's chief of staff, was by now practically
sleepwalking down the halls. Paulson had just updated him on the Gold-

man-Wachovia talks and asked him for his counsel. Should the government provide assistance? Wilkinson, in his stupor, said he thought that it sounded like a reasonable idea.

But a half hour later, after a cup of coffee and further reflection, Wilkinson changed his mind. He realized that such a deal would be a public relations nightmare at the worst possible time, just as they were trying to pass TARP. Paulson would lose all credibility; he would be accused of lining the pockets of his friends at Goldman; the "Government Sachs" conspiracy theories would flourish.

Wilkinson ran back into Paulson's office with Michele Davis.

"Hank, if you do this, you'll get killed," Wilkinson said frantically. "It would be fucking crazy."

———

Ben Bernanke was being piped in over the Polycom speakerphone in Geithner's conference room, where Jester and Norton from Treasury and Terry Checki, Meg McConnell, and William Dudley from the New York Fed were gathered around a conference table.

Warsh was reviewing the new terms of the Goldman-Wachovia agreement. Steel and Cohn had come back to him with a slight revision to the previous proposal, allowing for Goldman Sachs to take the first $1 billion of losses, per Warsh's suggestion. Cohn and Steel said they were committed to completing the deal that afternoon if the government would agree to provide assistance. The boards of both companies had been put on standby.

The general view in the room seemed to be that it was a good transaction: It would give Goldman a stable deposit base at the same time it provided Wachovia with a powerful investment bank and top-notch management.

But Geithner was quick to point out its drawbacks. "Does it make Goldman look weaker than they are?" he asked—the same question that Blankfein had raised earlier in the day. Geithner also wondered whether the Fed should be the one loaning the money. Since Wachovia's regulator was the FDIC, perhaps it ought to be the one to bear that burden.

Checki couldn't believe the gall of Goldman's request. "They're still driving these negotiations as though they have leverage," he said. But he opposed the merger for a different reason: He was concerned that neither side had enough time to make a thoughtful decision, referring to the situation as "the shotgun wedding syndrome."

Bernanke listened to the debate without comment.

Then Bill Dudley, a former Goldman man himself who thought the deal was unattractive for the government, also raised the same objection that Buffett had raised just hours earlier: It would prove a public relations disaster for the government.

"What are we doing here? Look at all of the connections you've got: Treasury and Steel and me. Goldman is everywhere. We have to be careful."

After Geithner and Bernanke called Paulson, all three agreed they just couldn't support the deal.

———

When Warsh delivered the news to Steel and Cohn, both men were flabbergasted. They had spent the last twenty-four hours trying to formulate an agreement at the behest of the government and were now being told it could not be carried out.

"I'm sorry, I understand, I'm just as frustrated as you are, we just don't have the money, we don't have the authorization," Warsh explained.

Steel, feeling particularly slighted, told Warsh that he felt as if he were running from one bride to another, trying to find the right marriage to save his firm. First Morgan Stanley, and now Goldman Sachs.

Cohn, realizing that the conversation was about to get testy, said, "I think I should step out."

"No, you should listen to this," Steel insisted, raising his voice for the first time. "You should sit here and listen to every goddamn word of this."

Anxiously talking into the speakerphone in the center of the table, Steel became even more irate. "What do you want me to do? Tell me what to do. You can't make this work, you don't like this, you don't like that. Do you want to do the Midtown deal?" he said, referring to Morgan Stanley. "Do you want me to call Citi? I've got to protect my shareholders. That's my job. Just tell me what the fuck you want me to do, because I'm tired of running in circles."

———

"I don't know if it's true, but we're hearing Goldman is announcing a deal with Wachovia in the next twenty-four hours," John Mack announced to the management team gathered in his office. He had just learned of the rumor from a director at the meeting with his board and was distressed by the possibility. After all, it had been only Friday that they were in merger negotiations that didn't seem to be going anywhere.

Taubman, the firm's head of investment banking, was horrified. *How could Goldman Sachs, Morgan Stanley's most bitter rival, be willing to take on all of Wachovia's toxic assets?* he thought to himself. *Hasn't Goldman seen the massive hole in Wachovia's balance sheet?* Then it dawned on him. "Those fuckers probably have a deal with the government!" he exclaimed to the group. "It makes no sense unless the government is bailing out Wachovia and taking back a bunch of bad assets!"

———

Paulson had gotten word that the Goldman-Wachovia deal was off, which put even more pressure on him to find a solution for Morgan Stanley. To him, JP Morgan was the obvious answer. While Jamie Dimon might have been resisting Paulson's overtures—Paulson had pressed the case with him several times already over the past day—Paulson now needed to apply some serious pressure.

"Jamie," Paulson said when he reached him, conferencing in Geithner and Bernanke. "I need you to really think about buying Morgan Stanley. It's a great company with great assets."

Dimon had just finished having an impromptu meeting with Gao of CIC, who had come to see him to explore whether JP Morgan would be willing to work together on a bid for Morgan Stanley, with CIC buying additional equity in the firm and JP Morgan providing a credit line. But the meeting hadn't gone anywhere.

Dimon, who had been anticipating that the government might try to foist the deal on him, was adamant.

"You've got to stop. This is not doable," he said intently. "It's not possible. I would do anything for you and for this country, but not if it's going to jeopardize JP Morgan.

"Even if you gave it to me, I couldn't do it," Dimon continued, explaining that he thought the deal would cost the bank $50 billion and countless job losses.

"I don't want to do it, and John doesn't want to do it," Dimon told him.

"Well, I might need you to do it," Paulson persisted.

Andrew Ross Sorkin

A few moments of silence passed until Dimon relented, but only slightly. "We'll consider it, but it's going to be tough," he said.

———

The tension inside Morgan Stanley's board meeting was becoming untenable. Roger Altman, the banker from Evercore who had been hired just twenty-four hours earlier to advise them, was telling them that they needed to think hard about selling the entire firm. He had painted a doomsday scenario, and it wasn't sitting well with several directors in the room, who had become convinced that Altman was trying to get them to do a deal simply so that he could collect a big fee.

During a break, Roy Bostock spoke with C. Robert Kidder, the firm's lead director: "We ought to fire that guy right now. Get him out of here. He is not helping." Others were concerned that given his close ties to the government—he was the former deputy Treasury secretary and was still considered very well connected—that he might leak information about the firm's health back to them. That, they thought, would explain why Geithner was putting so much pressure on Mack to do a deal. Though they did not know it, Altman had sent an e-mail to Geithner the night before telling him that he had gotten the assignment to work for Morgan, but he had not disclosed any of the details of the meeting.

Whether it was paranoia or just a lack of sleep, the discussion was becoming heated. Mack, who hadn't been consulted when Altman was hired, was even more upset about his being there than some of the board members. "I don't trust him," Mack announced after he kicked Altman out of the board meeting temporarily. He said he thought they should be using Morgan Stanley's own bankers to advise them if they really were going to sell the firm. He also told them he was worried about revealing the details of Morgan Stanley's negotiations with Mitsubishi in front of Altman, reminding the directors that Evercore had a partnership with Mizuho Financial Group of Japan, one of Mitsubishi's rivals.

"I don't know what this guy is up to," he said.

———

Geithner, still holding court from his office downtown, had become convinced that Morgan Stanley would fail if it didn't complete a deal by the time the markets opened on Monday. He had threatened Mack earlier in the day that he would deny his request to become a bank holding company unless he found a sizable investment or merged. "Being a naked bank holding company won't do it," he warned. Like Paulson, Geithner thought Mack was misguided in his belief that Mitsubishi would come through for them in time. "What's your Plan B? You need a Plan B," he had nearly screamed into the phone.

Not everyone at the Fed was in agreement with Geithner's insta-merger strategy, however. So unpopular was Geithner's single-mindedness about merging banks that afternoon that some CEOs began referring to him as "eHarmony," after the online dating service. "If we sell one more of these guys for a dollar," Kevin Warsh complained, "this whole freakin' thing is going to come undone."

———

At about 3:30 p.m., John Mack's assistant, Stacie Kruk, announced that Secretary Paulson was on the line. Mack took the call on the phone next to his couch. The New York Giants versus the Cincinnati Bengals game was playing on the TV behind him.

"Hi, John. I'm on with Ben Bernanke and Tim Geithner. We want to talk to you," Paulson said.

"Well," Mack said, "since you're all on the line, can I put my general counsel on?"

Paulson agreed, and Mack hit the speakerphone button after the television was muted.

"Markets can't open Monday without a resolution of Morgan Stanley," he said in the sternest way he knew. "You need to find a solution, we want you to do a deal."

Mack just listened, dumbstruck.

Bernanke, who was usually remote and silent in such situations, cleared his throat and added, "You don't see what we see. We're trying to keep the system safe. We really need you to do a deal."

"We've spent a lot of time working on this and we think you need to call Jamie," Geithner insisted.

"Tim, I called Jamie," Mack replied, clearly exasperated. "He doesn't want the bank."

"No, he'll buy it," Geithner said.

"Yes. For a dollar!" Mack exclaimed. "That makes no sense."

"We want you to do this," Geithner persisted.

"Let me ask you a question: Do you think this is good public policy?" Mack asked, clearly furious. "There are thirty-five thousand jobs that have been lost in this city between AIG, Lehman, Bear Stearns, and just layoffs. And you're telling me that the right thing to do is to take forty-five thousand to fifty thousand people, put them in play, and have twenty thousand jobs disappear? I don't see how that's good public policy."

For a moment, there was silence on the phone.

"It's about soundness," Geithner said impassively.

"Well, look, I have the utmost respect for the three of you and what you're doing," Mack said. "You are patriots, and no one in our country can thank you enough for that. But I won't do it. I just won't do it. I won't do it to the forty-five thousand people that work here."

With that, he hung up the phone.

———

At Goldman Sachs the mood was slightly less tense. "We're getting bank holding company," Blankfein, having just spoken with Geithner, announced as Cohn walked into his office. "It's going to happen." When the Federal Reserve faxed over the draft of the press release, he could see that one other institution, which was purposely left blank, would be granted the same status. *That must be Morgan Stanley*, he thought. His Friday-morning call to Mack must have worked.

Cohn, sitting down on Blankfein's couch, picked at an omelet, having not touched food all day. He could finally smile. They were finally out of the woods. Now all they needed to do was have the directors sign off on the execution of the application. They had set up a conference call with the entire board to start in five minutes.

When everyone was assembled on the line, Blankfein began, "I've finally got good news . . ."

———

When Gao returned to Morgan Stanley late that afternoon, he learned that the firm was engaged in merger talks with Mitsubishi. He had thought something was amiss earlier, because Mack had slowed down the negotiations, but he couldn't believe Mack was about to do a deal with the Japanese! He thought the U.S. government had already blessed an agreement with CIC, based on Paulson's conversation with Vice Premier Wang Qishan the night before. Furious, he pulled his entire team from

the conference room and marched out of the building without even saying good-bye.

———

The Morgan Stanley bankers were still waiting to find out if the Mitsubishi deal was a go. The Fed, they had learned, was going to grant them
bank holding company status, but Geithner was still insisting the firm
needed a big investment by Monday as a show of confidence in the company. Mitsubishi had sent over a proposal, a "letter of intent," to buy up
to 20 percent of the firm for as much as $9 billion. But Taubman and
Kindler knew that all they were getting was a letter; it wouldn't be an
ironclad contract, as they couldn't get a full deal turned around quickly
enough. But they were just hoping investors in the market would take
the Japanese at their word and have more faith in them than Paulson or
Geithner had.

As Kindler and Taubman were reviewing the letter, they laughed at all
the news coverage about their weekend of whirlwind merger talks. Various media outlets had the news backward or were reporting old rumors.
Gasparino declared on television that Morgan Stanley was about to do a
deal with either Wachovia or CIC. "The most fucking dangerous man on
Wall Street," Kindler sighed.

Upstairs Mack was on the phone with Mitsubishi's chief executive,
Nobuo Kuroyanagi, and a translator, trying to nail down the letter of
intent.

His assistant interrupted him, whispering, "Tim Geithner is on the
phone; he has to talk to you."

Cupping the receiver, he said, "Tell him I can't speak now, I'll call him
back."

Five minutes later, Paulson called. "I can't. I'm on with the Japanese,
I'll call him when I'm off," he told his assistant.

Two minutes later, Geithner was back on the line. "He says he has to
talk to you and it's important," Mack's assistant reported helplessly.

Mack was minutes away from reaching an agreement.

He looked at Ji-Yeun Lee, a banker who was standing in his office helping with the deal, and told her, "Cover your ears."

"Tell him to get fucked," Mack said of Geithner. "I'm trying to save my
firm."

———

"Thank God. We're out!" Jamie Dimon exclaimed as he ran across JP Morgan's executive floor into Jimmy Lee's office, where the management team had camped out, waiting for their next orders as they bided their time watching the Ryder Cup and the New York Giants game, chowing down on steaks from the Palm.

"Mack just called," Dimon said, breathing a sigh of relief. "They got $9 billion from the Japanese!"

———

At 9:30 p.m., the news hit the wires. Goldman Sachs and Morgan Stanley would become bank holding companies. It was a watershed event: The two biggest investment banks in the nation had essentially declared their business model dead to save themselves. The *New York Times* described it as "a move that fundamentally reshapes an era of high finance that defined the modern Gilded Age" and "a blunt acknowledgment that their model of finance and investing had become too risky."

CHAPTER NINETEEN

O n Monday, September 22, the day after Goldman Sachs became a bank holding company, Lloyd Blankfein, his face puffy with exhaustion, sat staring at a framed cartoon from Gary Larson's *The Far Side* on his office end table. The drawing features a father and son standing in their suburban front yard and gazing over a fence at their neighbor's house, where a line of wolves is in the process of entering the front door. "I know you miss the Wainwrights, Bobby," the caption reads, "but they were weak and stupid people—and that's why we have wolves and other large predators."

To Blankfein that pretty much summed up what had just happened to Wall Street: Had things worked out slightly different, Morgan Stanley, and perhaps even Goldman Sachs, could have ended up just like the Wainwrights.

Of the Big Five investment banks, his own and Morgan Stanley were the last ones standing, but Goldman's footing seemed increasingly unsteady. As the day wore on, Goldman's stock price, unlike Morgan Stanley's, was not stabilizing but continuing to plunge, falling 6.9 percent. Despite its having been designated a bank holding company—giving it virtually unlimited access to liquidity from the Federal Reserve—investors had suddenly become worried about whether Goldman would need more capital.

After rising for two days the week before on hopes that TARP would save the economy, the broader market also was now moving again in the wrong direction. As investors had begun digesting the plan, they had come to realize that Paulson was going to have to do a better job of selling it if it was, as he intended, to renew confidence in the economy. To many Americans who had suffered substantial losses in their 401(k) plans, Wall

Street simply didn't deserve to be saved. "It would be a grave mistake to say that we're going to buy up a bad debt that resulted from the bad decisions of these people and then allow them to get millions of dollars on the way out," Barney Frank bellowed the day before. "The American people don't want that to happen, and it shouldn't happen."

But the politics of the bailout was hardly a subject that was at the top of Blankfein's mind, given the more pressing concern of raising capital. He had assigned that task to Jon Winkelried, his co-president, who had put together a team over the weekend to reach out to potential investors in China, Japan, and the Persian Gulf. But their approach was scattershot, and they received only polite refusals from all of their potential targets.

On Monday night Byron Trott, wondering why there had been no news from New York, called Winkelried from his office in Chicago.

"It's been way too quiet since the weekend. What's going on?" he asked apprehensively.

Winkelried told him that they were going to begin another round of calling investors on Tuesday with a new proposal to sell shares in the firm. With the market still seesawing, he said, he didn't expect they'd be able to raise money from a single large source; given the conditions, it would have to come in smaller amounts from dozens of institutional investors.

"Hold on," Trott interrupted him. "You guys, you have to slow down here."

Trott, who was the firm's closest—and perhaps only—conduit to Warren Buffett, suggested that they consider approaching him one more time. Since the previous Thursday, Trott had gone to Buffett with a number of different proposals to invest in Goldman, but the ever-circumspect financier had declined them all. Blankfein had encouraged Trott to propose a standard convertible preferred deal, in which Buffett would receive preferred shares with a modest interest rate, which could be converted into common shares at about a 10 percent premium to Goldman's current stock price. But, as Trott had correctly predicted, there wouldn't be enough upside to interest the Oracle. "In a market like this there's no reason I can take the risk," Buffett told Trott.

On Tuesday morning, after consulting with Blankfein and the rest of the senior Goldman team, Trott called Buffett again with a new proposal.

Buffett's grandchildren were visiting Omaha, and as he was planning to take them to the local Dairy Queen (a chain owned by Berkshire), the conversation lasted no more than twenty minutes. Trott knew the only way Buffett would be willing to make an investment would be if he were offered an extraordinarily generous deal, which he now presented: Goldman would sell Buffett $5 billion worth of stock in the form of preferred shares that paid a 10 percent dividend. This meant that Goldman would be paying $500 million annually in exchange for the investment; Buffett would also receive warrants allowing him to buy up to $5 billion of Goldman shares in the future at the price of $115 a share, about 8 percent lower than their price that day. With those terms Goldman would be paying an even greater amount than what Buffett had asked of Dick Fuld back in the spring, a sum that Fuld had seemingly rejected.

Relying on his gut, as always, Buffett quickly agreed to the outlines of the deal. Trott called Winkelried, reaching him just as he emerged from the Grand Central terminal on his way to the United Nations, where President Bush was scheduled to address the Sixty-third General Assembly, to tell him the good news.

"I think Warren will do this!" Trott said excitedly.

"Okay, stay where you are," Winkelried told him. Trying to find a quiet spot on the congested, noisy sidewalks outside Grand Central, Winkelried called the office to set up a conference call with Goldman's brain trust— David Viniar, Gary Cohn, David Solomon, and Blankfein, who had flown down to Washington for the day for meetings with lawmakers.

Minutes later the group was assembled, and they began to discuss the Buffett deal. Just as important as the infusion of cash, they agreed, was the confidence that a Buffett investment would inspire in the market. Indeed, Winkelried said, the firm would be able to raise additional money from other investors on the back of Buffett's investment.

"Well, why wouldn't we do it?" Viniar wondered.

"We're done," Solomon said.

Trott immediately set up a call for Blankfein to speak directly with Buffett, and after the two briefly reviewed the transaction, Buffett suggested that Goldman get the papers in order and send them to him, so they could announce the deal that afternoon after the market closed.

Blankfein, who always liked to review every last detail, asked, "Would you like me to just do a download for you on things that I'm concerned about?"

"No, it's okay," Buffett replied calmly. "If I were worried, I wouldn't be doing this at all." With that he rounded up his grandchildren and headed for Dairy Queen.

Back at Broad Street, however, there was still one provision that troubled the group, a provision that Buffett had indicated would be a deal breaker: Goldman's top four officers could not sell more than 10 percent of their Goldman shares until 2011, or until Buffett sold his own, even if they left the firm. He had explained his rationale for this condition to Blankfein by saying, "If I'm buying the horse, I'm buying the jockey, too."

That stipulation would not be an issue for him, Cohn, or Viniar, Blankfein knew, but it would be a problem for Winkelried. Only forty-nine years old, he had recently been making noises about leaving Goldman and, while it was a secret within the firm, he was having his own personal liquidity crisis. Although Winkelried was debt-free, he was quickly running out of cash. Despite making $53.1 million in 2006 and about $71.5 million in 2007, most of it was in stock; in the meantime, he had been spending extraordinary sums. While he owned a 5.9-acre waterfront estate on Nantucket that he was preparing to put up for sale for $55 million, his real cash drain was Marvine Ranch, a horse farm he owned in Meeker, Colorado. Winkelried was a competitive "cutter" rider, and while the farm had won more than $1 million in prize money over the previous three years, it cost tens of millions of dollars to operate.

Blankfein called him personally and, after assuring him that the firm would help him find a way out of his financial troubles, Winkelried agreed to Buffett's condition. He was unhappy with the restriction, but he knew that the Buffett deal was best for Goldman.

By the next morning Goldman had managed to sell an additional $5 billion of shares to investors on the news of the Buffett deal, and its stock rose more than 6 percent.

Blankfein could finally relax. The wolves were no longer at the door.

———

"Josh, I cannot believe this is happening!" Paulson shouted into his cell phone at Josh Bolten, the White House chief of staff and the man who had helped hire him. "No one checked with me on this. Ah, and, if we are going to keep doing bullshit like this, you, ah, you are going to need a new Treasury secretary!"

Paulson, who had just concluded an entire afternoon of hearings on the Hill trying to persuade skeptical lawmakers to pass his TARP legislation, had just learned that John McCain, the Republican candidate for president, had announced that he was suspending his campaign to return to Washington to help work on the financial rescue plan. The crisis, which seemed only to be deepening, was now becoming part of the tactics of the presidential elections.

To Paulson, as depressed as he was exhausted, it was just the latest reminder of the uphill battle he faced in getting his legislation approved. McCain's return, he feared, would only galvanize the House Republicans opposed to the rescue proposal. If the Bush administration had no control over its presidential candidate—let alone the party itself—Paulson knew he was in trouble.

As Paulson paced in an anteroom at the Rayburn House Office Building, Bernanke, who had accompanied him to the hearings, became so uncomfortable with the tone of his conversation with Bolten that he left the room. He was hardly accustomed to officials screaming at each other, and worse, he couldn't abide the bare-knuckled behind-the-scenes fighting that is a staple of politics, especially in an election year.

In truth, support for TARP—which Joshua Rosner, a managing director at Graham, Fisher & Company, told the *New York Times* should stand for "Total Abdication of Responsibility to the Public"—was quickly waning in both parties. Democrats charged that it was a way for Paulson to line the pockets of his friends on Wall Street, while Republicans denounced it as just another example of government intervention run amok. Congressmembers on both sides of the aisle complained about the cost of the plan, with some questioning if it could be made in installments and others seeking to include limits on executive compensation in any legislation.

"What they have sent us is not acceptable," Christopher Dodd declared. "This is not going to work." Jack Kingston, a Republican congressman from Georgia, went so far as to publicly criticize Paulson as "a terrible communicator," complaining, "We're being asked to vote on the major piece of legislation of our lifetimes, and we haven't seen the bill."

Beyond the rhetoric, however, lawmakers as well as investors were starting to raise practical questions about how the process of buying troubled assets would actually work. How would the government pay for them? How would the prices be determined? What if certain parties wound up profiting at the expense of the taxpayers?

When Stephen Schwarzman, who had encouraged Paulson to announce a plan—any plan—finally saw the details of this one, he called Jim Wilkinson to get a message to Paulson.

"You announced the wrong plan!" Schwarzman told him.

"What do you mean?" Wilkinson asked.

"You won't practically be able to figure out a way to buy these assets in a short period of time to provide liquidity to the system without either screwing the taxpayers or screwing the banks," Schwarzman warned him. "And you won't be able to force people to sell!" He explained that most bank CEOs would prefer to leave their bad assets on their books at depressed prices rather than have to realize a huge loss. "And," he added, "each package of these assets is so highly complex that it's not like bidding for a bond; you have to do a lot of in-depth analysis, and that takes weeks to months, and meanwhile, if you do nothing for weeks to months, you're going to go back into crisis."

———

At around 4:00 p.m. on Thursday, September 25, leaders of both parties and of the relevant committees crowded around the large oval mahogany table of the stately Cabinet Room of the White House, joined by the presidential candidates, senators McCain and Obama. Seated at the middle of the throng were the president, Vice President Cheney, and Hank Paulson. The group had been assembled in an attempt to persuade House Republicans, who had been emboldened by McCain, to rejoin the negotiations and agree on a bailout.

"All of us around the table take this issue very seriously, and we know we've got to get something done as quickly as possible," Bush told the group. "If money isn't loosened up, this sucker could go down," he warned, referring to the nation's economy.

But the meeting quickly degenerated from a promising effort to reach a consensus into a partisan fracas after the House Republican leader, John Boehner of Ohio, announced that House Republicans would not support the bailout, but would instead propose an alternative that would involve insuring mortgages with a fund paid for by Wall Street. When Democrats protested that such a plan would do nothing to address the current crisis, arguments erupted throughout the room, followed by finger-pointing and shouting, a spectacle that Cheney sat watching with a smile.

Obama, in an attempt to reach a compromise, asked, "Well, do we need to start from scratch, or are there ways to incorporate some of those concerns?" But by then it was too late for any effort to find a middle ground, and the meeting ended with the various factions leaving the room without speaking to one another.

As the deflated Treasury team made their way to the Oval Office a staffer stopped to inform Paulson that the Democrats were gathering in the Roosevelt Room across the corridor.

"I need to find out what they're doing," Paulson mumbled, disappearing before some of the staff even realized he was no longer with them.

He marched into the middle of the scrum of Democrats, who were furious at the House Republicans' campaign to undermine the rescue plan. Paulson could see that it was only moments away from collapsing.

To break the tension, he went down on one knee before House speaker Nancy Pelosi.

"I beg you," he said in a heartfelt plea, backed by a chorus of chuckles from the congressmembers, "don't break this up. Give me one more chance to bring these people in."

Pelosi tried to repress a smile at the sight of the towering Treasury secretary genuflecting before her and, looking down at him, quipped, "I didn't know you were Catholic."

———

At 4:00 a.m. on Friday morning, Vikram Pandit, Citigroup's CEO, was puttering around his Upper East Side apartment, catching up on his e-mail. He had gotten only a few hours of sleep, having arrived home late after spending the day at the Wharton School in Philadelphia, where he had given a lecture in which he told the audience, "You have been great at picking exactly the right time to be at school."

His in-box was almost full, with e-mail traffic among his inner circle sharing the latest news: Hours earlier the Federal Deposit Insurance Corporation had swooped in to seize Washington Mutual, which held more than $300 billion in assets—making it the biggest bank failure in the nation's history. The FDIC had already run a mini-auction for WaMu, the largest of the savings and loans, requesting best bids a day before its announcement, just in case. The FDIC typically conducts seizures of troubled banks on Friday evenings, to allow regulators time over the following weekend to ready the institution to open under government oversight on Monday. But WaMu was deteriorating so rapidly—nearly $17 billion had been withdrawn in ten days—that the regulators had no choice.

Pandit, who had himself submitted an early bid for WaMu, learned that his rival, Jamie Dimon, had won the auction, paying $1.9 billion.

As Pandit made his way through the stream of e-mails, one from Bob Steel of Wachovia caught his eye. He knew that Steel had called his office earlier that week, and he imagined he knew the purpose of that call: Steel was probably interested in selling the firm. To Pandit, Wachovia was an attractive purchase because of its strong deposit base, which Citi, despite its mammoth size, lacked. But he knew instinctively that he would be interested in such a deal only if he could buy the company on the cheap.

"I'm sorry, I've been away," Pandit e-mailed Steel at 4:27 a.m. "But I'm back, call any time."

Minutes later, Steel, who was also awake, phoned him.

Having been abandoned at the altar the previous weekend by Goldman Sachs and Morgan Stanley—and with Kevin Warsh still pressuring him—Steel was eager to line up as many options as possible, suspecting that the upcoming weekend could well turn into another merger sprint. He had also reached out to Dick Kovacevich at Wells Fargo, whom he had run into in Aspen the previous weekend, and had scheduled a breakfast with him at the Carlyle Hotel on Sunday morning.

If everything worked out the way he hoped, he might well be able to set up an auction.

After the fiasco of Thursday's meeting, Paulson and the White House agreed that they needed to do everything possible to resume the talks on the bailout. "Time," Paulson warned Josh Bolten, "is running out."

By 3:15 p.m. on Saturday, September 27, Paulson and his Treasury team were heading down the hall of the Hill's Cannon House Office Building to conference room H-230, where they would meet with congressional leaders one more time, in hopes of fashioning a compromise.

Kashkari, in a huddle with the Treasury team before the gathering, reminded everyone that the biggest hurdle they faced was that Congress did not truly appreciate the severity of the economy's problems. "We've got to scare the shit out of the staff," he said, echoing Wilkinson's instruction to Paulson earlier in the week. "Let's not talk about the legislation," he urged, and suggested instead that they focus on the potentially devastating problems they would all face if the legislation wasn't passed.

When Paulson arrived in the conference room, which was across from Pelosi's office, he took note of the presence of Harry Reid, Barney Frank, Rahm Emanuel, Christopher Dodd, Charles Schumer, and their staffs; only the speaker herself was absent.

To underscore the significance and sensitive nature of the meeting, an announcement was made that all cell phones and BlackBerrys would be confiscated to avoid leaks. A trash can was used as a receptacle for the dozens of mobile devices labeled with congressional staffer names on yellow Post-Its.

As the meeting came to order, Paulson, following Kashkari's playbook, announced darkly, "You saw what happened earlier this week with Washington Mutual," and, with as much ominousness as he could muster, added, "There are other companies—including large companies—which are under stress as well. I can't emphasize enough the importance of this."

The stern-faced lawmakers listened attentively but immediately raised what they considered to be four major obstacles to the plan: oversight of the program, which the Democrats felt was severely lacking; limits on executive compensation for participating banks, a controversial provision that Paulson himself was convinced would discourage them from participating; whether the government would be better off making direct investments into the banks, as opposed to just buying their toxic assets; and whether the funds needed to be released all at once or could be parceled out in installments.

"Damn it," Schumer thundered, annoyed that he couldn't get a straight answer. "If you think you need $700 billion right away, you'd better tell us."

"I'm doing this for you as much as for me," Paulson replied, blanching at Schumer's aggressive tone. "If we don't do this, it's coming down on all our heads."

The conversation soon turned to executive compensation. While everyone in the room was aware of the potential political fallout over huge bonuses being paid out by firms requiring taxpayer rescue, it was Max Baucus, chairman of the Senate Finance Committee, who spoke to the issue. He made it abundantly clear that he was furious with Paulson for not having insisted on strict limits on compensation for the managements of banks that would take advantage of the program. In Baucus's view the executives should be entitled to next to nothing—and at the very minimum they should be forced to give up golden parachutes and other perks.

As Baucus railed on, raising his voice until he was virtually shouting at the Treasury staff, Paulson finally interrupted him with, "Let's not get emotional," and tried to explain his rationale. The reason he was loath to put in executive compensation limits, he said, was not because he wanted to protect his friends but because he believed the measure was impractical. Banks, he said, would have to renegotiate all of their compensation agreements, a process that could take months, preventing them from accessing the program.

Paulson's efforts to calm the group's nerves with practical reasoning, however, didn't appear to be working; other congressional leaders rushed in to express their own outrage, focusing now on the lack of oversight and accountability. While the three-page piece of legislation he had originally submitted the week before had since grown in size, it still contained little in the way of any watchdog provisions to guarantee that the program would be maintained properly. Paulson had been resisting the Democrats' demands to appoint a panel that would not only oversee the program, but also have the authority to determine how it operated and made decisions, as he feared that it would inevitably become politicized. "All we're talking about is having Groucho, Harpo, and Chico watching over Zeppo," said Frank to laughter.

The conversation dragged on into the night, as the staffers from Treasury and Congress tried to find a middle ground, with only the same sticking points raised again and again.

"It's impossible for us to go to hundreds of banks across the country and have them renegotiate all their employment contracts," Kashkari said, reiterating why they couldn't include more compensation curbs. "It's just going to take too long; it's impossible. So if they have golden parachutes, physically we can't do it."

One of Schumer's staffers proposed a different approach. "Well, why don't you just block new golden parachutes?"

"We hadn't thought of that," Kashkari admitted sheepishly.

It was the eureka! moment that finally seemed to break the impasse the group had reached. For the first time in days it appeared that with a few other compromises they could be near agreement on the terms of a deal. While the Democrats had backed down on the oversight component, they could console themselves with a victory of sorts on the executive compensation issue.

As his staffers continued to perform shuttle diplomacy among the various factions, trying to find some language on which they could finally settle, Paulson, looking deathly pale, retreated to Pelosi's office.

"You want us to go get the Hill doctor?" Harry Reid asked.

"No, no, no," Paulson said groggily. "I'll be fine."

Hurriedly pulling a trash can before him, he began having dry heaves.

———

Bob Steel and his lieutenant, David Carroll, entered the elegant Art Deco lobby of the Carlyle Hotel at 8:00 on Sunday morning, making their way to the elevators and to the suite of Dick Kovacevich, the chairman of Wells Fargo.

With the TARP legislation still publicly unresolved, Steel and Carroll had come to see Kovacevich in hopes of convincing him to buy Wachovia. For Steel it was an especially bitter pill to swallow; having left Treasury only two months earlier to become the CEO of the firm, he was now resigned to selling it. Much like AIG's Bob Willumstad, he simply had no good options available to him. Any attempt to turn around Wachovia in this environment, with its portfolio of subprime loans falling even more every day, was going to be increasingly difficult. Steel felt a deep sense of responsibility to find a buyer quickly, to obtain some value out of the business before the winds turned against him completely.

He was also under particular time pressure from the fact that both Standard & Poor's and Moody's had threatened to downgrade the firm's debt the following day. A downgrade could put even more pressure on the bank, whose stock had fallen 27 percent on Friday, further eroding confidence among customers, who had withdrawn some $5 billion that same day.

In his effort to encourage an auction, Steel had met with Pandit on Friday and Saturday, but the night before had received the bad news: Like Goldman Sachs the prior weekend, Citigroup would only buy the firm with government assistance, and even then Pandit said he was prepared to pay only $1 a share for it.

As Steel and Carroll sat down for breakfast in Kovacevich's suite, he could only hope he was going to get a more encouraging reception.

Kovacevich, a handsome sixty-four-year-old with silver just beginning to shade his temples, had built Wells Fargo into one of the best-managed banks in the country, establishing it as the dominant franchise on the West Coast and attracting Warren Buffett's Berkshire Hathaway as his largest single shareholder.

After a waiter poured coffee for the group, Kovacevich, who had flown from his home in San Francisco to New York expressly for this meeting, said he was very interested in making a bid for Wachovia without any government assistance and hoped to do so by the end of the day. But, he warned, in the straight-talking manner for which he was known, "This is not going to have a 'two-handle' in front of it."

Steel smiled. "Listen, Dick, let's not worry about price now," he replied, satisfied that even while Kovacevich was rejecting a $20 offer, his interest was sufficient that Steel would likely end up with a final number in the teens. "Let's see how this deal works, and once we know how it looks there will be a price that makes sense," he added.

Kovacevich said that his team would continue its due diligence, and he hoped to be able to get back to him later that day.

Steel, still smiling as he left the hotel, called his adviser, Peter Weinberg, and reported, "It was a good meeting. I think."

———

Sitting in his office Sunday morning Tim Geithner, habitually running his fingers through his thick hair, pondered his alternatives.

He had spoken to Citigroup the day before, when they had laid out a plan to buy Wachovia in concert with the U.S. government. The bank would assume $53 billion of Wachovia's subordinated debt and would cover as much as $42 billion of losses on its $312 billion portfolio; anything beyond that the government would absorb. In return for that protection, Citi would pay the government $12 billion in preferred stock and warrants. Geithner had always liked the idea of merging Citigroup and Wachovia, which he viewed as an ideal solution to each party's problems: Citigroup needed a larger deposit base and Wachovia clearly needed a larger, stronger institution. Even so, Geithner was still hopeful that Wells Fargo would pull through and be able to reach a deal without government involvement.

But now, having just gotten off a conference call with Kevin Warsh and Jeff Lacker of the Federal Reserve of Richmond, which regulates Wachovia, he had a new problem: Despite Kovacevich's indication to Steel just that morning that he wanted to reach an independent agreement, Kovacevich had called and stated that if he had to conclude the deal before Monday, he didn't feel comfortable moving forward without government assistance. He was too unsure of the firm's marks and couldn't take the risk.

There was now within the government a de facto turf battle over Wachovia, given the involvement of Richmond, with Warsh and Geithner playing deal makers. And Sheila Bair at the FDIC had yet to take part: If Wachovia really were to fail, it would be her jurisdiction.

Geithner and Warsh set up a conference call to coordinate their efforts with Bair, the fifty-four-year-old chairwoman of the FDIC and one of their least favorite people in government. They had always regarded Bair as a showboat, a media grandstander, a politician in a regulator's position whose only concern was to protect the FDIC, not the entire system. She was not, in their view, a team player. Geithner would frequently commiserate about Bair with Paulson, who shared a similar perspective about her. At times, Paulson had a genuine respect for her. "She comes to play," he regularly said to his staff, but added, "When she is surrounded by her people, when she's peacocking for other people or she's worried about the press, then she's going to be miserable."

Bair, who had just ended a conversation with Warren Buffett (who she was hoping could help her track down Wells Fargo's president, John

Stumpf), joined a conference call late Sunday with Geithner, Warsh, and Treasury's David Nason. Paulson, who was barred from talking to Steel, had tried to disentangle himself from this particular matter, expending his energy instead on TARP and receiving only irregular updates on the negotiation's progress from Nason.

When Geithner suggested Bair should help subsidize any deal for Wachovia, she resisted the proposal firmly, stating in a lengthy soliloquy that the only way she would get involved was if she were to take over the bank completely and then sell it.

When she finished, there was an awkward silence. "Right, right, right," Geithner said, almost mocking Bair.

Geithner countered that allowing the FDIC to take over Wachovia would have the effect of wiping out shareholders and bondholders, which he was convinced would only spook the markets. He was still furious with Bair for the way she had abruptly taken over Washington Mutual, which had had a deleterious effect on investor confidence. Given Paulson's ongoing public efforts to support the banking system, he told her, that option was a nonstarter. Then Geithner, looking for another jar of money, asked Nason if Treasury could contribute to the effort, which could eventually amount to more than $100 billion.

"We're still trying to get TARP passed," Nason replied briskly. "We can't be committing money."

———

At 7:00 p.m., Bob Steel, waiting in a conference room at Sullivan & Cromwell's Midtown offices, got a disturbing call from Kovacevich, who had been inexplicably out of touch for the past two hours and who had sounded oddly detached during their previous call.

Kovacevich now announced that he wasn't prepared to move forward without government assistance. "We don't make these kinds of loans, so we don't understand them," he explained. Steel, dumbfounded, thanked him, ended the call, and slumped down in his chair, wondering how he could have been rejected again. Citigroup was still on the sidelines, but he doubted they would raise their bid, especially if there was no competition. When he told his inner circle about the call with Kovacevich, he described it as "not an attractive fact."

At around 8:00 p.m., Rodgin Cohen heard a rumor that Citigroup had been talking to the FDIC, which only led him to suspect that Citi was trying to orchestrate an FDIC takeover of Wachovia, one similar to the deal that JP Morgan had made for Washington Mutual. Furious, he rang Ned Kelly, upon whom Pandit relied for strategy. Only days before, Kelly had been appointed head of global banking for the bank's institutional client business in a reshuffle that saw the departure of Sallie Krawcheck, who had once been one of the most powerful women on Wall Street.

"Okay, we need to talk," Cohen began testily.

"Rodge, look, I wasn't in touch with them, they just called me," a defensive Kelly insisted. "I still have the same deal on the table."

When Steel learned of their conversation he knew that he was, for all practical purposes, out of options, for Warsh had made it clear the bank couldn't open Monday without a deal. In a last-ditch plea to remain independent, he called Sheila Bair at 12:30 a.m. with a proposal: Would the FDIC consider guaranteeing some of Wachovia's most toxic assets in exchange for warrants in the bank?

At 4:00 a.m. Steel got the answer he had been dreading. Bair phoned to notify him that his bank had been sold to Citigroup by the government for $1 a share. The FDIC wouldn't be completely wiping out shareholders, she said; she had succumbed to pressure from Geithner and agreed to guarantee Wachovia's toxic assets after Citigroup accepted the first $42 billion of losses, declaring that the firm was "systemically important."

Paulson stood alone in his office, watching the congressional coverage of his bailout bill on C-SPAN. After some additional compromise on Sunday, legislation had been drafted that was acceptable to all the parties and was now being put to a vote.

Pelosi, standing on the floor of the House, had just given an impassioned speech about the need to pass the bill, but had also used the moment as an opportunity to assail the Bush administration, Paulson, and Wall Street. "They claim to be free market advocates, when it's really an anything-goes mentality," she said of the Bush administration. "No regulation, no supervision, no discipline. And if you fail, you will have a golden parachute, and the taxpayer will bail you out. . . . The party is over in that respect. Democrats believe in a free market. We know that it can create jobs, it can create wealth, it can create many good things in our economy. But in this case, in its unbridled form, as encouraged, supported, by the Republicans—some in the Republican Party, not all—it has created not jobs, not capital; it has created chaos."

Although a few members of Paulson's staff were loitering nervously outside his office, afraid to go in, Michele Davis had no such qualms and joined him, the two of them intently following the tally of yeas and nays at the bottom of the screen. Paulson expected the bill to pass without a problem, as the markets had already priced in its approval. Five minutes into the allotted fifteen-minute voting window, however, the number of nay votes began to rise consistently. He knew that the measure was still very unpopular with House Republicans, as well as with a number of liberal Democrats, and lawmakers facing tight reelection races did not want to give their opponents any ammunition with just five weeks before election day. There was still time, however, for Pelosi and the Democratic leadership to turn the vote around.

"They wouldn't have brought this bill to the floor if they didn't think it could pass, if they didn't have the votes lined up somewhere," Davis reassured him. Paulson said nothing and only continued to stare at the screen as the margin of no votes grew wider and wider.

Kevin Fromer, Treasury's legislative liaison, called anxiously from outside the House chamber. "This is going to fail."

"I know," Paulson mumbled dully. "I'm watching."

Finally, at 2:10 p.m., after an unusually long period of forty minutes to count the votes, the gavel came down: The bailout was rejected 228 to 205. More than two thirds of the Republican representatives had voted against it, as had a large number of Democrats. Traders and investors had been watching the coverage also and started a frantic wave of selling. Stock prices plunged, with the Dow Jones Industrial Average tumbling 7 percent, or 777.68 points, its biggest one-day point drop ever.

For a moment Paulson was speechless. His plan, which he believed might be the most important piece of legislation he could ever propose—his effort at avoiding a second Great Depression—had failed. As his staffers, seeking to comfort him and one another, silently gathered in his office, he said simply, "We've got to get back to work."

Within an hour he and his team were at the White House, meeting with the president in the Roosevelt Room and discussing plans for how to revive the bill.

Downstairs in the Treasury building, however, Dan Jester and Jeremiah Norton had their own ideas about the problem Paulson was facing. They had convinced themselves that the concept of buying up toxic assets was never going to work; the only way the government could truly make a difference would be to invest directly in the banks themselves. "This is crazy," Norton said of the TARP proposal as he walked into David Nason's office. "Do we really think this is the right approach?" Jester and Norton had made the case to Paulson before, but the politics of using government money to buy stakes in private enterprises, they knew, had gotten in the way. And once Paulson had gone public with his current plan it seemed as if it would be difficult for him to reverse course.

"If you feel that strongly, you need to tell Hank," Nason said to him. "You can tell him I'm onboard with you."

The next day Jester and Norton went to visit with Paulson. They laid out their case: Buying the toxic assets was too difficult; even if they ever figured out how to implement the program, it was unclear whether it would work. But by making direct investments in the banking system, Jester told him, they'd immediately shore up the capital base of the most fragile institutions. They would not have to play guessing games about how much a particular asset was worth. More important, Jester argued, most of these banks eventually would regain their value, so the taxpayer would likely be made whole. And, Jester continued, the current TARP proposal actually allowed Treasury to use it to make capital injections, even if it hadn't been advertised as such.

Paulson, who had become somewhat disillusioned with the time it was taking to design and implement TARP, was starting to come around to Jester's way of thinking. He had no idea how he'd sell it to the American public, and he knew that it would be anathema to the Bush administration, but he also knew it might be the most practical solution in a sea of bad options.

"Okay," he sighed. "Why don't you work something up? Let's see what this would look like."

———

As the sky grew dark, Bob Steel climbed the steps of Wachovia's corporate jet at Teterboro Airport in New Jersey to head back to Charlotte. He had spent virtually the entire week in back-to-back meetings with Citigroup to coordinate the details of the merger, which they planned to herald in a full-page newspaper ad on Friday, declaring: "Citibank is honored to enter into a partnership with Wachovia . . . the perfect partner for Citibank." While he was frustrated with the paltry final price of the deal, he was proud to have at least saved the firm from failure, and he knew that he had explored every possible option in trying to do so.

The government-orchestrated deal had been announced on Monday morning, but it still needed to be formally "papered over," and in the meantime, Citigroup was keeping Wachovia alive by loaning it $4.9 billion. A number of details were still to be worked out, but they expected to have a signed agreement within the next day. Steel had spent that afternoon at Citigroup discussing the postmerger fates of the most senior Wachovia executives. Before he left he had shaken hands with Pandit. "Looks like we're done," Pandit had said gladly.

As Steel's plane taxied down the runway his BlackBerry rang. It was Sheila Bair. "Hi, have you heard from Dick Kovacevich?"

"No, not since Monday morning," a puzzled Steel answered; the Wells Fargo CEO had called then to offer his congratulations on the deal with Citi. "Why?"

"I understand that he's going to be making a proposal for $7 in stock for the entire company—no government assistance."

"Wow," Steel replied, quickly trying to assess the ramifications of the surprise offer for his firm. Had Wells Fargo just jumped Citigroup's bid? Was the government, which had blessed the original deal, now reversing itself? "Sheila, I'm about to take off any second," he apologized. "You should call Jane Sherburne," he added, referring to Wachovia's general counsel.

Sometime after 9:00 p.m., just minutes after Steel's plane landed in Charlotte, Kovacevich phoned with the pitch that Bair had outlined earlier. Having just spoken with Sherburne and Rodgin Cohen, Wachovia's outside counsel, Steel had been instructed by them not to say anything that would indicate acceptance or rejection of the offer.

"I look forward to seeing the proposal," Steel told Kovacevich, and a minute later he received an e-mail with a merger agreement already approved by the Wells board.

It was as if Christmas had come early. Steel couldn't believe his luck: A deal at $7 a share, up from $1 a share—and without government assistance.

He called his office and scheduled an emergency board meeting by telephone for 11:00 p.m. Before the board call, Steel had a strategy discussion with Cohen. While he owed it to Wachovia shareholders to take the highest bid, he also recognized that he already had a deal with Citigroup— a deal that had kept the firm from failing. The term sheet that Wachovia had signed with Citigroup included an exclusivity provision that prevented the firm from accepting another offer.

"I'm going to be sued by somebody," Steel told Cohen.

"Pick your poison," Cohen replied drily.

To both of them, however, it was clear that there really was no choice: The board had to accept the higher bid and take its chances with a suit from Citigroup. Steel and Cohen realized that Wells Fargo had made its bid because of a little-noticed change in the tax law that had occurred on Tuesday, the day after the Citigroup deal. The new provision would allow Wells Fargo to use all of Wachovia's write-downs as a deduction against its own income, thus enabling the combined bank to save billions in future taxes.

Wachovia's board voted to accept the deal just after midnight. The Wells offer was for the entire company; it gave shareholders more; and it was clearly the deal preferred by regulators. (Citigroup's deal, while worth only $1 a share, would have left behind several Wachovia subsidiaries that could have additional value—possibly several dollars a share worth—but a precise number would have been difficult to determine.) It was after 2:00 a.m. by the time Wachovia's board had fairness opinions from advisers Goldman Sachs and Perella Weinberg, who had been on opposite sides of the negotiating table just a week before.

Steel called Kovacevich to tell him the news, and then dialed Bair's

BlackBerry, which she had instructed him to call instead of her home number so as not to wake her children.

"We're all approved," he told her.

"All right," Bair said, sounding relieved. "We will have to call Vikram first thing in the morning."

"Sheila, we're not waiting until the morning," Steel said resolutely. "We've done this; we've approved it. I think we have to call him now. I don't want him hearing this when he wakes up from someone else."

"You should do it," she said equally firmly.

"I think you should be on the phone, since you married us," he replied.

With Bair on the line, Steel conferenced in Jane Sherburne, and then he called Pandit, not surprisingly waking him.

"Bob, what's going on?" he asked groggily.

"Well, there's been an important development," Steel said carefully. "I'm on the phone with Sheila and Jane. Do you need a moment?"

"No, I'm fine," Pandit said, collecting himself. "What is it?"

"We received an unsolicited proposal from Wells Fargo for the entire company of Wachovia, $7 a share, no assistance, and a Wells Fargo board–approved doc that we've accepted. We think this is the right thing to do."

"Well, that's interesting," Pandit answered, a bit taken aback. "A better bid? Let me call Ned. Let's work with you, and let's see what we can do and get this thing resolved."

"No, no. You don't understand," Steel interrupted, pausing for a moment. "I've signed it already."

There was silence on the other end of the line. If Pandit hadn't been completely awake before, he was now. When he resumed speaking he was irate, the full force of Steel's news having registered with him.

"We have a deal! You know you can't do this, because we actually have an exclusive arrangement with you. You are not allowed to sign." Pandit, frustrated, appealed to Bair. "Madame Chairwoman?"

"Well, I can't get in the way of this," Bair replied, in her most official tones.

"This isn't just about Citi," Pandit explained to her. "There are other issues we need to consider. I need to speak to you privately."

Steel agreed to leave the conversation, and as soon as he hung up Pandit began pleading with Bair. "This is not right. It's not right for the country, it's just not right!"

But the decision, she made it abundantly clear, was final.

———

Stock prices were surging before the House began voting on the bailout bill for a second time on the afternoon of Friday, October 3. Its passage was eased after the Senate version of the legislation added a number of tax breaks that were otherwise due to expire. Another popular addition increased the amount in individual bank accounts insured by the FDIC to $250,000 from $100,000. What had begun as a three-page draft was now more than 450 pages of legislative legalese, which the Senate had approved after sundown on Wednesday.

Many of the House Democrats and Republicans who had opposed the measure on Monday had since been persuaded to switch their votes—some by appeals from the two presidential candidates or from the president, some by the added provisions in the bill, and others by the mounting signs that the financial crisis was dragging the economy down into a deep recession. A recent report indicated that 159,000 jobs had been lost in September, the fastest pace of monthly job cuts in more than five years. Stocks had slid sharply that week, and both the takeover of Washington Mutual and the desperate jockeying to secure a partner for Wachovia revealed that not only Wall Street was in trouble.

In the final House tally, thirty-three Democrats and twenty-four Republicans who had voted against the bill on Monday now approved it. That afternoon, President Bush signed the Emergency Economic Stabilization Act of 2008, which created the $700 billion Troubled Assets Relief Program, or TARP. "We have shown the world that the United States will stabilize our financial markets and maintain a leading role in the global economy," the president declared.

Of course, what none of the congressmembers nor the public knew was that TARP was being completely rethought within Treasury, as Jester, Norton, and Nason began developing plans to use a big chunk of the $700 billion to invest directly in individual banks.

Jester had flown back to his home in Austin for a brief respite, but he was constantly on his BlackBerry with Norton going over their various options. Norton and Nason, told by Treasury's general counsel, Bob Hoyt, that they could not hire an outside financial adviser because of the inherent conflicts, made a series of outbound calls to Wall Street bankers on an informal basis to bounce various ideas off them about how to implement a capital injection program. Their call list included a cast of characters that had become well known to them through the recent spate of weekend deal making: Tim Main and Steven Cutler of JP Morgan, Ruth Porat of Morgan Stanley, Merrill Lynch's Peter Kraus, and Ned Kelly of Citigroup, among others. They intentionally did not call anyone from Goldman Sachs, concerned that the conspiracy theory rumor mill was already in overdrive.

Norton and Nason asked them all the same questions: How would you design the program? Should the government seek to receive common or preferred shares in exchange for their investment? How big a dividend would banks be willing to pay for the investment? What other provisions would make such a program attractive, and what provisions would make it unappealing?

But Jester, Norton, and Nason knew they had precious little time to complete their planning. Even with TARP approved, the markets did not immediately respond by stabilizing. The Dow Jones Industrial Average, which had been up as many as 300 points before the start of the voting, closed down 157.47 points, or 1.5 percent. After the Wells Fargo deal for Wachovia was revealed, shares of Citigroup fell 18 percent, their sharpest decline since 1988. For the week, the Standard & Poor's 500 stock index was down another 9.4 percent.

———

"I'm the ugliest man in America," Dick Fuld, beside himself in a mix of sadness and anger, privately acknowledged to his team of advisers before they strode into a congressional hearing in Washington on Monday, October 6, that had been called to examine the failure of Lehman Brothers. The markets remained in turmoil, falling another 3.5 percent despite the passing of TARP, as investors continued to question whether the program would actually work.

As he entered, spectators were waving pink sign with handwritten scrawls proclaiming JAIL NOT BAIL and CROOK, and in case Fuld didn't fully comprehend how he was perceived, John Mica, a Republican congressman, announced, "If you haven't discovered your role, you're the villain today. You've got to act like a villain."

For the past several weeks Fuld had been in a depression deeper than any he'd ever experienced, pacing his home in Greenwich at all hours, taking calls from former Lehman employees who wanted either to scream at him or to cry. He continued to go to the office, but it was unclear even to him what he was doing there. He was, however, sufficiently self-aware to finally comprehend what had happened and to perceive the full extent of the vitriol that was now being directed at him. He wanted to be defiant, but he found he couldn't. He was at times saddened and angry—angry at himself, and increasingly angry at the government, especially at Paulson, whom he saw as having saved every firm but his. His beloved Lehman Brothers had died on his watch.

He now said as much to the congressmembers. "I want to be very clear," Fuld told the committee. "I take full responsibility for the decisions that I made and for the actions that I took." He added, "None of us ever gets the opportunity to turn back the clock. But, with the benefit of hindsight, would I have done things differently? Yes, I would have."

But his audience had little use for his contrition, peppering him instead with questions about his compensation. "Your company is now bankrupt, and our country is in a state of crisis," Representative Henry Waxman said. "You get to keep $480 million. I have a very basic question for you: Is that fair?"

"The majority of my stock, sir, came—excuse me, the majority of my compensation—came in stock," Fuld replied. "The vast majority of the stock I got I still owned at the point of our filing." In truth, while he had cashed out $260 million during that period, most of his net worth was tied up in Lehman until the end. His shares, once making him worth $1 billion, were now worth $65,486.72. He had already started working on plans to put his apartment and his wife's cherished art collection up for sale. It was a telling paradox in the debate about executive compensation: Fuld was a CEO with most of his wealth directly tied to the firm on a long-term basis, and still he took extraordinary risks.

As he spoke he struggled to gain any measure of empathy from his listeners, suggesting, "As incredibly painful as this is for all those connected to or affected by Lehman Brothers, this financial tsunami is much bigger than any one firm or industry." He also expressed his great frustrations—with hedge funds for spreading baseless rumors, with the Federal Reserve for not allowing him to become a bank holding company over the summer, and ultimately with himself.

For a moment, as his testimony was winding up, he looked as if he was about to break down, but he steadied himself, as he had done at home virtually every day prior to the hearing. The room fell silent as the congressmembers leaned forward in their chairs, waiting for him to speak.

"Not that anybody on this committee cares about this," Fuld said, putting his notes aside and surprising even his own lawyer by speaking so extemporaneously, "but I wake up every single night wondering, *What could I have done differently?*" On the verge of tears, he added, "In certain conversations, *what could I have said? What should I have done?* And I have searched myself every single night."

"This," he said gravely, "is a pain that will stay with me for the rest of my life." And, he continued, he was baffled by why the government went to extraordinary steps to save the rest of the system but hadn't done the same for Lehman.

"Until the day they put me in the ground," he said, as everyone in the chamber hung on his words, "I will wonder."

———

That Monday afternoon Hank Paulson received a private four-page, typed letter from his friend Warren Buffett. They had spoken over the weekend about Paulson's current predicament—namely, that even though his TARP plan had been approved by Congress, it was not passing muster on Wall Street, where investors were beginning to worry that it would be ineffectual. Paulson had confided in him that he was considering using TARP to make direct investment in banks. Buffett told him that before he went down that path, he had some ideas about how to make a program to buy up toxic assets work that he would put in a letter, which he said would spell out both the problems with the current plan and a solution.

In the letter, Buffett, perhaps one of the clearest and most articulate speakers on finance, first explained the shortcomings of Paulson's current plan:

"Some critics have worried that Treasury won't buy mortgages at prices close to the market but will instead buy at higher 'theoretical' prices that would please selling institutions. Critics have also questioned how Treasury would manage the mortgages purchased: Would Treasury act as a true investor or would it be overly influenced by pressures from Congress or the media? For example, would Treasury be slow to foreclose on properties or too bureaucratic in judging requests for loan forbearance?"

To address those problems, Buffett proposed something he called the "Public-Private Partnership Fund," or PPPF. It would act as a quasi-private investment fund backed by the U.S. government, with the sole objective of buying up whole loans and residential mortgage–backed securities, but it would avoid the most toxic CDOs. Instead of the government's doing this on its own, however, he suggested that it put up $40 billion for every $10 billion provided by the private sector. That way the government would be able to leverage its own capital. All proceeds "would first go to pay off Treasury, until it had recovered its entire investment along with interest. That having been accomplished, the private shareholders would be entitled to recoup both the $10 billion and a rate of interest equal to that received by Treasury." After that, he said, profits would be split three fourths to investors, one fourth to Treasury. His idea also had a unique way to protect taxpayers from losing money: Put the investors' money first in line to be lost.

Buffett said he was so excited about this structure that he had already spoken to Bill Gross and Mohamed El-Erian at PIMCO, who had offered to run the fund pro bono. He had also been in touch with Lloyd Blankfein, who had likewise offered to raise the investor money on a pro bono basis. Finally, Buffett added, "I would be willing to personally buy $100 million of stock in this public offering," which, he explained, "constitutes about 20 percent of my net worth outside of my Berkshire holdings."

After reading the letter, Paulson was intrigued. He was still starting to lean in favor of injecting capital directly into the banks, but he thought maybe a program modeled after portions of Buffett's proposal could be feasible as well. Paulson called Kashkari into his office; he had just named him interim assistant secretary for financial stability that morning, putting him in charge of the TARP plan. The appointment was already generating a firestorm, with accusations that Paulson was once again favoring his former Goldman Sachs employees. (At Goldman, meanwhile, none of the senior management seemed to know who Kashkari was, and some of them asked their assistants that morning to look though the computer system to find out.)

Paulson handed Kashkari Buffett's letter. "Call him."

———

"It is clearly a panic, and it's a panic around the world," John Mack, having flown to London, was telling his employees at their headquarters on Canary Wharf the morning of Wednesday, October 8. "So you think back how the regulators have done and what they have done—could they get ahead of this—you know it's pretty hard because you really didn't know how bad it was until it got worse…."

The stock market was cratering yet again amid renewed panic that the banking system—and the economy as a whole—were about to suffer further setbacks. Mack, who had gone to London in part to have dinner with his newest investors from Mitsubishi, was under perhaps the most pressure. He was exhausted, having spent much of the past week living on airplanes. In the wake of China Investment Corp.'s hasty departure from Morgan Stanley's building after Gao found out the firm was about to do a deal with the Japanese, Mack flew to Beijing to try to repair relations. It was a diplomatic mission, intended to calm frayed nerves and to avoid what seemed as if it might turn into a minor international incident, given that Paulson had quietly gotten involved in the talks with the Chinese government originally. Just as important, CIC was still a large investor in Morgan Stanley, and Mack wanted to placate his foreign partners.

But for now, Mack wasn't interested in anyone's hurt feelings. He was glued to his stock price, which had fallen 17 percent the day before, as investors grew nervous that Mitsubishi might renege on its deal. After a week and a half of diligence and regulatory approvals, the investment still had not been finalized, and as Morgan Stanley's stock price continued to drop, questions were raised about whether Mitsubishi would be better off simply walking away from the agreement. All they had on paper was a term sheet—no better than what Citigroup had signed with Wachovia. And Federal Reserve requirements wouldn't allow the firms to complete the deal until Monday, leaving Morgan Stanley exposed to the gyrations in the stock market—and the possibility that Mitsubishi could pull out—until then.

Earlier that day Mitsubishi had released a statement in Tokyo saying: "We have been made aware of rumors to the effect that MUFG is seeking not to close on our proposed investment in, and strategic alliance with, Morgan Stanley. Our normal policy is not to comment on rumors. Nevertheless, we wish to state that there is no basis for any such rumors."

That was all Mack needed to know; he trusted the Japanese and wanted to be confident that they wouldn't withdraw. In his gut, however, he couldn't help but be anxious.

———

Hank Paulson was about to officially change his mind.

It was Wednesday, October 8, and Ben Bernanke and Sheila Bair were on their way to meet with him in his office at 10:15 a.m.

He had finally determined that Treasury should make direct investments in banks, sufficiently persuaded by a growing chorus both inside and outside of Treasury to do so.

"We can buy these preferred shares, and if a company becomes more profitable, you will get a share of that as well," Barney Frank said during a speech championing the idea of taxpayers becoming shareholders. Chuck Schumer was also in favor of the idea, stating, "When the market recovers, the federal government would profit."

But perhaps the greatest indication that the concept was feasible came from abroad: The United Kingdom had announced plans to invest $87 billion in Barclays, the Royal Bank of Scotland Group, and six other banks in an effort to instill confidence after a near Lehman-like meltdown confronted them. In exchange, British taxpayers would receive preferred shares in the banks (including annual interest payments) that were convertible into common shares, so that if the banks' prospects improved—and their shares rose—taxpayers would benefit. Of course, the plan was also a huge gamble, for the reverse was also true: If the banks faltered after the investment was made, a great deal of money stood to be lost.

Paulson and President Bush had been briefed by Gordon Brown on these plans on Tuesday morning at 7:40 by phone in the Oval Office. Now that the formal announcement had been made, Brown was being praised for his judgment to step in so decisively—often in favorable contrast to

Paulson. "The Brown government has shown itself willing to think clearly about the financial crisis, and act quickly on its conclusions. And this combination of clarity and decisiveness hasn't been matched by any other Western government, least of all our own," Paul Krugman, the economist and *New York Times* columnist, wrote days later.

With the G7 ministers scheduled to be in Washington for the long Columbus Day weekend, Paulson began to think that he should take advantage of the occasion to once and for all make a bold move to stabilize the system. Still, he knew it could be unpopular politically. After he broached the idea with Michele Davis a week earlier, she only looked at him with a sense of bafflement and remarked, "There's no way you're going to say that publicly."

Paulson had been discussing his shifting views with Bernanke, who had been a fan of capital injections from the start, and they were now in agreement. But they had been thinking about another program to go hand in hand with such an announcement: a broad, across-the-board program to guarantee all current and future unsecured debts of the banks. It would essentially remove any anxiety among investors who loan money to banks that they could ever get wiped out. By Bernanke's estimation, announcing capital injections and a broad guarantee would be an effective enough economic cocktail to finally turn things around.

But first they needed the money to effectuate such a guarantee program, which is where Bair came in. They felt that the FDIC was the only agency with such powers, and that the guarantee would fall within the agency's mission.

Paulson and Bernanke, sitting in Paulson's office, now walked Bair through the concept. The FDIC, they explained to her, would essentially be offering a form of insurance for which the banks would pay by being assessed a fee. The FDIC, Paulson argued, could even end up making money if the assessments outweighed the amount of payouts.

Bair instantly recoiled, doing the math in her head to assess the extraordinary strain such a guarantee could put on the FDIC's fund.

"I can't see us doing that," she replied.

———

Morgan Stanley's Walid Chammah woke up Saturday morning deathly afraid that his firm was going to go out of business. Its stock price had continued to fall, closing on Friday at $9.68—its lowest level since 1996. Hedge funds and other clients were again pulling money out. Dick Bove, an influential analyst at Ladenburg Thalmann, was comparing Morgan Stanley to Lehman Brothers and Bear Stearns. "The focus on Morgan Stanley is to change the ending," Bove wrote in a note to clients. "In sum, one must hold one's breath at the moment and hope that this is a different movie."

Chammah had canceled a talk he was scheduled to give at Duke's business school so he could stay in New York to try to shore up morale at the firm. That Friday he walked every floor in Morgan Stanley's headquarters, stopping to reassure fretful employees and giving a speech on the trading floor. "This firm has been around for seventy-five years and will be around for another seventy-five years," he proudly told the traders. To work his way down from the fortieth floor to the second took him three and a half hours. When he got back to his office he was emotionally drained, practically in tears.

It had been a difficult day for one other reason: Rumors were by now rampant that Mitsubishi was going to renege on its deal. No one at Morgan Stanley had received the slightest indication that they were even thinking of doing so—indeed, Mitsubishi had confirmed that they intended to honor the commitment—but the uncomfortable truth was that withdrawing might actually be the right business decision.

"They're going to recut. They just have to," Robert Kindler told Paul Taubman that afternoon. "When are they going to call? It's a no-brainer." They braced themselves for a call from Mitsubishi's adviser, Lazard.

And everyone inside Morgan Stanley knew what Mitsubishi's pulling out would mean: a run on the bank all over again, and, just possibly, the end of the firm.

With Mack flying back from London that day, it had been left to Chammah to hold the firm together in the face of that anxious speculation. His wife, who had been watching the financial news on television, called him at the office. "Are you okay?" she asked.

"I'm fine," he said serenely, trying not to betray his concern.

"You are too, *too* calm," she observed. "Are you taking Valium or something?"

Chammah had planned to go to Washington early on Saturday for a series of meetings with Mack and the G7 leaders, but decided to remain in New York throughout the morning in case there was any word from the Japanese. At noon, sufficiently satisfied that if they were going to drop the deal they would have contacted him by now, he headed to LaGuardia to hop a Delta shuttle. As he was walking down the Jetway, his cell phone went off. *Oh, shit,* Chammah thought, *here it comes.*

The call was indeed from Mitsubishi's banker, but to Chammah's surprise they reaffirmed their intention to go forward with the deal—but did add that they wished to renegotiate for more favorable terms that would give them preferred shares instead of common ones.

"Are you still prepared to close on Monday?" Chammah asked.

The answer was yes. A smile came over Chammah's face. For a moment, the deal maker in him injected, "Is there a reason for $9 billion? Could it be larger?" In other words, he was asking if, since they were reopening the negotiations anyway, Mitsubishi would like to buy even more of the firm. But he knew he was getting ahead of himself.

Rob Kindler, who had flown to Cape Cod, had just sent an e-mail to Ji-Yeun Lee back at the office. "Is all quiet?" he asked.

Two minutes later, he got the reply: "It was until an hour ago. Call me."

Kindler flew back to New York as Chammah and Taubman rounded up the troops. It was imperative that they find a way to close this deal by Monday.

By Sunday, they had revised terms—the deal had become more expensive for Morgan Stanley, but they were just happy to still have an investor. Mitsubishi would buy $7.8 billion of convertible preferred stock with a 10 percent dividend and $1.2 billion of nonconvertible preferred stock with a 10 percent dividend.

There remained one complicating factor: Monday was Columbus Day, and since banks in both the United States and Japan were closed, a normal wire transfer was not possible.

"How the fuck are we going to get this thing done?" Kindler, now back at headquarters, asked aloud.

Taubman had a thought: "They could write us a check," he said. Taubman had never heard of anyone writing a $9 billion check, but, he imagined, given the state of the world, anything was possible.

At 10:00 on Sunday morning, October 12, Hank Paulson, dressed casually, took his place at the table in the large conference room across from his office. The room was overflowing with the government's top financial officials and regulators. Ben Bernanke had arrived, as had Sheila Bair. Tim Geithner had flown down the day before to join the group. John Dugan, the comptroller of the currency, was present, as was Joel Kaplan, deputy chief of staff for policy at the White House. Paulson's inner circle—including Nason, Jester, Kashkari, Davis, Wilkinson, Ryan, Fromer, Norton, Wilson, and Hoyt—had also taken their seats, though some of them had to be "back-benched" in chairs against the walls, because there was no room for them around the table.

Paulson had called this meeting to coordinate the final details of a series of steps he had been working on to finally stabilize the system, and he wanted to go public with them. Sunday's meeting was the second such gathering of this group; many of them had met the day before at 3:00 p.m. to sketch out the outlines of the plan.

The multipart plan—which included the Treasury, Federal Reserve, and FDIC—was, as Paulson described it even that day, "unthinkable." Based on the work of Jester, Norton, and Nason, he wanted to forge ahead and invest $250 billion of the TARP funds into the banking system. The group had settled on the general terms: Banks that accepted the money would pay a 5 percent interest payment. Paulson had decided that if the amount was any higher, like the 10 percent cost that Buffett had charged Goldman, banks would be unlikely to participate. Still, the rate would eventually become more expensive, rising to 9 percent after the first five years.

Much of the debate about the program that morning was less about the numbers than the approach. "In the history of financial crisis in the U.S., you need to do three things: You need to harden the liabilities; you need to import equity; and you need to take out bad assets. This is one part of that plan," Geithner said, to sell the group on the need for capital injections.

He had suggested that the only way to make the program palatable to the weakest banks would be if the strongest banks accepted the money as well, "to destigmatize" participation in the program, and perhaps even mask the problems of the most endangered firms. Not everyone was in agreement on this point. "Let's not destroy the strong to convince the world that the weak aren't so weak," Bernanke commented. There was the issue of using the TARP money efficiently; if it was directed to otherwise healthy companies, that would mean less money would be available to those institutions that needed it most. Before the meeting Geithner had had a conversation on this same topic with Kevin Warsh, who told him the stigma argument was a red herring. "There's no fooling these markets. You aren't going to fool them into thinking that everybody is equally good, bad, or indifferent."

Still, Geithner, along with Paulson, quickly prevailed on the group that the only way the program could become effective would be if they could persuade the biggest banks—banks like Goldman Sachs and Citigroup—to accept the money. As they started sketching out a list of firms they wanted to persuade to sign up on day one, with plans to invite them to Washington on Monday to propose that they accept the investment, a question was raised about whether they should make the program available to insurance companies. David Nason suggested they invite MetLife to be a charter TARP participant.

"How are we going to do that?" Geithner asked.

"Well, you regulate them, Tim," Nason said, to knowing smiles in the room.

The debate about capital injections was playing out against the backdrop of Paulson's own ongoing worries about the fate of Morgan Stanley. He had been back and forth on the phone with Mack, who he knew was trying to clinch a renegotiated deal. But he had also learned that the Japanese had reached out to the Federal Reserve, seeking assurances that the U.S. government wasn't planning to come in and make an investment in Morgan Stanley after it did—fearing that if it did, it would wipe out all shareholders. When Warsh first called Geithner to tell him the news, his reaction was simple: "Fuck!" That afternoon they worked to write a letter to the Japanese government assuring them that Mitsubishi would not be negatively impacted any more than other shareholders by any future government intervention in the firm. Of course, Morgan Stanley was unaware of the government's plans—or the extent of the back-channel conversations taking place between the governments to orchestrate the deal.

Perhaps the biggest fireworks that weekend concerned the one unresolved portion of the plan that Paulson was still hoping to announce: the FDIC guarantee of all current and future unsecured debts of the banks and bank holding companies. He and Bernanke had had lengthy discussions with Bair about the subject. At first, she had offered a compromise: The FDIC would provide the guarantee, but only to banks—not bank holding companies—which left firms like Goldman Sachs and Morgan Stanley still exposed. But Bair seemed to be coming around; Paulson had put the full-court press on her, at one point taking her aside in his office and telling her, "I'll make sure you get the credit." For her part, she thought Paulson was under enormous political pressure to put the program into place, in part because a number of European governments were putting together similar facilities. The guarantee would end up being perhaps the largest—though an often overlooked—part of the program. It put the government on the hook for potentially hundreds of billions, if not more, in liabilities, providing the ultimate safety net for the banking system.

Nason and Paulson had been debating the guarantee issue all week. To Nason, it represented the "biggest policy shift in our history." He told Paulson, "This is an enormous decision. It must be debated in front of everyone so that everyone's nodding their heads in agreement."

At one of the meetings that weekend, Geithner, who supported the guarantee, debated the issue with Nason, who played devil's advocate but also had his own misgivings about the larger implications of the government's effectively providing an unlimited backstop for an entire industry.

Still, Geithner finally prevailed, and Bair agreed to the plan.

The final piece of business would be to coordinate how they could invite the banks to Washington and what would be the best way to encourage them to accept the TARP money. There was agreement that if they could assemble all the CEOs in one room, the peer pressure would be so great that they'd be inclined to go along with the proposal.

After deciding on a list of prospective banks, it fell to Paulson to call them. (He had gotten out of making the calls for the Lehman weekend, so it was his turn.)

At 6:25 p.m. he returned to his office and began reaching out. His message was simple. He would tell the CEOs to come to Washington, but he would do everything he could to avoid providing any specific details about the reason for the invitation.

Lloyd Blankfein, at a client dinner Sunday night at the Ritz-Carlton in Washington for the International Monetary Fund weekend, made eye contact with Gary Cohn, and they both walked to the corner of the room.

"Hank just called," Blankfein said in a hushed tone, "and told me I have to be at Treasury tomorrow at three p.m."

"For what?" Cohn asked.

"I don't know."

"What did he tell you?" Cohn said, confused.

"I pushed him, trust me, I pushed him," Blankfein replied. "The only thing he told me is I'd be 'happy.'"

"That scares me," Cohn said.

"I knew it would really warm the cockles of your heart," Blankfein said with a laugh.

———

Ken Lewis was in his kitchen at his home in Charlotte on Sunday night, getting ready for dinner, when Paulson called.

"Ken," Paulson said with no introduction. "I need you to come to Washington tomorrow for a meeting at three p.m."

"Okay," Lewis said. "I'll be there. What's this about?"

"I think you're going to like it," Paulson said, so vaguely that Lewis knew not to follow up.

———

At 7:30 a.m. on Monday, October 13, 2008, Rob Kindler was sitting in a conference room at Wachtell Lipton. He looked like hell, unshaven and still in his vacation khakis and flip-flops. He hadn't slept in at least a day. He had come to Wachtell to personally pick up the check that he understood Mitsubishi would be delivering. With John Mack in Washington, it was left to him to complete the deal. He was somewhat anxious, for even though Mitsubishi had agreed to all the terms of the deal, he had never seen a physical check with nine zeros on it. He didn't even know if it was possible. Maybe it would come as several checks?

Kindler was expecting a low-level employee from Mitsubishi to deliver the final payment when he learned from Wachtell's receptionist that a contingent of senior Mitsubishi executives, dressed in impeccable dark suits, had just arrived in the building's lobby and was on its way upstairs.

Kindler was embarrassed; he looked like a beach bum. He ran down the hall and quickly borrowed a suit jacket from a lawyer—but as he was buttoning the front he heard a loud tear. The seam on the back of the jacket had ripped in half. The Wachtell lawyers could only laugh.

Takaaki Nakajima, general manager for the Bank of Tokyo–Mitsubishi UFJ, along with a half dozen Japanese colleagues, arrived for what they thought was going to be a deal-closing ceremony.

"I didn't know you were coming," Kindler said apologetically to the bemused Japanese. "If I did, I would have had John Mack here."

Nakajima opened an envelope and presented Kindler with a check. There it was: "Pay Against this Check to the Order of Morgan Stanley. $9,000,000,000.00." Kindler held it in his hands, somewhat in disbelief, clutching what had to be the largest amount of money a single individual had ever physically touched. Morgan Stanley, he knew, had just been saved.

Some of the Japanese started snapping pictures, trying their best to capture the eye-popping amount on the check.

"This is an honor and a great sign of your faith and confidence in America and Morgan Stanley," Kindler said, trying to play the role of statesman in his disheveled state. "It's going to be a great investment."

As the Japanese group turned to leave, Kindler, grinning from ear to ear, tapped out a BlackBerry message to the entire Morgan Stanley management team at exactly 7:53 a.m.

The subject line: "We Have The Check!!!!!!"

The body of the message was two words:

"It's Closed !!!!!!!!"

CHAPTER TWENTY

"Secretary Paulson's office. Please hold," Christal West said into her phone from outside Hank Paulson's office.

It was only 8:00 a.m., but she was already overwhelmed with calls. Paulson's decision to invite the "Big 9" Wall Street firms to Washington, without giving them any hint of what the agenda might be, wasn't going over particularly well.

"Nick Calio just called me," she typed in an e-mail to Paulson's inner circle of advisers, referring to Citigroup's top lobbyist. "I told him what I told Thain's office—that he should come and that no other information would be given out ahead of time . . . and that everyone had confirmed their attendance with HMP last night."

Heather Wingate, another Citigroup lobbyist, was on the phone, likewise trying to determine the purpose of the meeting. She had just received an e-mail from her boss, Lewis B. Kaden, a vice chairman at Citigroup, asking her to "find out as soon as possible what Paulson's invite to VP [Vikram Pandit] for meeting at Treasury this afternoon is about? If this is a briefing of industry group, I don't think VP can go back to DC. If it is something else we need to know."

Ah, Pandit! Paulson's assistant knew just how her boss felt about him: He could be a difficult one.

Jeffrey Stoltzfoos, a senior adviser at Treasury, took Wingate's call, and immediately followed up with another e-mail to the team, complaining, "Apparently Vikram is trying to decide whether to come to DC or send someone in his place. I did not offer additional information to Heather, but I did let her know that we would call her or someone else within Citi to discuss."

Wall Street executives weren't the only ones who were confused invitees; the White House, too, was left out of the loop about the details of Paulson's summons. "Is it one meeting or nine meetings?" Joel Kaplan, White House deputy chief of staff for policy, asked Jim Wilkinson by e-mail.

The gathering "will be a large meeting but also expecting smaller break-out meetings to make the case," Wilkinson replied minutes later from his BlackBerry.

It fell on West to see to it that all went smoothly. This was perhaps the most important meeting in history that had ever been held at the Treasury Building, and she was the coordinator. She shot an e-mail message down to Stafford Via, a senior adviser at Treasury: "We do need to figure out logistics. I think we need someone down outside the gate and just inside the door to direct them up to the 3rd Floor. Also, we can use the small conference rooms and diplomatic reception room for hold rooms if needed."

She called the Secret Service to see if they would close down Hamilton Place, for with all the photographers expected to show up, the event could well turn into a zoo. She got a firm no.

At 9:19 a.m., she sent an e-mail to the assistants of all nine Wall Street CEOs, with instructions about what they should do after being dropped off at Fifteenth Street and Hamilton Place: "They should proceed on foot down Hamilton Place to the Gate to enter the building. They will need to show photo id (a driver's license would be fine)." As she raced through what she needed to get done, West realized that she was missing one last thing. She had gotten the Social Security numbers and dates of birth of everyone but Ken Lewis, which she needed to get him cleared through Secret Service. She tried his office three times, but when no one picked up she decided to call his home. "I just spoke with Mr. Lewis's wife and have his DOB and SSN," she wrote moments later to Lewis's assistant.

To almost no one's surprise but everyone's disappointment, news of the secret meeting started to leak. "I guess my invitation got lost in the mail," Cam Fine, president of the Independent Community Bankers of America, wrote to Jeb Mason, the handsome Texan who was the Treasury Department's liaison to the business community. "We do represent 5,000 banks with over one trillion in assets," he wrote, adding a smiley emoticon. "A little financial humor Jeb—laugh a little."

Despite West's best efforts, confusion still reigned. "Do you have a list of market participants attending the 3pm meeting?" Calvin Mitchell, head of communications for Geithner, wrote Wilkinson. "Are you guys confirming yet who's invited?"

Even an hour before the meeting the CEOs were still trying to sniff out what was really up. "Any ideas what the topics will be for the 3pm meeting with the CEOs?" Steven Berry, Merrill's government relations person, e-mailed Wilkinson. "Thain was asking. Also room number? I will see Thain in about 15 min."

A little after 2:00 p.m., Ben Bernanke, Tim Geithner, and Sheila Bair assembled in Paulson's office, their last chance to get on the same page before the big meeting. Paulson, his sleeves rolled up, took up in his usual chair in the corner, slumping just enough to suggest that he was pining for an ottoman. Geithner took the seat next to him; Bair settled on the blue velvet sofa; and Bernanke found a chair across from him. They were about to do what Paulson had been describing as "the unthinkable," and their tension in the face of it was evident. Paulson himself looked visibly pained.

"Okay," he said, "has everyone seen the talking points?" Paulson waved the printed page with its half dozen bulleted items before them all, and continued, "Let's run through this."

First, he explained, he would introduce everyone. Then, he said, he'd highlight the three pieces of the program: commercial paper; FDIC; and TARP, the acronym that would soon become synonymous with the word "bailout," and one that he clearly had a hard time saying.

"Then I'll hand it over to you guys," Paulson said, nodding in the direction of Bernanke and Geithner, who then rehearsed their lines about the commercial paper program. "From there, Sheila will take it," he instructed, still annoyed with her for all of her complaining the night before about the loan-guarantee program.

Finally, they got to the key provision: the equivalent of welfare checks, earmarked for the biggest banks in the nation.

Paulson read the talking point aloud: "To encourage wide participation, the program is designed to provide an attractive source of capital, on identical terms, to all qualifying financial institutions. We plan to announce the program tomorrow—and that you nine firms will be the initial participants. We will state clearly that you are healthy institutions, participating in order to support the U.S. economy."

They all knew that line was wishful thinking. Bernanke and Geithner had talked earlier in the day about whether the sum would be sufficient to sustain even one troubled bank, Citigroup, the nation's largest, let alone solve a full-fledged financial crisis. Geithner, for one, had been especially anxious that Citigroup, as he had been saying for weeks, "was next."

Then they got to the question that Geithner and Paulson had been debating all day: How forceful could they be? Geithner had prevailed upon Paulson earlier to make accepting the TARP money as close to a requirement for the participants as possible. "The language needs to be stronger," Geithner urged him. "We need to make clear that this is not optional," Paulson agreed.

The new talking-point language reflected Geithner's changes. "This is a combined program (bank liability guarantee and capital purchase). Your firms need to agree to both," it stated. "We don't believe it is tenable to opt out because doing so would leave you vulnerable and exposed."

Just to drive home the point, one of the talking points warned, "If a capital infusion is not appealing, you should be aware that your regulator will require it in any circumstance."

They had already tried to game out which of the CEOs would be resistant. Pandit might be tough, but he'd take it, Paulson thought. Dimon was in the bag. Blankfein might get snippy, but he wouldn't get in the way. Mack needed the money, so that should be easy. Lewis might put up a fight. The biggest wild card was Dick Kovacevich of Wells Fargo: Would he be the one to derail it?

Paulson recounted how much trouble it had been just trying to get him to show up. "I could hardly get him on the airplane," he told the group, who looked at him with a mixture of amusement and astonishment. "I just said, 'Listen, the secretary of Treasury, the chairman of the Fed, the FDIC want you here! You better get here!'" Everyone laughed, but got right back to business.

"David," Paulson said, pointing to David Nason, "will walk through the numbers." And Bob "will go over the comp issues," meaning the delicate conversation about the industry's famously extravagant way of compensating, or paying, its medium to big producers.

After that, Paulson explained, the plan was to sequester all the CEOs in separate rooms. "We let them think it over. They can talk to their boards. And we can answer their questions if they have them," he said. "And then we'll reconvene at 6:30 p.m."

"Let's hope this works," Paulson said encouragingly, as the group got ready to march down the hallway to, if not the biggest meeting of their careers, certainly the most historic.

Outside the Treasury building every attempt that had been made to keep tight control over the meeting had become moot. Jamie Dimon had arrived at 2:15 p.m., some forty-five minutes early, and casually ambled down Hamilton as the group of camped-out photographers snapped picture after picture. "He caught us off guard!" Brookly McLaughlin, one of the press staffers, wrote to her colleague, who was trying to coordinate the logistics from her BlackBerry. Ronald Logue of State Street Bank showed up ten minutes later; Robert Kelly of Bank of New York and Blankfein arrived at 2:43; then Mack and Pandit. At 2:53, Lewis was still missing. Christal West was getting nervous until he finally arrived, with five minutes to spare, sneaking in through Paulson's private entrance at the side of the building.

At 2:59 Christal West sent an e-mail to the group: "They're all in."

The centerpiece of the secretary's imposing conference room is a twenty-four-foot-long mahogany table buffed to a high shine, with a Gilbert Stuart portrait of George Washington looming over it from one side of the room and a portrait of Salmon P. Chase, the secretary of the Treasury during Lincoln's administration and the man responsible for putting the words "In God We Trust" on U.S. currency, from the other. Five chandeliers, lit by gas, hang from the vaulted rose-and-green ceiling. On the back of each of the twenty leather and mahogany chairs positioned around the table is the U.S. insignia in the configuration of the sign for the dollar.

The nine CEOs had already taken their seats, arranged alphabetically behind placards with their names, when Paulson, Geithner, Bernanke, and Bair entered. It was the first time—perhaps the only time—that the nine most powerful CEOs in American finance and their regulators would be in the same room at the same time.

"I would like to thank all of you for coming down to Washington on such short notice," Paulson began, in perhaps the most serious tone he had yet taken with them individually during the dramatic events of the previous weeks. "Ben, Sheila, Tim, and I have asked you here this afternoon because we are of the view that the United States needs to take strong, decisive action to arrest the stress in our financial system."

Blankfein, who was sitting directly across from Paulson, quickly turned solemn, while Lewis leaned forward to hear better.

"Over the recent days we have worked hard to come up with a three-part plan to address the turmoil," Paulson explained.

Just as they had rehearsed, Geithner and Bernanke now took the group through the new commercial paper facility, followed by Bair's explanation of the FDIC's plan to guarantee bank debt. Paulson saved the key announcement for himself.

"Through our new TARP authority, Treasury will purchase up to $250 billion of preferred stock of banks and thrifts prior to year-end," he said, with the gravity due the unprecedented measure. "The system needs more money, and all of you will be better off if there's more capital in the system. That's why we're planning to announce that all nine of you will participate in the program."

Paulson explained that the money would be invested on identical terms for each bank, with the strongest banks in the country taking the money to provide cover to the weaker banks that would follow suit. "This is about getting confidence back into the system. You're the key to that confidence."

"We regret having to take these actions," he reiterated, and in case there was any confusion, he underscored the fact that he expected them to accept the money whether they wished to or not. "But let me be clear: If you don't take it and you aren't able to raise the capital that they say you need in the market, then I'm going to give you a second helping and you're not going to like the terms on that."

The bankers sat stunned. If Paulson's aim had been to shock and awe them, the tactic had worked spectacularly well.

"This is the right thing to do for the country," he said in closing.

Geithner now read off the amount that each bank would receive, in alphabetical order. Bank of America: $25 billion; Citigroup: $25 billion; Goldman Sachs: $10 billion; JP Morgan: $25 billion; Morgan Stanley: $10 billion; State Street: $10 billion; Wells Fargo: $25 billion.

"So where do I sign?" Dimon said to some laughter, trying to relieve the tension, which had not dissipated now that the bankers had learned why they had been summoned.

At 3:19 p.m. Wilkinson, who was sitting in the back of the room after inviting himself to the meeting, got an e-mail on his BlackBerry from Joel Kaplan, who was desperate to give President Bush some intelligence. "Gimme quick update—how is the reaction?"

He didn't know how to reply, as the outcome was not at all certain.

Dick Kovacevich, for one, was obviously not pleased to have been given this ultimatum. He had had to get on a flight—a commercial flight, no less—to Washington, a place he had always found contemptible, only to be told he would have to take money he thought he didn't need from the government, in some godforsaken effort to save all these other cowboys?

"I'm not one of you New York guys with your fancy products. Why am I in this room, talking about bailing you out?" he asked derisively.

For a moment no one said a word, and then the room suddenly broke out in pandemonium, with everyone talking over one another until Paulson finally broke in.

Staring sternly at Kovacevich, Paulson told him, "Your regulator is sitting right there." John Dugan, comptroller of the currency, and FDIC chairwoman Sheila Bair were directly across the table from him. "And you're going to get a call tomorrow telling you you're undercapitalized and that you won't be able to raise money in the private markets."

Thain jumped in with his own question: "What kind of protections can you give us on changes in compensation policy?"

Although his new boss, Lewis, couldn't believe Thain's nerve in posing the question, it was nonetheless the one that everyone present wanted to ask. Would the government retroactively change compensation plans? Could they? What would happen if there was a populist outcry? After all, the government would now own stakes in their companies.

Bob Hoyt, Treasury's general counsel, took the question. "We are going to be producing some rules so that the administration will not unilaterally change its view," he said. "But you have no insulation if Congress wants to change the law."

Lewis, increasingly frustrated, could see the conversation needed to move along and stated, "I have three things to say. There's obviously a lot to like and dislike about the program. I think given what's happening, if we don't have a healthy fear of the unknown, then we're crazy."

Second, "if we spend another second talking about compensation issues, we've lost our minds!"

And finally, he said adamantly, "I don't think we need to be talking about this a whole lot more," adding, "We all know that we are going to sign."

Still, Kovacevich kept stirring in his seat. *This is practically socialism!*

As Bernanke cleared his throat, the room fell silent again.

"I don't really understand why there needs to be so much tension about this," he said in his professorial way. He explained that the country was facing the worst economy since the Great Depression and pleaded with them to think about "the collective good. Look, we're not trying to be intimidating or pushy. . . ."

Paulson gave him a look as if to suggest, *Yes, in fact, I am being pushy!*

John Mack, who had been sitting silently for most of the meeting, turned to Geithner and said, "Give me the paper." Taking a pen from his breast pocket he signed the document and, with a flick of his finger, sent it sliding back across the table. "Done," he exclaimed, thus unceremoniously certifying what Paulson hated calling a bailout.

"But you didn't write your name in," Geithner pointed out. "*You* write it in," Mack instructed, and Geithner penned the words "MORGAN STAN-LEY" in block letters at the top. "And you didn't put the amount in," Geithner protested.

"It's $10 billion," Mack replied nonchalantly.

Thain, looking at Mack in dismay, said, "You can't sign that without your board."

"No?" Mack replied. "My board's on twenty-four-hour notice. They'll go along with it. And if they don't, they'll fire me!"

Blankfein indicated that he, too, needed to speak with his board. "I don't feel authorized to do that on my own," he said, with everyone else agreeing that they, too, would need to go through proper channels.

Dimon stood up, walked to the corner of the room near the window, and decided that he was going to convene a board meeting by phone right then and there. He called his assistant, Kathy, and told her to get the directors on the line. The other CEOs dispersed to separate conference rooms to call their offices.

At 4:01 Wilkinson finally replied to Kaplan's e-mail. "We are there except for one," he wrote, referring to Wells Fargo. "This deal will get done."

Outside in the hallway, a huge grin was on Pandit's face. "We just got out. They're going to give us $25 billion, and it comes with a guarantee," he said into the cell phone, sounding as if he had just won the Powerball lottery.

Mack, having already signed the agreement, called Roy Bostock, one of Morgan Stanley's board members, hoping he could help calm the waters with the other directors over his impetuous decision.

"I want to give you a heads-up," he told him. "We're going to be having a board call in about twenty minutes or so. It's going to be to approve accepting $10 billion in TARP money," he said, before pausing. "But I already have."

Bostock knew what was being asked of him. "I understand. The board will not throw an ax in the wheel here."

When the Morgan Stanley call finally began, Bostock started by saying, "John, we didn't have any choice but for you to sign that. It was the right thing to do." Bostock called for a vote before there could be much discussion. "I'm in favor," he began.

In stark contrast, Dimon's tone when he spoke to his own board was bleak. "This is asymmetrically bad for JP Morgan," he said, whispering into his cell phone. In other words, the money would help the weaker banks catch up to them. "But we can't be selfish. We shouldn't stand in the way."

At 5:38, Bob Hoyt, while collecting the signed papers, shot an e-mail to the team, "On my way—that's 5 down, 4 to go."

Paulson, Geithner, Bernanke, and Bair sat in Paulson's office, waiting. With the exception of Kovacevich's grumbling, the meeting had gone well, much better than they had anticipated. They had effectively just nationalized the nation's financial system, and no one had had to be removed from the room on a stretcher. Paulson, running his fingers over his stomach, as he always did when he was deep in thought, still couldn't believe he had pulled it off.

Paulson had just gotten off the phone with Barack Obama—then the presidential front-runner—who had just finished up a speech about the economy in Toledo, Ohio, to tell him the news. He then tried John McCain, but couldn't get through.

At 6:23 p.m. Wilkinson wrote to the team, "8 out of 9 are in. . . . [S]tate [S]treet is just waiting on board. . . . [W]e are basically done."

Two minutes later, at 6:25 p.m., Wilkinson triumphantly reported the final tally from his BlackBerry: "We now have 9 out of 9."

Kaplan, at the White House, replied, "Awesome."

David Nason carried the signed papers down the hallway to Paulson.

Standing in the doorway of the secretary's office, Nason paused for a moment as Paulson and his half dozen senior staffers took a minute to appreciate the significance of the moment.

"We just crossed the Rubicon," he said.

EPILOGUE

In the span of just a few months, the shape of Wall Street and the global financial system changed almost beyond recognition. Each of the former Big Five investment banks failed, was sold, or was converted into a bank holding company. Two mortgage-lending giants and the world's largest insurer were placed under government control. And in early October, with a stroke of the president's pen, the Treasury—and, by extension, American taxpayers—became part owners in what were once the nation's proudest financial institutions, a rescue that would have seemed unthinkable only months earlier.

Wiring tens of billions of dollars from Washington to Wall Street, however, did not immediately bring an end to the chaos in the markets. Instead of restoring confidence, the bailout had, perversely, the opposite effect: Investors' emotions and imaginations—the forces that John Maynard Keynes famously described as "animal spirits"—ran wild. Even after President Bush signed TARP into law, the Dow Jones Industrial Average went on to lose as much as 37 percent of its value.

But there was another kind of fallout, too—one that had a far more profound effect on the American psyche than did the immediate consequences of the dramas being played out daily on Wall Street. In the days and weeks that followed the first payouts under the bailout bill, a national debate emerged about what the tumult in the financial industry meant for the future of capitalism, and about the government's role in the economy, and whether that role had changed permanently.

A year later such concerns remain very much at the forefront of the national conversation. As this book was going to press, a raucous public outcry, complete with warnings about creeping socialism, questioned the government's role not just in Wall Street, but in Detroit (since the bank rescue, the government also supplied billions of dollars in aid to two automotive giants, General Motors and Chrysler, to restructure in bankruptcy court) and in the health care system. Washington has also named an overseer, popularly known as a "pay czar," to review compensation at the nation's bailed-out banks.

One unexpected result of this new federal activism was that traditional political beliefs had been turned on their head, with a Republican president finding himself in the unaccustomed position of having to defend a hands-on approach. "The government intervention is not a government takeover," President Bush asserted on October 17, 2008, as he sought to counter his critics. "Its purpose is not to weaken the free market. It is to preserve the free market."

Bush's statement seemed to sum up the paradox of the bailout, in which his administration and the one that followed decided that the free market needed to be a little less free—at least temporarily.

In some respects, Hank Paulson's TARP was initially a victim of his own aggressive sales pitch. While the program was fundamentally an attempt to stabilize the financial system and keep conditions from growing worse, in order to win over lawmakers and voters it had been presented as a turnaround plan. From the vantage point of consumers and small-business owners, however, the credit markets were still malfunctioning. After hundreds of billions of dollars had been set aside to rescue banks, many Americans still couldn't obtain a mortgage or a line of credit. For them the turnaround that had been promised didn't come soon enough.

Even with the help of cash infusions some of the country's major banks continued to falter. Citigroup, the largest American financial institution before the crisis, devolved into what Treasury officials began referring to as "the Death Star." In November 2008 they had to put another $20 billion into the financial behemoth, on top of the original $25 billion TARP investment, and agreed to insure hundreds of billions of dollars of Citi's assets. In February 2009 the government increased its stake in the bank from 8 percent to 36 percent. The bank that only a decade earlier had spearheaded a push toward deregulation was now more than one third owned by taxpayers.

Even among those who continued to believe in the bailout concept, there were lingering questions about how well Washington had acquitted itself, with the loudest debate focusing on one deal in particular.

In early 2009 the Bank of America–Merrill Lynch merger became the subject of national controversy when BofA announced that it needed a new $20 billion bailout from the government, becoming what Paulson declared "the turd in the punchbowl." When it later emerged that Merrill had paid its employees billions of dollars in bonuses just before the deal closed, the public outrage led to a series of investigations and hearings that embarrassingly pulled back the curtain on the private negotiations that took place between the government and the nation's financial institutions.

The September sale of Merrill Lynch to Bank of America had been presented as a way to save Merrill. But in the several months that it took the deal to close, Merrill's trading losses ballooned, its asset management business weakened, and the firm had to take additional write-downs on its deteriorating assets. The public wasn't informed about these mounting problems, however, and on December 5, shareholders of both companies voted to approve the deal at separate meetings.

Behind the scenes, Ken Lewis threatened to withdraw from the deal, but Paulson and Bernanke pressed him to complete it or risk losing his job.

As details of the drama leaked out John Thain became a quick casualty, with Ken Lewis firing him in his own office. He was soon recast from the hero who had saved Merrill into the source of its troubles, despite indications that Bank of America was aware of the firm's problems and chose not to disclose them. Additional criticism was leveled at Thain when it emerged that he had asked the outgoing Merrill board for as much as a $40 million bonus. "That's ludicrous!" shouted John Finnegan, the Merrill director who was on its compensation committee, when a human resources representative made the request. Thain has said that he knew nothing about it, and by the time a discussion about his compensation reached the full board, he had withdrawn any request for a bonus.

Nowhere was the public backlash more severe, however, than it was against American International Group. AIG had become an even greater burden than anyone expected, as its initial $85 billion lifeline from taxpayers eventually grew to include more than $180 billion in government aid. Geithner's original loan to AIG, which he had said was fully collateralized, quickly looked to be no sounder an investment than a mortgage lender's loan to a family with bad credit and no ability to ever pay it back.

Now that taxpayers were owners of AIG, lawmakers complained loudly about a $440,000 retreat for their independent insurance agents at the St. Regis Monarch Beach resort in Dana Point, California, and an $86,000 partridge-hunting trip in the English countryside. But the greatest ire was reserved for reports of millions of dollars in bonuses being awarded to AIG executives, as protesters swarmed its headquarters and its officials' homes. President Obama asked, "How do they justify this outrage to the taxpayers who are keeping the company afloat?" while on his television program Jim Cramer ranted, "We should hound them in the supermarket, we should hound them in the ballpark, we should hound them everywhere they are."

The widespread criticism gave rise to considerations about how to continue operating the business: Should decisions about how the company spent its money be made in reaction to popular opinion or with the goal of achieving profits? Edward Liddy, AIG's new CEO, so frustrated with trying to serve two masters, left the company within eleven months of joining it.

There was also the issue of exactly how the AIG bailout money was used. More than a quarter of the bailout funds left AIG immediately and went directly into the accounts of global financial institutions like Goldman Sachs, Merrill Lynch, and Deutsche Bank, which were owed the money under the credit default swaps that AIG had sold them and through their participation in its securities lending program. To some extent this disbursement only bolstered the argument of critics who decried Paulson's rescue as a bailout by Wall Street for Wall Street. (It didn't help that foreign banks received some of the indirect aid, even though foreign governments hadn't contributed to the rescue plan.)

Because Goldman Sachs was the largest single recipient of the AIG payments, receiving $12.9 billion, much of the anger quickly settled on it, as theories proliferated about what strings the firm might have pulled behind the scenes given its ties to Paulson and Treasury's cast of Goldman alumni. In particular, the Goldman connection to AIG suggested to some that it was the reason that Treasury—or what people had started calling "Government Sachs"—had chosen to rescue the insurance giant and not Lehman. Goldman disputed claims that it benefited from the AIG rescue, contending that it had been "always fully collateralized and hedged" in its exposure to the insurance company. (In fairness, it does appear that the firm had been so, despite a lingering whisper campaign to the contrary. And the $12.9 billion headline number is somewhat misleading; $4.8 billion of the amount transferred to Goldman was in exchange for securities that it had been holding.) That's not to say Goldman did not have a vested interest in seeing AIG rescued, but the facts are slightly more complex than have often been presented by the media.

The news reports, however, kept feeding off one another and therefore missed the underlying truth: Paulson himself had had very little to do with the rescue of AIG; it was, rather, orchestrated by Geithner (and executed, in part, by Treasury's Dan Jester). While the fact has often been overlooked, Geithner, by his very nature—as has been demonstrated throughout this book and in his subsequent policies as Treasury secretary—is as much a proactive deal maker as Paulson, if not more so.

Still, the conspiracy theories kept coming, and the narratives grew more elaborate. "Is Goldman Sachs Evil?" asked the cover of *New York* magazine. The writer Matt Taibbi created a new popular metaphor for the firm, describing Goldman in a *Rolling Stone* article as a "great vampire squid wrapped around the face of humanity, relentlessly jamming its blood funnel into anything that smells like money."

Months after the TARP infusion, Goldman reported a profit of $5.2 billion for the first half of 2009. In June the firm paid back the $10 billion of TARP money, and in July paid $1.1 billion to redeem the warrants that were issued to the government as part of the TARP infusion. For Goldman, even as a bank holding company, it was back to business as usual.

The real question about Goldman's success, which could be asked about other firms as well, is this: How should regulators respond to continued risk taking—which generates enormous profits—when the government and taxpayers provide an implicit, if not explicit, guarantee of its business? Indeed, in Goldman's second quarter of 2009, its VaR, or value at risk, on any given day had risen to an all-time high of $245 million. (A year earlier that figure had been $184 million.) Goldman's trades have so far paid off, but what if it had bet the wrong way? For better or worse, Goldman, like so many of the nation's largest financial institutions, remains too big to fail.

———

Could the financial crisis have been avoided? That is the $1.1 trillion question—the price tag of the bailout thus far.

The answer to that question is "perhaps." But the preemptive strike would probably have had to come long before Henry Paulson was sworn in as secretary of the Treasury in the spring of 2006. The seeds of disaster had been planted years earlier with such measures as: the deregulation of the banks in the late 1990s; the push to increase home ownership, which encouraged lax mortgage standards; historically low interest rates, which created a liquidity bubble; and the system of Wall Street compensation that rewarded short-term risk taking. They all came together to create the perfect storm.

By the time the first signs of the credit crisis surfaced, it was probably already too late to prevent a crash, for by then a massive correction was inevitable. Still, it is reasonable to ask whether steps could have been taken even at that late stage to minimize the damage. Hank Paulson had, after all, been predicting a problem in the markets since the first summer he joined the Bush administration. Likewise, as chairman of the New York Fed, Tim Geithner had also warned for years that the interconnectedness of the global financial markets may well have made them more vulnerable to a panic, not less. Should these men have done more to prepare for an actual crisis?

To his credit, Paulson did speak openly for months about formalizing the government's authority to "wind down" a failing investment bank. He never made that request directly to Congress, however, and even if he had, it's doubtful he could have gotten it passed. The sad reality is that Washington typically tends not to notice much until an actual crisis is at hand.

That, of course, raises a more pointed question: Once the crisis was unavoidable, did the government's response mitigate it or make it worse?

To be sure, if the government had stood aside and done nothing as a parade of financial giants filed for bankruptcy, the result would have been a market cataclysm far worse than the one that actually took place. On the other hand, it cannot be denied that federal officials—including Paulson, Bernanke, and Geithner—contributed to the market turmoil through a series of inconsistent decisions. They offered a safety net to Bear Stearns and backstopped Fannie Mae and Freddie Mac but allowed Lehman to fall into Chapter 11, only to rescue AIG soon after. What was the pattern? What were the rules? There didn't appear to be any, and when investors grew confused—wondering whether a given firm might be saved, allowed to fail, or even nationalized—they not surprisingly began to panic.

Tim Geithner admitted as much in February 2009, acknowledging that "emergency actions meant to provide confidence and reassurance too often added to public anxiety and to investor uncertainty."

Of course, there are many people on Wall Street and elsewhere who argue to this day that it was the government's decision to let Lehman fail that was its fundamental error. "On the day that Lehman went into Chapter 11," Alan Blinder, an economist and former vice chairman of the Federal Reserve, said, "everything just fell apart."

It is, by any account, a tragedy that Lehman was not saved—not because the firm deserved saving but because of the damage its failure ultimately wreaked on the market and the world economy. Perhaps the economy would have crumbled anyway, but Lehman's failure clearly hastened its collapse.

CEO Richard Fuld did make errors, to be sure—some out of loyalty, some out of hubris, and even some, possibly, out of naïveté. But unlike many of the characters in this drama, whose primary motive was clearly to save themselves, Fuld seems to have been driven less by greed than by an overpowering desire to preserve the firm he loved. As a former trader whose career was filled with any number of near-death experiences and comebacks, he remained confident until the end that he could face down this crisis, too.

Despite claims to the contrary by Paulson, it seems undeniable that the fear of a public outcry over another Wall Street rescue was at least a factor in how he approached Lehman's dilemma. One person involved in the government's deliberations that weekend, in a remarkably candid moment, told me that the fact that the UK government indicated that it would face a major struggle to approve a deal with Barclays was "actually a strange coincidence," because "we would have been impeached if we bailed out Lehman."

While hindsight suggests that the federal government should have taken some action to prop up Lehman—given the assistance it was prepared to offer the rest of the industry once it began to face calamity—it is also true that the federal government did lack an established system for winding down an investment bank that was threatened with failure. Paulson, Geithner, and Bernanke were forced to resort to what MIT professor Simon Johnson has called "policy by deal."

But deals, unlike rules, have to be improvised—and the hastier ones tend by their very nature to be imperfect. The deals hatched in sleepless sessions at the Federal Reserve Bank of New York or at Treasury were no different. They were products of their moment.

In truth, while unnoticed, it wasn't the fate of the U.S. operations of Lehman Brothers that caused the white-knuckled panic that quickly spread throughout the world. To its credit, the Fed wisely decided to permit Lehman's broker-dealer to remain open after the parent company filed for bankruptcy, which allowed for a fairly orderly unwinding of trades in the United States. Outside the country, however, there was pandemonium. Rules in the United Kingdom and Japan forced Lehman's brokerage units there to shut down completely, freezing billions of dollars of assets held by investors not just abroad, but perhaps more important, here in the United States. Many hedge funds were suddenly left short of cash, forcing them to sell assets to meet margin calls. That pushed down asset prices, which only sparked more selling as the cycle fed on itself.

Washington was totally unprepared for these secondary effects, as policy makers had seemingly neglected to consider the international impact of their actions—an oversight that offers a strong argument for more effective global coordination of financial regulations.

Subsequently, Paulson, in trying to defend his decisions, managed to muddy the waters by periodically revising his reasons for not having saved Lehman. In a January 4, 2009, op-ed piece in the *New York Times*, Michael Lewis and David Einhorn wrote: "At first, the Treasury and the Federal Reserve claimed they had allowed Lehman to fail in order to signal that recklessly managed Wall Street firms did not all come with government guarantees; but then, when chaos ensued, and people started saying that letting Lehman fail was a dumb thing to have done, they changed their story and claimed they lacked the legal authority to rescue the firm."

Once the Barclays deal failed, it appears that the United States government truly did lack the regulatory tools to save Lehman. Unlike the Bear Stearns situation, in which JP Morgan was used as a vehicle to funnel emergency loans to Bear, there was no financial institution available to act as conduit for government loans to Lehman. Because the Fed had already determined that Lehman didn't have sufficient collateral to borrow against as a stand-alone firm, there were effectively no options left.

Still, these explanations don't address the question of why Paulson and the U.S. government didn't do more to keep Barclays at the table during negotiations. In the series of hectic phone calls with British regulators on the morning of Sunday, September 14, 2008, neither Paulson nor Geithner ever offered to have the government subsidize Barclays' bid, helping reduce the risk for the firm and possibly easing the concerns of wary politicians in Britain.

In Paulson's view, Barclays' regulators in the UK would never have approved a deal for Lehman within the twelve-hour period in which he believed a transaction would have had to be completed. From that perspective, further negotiations would only have been a waste of precious time. Paulson may be correct in his conclusions, but it is legitimate to ask whether he pulled the plug too early.

It will likely be endlessly debated whether Paulson's decisiveness throughout the crisis was a benefit or a detriment, but the argument can also be made that any other individual in Paulson's position—in a lame-duck administration with low and dwindling popular support—might have simply frozen and done nothing. It is impossible to argue he didn't work hard enough. And a year later, it appears that many of the steps he took in the midst of the crisis laid the groundwork for the market's stabilization, with the Obama administration, Geithner, and Bernanke often taking credit for the reversal. Thus far, many of the biggest banks that accepted TARP funds have returned it, taxpayers have made $4 billion in profit. However, that does not account for the hundreds of millions of dollars directed at firms like AIG, Citigroup, and elsewhere that may never get paid back.

Barney Frank perfectly articulated the dilemma that will likely haunt

Paulson as historians seek to judge his performance. "The problem in politics is this: You don't get any credit for disaster averted," he said. "Going to the voters and saying, 'Boy, things really suck, but you know what? If it wasn't for me, they would suck worse.' That is not a platform on which anybody has ever gotten elected in the history of the world."

———

To attempt to understand how the events of September 2008 occurred is, of course, an important exercise, but only if its lessons are used to help strengthen the system and protect it from future crises. Washington now has a rare opportunity to examine and introduce reforms to the fundamental regulatory structure, but it appears there is a danger that this once-in-a-generation opportunity will be squandered.

Unless those regulations are changed radically—to include such measures as stricter limits on leverage at large financial institutions, curbs on pay structures that encourage irresponsible risks, and a crackdown on rumormongers and the manipulation of stock and derivative markets—there will continue to be firms that are too big to fail. And when the next, inevitable bubble bursts, the cycle will only repeat itself.

The financial industry had always been intended to be something of an unseen backroom support for the broader economy, helping new businesses get off the ground and mature companies adapt and expand. Yet in the years leading up to the crisis, the finance sector itself became the front room. The goal on Wall Street became to generate fees for themselves as opposed to for their clients. As this book went to press, the handful of proposals that have been introduced to put the financial system back in its right place and rein in risk have seemed tepid and halfhearted, at best. Relieved that the worst is supposedly behind us, the Obama administration seems to have moved on to other priorities.

Meanwhile, Wall Street, bent but not broken, rumbles on in search of new profits. Risk is being reintroduced into the system. Vulture investing is back in vogue again, with everyone raising money in anticipation of the collapse of commercial real estate and the once-in-a-lifetime bargains that might be available as a result. Perhaps most disturbing of all, ego is still very much a central part of the Wall Street machine. While the financial crisis destroyed careers and reputations, and left many more bruised and battered, it also left the survivors with a genuine sense of invulnerability at having made it back from the brink. Still missing in the current environment is a genuine sense of humility.

As this behind-the-scenes tale has, I hope, illustrated, in the end, whether an institution—or the entire system—is too big to fail has as much to do with the people that run these firms and those that regulate them as it does any policy or written rules. What happened during this period will be studied for years to come, perhaps even by a new generation of bankers and regulators facing similar challenges.

When the post-bailout debate was still at its highest pitch, Jamie Dimon sent Hank Paulson a note with a quote from a speech that President Theodore Roosevelt delivered at the Sorbonne in April 1910 entitled "Citizenship in a Republic." It reads:

> It is not the critic who counts: not the man who points out how the strong man stumbles or where the doer of deeds could have done better. The credit belongs to the man who is actually in the arena, whose face is marred by dust and sweat and blood, who strives valiantly, who errs and comes up short again and again, because there is no effort without error or shortcoming, but who knows the great enthusiasms, the great devotions, who spends himself for a worthy cause; who, at the best, knows, in the end, the triumph of high achievement, and who, at the worst, if he fails, at least he fails while daring greatly, so that his place shall never be with those cold and timid souls who knew neither victory nor defeat.

It was a remarkable quote for Dimon to have chosen. While Roosevelt's words described a hero, they were deeply ambiguous about whether that hero succeeded or failed. And so it is with Paulson, Geithner, Bernanke, and the dozens of public- and private-sector figures who populate this drama. It will be left to history to judge how they fared during their own time "in the arena."

AFTERWORD

The people on Wall Street still don't get it. They don't get it. They're still puzzled: Why is it that people are mad at the banks? Well, let's see. You guys are drawing down ten-, twenty-million-dollar bonuses after America went through the worst economic year that it's gone through in decades, and you guys caused the problem. And we've got ten percent unemployment. Why do you think people might be a little frustrated?

—President Barack Obama, December 7, 2009

Nearly three years have passed since the peak of the financial crisis, but the debate over its ultimate causes and the decisions that were made during those sleepless days in September 2008 to rescue the financial system is still raging. Disputes about how to fix the banking industry to prevent another crisis from occurring have become a fixture of global conversation. Although legislation to reform the financial industry was approved by Congress and signed by the president, questions persist about whether it went far enough. Indeed, the phrase "too big to fail" has become as common on Main Street as it is on Wall Street, as everyone from small businessmen to farmers finally have come to understand the dangers of a financial sector that has grown so large and interconnected.

The debate has been spurred, at least in part, by an ongoing disconnect between the public and the financial industry that, despite the damage left in the wake of the crisis, seemed to quickly return to business as usual while the rest of the nation struggled.

While unemployment in the United States hovered at almost 10 percent for much of 2009, Wall Street banks were seemingly minting money again. Goldman Sachs announced a record profit that year of $13.4 billion, due in large part to trading for its own account. The firm paid out $16.2 billion in bonuses, the equivalent of $498,000 per employee. Even troubled firms, like Citigroup and Bank of America, were successful enough that they hastened to pay back their TARP money, at least in part so that they, too, could reward their employees with large bonuses without the restrictions imposed if they had still owed money to the government.

In Washington, the rift between Wall Street and the public grew as legislation to reform the financial industry slowly wound its way through the House of Representatives and Senate. Despite lip service by many of the industry's leaders to support reform, Wall Street swarmed Washington with some 1,400 lobbyists, paying the top ten lobbying firms $30 million to push back on most of the significant reform efforts.

The president, meanwhile, channeling the public's rage, took to chastising the financial industry publicly. "I did not run for office to be helping out a bunch of fat-cat bankers on Wall Street," he told CBS's *60 Minutes*.

Although many Wall Street bankers, like Jamie Dimon, had supported President Obama's election—*The New York Times* called him "President Obama's favorite banker"—he and others in the industry felt that the president had begun to use Wall Street as a convenient target to score political points.

The relationship between the financial industry and Washington started to deteriorate in earnest late January 2010. Two days after the Democrats surprisingly lost an election in Massachusetts for the late Ted Kennedy's former Senate seat, President Obama, seemingly out of nowhere, announced a sweeping plan to overhaul Wall Street.

"I'm proposing a simple and common-sense reform, which we're calling the 'Volcker Rule'—after this tall guy behind me," Obama announced, referring to Paul Volcker, the former chairman of the Federal Reserve. "Banks will no longer be allowed to own, invest, or sponsor hedge funds, private equity funds, or proprietary trading operations for their own profit, unrelated to serving their customers. If financial firms want to trade for profit, that's something they're free to do. Indeed, doing so—responsibly—is a good thing for the markets and the economy. But these firms should not be allowed to run these hedge funds and private equities funds while running a bank backed by the American people."

The proposal, which would have a profound effect on the way the industry worked, was greeted with cheers from critics of the financial sector, but with dismay from those within it. "For a lot of Wall Street people, it was like, 'Okay, first you slap us in the face, now you kick us in the balls. Enough is enough. I mean, we're done,'" one banking CEO complained.

The choice was especially surprising because for many months Volcker, whom Obama had asked to chair the President's Economic Recovery Advisory Board, had effectively been ignored by other members of the administration, like Timothy Geithner, the Treasury secretary.

Volcker had been the most outspoken member of Obama's inner circle about the need for reform. To him, Wall Street had grown far too complicated with fancy new products like collateralized debt obligations and had veered away from its core purpose of helping the economy through responsible lending.

At a gathering of bank CEOs in late 2009, he famously chided its leaders.

"Wake up, gentlemen," he declared. "I wish that somebody would give me some shred of neutral evidence about the relationship between financial innovation recently and the growth of the economy, just one shred of information." He added, "The most important financial innovation that I have seen the past twenty years is the automatic teller machine. That really helps people."

In early June 2010 Warren Buffett was subpoenaed to testify before the Financial Crisis Inquiry Commission. The commission, which had been appointed by the president, had been mandated "to examine the causes of the financial crisis that has gripped the country and to report our findings to the Congress, the President, and the American people."

As part of its investigation, it summoned Buffett to a hearing about the role of rating agencies, including Moody's, of which his Berkshire Hathaway was the largest shareholder.

But the commission wasn't strictly interested in Buffett's views on the agencies. What the panelists, like much of the public, really wanted to know was who exactly was to blame for the crisis.

Buffett's response spoke to the essential truth of both the boom—which was fueled by speculation in the housing market—and the bust:

When there's a delusion, a mass delusion, you can say everybody is to blame. I mean, you can say I should have spotted it, you can say the Feds should have spotted it, you can say the mortgage brokers should have, Wall Street should have spotted it and blown the whistle.

I'm not sure if they had blown the whistle how much good it would have done. People were having so much fun.

And it's a little bit like Cinderella at the ball. People may have some feeling that at midnight it's going to turn to pumpkin and mice, but it's so darn much fun, you know, when the wine is flowing and the guys get better looking all the time and the music sounds better and you think you'll leave at five of twelve and all of a sudden you look up and you see there are no clocks on the wall and—bingo, you know? It does turn to pumpkins and mice. It's hard to blame the band. It's hard to blame the guy you're dancing with.

There's plenty of blame to go around. There's no villain.

However accurate his assessment, Buffett's answer was hardly satisfying to those still eager for the sight of some executive—any executive—being hauled away in handcuffs.

Despite months of effort, however, a viable culprit had yet to be identified. In March 2010, a court-appointed examiner in the bankruptcy of Lehman Brothers, Anton R. Valukas, issued a report that, at over 2,200 pages and a cost of more than $36 million, was the closest thing to an autopsy of Lehman. The report had been highly anticipated by the Justice Department and Securities and Exchange Commission, whose own probes had stalled. Despite the voluminous amount of information it had gathered, however, it did not appear to have produced a smoking gun, for while it raised questions about the firm's behavior, it also appeared to exonerate its board.

Mr. Valukas stated that, while Lehman's directors should have exercised greater caution, they did not cross the line into "gross negligence." Instead, he concluded, "Lehman was more the consequence than the cause of a deteriorating economic climate."

The report did, however, include some new revelations that could still lead to government action. Its most interesting and controversial discovery concerned an accounting practice called Repo 105, which the public was learning about for the first time. As the report explained it, "Lehman did not disclose . . . that it had been using an accounting device (known within Lehman as 'Repo 105') to manage its balance sheet—by temporarily removing approximately $50 billion of assets from the balance sheet at the end of the first and second quarters of 2008. . . .Lehman's own accounting personnel described Repo 105 transactions as an 'accounting gimmick' and a 'lazy way of managing the balance sheet as opposed to legitimately meeting balance sheet targets at quarter end.'"

The report found that there were "colorable claims" (a legalism for a civil case) against certain members of Lehman's management—Richard Fuld, Chris O'Meara, Erin Callan, and Ian Lowitt—for breaching "their fiduciary duties by exposing Lehman to potential liability for filing materially misleading periodic reports" and against Lehman's auditor, Ernst & Young, for "being professionally negligent in allowing those reports to go unchallenged."

In particular, the report said of Fuld that, "There is sufficient credible evidence to support a determination that Fuld's failure to make a deliberate decision about Lehman's disclosure obligations was grossly negligent or demonstrated a conscious disregard of his duties."

For his part, Fuld (who has since returned to work by setting up a small advisory firm several blocks from Lehman's old headquarters) insisted he was unaware of Repo 105. "I have absolutely no recollection whatsoever of hearing anything about or seeing documents related to Repo 105 transactions while I was the CEO of Lehman."

Outside of his home in Sun Valley, the week before the first anniversary of Lehman's collapse, he said, "You know what, people are saying all sorts of crap, and it's a shame that they don't know the truth, but they're not going to get it from me." He added, "You know Freud in his lifetime was challenged, but you know what he always said: 'You know what, my mother loves me.' And you know what, my family loves me, and I've got a few close friends who understand what happened, and that's all I need."

As of this writing, several government investigations into Lehman remain ongoing, though it is unclear how they will be resolved.

Despite serving for so long as the public face of the crisis, Fuld and Lehman were relegated to the background as the spotlight seemed to turn again onto Goldman Sachs, the firm that had managed to weather the crisis more successfully than its peers. While its success had long made it the target of the public's ire, it only exacerbated the situation with a number of ill-considered gaffes, the most notable of which was an off-handed joke Lloyd Blankfein made to a reporter that he was just a banker "doing God's work."

That comment led to an enormous amount of scorn being heaped on the firm as it demonstrated the emerging disconnect between Wall Street and Main Street, quickly becoming a running punch line on late-night television. Warren Buffett, a longtime Goldman fan, observed of the public outrage, "I mean, they're going to rewrite Genesis and have Goldman Sachs offering the apple."

In April 2010 the Securities and Exchange Commission brought its only major case against Wall Street since the crisis, filing securities fraud charges against Goldman Sachs and one of its employees, Fabrice Tourre, a vice president, accusing them of selling securities that were intended to fail. The suit alleged that Goldman had created a synthetic CDO purposely filled with low-quality mortgages on behalf of one of its clients, Paulson & Co., a hedge fund that had made $3.7 billion by shorting the mortgage market. Paulson (unrelated to Henry M. Paulson Jr.) had likewise planned to short the CDO in question, called Abacus. The SEC asserted that Goldman had purposely not disclosed to buyers of Abacus that Paulson had helped create it with the goal of having it fail. The investors who bet it would rise in value wound up losing $1 billion.

Despite the headline-grabbing claims, legal experts described the case as "thin," and raised questions about whether it was politically motivated to help gain support for the president's financial regulatory reform bill. The SEC's five commissioners had voted along party lines, 3–2, to pursue the case.

For its part, Goldman, which claimed it was blindsided by the suit, originally said it planned to defend itself and that it, too, lost money on the Abacus deal. The firm stated that it had disclosed all of the material information that an investor would have needed to properly evaluate the deal, including which mortgages were being referenced in the CDO.

The public drubbing that Goldman took may have proved too much to bear: The firm settled the case for a record $550 million without admitting or denying guilt.

Irrespective of the merits of the suit, it did offer the American public a window into the world of how investment banks really work and the various conflicts of interest that seem to be embedded into their business model.

Senator Carl Levin quizzed Goldman's CFO, David Viniar, at one of many hearings about the financial crisis. During a heated exchange, Levin asked Viniar why Goldman had sold a CDO called Timberwolf to its clients, even though it was betting against the security itself. Levin had found an e-mail in which one Goldman colleague had observed to another, "Boy that timeberwof [*sic*] was one shitty deal."

When asked about that assessment, Viniar only made the situation worse by responding, "I think that's very unfortunate to have on e-mail." (After lots of laughter in the gallery, he tried to correct himself. "Please don't take that the wrong way, " he added. "I think it's very unfortunate for anyone to have said that in any form.")

Another sequence of e-mails uncovered since the height of the crisis revealed that Washington Mutual's CEO, Kerry Killinger, had been nervous about doing business with Goldman precisely because of such conflicts.

"I don't trust Goldy on this," Killinger wrote to a colleague. "They are smart, but this is swimming with the sharks. They were shorting mortgages big time while they were giving CfC [Countrywide Financial Corporation] advice."

The Goldman suit also brought into stark relief larger questions about the dangers of derivatives and whether they had much social utility. What the public learned was that many derivatives like synthetic CDOs were simply bets without anything underlying them. Nobody was able to get a mortgage as a result of the sale of synthetic CDOs. An investor in a synthetic CDO is simply gambling on what is going to happen to a series of mortgages that he doesn't even own.

"Synthetics became the chips in a giant casino, one that created no economic growth even when it thrived, and then helped throttle the economy when the casino collapsed," Senator Levin said.

Despite the attacks against it, however, many of Goldman's clients rushed to its defense, denouncing the outrage in Washington and elsewhere as politically motivated.

"People need to tone down the rhetoric around financial services and stop the populism and be adults," Jeffrey Immelt, CEO of General Electric, stated. Warren Buffett was even more vociferous in his defense of Gold-man and, specifically, of the Abacus deal.

"I don't have a problem with the Abacus transaction at all, and I think I understand it better than most," said Buffett, whose Berkshire still held a $5 billion stake in Goldman. "For the life of me, I don't see whether it makes any difference whether it was John Paulson on the other side of the deal, or whether it was Goldman Sachs on the other side of the deal," he observed, adding, "It's very strange to say, at the end of the transaction, that if the other guy is smarter than you, that you have been defrauded. It seems to me that that's what they are saying."

———

For all the anger directed at Wall Street, there was still a portion left over for the government and its own handling of the crisis. A U.S. Congressional Oversight Panel report was critical of the roles of Henry M. Paulson, Ben Bernanke, and Timothy Geithner. In particular, it took issue with their decision to bail out AIG which, the report contended, "demonstrated that Treasury and the Federal Reserve would commit taxpayers to pay any price and bear any burden to prevent the collapse of America's largest financial institutions and to assure repayment to the creditors doing business with them."

The Federal Reserve also came under scrutiny for being too close to Wall Street, as members of Congress questioned whether the agency had acted appropriately in making some of its secret middle-of-the-night decisions and whether more disclosure was necessary. Several congressmen, led by Ron Paul, sought to audit the Fed, which Ben Bernanke resisted, adamant that the Fed remain independent of political interference. As of this writing, it appears that proponents of regular audits have backed down in their demands.

Paulson, who published his own account of the financial crisis, *On the Brink: Inside the Race to Stop the Collapse of the Global Financial System,* in February 2010, spent much of the year traveling the globe, in part to defend his actions. "We did things that were unpopular at the time, are even more unpopular today as the public has gotten angry," he acknowledged. In explaining his actions, he said, "I didn't think a lot about theory. I just understood how bad it could be. And so I just felt like I was racing against time with inadequate tools and authorities, to try to stave off disaster."

The Paulsons recently sold their Washington, D.C., home and moved back to the home they bought in the 1970s in Barrington, Illinois. Since completing his book, Paulson has not yet announced what he might do next.

Timothy Geithner, who has done very little redecorating of Paulson's former office since becoming Treasury secretary, spent the past two years trying to push through and executing upon the new regulatory reform legislation. He has been credited with helping stabilize the economy, but he continued to be criticized for not pressing for harsh enough regulatory legislation to fundamentally alter the sector. That led to charges he was too close to the financial industry. In Washington, his critics spread false rumors that Geithner once worked at Goldman Sachs. The rumor was so pervasive that the wife of Rahm Emanuel, the White House chief of staff, once said to Geithner at a dinner that he "must be looking forward to going back to that nice spot you have waiting for you at Goldman."

Perhaps surprisingly, despite all the public condemnation for the "bailouts," the prevailing wisdom has become that they worked—albeit more slowly than some people had hoped.

Today, the economy has clearly stabilized and unemployment rates have steadily gotten better. Bank lending has returned, though still not nearly to the levels of 2007. Companies like AIG are seemingly back on their feet.

Almost shockingly, the government is expected to book a profit of more than $20 billion on TARP, including its investment in A.I.G. (Jimmy Lee may owe Jamie Dimon $10 to settle their bet about whether the government would get its money back.)

One question remains: nearly three years after the greatest financial crisis of modern times, are we any closer to solving the Too Big to Fail conundrum?

Yes—and no.

The new reform legislation goes a long way toward fixing the way certain parts of Wall Street are regulated. The government has added a new Consumer Financial Protection Bureau to be a watchdog over how mortgages and other products are sold by banks. It is also putting together a systemic risk council made up of various agencies to better share information in hopes of being able to spot a potential crisis before it turns into a real one. In addition, the legislation pushes derivative trading at big banks into better-capitalized subsidiaries. And the government will finally be given resolution authority so it can wind down a big investment bank or insurance company—as in the case of Lehman or AIG—without the risks associated with a bankruptcy that could cascade through the system.

But the legislation still didn't go far enough. It has no provisions to deal with Fannie Mae and Freddie Mac, which have cost taxpayers some $130 billion. Derivatives will still be allowed to live, at least partially, in an opaque world. And big banks are even bigger and they are still as interconnected as ever. Given the many mergers by the biggest banks, some of these institutions have been dubbed "Too Big to Manage."

Early in the process Senator Bernie Sanders of Vermont responded to the legislation's shortcomings by introducing the "Too Big to Fail, Too Big to Exist Act," giving the government power to break up systemically important institutions. Senators Maria Cantwell of Washington and John McCain of Arizona, meanwhile, introduced a bill to reinstate Glass-Steagall. Neither proposal gained much enthusiasm, in part because of arguments made by the industry that it would make the United States less competitive in the global marketplace.

"The fact is that some businesses require size in order to make necessary investments, take extraordinary risks, and provide vital support globally," Jamie Dimon said. "America's largest companies operate around the world and employ millions. This includes companies that can make huge investments—as much as $10 billion to $20 billion a year—and compete in as many as fifty to one hundred countries to assure America's long-term success."

Perhaps the most disquieting development that has taken place postcrisis hasn't been on Wall Street or in Washington. It is that the phrase "too big to fail" is no longer being associated with banks alone. It is now being used to describe municipalities and countries that, like many home borrowers, have become overleveraged. Much recent concern has focused on Greece, but Spain, Italy, Portugal, and Ireland are all considered vulnerable. In the United States, worries persist about whether the state of California will ultimately meet its day of reckoning.

———

"We cannot control ourselves. You have to step in and control The Street."

John Mack, standing next to his wife, Christie, made this remarkably candid and poignant comment about the need for regulation in the fall of 2009, just a month after *Too Big to Fail* was originally published. Mack had been sitting in the audience of a panel on the financial crisis on which I was appearing when he surprised the group by offering a viewpoint that was contrary to that of most of his peers, who had been lobbying against any serious reform.

Mack offered an anecdote about why Wall Street's culture—and perhaps our global culture of risk taking—would make self-policing nearly impossible.

At the height of the economic boom, he recounted, he had turned down an opportunity to make a highly leveraged loan, which would have likely included enormous fees, out of fear that it would later blow up.

"I missed a piece of business," he acknowledged. "I can live with that, but as soon as I hung up the phone someone else put up ten times leverage."

It is the ultimate truism: In the race for profits on Wall Street and elsewhere—and perhaps more important, as a matter of personal pride—someone is always willing to stick his neck out just a little farther than the next guy.

While that sort of heedless risk-taking has led to lucrative returns for many financiers in recent decades, the vulnerabilities in the financial system that have been exposed by the crisis must at some point lead to an accounting—not only of the practices that have become common on Wall Street but of the principles that underlie them. As Harvard's Elizabeth Warren, chair of the Congressional Oversight Panel, has observed, "This generation of Wall Street CEOs could be the ones to forfeit America's trust. When the history of the Great Recession is written, they can be singled out as the bonus babies who were so shortsighted that they put the economy at risk and contributed to the destruction of their own companies. Or they can acknowledge how Americans' trust has been lost and take the first steps to earn it back."

Andrew Ross Sorkin
March 31, 2011

ACKNOWLEDGMENTS

This book had its origins in the wee hours of the morning of Monday, September 15, 2008. I had just gotten home at about 2:30 a.m. after working flat out for days with my colleagues at the *New York Times* as we sought to report all of the details of what has become perhaps the most storied weekend in our economic history. When I walked in the door I was still in shock, having just finished writing the paper's lead article that morning: Lehman Brothers had officially filed for bankruptcy protection, Merrill Lynch was sold to Bank of America, and American International Group was teetering.

Desperate to talk to someone about what had just happened, I woke up my wife, Pilar Queen, to share the news with her. "You're not going to believe this," I said, as I recounted all of the dramatic details. "It's like a movie!"

Pilar looked at me for a split second, and before pulling the sheets back around herself and going back to sleep, she said, *"No*, it's like a book."

For the entire week after that conversation I resisted even considering the idea of writing a book. I was overwhelmed with my reporting for the paper, and the thought of ever writing more than a few thousand words at once frankly scared me. But Pilar was persistent, nudging me gently but firmly, and ultimately persuading me to take on the task, believing that I was capable of doing so even when I didn't. For virtually the next 365 days she encouraged me through the completion of this project—one that often felt like trying to sprint for the duration of an entire marathon.

I also owe a special thank-you to my parents, Joan and Larry Sorkin, and to my sister, Suzie. Whatever success I've had in my life has been a direct result of their love and support. When I was in high school they would all anxiously hover over me as I struggled to write my term papers;

to them—and to me—the very idea that I would end up writing a book is more than a little inconceivable.

There is one important family member I need to mention who didn't get to read this book—or witness the climax of the financial crisis. Up until the Friday of "Lehman Weekend"—September 12, 2008—I was fortunate enough to have all four of my grandparents. But that Friday my grandfather Sidney Sorkin passed away at ninety-one years old. He had always been a voracious reader, and I felt that he would have urged me to continue to cover the events of that weekend as I grieved his death.

I have been encouraged throughout my life by my three other grandparents, Chester and Barbara Ross and Lilly Sorkin—all proudly over the age of ninety—who have also been tremendous sources of support over the past year.

Writing a book can be an isolating experience, but I was helped through it by so many dear friends at various points in the process that I never felt alone. I owe a special debt of gratitude to Jeff Cane, my former longtime editor at the *Times*, who has an encyclopedic knowledge of Wall Street and offered his assistance from the very beginning. My pal Jim Impoco, another of my favorite former editors at the *Times*, offered keen suggestions throughout, as did Hugo Lindgren, a brilliant editor at *New York* magazine (and another former Timesman). Michelle Memran, researcher and fact-checker extraordinaire, tracked down the most obscure details and made the most meticulous time lines imaginable, helping me keep track of a very complicated plot. In the final weeks of the project, Pam Newton, another researcher, tirelessly located people on various continents. These friends worked at all hours, often sacrificing time with their families, to help me see this project through.

One of the reasons I wrote this book at all was that I was lucky enough to have as my editor Viking's Rick Kot, who edited my favorite business book of all time, *Barbarians at the Gate*. Rick was a good friend before this project, and he's an even better friend now. He hustled to make this book work under enormous time pressure, and his deft editing improved every page. His assistant, Laura Tisdel, was also remarkable, simultaneously juggling a dozen moving parts at the same time. Clare Ferraro, Viking's president, believed in the vision of this project from the moment I walked in the door to pitch it. I am also indebted to the rest of the Viking team, who worked around the clock to make this book happen: Rachel Burd, Carla Bolte, Pat Lyons, Fabiana Van Arsdell, Paul Buckley, Jennifer Wang, Carolyn Coleburn, Yen Cheong, Louise Braverman, Linda Cowen, Alex Gigante, Melanie Belkin, Jane Cavolina, Norina Frabotta, Susan Johnson, John Jusino, Michael Burke, Martha Cameron, Beth Caspar, Hilary Roberts, Jackie Véissid, Christina Caruccio, and Noirin Lucas.

My agent, David McCormick, did everything a good agent should do—only better. I'm also grateful to P. J. Mark, who handled the international sales of this project, and Leslie Falk. I must also thank Matthew Snyder, my film agent at Creative Artists Agency, who has been with me since 2001.

I would be remiss if I did not acknowledge my extraordinary colleagues at the *Times*, many of whom generously offered their editorial guidance—and, more important, emotional support—whenever I was on the verge of mental and physical exhaustion, which was more often than I'd like to admit. I'm especially grateful to Jenny Anderson, Liz Alderman, Alex Berenson, Adam Bryant, Eric Dash, Charles Duhigg, Geraldine Fabrikant, Mark Getzfred, David Gillen, Diana Henriques, David Joachim, P. J. Joshi, Kevin McKenna, Dan Niemi, Joseph Nocera, Floyd Norris, Winnie O'Kelley, Cass Peterson, Tim Race, and Louise Story. I'd also like to single out a special group of people at the *Times* who have become a very important part of my life: the team behind DealBook, an online financial report I started in 2001. My good friends and trusted partners, Peter Edmonston, Michael J. de la Merced, and Liza Klaussmann, are largely responsible for much of our early success. As our team has grown, it has also been a pleasure to work with Zachery Kouwe, Steven M. Davidoff, Jack Lynch, Cyrus Sanati, and Chris V. Nicholson.

I'd also like to acknowledge my friends at CNBC, especially the *Squawk Box* team and the old *Kudlow & Cramer* crew, which put me on television when I was twenty-five years old and had no business being in front of a camera.

A handful of friends from various parts of my life who supported this project and my career also deserve thanks: David Berenson, Dan Bigman, Graydon Carter, Cynthia Colonna, Alan Cowell, David Faber, David Goodman, Warren Hoge, Mark Hoffman, Laura Holson, Ben Hordell, Joe Kernen, the Malman family, the Queen family, Carl Quintanilla, Anita

Raghavan, Dan Richenthal, Becky Quick, Charlie Rose, Seth and Shari Saideman, the Schneiderman family, Alixandra Smith, Doug Stumpf, Matt and Melissa Sussberg, Jonathan Wald, the Weinberg family, Josh and Lauren Wolfe, and Michael Wolff. I'm sure I have inadvertently left out more than one person on this list, for which I apologize in advance. (I have purposely not included anyone who could possibly be confused as a source for this book.)

Perhaps my biggest thank-you goes to my employer, the *New York Times*. I first started at the paper when I was eighteen years old, back in the spring of 1995, pretty much by accident. Stuart Elliott, the paper's advertising columnist, whom I read religiously, was crazy enough to let me in the building. An editor, Felicity Barringer—unaware of my age—took a gamble and assigned me a story. Glenn Kramon, the business editor, was trusting enough to let me stay and later to hire me when I graduated from college and send me to London. Larry Ingrassia, the current business editor, not only kept me around, but gave me a column—always going above and beyond to support me. And Bill Keller, the paper's executive editor (and Joe Lelyveld before him, when I originally joined the paper) allowed—even encouraged—all of this to happen. I owe my career to these people.

I am especially thankful to Larry and Bill—as well as to managing editors John Geddes and Jill Abramson—for generously giving me the time to write this book. I must also thank two people on the other side of the "wall": Arthur Sulzberger Jr., the paper's publisher, and Martin Nisenholtz, senior vice president of digital operations. Both of them have not only encouraged my career in journalism but have also supported my entrepreneurial efforts to help the paper.

Finally, this book would not have been possible without the hundreds of people on Wall Street, in Washington, and elsewhere who generously sacrificed their time to share their insider accounts to help me tell this important story. As I promised them, I have identified none of them by name here, but they know who they are. And they know how truly grateful I am.

NOTES AND SOURCES

When I first began this project I could have never imagined the twists and turns the reporting process would take. Relying on the many relationships I had developed on Wall Street and in Washington over the past decade as a reporter at the *New York Times*, I set about trying to reconstruct the record, pressing my sources to re-create hundreds of meetings and phone calls. Some participants were generous with their time; others were more reluctant, as the economic crisis remained an open wound.

But happily hundreds of participants did agree to speak with me, some for as long as ten hours. One CEO, whom I have known for several years, arrived at our first meeting with meticulous handwritten notes from the big weekend at the Fed, and had even drawn an illustration of where all the participants sat around the table. "I'm giving you them for the same reason I took them," he explained. "This was history in the making." Another source provided videotape recordings of several internal meetings, while others, often after some cajoling, allowed me to view their calendars or e-mail archives. The greatest challenge I faced, oddly enough, was dealing with what often felt like too much information. In trying to reconcile five different versions of a meeting, for instance—from people who were in a sleepless haze at the time—I often found myself repeatedly going back to the same sources to confirm even the tiniest details.

To aid in my reporting, I tried to rely as often as possible on the written record, and I was lucky to have found sources who often took incredible notes or provided access to internal documents, e-mails, presentations, scripts, etc. I also relied upon government documents that I obtained through Freedom of Information Act requests. Both Henry Paulson's and Tim Geithner's calendars helped provide key dates and times. However, it is worth noting that both of those calendars—like diaries I was provided by others—often contained errors about dates or specific meetings.

It was clear from the very beginning of this project that no matter how eager I was to interview these participants on the record, I was not going to get very far if I truly wanted to capture the personal, behind-the-scenes machinations of this dramatic period. As I indicated in the author's note at the beginning of this volume, the majority of subjects interviewed took part only on the condition that they not be revealed as a source, though I was free to capture their contemporaneous words and feelings in the text as they remembered them.

Even in conversations that appear to be between only two people, it is remarkable how many others may have been privy to them. For example, many of the calls conducted by CEOs and government officials took place on speakerphone, sometimes with a dozen people listening in. Other times, a detailed description of a conversation might have been sent by e-mail immediately afterward by one of the participants to a colleague, and forwarded to others.

It is worth noting that much of the dialogue that appears in this book came from the best recollections of participants. As a result, it should be said that the dialogue cannot be considered to be the same as an exact transcript. I have sought out as many sources as possible for confirmation, especially for particularly memorable remarks, but the dialogue is only as good as the memories of those who recalled it.

I have also relied on a treasure trove of reporting by my peers in the business press, who, it must be said, did a remarkable job covering these events in real time, and I have sought to credit them in the notes that follow. Even in instances where I have confirmed the information independently, I have still tried to identify the news article that reported the information first, though I am sure I have inadvertently overlooked some publication or article that may have broken a piece of news or detail that is included in this volume.

Some of the best reporting that took place during this period, I am proud to say, came from my colleagues at the *New York Times*. But I must also acknowledge the excellent reporting by the Associated Press, Bloomberg, *BusinessWeek*, CBS's *60 Minutes*, CNBC, *Forbes, Fortune, Institutional Investor*, Reuters, the *Washington Post*, and the *Wall Street Journal*. Among others, I'd like to single out two remarkable reporters at the *Wall Street Journal* who I found myself citing frequently: Susanne Craig, who led that paper's coverage of Lehman's collapse, and Deborah Solomon, whose Washington coverage was first rate.

Finally, any fact or piece of dialogue not cited in the notes below came from one or more of my confidential sources or documentary evidence that was provided to me.

PROLOGUE

1 **"Lehman Races Clock"**: Susanne Craig, Deborah Solomon, Carrie Mollenkamp, and Matthew Karnitschnig, "Lehman Races Clock; Crisis Spreads," *Wall Street Journal*, September 13, 2008.

4 **Goldman Sachs, ranked at the top of the five leading brokerages**: Harper, "Wall Street Bonuses Hit Record," Bloomberg.

4 **Blankfein, alone took home $68 million**: In addition to his salary, Blankfein earned a $67.9 million bonus in 2007—"the biggest ever for a top Wall Street executive." Christine Harper, "Wall Street Bonuses Hit Record $39 Billion for 2007," Bloomberg, January 17, 2008; Susanne Craig, Kate Kelly, and Deborah Solomon, "Goldman Sets Plan to Escape U.S. Grip," *Wall Street Journal*, April 14, 2009.

4 **"The whole world is moving"**: Louis Uchitelle, "The Richest of the Rich, Proud of a New Gilded Age," *New York Times*, July 15, 2007.

5 **"ate their own cooking"**: As Emanuel Derman, of hedge fund Prisma Capital Partners, noted: "These guys ate their own cooking; they didn't just pass it on to clients." Paul Barrett, "What Brought Down Wall Street?" *BusinessWeek*, September 19, 2008.

5 **"The sudden failure or abrupt withdrawal"**: Charles A. Bowsher, comptroller general of the United States, said this on May 18, 1994, before the Senate Committee on Banking, Housing, and Urban Affairs. http://www.gao.gov/products/GGD-94-133.

5 **"The impact on the broader economy"**: "Chairman Bernanke Testifies Before Joint Economic Committee," U.S. Fed News, March 28, 2007.

5 **Bear Stearns' hedge funds failing**: In July 2007, the High-Grade Structured Credit Strategies Fund and the High-Grade Structured Credit Strategies Enhanced Leverage Fund caved in. Kate Kelly, "Barclays Sues Bear Over Failed Funds," *Wall Street Journal*, December 20, 2007.

6 **BNP Paribas:** "BNP Paribas Freezes Funds Amid Subprime Concern," Bloomberg, August 10, 2007.

CHAPTER ONE

9 **the twelve-acre estate:** His Greenwich property, worth an estimated $11 million, has a home with twenty rooms, eight bedrooms, a tennis court, a squash court, and a pool house. It's one of five Richard Fuld owns. Steve Fishman, "Burning Down His House," *New York*, December 8, 2008.

9 **supposed to be in India:** Susanne Craig, "Lehman Finds Itself in Center of a Storm," *Wall Street Journal*, March 18, 2008.

11 **rumors were rampant that ING:** Ibid. When asked about these rumors, an ING spokeswoman said the company would continue to offer funds but will be looking "more carefully at risk and collateral."

11 **Gregory, who lived in Lloyd Harbor:** Lloyd Harbor was Gregory's primary address, but he owned several other properties, including a 2.5-acre oceanfront estate in Bridgehampton and an apartment at 610 Park Avenue on Manhattan's Upper East Side. See Michael Shnayerson, "Profiles in Panic," *Vanity Fair*, January 2009.

11 **helicopter for his daily commute:** Ibid.

11 **missed his son's lacrosse game:** Craig, "Lehman Finds Itself," *Wall Street Journal*.

12 **"Do we have some stuff"**: Fuld, as quoted by the *Financial Times*: "Do we have some stuff on the books that would be tough to get rid of? Yes," he said, referring to commercial and residential mortgage assets. "Am I worried about it? No. If you have some repricing of these things will we lose some money? Yes. Is it going to kill us? Of course not." Ben White, "A Fighter on the Ropes," *Financial Times*, June 14, 2008.

12 **He had led Lehman through the tragedy and subsequent disruptions of 9/11**: A few days after 9/11, with Fuld leading the way, the firm relocated to the Sheraton Manhattan hotel in Midtown, where desks replaced beds and the cocktail lounge became the global finance group's base of operations. Eight months later, in April 2002, Lehman moved into its new headquarters. See Andy Serwer, "The Improbable Power Broker: How Dick Fuld Transformed Lehman from Wall Street Also-Ran to Super-Hot Machine," *Fortune*, April 17, 2006.

12 **buying this new tower from Morgan Stanley**: In October 2001, Morgan Stanley sold its office building, located on Broadway and West Forty-ninth Street, to Lehman Brothers for $700 million. Charles V. Bagli, "Morgan Stanley Selling Nearly Completed Office Tower to Lehman for $700 Million," *New York Times*, October 9, 2001.

13 **"We've been characterizing Lehman Brothers"**: Joe Kernen, *Squawk Box*, CNBC, March 17, 2008.

13 **DBS Group Holdings**: The memo, however, didn't mention closing any existing accounts with the firms. Patricia Kowsmann, "DBS Not Entering New Positions with Lehman–Sources," Dow Jones Newswires, March 17, 2008.

13 **Moody's reaffirmed its A1 rating**: Craig, "Lehman Finds Itself," *Wall Street Journal*.

14 **"It's paving the road with cheap tar"**: Fuld, as quoted by Yalman Onaran and John Helyar, "Lehman's Last Days," *Bloomberg Markets*, January 2009.

15 **"Lehman may have to follow Bear into the confessional"**: McCarty, as quoted by David Cho and Neil Irwin, "Crises of Confidence in the Markets; Federal Reserve's Rescue of Bear Stearns Exposes Cracks in Financial System," *Washington Post*, March 18, 2008.

15 **"Bear Stearns's demise"**: Ibid.

15 **"I don't think we're going bust this afternoon"**: This was reported by Andrew Gowers, and while attributed to "the boss" in the *Sunday Times* of London, "the boss" on the line is actually Jeremy Isaacs, Lehman's CEO for Europe and Asia, not Dick Fuld. See Andrew Gowers, "The Man Who Brought the World to Its Knees EXPOSED," *Sunday Times* (London), December 14, 2008.

16 **"I don't care who you are"**: Fuld, as reported by Gary Silverman and Charles Pretzlik, "Richard Fuld—A Cunning Player Shows His Hand," *Financial Times*, August 17, 2001.

16 **As he fumed to the *Washington Post***: Ianthe Jeanne Dugan, "Battling Rumors on Wall St.; Lehman Brothers Chairman Launches Aggressive Defense," *Washington Post*, October 10, 1998.

17 **"We learned we need a lot of liquidity"**: Fuld, in an interview with Craig, "Lehman Finds Itself," *Wall Street Journal*.

17 **white paper he presented in Davos**: Russo's presentation, titled "Credit Crunch: Where Do We Stand?," was originally given at the Group of Thirty meeting on November 30, 2007. He updated the paper for the World Economic Forum in January 2008. See http://www.group30.org/pubs/pub_1401.htm.

17 **for $21 million were finished**: A broker told the *New York Post*: "It's got great bones, but it needs tons of work," estimating that the renovation of Fuld's apartment would cost $10 million more. See "$21 Million Wreck," *New York Post*, February 6, 2007.

18 **he joined the Reserve Officers' Training Corps**: Fuld's ROTC recruitment has been reported previously by various publications, including the *Wall Street Journal* and *Fortune*, but this scene between Fuld and his sergeant, to the author's knowledge, has never been published before.

19 **United Merchants & Manufacturers**: "Jacob W. Schwab, 89, Textile Manufacturer," *New York Times*, March 30, 1982.

19 **Fuld's Lehman internship**: Justin Schack, "Restoring the House of Lehman," *Institutional Investor—Americas*, May 12, 2005; Tom Bawden, "Bruiser of Wall St Dick Fuld Looked After His People, But Didn't Know When to Quit," *The Times* (London), September 16, 2008; Annys Shin, "Capitol Grilling for Lehman CEO," *Washington Post*, October 7, 2008.

19 **"I truly stumbled into investment banking"**: Schack, "Restoring the House," *Institutional Investor.*

19 **magnificent 1907 Italian Renaissance building**: Ann Crittenden, "Lehman's Office Move Marks End of an Aura," *New York Times*, December 20, 1980.

20 **"He didn't let his emotions get the best of his judgment"**: Edward Robinson, "Lehman's Fuld, a Survivor, Now Eyes Investment Banking Business," *Bloomberg Markets*, July 2008.

20 **Glucksman, who died in 2006**: Diana B. Henriques, "Lewis Glucksman, Veteran of a Wall St. Battle, Dies at 80," *New York Times*, July 8, 2006.

21 **Lehman's history**: Charles Geisst, *The Last Partnership: Inside the Great Wall Street Dynasties* (New York: McGraw-Hill, 2001), 49–51; Auletta, *Greed and Glory On Wall Street*, 27–30.

21 **commercial paper-trading operation**: Keith Dovkants, "The Godfather, a Man They Call the Gorilla and How a Banking Legend Was Lost," *Evening Standard* (London), September 16, 2008.

21 While this anecdote has been reported previously, the scene and dialogue between Kaplan and Fuld have been reported newly by this author. A brief mention of this event was previously reported by Fishman, "Burning Down His House," *New York.*

23 **"The Gorilla," a nickname . . . stuffed gorilla**: Susanne Craig, "Trading Up: To Crack Wall Street's Top Tier, Lehman Gambles on Going Solo," *Wall Street Journal*, October 13, 2004; Schack, "Restoring the House of Lehman," *Institutional Investor—Americas*; Louise Story, "At Lehman, Chief Exudes Confidence," *New York Times*, June 17, 2008.

23 **"I was one of those people who didn't want to disappoint Dick"**: Fishman, "Burning Down His House," *New York.*

23 **the "Huntington Mafia"**: Shnayerson, "Profiles in Panic," *Vanity Fair.*

24 **"Fucking bankers!"**: Auletta, *Greed and Glory*, 118.

24 **Glucksman, Peter Lusk's office**: David Patrick Columbia, "Highs and Lows," *New York Social Diary*, January 27, 2009.

24 **Glucksman ousting Peterson**: Ken Auletta, "Power, Greed and Glory on Wall Street: The Fall of the Lehman Brothers," *New York Times Magazine*, February 17, 1985.

25 **"That's kind of like talking about my first wife"**: Robinson, "Lehman's Fuld," *Bloomberg Markets*, July 2008.

25 **Shearson/American Express acquiring Lehman**: Robert J. Cole, "Shearson to Pay $360 Million to Acquire Lehman Brothers," *New York Times*, April 11, 1984.

25 **"I loved this place"**: Ken Auletta, "The Fall of Lehman Brothers: The Men, the Money, the Merger," *New York Times*, February 24, 1985.

25 **"It was like a ten-year prison sentence"**: Peter Truell, "Market Place: Is Lehman Ready to Take the Plunge?" *New York Times*, June 3, 1997.

25 **"Stay together, and you will continue to do great things"**: Glucksman's quote, as well as his pencil demonstration, from Robinson, "Lehman's Fuld," *Bloomberg Markets.*

26 **Fuld pushed out Pettit**: Peter Truell, "Pettit Resigns as President of Lehman Brothers," *New York Times*, November 27, 1996; Peter Truell, "Christopher Pettit Dies at 51; Ex-President of Lehman Bros.," *New York Times*, February 19, 1997.

26 **"You're the best business fixer I have"**: Fishman, "Burning Down His House," *New York.*

26 **Fuld began by slashing payroll**: And brokers, too. Fuld noted, "Within a week or 10 days we fired 60% of the 550 brokers [who] weren't representing the firm." He shaved expenses from $1.25 billion to under $1 billion and fired nearly two thousand people. See "Take Notice, It's Lehman," *US Banker*, May 1, 2001.

26 **"Inside" to Fuld's "Mr. Outside"**: Fishman, "Burning Down His House," *New York.*

26 **"I want my employees to act like owners"**: Schack, "Restoring the House of Lehman," *Institutional Investor.*

27 **point system similar to the one that he used to reward his son**: *Wall Street Journal*, October 14, 2005.

27 **his vacation with James Tisch: "Ben, lead the way"**: Schack, "Restoring the House of Lehman," *Institutional Investor.*

28 **"Every day is a battle"**: Fishman, "Burning Down His House," *New York.*

28 **"I tried to train investment bankers"**: Robinson, "Lehman's Fuld," *Bloomberg Markets.*

28 **Gregory's $34 million, Fuld's $40 million**: Yalman Onaran, "Lehman Brothers Paid CEO Fuld $40 Million for 2007," Bloomberg News, March 5, 2008.

29 **people inside Lehman referred to as a "Joeicide":** Fishman, "Burning Down His House," *New York*.

29 **"People need broad experience":** Ibid.

29 **Callan history, early career:** Susanne Craig, "Lehman's Straight Shooter," *Wall Street Journal*, May 17, 2008.

30 **"Would it be weird for someone like to me to work on Wall Street?":** From a profile of Callan in NYU Law School's alumni newsletter, "Erin Callan, '90: Chief Financial Officer, Lehman Brothers Holdings Inc.," April 2008. See http://www.law.nyu.edu/alumni/almo/pastalmos/20072008almos/erincallanapril/index.htm

30 **Citadel Investment Group, she orchestrated the sale of $500 million worth of five-year bonds:** Pierre Paulden, "Rainmakers—Alpha Female," *Institutional Investor*, June 2007.

31 **her personal shopper at Bergdorf Goodman:** Craig, "Lehman's Straight Shooter," *Wall Street Journal*.

31 **negotiations to buy her dream home:** According to New York City housing records, Callan signed both her deed and mortgage on April 16, 2008. Lysandra Ohrstrom, "15 CPW Alert! Lehman Lady Lands $6.5 M. Pad," *New York Observer*, April 25, 2008.

31 **15 Central Park West:** James Quinn, "Sting Rubs Shoulders with Giants of Finance at $2bn Apartments," *Daily Telegraph* (London), February 2, 2008; Christina S. N. Lewis, "Private Properties," *Wall Street Journal*, October 3, 2008.

31 **borrow $5 million to pay for the $6.48 million space:** According to New York City housing records she took out a $5 million mortgage. Also see DealBook, "Lehman's C.F.O. Checks into 15 C.P.W.," *New York Times*, April 29, 2008.

31 **"I don't want to make too much of words":** Matt Lauer interview with Treasury secretary Henry Paulson, *Today*, NBC, March 18, 2008.

32 **quoting from the front page of the *Wall Street Journal*:** Robin Sidel, Greg Ip, Michael M. Phillips, and Kate Kelly, "The Week That Shook Wall Street," *Wall Street Journal*, March 18, 2008.

33 **Goldman, Lehman first-quarter earnings:** Jenny Anderson, "Swinging Between Optimism and Dread on Wall Street," *New York Times*, March 19, 2008.

33 **"Lehman kind of confounded the doomsayers":** "Lehman Lifts Mood, and So Does Goldman," *International Herald Tribune*, March 19, 2008.

33 **"all in all solid":** Susanne Craig and David Reilly, "Goldman, Lehman Earnings: Good Comes from the Bad," *Wall Street Journal*, March 19, 2008.

34 **"There's no question the last few days":** Callan, from transcripts of the Lehman Conference Call: Lehman Brothers Holdings Inc. (LEH) F1Q08 Earnings Call, March 18, 2008.

34 **"You did a great job, Erin":** Ibid.

35 **The stock would end the day up:** Anderson, "Swinging Between Optimism and Dread," *New York Times*; Rob Curran, "Lehman Surges 46% As Brokers Rally Back," *Wall Street Journal*, March 19, 2008.

35 **"The only complaint I have":** Patricia Sellers, "The Fall of a Wall Street Highflier," *Fortune*, March 8, 2010.

35 **she slapped him a high five:** Curran, "Lehman Surges 46%," *Wall Street Journal*.

35 **"I still don't believe any of these numbers":** Alejandro Lazo and David Cho, "Financial Stocks Lead Wall Street Turnabout," *Washington Post*, March 19, 2008.

CHAPTER TWO

36 **"That makes me want to vomit!":** A version of this story was previously reported by Kelly, *Street Fighters*, 204.

36 **raise the price to $10:** Kate Kelly, "The Fall of Bear Stearns: Bear Stearns Neared Collapse Twice in Frenzied Last Days," *Wall Street Journal*, May 29, 2008.

37 **"I could see something nominal, like one or two dollars per share":** Kelly, *Street Fighters*, 205.

37 **government's offer to backstop $29 billion of Bear's debt:** A week later, to limit exposure, the Fed revised its offer to $29 billion. See Robin Sidel and Kate Kelly, "J.P. Morgan Quintuples Bid to Seal Bear Deal," *Wall Street Journal*, March 25, 2008.

37 **Bear's shareholders and employees had practically revolted:** Ibid.

37 "This isn't a shotgun marriage": Moldaver, as reported by Kelly, "The Fall of Bear Stearns," *Wall Street Journal*.

38 "All these years of deregulation by the Republicans": Maura Reynolds and Janet Hook, "Critics Say Bush Is Out of Touch on the Economy," *Los Angeles Times*, March 18, 2008.

38 Paulson advising Bush on his Economic Club speech: Kelly, *Street Fighters*, 34.

39 "You may need a bailout, as bad as that sounds": Ibid.

39 worked in the Nixon White House: In 1972, after two years as a Pentagon aide, Paulson assisted John Ehrlichman, Nixon's domestic policy chief, who would later be jailed for his role in Watergate. See "The Quiet Ascendancy of Hank Paulson," *Institutional Investor*, July 1, 1998.

39 "I will get down here and": David Cho, "A Skeptical Outsider Becomes Bush's 'Wartime General,'" *Washington Post*, November 19, 2008.

39 pushing especially hard for Paulson: See Fred Barnes, "Bolten's White House: And Why Hank Paulson, the Former Goldman Sachs Chief, Is the New Treasury Secretary," *International Economy*.

40 had been a "pioneer" for Bush: Landon Thomas Jr., "Paulson Comes Full Circle," *New York Times*, May 31, 2006; Terence Hunt, "Treasury Secretary Snow Resigns, Replaced by Goldman Sachs Chairman Henry M. Paulson," Associated Press, May 30, 2006.

40 "You started with Nixon": Paulson, *On the Brink*, 19.

40 "This is a failed administration": Ellis, *The Partnership*, 662.

40 "I love my job": Susanne Craig, "Boss Talk: Goldman CEO Tackles Critics, Touchy Issues," *Wall Street Journal*, April 26, 2006.

41 "Fear is the fountain of sickness": Eddy, *Science and Health*, 391–92.

42 He demanded assurances, in writing: Cho, "A Skeptical Outsider," *Washington Post*.

42 same status in the cabinet as Defense and State: Deborah Solomon, "Bush Taps Paulson as Treasury Chief—Goldman CEO Is Promised More Power Than Snow," *Wall Street Journal*, May 31, 2006.

42 "As a prudential matter, I will not participate": From the six-page "Ethics Agreement of Henry M Paulson Jr.," dated June 19, 2008.

42 some 3.23 million shares: "Paulson to Sell His Goldman Shares," Bloomberg News, June 22, 2006.

44 "Given how [Hank] moved from a low-ranking position": Valerie Shanley, "Profile: Hank Paulson," *Sunday Tribune* (Dublin), September 14, 2008.

45 Goldman Sachs was in turmoil: "Goldman Seeking Capital Investment; Firm Beset by Falling Profits, Departing Partners," Bloomberg, September 16, 1994.

46 "Hank, nothing could please me more": Ellis, *The Partnership*, 541.

46 cutting expenses by 25 percent: Emily Thornton, "Wall Street's Lone Ranger," *BusinessWeek*, March 4, 2002.

46 became co-chief executive in June 1998: Paulson was named Goldman's co–chief executive and co-chairman on June 1, 1998—less than two weeks before Goldman voted to go public. "Goldman Sachs Promotes Paulson, Takes Step Toward Public Offering," Dow Jones, June 1, 1998.

46 $300 million as part of a Wall Street bailout of Long-Term Capital: Lowenstein, *When Genius Failed*, 215.

46 Goldman pulling its IPO: Patrick McGeehan, "Goldman Shelves Plan to Go Public—Unsettled Markets Cited as Chief Cause," *Wall Street Journal*, September 29, 1998.

46 retired from Goldman's powerful executive committee: At the end of October, Goldman announced that Zuckerberg would retire at the end of its fiscal year (November). Anita Raghavan, "Zuckerberg, Goldman's Vice Chairman, to Retire as the Guard Changes at Firm," *Wall Street Journal*, October 23, 1998.

47 Corzine had tears in his eyes: Ellis, *The Partnership*, 609–13.

47 trading debut in a $3.66 billion offering: On May 4, 1999, after a seven-month delay, Goldman went public—selling an oversubscribed 69 million shares for $53 each—and officially ending its 130 years as a private partnership. "Goldman Sachs Shares Soar in Long-Awaited Trading Debut," Dow Jones, May 4, 1999.

48 a $4.3 million home: Marc Gunther, "Paulson to the Rescue," *Fortune*, September 29, 2008.

48 **oversaw a department of 112,000:** Ibid.

49 **refurbishment of the building's basement gym:** Gunther, "Paulson to the Rescue," *Fortune*.

49 **"When there is a lot of dry tinder":** Paulson used similar language in an interview he later did with *60 Minutes* correspondent Scott Pelley: "You know, we are about due for some kind of market turbulence," he told the news program. "I didn't expect quite this. But I said to the team, as we worked, 'You never know, when there's a lot of dry tinder out there, you never know what spark is gonna light the tinder.'" *60 Minutes*, CBS News transcripts, September 28, 2008.

49 **"We have these periods every six, eight, ten years":** Daniel Gross, "The Captain of the Street," *Newsweek*, September 29, 2008.

49 **"wind-down authorities":** At a September hearing on U.S. credit markets, Paulson said, "We were not left with the authorities we needed fully to protect the system and the taxpayer, because we have wind-down authorities, where the insurance or, you know, savings depositors, FDIC insurance—in 75 years, you know, we haven't had a saver with FDIC insurance lose a penny." See "Senate Committee on Banking, Housing and Urban Affairs Holds Hearing on U.S. Credit Markets," Congressional Quarterly transcripts wire, September 23, 2008.

54 **Good Housekeeping Seal of Approval:** John Helyar and Yalman Onaran, "Fuld Sought Buffett Offer He Refused as Lehman Sank," Bloomberg News, November 10, 2008.

CHAPTER THREE

58 **an agitated Timothy F. Geithner took the escalator:** Geithner's plane left LaGuardia Airport at 7:00 p.m., arriving in D.C. at approximately 8:20 p.m. on Wednesday, April 2, 2008. Geithner's daily schedules at the New York Fed can be viewed online at the *New York Times* Web site. See http://documents.nytimes.com/geithner-schedule-new-york-fed#p=1.

59 **"The most important risk is systemic":** "Testimony Before the U.S. Senate Committee on Banking, Housing, and Urban Affairs, Washington, D.C.," April 3, 2008. See http://www.newyorkfed.org/newsevents/speeches/2008/gei080403.html.

59 **the $29 billion government backstop:** A week after the deal, J.P. Morgan agreed to cover $1 billion of Bear Stearns' losses, lowering the Fed's backstop to $29 billion. Robin Sidel and Kate Kelly, "J.P. Morgan Quintuples Bid to Seal Bear Deal," *Wall Street Journal*, March 25, 2008.

59 **comparing the Bear rescue unfavorably:** "I have reached a certain age where I can remember quite a few things, and there are some resemblances between the present situation, I'm afraid, and the early 1970s," said Paul Volcker, in a speech to the Economic Club of New York on April 8, 2008. See http://econclubny.org/files/Transcript_Volcker_April_2008.pdf.

59 **"Ford to City: Drop Dead":** On October 30, 1975, this *New York Daily News* headline appeared on the front page, a day after President Gerald Ford said publicly that there would be no federal bailouts for a near bankrupt New York. Ford later lamented that he had never actually used the words "drop dead" in his speech. Sam Roberts, "Infamous 'Drop Dead' Was Never Said by Ford," *New York Times*, December 28, 2006.

61 **after announcing a record loss:** On Sunday, November 4, 2007, Citigroup held an emergency board meeting, which revealed that there could be up to $11 billion in additional subprime write-downs. Later that day Citi installed Robert Rubin as chairman and released this statement from Prince: "It is my judgment that given the size of the recent losses in our mortgage-backed securities business, the only honorable course for me to take as chief executive officer is to step down. This is what I advised the board." Jonathan Stempel and Dan Wilchins, "Citigroup CEO Prince Expected to Resign," Reuters, November 4, 2007; Tomoeh Murakami Tse, "Citigroup CEO Resigns," *Washington Post*, November 5, 2007.

61 **"I'm not the right choice":** Jo Becker and Gretchen Morgenson, "Member and Overseer of Finance Club," *New York Times*, April 27, 2009.

61 **making $398,200 a year:** Geithner's salary in 2008 has been reported as being $411,200, but this figure also includes the first two weeks of 2009. Scott Lanman, "Geithner Nomination Takes Top Fed Wall Street Liaison," Bloomberg News, November 24, 2008; Robert Schmidt, "Geithner Takes Salary Cut to Run Treasury, Gets Fed Severance," Bloomberg News, January 27, 2008.

61 **his monthly $80 haircut:** Joseph Berger, "Suddenly, There's a Celebrity Next Door," *New York Times*, January 2, 2009.

62 **punctuating his sentences with "fuck":** "A Reassuring Figure for Treasury," *The Economist*, November 22, 2008.

62 **"He's twelve years old!":** Robert Rubin recalled Pete Peterson telling him this after meeting Timothy Geithner. Peterson, when later asked about the comment, only remembered saying that Geithner looked young. Greg Ip, "Geithner's Balancing Act—The Fed's Go-to Man for Financial Crises Takes on Hedge Funds," *Wall Street Journal*, February 20, 2007.

62 **summoning the chief executives:** Lowenstein, *When Genius Failed*, 216; Victoria Thieberger, "Fed's McDonough a Cool Head in Financial Storms," Reuters, January 16, 2003.

63 **Geithner's beginnings:** Gary Weiss, "The Man Who Saved (or Got Suckered by) Wall Street," *Condé Nast Portfolio*, June 2008; Yalman Onaran and Michael McKee, "In Geithner We Trust Eludes Treasury as Market Fails to Recover," Bloomberg News, February 25, 2009; Daniel Gross, "The Un-Paulson," *Slate*, November 21, 2008.

63 **published a number of incendiary stories:** Peter S. Canellos, "Conservatives Sour on 'Rebel Media,'" *Boston Globe*, April 19, 2007.

63 **Geithner played conciliator:** Onaran and McKee, "In Geithner We Trust," Bloomberg News.

63 **recommendation from the dean at Johns Hopkins:** George Packard, then dean of Johns Hopkins, recommended Geithner to Brent Scowcroft, then vice chairman of Kissinger Associates, which led to his research job. Deepak Gopinath, "New York Fed's Geithner Hones Skills for Wall Street," *Bloomberg Markets*, April 22, 2004.

63 **a very favorable impression on the former secretary of state:** "He doesn't try to walk into a room and take it over," Kissinger once said about Geithner. "He prevails with the power of his argument." Candace Taylor, "Quiet NY Fed Chief Makes Loud Moves," *New York Sun*, March 31, 2008.

64 **"The Committee to Save the World":** *Time*'s headline for its February 15, 1999, cover, which featured the faces of Treasury secretary Robert Rubin, Fed chairman Alan Greenspan, and Treasury deputy Larry Summers.

64 **On Thanksgiving Day, Geithner called Summers:** Jon Hilsenrath and Deborah Solomon, "Longtime Crisis Manager Pleases Wall Street, Mystifies Some Democrats," *Wall Street Journal*, November 22, 2008.

65 **"Tim's controlled, consistent, with very good ground strokes":** Onaran and McKee, "In Geithner We Trust," Bloomberg News.

65 **New York Fed is the only one whose president is a permanent member:** "The Federal Open Market Committee includes seven members of the Board of Governors and five Reserve Bank presidents. While the president of the Federal Reserve Bank of New York serves on a continuous basis, the other 11 Reserve presidents serve rotating one-year terms beginning January 1 of each year." http://www.federalreserve.gov/FOMC/.

65 **the annual salary of the New York Fed president:** The Fed chairman's salary in 2008 was $191,300. http://www.federalreserve.gov/generalinfo/faq/faqbog.htm.

65 **"These changes appear to have made the financial system":** Geithner, from his "Remarks at the Global Association of Risk Professionals 7th Annual Risk Management Convention & Exhibition in New York City, February 28, 2006." http://www.ny.frb.org/newsevents/speeches/2006/gei060228.html.

66 **his deputy, Steel, would be there in his place:** "I very much appreciate the opportunity to appear before you today to represent Secretary Paulson and the U.S. Treasury Department," Steel said on April 3, 2008. "As you know, Secretary Paulson is on a long-scheduled trip to China." Steel's full speech is available at http://www.ustreas.gov/press/releases/hp904.htm.

67 **underwriting more than 40 percent of all mortgages:** Bethany McLean, "Fannie Mae's Last Stand," *Vanity Fair*, February 2009; Carol D. Leonnig, "How HUD Mortgage Policy Fed the Crisis," *Washington Post*, June 10, 2008.

67 **"Their securities move like water":** Justin Fox, "Hank Paulson," *Time*, August 11, 2008.

67 **The two men had known each other since 1976:** Brendan Murray and John Brinsley, "Paulson's Surrogate Steel Sees 'Initial' Progress in Markets," Bloomberg News, March 19, 2008.

67 **Steel came from a modest background:** Rick Rothacker, Stella M. Hopkins, and Christina Rexrode, "Wachovia's New CEO Is Pro in Crisis Control," *Charlotte Observer*, July 13, 2008.

69 **"Was this a justified rescue":** Dodd's question as well as succeeding statements from Ber-

nanke, Steel, and Geithner are taken directly from official Fed transcripts from the first half of the hearing. See "Panel I of a Hearing of the Senate Banking, Housing and Urban Affairs Committee," Federal News Service, April 3, 2008.

71 **"Buying a house is not the same as buying a house on fire"**: When asked about the logic behind Bear's $2-a-share price, Dimon said: "I tell people that buying a house is not the same as buying a house on fire." "Panel II of a Hearing of the Senate Banking, Housing and Urban Affairs Committee," Federal News Service, April 3, 2008.

71 **cancel the office's newspaper subscriptions to cut costs**: Dimon "obsesses over spending at the granular level," so much so that he once told a vice president, who was listing the company's print subscriptions, "You're a businessman; pay for your own *Wall Street Journal*." See Ken Kurson, "Jamie Dimon Wants Respect," *Money*, February 2002.

71 **"has suddenly become the most talked about"**: Eric Dash, "Rallying the House of Morgan," *New York Times*, March 18, 2008.

71 **"quickly becoming Wall Street's banker of last resort"**: Robin Sidel, "In a Crisis, It's Dimon Once Again," *Wall Street Journal*, March 17, 2008.

71 **"All hail Jamie Dimon!"** Andrew Bary, "The Deal—Rhymes With Steal—of a Lifetime," *Barron's*, March 24, 2008.

72 **"I want to be rich"**: Leah Nathans Spiro, "Ticker Tape in the Genes," *BusinessWeek*, October 21, 1996.

72 **"I think you're wrong!"** Shawn Tully, "In This Corner! The Contender," *Fortune*, March 29, 2006.

73 **which his mother showed to Weill**: Leah Nathans Spiro, "Smith Barney's Whiz Kid," *BusinessWeek*, October 21, 1996.

73 **"Can I show it to people here?"** As Monica Langley reported: "Sandy liked the paper enough that he sent Jamie a note: 'Terrific paper. Can I show it to people here?'" Langley, *Tearing Down the Walls*, 50.

73 **"I won't pay you as much"**: Ibid., 74.

73 **"Jews are going to take over American Express!"**: Ibid., 71.

73 **watching Weill sleep off his martini lunches**: Ibid., 103.

73 **the $1.65 billion acquisition of Primerica**: Robert J. Cole, "2 Leading Financiers Will Merge Companies in $1.65 Billion Deal," *New York Times*, August 30, 1988.

74 **A $1.2 billion purchase of Shearson**: Dana Wechsler Linden, "Deputy Dog Becomes Top Dog," *Forbes*, October 25, 1993.

74 **"You're a fucking asshole!"**: Langley, *Tearing Down the Walls*, 201.

74 **$4 billion deal for Travelers**: Greg Steinmetz, "Primerica, Travelers Seal Merger Pact; Takeover May Speed Insurer's Recovery," *Wall Street Journal*, September 24, 1993.

74 **"Promote her"**: Langley, *Tearing Down the Walls*, 241.

74 **"Now we can be father and daughter again"**: Ibid., 254.

74 **the $83 billion merger with Citicorp**: Announced as a $70-billion merger Monday morning, by the day's end Travelers had soared 18 percent and Citicorp 27 percent, bringing the merger's value up to $83 billion. Langley, *Tearing Down the Walls*, 289–93. Michael Siconolfi, "Citicorp, Travelers Group to Combine in Biggest-Ever Merger," *Wall Street Journal*, April 7, 1998.

75 **"It's bad enough how you treat me"**: Langley, *Tearing Down the Walls*, 314.

75 **"Don't you ever turn your back on me while I'm talking!"**: Roger Lowenstein, "Alone at the Top," *New York Times Magazine*, August 27, 2000.

75 **summoned Dimon to the corporate compound in Armonk**: Timothy L. O'Brien and Peter Truell, "Downfall of a Peacemaker," *New York Times*, November 3, 1998.

76 **the Internet retailer Amazon**: Duff McDonald, "The Heist," *New York*, March 24, 2008.

76 **Dimon brought in his own team of expense cutters**: Shawn Tully, "In This Corner! The Contender," *Fortune*, March 29, 2006.

76 **"fortress balance sheet"**: Jamie Dimon representing JP Morgan Chase at the Credit Suisse Group Financial Services Forum, February 7, 2008.

77 **celebrating his fifty-second birthday over dinner**: Alistair Barr, "Dimon Steers J.P. Morgan Through Financial Storm," MarketWatch.com, December 4, 2008.

78 **"This wasn't a negotiating posture"**: "Panel II of a Hearing of the Senate Banking, Housing and Urban Affairs Committee," Federal News Service, April 3, 2008.

78 **"I am very troubled by the failure of Bear Stearns"**: "Panel I of a Hearing of the Senate Banking, Housing and Urban Affairs Committee," Federal News Service, April 3, 2008.

CHAPTER FOUR

79 **private dinner to mark the end of a G7 summit**: Treasury provided a list of dinner attendees to the press that Friday. Lehman's Fuld was listed alphabetically between Larry Fink of BlackRock and John Mack of Morgan Stanley. "Attendees for G7 Outreach Dinner with Banks," Reuters, April 11, 2008.

79 **it would raise $4 billion**: Jenny Anderson, "Trying to Quell Rumors of Trouble, Lehman Raises $4 Billion," *New York Times*, April 2, 2008.

79 **"We're closer to the end than the beginning"**: Joseph A. Giannone, "Goldman CEO Says Credit Crisis in Later Stages," Reuters, April 10, 2008.

81 **a new IMF Report**: International Monetary Fund, "Global Financial Stability Report," April 2008, 50.

81 **staggering amount of leverage—the amount of debt to equity**: "At the end of the first quarter in 2008, the leverage ratios at Morgan Stanley, Lehman Brothers, Merrill Lynch, and Goldman Sachs were 31.8, 30.7, 27.5, and 26.9, respectively, compared with an average of 8.8 for all U.S. commercial banks and savings institutions." Senate Joint Economic Committee, "Financial Meltdown and Policy Response," September 2008.

81 **"Isn't there something you can do to order us not to take all of these risks?"**: Paulson, *On the Brink*, 70.

82 **"You are all bright people"**: Paulson, *On the Brink*, 130.

82 **"Just finished the Paulson dinner"**: "Hearing on Causes and Effects of the Lehman Brothers Bankruptcy," House of Representatives Committee on Oversight and Government, October 6, 2008. See http://oversight.house.gov/story.asp?ID=2208.

84 **"Break the Glass: Bank Recapitalization Plan"**: Author obtained a copy of the proposal from a confidential source.

84 **Kashkari background**: Deborah Solomon, "U.S. News: Paulson to Tap Adviser to Run Rescue Program," *Wall Street Journal*, October 6, 2008.

85 **chairman of the Federal Reserve on February 1, 2006**: Bernanke's first day fell on the first of the month; his swearing-in ceremony took place the following Monday. "Our mission as set forth by the Congress is a critical one," Bernanke said at his Fed ceremony. Jeannine Aversa, "At Ceremonial Swearing-in, New Fed Chief Bernanke Vows to Work with Congress," Associated Press, February 6, 2006.

85 **Bernanke's beginnings**: John Cassidy, "Anatomy of a Meltdown," *New Yorker*, December 1, 2008; Roger Lowenstein, "The Education of Ben Bernanke," *New York Times Magazine*, January 20, 2008; Larry Elliott, "Ben Bernanke," *Guardian*, June 16, 2006; Mark Trumbull, "Backstory: Banking on Bernanke," *Christian Science Monitor*, February 1, 2006; Ben White, "Bernanke Unwrapped," *Washington Post*, November 15, 2005.

86 **Anna Friedmann, a Wellesley College student whom he married**: John Cassidy, *New Yorker*, December 1, 2008.

87 **"econometrics" research**: Lowenstein, "The Education of Ben Bernanke," *New York Times Magazine*, January 20, 2008.

87 **planned to take a vacation**: Ibid.

87 **interest rate unchanged at 5.25 percent**: "Fed Keeps Rates Steady," Dow Jones, August 7, 2007.

87 **"The committee's predominant policy concern"**: "Text of Federal Reserve's Interest Rate Decision," Dow Jones Capital Markets Report, August 7, 2007.

87 **"They're nuts! They know nothing!"**: "Ben Bernanke needs to open the discount window. . . . He is being an academic! This is no time to be an academic. Open the darn discount window! . . . My people have been in this game for 25 years. And they are losing their jobs and these firms are going to go out of business, and he's nuts! They're nuts! They know nothing! . . . The Fed is asleep." Jim Cramer, *Street Signs*, CNBC, August 3, 2007.

88 **BNP Paribas announced that it was halting investors from withdrawing**: As of August 7, after declining 20 percent in just under two weeks, the funds had some €1.6 billion ($2.2 billion) left in assets. Sebastian Boyd, "BNP Paribas Freezes Funds as Loan Losses Roil Markets," Bloomberg News, August 9, 2007.

88 **"The complete evaporation of liquidity"**: Ibid.

88 **bigger cash infusion than the one that had followed**: On September 12, 2001, a day after the attacks, the European Central Bank (ECB) injected a record €69.3 billion. "ECB Injects 95 billion Euros Into Money Supply Amid US Subprime Worries," Agence France-Presse, August 9, 2007.

88 **"unprecedented disruptions"**: Countrywide's SEC filing late Thursday said it had adequate funding liquidity but added, "[T]he situation is rapidly evolving and the impact on the company is unknown." Randall W. Forsyth, "Why the Blowup May Get Worse," *Barron's*, August 13, 2007.

88 **"Every banker knows that if he has to prove"**: Bagehot, *Lombard Street*, 69.

89 **reversed his earlier decision**: On Friday, August 17, 2001, the Fed issued a statement lowering the rate on discount window borrowings, which buoyed the market. "S&P 500 Futures Sharply Higher on Fed Statement," Dow Jones, August 17, 2007.

89 **"at this point, the troubles in the subprime sector"**: Bernanke delivered this speech via satellite to attendees of the 2007 International Monetary Conference in Cape Town, South Africa. See Ben Bernanke, "The Housing Market and Subprime Lending," June 5, 2007. See http://www.federalreserve.gov/newsevents/speech/bernanke20070605a.htm.

90 **"I've got some fairly heavy background in mathematics"**: Faber, *And Then the Roof Caved In*, 95.

93 **was also a die-hard Sox fan**: Stanley Reed, "Barclays: Anything But Stodgy President Bob Diamond has turned the once-troubled investment banking unit into a powerhouse," *BusinessWeek*, April 10, 2006.

93 **they joined the board of Barclays at the same time**: On June 1, 2005, Robert Diamond Jr., chief executive of investment banking and investment management, joined the board as an executive director, while Robert Steel, former vice chairman of Goldman Sachs, joined as a nonexecutive director. "Barclays PLC—Directorate Change," Regulatory News Service, May 27, 2005.

95 **Diamond had so abruptly left Morgan Stanley . . . in 1992**: "'Coach' Proud of His Trading Floor Origins," *Financial News*, December 4, 2000.

95 **losing an expensive bidding war for Dutch bank ABN AMRO**: Seven months after its initial bid for ABN AMRO, and following a battle involving investors in China, Singapore, the Royal Bank of Scotland, and even Bank of America, Barclays withdrew its bid for the Dutch bank on October 5, 2007. Carrick Mollenkamp, "Barclays's CEO Shifts to Plan B—U.K. Bank Pursues Emerging Markets as ABN Bid Fails," *Wall Street Journal*, October 6, 2007.

CHAPTER FIVE

96 **breakfast meeting with Dick Fuld**: Took place on Thursday, April 2, 2008.

97 **counted as one of his best friends Eliot Spitzer**: When the prostitution scandal broke, Cramer had this to say about his Harvard Law School pal: "Eliot's one of my oldest friends, so is Silda. You know, look, I hope it's not true. You know, I read it like you did—I hope it's not true. . . . Eliot's my friend. So he's my friend, he'll be my friend after." "DealBook: Wall Street on Spitzer: 'There Is a God,'" *New York Times*, March 10, 2008.

97 **the uptick rule**: After the rule's repeal on July 6, 2007, Cramer continuously lamented the loss on his show *Mad Money*. "Cramer Is Uptick'd Off" and "Out with Cox, in with Uptick Rule," *Mad Money*, CNBC, May 4, 2009, November 21, 2008.

99 **"unbelievable portfolio from Peloton"**: Founded in 2005 by Ron Beller and Geoffrey Grant, the London hedge fund Peloton Partners was forced into a fire sale in February 2008. Cassell Bryan-Low, Carrick Mollenkamp, and Gregory Zuckerman, "Peloton Flew High, Fell Fast," *Wall Street Journal*, May 12, 2008.

101 **people pay as much as $3,250**: Hugo Lindgren, "The Confidence Man," *New York*, June 23, 2008.

101 **Tomorrow's Children Fund**: Ira W. Sohn conference proceeds go to this fund, which helps children with serious blood disorders and cancer (Sohn, a trader, died of cancer at twenty-nine). See http://www.atcfkid.com/.

101 **"We start by asking why a security is likely to be misvalued in the market"**: Einhorn, *Fooling Some of the People All of the Time*, 14.

101 **"The Nonrecurring Room"**: Jesse Eisinger, "Diary of a Short-Seller," *Condé Nast Portfolio*, May 12, 2008.

102 **had announced that it was stopping investors**: At 2:30 a.m. on August 9, Dow Jones posted a press release from BNP Paribas: "The complete evaporation of liquidity in certain market segments of the US securitisation [sic] market has made it impossible to value certain assets fairly regardless of their quality or credit rating. The situation is such that it is no longer pos-

sible to value fairly the underlying US ABS assets in the three above-mentioned funds. We are therefore unable to calculate a reliable net asset value ('NAV') for the funds." See "BNP Paribas Unit to Suspend NAV Calculation of Some Funds," Dow Jones, August 9, 2007.

102 **code named "The Credit Basket":** Lindgren, "The Confidence Man," *New York*.

102 **"It is early, and we don't give guidance on future periods":** Chris O'Meara, Lehman's Chief Financial Officer, from the "Q3 2007 Lehman Brothers Holdings Inc. Earnings Conference Call," September 18, 2007.

103 **"This is crazy accounting":** Lindgren, "The Confidence Man," *New York*.

104 **"Lehman is not that materially different from Bear Stearns":** David Einhorn, "Private Profits and Socialized Risk," Grant's Spring Investment Conference, April 8, 2008.

105 **"I can only feel that you set me up":** Einhorn's exchange with Callan reported by Susanne Craig, "Finance Chief Is Demoted," *Wall Street Journal*, June 13, 2008.

105 **"This is classic value":** "Stock Picks from Sohn Investment Conference," Reuters, May 23, 2008.

106 **shares of Allied plunged nearly 11 percent:** Stephen Taub, "Speaking Candidly," *Alpha*, May 2005.

106 **the Securities and Exchange Commission started investigating him:** Lindgren, "The Confidence Man," *New York*.

106 **"One of the key issues I raised about Allied":** This and all succeeding speech quotes by David Einhorn of Greenlight Capital are from his "Accounting Ingenuity" speech at the Ira W. Sohn Investment Research Conference, May 21, 2008.

CHAPTER SIX

109 **"Who talked?":** Susanne Craig, "Lehman Struggles to Shore Up Confidence," *Wall Street Journal*, September 11, 2008.

109 **"Losses Push Lehman to Weigh Raising New Capital":** Susanne Craig, "Losses Push Lehman to Weigh Raising New Capital," *Wall Street Journal*, June 3, 2008.

110 **it had tapped the Federal Reserve's discount window:** Lehman emphatically denied the rumors on June 3, 2008, referencing its previous quarter, which had ended with more than $40 billion of liquidity. Joe Bel Bruno, "Lehman Brothers Treasurer: Firm Did Not Tap Fed Discount Window to Avert Cash Problems," Associated Press, June 3, 2008.

110 **stock was pummeled:** Ibid. Lehman's shares fell 15 percent in the afternoon of Tuesday, June 3, after Lehman liquidity rumors surfaced.

112 **"Lehman's straight shooter":** Susanne Craig, "Lehman's Straight Shooter," *Wall Street Journal*, May 17, 2008.

112 **"The Most Powerful Woman on Wall Street":** Jesse Eisinger, "Diary of a Short-Seller," *Condé Nast Portfolio*, April 2008.

113 **Lehman's deal with Woori:** Hae Won Choi, "Woori Sets Pact with Lehman to Cut Bad Debt," *Wall Street Journal Asia*, September 6, 2002; Donald Kirk, "No Pause for Woori," *Institutional Investor*, July 1, 2002.

113 **having judged his credentials inadequate, had tried unsuccessfully to stop it:** In June 2008, instead of settling in to his new office at KDB, Min spent several days addressing complaints and protests from KDB trade union workers enraged about his appointment. Song Jung-A, "Man Behind Doubts Rise over KDB's Push for Global Status," *Financial Times*, September 2, 2008.

113 **he sang a song called "Leopard in Mt. Kilimanjaro":** Kim Yeon-hee, "KDB's CEO: A Leopard on the Hunt for Lehman," Reuters, September 5, 2008.

114 **"Korea situation sounds promising":** Goldfarb's e-mail, sent May 26, 2008, was made available from the House Oversight and Government Reform Committee's investigation on the "Causes and Effects of the Lehman Brothers Bankruptcy." See "Lehman Brothers Email Regarding Punishing Short Seller," http://oversight.house.gov/story.asp?ID=2208.

114 **set off for Korea:** According to flight records obtained by the *Wall Street Journal*. See Craig, "Lehman Struggles to Shore Up Confidence," *Wall Street Journal*, September 11, 2008.

114 **The Shilla:** http://www.shilla.net/en/seoul/.

114 **Hana Financial, which was also considering an investment:** Hana Financial Group was one

of several top South Korean banks (Shinhan, Woori) reportedly contemplating a Lehman bid. The company, however, publicly "denied any interest in joining a consortium bidding for Lehman Shares." Kim Yeon-hee, "KDB Confirms Lehman Talks; Korea Bank Shares Fall," Reuters, September 1, 2008.

116 **Matthew Lee . . . sent a letter:** Report of the Examiner in the Chapter 11 proceedings of Lehman Brothers Holdings by Anton R. Valukas, chairman of Jenner & Block. See: http://lehmanreport.jenner.com/.

117 **"Basically window dressing":** Report of the Examiner in the Chapter 11 proceedings of Lehman Brothers Holdings by Anton R. Valukas, chairman of Jenner & Block. See: http://lehmanreport.jenner.com/.

117 **"I am very aware. . . . It is another drug we r on":** Report of the Examiner in the Chapter 11 proceedings of Lehman Brothers Holdings by Anton R. Valukas, chairman of Jenner & Block. See: http://lehmanreport.jenner.com/.

117 **"not to make any remarks":** Lehman's five-page severance agreement with Matthew Lee was signed on June 18.

118 **bringing in $3.9 billion in revenue:** Lehman's investment banking net revenues rose from $3.2 billion in 2006 to $3.9 billion in 2007, a 24 percent increase, according to the company's 10-K filing with the Securities and Exchange Commission on January 29, 2008.

120 **Over at Neuberger Berman:** Lehman sealed its $2.6 billion purchase of Neuberger Berman on October 31, 2003.

120 **demanding that top Lehman managers forgo bonuses:** Vale, Walker, and Fuld's e-mail string is available under "Lehman Brothers Email Regarding Suspending Executive Compensation," House Oversight and Government Reform Committee's investigation, http://oversight.house.gov/story.asp?ID=2208.

121 **Few seemed to flaunt their personal wealth as much as he did:** Michael Shnayerson, "Profiles in Panic," *Vanity Fair,* January 2009; Christina S. N. Lewis, "Hot Words in Finance: 'For Sale,'" *Wall Street Journal,* January 16, 2009.

122 **He gave generously to charities:** Shnayerson, "Profiles in Panic," *Vanity Fair*; "Spelman Receives $10 Million Gift," *Jet,* November 19, 2007.

123 **he used it to ram through deals much more quickly:** About Walsh, Aby Rosen told the *New York Times:* "He was fast. . . . He doesn't try to kill you or retrade. To be honest, there are very few people in the industry you can say that about." See Devin Leonard, "How Lehman Brothers Got Its Real Estate Fix," *New York Times,* May 3, 2009; Dana Rubinstein, "Mark Walsh, Lehman's Unluckiest Gambler," *New York Observer,* October 1, 2008.

124 **her input was virtually nil:** See Nick Mathiason, Heather Connon, and Richard Wachman, "Banking's Big Question: Why Didn't Anyone Stop Them?" *Observer* (London), February 15, 2009.

125 **Lehman paid nearly $100 million for Grange Securities:** Chris Wright, "Can Lehman Build on Grange?" *Euromoney,* July 2007.

125 **Had there been a sound reason for acquiring Eagle Energy:** In 2006, Lehman purchased one third of Eagle Energy and agreed to buy the remaining two thirds a year later. "Lehman Buys Rest of Energy Marketing Co. Eagle Energy," Reuters, May 9, 2007.

125 **deals that did concern him were the ones that Lehman had failed to get:** Leonard, "How Lehman Brothers Got Its Real Estate Fix," *New York Times.*

126 **"I am very disappointed":** On the morning of June 9, Fuld said: "I am very disappointed in this quarter's results. Notwithstanding the solid underlying performance of our client franchise, we had our first-ever quarterly loss as a public company. However, with our strengthened balance sheet and the improvement in the financial markets since March, we are well-positioned to serve our clients and execute our strategy." See "Lehman Brothers Announces Expected Second Quarter Results," Reuters, June 9, 2008.

126 **Lehman's second-quarter earnings:** Susanne Craig and Tom Lauricella, "Big Loss at Lehman Intensifies Crisis Jitters," *Wall Street Journal,* June 10, 2008; "Preliminary 2008 Lehman Brothers Holdings Inc. Earnings Conference Call," June 9, 2008.

126 **"Dick Fuld is Lehman":** George Ball, "Lehman's $2.8B Loss," *Squawk Box,* CNBC, June 9, 2008.

126 **"Are you saying 'I told you so'":** Carl Quintanilla, "Lehman's Q2 Loss," *Squawk Box,* CNBC, June 9, 2008.

127 **an e-mail to Fuld from Benoît D'Angelin:** See "Lehman Brothers Email Regarding Lack of

Accountability," House Oversight and Government Reform Committee's investigation, http://oversight.house.gov/story.asp?ID=2208.

129 **So she sent Fuld a two-sentence e-mail:** Read to the author by a confidential source.

130 **Fuld met with the investment bankers for lunch on Wednesday, June 11:** Previously referenced by Steve Fishman, "Burning Down His House," *New York*, December 8, 2008, as well as Susanne Craig, "Lehman Shuffles 2 Key Jobs in Bid to Restore Confidence—Finance Chief Is Demoted; 'Wall Street Wants a Head,'" *Wall Street Journal*, June 13, 2008.

133 **Gasparino hectoring Lehman's spokesperson:** Dealbreaker.com posted a series of Gasparino's taped voicemail messages to Kerrie Cohen. "Charlie Gasparino Leaves The Greatest Voicemail(s) of All Time," September 22, 2008. http://dealbreaker.com/2008/09/charlie-gasparino-leaves-the-g.php.

133 **"Our credibility has eroded":** Yalman Onaran, "Lehman Drops Callan, Gregory; McDade Named President," Bloomberg News, June 12, 2008.

CHAPTER SEVEN

135 **"Lehman is not a Bear Stearns situation":** "BlackRock's Fink Says Lehman Not Another Bear—CNBC," Reuters, June 11, 2008.

135 **Fleming had helped broker a 2006 deal to merge Merrill's $539 billion asset-management business:** On February 15, 2006, Merrill Lynch agreed to sell its investment managers business to BlackRock in exchange for a 49.8 percent stake in the combined company. "Given its complexity, the transaction was put together quickly, helped by the close friendship that Mr. Fleming, who took BlackRock public at a price of $14, and Mr. Fink enjoy." Landon Thomas Jr., "On the Menu for Breakfast: $1 Trillion," *New York Times*, February 16, 2006.

136 **"Everyone is shrinking their balance sheet":** Joseph A. Giannone, "Merrill CEO Wants Ongoing Fed Access, Rules Reform," Reuters, June 10, 2008.

136 **"We all have concerns about what we read in the papers":** Joe Bel Bruno, "Merrill CEO Sees More Industry Consolidation," Associated Press, June 10, 2008.

137 **Merrill's shares down 32 percent for the year:** Tenzin Pema, "Merrill Lynch Outlook Cut at JP Morgan," Reuters, June 11, 2008.

137 **who was sometimes referred to as "I-Robot":** "Stiff, cerebral and intimidating, John Thain is not a 'people person.' Behind his back his nickname is 'I Robot.'" See Dominic Rushe, "The IRobot Rides In to Sort Out Merrill Lynch," *Sunday Times* (London), November 18, 2007.

137 **Fink, ironically, had lead the exchange's search committee that selected him:** Kate Kelly, Greg Ip, and Ianthe Jeanne Dugan, "For NYSE, New CEO Could Be Just the Start," *Wall Street Journal*, December 19, 2003.

137 **shutting the wood-paneled Luncheon Club and firing the exchange's barber:** Asked about his firing of the NYSE barber, a kindly old man who made $24,000 a year, Thain said: "The barber was a very nice guy who'd been there for a very long time. . . . [I]t's difficult to argue that a publicly traded company needs to have its own barber." Gary Weiss, "The Taming of Merrill Lynch," *Portfolio*, May 2008.

137 **when he interned at Procter & Gamble:** Justin Schack, "The Adventures of Superthain," *Institutional Investor—Americas*, June 14, 2006.

138 **"When he made conversation":** Lisa Kassenaar and Yalman Onaran, "Merrill's Repairman," *Bloomberg Markets*, February 2008.

138 **"Would it hurt you to suck up to me once in a while?":** Ibid.

138 **"So, I think you said before that you're comfortable":** Deutsche Bank analyst Mike Mayo, asked Thain during a conference call. "John A. Thain, Chairman and Chief Executive Officer–Merrill Lynch, to Participate in a Conference Call Hosted by Deutsche Bank on June 11—Final," Fair Disclosure Wire, June 11, 2008.

138 **"At the end of last year when we were looking to":** Ibid.

138 **having heard him repeatedly say, "We have plenty of capital":** On March 8, 2008, Thain told France's *Le Figaro*: "Today I can say that we will not need additional funds. These problems are behind us. We will not return to the market." To the Japanese *Nikkei Report* on April 3, he said: "We have plenty of capital going forward, and we don't need to come back into the equity market." At a news conference in Mumbai on May 7: "We have no present inten-

tion of raising any more capital." See Nick Antonovics, "Merrill CEO Says Won't Need More Capital," Reuters, March 8, 2008; "Full Text of Interview with Merrill Lynch CEO John Thain," *Nikkei Report*, April 4, 2008; John Satish Kumar, "Credit Crunch: Merrill's Thain Backs Auction-Rate Securities," *Wall Street Journal*, May 8, 2008.

138 **as "the most vulnerable brokerage after Lehman":** Reinhardt Krause, "Lehman Bros. Extends Slide as Wall St. Doubts Future," *Investor's Business Daily*, June 13, 2008.

139 **For a single day John Thain had the job he had wanted for his entire career:** Kassenaar and Onaran, "Merrill's Repairman," *Bloomberg Markets*. Craig Horowitz, "The Deal He Made," *New York*, July 10, 2005.

139 **At Robert Hurst's Fifth Avenue apartment:** Ellis, *The Partnership*, 613.

139 **Corzine off skiing in Telluride, Colorado:** Ibid.

139 **Thain, a longtime lieutenant and friend of Corzine:** Ibid. Corzine had long been an ally of Thain's, helping him secure the chief financial officer job in 1994 and later a spot on the executive committee. They went skiing together in Colorado and dined out with their wives in Manhattan. Thain was the trustee-designate for the Corzines' children's trusts. See also Noam Scheiber, "The Brain in Thain," *New York*, January 8, 2007.

139 **Thain was the one to have to break the news to him:** Ibid.

139 **"Jon has decided to relinquish the CEO title":** Ibid.

139 **accumulating several hundred million dollars in stock from the IPO:** After Goldman's IPO, Thain's 3.1 million shares were worth about $171 million. Kimberly Seals McDonald, "Goldman's Bounty—Top Execs Will Pocket up to $869m in IPO," *New York Post*, April 13, 1999; Erica Copulsky, "Goldman Notifies Top Non-Partners of Payout Formulas," *Investment Dealers Digest*, May 3, 1999.

140 **he bought a ten-acre property in Rye:** Charlie Gasparino, "John Thain's $87,000 Rug," *Daily Beast*, January 22, 2009.

140 **determined to take a two-week trip to Vail at Christmastime:** Susanne Craig and Dan Fitzpatrick, "Merrill Architects Criticized," *Wall Street Journal*, January 20, 2009.

140 **he took Thain out to dinner:** Ellis, *The Partnership*, 660.

140 **leaving to become CEO at the New York Stock Exchange:** While Thain's NYSE appointment was confirmed on December 18, 2003, his first day was not until January 15, 2004. "Recap of Stories on NYSE Naming Goldman's Thain As CEO," Dow Jones, December 18, 2003.

141 **was paid a $15 million signing bonus:** Cardiff de Alejo Garcia, "Financial News: Thain to Get up to $11M from Restricted Shares," Dow Jones, September 16, 2008.

141 **raised $12.8 billion from the sovereign wealth funds:** Other investors in this group include Japan's Mizuho bank group and the Korea Investment Corp. Jed Horowitz, "Merrill Seeks Intl Investments for Itself, Clients: Pres," Dow Jones, February 6, 2008.

141 **He also went about slashing costs:** Susanne Craig, "The Weekend That Wall Street Died," *Wall Street Journal*, December 29, 2008.

141 **flowers that were costing the firm some $200,000:** Ibid.

142 **a signing bonus of $39.4 million, even though Montag wouldn't begin work:** An SEC filing revealed that in addition to Montag's $600,000 annual salary, Merrill agreed to pay him a bonus of $39.4 million in cash and stock-based compensation for fiscal year 2008, which he would receive in January 2009. "Merrill Lynch to Pay New EVP Montag $600,000 Salary," Dow Jones Corporate Filings Alert, May 2, 2008.

142 **Thain would hire Peter Kraus:** Kevin Kingsbury, "Kraus the Latest Ex-Goldman Hire at Merrill," Dow Jones, May 5, 2008; Heidi N. Moore, "Merrill's Kraus Gets $25M, Then Leaves," Dow Jones, December 22, 2008.

142 **And then there was his office:** Charlie Gasparino, "John Thain's $87,000 Rug," *Daily Beast*, January 22, 2009.

142 **angling for the Treasury Secretary post if John McCain:** Louise Story and Julie Creswell, "Love Was Blind," *New York Times*, February 8, 2009.

143 **"It's kind of 'Raise as you go'":** Fair Disclosure Wire, June 11, 2008.

143 **Thain and O'Neal breakfast:** During breakfast between John Thain and Stan O'Neal, Thain pressed him to give him some guidance about his views on the management team. O'Neal replied, "The only person you ought to watch out for is Bob McCann." McCann was the head of the firm's brokerage business and the two had a long-standing mutual distrust.

144 **Merrill's $27 billion in CDO and subprime:** In November 2007, Merrill announced that its

total exposure to subprime mortgages and collateralized debt obligation was $27.2 billion. UBS analyst Glenn Schorr said that hiring Thain "doesn't change the fact that Merrill has $27 billion of CDO/subprime exposure and is likely facing further write-downs in the near term." "Thain to the Rescue," *Investment Dealers Digest,* November 19, 2007.

144 **[O'Neal rise]:** John Cassidy, "Subprime Suspect: The Rise and Fall of Wall Street's First Black C.E.O.," *New Yorker,* March 31, 2008; David Rynecki, "Can Stan O'Neal Save Merrill?" *Fortune,* September 30, 2002.

144 **Merrill's beginnings, Wheaties, "Bullish on America":** "Charles Merrill, Broker, Dies, Founder of Merrill Lynch Firm," *New York Times,* October 7, 1956; "Advertising: Jackpot," *Time,* August 20, 1951; Joseph Nocera, "Charles Merrill," *Time,* December 7, 1998; Suzanne Woolley, "A New Bull at Merrill Lynch," *Money,* March 1, 2002; Helen Avery, "Merrill Shrugs Off the Herd Mentality," *Euromoney,* August 1, 2004.

145 **"I think this is a great firm":** Charles Gasparino, "Bull by the Horns," *Wall Street Journal,* November 2, 2001.

146 **"Ruthless," O'Neal would tell associates, "isn't always that bad":** David Rynecki, "Putting the Muscle Back in the Bull," *Fortune,* April 5, 2004.

146 **O'Neal's top management team as "the Taliban" and calling O'Neal "Mullah Omar":** Ibid.

147 **acquired one of the biggest subprime mortgage lenders in the nation, First Franklin:** Erick Bergquist, "Merrill Wins Bidding for First Franklin," *American Banker,* September 6, 2006.

147 **left Merrill in February 2006:** Avital Hahn, "Leading CDO Team Breaks into Two; Ricciardi Joins Cohen Brothers as CEO," *Investment Dealers Digest,* February 27, 2006.

147 **"whatever it takes":** Kim, as three people heard and remembered him saying. Serena Ng and Carrick Mollenkamp, "Merrill Takes $8.4 Billion Credit Hit," *Wall Street Journal,* October 25, 2007.

147 **replaced by thirty-nine-year-old executive Osman Semerci:** Bradley Keoun, "Merrill Names Semerci, D'Souza to Run FICC, Equities," *Bloomberg,* July 25, 2006.

148 **Kim took home $37 million:** SEC filing disclosed a $14.45 million cash bonus and a $22.2 million stock incentive bonus, in addition to his salary of $350,000. See Nicolas Brulliard, "Merrill Lynch Exec VP Fleming Gets $20.4M Stk Bonus," *Dow Jones Corporate Filings Alert,* January 24, 2007.

148 **Semerci, more than $20 million:** Louise Story, "Bonuses Soared on Wall Street Even as Earnings Were Starting to Crumble," *New York Times,* December 19, 2008.

148 **Fleming and Fakahany sent a letter to Merrill's directors:** Cassidy, "Subprime Suspect," *New Yorker.*

148 **O'Neal sent an overture to Wachovia about a merger:** Jenny Anderson and Landon Thomas Jr., "Merrill's Chief Is Said to Float a Bid to Merge," *New York Times,* October 26, 2007.

149 **"I wouldn't hire Stan to wash windows":** Cassidy, "Subprime Suspect," *New Yorker.*

CHAPTER EIGHT

151 **remained close in the decade since Dimon had been forced out:** Regarding Citigroup, Dimon told *New York* magazine: "I left ten years ago. . . . No, I didn't leave, I was fired. I was kicked out of the nest." Duff McDonald, "The Heist," *New York,* March 24, 2008.

151 **A glass cabinet displayed replicas of two wood-handled pistols:** Crisafulli, "Replicas of the famous pistols are displayed in the JPMorgan lobby, while the originals—curious icons of the bank's storied past—are displayed on the executive floor," *The House of Dimon,* 7.

151 **Like Dimon, Willumstad had been outmaneuvered by Weill:** He announced his departure in July but didn't officially step down until September 5, 2005. David Enrich, "Citigroup Pres Willumstad to Step Down in Sept," *Dow Jones,* July 14, 2005.

151 **Brysam Global Partners:** Brysam began business at the end of January 2007. "Willumstad and Magner Establish Private Equity Firm that Will Focus on Financial Services Investments in Emerging Markets," *Business Wire,* January 22, 2007.

151 **His partner, Marge Magner, was another Citigroup exile:** With Citigroup since 1987, Magner had most recently been chairman and CEO of the company's Global Consumer Group. Mark McSherry and Jonathan Stempel, "Citigroup's Consumer Chief Magner to Leave," *Reuters,* August 22, 2005.

151 **He was the chairman of the board of American International Group:** Willumstad first joined AIG's board as a director in early 2006. Later that year Frank Zarb, acting as interim chairman, suggested him for the job. Emily Thornton and Jena McGregor, "A Tepid Welcome for AIG's New Boss," *BusinessWeek*, June 30, 2008.

152 **Willumstad's beginnings:** Lynnley Browning, "A Quiet Banker in a Big Shadow," *New York Times*, March 10, 2002.

152 **at a conference in Boca Raton:** Gillian Tett, "The Dream Machine," *Financial Times*, March 25, 2008.

152 **blitzkrieg of acquisitions:** Commercial Credit acquired Primerica, Shearson, and Travelers in 1993, Aetna's property and casualty business in 1996, Salomon Brothers in 1997, culminating with Citigroup in 1998. Shawn Tully, "The Jamie Dimon Show," *Fortune*, July 22, 2002.

154 **Removing Sullivan, installing Willumstad:** Liam Pleven, Randall Smith, and Monica Langley, "AIG Ousts Sullivan, Taps Willumstad as Losses Mount," *Wall Street Journal*, June 16, 2008.

154 **in a small office in Shanghai:** Shelp, *Fallen Giant*, 17–28, 153–60; Brian Bremner, "AIG's Asian Connection; Can It Maintain Its Strong Growth in the Region?" *BusinessWeek*, September 15, 2003.

154 **market value of $300 million:** Carol J. Loomis, "AIG: Aggressive. Inscrutable. Greenberg," *Fortune*, April 27, 1998.

154 **with a market value of just under $80 billion:** At the end of AIG's second quarter (August 2008), it had over $1 trillion in assets and about $78 billion in shareholders equity. Matthew Karnitschnig, Liam Pleven, and Peter Lattman, "AIG Scrambles to Raise Cash, Talks to Fed," *Wall Street Journal*, September 15, 2008.

155 **Greenberg's upbringing:** Reports conflict on Greenberg's age at the time of his father's death. This author has chosen to go with the age listed in Shelp, *Fallen Giant*, 95–96.

155 **Greenberg talked his way into a job as a $75-a-week insurance underwriting trainee:** "On a whim, he wandered into the offices of Continental Casualty in lower Manhattan in 1953 and talked his way into the office of the personnel director. Greenberg thought the man was excessively rude, so he stormed into the office of a vice president and told him that Continental's personnel director was a 'jerk.' He was rewarded with a job as a $75-a-week underwriting trainee. Before the end of the decade, he was Continental's assistant vice president in charge of accident and health insurance." See Devin Leonard, "Greenberg & Sons," *Fortune*, February 21, 2005.

155 **C.V. Starr's story and AIG:** Ibid.; Monica Langley, "Eastern Front: AIG and Fired Chief Greenberg Cross Paths Again—in China." *Wall Street Journal*, December 2, 2005; Shelp, *Fallen Giant*, 95–102.

156 **"Sit down, Gordon, and shut up":** Shelp, *Fallen Giant*, 104.

156 **He drove himself relentlessly:** *Fortune* reported that Greenberg installed a StairMaster on the corporate jet as well, to keep fit in flight. Leonard, "Greenberg & Sons," *Fortune*.

156 **He showed little affection for anyone:** As he told Cindy Adams, "You learn fast who your friends are. Some I considered close became a lot less close. They separated quickly. Many you think loyal are suddenly not and you find out during adversity. . . . But Snowball gives me extra love. She sleeps with me. Puts her head on my shoulder." Cindy Adams, "Ex-AIG Executive on Friends, Family," *New York Post*, October 25, 2005.

156 **Jeffrey, Evan Greenberg:** Albert B. Crenshaw, "Another Son of CEO Leaves AIG," *Washington Post*, September 20, 2000; Christopher Oster, "Uneasy Sits the Greenbergs' Insurance Crown," *Wall Street Journal*, October 18, 2004; Diane Brady, "Insurance and the Greenbergs, like Father like Sons," *BusinessWeek*, March 1, 1999.

157 **AIG agreed to pay $10 million:** According to an SEC press release: "AIG developed and marketed a so-called 'non-traditional' insurance product for the stated purpose of 'income statement smoothing,' i.e., enabling a public reporting company to spread the recognition of known and quantified one-time losses over several future reporting periods. . . . AIG issued the purported insurance policy to Brightpoint for the purpose of assisting Brightpoint to conceal $11.9 million in losses that Brightpoint sustained in 1998." U.S. Securities and Exchange Commission, "AIG Agrees to Pay $10 Million Civil Penalty," September 11, 2003. http://www.sec.gov/news/press/2003-111.htm.

157 **AIG agreed to pay $126 million to settle:** "In consenting to settle the Commission's action

and related, criminal charges, AIG has agreed to pay disgorgement, plus prejudgment interest, and penalties totaling $126,366,000." *Securities and Exchange Commission v. American International Group, Inc.,* Litigation Release No. 18985, November 30, 2004. See http://www.sec.gov/litigation/litreleases/lr18985.htm.

157 **deferred prosecution agreement:** Pamela H. Bucy, "Trends in Corporate Criminal Prosecutions Symposium: Corporate Criminality: Legal, Ethical, and Managerial Implications," *American Criminal Law Review,* September 22, 2007.

157 **"Dr. Strangelove of Derivatives":** Lynnley Browning, "AIG's House of Cards," *Portfolio,* September 28, 2008.

158 **Warren Buffett called them weapons of mass destruction:** In the past he had referred to them as "time bombs" and "financial weapons of mass destruction." Clare Gascoigne, "A Two-Faced Form of Investment—the Culture of Derivatives," *Financial Times,* May 3, 2003.

158 **Sosin fled to AIG:** Sosin signed a joint venture agreement with AIG on January 27, 1987, and shortly recruited the ten men who would join his team, which already included Drexel's Randy Rackson and Barry Goldman as partners. See Robert O'Harrow Jr. and Brady Dennis, "The Beautiful Machine," *Washington Post,* December 29, 2008.

158 **traders got to keep some 38 percent of the profits:** Ibid. AIGFP reportedly kept 38 percent of the profits, with AIG retaining 62 percent. The *Washington Post* noted that Greenberg later said this figure was 65 percent.

158 **"You guys up at FP ever do anything to my Triple-A rating":** Ibid.

158 **formed a "shadow group":** Ibid. Randall Smith, Amir Efrati, and Liam Pleven, "AIG Group Tied to Swaps Draws Focus of Probes," *Wall Street Journal,* June 13, 2008.

159 **BISTRO and JP Morgan:** Gillian Tett, "The Dream Machine," *Financial Times,* March 24, 2006; Jesse Eisinger, "The $58 Trillion Elephant in the Room," *Portfolio,* November 2008.

159 **"How could we possibly be doing so many deals?":** Brady Dennis and Robert O'Harrow Jr., "Downgrades and Downfall," *Washington Post,* December 31, 2008.

160 **"It is hard for us, without being flippant":** Ibid.

160 **"does not rely on asset-backed commercial paper":** "American International Group Investor Meeting—Final," Fair Disclosure Wire, December 5, 2007.

161 **In 2007 one of its biggest clients, Goldman Sachs, demanded:** Serena Ng, "Goldman Confirms $6 Billion AIG Bets," *Wall Street Journal,* March 21, 2009.

161 **"It means the market's a little screwed up":** AIG investor meeting, Fair Disclosure Wire, December 5, 2007.

161 **"We have, from time to time, gotten collateral calls from people":** Ibid.

162 **Greenberg's forced resignation, Spitzer's criminal threat:** According to the *Wall Street Journal,* Spitzer threatened AIG's board with criminal charges unless it dismissed Greenberg. He was forced out as chairman and CEO on March 14, 2005. Spitzer filed a civil fraud suit against the firm in May, accusing AIG of "sham transactions." James Freeman, "Eliot Spitzer and the Decline of AIG," *Wall Street Journal,* May 16, 2008; Daniel Kadlec, "Down . . . But Not Out," *Time,* June 20, 2005.

162 **AIG's $500 million boost:** James Bandler, "Hank's Last Stand," *Fortune,* October 13, 2008.

162 **He immediately contacted PricewaterhouseCoopers:** Theo Francis and Diya Gullapalli, "Insurance Hazard: Pricewaterhouse's Squeeze Play," *Wall Street Journal,* May 3, 2005.

164 **consulting contract, at the rate of $1 million a month:** Gretchen Morgenson, "Behind Biggest Insurer's Crisis, a Blind Eye to a Web of Risk," *New York Times,* September 28, 2008; Carrick Mollenkamp, Serena Ng, Liam Pleven, and Randall Smith, "Behind AIG's Fall, Risk Models Failed to Pass Real-World Test," *Wall Street Journal,* November 3, 2008.

164 **a $7.8 billion loss:** Liam Pleven, "AIG Posts Record Loss, As Crisis Continues Taking Toll," *Wall Street Journal,* May 9, 2008.

164 **International Lease Finance Corp. was pushing for a split:** J. Lynn Lunsford and Liam Pleven, "AIG Leasing Unit Mulls Split-Up," *Wall Street Journal,* May 12, 2008.

164 **"I am as concerned as millions of other investors":** Liam Pleven and Randall Smith, "Financial Rebels with a Cause: AIG—Hank Greenberg, Who Built the Giant Insurer, Steps Up His Attack," *Wall Street Journal,* May 13, 2008.

165 **"steps that can be taken to improve":** Liam Pleven and Randall Smith, "Big Shareholders Rebel at AIG—Letter to the Board Cites Problems with Senior Management," *Wall Street Journal,* June 9, 2008.

165 **to meet with the three investors: Ibid.** Francesco Guerrera and Julie MacIntosh, "AIG removes Sullivan as chief executive," *Financial Times*, June 15, 2008.

165 **The company had paid Manchester United $100 million:** "Manchester United Signs Shirt Deal with American Insurance Giant," Associated Press, April 6, 2006.

166 **"AIG Offers Empathy, Little Else":** Liam Pleven and Randall Smith, "AIG Offers Empathy, Little Else—Some Shareholders Left Wanting More After Insurer's Slips," *Wall Street Journal*, May 15, 2008.

166 **an additional $10 billion in new collateral:** Randall Smith, Amir Efrati, and Liam Pleven, "AIG Group Tied to Swaps Draws Focus of Probes," *Wall Street Journal*, June 13, 2008; Liam Pleven, "AIG's $5.4 Billion Loss Roils the Markets— Investors Impatient on New CEO's Plan as Problems Attack the Complex Insurer," *Wall Street Journal*, August 8, 2008.

167 **The two men agreed to have dinner together:** Liam Pleven, "Two Financial Titans Put on Best Face," *Wall Street Journal*, June 17, 2008; Lilla Zuill, "New AIG Chief and Ex-CEO Greenberg Set to Meet Thursday," Reuters, June 18, 2008.

CHAPTER NINE

168 **Oil, most crucially, was going for $140 a barrel:** A record for oil futures in Russia, this price was predicted to rise—and it did—hitting $147 in July. "Russia's Crude Money Box," *International Securities Finance*, June 26, 2008.

168 **Russia was pumping out millions of barrels a day:** The International Energy Agency said that as of June 11, 2008, Russia was producing 9.5 million barrels of oil per day. Jason Bush, "Prime Minister Putin Primes the Pump," *BusinessWeek*, June 30, 2008.

169 **who had coined the appellation for those four economies:** Goldman's chief economist Jim O'Neill, leading a team from the firm, created the acronym in 2001, when they were making growth predictions about the four emerging markets. See Dominic Elliott, "Fundamentals Drive the 'BRIC' Rebound," *Wall Street Journal*, July 27, 2009.

169 **defaulting on the nation's debt:** "On August 13, with dollars fleeing the country, its reserves dwindling, its budget overtapped, and the price of oil, its chief commodity, down 33 percent, the government imposed controls on the ruble." Lowenstein, *When Genius Failed*, 140–45.

169 **Long-Term Capital Management: Ibid.**

169 **"I really think we are a little better":** Bethany McLean, "The Man Who Must Keep Goldman Growing," *Fortune*, March 17, 2008.

170 **They had bet against something called the ABX Index:** Chris Blackhurst, "The Credit Crunch Genius Who Masterminded a £2 billion Jackpot," *Evening Standard* (London), December 18, 2007.

170 **"I don't speak Russian":** Ellis, *The Partnership*, 37.

170 **Yeltsin's new government named the firm its banking adviser:** "Russia Hires Goldman Sachs as Adviser," *Washington Post*, February 18, 1992.

170 **Goldman pulled out of the country in 1994 but would eventually return:** Joseph Kahn and Timothy L. O'Brien, "For Russia and Its U.S. Bankers, Match Wasn't Made in Heaven," *New York Times*, October 18, 1998.

170 **Adolf Hitler had planned to hold his victory celebration there:** Hitler had chosen Astoria's Winter Garden ballroom for his victory ball, scheduled for November 7, 1941, but Germany's summer invasion of the Soviet Union didn't go as planned. Stacks of invitations were later discovered in Berlin's Nazi headquarters after the war. Corinna Lothar, "Gem of the North— St. Petersburg Reclaims Its Glory as Russia's 'Window to the West,'" *Washington Times*, December 27, 2003.

172 **short, fat, bearded guy who wore tube socks:** Jenny Anderson, "Goldman Runs Risks, Reaps Rewards," *New York Times*, June 10, 2007.

172 **Blankfein's beginnings:** Neil Weinberg, "Sachs Appeal," *Forbes*, January 29, 2007; Ellis, *The Partnership*, 669; Bethany McLean, "The Man Who Must Keep Goldman Growing," *Fortune*, March 17, 2008; Susanne Craig, "How One Executive Reignited Goldman's Appetite for Risk," *Wall Street Journal*, May 5, 2004.

172 **dating a Wellesley student from Kansas City, he took a summer job at Hallmark:** Ellis, *The Partnership*, 707.

172 **"If we don't show up Monday it's because we've hit the jackpot"**: Craig, "How One Executive Reignited," *Wall Street Journal*, May 5, 2004.

172 **"prelife crisis"**: Ibid.

173 **taking a job as a salesman of gold coins and bars, she cried**: Ibid. Also see "Laura Jacobs Engaged to Lloyd C. Blankfein," *New York Times*, May 15, 1983.

173 **the firm acquired J. Aron in late October 1981**: On October 29, 1981, Goldman Sachs announced its acquisition of J. Aron & Company for an undisclosed amount (at the time industry experts said it was "slightly more than $100 million"). H. J. Maidenberg, "Goldman Sachs Buys Big Commodity Dealer," *New York Times*, October 30, 1981.

173 **they pounded their desks with their fists and threw their**: Endlich, *Goldman Sachs*, 96.

173 **"You can call yourself contessa, if you want"**: Bethany McLean, "Rising Star: Lloyd Blankfein, Goldman Sachs," *Fortune*, February 6, 2006.

173 **Winkelman first noticed Blankfein**: Craig, "How One Executive Reignited," *Wall Street Journal*.

174 **"We've never seen it work to put"**: Ellis, *The Partnership*, 266.

174 **structuring a trade that allowed a Muslim client to obey the Koran's proscriptions**: Craig, "How One Executive Reignited," *Wall Street Journal*.

174 **Winkelman was crushed when he was passed over for Corzine**: Adrian Cox and George Stein, "Winkelman, Denied Top Goldman Job, Seeks to Fix Refco," Bloomberg News, October 24, 2005.

174 **he announced that he had selected Blankfein as his replacement**: Jenny Anderson, "Blankfein Next in Line at Goldman," *New York Post*, December 19, 2003; Kate Kelly, Greg Ip, and Ianthe Jeanne Dugan, "For NYSE, New CEO Could Be Just the Start," *Wall Street Journal*, December 19, 2003.

174 **"Legally, we would be buying Morgan"**: Ellis, *The Partnership*, 639.

175 **Gramm-Leach-Bliley Act**: Barbara A. Rehm, "Commerce, a Reform Gem, in Fed's Hands," *American Banker*, November 9, 2000.

177 **collateral dispute with AIG**: Serena Ng, "Goldman Confirms $6 Billion AIG Bets," *Wall Street Journal*, March 21, 2009.

177 **Dmitry Medvedev had recently been elected to succeed him**: Medvedev was elected Russia's president on Sunday, March 2, 2008, after Putin had officially endorsed him in December. Peter Finn, "Putin's Chosen Successor, Medvedev, Elected in Russia; Power-Sharing Is Main Focus After a Crushing Win," *Washington Post*, March 3, 2008.

178 **visiting the Persian Gulf states; attending the Group of Eight meeting of finance ministers in Osaka**: Paulson's trip began at the end of May with Saudi Arabia, Qatar, and the United Arab Emirates. In Abu Dhabi, he delivered a speech on the importance of open investment and then headed off to Osaka, where he met with Japanese finance minister Fukushiro Nukaga, before the G8 conference began. "Treasury Secretary Paulson to Travel to the Middle East," Department of the Treasury Press Releases/Statements, May 28, 2008; "Nukaga, Paulson Set to Meet Ahead of G-8 Finance Ministers' Talks," Japan Economic Newswire, June 13, 2008.

178 **"To address the perception that some institutions"**: "Remarks by U.S. Treasury Secretary Henry M. Paulson, Jr. on the U.S., the World Economy and Markets before the Chatham House," July 2, 2008. See http://www.treas.gov/press/releases/hp1064.htm.

179 **Spaso House**: See moscow.usembassy.gov/spaso.html.

179 **private sessions with Medvedev and Putin**: David Lawder, "Paulson in Russia to Meet with Medvedev, Putin," Reuters, June 29, 2008.

179 **"best practices"**: "Putin—No Sovereign Wealth Fund in Russia Yet," Reuters, June 30, 2008.

CHAPTER TEN

181 **rehire Michael Gelband and Alex Kirk**: See Susanne Craig, "Gelband, Kirk Rejoin Lehman in Shake-Up," *Wall Street Journal*, June 25, 2008; Jed Horowitz, "Lehman's New President McDade Brings in His Own Team," Dow Jones, June 25, 2008.

182 **classmates at the University of Michigan Business School**: Susanne Craig, "Lehman Vet Grapples with the Firm's Repair," *Wall Street Journal*, September 4, 2008.

182 **on Little St. Simons Island:** According to Paulson's calendar, he left Dulles Airport at 8:00 a.m. on Friday, July 4, 2008, headed for Georgia, where he would "remain overnight" for three nights.

183 **Paulsons bought up three quarters of the ten-thousand-acre property:** Mary Jane Credeur, "Paulson's Georgia Investment Rises as Blind Trust Becomes Joke," *Bloomberg News*, January 14, 2008.

183 **"The U.S. economy is . . . facing a trio of headwinds":** From Paulson's speech in London on the U.S., the world economy and markets, July 2, 2008. See http://www.treas.gov/press/releases/hp1064.htm.

183 **brother, Richard Paulson, worked as a fixed-income salesman in Lehman's Chicago office:** Anita Raghavan, "Paulson Brothers on Either Side of Lehman Divide," *Forbes*, September 12, 2008.

184 **reporting a $708 million loss:** After restating its first quarterly loss since 2001 (it had mistakenly reported $393 million), Wachovia ousted Ken Thompson as chairman and—a month later—as CEO. See David Mildenberg and Hugh Son, "Wachovia Ousts Thompson on Writedowns, Share Plunge," *Bloomberg News*, June 2, 2008.

184 **flown back home on a private chartered jet to Dulles Airport:** According to his calendar, Paulson left Georgia at 2:00 p.m. on Monday, July 7, arriving back in Washington, D.C., at 3:42 p.m.

184 **Freddie tumbled as much as 30 percent:** On Monday, July 7, 2008, Fannie Mae shares fell $3.04, or 16.2 percent, to $15.74, their lowest since 1992, while Freddie stock was down $2.59, or 17.9 percent, to $11.91, its lowest since 1993. See James R. Hagerty and Serena Ng, "Mortgage Giants Take Beating on Fears over Loan Defaults," *Wall Street Journal*, July 8, 2008.

184 **Fannie shares slid 16.2 percent:** Ibid.

184 **wrote that revised accounting rules might require Fannie and Freddie to raise:** Harting Report released on Monday, July 7, 2008. Aaron Lucchetti, "How Fannie/Freddie Selldown Went Down," *Wall Street Journal*, July 12, 2008.

185 **"the closest thing I've seen to a holy war":** In February 2007, Paulson told the House of Representatives' budget committee: "I feel very strongly that we need a regulator that's independent, got more muscle, and a number of other changes. . . . I also know people feel very strongly on both sides of this issue. I've never witnessed anything quite like this. It's the closest thing I've seen to a holy war." "US House to Have GSE Bill by End-Mar," Reuters, February 7, 2007.

186 **"we are the equivalent of a Federal Reserve system for housing":** Franklin Raines, as reported by David A. Vise, "The Financial Giant That's in Our Midst," *Washington Post*, January 15, 1995.

186 **55 percent of the $11 trillion U.S. mortgage market:** Shannon D. Harrington and Dawn Kopecki, "Fannie, Freddie Downgraded by Derivatives Traders," *Bloomberg*, July 9, 2008.

186 **"In moving, even tentatively, into this new area of lending":** Steven A. Holmes, "Fannie Mae Eases Credit to Aid Mortgage Lending," *New York Times*, September 30, 1999.

186 **"[We] always won, we took no prisoners":** Mudd wrote this in a note to Franklin Raines in November 2004. See James Tyson, "Fannie, Freddie Retreat as Mortgage Bonds Mutate," *Bloomberg News*, September 6, 2006.

187 **Bush administration lowered the amount of capital:** Damian Paletta and James R. Hagerty, "U.S. Puts Faith in Fannie, Freddie," *Wall Street Journal*, March 20, 2008.

187 **"Congress ought to recognize":** Dawn Kopecki and Shannon D. Harrington, "Fannie, Freddie Tumble on Bailout Concern, UBS Cut," *Bloomberg*, July 10, 2008.

188 **"You're not going to like this conversation":** Portions of this exchange, including Fuld having heard "a lot of noise," were first reported by Kate Kelly and Susanne Craig, "Goldman Is Queried About Bear's Fall," *Wall Street Journal*, July 16, 2008.

189 **"There's blood in the water, let's go kill someone!":** According to a former Morgan Stanley trader, Frank Partnoy, from his book *Fiasco*, 99.

189 **"I see that again, and you're fired":** Michael Carroll, "Morgan Stanley's Global Gamble," *Institutional Investor*, March 1, 1995.

189 **House Financial Services Committee hearing:** "Systemic Risk and the Financial Markets" hearing, with witnesses Henry Paulson and Ben Bernanke, held on July 10, 8. See http://financialservices.house.gov/hearing/hr008.shtml.

189 "We're going to need broader emergency authorities": Ibid.

190 some confusion about tracking down Greenspan's home phone number: First reported by Deborah Solomon, "The Fannie & Freddie Question—Treasury's Paulson Struggles with the Mortgage Crisis," *Wall Street Journal*, August 30, 2008.

191 "considering a plan to have the government take over": Stephen Labaton and Steven R. Weisman, "U.S. Weighs Takeover Plan for Two Mortgage Giants," *New York Times*, July 11, 2008.

191 It had already been a long morning for Paulson: Paulson's calendar.

191 "Today our primary focus is supporting Fannie Mae": Brendan Murray, "Paulson Backs Fannie, Freddie in Their 'Current Form,'" Bloomberg News, July 11, 2008.

192 briefed Bush on the Fannie and Freddie situation: Later that morning, at the Department of Energy, Bush said: "I want to thank the members of my economic team for assembling here at the Department of Energy. Secretary Bodman, thank you for hosting us. First of all, Secretary Paulson came by this morning to brief me on the financial markets. Freddie Mac and Fannie Mae are very important institutions. You spent a fair amount of time discussing these institutions. He assured me that he and Ben Bernanke will be working this issue very hard." Office of the Press Secretary, "President Bush Meets with Economic Team," July 11, 2008, 11:38 a.m. EDT.

192 Paulson had a call with Sheila Bair: Verified from his calendar.

192 FDIC was about to seize IndyMac: On Friday, July 11, 2008, the Office of Thrift Supervision closed IndyMac Bank, F.S.B, with total assets of $32.01 billion, transferring its operations to the FDIC. "OTS Closes IndyMac Bank and Transfers Operations to FDIC," July 11, 2008. See http://www.fdic.gov/news/news/press/2008/pr08056.html.

195 "We have a new kind of bank": James Surowiecki, "Too Dumb to Fail," *New Yorker*, March 31, 2008.

195 "We're giving serious consideration to becoming a bank holding company": Fuld's plea to become a bank holding company was first reported by Julie MacIntosh and Francesco Guerrera, "Lehman Failed to Convince Fed Officials over Survival Strategy," *Financial Times*, October 6, 2008; and subsequently reported by Julie Creswell and Ben White, "The Guys from 'Government Sachs,'" *New York Times*, October 19, 2008.

196 "As long as I am alive this firm will never be sold": Susanne Craig, Jeffrey McCracken, Aaron Lucchetti, and Kate Kelly, "The Weekend That Wall Street Died," *Wall Street Journal*, December 29, 2008.

196 he came close to buying Lazard: See Cohan, *The Last Tycoons*, 517–20.

196 About Greg Curl: Zachary R. Mider, "Lewis Turns to Tomato-Growing 'Unknown Genius' on Merrill Deal," Bloomberg News, September 24, 2008.

197 "Okay, you can fight him": Daniel S. Morrow, "Kenneth Lewis Oral History," Computerworld Honors Program International Archives, May 3, 2004. See www.cwhonors.org/archives/histories/Lewis.pdf.

199 "No, we wouldn't use our *petty cash* to buy an investment bank": Heidi N. Moore, "Ken Lewis Tells Investment Bankers All Is Forgiven," WSJ Blog/Deal Journal, June 11, 2008.

200 Paulson, unshaven and wearing jeans, was pacing the halls and pestering his staff: This scene was first reported by Deborah Solomon, who quoted Wilkinson as saying: "[Y]ou need to leave us alone so we can do our jobs." Author's subsequent reporting revealed slightly different wording. See Deborah Solomon, "The Fannie & Freddie Question—Treasury's Paulson Struggles with the Mortgage Crisis," *Wall Street Journal*, August 30, 2008.

200 take a quick bike ride: Ibid.

201 "Fannie Mae and Freddie Mac play a central role": "Paulson Announces GSE Initiatives," press release, Department of the Treasury, July 13, 2008. See http://www.treas.gov/press/releases/hp1079.htm.

201 "Our proposal": "Part I, Part II of a Hearing of the Senate Banking, Housing and Urban Affairs Committee," Federal News Service, July 15, 2008.

203 SEC to begin cracking down on improper short selling: The SEC issued an emergency diktat to halt "unlawful manipulation through 'naked' short selling," which was set to start that Monday, July 21, 2008, and expire after thirty days. Kara Scannell and Jenny Strasburg, "SEC Moves to Curb Short-Selling," *Wall Street Journal*, July 16, 2008.

204 **Lehman's board:** Dennis K. Berman, "Where Was Lehman's Board?" WSJ Blog/Deal Journal, September 15, 2008.

205 **Ken Wilson was standing in line at Westchester County Airport:** Susanne Craig, "In Ken Wilson, Paulson Gets Direction from the Go-To Banker of Wall Street," *Wall Street Journal,* July 22, 2008.

206 **On the evening of July 21, Paulson arrived for a dinner:** From Paulson's July calendar, with dinner scheduled from 6:45 to 8:30 p.m.

CHAPTER ELEVEN

209 **"to conduct a thorough strategic":** "American International Group Names Robert B. Willumstad Chief Executive Officer," transcript of an AIG board conference call, June 16, 2008.

210 **reported $5.4 billion loss:** Liam Pleven, "AIG Posts $5.4 Billion Loss as Housing Woes Continue," *Wall Street Journal,* August 7, 2008.

210 **Geithner had greeted him with his usual firm, athletic handshake:** According to Geithner's calendar, they were scheduled to meet from 9:30 to 10:30 a.m. on Tuesday, July 29, 2008.

212 **Morgan Stanley would receive a token payment of $95,000:** Aaron Lucchetti, "The Fannie-Freddie Takeover: Two Veterans Led Task for Morgan Stanley," *Wall Street Journal,* September 8, 2008.

213 **"Either investors are going to be massively diluted":** Al Yoon, "Freddie Posts 4th Straight Qtrly Loss, Slashes Dividend," Reuters, August 6, 2008.

214 **Freddie's reported loss of $821 million:** Ibid.

214 **In the first week of August; On that Monday:** These meetings took place on August 4 and 5.

214 **Min Euoo Sung arrived in Manhattan from Seoul:** Lehman's "secret meetings" with KDB were reported by Henny Sender and Francesco Guerrera, "Lehman's Secret Talks to Sell 50% Stake Stall," *Financial Times,* August 20, 2008.

219 **"In the event the slow erosion of confidence turns into a rout":** Donald Kohn's e-mail to Ben Bernanke was released as part of the Report of the Examiner in the Chapter 11 proceedings of Lehman Brothers Holdings by Anton R. Valukas, chairman of Jenner & Block. See: http://lehmanreport.jenner.com/.

219 **Fuld owned ninety-seven acres in the area:** "Lehman Brothers CEO Is Local Land Baron," *Idaho Mountain Express,* September 24, 2008.

221 **"A bubble, once 'pricked'":** Ben Bernanke and Mark Gertler, "Monetary Policy and Asset Price Volatility," Federal Reserve Bank of Kansas City's Economic Symposium, Jackson Hole, Wyoming, 1999. See http://www.kc.frb.org/Publicat/sympos/1999/S99gert.pdf.

221 **"the Bernanke doctrine":** John Cassidy, "Anatomy of a Meltdown," *New Yorker,* December 1, 2008.

221 **"It is not the responsibility of the Federal Reserve":** Ben Bernanke, "Housing, Housing Finance, and Monetary Policy," Federal Reserve Bank of Kansas City's Economic Symposium, Jackson Hole, Wyoming, August 31, 2007. See http://www.federalreserve.gov/newsevents/speech/bernanke20070831a.htm.

222 **One day a little Dutch boy:** Alan S. Blinder, "Discussion of Willem Buiter's, 'Central Banks and Financial Crises,'" Federal Reserve Bank of Kansas City's Annual Economic Symposium," Jackson Hole, Wyoming, August 23, 2008. See http://www.kc.frb.org/publicat/sympos/2008/blinder.08.25.08.pdf.

222 **"statutory resolution regime for nonbanks":** Ben Bernanke, "Reducing Systemic Risk," Federal Reserve Bank of Kansas City's Annual Economic Symposium," Jackson Hole, Wyoming, August 22, 2008.

223 **Moody's cut its ratings:** Jody Shenn, "Fannie, Freddie Preferred Stock Downgraded by Moody's," Bloomberg News, August 22, 2008.

224 **having shorted subprime before anyone else:** Andy Kessler, "The Paulson Plan Will Make Money for Taxpayers," *Wall Street Journal,* September 25, 2008.

224 **Paulson had heard rumors when he was in China:** Paulson, *On the Brink,* 161. Paulson's account was later denied by a Russian spokesman. "Russia at that time was a country that invested huge funds in these organizations and was not interested in rocking these institutions," Dmitry Peskov reportedly said to the Russian state-run news agency RIA Novosti.

228 **analyst report issued by Goldman Sachs raising questions about the firm:** Hugh Son, "AIG Falls as Goldman Says a Capital Raise Is 'Likely,'" Bloomberg News, August 19, 2008.

228 **As the company had warned in an SEC filing:** Figures are from AIG's 10-Q filing on August 6, 2008.

229 **AIG owning seventy-one state-regulated insurance subsidiaries:** AIG issued a press release on September 18, 2008, assuring policyholders that their protection was a top priority. "The 71 state-regulated insurance companies within AIG did not receive a bailout; they are financially solvent," it said. "The federal bailout of the non-insurance portions of AIG does not negatively change the solvency strength of its insurance subsidiaries." http://www.aig.com.

231 **"rather than letting these conditions fester":** "The result has been that they have been unable to provide needed stability to the market. They also find themselves unable to meet their affordable housing mission. Rather than letting these conditions fester and worsen and put our markets in jeopardy, FHFA, after painstaking review, has decided to take action now." "Fhfa Director Lockhart Issues Statement on Safety and Soundness Concerns," U.S. Fed News, September 7, 2008.

231 **Treasury's takeover terms:** Rebecca Christie and John Brinsley, "U.S. Takeover of Fannie, Freddie Offers 'Stopgap,'" Bloomberg News, September 8, 2008.

232 **"any action we take":** As Obama told reporters in Indiana on September 6, 2008. See http://www.msnbc.msn.com/id/26577811/.

CHAPTER TWELVE

234 **Reuters headline:** Kim Yeon-hee and Chris Wickham, "Eyes on Lehman Rescue as Korea Lifeline Drifts," Reuters, September 8, 2008.

234 **had held a briefing with reporters:** Ibid.; Susanne Craig, Diya Gullapali, and Jin-Young Yook, "Korean Remarks Hit Lehman," *Wall Street Journal*, September 9, 2008.

234 **Shares of Lehman dropped precipitously:** Joe Bel Bruno, "Lehman Shares Plunge 30 percent on Report that Talks with Korea Development Bank Ended," Associated Press, September 9, 2008.

234 **annual banking conference:** The Lehman Brothers Global Finance Services Conference was held at New York's Hilton Hotel from September 8–10, 2008. Wachovia CEO Robert Steel presented on Tuesday, September 9, according to the press release: "Wachovia CEO Robert K. Steel to Present at Lehman Conference," PR Newswire, September 3, 2008.

234 **"Here we go again":** Fuld, as quoted in an article by John Helyar and Yalman Onaran, "Fuld Sought Buffett Offer He Refused as Lehman Sank," Bloomberg News, November 10, 2008.

234 **"Time Running Out for Lehman":** "Stocks to Watch," CNBC, September 9, 2008.

235 **"We've got to act fast":** John Helyar and Yalman Onaran, "Fuld Sought Buffett Offer He Refused as Lehman Sank," Bloomberg News, November 10, 2008.

235 **meeting with Jamie Dimon:** According to official calendars obtained from the Department of the Treasury, this meeting was scheduled for 8:30 a.m. on September 9, 2008, and was one of several listed on Paulson's calendar.

236 **"[A]ll he wanted was the bazooka":** Alison Vekshin, "Dodd Plans Senate Hearing on Fannie, Freddie Takeover," Bloomberg News, September 8, 2008.

236 **"Secretary Paulson knew more than he was telling us":** From a statement issued by Bunning on September 8, 2008, titled "Bunning Rips Bailout of Fannie and Freddie."

238 **Lehman's stock had plunged 38 percent:** Joe Bel Bruno, "Lehman Shares Plunge 30 Percent on Report That Talks with Korea Development Bank Ended," Associated Press, September 9, 2008.

239 **AIG's lawyers and advisers:** Scott Pegram, "Davis Polk, Weil Gotshal, Sullivan, Simpson Work on AIG Restructuring," *New York Law Journal*, March 5, 2009.

239 **including Rodgin Cohen:** Matthew Karnitschnig and David Enrich, "A Lawyer for All Wall Street Navigates Tempestuous Times," *Wall Street Journal*, October 9, 2008.

239 **Two documents given to Geithner:** Obtained by author from confidential source.

240 **Jester hadn't been required to sell all his Goldman stock:** Greg Farrell and Stephanie Kirch-

gaessner, "Goldman links to US Treasury Raise Questions," *Financial Times,* October 12, 2008.

240 **$3.9 billion loss:** On the morning of Wednesday, September 10, Lehman announced its preliminary third-quarter earnings and an estimated net loss of $3.9 billion. See "Lehman Brothers Announces Preliminary Third Quarter Results and Strategic Restructuring," PR Newswire, September 10, 2008.

241 **"'I would much rather have partners that are really, really smart motherfuckers than guys that I like'":** Mr. Briger confirmed making such an observation but disputes using the word "motherfucker" despite the accounts of several other sources who either heard it directly or in the retelling from Alex Kirk after he ran down the hall.

247 **"The stock is coming down":** Dick Bove to Erin Burnett, *Streets Signs,* "LEH Shares Down," CNBC, September 9, 2008.

248 **"This is coming directly from Paulson":** This quote is one of only a few that caused confusion and consternation among various sources. All the sources for this scene agree that this was the comment that McDade made at the time, based on his conversation with Fuld. It is also clear that Paulson spoke to both Blankfein and Fuld about how the two firms should talk to each other and about a sale of Lehman's real estate assets. It is also clear that David Viniar, Goldman's CFO, placed a call to Dan Jester earlier in the day seeking help to orchestrate negotiations, which is detailed in an earlier scene. Paulson's calendar cites a series of phone calls between Paulson and Fuld and Paulson and Blankfein that day, with at least one in rapid succession back to back from each other. Furthermore, multiple sources privy to both of those conversations say that Paulson suggested that Fuld hold discussions with Goldman, as one of many options. So far, nothing is in dispute. What is confusing is why Fuld is under the impression that Goldman is working for the government. There is no evidence that was the case and no evidence that Paulson said so directly. What appears most likely is that there was a miscommunication, with Fuld making certain assumptions and Goldman, during its phone calls with McDade and Kirk, doing little to disavow these views until Wednesday morning, when clarity was required to execute the confidentiality agreement to begin due diligence.

248 **Ken Lewis:** Shawn Tully, "Meanwhile, Down in Charlotte . . . ," *Fortune,* October 13, 2008.

CHAPTER THIRTEEN

253 **The lead of the *New York Times:*** Jenny Anderson and Ben White, "Wall Street's Fears on Lehman Bros. Batter Markets," *New York Times,* September 10, 2008.

253 **"Some may worry that Treasury":** Ibid.

253 ***Wall Street Journal* noted:** "The firm's situation differs markedly from that of Bear Stearns, which was taken over earlier this year after it ran into a liquidity crisis. Unlike Bear Stearns, Lehman has access to new Federal Reserve facilities that can provide short-term funding when the markets won't, in addition to the ability to exchange illiquid assets for safer securities such as Treasurys." Susanne Craig, Randall Smith, Serena Ng, and Matthew Karnitschnig, *Wall Street Journal,* September 10, 2008.

253 **reduced the amount of business:** On September 16, 2008, GLG Partners issued the following statement regarding Lehman Brothers: "With respect to Lehman, GLG last week transferred substantially all of the remaining positions of the GLG Funds to other prime brokers. The majority of these transfers have already settled and we expect the remainder to settle shortly. We believe the residual exposure of the GLG Funds to Lehman will not be material. Lehman is also a shareholder in GLG, owning approximately 33.7 million shares, through Lehman (Cayman Islands), a Cayman Islands company, about 13.7 per cent of the total GLG stock outstanding."

255 **"That's it? That's fucking it?":** McDonald and Robinson, *A Colossal Failure of Common Sense,* 314.

255 **"The firm remains committed":** From a press release issued by Lehman that morning. "Lehman Brothers Announces Preliminary Third Quarter Results and Strategic Restructuring," September 10, 2008.

256 **Herlihy had worked on nearly every deal Bank of America had orchestrated:** "Bailout Lawyer Optimistic Worst Is Over," WSJ Blog/Deal Journal, October 16, 2008.

257 **forecast a third-quarter loss of $3.9 billion:** Ben White, "With Big Loss Forecast, Lehman to Spin Off Assets," *New York Times,* September 11, 2008.

257 **"In light of these last two days":** Lehman Brothers preliminary F3Q08 Earnings Call Transcript, September 10, 2008.

258 **"The real estate held-for-sale portfolio":** Ibid.

259 **"To the extent you might need $7 billion":** Ibid.

260 **"The Bungalow":** "HSBC's Canary Wharf headquarters towers over that of Barclays. So much so that HSBC workers have christened their neighbour's building 'the bungalow.' A spokesman for Barclays retorts: 'Size is not our objective—growth is.' Touche." Dominic Walsh, "Barclays Bungalow; City Diary," *Times* (London), July 8, 2006.

261 **having both vied for the top job in 2003:** Grant Ringshaw, "Barclays' Odd Couple John Varley and Bob Diamond," *Sunday Times,* (London), February 17, 2008.

261 **In 2007, Diamond earned $42 million to Varley's $8.4 million:** "Barclays' Diamond Gets 21 Million Pounds in Pay and Bonus," Reuters, March 27, 2008; Ben Livesey and Jon Menon, "Barclays Pays Diamond Five Times More than CEO Varley," March 26, 2007.

261 **"Bob Diamond 3, John Varley 0":** Ringshaw, "Barclays' Odd Couple," *Sunday Times* (London).

263 **trying to buy ABN AMRO:** After a harrowing nine-month takeover battle, Barclays withdrew its bid of €67.5 billion for ABN AMRO in October 2007, finally conceding to a consortium led by the Royal Bank of Scotland. Julia Werdigier, "Barclays Withdraws Bid to Take Over ABN Amro," *New York Times,* October 6, 2007.

264 **been on the phone with Tim Geithner and Hank Paulson twice about it:** From Geithner's calendar for Wednesday, September 10, 2008.

265 **"Unless I've missed something":** Brian Blackstone, "Ex-Fed Official Poole: Fed Not Defining Post-Bailout World," Dow Jones, September 10, 2008.

266 **Any hope that the SpinCo plan was going to turn Lehman's fortunes around:** Susanne Craig, Randall Smith, Serena Ng, and Matthew Karnitschnig, "Lehman Faces Mounting Pressures," *Wall Street Journal,* September 10, 2008.

267 **announced his plans to "retire" from the firm:** Mark Kleinman, "Jeremy Isaacs to Step Down at Lehman," *Daily Telegraph,* September 7, 2008.

267 **$5 million severance:** Danny Fortson, "Five Lehman Chiefs Coop $100m Days Before Collapse," *Sunday Times* (London), October 12, 2008.

267 **"engage in detrimental activity":** From Exhibit A of Lehman's "Termination Arrangements for Executives" in a section called "Restrictive Covenants." Document was made public by the House Oversight and Government Reform Committee and is available online under "Materials for Lehman Brothers Compensation Meeting," http://oversight.house.gov/story.asp?ID=2208.

269 **pocketing some $540 million from an investment in Shinsei Bank:** Matthew Miller, "Cash Kings," *Forbes,* October 9, 2006.

269 **town house on the Upper East Side for $53 million:** Zachery Kouwe, "Sallie's Suitor—Flowers' Power: Art of the Deal," *New York Post,* October 7, 2007.

270 **Goldfield happened to be the banker depicted:** Roger Lowenstein, *When Genius Failed,* 170–85.

270 **Greenberg . . . bought millions of preferred shares:** In June 2008, Lehman sold $6 billion in common and preferred shares to a group of investors, which included Hank Greenberg. Greenberg would not disclose how much he spent. Lavonne Kuykendall, "Greenberg: Lehman 'A Great Franchise,' Now Has Enough Capital," Dow Jones, June 10, 2008.

270 **"Management did not successfully put to rest":** Patrick M. Fitzgibbons, "Lehman in Sale Talks as Survival Questioned—Sources," Reuters, September 11, 2008.

271 **"The change in rating agency posture":** Alistair Barr, "Treasury, Fed Reportedly Helping as Deal Sought by This Weekend," MarketWatch.com, September 11, 2008.

271 **"He is as feisty as ever":** Louise Story, "Tough Fight for Chief at Lehman," *New York Times,* September 11, 2008.

272 **buy Chicago's LaSalle Bank from ABN:** "ABN AMRO Shareholders Vote in Favor of Sale, Breakup," Dow Jones, April 26, 2007.

273 **It is with deep regret:** Letter obtained by author.

274 **had just gotten off the phone with Geithner:** The *Wall Street Journal* reported that Willumstad made his first call to Geithner on Thursday, but they didn't actually speak on the phone until Friday morning. Author's subsequent reporting places the phone conversation on Thursday morning. See Monica Langley, Deborah Solomon, and Matthew Karnitschnig, "Bad Bets and Cash Crunch Pushed Ailing AIG to Brink," *Wall Street Journal,* September 18, 2008.

275 **If the agency cut AIG's credit rating by even one notch, it could trigger a collateral call of $10.5 billion:** Greg Farrell, Aline van Duyn, and Nicole Bullock, "S&P in Warning after AIG Shares Plunge," *Financial Times,* September 12, 2008.

274 **The cost to insure the debt of AIG:** Lilla Zuill, "AIG Woes Knock Its Market Value Below Peers," Reuters, September 11, 2008.

274 **Hank Greenberg, being deposed that day:** In the midst of settling a Delaware shareholder suit for $115 million, Greenberg began his deposition with Andrew Cuomo for a civil fraud lawsuit, which would stretch over the next several days. Amir Efrati, "Greenberg Settles AIG Shareholder Case," *Wall Street Journal,* September 12, 2008.

274 **"What the hell are you people waiting for?":** James Bandler, "Hank's Last Stand," *Fortune,* October 7, 2008.

275 **If the agency cut AIG's credit rating:** Mary Williams Walsh and Jonathan D. Glater, "Investors Turn Gaze to A.I.G.," *New York Times,* September 12, 2008

276 **Texaco trucks and Eastern Airlines jets:** Stephen Labaton, "Bankruptcy Bar: Never So Solvent," *New York Times,* April 1, 1990.

276 **he billed clients nearly $1,000 an hour:** Jonathan D. Glater, "The Man Who Is Unwinding Lehman Brothers," *New York Times,* December 14, 2008.

276 **He had grown up in the Gravesend neighborhood of Brooklyn:** Ibid.; Labaton, "Bankruptcy Bar," *New York Times.*

277 **"Bankruptcy," he once said, "is like dancing":** Ibid.

284 **"Fuld is a friend. Try to help, but don't bail Lehman out":** Paulson, *On the Brink,* 181.

286 **"With a beleaguered Lehman":** Jessica Papini, "Possible Govt Backstop for Lehman Buy Has Two Prior Models," Dow Jones, September 11, 2008.

287 **"Federal officials currently":** Efrati, "Greenberg Settles," *Wall Street Journal.*

287 **"But while the Treasury Department":** Walsh and Glater, "Investors Turn Gaze to A.I.G.," *New York Times.*

287 **"At least in the Bear case":** "Lehman's Fate," *Wall Street Journal,* September 12, 2008.

288 **"Source: There will be no government money":** Steve Liesman to David Faber, *Faber Report,* CNBC, September 12, 2008.

290 **"Lehman is going down":** Susanne Craig, Jeffrey McCracken, Aaron Lucchetti, and Kate Kelly, "The Weekend that Wall Street Died," *Wall Street Journal,* December 29, 2008.

290 **"We're not Lehman":** Ibid.

291 **"concerns about AIG's ability to shed":** "AIG Shares Fall 20 Percent On Mortgage Woes," Reuters, September 12, 2008.

CHAPTER FOURTEEN

299 **he had given her some $4,600 in donations:** On February 21, 2007, Lloyd Blankfein made two contributions, of $2,300 each, to Hillary Clinton's Presidential Campaign. See http://www.opensecrets.org.

300 **after testifying at a hearing for the Committee on Energy and Natural Resources:** "Summit to Consider How to Achieve a More Secure, Reliable, Sustainable, and Affordable Energy Future for the American People." Friday, September 12, 2008.

302 **BofA shares closed that day at $33.74:** Bank of America rose $.68 or 2.1 percent, to $33.74 on Friday, September 12, 2008. "Finance Companies Shares Mixed at the Close of Trading," Associated Press, September 12, 2008.

303 **"a quality which, for lack of a better word, I can best describe as epic."** Christopher Gray, "Mix of Limestone and Sandstone, in Florentine Style," *New York Times,* November 11, 2001.

303 **a three-level vault:** www.newyorkfed.org.

303 **Emergency meeting at NY Fed:** Evan Thomas and Michael Hirsh, "Paulson's Complaint," *Newsweek,* May 16, 2009.

305 "He is in denial," Paulson continued: Author obtained notes from the emergency meeting at the New York Federal Reserve.

305 "There is no political will for a federal bailout": Deborah Solomon, Dennis K. Berman, Susanne Craig, and Carrick Mollenkamp, "Ultimatum by Paulson Sparked Frantic End," *Wall Street Journal*, September 15, 2008.

306 "I assume we are going to talk about AIG?": Tett, *Fool's Gold*, 233.

306 "Stop being such a jerk": Kate Kelly, "The Fall of Bear Stearns," *Wall Street Journal*, May 29, 2008.

309 Fuld swallowed his pride and dialed Lewis's home in Charlotte: According to the *Wall Street Journal*, Fuld placed the call to Lewis on the afternoon of Sunday, September 14, 2008. Subsequent reporting by the author has revealed that the call was actually made on the evening of Friday, September 12, 2008. See Susanne Craig, Jeffrey McCracken, Aaron Lucchetti, and Kate Kelly in "The Weekend That Wall Street Died," *Wall Street Journal*, December 29, 2008.

310 the same home he had purchased in 1958 for $31,500: Roger Lowenstein, "King Midas—Warren Buffett," *Independent on Sunday*, February 18, 1996.

319 David Bonderman of Texas Pacific Group: Riva D. Atlas and Edward Wong, "Texas Pacific Goes Where Others Fear to Spend," *New York Times*, August 25, 2002.

319 watched his investment lose virtually all of its value in less than half a year: Peter Lattman, "WaMu Fall Crushes TPG," *Wall Street Journal*, September 27; Geraldine Fabrikant, "WaMu Tarnishes Star Equity Firm," *New York Times*, September 27, 2008.

320 Paulson hated Flowers, and the antipathy was mutual: Peter Truell and Joseph Kahn, "Goldman Sachs Nears Decisive Talks on Going Public," *New York Times*, June 2, 1998.

324 "Urgent. Code name: Equinox": Craig, McCracken, Lucchetti, and Kelly, "The Weekend that Wall Street Died," *Wall Street Journal*. For a more detailed account of Weil Gotshal's involvement in the Lehman bankruptcy, see Ben Hallman, "A Moment's Notice; Weil Gotshal Put Together the Largest Bankruptcy in U.S. History in Record Time." *American Lawyer*, December 1, 2008.

329 "If we do that": Cohan, *House of Cards*.

332 Eric R. Dinallo: Matthew Karnitschnig, Liam Pleven, and Peter Lattman, "AIG Scrambles to Raise Cash, Talks to Fed," *Wall Street Journal*, September 15, 2008.

335 Merrill had just sold $8.55 billion of convertible stock: "Thain Gains $2 Mln on Merrill Lynch Share Purchase," Reuters, July 31, 2008.

335 the restaurant plays host to Wall Street bigwigs over lunch: Landon Thomas Jr. "Make Your Best Offer and Pass the Parmesan, Please," *New York Times*, October 2, 2005.

338 the "good bank": Cohan, *House of Cards*, 445.

339 "How much equity do you need to raise": This exchange between Gary Shedlin and Michael Klein was first reported in William D. Cohan's article for *Fortune* magazine, soon followed up in his book, *House of Cards*. According to Cohan, "Shedlin confirmed the exchange to *Fortune*; Klein did not respond to requests to be interviewed." See William D. Cohan, "Three Days That Shook the World," *Fortune*, December 16, 2008.

339 lost $20 billion more than anyone had recorded: Eric Dash and Andrew Ross Sorkin, "Throwing a Lifeline to a Troubled Giant," *New York Times*, September 18, 2008.

CHAPTER FIFTEEN

342 "I don't think I can take another day of this": The "Goldman aide" referenced in the *Wall Street Journal* is Greg Palm, Goldman's general counsel. Susanne Craig, Jeffrey McCracken, Aaron Lucchetti, and Kate Kelly, "The Weekend That Wall Street Died," *Wall Street Journal*, December 29, 2008.

342 not-so-subtle reference to John Whitehead: John C. Whitehead, *A Life in Leadership: From D-Day to Ground Zero: An Autobiography*, New York: Basic Books, 2005.

342 "Certain Deal Issues": Author obtained copy of document.

343 had posed a decade earlier: "Merrill's Mr. Allison, reading from a handwritten sheet, spelled out the terms. 'We think we need $4 billion to assure the fund can withstand any concerted attack by others against its positions.' Sixteen firms were asked to pitch in $250 million." Michael Siconolfi, Anita Raghavan, and Mitchell Pacelle, "All Bets Are Off: How the Salesmanship and Brainpower Failed at Long-Term Capital," *Wall Street Journal*, November 16, 1998.

343 "What the fuck are you doing?": Lowenstein, *When Genius Failed*, 203.

343 he had contributed only $100 million: *Wall Street Journal*, November 16, 1998.

344 Merrill's market capitalization: According to Standard & Poor's, Merrill's market capitalization for Friday, September 12, 2008, was $26.1 billion. "Five Facts About Merrill Lynch and Bank of America," Reuters, September 14, 2008.

345 "It looks like we may have the outlines of a deal around the financing": William D. Cohan, "Three Days," *Fortune*.

345 tapped out a message on his BlackBerry to Michael Gelband: A version of this anecdote was reported by Steve Fishman, "Burning Down His House," *New York*, December 8, 2008.

345 McCarthy, meanwhile, in London . . .: Nick Mathiason, "Three Weeks That Changed the World," *The Observer*, December 28, 2008.

347 FSA's refusal to waive shareholder-approval requirements: As reported by Bloomberg, Barclays spokesman Leigh Bruce said: "The only reason it didn't happen is that there was no guarantee from the U.S. government, and a technical stock-exchange rule required prior shareholder approval for us to make a similar guarantee ourselves. We didn't have that approval, so it wasn't possible for us to do the deal. No U.K. bank could have done it. It was a technical rule that could not be overcome." John Helyar and Yalman Onaran, "Fuld Sought Buffett Offer He Refused as Lehman Sank," Bloomberg, November 10, 2008.

349 editorial in the *Sunday Telegraph*: Mark Keinman, "Barclays Should Be Wary of the Gorilla in Its Midst," *Sunday Telegraph*, (London), Sep 14, 2008.

351 "We lost the patient": James. B. Stewart, "Eight Days: The Battle to Save the Financial System," *The New Yorker*, September 21, 2009.

353 "What if the system collapses?": Paulson, *On the Brink*, 215. Paulson rarely publically acknowledges his faith nor his most intimate conversations with his wife. This anecdote, as described by him in his memoir, was perhaps the most revealing he has ever been about his religion and his emotional state that weekend.

352 "Those of you who do not want to assist a Barclays deal": Author received notes from this meeting, with Paulson's remarks dictated, as well as Geithner's proposal to create a $100 billion emergency fund for the three remaining investment banks.

353 Thain had had coffee with Ken Lewis that morning: Referenced by Craig, McCracken, Lucchetti, and Kelly in "The Weekend that Wall Street Died," *Wall Street Journal*, December 29, 2008.

354 "Couldn't have gone more poorly": Diamond's e-mail exchange read to author.

355 "We've got a good deal in hand": Greg Fleming's words to Peter Kraus were first reported in the *Wall Street Journal* and differ slightly from the author's subsequent reporting. According to the *WSJ*, Fleming said: "We have a great deal in hand, and need to finish doing this deal." Susanne Craig, Jeffrey McCracken, Aaron Lucchetti, and Kate Kelly, "The Weekend That Wall Street Died," *Wall Street Journal*, December 29, 2008.

356 together they had prepared an offer for the company: Zachary R. Mider and Erik Holm, "Allianz, Flowers Said to Have Bid for AIG Before Fed Takeover," Bloomberg, September 17, 2008.

356 The company's actual market value on Friday had been about $31 billion: "With a market value of $31 billion on Friday, based on an intraday low of $11.49, it now trails some other insurers, including AXA SA. The shares slipped further after the closing bell, following a warning from Standard & Poor's that it may cut AIG's ratings." Lilla Zuill, "AIG Could Hold Investor Call as Soon as Mon," Reuters, September 12, 2008.

357 "I don't approve of": Dr. Paul Achleitner of Allianz denies having made these comments. However, several eyewitnesses confirmed that these were the words he used.

358 Dannhauser grabbed three senior partners: Ben Hallman, "A Moment's Notice for Lehman," *American Lawyer*, December 16, 2008.

359 Roberts took a call from a partner: Ibid.

359 "You don't understand the consequences": Ibid.

362 "All trades conducted will be done": Author obtained copy of Fed memo.

362 "The extraordinary trading session held today": Jennifer Ablan, "Pimco's Gross Sees Tsunami of Risk if Lehman Fails," Reuters, September 14, 2008.

363 "a group of global commercial and investment banks": From Morgan Stanley press release, issued September 14, 2008.

364 He had received bids for it on Friday from two separate private-equity firms, Bain Capital and TPG: Christine Williamson, "Walker Rises from Ashes of Lehman Brothers Firestorm," *Pensions & Investments*, October 13, 2008.

365 Diamond's cell phone rang: First reported by Aleksandrs Rozens, "Who Dares Wins; Barclays' Diamond Leads Team to Snare One of Wall Street's Most Storied Investment Banks," *Investment Dealers Digest*, January 19, 2009.

369 Thomas Cruikshank, who had led the oil services company Halliburton: Cruikshank served as the chairman and CEO of Houston-based Halliburton from 1989 to 1995, after which Dick Cheney assumed his position. He had been on Lehman's board of directors for twelve years when the company filed for bankruptcy. Hillary Durgin, "Halliburton—On the Offensive," *Houston Chronicle*, October 5, 1997.

370 Known as "Dr. Doom": Karen Pennar, "Dr. Doom and Dr. Gloom Are Still Prescribing Caution," *BusinessWeek*, October 17, 1988.

370 "providing only tepid oversight": From a speech Kaufman gave at a conference in Philadelphia in April 2008. "Credit Crisis a 'Global Calamity'—Kaufman," Reuters, April 18, 2008.

371 Mayor Michael Bloomberg: Azi Paybarah, "Bloomberg and Schwarzenegger (and Sheekey?) Together Again," *New York Observer*, January 16, 2008.

372 "My goodness. I've been in the business": Andrew Ross Sorkin, Jenny Anderson, and Eric Dash, "A Buyer for Merrill," *New York Times*, September 16, 2008.

372 "Words cannot express the sadness": Carrick Mollenkamp, Susanne Craig, Jeffrey McCracken, and Jon Hilsenrath, "The Two Faces of Lehman's Fall," *Wall Street Journal*, October 6, 2008.

372 $5.8 billion in "incentive compensation": A complaint later filed by the SEC against Bank of America revealed that the bank had "contractually authorized" Merrill to pay billions in discretionary bonuses—not to exceed $5.8 billion—to its employees. SEC press release, "SEC Charges Bank of America for Failing to Disclose Merrill Lynch Bonus Payments," Washington, D.C., August 3, 2009. See http://www.sec.gov/news/press/2009/2009-177.htm.

373 "BAC Update": http://online.wsj.com/public/resources/documents/FedbofaDocs.pdf.

374 "fairness opinion": Zachary R. Mider, "Lewis Turns to Tomato-Growing 'Unknown Genius' on Merrill Deal," Bloomberg, September 24, 2008.

374 Flowers and Fox-Pitt would earn a combined $20 million: From Bank of America's SEC filing.

CHAPTER SIXTEEN

376 "CRISIS ON WALL STREET AS LEHMAN TOTTERS": Carrick Mollenkamp, Susanne Craig, Serena Ng, and Aaron Lucchetti, "Crisis on Wall Street as Lehman Totters, Merrill Is Sold, AIG Seeks to Raise Cash," *Wall Street Journal*, September 15, 2008.

376 Lehman formally filed for bankruptcy at exactly 1:45 that morning: Legal documents show that Lehman filed a voluntary petition under Chapter 11 with the United States Bankruptcy Court for the Southern District of New York on Monday morning at 1:45 a.m. See www.lehman-docket.com; Peg Brickley, "Lehman Makes It Official in Overnight Chapter 11 Filing," *Wall Street Journal*, September 15, 2008.

376 "Everybody's prepared this time": Annelena Lobb, "A Chaotic Sunday Opens Wall Street's Week," *Wall Street Journal*, September 15, 2008.

377 sent out a note to his clients: "Analysts' View 3—Lehman Files for Bankruptcy, Merrill to be Sold," Reuters, September 15, 2008.

379 a mogul unto himself: Landon Thomas Jr., "Banker, Loan Maestro Jimmy Lee Switched Suspenders for Sweaters," *New York Observer*, December 24, 2001.

379 finance some of the biggest deals in history: Ibid. Beginning in the late seventies at Chemical Bank, Lee raised hundreds of billions for companies on the brink, such as IBM, General Motors, Seagram, Nextel, and AT&T, to name a few. Robert Lenzner, "Jimmy's List," *Forbes*, April 17, 2000.

381 they were angry: Aleksandrs Rozens, "Death of an Era: Within the Span of Several Days, Wall Street Loses Two Titans," *Investment Dealers Digest*, September 22, 2008.

381 Wall of Shame: Ibid.; McDonald and Robinson, *A Colossal Failure of Common Sense*, 317.

381 "Dumb and Dumber," "Voting in Braille Only": Ibid.

382 **Geithner's phone conference with Dimon, Blankfein:** According to Geithner's calendar, the call was scheduled from 10:00 to 10:15 a.m. that Monday.

383 **relatively uneventful press conference of Bank of America and Merrill Lynch:** A press release on Bank of America's Web site early Monday morning announced the merger with Merrill Lynch, and also that Lewis and Thain would be hosting a press conference at 10:00 a.m. in the auditorium at Bank of America's New York City headquarters. See http://www. bankofamerica.com/merrill/.

384 **formally agreed to allow AIG to use some of its regulated insurance company assets:** In a press conference at noon on Monday, September 15, New York governor Paterson said that he had given Eric Dinallo "authorization, such that AIG can access $20 billion of its assets through its subsidiaries for the purpose of posting these assets as collateral to provide liquid cash in order to run the day-to-day operations of the parent company." States News Service, "Transcript: Governor Paterson Press Conference on AIG—September 15, 2008," September 15, 2008.

385 **Geithner called and told him he should be at this meeting instead:** Paterson thanked Dinallo in his speech, acknowledging that he was presently meeting with Federal Reserve officials.

385 **to discuss the fate of the insurers Ambac and MBIA:** Susanne Craig and Liam Pleven, "Credit Crunch: Good Plan, but Who Will Pay?" *Wall Street Journal,* January 30, 2008.

388 **"I hope you all had an enjoyable weekend":** Paulson's comments to the press, and their questions, were taken from transcripts released by the White House. "White House Conducts Press Briefing, Sept. 15," 1:42 p.m. EDT. US Fed News, September 15, 2008.

392 **"It is oddly reassuring that the Treasury Department . . . let Lehman Brothers fail":** "Wall Street Casualties," *New York Times,* September 16, 2008.

393 **"Stocks Plunge as Crisis Intensifies":** Glenn Kessler and David S. Hilzenrath, "Stocks Plunge as Crisis Intensifies; AIG at Risk; $700 Billion in Shareholder Value Vanishes," *Washington Post,* September 16, 2008.

393 **The Dow Jones Industrial Average had slumped 504.48 points:** The Dow dropped 504.5 points on Monday. Alex Berenson, "Wall St.'s Turmoil Sends Stocks Reeling," *New York Times,* September 16, 2008.

396 **Fed had kept Lehman's broker-dealer in the United States open:** According to Lehman's official press release issued that Monday, the company was "exploring the sale of its broker-dealer operations" and its subsidiaries, including Neuberger Berman, LLC, and Lehman Brothers Asset Management, would "not be subject to the bankruptcy case of its parent." See http://www.lehman.com/press/pdf_2008/091508_lbhi_Chapter11_announce.pdf.

397 **as was the case with Ramius Capital:** Cassell Bryan-Low, "Crisis on Wall Street: Funds Assess Lehman (Gulp!) Exposure," *Wall Street Journal,* September 26, 2008.

397 **he presided over the FOMC meeting at the Federal Reserve in Washington:** The meeting was held in the offices of the Board of Governors of the Federal Reserve System in Washington, D.C., on Tuesday, September 16, 2008 at 8:30 a.m. See http://www.federalreserve.gov/ FOMC.

397 **Federal Reserve Act, Section 13, point 3:** www.federalreserve.gov/aboutthefed/section13. htm.

398 **"regulatory capital relief":** From AIG's 10-Q filing, August 6, 2008: "Approximately $307 billion of the $441 billion in notional exposure on AIGFP's super senior credit default swap portfolio as of June 30, 2008, was written to facilitate regulatory capital relief for financial institutions primarily in Europe."

398 **AIG's vast insurance empire:** A "strictly confidential" AIG presentation draft, dated February 26, 2009, entitled, "AIG: Is the Risk Systemic?" states that "AIG has written more than 81 million life insurance policies to individuals worldwide" at a face value of $1.9 trillion, with more than $12 billion in claims paid in 2008.

400 **he knew the top people in the industry:** Susanne Craig, "In Ken Wilson, Paulson Gets Direction From the Go-To Banker of Wall Street," *Wall Street Journal,* July 22, 2008.

400 **telling the press that he planned to mount a proxy contest:** "Hank Greenberg: Plans Fight for Control or Buyout of AIG," Dow Jones Newswires, September 16, 2008.

400 **Dear Bob:** The full text of Hank Greenberg's letter to Robert Willumstad, dated September

16, 2008, can be viewed online at http://online.wsj.com/public/resources/documents/AIG09162008.pdf.

403 **He and Ben Bernanke had scheduled a meeting with President Bush:** According to the *Wall Street Journal*, this meeting took place at 3:30 p.m. See Monica Langley, Deborah Solomon, and Matthew Karnitschnig, "Bad Bets and Cash Crunch Pushed Ailing AIG to Brink," *Wall Street Journal*, September 18, 2008.

404 **"Well, you finally get your chance":** Richard Beattie's remarks to Robert Willumstad, as first reported in *Fortune* magazine. James Bandler, "Hank's Last Stand," *Fortune*, October 7, 2008.

404 **the government was taking a large ownership stake—79.9 percent:** Matthew Karnitschnig, Deborah Solomon, Liam Pleven, and Jon E. Hilsenrath, "U.S. to Take Over AIG in $85 Billion Bailout," *Wall Street Journal*, September 16, 2008.

404 **"Paulson is handling this the same way he did Fannie, Freddie, and Bear":** Monica Langley, Deborah Solomon and Matthew Karnitschnig, "Bad Bets and Cash Crunch," *Wall Street Journal*, September 18, 2008.

404 **the London Interbank offered rate:** Known as LIBOR, this is the average interest rate charged when banks borrow unsecured funds from one another, whether it's an overnight or a long-term loan. In the United States, LIBOR maturities used in pricing loans most commonly include one, three, six, and twelve months. On Wednesday, September 17, 2008, the three-month LIBOR jumped 19 basis points, to 3.0625 percent, its biggest jump since September 1999. Lisa Twaronite, "Three-Month Libor Marks Biggest Jump in Nine Years," MarketWatch.com, September 17, 2008.

406 **"I won't be working for the federal government":** Willumstad, as quoted in Bandler, "Hank's Last Stand," *Fortune*.

407 **a Maine insurer that had fought off an effort by Allstate:** Laura Jereski, "We Understand Risk" (UNUM Corp.), *Forbes*, March 20, 1989.

407 **AIG had invested $1.35 billion in Blackstone:** Peter Truell, "AIG Will Put $1.35 Billion into Blackstone," *New York Times*, July 31, 1998.

407 **Greenberg's office on Park Avenue:** A year after his ouster from AIG in 2005, Greenberg relocated his office to the seventeenth floor of Citigroup's headquarters, at 399 Park Avenue. See Diane Brady, "Hank at War," *BusinessWeek*, March 27, 2006.

407 **"He's going on *Charlie Rose* to talk about AIG":** During that week, Hank Greenberg appeared on two consecutive episodes of *Charlie Rose*. The first was simply to discuss AIG's crisis, and the second to speak about the federal bailout. See *The Charlie Rose Show*, "More Crises on Wall Street," September 16, 2008, and "Former AIG Chair Discusses Bail Out," September 17, 2008.

409 **The gathering had been hastily organized:** Langley, Solomon, and Karnitschnig, "Bad Bets and Cash Crunch," *Wall Street Journal*.

410 **had sent him an e-mail:** A facsimile of Herzog's e-mail appeared in *Fortune*, where this was first reported. Carol J. Loomis, "AIG's Rescue Has a Long Way to Go," *Fortune*, December 29, 2008.

CHAPTER SEVENTEEN

412 **"Reserve Primary Fund, had broken the buck":** It was the first time in fourteen years that a fund's net asset value had fallen below $1, or "broken the buck." Particularly unsettling was the fact that the Primary Fund's owner, the Reserve Management Corporation, invented the money fund in 1970. See Christopher Condon, "Reserve Primary Money Fund Falls Below $1 a Share," Bloomberg, September 16, 2008.

413 **4.04 percent annual return:** According to Morningstar Inc., the Reserve Primary Fund posted a return of 4.04 percent over a twelve-month period, versus a 2.75 percent average among more than twenty-one hundred money market funds it tracks. See Binyamin Appelbaum, "Beyond Wall St., Losses Spill Over," *Washington Post*, September 18, 2008; Eleanor Laise, "Market Rescue: Money Funds Offer More Detail," *Wall Street Journal*, September 20, 2008.

413 **$785 million in Lehman paper:** Steve Stecklow and Diya Gullapalli, "A Money-Fund Man-

ager's Fateful Shift: Bruce Bent Shunned Corporate Debt for Years—Then Bought Some of Lehman's," *Wall Street Journal,* December 8, 2008.

413 "Goldman, Morgan Now Stand Alone": Aaron Lucchetti and Robin Sidel, "Dow Industrials Take a 504.48-Point Dive—Goldman, Morgan Now Stand Alone; Fight On or Fold?," *Wall Street Journal,* September 16, 2008.

415 "For seven years, I've said": Lewis, during a conference call that Monday to discuss the Merrill merger. Joseph A. Giannone, "Goldman, Morgan Stanley Face Biggest Market Test," Reuters, September 16, 2008.

415 had been given a big promotion by Mack: Pandit joined Morgan Stanley as an associate in 1983. Seventeen years later, with Mack at the helm, he became president of investment banking. Joe Hagan, "The Most Powerless Powerful Man on Wall Street," *New York,* March 9, 2009.

415 With $62.6 billion in assets: On Friday, September 12, 2008, the Primary Fund's assets had been about $62 billion. Diya Gullapalli, Shefali Anand, and Daisy Maxey, "Money Fund, Hurt by Debt Tied to Lehman, Breaks the Buck," *Wall Street Journal,* September 17, 2008.

416 "They pretended they were drawing a line in the sand": Nouriel Roubini, quoted in Emily Kaiser, "After AIG Rescue, Fed May Find More at Its Door," Reuters, September 17, 2008.

417 Wachovia's 2006 acquisition of Golden West: On May 7, 2006, Wachovia announced plans to purchase Golden West Financial Corp., based in Oakland, California, for $25.5 billion. Investors, however, failed to embrace the merger, and Wachovia's shares took a dive. Jonathan Stempel, "Wachovia CEO—No More Big Mergers After Golden West," Reuters, June 14, 2006.

417 "The past several months have been": Serena Saitto and Yalman Onaran, "Fuld Tells Lehman Employees He Feels 'Horrible' for Their Pain," Bloomberg, September 17, 2008.

418 "the war situation has developed": Broadcast at noon on August 15, 1945, Hirohito continued with, "while the general trends of the world have turned against her interest.'" Andrew Roberts, "The Debt Japan Owes These Men," *Daily Mail* (London), September 17, 1993.

418 graduates of Duke and members of the university board: Steel retired from the board in May 2009. See http://trustees.duke.edu/.

419 "One Firm, One Team, Bribe a Leader": See http://www.dealbreaker.com/robert_kindler/.

420 portrait of Alexander Hamilton: Andy Serwer, "Mr. Paulson Goes to Washington," *Fortune,* November 27, 2006.

420 Duer could not cover his debts, setting off a panic: Chernow, *Alexander Hamilton,* 293.

421 "Nothing is breaking our way": James B. Stewart, "Eight Days: The Battle to Save the Financial System," *The New Yorker,* September 21, 2009.

421 "Free Market Day": Frank quipped at a hearing held on Wednesday, two days after Lehman filed for bankruptcy. "Barney Frank Celebrates Free Market Day," *Wall Street Journal,* September 17, 2008.

421 Senator Jim Bunning, a Republican from Kentucky: Ted Barrett, Deirdre Walsh, and Brianna Keilar, "AIG Bailout upsets Republican lawmakers," CNN.com, September 17, 2008.

421 Richard Shelby, Republican from Alabama: Ibid.

421 The Gold Reserve Act of 1934: See http://www.treas.gov/offices/international-affairs/esf/.

423 "DB: A Solid Counterparty": Aaron Lucchetti, Randall Smith, and Jenny Strasburg, "Morgan Stanley in Talks with Wachovia, Others," *Wall Street Journal,* September 18, 2008.

425 set up a series of phone calls for Mack, who also contacted Chuck Schumer and Hillary Clinton: First reported by Emily Thornton, "Morgan Stanley's John Mack Swings into Action," BusinessWeek.com, September 17, 2008.

426 "I know all of you are watching our stock price today": "Morgan Stanley Memo: 'There Is No Rational Basis for the Movements in Our Stock,'" WSJ Blog/Deal Journal, September 17, 2008.

427 "This memorandum provides a waiver. . . .": Author obtained copy of memo from a FOIA request. Paulson disclosed receiving a waiver for the first time during a congressional hearing on July 16, 2009. "Paulson's Calls to Goldman Tested Ethics," *New York Times,* August 9, 2009.

428 "Stop the insanity—we need a time out": Author obtained copy of Schorr's e-mail.

430 "It's one thing to complain": Susan Pulliam, Liz Rappaport, Aaron Lucchetti, Jenny Stras-

burg, and Tom McGinty, "Anatomy of the Morgan Stanley Panic," *Wall Street Journal*, November 24, 2008.

431 **"Morgan Stanley applauds Attorney General Cuomo":** Press release, September 18, 2008. Find full text in Press section of Morgan Stanley's company Web site, http://www.morgan stanley.com.

432 **"There are no atheists in foxholes":** Peter Baker, "A Professor and a Wall Street Deal Maker Bury Old Dogma on Free Markets," *New York Times*, September 21, 2008.

432 **Resolution Trust Corporation:** Lee Davidson, "The Resolution Trust Corporation and Congress, 1989–1993," 18, no. 2, *FDIC Banking Review*, 2006.

432 **L. William Seidman:** Greenspan, *The Age of Turbulence*, 116.

432 **"This new governmental body":** Excerpt of an editorial written by Nicholas F. Brady, Eugene A. Ludwig, and Paul A. Volcker, "Resurrect the Resolution Trust Corp.," *Wall Street Journal*, September 17, 2008.

433 **"As Fears Grow, Wall St. Titans":** Ben White and Eric Dash, "As Fears Grow, Wall St. Titans See Shares Fall," *New York Times*, September 17, 2008.

433 **"We need a merger or we're not going to make it":** An appended editors' note in the *New York Times* on September 17, 2008, said that both Morgan Stanley and Citigroup "vigorously" denied that Mack had ever made this comment.

433 **Sulzberger family pulled its money from Morgan Stanley:** Sarah Ellison, "New York Times Controlling Family Moves Assets from Morgan Stanley," *Wall Street Journal*, February 3, 2007.

435 **Morgan Stanley's unfailingly bearish economist:** Sarah McBride, "Bearish Economist Roach Says U.S. Caused Global Recession," *Wall Street Journal Asia*, July 13, 2001.

436 **George Soros acolyte worth more than $3.5 billion:** That week, Stanley Druckenmiller had been ranked 105 on *Forbes*'s annual list of the four hundred richest Americans, with a net worth of $3.5 billion. "The Forbes 400 List," *Forbes*, September 17, 2008.

438 **send out a companywide e-mail:** Author obtained copy of e-mail.

439 **Congress to increase the debt ceiling:** The "debt ceiling" was a political hot potato that would require Congress to vote to increase the amount of debt the country could take on, and Congress had just increased the amount to $10.615 trillion in July.

441 **"The market is trading under the assumption":** "European Shares Rise after Central Bank Plan, Asia Losses," Agence France-Presse, September 18, 2008.

441 **FSA announcing temporary ban on short selling:** David Prosser, "Hedge Funds' Misery as FSA Bans Short-selling on 32 Firms," *Independent*, September 20, 2008.

442 **"The Star-Spangled Banner":** *New York Times*, October 2, 2008.

442 **"Treasury, Fed Weighing Wider Plan":** Alison Vekshin, "Treasury, Fed Weighing Wider Plan to Ease Crisis, Schumer Says," Bloomberg, September 18, 2008.

442 **Charlie Gasparino of CNBC reported what he was hearing from his sources on Wall Street:** "Treasury Secretary Hank Paulson is working on an RTC-type solution to the financial crisis, reports CNBC's Charlie Gasparino," CNBC, September 18, 2008.

443 **"Mr. Secretary, . . . we would like to meet with you":** On September 28, Pelosi relayed her phone conversation with Paulson to CBS's *60 Minutes* anchor Scott Pelley. Pelley also interviewed Paulson on the show. "Secretary Paulson Details the Federal Bailout," *60 Minutes*, CBS, September 28, 2008.

445 **The notion of becoming a bank holding company:** Jon Hilsenrath, Damian Paletta, and Aaron Lucchetti, "Goldman, Morgan Scrap Wall Street Model, Become Banks in Bid to Ride Out Crisis," *Wall Street Journal*, September 22, 2008.

445 **to meet with the congressional leadership at Nancy Pelosi's office:** The meeting took place on the second floor of the Capitol, in a conference room beside Pelosi's personal suite. Carl Hulse and David M. Herszenhorn, "Behind Closed Doors, Warnings of Calamity," *New York Times*, September 20, 2008.

446 **"I spent my career as an academic studying great depressions":** Bernanke, as quoted by Wessel, *In FED We Trust*, 203.

446 **noticeably gulped:** As Schumer himself told the *New York Times*, "When you listened to him describe it, you gulped." David M. Herszenhorn, "Congressional Leaders Stunned by Warnings," *New York Times*, September 19, 2008.

446 **"What about the home owner?":** Wessel, *In FED We Trust*.
446 **Richard Shelby disapprovingly characterized:** "If we say 'whatever it takes,' that means there's a blank check of the treasury, future generations, to pay for the mistakes of a lot of people."
446 **"If it doesn't pass, then heaven help us all":** Deborah Solomon, Liz Rappaport, Damian Paletta, and Jon Hilsenrath, "Shock Forced Paulson's Hand," *Wall Street Journal*, September 20, 2008.
446 **"Do you know what you are asking me to do?":** *New York Times*, September 20, 2008.
447 **"I think we need to do this":** McConnell, a Republican senator from Kentucky and Republican leader of the Senate, who often spars with Reid on the Senate floor, "reached over to assure his colleague they could work it out." *New York Times*, September 20, 2008.
447 **put in place a ban on shorting financial stocks:** The SEC issued a press release on the morning of Friday, September 19, that read: "Given the importance of confidence in financial markets, the SEC's action halts short selling in 799 financial institutions. The SEC's emergency order . . . will be immediately effective and will terminate at 11:59 p.m. ET on Oct. 2, 2008. The Commission may extend the order beyond 10 business days if it deems an extension necessary in the public interest and for the protection of investors, but will not extend the order for more than 30 calendar days in total duration." See http://www.sec.gov/news/press/2008/2008-211.htm.
447 **"While this is all politically pleasing":** Chanos, as reported by Kara Scannell, Deborah Solomon, Craig Karmin, and Gregory Zuckerman, "SEC Is Set to Issue Temporary Ban Against Short Selling," *Wall Street Journal*, September 19, 2008.
447 **Merrill Lynch had bought insurance covering $150 million:** On September 17, Merrill bought insurance to cover $106.2 million in Morgan Stanley debt and returned the following day, September 18, to buy protection on another $43 million of debt, according to trading documents obtained by the *Wall Street Journal*. Susan Pulliam, Liz Rappaport, Aaron Lucchetti, Jenny Strasburg, and Tom McGinty, "Anatomy of the Morgan Stanley Panic—Trading Records Tell Tale of How Rivals' Bearish Bets Pounded Stock in September," *Wall Street Journal*, November 24, 2008.
447 **Citigroup, Deutsche Bank, UBS, AllianceBernstein, and Royal Bank of Canada:** Ibid.
448 **Wei Sun Christianson:** In December 2007, Christianson played a major role in negotiating Morgan Stanley's $5.6 billion deal with China Investment Corp., which gave CIC a 9.9 percent stake in the company. See Jason Leow and Rick Carew, "Wei Sun Christianson and How Morgan Deal Got Boost in China—Longtime Mack Aide from Beijing Lends Stature, Ties to Region," *Wall Street Journal Asia*, December 21, 2007.
448 **CIC already held a 9.9 percent stake in Morgan Stanley:** When Morgan Stanley announced a loss of $3.59 billion at the end of 2007, the state-owned China Investment Corp. (CIC) invested five-billion-dollars in the company, giving it a 9.9 percent stake. "China Fund Grabs Big Stake in Morgan Stanley," AFP, December 2007.
448 **he'd be interested in buying up to 49 percent of the firm:** Christine Harper, "Morgan Stanley Said to Be in Talks with China's CIC," Bloomberg, September 18, 2008.
448 **investments, in Blackstone:** When Blackstone went public in June 2007, CIC invested $3 billion—giving it a 9.9 percent stake in the company. Since then shares had fallen by nearly 45 percent, to $17.13 in late August, giving CIC a paper loss of more than $1.3 billion. Allen T. Cheng, "Inside the CIC," *Institutional Investor—America*, September 10, 2008.

CHAPTER EIGHTEEN

449 **"the illiquid assets":** "Text of Paulson's News Conference Friday," Associated Press, September 19, 2008.
451 **Wachovia's $120 billion mortgage portfolio:** As part of its 2006 purchase of Golden West Financial Corp., Wachovia inherited a $120 billion adjustable-rate home-loan portfolio, the bulk of which comes from California and Florida, two of the hardest-hit housing markets in the country. Dan Fitzpatrick, Alex Roth, and David Enrich, "With Wachovia Sale Looking Likely, a Makeover for Charlotte, U.S. Banking," *Wall Street Journal*, September 29, 2008.
451 **Bob Steel had estimated that figure at 12 percent:** Speaking at the Lehman Brothers Finan-

cial Services Conference on Tuesday, September 9, Steel said Wachovia still expects losses equal to 12 percent, though he said, "it's still early days." See "Wachovia Keeps Mortgage Loss View," stock downgraded, *AFX Asia,* September 9, 2008.

454 **his firm would not be making any investments:** "We won't be investing in U.S. banks under current circumstances," Ryosuke Tamakoshi said in Tokyo on Tuesday, September 16, 2008. Takahiko Hyuga, Shingo Kawamoto, and Komaki Ito, "Japan Banks, Insurers Have $2.4 Billion Lehman Risk," Bloomberg, September 17, 2008.

456 **Gao reiterated his interest in buying 49 percent of Morgan Stanley:** Christine Harper, "Morgan Stanley Said to Be in Talks with China's CIC," Bloomberg, September 18, 2008.

457 **the sale of Lehman Brothers to Barclays:** Ben White and Eric Dash, "Barclays Reaches $1.75 Billion Deal for a Lehman Unit," *New York Times,* September 18, 2008.

457 **"You may approach":** The dialogue between Judge Peck and Harvey Miller was taken from the official court transcript, dated September 19, 2008.

463 **Merging the "Houses of Morgan":** Chernow, *The House of Morgan,* 591.

464 **"URGENT and Confidential":** Author obtained copy of e-mail.

466 **chose Roger Altman:** Morgan Stanley's independent board members chose to hire Roger Altman as their adviser, but he only narrowly won the assignment over Christopher Lawrence, a banker at Rothschild.

468 **"Decisions by the Secretary pursuant to the authority":** "Text of Draft Proposal for Bailout Plan," *New York Times,* September 20, 2008.

472 **"You know, there's a chance I could lose the firm":** Mack later recounted this story to Bloomberg: "I said to my wife, when things were really crazy, 'You know, there's a chance I will lose this firm. But I would rather be doing this than sitting on a beach reading a book.'" See Lisa Kassenaar and Christine Harper, "Mack Tells Wife He May Lose Firm Before Brokerage Bid," Bloomberg, January 26, 2009.

473 **the headline "King Henry":** *Newsweek,* September 29, 2008.

473 **a quote from Governor Jon Corzine:** "There hasn't been a consistent pattern. . . . We save Bear Stearns but not Lehman. The market is going to have a hard time sorting through what the underlying principle is." Daniel Gross, "The Captain of the Street; Treasury Secretary Hank Paulson Has a Radical Game Plan for Beating America's Financial Crisis," *Newsweek,* September 29, 2008.

474 **"If you were in your old job":** Tom Brokaw, *Meet the Press,* NBC, September 21, 2008.

476 **"He understands Berkshire far better":** Buffett, from his 2003 chairman's letter. See the annual report at http://www.berkshirehathaway.com/2003ar/2003ar.pdf.

477 **it had used Morgan Stanley as an adviser:** "MUFG's unsolicited bid, arranged by Morgan Stanley as its financial advisor, also illustrates how conservative Japanese companies are adapting to the cut and thrust of U.S. M&A." Yuka Hayashi and Alison Tudor, "MUFG offers to buy UnionBanCal," *Wall Street Journal Asia,* August 13, 2008.

485 **Mitsubishi agreeing to buy up to 20 percent:** Louise Story, "Morgan Stanley Secures Japan Deal; Mitsubishi UFJ to Pay $9 billion for 21% Stake in U.S. Firm," *New York Times,* October 1, 2008.

486 **At 9:30 p.m., the news hit the wires:** On September 21, 2008, the Federal Reserve released the following: "The Federal Reserve Board on Sunday approved, pending a statutory five-day antitrust waiting period, the applications of Goldman Sachs and Morgan Stanley to become bank holding companies." See http://www.federalreserve.gov/newsevents/press/bcreg/20080921a.htm.

CHAPTER NINETEEN

488 **"It would be a grave mistake":** Representative Barney Frank, appearing on *Face the Nation,* CBS, September 21, 2008.

488 **Trott called Buffett again:** Chris Blackhurst, "Billionaire Buffett and the Only Banker He Trusts," *Evening Standard* (London), September 25, 2008.

489 **Buffett buying $5 billion in Goldman Stock:** Susanne Craig, Matthew Karnitschnig, and Aaron Lucchetti, "Buffett to Invest $5 Billion in Goldman," *Wall Street Journal,* September 24, 2008.

490 **Winkelried's salary:** Joseph McCafferty, "Goldman Execs Earn $70M Plus," Directorship

.com; Joseph A. Giannone, "Goldman Buys $58 mln Winkelried, Palm Fund Stakes," Reuters, March 30, 2009.

490 **Winkelried selling Nantucket property:** According to the Town of Nantucket's tax assessor's office, Winkelried purchased 4.18 acres for $5 million in January 1999 and another 1.7 acres for $1.95 million later that September. Peter B. Brace, "Goldman Sachs Executive Selling 5.9 Acres on Nantucket for $55 million," *Daily News Tribune*, October 10, 2008; Christine Harper and Sharon L. Lynch, "Goldman's Winkelried Lists Nantucket Estate for $55 Million," Bloomberg, October 10, 2008.

491 **"Total Abdication of Responsibility to the Public":** Andrew Ross Sorkin, "DealBook: Power Grab and a Roll of the Dice," *New York Times*, September 24, 2008.

491 **"What they have sent us is not acceptable":** "U.S. Lawmaker Dodd Says Treasury Plan 'Unacceptable,'" Reuters, September 23, 2008.

491 **"a terrible communicator":** Charles Babington and Julie Hirschfeld Davis, "Simmering GOP Upset They Were Kept in the Dark; Political Meltdown Came on the Heels of Financial One," Associated Press, September 27, 2008.

492 **"All of us around the table":** Press releases and documents, "Bush Pushes Financial Plan with Congressional Leaders, Candidates," Voice of America, September 26, 2008.

492 **"If money isn't loosened up":** David M. Herszenhorn, Carl Hulse, and Sheryl Gay Stolberg, "Talks Implode During a Day of Chaos; Fate of Bailout Plan Remains Unresolved," *New York Times*, September 25, 2008.

493 **"Well, do we need to start from scratch":** Nedra Pickler, "Obama Says More Work Needed for Deal," Associated Press, September 25, 2008.

493 **"I didn't know you were Catholic":** David M. Herszenhorn, Carl Hulse, and Sheryl Gay Stolberg, "Crunch Time as Washington Battles Impasse," *New York Times*, September 27, 2008.

493 **"You have been great at picking":** "'In the Eye of the Storm': Citi CEO Vikram Pandit Sees a Difficult Recovery Ahead," Knowledge@Wharton, October 2, 2008. See: http://knowledge.wharton.upenn.edu/article.cfm?articleid=2068.

494 **WaMu . . . paying $1.9 billion:** FDIC Press Release, "JPMorgan Chase Acquires Banking Operations of Washington Mutual," September 25, 2008. http://www.fdic.gov/news/news/press/2008/pr08085.html.

495 **"You saw what happened earlier":** Deborah Solomon, Damian Paletta, and Greg Hitt, "US Seals Bailout Deal," *Wall Street Journal*, September 29, 2008.

495 **"Damn it. . . . If you think you need":** Ibid.

496 **"Let's not get emotional":** Ibid.

496 **"All we're talking about is having Groucho":** Ibid.

498 **Wachovia threatened to downgrade the firm's debt:** David Enrich and Matthew Karnitschnig, "Citi, U.S. Rescue Wachovia—Latest Shotgun Deal Creates Nation's Third-Largest Bank," *Wall Street Journal*, September 30, 2008.

499 **Citigroup acquiring Wachovia, Fed help:** Ibid. See also Eric Dash and Andrew Ross Sorkin, "Citigroup to Acquire Banking Operations of Wachovia; Crisis on Wall Street," *New York Times*, September 30, 2008.

501 **"They claim to be free market advocates":** Pelosi delivered this speech from the House floor on September 29, 2008. "Speaker Pelosi Speaks in Support of Emergency Economic Stabilization Act of 2008," US Fed News, September 30, 2008.

502 **"They wouldn't have brought this bill":** Michele Davis, appearing on PBS's *Frontline*, April 9, 2009.

502 **bailout was rejected 228 to 205:** "US Bailout Plan Rejected," *Nation*, September 29, 2008.

504 **"Citibank is honored to enter into a partnership":** From an ad that ran in *USA Today* that Friday, according to David Enrich and Dan Fitzpatrick, "Wachovia Chooses Wells Fargo, Spurns Citi," *Wall Street Journal*, October 4, 2008.

507 **Increasing FDIC insurance on new bailout bill:** Meena Thiruvengadam, "Some Ex-FDIC Officials See No Reason to Hike Insurance Limit," Dow Jones Newswires, October 3, 2008.

507 **"We have shown the world that the United States":** David M. Herszenhorn, "Bailout Plan Wins Approval; Democrats Vow Tighter Rules," *New York Times*, October 3, 2008.

509 **"If you haven't discovered your role":** "The Guilty Men of Wall Street," *Economist*, October 14, 2008.

509 **"I want to be very clear":** From transcripts of Fuld's testimony on the causes and effects of

the Lehman Brothers bankruptcy, Hearing of the House Oversight and Government Reform Committee, chaired by Representative Henry Waxman, Monday, October 6, 2008.

509 **"Your company is now bankrupt":** Ibid.

509 **"the majority of my compensation":** Ibid.

510 **"Not that anybody on this committee cares about this":** Ibid.

511 **"Some critics have worried that Treasury":** Author obtained Buffett's letter to Paulson from a confidential source.

513 **"We have been made aware of rumors":** "MUFG Issues Statement Regarding Transaction with Morgan Stanley," Business Wire, October 8, 2008.

513 **"We can buy these preferred shares":** Representative Barney Frank said to taxpayers in Providence, Rhode Island, on October 8, 2008. Glenn Somerville, "Treasury Says Has Power to Inject Bank Capital," Reuters, October 9, 2008.

513 **UK to invest $87 billion in Barclays:** Banks eligible to participate included Abbey, Barclays Plc, HSBC Holdings Plc, Lloyds TSB Group Plc, Royal Bank of Scotland (RBS, HBOS), Nationwide Building Society, and Standard Chartered Plc. Ben Livesey and Jon Menon, "U.K. to Inject About $87 Billion in Country's Banks," Bloomberg News, October 8, 2008.

514 **"The Brown government has shown itself":** Paul Krugman, "Gordon Does Good," October 12, 2008.

521 **"We Have The Check!!!"** Author obtained copy of Kindler's e-mail to Morgan Stanley staffers from a confidential source.

CHAPTER TWENTY

522 **"Nick Calio just called me":** This and all following e-mails cited were obtained by Judicial Watch, a public interest group, in response to Freedom of Information Act requests it filed on October 16, 2008. For the first batch of e-mails see http://www.judicialwatch.org/files/documents/2009/TreasuryDocsPart1.pdf.

524 **A little after 2:00 p.m.:** Confirmed by Christal West's e-mail, sent at 10:55 a.m. on Monday, October 13, 2008: "There will be a principals only Meeting today prior to the 3:00 pm meeting with CEOs. . . . Principals Meeting 2:15 pm–3:00 pm Hank's Office (Room 3330)."

524 **"To encourage wide participation":** From "Talking Points" documents, also obtained by Judicial Watch.

524 **Meeting background:** Nina Easton, "How the Bailout Bashed the Banks," *Fortune*, June 22, 2009.

526 **"They're all in":** This and all succeeding e-mails to the end of this chapter come from the second batch of FOIA-requested e-mails, courtesy of Judicial Watch. See http://www.judicialwatch.org/files/documents/2009/TreasuryDocsPart2.pdf

527 **Geithner now read off the amounts:** In its FOIA request, Judicial Watch also obtained signed contracts from the banks, with accepted allotments written in ink by the CEOs. See http://www.judicialwatch.org/files/documents/2009/Treasury-ParticipationCommitment.pdf.

EPILOGUE

533 **"animal spirits":** In his 1936 book, *The General Theory of Employment, Interest and Money*, John Maynard Keynes wrote: "Even apart from the instability due to speculation, there is the instability due to the characteristic of human nature that a large proportion of our positive activities depend on spontaneous optimism rather than mathematical expectations, whether moral or hedonistic or economic. Most, probably, of our decisions to do something positive, the full consequences of which will be drawn out over many days to come, can only be taken as the result of animal spirits—a spontaneous urge to action rather than inaction, and not as the outcome of a weighted average of quantitative benefits multiplied by quantitative probabilities," p. 161.

534 **"pay czar":** On June 10, in lieu of his much contested pay caps, Obama appointed Kenneth Feinberg to oversee and modify executive salaries and bonuses. Deborah Solomon, "Pay Czar Gets Broad Authority over Executive Compensation," *Wall Street Journal*, June 11, 2009.

534 "The government intervention is not a government takeover": President George W. Bush, "Remarks to the United States Chamber of Commerce," Weekly Compilation of Presidential Documents, October 17, 2008.

534 Government increasing Citigroup stake/funds: Eric Dash, "U.S. Agrees to Raise Its Stake in Citigroup," *New York Times,* February 28, 2009.

535 "the turd in the punchbowl": According to an undisclosed official's handwritten notes taken during a conference call in January 2009. Michael R. Crittenden and Jon Hilsenrath, "Bernanke Blasted in House—Political Heat Mounts on Fed as Grilling over BofA Shows Ire at Its Interventions," *Wall Street Journal,* June 26, 2009.

535 Shareholders voting for BofA–Merrill deal: Ieva M. Augstums and Stephen Bernard, "Merrill Lynch, Bank of America Shareholders Approve BofA's Purchase of the Investment Bank," Associated Press, December 5, 2008.

536 "How do they justify this outrage?": Michael D. Shear and Paul Kane, "Anger Over Firm Depletes Obama's Political Capital," *Washington Post,* March 17, 2009.

536 "We should hound them in the supermarket": A few days after Cramer's rant, AIG's new chief, Edward Liddy, sent him a letter demanding a retraction and an apology to AIG employees. "It is one thing to criticize the executive leadership of AIG—that's fair commentary," he wrote. "But it is way out of bounds to incite people to confront and harass other AIG employees." Shortly after, Cramer apologized on his show: "Sorry, regular AIG guys. I did not mean you." Heidi N. Moore, "AIG CEO Demands Apology from Mad Money's Jim Cramer," WSJ/Deal Journal, October 20, 2008.

537 "Is Goldman Sachs Evil?": Joe Hagen, "Is Goldman Sachs Evil? Or Just Too Good?" *New York,* July 26, 2009.

537 "great vampire squid wrapped": Matt Taibbi, "The Great American Bubble Machine," *Rolling Stone,* July 13, 2009.

537 Goldman reported a profit of $5.2 billion: On April 13, Goldman reported net earnings of $1.81 billion for its first quarter. Three months later, its second-quarter earnings soared to $3.44 billion. See http://www2.goldmansachs.com.

537 Goldman's VaR rising to record high: Christine Harper, "Goldman Sachs VaR Reaches Record on Risks Led by Equity Trading," Bloomberg, July 15, 2009.

539 "emergency actions meant to provide confidence": Department of the Treasury press release, "Secretary Geithner Introduces Financial Stability Plan," February 10, 2009. See http://www.treasury.gov/press/releases/tg18.htm.

539 Alan Blinder: "After the fact, it is extremely clear that everything fell apart on the day Lehman went under."

540 "policy by deal": Simon Johnson, "Systemic Risk: Are Some Institutions Too Big to Fail and If So, What Should We Do About It?" Testimony before the U.S. House of Representatives Committee on Financial Services during hearing held July 21, 2009. The phrase was originally coined as "regulation by deal" by Steven Davidoff and David Zaring in their paper Regulation by Deal: The Government's Response to the Financial Crisis. 61 Admin, L. Rev. 463, 2009.

540 "At first, the Treasury": Michael Lewis and David Einhorn, "The End of the Financial World as We Know It," *New York Times,* January 4, 2009.

542 "The problem in politics is this": From a Barney Frank interview on CBS's *60 Minutes* that first aired on December 11, 2008.

543 It is not the critic: Theodore Roosevelt, "Citizenship in a Republic: 'Man in the Arena.'" Speech at the Sorbonne, Paris, April 23, 1920.

AFTERWORD

545 *"The people on Wall Street still don't get it"*: *60 Minutes,* CBS News transcripts, December 7, 2009.

545 unemployment in the United States hovered at almost 10 percent for much of 2009: U.S. Bureau of Labor Statistics.

545 Goldman Sachs announced a record profit: Goldman Sachs earnings report, January 21, 1010.

546 Wall Street swarmed Washington with some 1,400 lobbyists: Not only were they lobbyists

600	 | 	*Notes and Sources*

for the financial industry, but they formerly worked for lawmakers and federal agencies. Public Citizen and the Center for Responsive Politics, June 4, 2010.

546 **paying the top ten lobbying firms $30 million:** The Center for Public Integrity, June 8, 2010.

546 **"I did not run for office to be helping out a bunch of fat-cat bankers on Wall Street":** *60 Minutes*, CBS News transcripts, December 7, 2009.

546 **"President Obama's favorite banker":** Jackie Calmes and Lousie Story, "Washington, One Bank Chief Still Holds Sway," *New York Times*, July 18, 2009.

546 **"I'm proposing a simple and common-sense reform, which we're calling the 'Volcker Rule' ":** President Obama, the White House, Office of the Press Secretary, January 21, 2010.

546 **"For a lot of Wall Street people, it was like, 'Okay, first you slap us in the face' ":** John Heilemann, "Obama Is from Mars, Wall Street Is from Venus," *New York Magazine*, May 22, 2010.

547 **"I wish that somebody would give me some shred of neutral evidence about the relationship between financial innovation recently and the growth of the economy":** Paul Volcker: "Think More Boldly," *Wall Street Journal*, December 14, 2009.

547 **"When there's a delusion, a mass delusion, you can say everybody is to blame":** Warren Buffett, CNBC transcript, May 3, 2010.

548 **Anton R. Valukas, issued a report that, at over 2,200 pages and a cost of more than $36 million, was the closest thing to an autopsy of Lehman:** The report is available online: http://lehmanreport.jenner.com/.

549 **"I have absolutely no recollection whatsoever of hearing anything about or seeing documents related to Repo 105 transactions while I was the CEO of Lehman":** Richard S. Fuld Jr., prepared statement before the U. S. House of Representatives Committee on Financial Services, April 20, 2010.

549 **"You know what, people are saying all sorts of crap":** Clare Baldwin, "On Dick Fuld's Trail, No Dinner but I Got Hugged," Reuters, September 7, 2009.

550 **"doing God's work":** John Arlidge, "I'm Doing 'God's Work.' Meet Mr. Goldman Sachs," *Sunday Times*, November 8, 2009.

550 **"I mean, they're going to rewrite Genesis and have Goldman Sachs offering the apple":** Warren Buffett, CNBC transcripts, April 16, 2010.

550 **In April 2010 the Securities and Exchange Commission brought its only major case against Wall Street since the crisis:** *SEC v. Goldman Sachs & Co. and Fabrice Tourre.*

550 **legal experts described the case as "thin":** Kian Abouhossein, a banks analyst at JPMorgan told the *Financial Times* on April 21, 2010, "The SEC has a very weak case, but for the business, for shareholders, the best thing is probably to settle. If they settle, they can start silencing the debate about reputational damage and share price damage."

551 **"Boy that timeberwof [sic] was one shitty deal":** The Goldman e-mail had been subpoenaed by the U.S. Senate Permanent Subcommittee on Investigations. It is available, along with other internal Goldman e-mails: http://levin.senate.gov/newsroom/supporting/2010/PSI.Exhibits.pdf.

551 **"I think that's very unfortunate to have on e-mail":** David Viniar, CSPAN, April 27, 2010.

551 **"I don't trust Goldy on this":** The e-mail had been subpoenaed by the U.S. Senate Permanent Subcommittee on Investigations. It is available: http://levin.senate.gov/newsroom/supporting/2010/PSI.Exhibits.pdf.

551 **"People need to tone down the rhetoric around financial services and stop the populism and be adults":** Transcript, 92nd St. Y Captains of Industry Event, May 6, 2010.

552 **"I don't have a problem with the Abacus transaction at all":** Andrew Ross Sorkin, "From Buffett, Thought-out Support for Goldman," *New York Times*, May 3, 2010.

552 **"I didn't think a lot about theory. I just understood how bad it could be":** Henry M. Paulson, promoting his book on *CBS Sunday Morning*, January 31, 2010.

553 **"must be looking forward to going back to that nice spot you have waiting for you at Goldman":** John Heilemann, "Obama Is from Mars, Wall Street Is from Venus," *New York Magazine*, May 22, 2010.

554 **"The fact is that some businesses require size":** Jamie Dimon's letter to investors in JPMorgan Chase's annual report from 2010.

555 **"We cannot control ourselves":** John Mack made this comment at a *Vanity Fair*/Bloomberg

News panel discussion on media coverage of the financial crisis on November 18, 2009. Michael J. Moore, "Morgan Stanley's Mack Welcomes Regulation by Fed," Bloomberg News, November 19, 2009.

555 **"This generation of Wall Street CEOs could be the ones to forfeit America's trust"**: Elizabeth Warren, "Wall Street's Race to the Bottom," *Wall Street Journal*, February 9, 2010.

BIBLIOGRAPHY

Auletta, Ken. *Greed and Glory on Wall Street: The Fall of the House of Lehman*. New York: Random House, 1986.

Bagehot, Walter. *Lombard Street: A Description of the Money Market*. New York: Charles Scribner & Sons, 1897.

Chernow, Ron. *Alexander Hamilton*. New York: Penguin Press, 2004.

————. *The House of Morgan: An American Banking Dynasty and the Rise of Modern Finance*. New York: Grove Press, 2001.

Cohan, William D. *House of Cards: A Tale of Hubris and Wretched Excess*. New York: Random House, 2009.

————. *The Last Tycoons: The Secret History of Lazard Frères & Co*. New York: Doubleday, 2007.

Crisafulli, Patricia. *The House of Dimon: How Jamie Dimon Rose to the Top of the Financial World*. New York: Wiley, 2009.

Eddy, Mary Baker. *Science and Health with Key to the Scriptures*. Boston: The Christian Science Board of Directors, 2000.

Einhorn, David. *Fooling Some of the People All of the Time: A Long Short Story*. New York: Wiley, 2008.

Ellis, Charles D. *The Partnership: The Making of Goldman Sachs*. New York: Penguin Press, 2008.

Endlich, Lisa. *Goldman Sachs: The Culture of Success*. New York: Touchstone, 1999.

Faber, David. *And Then the Roof Caved In: How Wall Street's Greed and Stupidity Brought Capitalism to Its Knees*. New York: Wiley, 2009.

Friedman, Milton, and Anna Jacobson Schwartz. *A Monetary History of the United States, 1867–1960*. Princeton: Princeton University Press, 1963.

Greenspan, Alan. *The Age of Turbulence: Adventures in a New World*. New York: Penguin Press, 2007.

Kelly, Kate. *Street Fighters: The Last 72 Hours of Bear Stearns, the Toughest Firm on Wall Street*. New York: Portfolio, 2009.

Langley, Monica. *Tearing Down the Walls: How Sandy Weill Fought His Way to the Top of the Financial World . . . and Then Nearly Lost It All*. New York: Simon & Schuster, 2003.

Lowenstein, Roger. *When Genius Failed: The Rise and Fall of Long-Term Capital Management*. New York: Random House Trade Publishing, 2000.

McDonald, Lawrence G., and Patrick Robinson, *A Colossal Failure of Common Sense: The Inside Story of the Collapse of Lehman Brothers*. New York: Crown Business, July 2009.

Partnoy, Frank. *Fiasco: The Inside Story of a Wall Street Trader*. New York: Penguin, 1999.

Paulson, Henry M. Jr. *On the Brink: Inside the Race to Stop the Collapse of the Global Financial System*. New York: Business Plus, February 2010.

Schroeder, Alice. *The Snowball: Warren Buffett and the Business of Life*. New York: Bantam Books, 2008.

Shelp, Ronald. *Fallen Giant: The Amazing Story of Hank Greenberg and the History of AIG*. New York: Wiley, 2006.

Strauss, Barry. *The Battle of Salamis: The Naval Encounter That Saved Greece—and Western Civilization*. New York: Simon and Schuster, 2004

Tett, Gillian. *Fool's Gold: How the Bold Dream of a Small Tribe at J.P. Morgan Was Corrupted by Wall Street Greed and Unleashed a Catastrophe*. New York: Free Press, 2009.

Wessel, David. *In FED We Trust: Ben Bernanke's War on the Great Panic.* New York: Crown Business, 2009.

Whitehead, John C. *A Life in Leadership: From D-Day to Ground Zero: An Autobiography.* New York: Basic Books, 2005.

Woodward, Bob. *Maestro: Greenspan's Fed and the American Boom.* New York: Simon & Schuster, 2001.

INDEX